Roots of the Classical

Roots of the Classical

The Popular Origins of Western Music

PETER VAN DER MERWE

OXFORD
UNIVERSITY PRESS

OXFORD
UNIVERSITY PRESS

Great Clarendon Street, Oxford, OX2 6DP

Oxford University Press is a department of the University of Oxford.
It furthers the University's objective of excellence in research, scholarship,
and education by publishing worldwide in

Oxford New York

Auckland Bangkok Buenos Aires Cape Town Chennai
Dar es Salaam Delhi Hong Kong Istanbul Karachi Kolkata
Kuala Lumpur Madrid Melbourne Mexico City Mumbai Nairobi
São Paulo Shanghai Taipei Tokyo Toronto

Oxford is a registered trade mark of Oxford University Press
in the UK and certain other countries

Published in the United States
by Oxford University Press Inc., New York

British Library Cataloguing in Publication Data
Data available

Library of Congress Cataloging-in-Publication Data
Data available

ISBN 0-19-816647-8

1 3 5 7 9 10 8 6 4 2

Typeset by Figaro, Launton, OX26 5DG
Music examples prepared by the author
Printed in Great Britain
on acid-free paper by
Biddles Ltd.,
Guildford & King's Lynn

Preface

I have built a House, where I intended but a Lodge: Yet with better
Success than a certain Nobleman, who, beginning with a Dog-kennil
never liv'd to finish the Palace he had contriv'd.

John Dryden, *Fables Ancient and Modern* (1700)

I wish I could point to some dramatic originating impulse for this book, some
humble equivalent of Newton's apple, Watt's kettle, or those 'barefooted fryars',
singing Vespers in the temple of Jupiter on the ruins of the Capitol, who started
Gibbon off on *The Decline and Fall of the Roman Empire*. As it is, all I can offer is a
question which was already troubling me as a music student in 1967, namely: why
does Johann Strauss sound so different from Beethoven? Or, more generally: why
does light or popular music sound so different from classical music, even when
based on the same patterns? The answer, which I suppose must have been dawning
on me by about 1970, was that the patterns are not really the same. I did not know
that the task of working out just how different they are would occupy me for the
next quarter of a century.

The first fruit of this labour, *Origins of the Popular Style* (hereinafter *Origins*),
was published in 1989. In it, I attempted to trace the patterns of twentieth-century
popular music to their sources. Inevitably, it was mostly concerned with North
America, but there was also a substantial section on the light music of nineteenth-
century Europe. This part of the book never quite satisfied me, and it is out of that
germ of dissatisfaction that the present volume has grown. At first, I fondly imagined that 20,000 words or so would be enough to plug the gap, but this modest
essay relentlessly expanded until it embraced, or at least touched on, almost the
entire body of European music from the fifteenth to the early twentieth century.

In going back to the European classics, I was reverting to my earliest intellectual
passion. Long before acquiring my first popular music scores, I had possessed a
small library of Bach, Beethoven, Mozart, and Brahms, and I can vividly recall the
embarrassment that the gaudy covers of the former caused among the sober greys
and buffs of the latter, like pornographic magazines in the vestry. Then, for reasons
mysterious even to myself, this initially mild interest in popular music grew into an

obsession. By the mid-1970s it was occupying me almost exclusively. For fifteen years I all but abandoned the classics, though with an inward promise to come back to them one day.

When I did so, some fifteen years ago, it was with the feelings of the anthropologist who, returning from a long stay in New Guinea, is astonished by the tribal customs of London, Paris, or New York. In the present book, Western classical music is approached rather in the spirit of the ethnomusicologist, or, better, the old-style 'comparative musicologist'. The 'roots' I have attempted to dig up are of two kinds: on the one hand, social and historical; on the other, abstract and theoretical—in the words of the *Oxford English Dictionary*, the 'bottom or real basis, the inner or essential part'. A project so wide-ranging inevitably raises problems of selection. One lot of critics will remark that 'this is really two books, if not three or four'. Another will complain that 'it is strange to see no mention of —'. Both will be right. Two topics in particular have been neglected: religious music, especially after 1600, and rhythm, which is entirely subordinate to melody and harmony.

A publisher's reader described an early, much shorter draft of this book as 'ambitious in the extreme'. He was wrong. The present volume is at least twice as ambitious—so much so as to encroach on the limits of the utmost possible erudition. This is no academic mock modesty. In these days of micro-specialities, when third- or fourth-rate composers are the subjects of doctoral theses (if not learned journals), a book such as this is bound to be scrutinized by readers who know far more about any individual detail than I do. But, as Bertrand Russell observed in the preface to his *History of Western Philosophy*: 'If there is any unity in the movement of history, if there is any intimate relation between what goes before and what comes later, it is necessary, for setting this forth, that earlier and later periods should be synthesized in a single mind.'

That must be my excuse too.

P.V.d.M.

Pietermaritzburg,
January 2003

Acknowledgements

As what the academic fraternity is pleased to call an 'amateur' scholar, I have contracted an especially large number of debts in writing this book. My thanks go to the following:

The Ernest Oppenheimer Memorial Trust, for financing a three-month stay at Wolfson College, Oxford in 1992 and a shorter trip to England four years later. Without the research undertaken on those two occasions, the factual support for my theories would be a great deal more rickety than it is.

The Natal Society Foundation Trust, for easing the final labours on this book with a generous grant.

Innumerable friends and acquaintances, for general encouragement and often also practical help. Most must remain nameless, but I should at least mention my colleagues at the Natal Society Library: Jane Bentley, Saragh McCrudden-Parfitt, Lois du Toit, and John Morrison, the last of whom gave expert advice on the delicate art of approaching official bodies.

Another colleague, Nomvula Kuzwayo, for transcribing, with her friend Ketsiwe Dlamini, the Swazi song quoted on page 40. Also Irina Guschina, for help with various bits of Russian, and Milada Pešek for translating the little Slovak song on page 34.

My friends in England: Rosemarie Finch, Nick Hollinghurst, Hubert and Shirley Elffers, and those fellow pioneers in the study of popular music, Wilfrid Mellers and Philip Tagg. All of them provided not only help and encouragement, but also accommodation. Also Tim Crawford, for lending me his copy of Joan Ambrosio Dalza's lute music, and the late Arthur Jacobs, for unfailing friendship and assistance.

Two American friends: Anatole Leikin, who provided invaluable information on octatonic scales, monotertial relationships, and other arcana of east European music, and Orly Krasner, whose letters have been a constant source of amusement and encouragement.

Finally, Bruce Phillips, head until 1998 of the Music Books Department at the Oxford University Press. At least for me, he was the ideal editor, endlessly patient and helpful far beyond the call of duty. In an increasingly philistine and impersonal world, his department remained a bastion of gentlemanly publishing. For that, he will always have my gratitude.

Contents

List of Figures

List of Tables

A Note on Terminology and Notation

A man coynes not a new word without some perill, and lesse fruit; for if it happen to be received, the praise is but moderate; if refus'd, the scorn is assur'd.

Ben Jonson, *Timber, or Discoveries Made upon Men and Matter*, 622

GENERAL VOCABULARY

New thought demands new words. Unavoidably—and I wish it could have been avoided—this book contains both many neologisms and many familiar terms employed in a special sense. All these are defined in the Glossary.

In addition to such technicalities, there are the problems faced by any cultural historian in designating historical periods, artistic genres, social or ethnic groups, and the like. At the cost of a certain clumsiness, I have generally preferred neutral indications of period to words like 'Renaissance', 'Baroque', or (especially) 'Romantic'.

Musical class distinctions have been an endless source of trouble, involving as they do such exasperating but indispensable words as 'folk', 'popular', and 'classical'. In particular, there seems to be no satisfactory term for music of—shall we say—a certain loftiness of brow. 'Art' or 'cultivated music' is about the best I could do.

In the absence of qualification, 'music' means European 'art' music, 'folk music' means 'European folk music', and so on. This is an entirely Eurocentric book. On the other hand, ethnic and geographical designations are generally to be understood in a broad sense. Unless the contrary is stated, 'German', for instance, includes 'Austrian'.

MUSICAL SYMBOLISM WITHIN THE TEXT

More important than any verbal novelties is the symbolic language used to describe musical patterns within the text. This may be either numerical or alphabetical.

Numerical symbolism

This is essentially the solmization familiar to many musical cultures, for example, Guido d'Arezzo's 'ut, re, mi . . .' (later 'do, re, mi . . .', or, anglicized, 'doh, ray, me . . .'), the Indian 'sa, ri, ga . . .', etc., but with syllables replaced by figures. Thus, 'do, re, mi . . .' becomes the Schenkerian $\hat{1}, \hat{2}, \hat{3}$ . . . or simply 1, 2, 3 . . . (as used e.g. by Deryck Cooke in *The Language of Music*), or, in the notation of this book, *1, 2, 3* . . . Here, as elsewhere, the italics indicate relative rather than absolute pitch.

In all such systems, a heptatonic mode is grouped round a single focus, whether this happens to be called 'ut', 'do', 'doh', '$\hat{1}$', '1', or '*1*'. This leaves two important types of melodic pattern unprovided for:

1. Those with more than one focus to the octave: the same cadence, for example, may occur on both tonic and dominant in the forms 'ray–doh' and 'lah–soh'.
2. Those with no focus at all.

In type (1), it is useful to have some way of indicating the replicated pattern without specifying its position within the mode. For this I use italicized lower-case roman numerals. Thus, ray–doh and lah–soh are both special cases of *ii–i*.

To indicate the harmony, I have retained the traditional capital roman numerals: I, the tonic triad, V, the dominant, etc. For further details, see 'Chord Symbols' below.

All numerical systems, whether roman or arabic, are modelled on the major scale, e.g. *iii* is always a major third above *i*. Chromatic inflections are shown by placing sharps, flats, or naturals after the numbers: IV♯, 6♭, *iii*♮. Superscript plus and minus signs indicate respectively the octaves above and below. Thus, *5–1* stands for the fall of a fifth, but *5–1*⁺ for the rise of a fourth; *1–6*, for the rise of a major sixth, *1–6*⁻ for the fall of a minor third.

Alphabetical notation

For type 2, where a focus is lacking (or we prefer to ignore it), Zoltán Kodály used what he called 'relative solmization'—really just the 'movable-doh' sol-fa familiar to English-speaking countries. (For a brief account, see Ernő Lendvai, *the Workshop of Bartók and Kodály*, 760–1.) A neater way (used e.g. by Vaughan Williams in recording the patterns of folk melody) is to use the letter names *a, b, c* . . .:

Relative solmization	Equivalent alphabetical symbol
la	a
ta	$b\flat$
ti	b
do	c
di	$c\sharp$
re	d
ma	$e\flat$
mi	e
fa	f
fi	$f\sharp$
so	g
si	$g\sharp$

These 'movable' letter names are to the 'fixed' type what 'movable-doh' sol-fa is to the 'fixed-doh' system of the Romance languages.

Broadly the same conventions apply to this alphabetical notation as to its numerical relatives. Accidentals and superscript pluses and minuses are used in the same way. Melodic patterns are printed in lower case, harmonic patterns in capitals: thus, c is a note, but C a chord. Italicization, as always, indicates relativity.

Apart from its general neatness, this alphabetical shorthand has several advantages over solmization. For anyone familiar with the English note names (or those of other Germanic languages), it is much easier to follow. It permits any conceivable chromatic inflection, not merely 'ta', 'di', 'ma', 'fi', and 'si'. It makes discussion of key relationships much easier: e.g. a modulation from A♭ minor to B minor (enharmonically equivalent to C♭ minor), instead of being 'from an initial minor key to the minor key a minor third higher', becomes simply 'from A minor to C minor'. It may be reflected in musical notation as follows:

For this last purpose (among others), the musical examples in this book have been so transposed as to tally with the descriptions in the text. This generally (though not quite invariably) means that they appear in the keys of C major, C minor, or A minor. This type of transposition, though likely to provoke resistance from some readers, is an old practice among ethnomusicologists (who, however, usually prefer G to C). In fact, it is not so much transposition as restatement of the music in a different and clearer form of notation, and probably the most powerful single aid to the understanding of melodic and harmonic progressions.

Chord symbols

1. Round brackets indicate optional features: e.g. C(m) means the chord of either C major or C minor, $1^{(+)}$ the tonic note in either the upper or lower octave.

2. Melodic and harmonic symbols may be combined: e.g. $3/V7$ indicates a dominant seventh chord with the third degree of the major scale in the top part—in other words, a 'dominant thirteenth'.

3. Square brackets indicate that a progression is to be treated as a unit. Thus, $6–5/$I means a progression from the note 6 (in any or no harmonization) to the chord $5/$I; but $[6–5]/$I means that the whole $6–5$ progression is to take place over the chord I.

Cadences

An arrow indicates a cadence, harmonic or melodic, e.g. V$\rightarrow$$I$ or $2$$\rightarrow$$1$.

Rhythm

1. Progressions may be measured or unmeasured. In measured progressions, each rhythmic unit is of equal length and stands alone. Here, dashes connect notes or chords belonging to the same unit: e.g. in I IV I–V I the I–V occupies the same time (probably a bar or two) as each of the other three chords. In unmeasured progressions, dashes connect *all* the notes or chords, e.g. *a–g–e*, I–IV–V.

2. A break within a progression may be indicated by a single raised dot, or, if more pronounced, by two vertically aligned dots: e.g. I · I : IV I.

A Note on the Musical Examples

The musical examples are of two types: (1) quotations of actual music, and (2) schematic 'diagrams' of progressions, etc.

MUSICAL QUOTATIONS

Where these have been transposed, the interval is given at the end of the caption, e. g. 'up a tone' means that the example is a tone higher than the original. In addition, note the following:

1. Dates are provided for most quotations. I must disclaim any deep research for these, most of which have simply been drawn from the handiest source; in any case, it is often impossible to ascertain the exact year of composition. When a period covers more than one year (e.g. 1856–8), this usually means that the work was composed at some time during that period, rather than that it occupied the whole of it. In dubious cases I have preferred later dates, on the grounds that the work must at least have been in existence by then.

2. Bar numbers are included in most headings, e.g. 'Schoenberg, *Verklärte Nacht*, bars 231–5'. These are not to be confused with the numbers printed below most of the staves. It is the latter that are referred to in the text, e.g. 'in bars 3–5 of Ex. . . .'.

3. Repeat marks with four instead of two dots indicate indefinite repetition.

4. A few liberties have been taken with the rhythmic notation, especially the beaming together of separate notes in vocal music. I have, however, been careful to avoid anything that would make a difference in performance.

5. Full-sized notes are to be taken literally. Small notes serve to sketch in the harmony, or, in one or two examples, to set off melodic figures that rise above the Melody proper.

6. Most octave doublings have been omitted.

7. So have some of the more otiose marks of expression.

8. In marks of expression, etc., square brackets indicate editorial additions,

usually transferred from earlier in the movement; e.g. 'Andante [più mosso]' means that the original direction 'Andante' has been followed at some point by a 'più mosso'. Round brackets, as in 'Allegretto grazioso (Quasi Andantino)' from the second movement of Brahms's Second Symphony, are original.

9. In tempo directions, words of songs, etc., I have tried to keep to the original spelling and punctuation. Hence some inconsistencies, especially in German.

10. More important omissions (e.g. of words or orchestral parts) have been duly noted.

11. Octave signs above or below the stave apply only to the melodic lines closest to them. Transpositions affecting all the notes on the stave are indicated by clef.

12. The principles governing the transcription of lute tablature are set out in the note on Ex. 6.7 in the List of Musical Examples.

SCHEMATIC EXAMPLES

1. Stemless black blobs indicate melody; semibreves ('whole notes'), harmonic chords; breves ('double notes'), keynotes or drones.

2. Normal-sized black blobs predominate over smaller ones.

3. Any chord or key remains in force until cancelled by a new chord or key.

In general, I have aimed to present these examples as concisely as possible. For this purpose 'guitar notation' (that is, on one stave with the notes an octave higher than usual) has proved to be invaluable. I should, however, add that the presentation of an example—whether on one, two, or even more staves—is purely a matter of convenience, and has nothing to do with its importance.

Abbreviations

FVB	*Fitzwilliam Virginal Book*
New Grove	*The New Grove Dictionary of Music and Musicians*, ed. Stanley Sadie (London: Macmillan, 1980)
New Grove II	*The New Grove Dictionary of Music and Musicians*, 2nd edn., ed. Stanley Sadie and John Tyrrell (London: Macmillan, 2001)
NOHM	*The New Oxford History of Music*. i: *Ancient and Oriental Music*, ed. Egon Wellesz (London: Oxford University Press, 1957); ii: *Early Medieval Music up to 1300*, ed. Dom Anselm Hughes, rev. edn. (London: Oxford University Press, 1955); iii: *Ars Nova and the Renaissance, 1300–1540*, ed. Dom Anselm Hughes and Gerald Abraham (London: Oxford University Press, 1960); x: *The Modern Age, 1890–1960*, ed. Martin Cooper (London: Oxford University Press, 1974)
OED	*The Oxford English Dictionary*, 2nd edn., ed. J. A. Simpson and E. S. C. Weiner (Oxford: Clarendon Press, 1989)

Introduction

The word 'roots', as used in the title of this book, is trite, shopworn, and, worst of all, patronizing. But it does at least have the merit of reminding us that cultural traditions are organic growths. Like plants, they need nourishment from below, and without that nourishment they die.

A worthy truism, one might think. Yet it is astonishing how little use conventional musicology has for roots. Even today, the history of Western classical music is largely a list of famous names. It is true that the list has grown longer. A century ago, almost the only generally recognized influences on the young Beethoven were Haydn and Mozart. Nowadays they have been joined by C. P. E. Bach, J. C. Bach, Baillot, Berton, Catel, Cherubini, Clementi, Dussek, Förster, Gluck, Gossec, Grétry, Kreutzer, Méhul, Viotti, and no doubt many others who have eluded me. This is an improvement, but still a list of names. The great anonymous either receive no mention at all, or merely a passing comment.

To be sure, critics often remark on the popular element in classical music. Here, for instance, is Martin Cooper on Beethoven:

Nobody ... has been able to deny the 'Joy' theme [in the finale of the Ninth Symphony] ... a popular character that no subsequent composer has ever quite achieved . . . We may explain this in a general sense by the fact that Beethoven himself remained, certainly physically and in many ways emotionally, an unsophisticated man of the people who knew by instinct the stimulus to which simple listeners respond.[1]

And here is Hans Gál on Schubert: 'anyone who is familiar with this down-to-earth yet flexible idiom [Viennese German] will detect it, translated into musical terms, in his melody, and not just in dance tunes, whose popular background is obvious, but sometimes in his most sublime utterances'.[2] And Jeremy Siepmann on Chopin: 'The near-universal appeal of his music, to listeners ranging from the novice to the near-omniscient, derives in part from a unique combination of sophistication and a deep-rooted, wholly uncondescending sense of the popular.'[3]

[1] *Beethoven: The Last Decade, 1817–1827*, 327.
[2] *Franz Schubert and the Essence of Melody*, 25.   [3] *Chopin*, 172.

And Cooper, again, on Bizet's 'instinct, which can only be called classical, for the effortless conversion of raw vulgarities into the material for a serious work of art'.[4]

This is all very well, but where did the popular element come from? What were its distinguishing features? What were the mechanics of the process of 'conversion'? Such questions are hardly considered, let alone answered. On points such as these, even studies of overtly nationalistic composers like Grieg, Musorgsky, or Falla seldom get further than generalities.

One is bound to ask why. The usual and most honourable explanation is ignorance. To go further would be to trespass on the territory of the ethnomusicologists, who themselves pay little attention to classical music. At least in the English- and German-speaking worlds, the two disciplines have always been separate, springing from different nineteenth-century origins, practised by different groups, and espousing different ideals. Whereas ethnomusicology aspires to be a science, 'classical' musicology often seems more like a form of religious devotion:

> it is idle to say that these men [Homer, Dante, Shakespeare, Raphael, Dürer, and Beethoven] undervalued the religion in which they held the priesthood. Only they knew that its Theology was on broad, simple lines, that its gospel consisted of truths which could find a ready echo in the heart of the world; that its temple was one in which the humblest worshipper could find his appointed place.[5]

No one would now write like that, but even today musicology retains a devotional aura. Criticism and analysis are forms of homage; the works of the great masters are sacred texts, approached in a spirit of exegetical piety; the masters themselves transcend the merely human. At the very least, musicologists see themselves as concerned with only the *best* music. As one of them has put it: 'There are, at bottom, just two tests for the worthiness of a musicological undertaking: (1) that it be concerned with first-class music; and (2) that it be concerned with a first-class problem.'[6]

A first-class problem, yes. But why only first-class music? Is it not possible that second-class, mediocre, or downright bad music may be equally worthy of the scholar's attention? Is it not even possible that, without a knowledge of the worse, one can never fully understand the better? Homage-musicology inevitably denies, or at least plays down, the communal nature of art. Music demands the cooperation of whole classes of people: composers, performers, instrument makers, teachers, administrators, publishers, and many more, none of whom could work effectively without the support of their own sustaining tradition. That of the composer is distinguished both in being unusually creative and (by a familiar paradox) unusu-

[4] 'Stage Works: 1890–1918', 154.

[5] Sir Henry Hadow, *Studies in Modern Music, Second Series* (1895), 7.

[6] Kenneth J. Levy, in the Foreword to Oliver Strunk, *Music in the Byzantine World*; quoted by Joseph Kerman in *Musicology*, 45.

ally destructive. At least since the days of the troubadours, Western society has expected its composers to be original; but even without this inducement there is a seemingly inexorable tendency for musical forms to become bigger, subtler, more elaborate. Obviously, there are limits to this process. Every refinement, every complexity, every increase in size places a strain on the original form, till progress can go no further.

What then happens has been well described by the French phrase *reculer pour mieux sauter*, 'drawing back the better to leap': in essence, a return to an earlier—often very much earlier—stage of evolution, in order to follow a new line of development. This process is not confined to music, or even to the arts. Indeed, some people (notably Arthur Koestler, who was particularly fond of the phrase)[7] believe it to be a feature of all evolution. It does, however, seem to be particularly characteristic of music. The Renaissance, Baroque, Classical, and Romantic movements all began with a reaction towards simplicity.

Of course, it would be wrong to see Western music as purely a matter of boom and bust. Music renews itself by small retreats as well as large. Even as a form develops, new complexities will be compensated for by new simplicities. The latter are not always of popular origin; nor, for that matter, does popular origin necessarily imply simplicity. Still, the trend is in that direction; and this, too, seems to be especially characteristic of music. With the exception of dancing, it is the most instinctive of the arts. But it is also the most abstract, and perhaps it is this unique combination that makes it both unusually receptive to popular influences and unusually dependent on them.

The result may be an entire tune, a drone, an ostinato, a chord, mode, or scale—in fact any conceivable musical pattern. But, whatever it is, there is a good chance that classical theory will fail to account for it. And this brings us to the third reason for the scholarly reluctance to examine popular roots. To do so is to enter a terrifying theoretical wilderness where the old rules no longer apply. New, wider-ranging rules are needed. If the analysis of music aims to be a science—and if not, what is its point?—it must 'search for laws with an unlimited realm of validity'.[8]

Now, there is melody without harmony, but there is no such thing as harmony without melody. The inescapable conclusion is that the laws of harmony must be sought in melody. But how is this to be done? At least since the days of William of Occam, it has been a maxim that the complex must be explained in terms of the simple. The first step, then, is to examine the simplest forms of melody. The next is to identify the processes by which these are built into more complex melody. Only then can we go on to harmony.

---

[7] See e.g. 'Draw Back to Leap', in *The Ghost in the Machine*, ch. 12.

[8] Karl Popper, *The Poverty of Historicism*, 103.

Fortunately there is a wealth of material to explore: the chants of small children; the songs and dance tunes of primitive peoples, as collected and analysed by generations of musicologists; and, in Western Europe, written records of popular music going back almost a millennium. For the purposes of evolutionary musicology, this is more than enough.

At the same time, a serious search for 'laws with an unlimited realm of validity' compels us to go beyond music itself, to the general theories of language and complex systems; and here, too, we are fortunate enough to have a mass of work to draw on.

In all this the emphasis must be on the abstract rather than the personal. As far as this book is concerned, the function of the composer, no matter how eminent, is to develop and transmit musical patterns. Nothing could be further from my intention than to 'debunk' the great masters. On the contrary, having spent well over a decade in the intensive study of their works, I am more than ever impressed by their greatness. But I have come to the conclusion that their originality has been misunderstood. Their task was not to invent patterns, but to elaborate and combine them; above all, to reconcile the directness of popular music with the sophistication of high art.

The chapters that follow fall into three broad sections. Part One, 'The Melodic Foundations', deals with the psychological basis, first of music in general and then of melody and harmony in particular. Then follows a more or less chronological history of popular influences on Western music from the late Middle Ages to the early twentieth century. This falls into two broad phases: Part Two, 'The Harmonic Revolution', which traces the development of classical tonality, and Part Three, 'The Melodic Counter-Revolution', which goes on to show how this same tonality was modified and subverted from the late eighteenth century on.

PART ONE

The Melodic Foundations

1 The Subtle Mathematics of Music

Life is not an illogicality; yet it is a trap for logicians. It looks just a little more mathematical and regular than it is; its exactitude is obvious, but its inexactitude is hidden; its wildness lies in wait

G. K. Chesterton[1]

At an open-air service on the island of Skye, Ralph Vaughan Williams once heard a sermon in Gaelic, a language he did not understand. As he later explained, this ignorance enabled him to devote all his attention to the tones of the preacher's voice: 'The fact that he was out of doors forced him to speak loud, and that, coupled with the emotional excitement which inspired his words, caused him gradually to leave off speaking and actually, unconsciously of course, to sing.'[2] At first the preacher was content with a monotone, but as his excitement grew he gradually developed certain clearly defined melodic formulas, which Vaughan Williams quotes in musical notation as e–a–b–a, a–b–c^+–b–a, and a–b–a–g–a.[3]

He was probably mistaken in assuming that this gradual heightening of speech into song was unconscious, but perfectly justified in drawing a connection between musical pattern and emotional emphasis. Not only preachers and orators, but all human beings incline towards song when excited. Similar forms of oratory might have been observed in Africa, in the southern United States, and in many other parts of the world. What is much more remarkable, these speech tunes bear a strong family likeness to one another, regardless of language or culture. Again and again we find the same limited set of rhythms and intervals, expressible in the same simple mathematical ratios.

This proves the closeness of speech to song and the impossibility of drawing a clear distinction between the two. It proves, too, the fundamental importance

[1] 'The Paradoxes of Christianity' (third sentence), in *Orthodoxy*.

[2] *The Making of Music*, ch. 2, 'What is Music?' (in *National Music and Other Essays*), 207.

[3] In another passage, evidently referring to the same incident, Vaughan Williams gives the notes as being 'a, b, a, g, a, with an occasional drop down to e'. See *National Music and Other Essays*, ch. 2, 'Some Tentative Ideas on the Origins of Music', 17.

of certain melodic and rhythmic patterns, and the mathematical nature of these patterns. Finally—and surprisingly—it proves that music is emotional not *in spite of*, but *because of*, its mathematical nature. It is a language for communicating emotion, largely, though far from entirely, by means of mathematics. As Leibniz observed, it is a form of subconscious computation.[4] And if, as most linguists now believe, verbal language has a 'universal grammar' instinctively understood by every infant, the same must surely be true of music. There is, however, one important respect in which the language of music differs from that of words: its 'vocabulary' is self-explanatory. No one ever had to look up the meaning of a cadence in a dictionary.

THE EVOLUTION OF SYMMETRY

How did human beings develop the capacity to communicate in this astonishing way? Unfortunately, our remote ancestors are beyond direct observation. But by putting together what we know of rudimentary music or near-music, as performed by human infants, primitive peoples, monkeys, and apes, we can get a fair idea of what happened. Here an important study is *The Dancing Chimpanzee* by Leonard Williams, who, as both a musician and an expert on animal behaviour, is in a good position to evaluate the musical abilities of our ape-like ancestors.

His verdict is unequivocal. Chimpanzees do *not* dance. Nor do they, or other apes or monkeys, sing, or drum in any musical sense. On a purely emotional level, such behaviour may be the ancestor of true music or dance, but it lacks an essential intellectual component. What is absent is any feeling for what scientists call 'symmetry': that property, 'by virtue of which something is effectively unchanged by a particular operation'.[5] In the everyday sense of the word, that operation takes place around a central axis. Thus, a building is 'symmetrical' if we can mentally draw a line down the middle, take one of the halves, reverse it, and fit it precisely over the other half. But in the broader scientific sense, this reversal is optional. An ornamental pattern of roses or flying ducks is equally symmetrical, in that any given rose or duck will fit perfectly over any of its fellows.

Moreover, symmetry exists in time as well as space. A rock (or any other object) exhibits temporal symmetry if it remains precisely the same on Tuesday as it had been on Monday. The most symmetrical objects and processes are also the simplest: a straight line or circle; a plane or sphere; an evenly sustained note; a regular

---

[4] His precise words, in a letter to Christoph Goldbach (1712), are: 'musica est exercitium arithmeticae occultum nescientis se numerare animi' ('music is a secret exercise of the mind in which it computes without being aware of doing so'). See Rudolph Haase, 'Leibniz, Gottfried Wilhelm', *New Grove II*, xiv. 500.

[5] *OED* xvii. 456, article on 'symmetry', definition 3.b.(*a*).

pulse. In every case, we can mentally detach any part of the whole, put it down anywhere else, and get a perfect fit.[6]

In this special sense, a thing must be symmetrical to exhibit exact proportions. This is what enables us to say that two sides of a square are the same length, for instance, or that one note goes on for twice as long as another. Where the sense of symmetry is lacking—as, for instance, in comparing the roughness of different fabrics—we can make no such precise comparison. And here we may notice how rare this ability is. Symmetry can be perceived by sight, by hearing, and by the sense of time—and that is all. At least in human beings, it is inaccessible to the more ancient senses of touch, taste, and smell. Even our eyes and ears can detect it only in certain circumstances: in length, breadth, and depth, but not in area or colour; in pitch, but not in volume or timbre. In the entire sensory world, it occurs in only three properties: spatial dimension, melodic pitch, and rhythm. The first of these belongs to the eye, the second to the ear, and the third again mainly to the ear. Other senses may perceive rhythm—in the silent beating of a bird's wings, in a regular stroking of the skin—but never with the same mathematical precision.

Moreover, the symmetry of space is much simpler than the symmetry of sound. Any 'subconscious computations' we make while contemplating classical architecture, or abstract decorative design, are vague and rudimentary indeed compared with those of music, the symmetrical art *par excellence*. We may guess that it was the gradually developing sense of symmetry that transformed the unmelodic cries and arrhythmic movements of our remote ancestors into music and dance. Most likely the perception of symmetry in all the senses arrived as part of a single evolutionary package, together with the ability to reason. At all events, the gradual transition from the non-musical to the musical did not deprive these instinctive actions of their emotional content, but rather gave to that content a partially mathematical expression. A striking example, cited by Williams, is the development of cries similar to those of the woolly monkey into the 'tumbling strains' of certain primitive peoples.[7] The descending contour, wide range (up to two octaves, in the case of the monkey), and background of strong emotion are all the same. But, even at its wildest, the human cry has something that its simian equivalent lacks: it is symmetrical, and therefore musical.

And, if the emotion is expressed through mathematics, it is equally true that the mathematics is controlled by emotion. The simplest patterns of all, those of musical rhythm, are interpreted against the background of the beat, that regular, moderate pulse that first began to be impressed on the human brain when our remote ancestors learnt to walk on their hind legs. (At least, that is the most likely explanation.

---

[6] For a wide-ranging and readable discussion of symmetry in nature, see Ian Stewart and Martin Golubitsky, *Fearful Symmetry*.

[7] Quoted in musical notation in *The Dancing Chimpanzee*, 77.

The fashionable theory that it derives *principally* from the heartbeat is much less plausible.) This beat may be speeded up or slowed down; it may be subdivided, multiplied, syncopated. But through all these changes it remains a norm. We carry in our heads both a 'tempo giusto' (estimated by Curt Sachs at between 76 and 80 pulses a minute)[8] and what might be called a 'ritmo giusto' of regularly alternating strong and weak beats. All else is felt to be a transformation of this.

In the same way, the pitch ratios of melody are perceived with a uniquely human bias. Just as our bipedal gait is the source of all rhythm, so the arbiter of all melodic propriety is the human voice. Like the woolly monkey, we find it more natural to fall than rise in singing. We also prefer fairly narrow intervals, ranging from the major second to the perfect fourth. Intervals outside this range, while quite possible, are felt to be just a trifle abnormal, so that the octave and fifth are in some ways less fundamental to human melody than the acoustically more complex major or minor third.

Harmony, too, has its norms, derived from the bottom five notes of the harmonic series, which together make up the major triad. Chords within this range are felt to be euphonious; those outside (notwithstanding a barrage of propaganda to the contrary), increasingly discordant.

SHAPES, PATTERNS, AND FIGURES

The ratios of music, though mathematical, are also subjective. Only intermittently do they exist in nature. But that does not bother us in the least. We are content to apply to the approximations actually heard a set of ideal ratios carried in our heads. Rhythms in the ratio of $2.017 : 1.103 : 0.972$, let us say, are construed as being 're-ally' ♩ ♪♪; vibrations in the ratio of $2 : 3.14$ as 'really' a perfect fifth.

What are we to call such an ideal pattern? It has something in common with Kant's 'schema', intimidatingly defined by the *Oxford English Dictionary* as 'any one of certain forms or rules of the "productive imagination" through which the understanding is able to apply its "categories" to the manifold of sense-perception in the process of realizing knowledge or experience'.[9] But there is an important difference. Kant believed that true reality—'the thing in itself'—is unknowable; all we have to go on is the schema. In music, we are aware of both 'the sound in itself' *and* the schema. In fact, much of our enjoyment derives from comparing the two—in noticing, for instance, how the performer's subtle rubato diverges from metronomic regularity. In *Origins*, I used the term 'matrix' for the musical schema,

---

[8] See *Rhythm and Tempo*, 32.   [9] *OED* xiv. 615, article on 'schema', definition 1.a.

not without misgivings that have since grown steadily worse. For the present volume, I decided on the simple term 'pattern'.

Such patterns reside in the head of the listener. They should be distinguished both from what I call 'figures'—what we actually hear—and also from mere 'shapes', which lack their intellectual and emotional significance. Two notes a perfect fifth apart, for instance, make up a shape; but once we begin to think of the lower as a tonic and the upper as a dominant (though probably without being aware of those terms), they turn into a pattern. No clear line separates shapes from patterns. In the course of musical evolution, shapes are constantly combining into patterns, and patterns dissolving into shapes.

Nevertheless, the distinction between the two is crucial, and its neglect leads to some dangerous fallacies. The publisher Ernst Roth tells us how, among Schoenberg's early followers, the theorist Erwin Stein held the position of 'official panegyrist and publicist'. 'His 1924 article on "New Formal Principles" had among the initiates almost the same standing as Albert Einstein's first few pages about relativity in physics.'[10] Here is an extract from that article, on the vast possibilities of atonal harmony:

Whereas the old harmony teaching knew only a few dozen chords which, transposed on to the various degrees of the scale, amount to a mere few hundred, every possible combination of the twelve tones is possible. Hence we dispose of 55 different three-part chords, 165 four-part, 330 five-part, 462 six- and seven-part, 330 eight-part, 165 nine-part, 55 ten-part, 11 eleven-part and 1 twelve-part—altogether over 2,000 chords, and 4,000 when transposed on to other degrees of the semitonic scale.[11]

Alas! The few dozen old chords are patterns, but the thousands of new ones are only shapes.

MUSICAL HIERARCHIES

To observe pattern recognition at its most basic, one must reduce music to the regular, unaccented, toneless pulse of a ticking clock—supposing, that is, one manages to find a clock that still ticks. As Percy Scholes pointed out long ago:

It appears that the human ear demands of music the perceptible presence of a unit of time—the feeling of a metronome audibly or inaudibly ticking in the background . . . And, the ticks being felt, it is a further necessity that they shall be grouped into twos or threes. Indeed, the mind cannot accept regularly recurring sounds without supplying them with

[10] *The Business of Music*, 153.

[11] First published as 'Neue Formprinzipien' in the avant-garde magazine *Anbruch*. Quoted in this translation by Cecil Gray in *Predicaments*, 171.

some grouping, if they have not already got it: in listening to a clock ticking the mind hears either *tick*-tack or *tick*-tack-tack; this is so definite that it is hard to believe that the ticking is really quite accentless, yet that this effect is purely subjective is seen in the fact that a very slight conscious effort turns the effect from the one grouping to the other and then back again.[12]

This simple observation brings out several important points. The first is that, simple as this bare ticking may seem, its musical potential is far greater than that of a sustained note. Such a note would be purely symmetrical, in the sense explained above. The alternation between tick and intervening silence introduces an element of asymmetry into the scheme that makes it much more interesting. As at every other level of musical complexity, interest and beauty are generated, not by symmetry or asymmetry alone, but by a conflict between the two.

On this simple sound-shape, as Scholes points out, the ear superimposes a purely subjective asymmetry of its own: '*tick*' (silence) 'tack' (silence) '*tick*' (silence) 'tack' (silence) . . . Notice that the accented *tick* comes first. One *could* switch the order round to 'tick *tack* tick *tack* . . .', but there would be something forced in this. Once again, the '*tick* tack' pattern is rooted in human psychology rather than mathematical abstraction. The accent comes first because effort naturally precedes relaxation. It is for essentially the same reason that the cries of the woolly monkey (and the tunes of primitive peoples) proceed from high to low.

This still leaves the question of why we feel impelled to impose the '*tick* tack' pattern at all. The answer lies in the instinctive human need for perceptual hierarchy. Like symmetry, this is confined to the senses of sight and hearing, but with a difference. Broadly speaking, visual hierarchies already exist in nature—in trees, clouds, rivers, rocks, and a thousand other natural features—and are merely discerned by the eye. Aural hierarchies are *read into* sounds by the ear.

So, as we read those accents into the even pulses of the clock, we are arranging them in a two-level hierarchy, with the accented '*ticks*' on top (as it were) and the unaccented 'tacks' at the bottom. This separation into closely connected 'levels' is what distinguishes the true hierarchy from the simple combination, such as is perceptible to the other senses. On entering a church, we may be conscious of the odours of stone, wood, incense, leather, and paper, but this ecclesiastical medley is not a hierarchy. The scent of wood, for instance, may be fainter than that of stone, but lacks the essential hierarchic property of being *part of* it. The test is always: what can be removed from what? The part can be removed from the whole, but the whole cannot be removed from the part. You can prune a twig from a branch, but not a branch from a twig. This proves both that they are hierarchically related, and that the branch is on a higher level than the twig.

[12] *The Oxford Companion to Music*, 'Rhythm: 3. Rhythm as "Grouping" ', 878.

Applying the same test to the ticking of the clock, we find that we can mentally suppress the unaccented 'tacks', but not the accented '*ticks*'. The former is of course a fundamental rhythmic procedure, the equivalent of replacing | ♩♩ | with | ♩ |. The attempt to do the opposite—to suppress the upper level of the rhythmic hierarchy—has interesting consequences, to which we shall return. For the moment, let us observe that there is no need to limit ourselves to two levels. If we silence or ignore the 'tacks', the remaining '*ticks*' will again group themselves into twos, and this process can then be repeated, if not *ad infinitum*, at least to the point where successive pulses are too far apart to be grouped at all, while in the opposite direction pulses can be subdivided to the point where they merge into a drum roll. Experiment with a metronome shows that the grouping instinct operates comfortably at the rate of between 40 and 400 pulses per minute, becoming gradually stronger as the tempo increases. At a rate of about 320 pulses per minute, it is quite possible to hear the four hierarchic levels depicted in Fig. 1.1.

FIG. 1.1. Four levels of rhythmical pulses

Self-similarity

This rhythmic hierarchy has an important and interesting property: it is 'self-similar'. Indeed, a simpler case of self-similarity could hardly be conceived. Self-similarity is usually defined as the similarity of the part to whole, but, as we have just seen, there is not always a clear-cut 'whole'. Hierarchic systems may be open at the top, at the bottom, or (as here) at both ends. A more satisfactory definition might therefore be 'similarity of form or function across hierarchic level'. In this case, every level has exactly the same form—a series of evenly spaced pulses—but on a different scale.

As a feature of hierarchic systems, self-similarity is perceptible only to the senses of hearing and sight. In this it resembles symmetry, though it is important to understand that symmetry is not essential to it. Countless natural examples of self-similarity—mountains, coastlines, ferns, leafless trees, the branching networks of the vascular or nervous systems—are not symmetrical, or at least not in this strict sense (the term 'average symmetry' is sometimes used). The combination of self-similarity with symmetry is found predominantly, perhaps even exclusively, in creations of the human mind; and even there its scope is severely limited, since it depends on a delicate combination of simplicity and sophistication.

For it is precisely the simplest patterns that are most easily repeated across hierarchic levels. Consider again that ticking clock. As Scholes remarks, it is not necessary to group the ticks in twos. Threes will do just as well, but in that case our ability to pile up self-similar levels is greatly restricted. In practice two is the limit, as in 9/8 time, with three—a hypothetical 27/8 time—just conceivable as a *tour de force*.[13] More irregular groupings, such as the 5/8 or 7/8 metres that occur quite naturally in many musical cultures, are even more restricted, being confined to a single level. There is no such thing as 25/8 or 49/8 time.

In contrast, the self-similar grouping of duple pulses can multiply to an astonishing degree. They attained probably their greatest heights in the early eighteenth century, notably in the works of J. S. Bach. The Allemande from the 'English' Suite No. 1 in A, for instance, consists, without repeats, of thirty-two common-time bars of evenly flowing semiquavers, sometimes subdivided into demisemiquavers (or thirty-second notes, for the benefit of American readers). This makes a staggering total of ten levels, or eleven if one observes the repeats.

MUSIC AS ORGANISM

A page or two back we encountered the question of what would happen if one suppressed the strong '*ticks*' rather than the weak 'tacks'. This is not something that can easily be done with an actual clock, so let us imagine, rather, that the ticks are produced by two metronomes acting in alternation: the 'tick' and 'tack' metronomes, as we may call them. The 'tick' metronome is fitted with a volume control, so adjusted that its 'ticks' at first match the 'tacks' in loudness. Now let us gradually turn down the volume. As it sinks, a new pattern challenges our preconceived one. The 'tacks' at first strike us as off-beat sforzandos, but later, as the 'ticks' recede into inaudibility, as main beats. In other words, the 'tacks' have turned into 'ticks'. A hierarchic level has successfully rebelled against its immediate superior.

This may seem a fancifully metaphorical way of putting it. After all, these sounds are not alive. No—but we human listeners are, and we are inveterate personifiers. In placing the accent at the start of the group—'*tick* tack' instead of 'tack *tick*'—we are, in effect, turning the pulses into tiny organisms, which must relax after effort. And if we can breathe life into these irreducibly primitive patterns, could we not do the same for more complex ones? Can chords, modes, or keys behave as if alive?

On this question, musical theorists have long been sharply divided. One school

[13] For an example of '27/8' time (written as 9/16) see the last movement of Beethoven's Piano Sonata in C minor, Op. 111, variation 4. Notice that he is careful to build up this complex rhythm incrementally, first dividing the pulses into 3s, then 9s, and finally 27s.

of thought will have none of this cloudy anthropomorphism, preferring to draw its metaphors from the hard, practical world of engineering: 'pivot chord', 'bridge passage', 'harmonic foundation', 'melodic superstructure', 'rhythmic framework', and the like. But another school, particularly strong in Germany about a century ago, regards the biological view as almost self-evident. Thus, we find Schoenberg observing that

Every chord . . . that is set beside the principal tone has at least as much tendency to lead away from it as to return to it. And if life, if a work of art is to emerge, then we must engage in this movement-generating conflict. The tonality must be placed in danger of losing its sovereignty; the appetites for independence and the tendencies toward mutiny must be given opportunity to activate themselves . . .[14]

And in much the same way, Schenker

continually admonishes us to see tones as creatures. 'We should learn to assume in them biological urges as they characterize living beings.' Each tone, he argues, has its own 'egotism' and, as the bearer of its generations, strives to exert its will as the tonic, as the strongest scale step, by struggling 'to gain the upper hand' [*Lebenskräfte reichen*] in its relationships with others.[15]

These notions, so fantastic-seeming to those used to the engineering model of musical analysis, belong to the venerable German tradition of *Naturphilosophie*. Beginning in the late eighteenth century as a reaction against the mechanistic universe of Newton and Descartes,[16] this was from the first the antithesis of the conventionally scientific, concerned as it was with wholes rather than parts, becoming rather than being, qualities rather than quantities. Where the Newtonian tradition had treated living creatures as machines, the *Naturphilosophen* were inclined to treat the inanimate world as alive.

In such an attitude the dangers of pantheistic mumbo-jumbo are all too evident. Nature philosophy has had a bad press, deservedly on the whole. Yet its ideas have never ceased to appeal to a long line of dreamers, misfits, cranks, and occasionally geniuses. Among the works in which something of its spirit lives on are D'Arcy Thompson's *On Growth and Form* (1917), Smuts's *Holism and Evolution* (1926), Koestler's *The Act of Creation* (1964), and Mandelbrot's *The Fractal Geometry of Nature* (1983). Often under heavy disguise, *naturphilosophische* ideas persisted through the holism of the 1920s; the Gestalt psychology of the 1930s and 1940s;

---

[14] *Theory of Harmony*, 151.

[15] Eugene Narmour, *Beyond Schenkerism*, 35. This passage is accompanied by footnote references to Schenker's *Harmony*, 6, 30, 29, 256, and 84.

[16] The seminal works were Goethe's *Versuch die Metamorphose der Pflanzen zu erklären* (*Attempt to Explain the Metamorphosis of Plants*, 1790) and Schelling's *Ideen zu einer Philosophie der Natur* (*Ideas on a Philosophy of Nature*, 1797). It was the latter who introduced the term *Naturphilosophie*.

the general systems theory of the 1950s and 1960s; and, most vigorously of all, the chaos theory of the 1970s and 1980s and the complexity theory of the 1990s.[17] Subjected to scientific discipline, the intuitions of the nature philosophers have made important (if seldom acknowledged) contributions to many branches of learning, including, as we have seen, musicology. The present study owes much to them, in both their recent and earlier guises.

I must acknowledge a special debt to Koestler. Unusually for a central European Jewish intellectual, he seems not to have been particularly musical, so it is ironic that, of all the arts, music is probably the one that most fully bears out his ideas. And, quite apart from this, his now almost forgotten non-fiction works are still good reading. Time and again, one comes upon ideas that have since become fashionable. Independently of Thomas Kuhn, he developed a theory of 'paradigm shifts';[18] and, long before Richard Dawkins, a theory of 'memes':

New ideas are thrown up spontaneously like mutations; the vast majority of them are use-less crank theories, the equivalent of biological freaks without survival-value. There is a constant struggle for survival between competing theories in every branch of the history of thought. The process of 'natural selection', too, has its equivalent in mental evolution: among the multitude of new concepts which emerge only those survive which are well adapted to the period's intellectual *milieu*.[19]

Since the present volume is a study of musical 'memes', it is only right that I should quote this passage, written almost two decades before Dawkins coined the term.[20]

Although Koestler did occasionally mention the *Naturphilosophen*, he seems to have been unaware (or unwilling to acknowledge) how much he owed to them. In particular, he was preoccupied throughout his life by the nature of hierarchies, and more generally by the relation of parts to wholes. One of his insights was that most hierarchies have no natural top or bottom. In such cases, there is no definite whole, and therefore no clear-cut relation between the whole and its part. To resolve this difficulty, he invented the word 'holon' for a hierarchic component.[21]

---

[17] Eric Hobsbawm points out the links between 'chaos' theory and nature philosophy in *Age of Extremes*, 541–2 n. For a brief account of nature philosophy itself, see the same author's *The Age of Revolution*, 355–7.

[18] The Kuhnian 'paradigm', for those not yet acquainted with it, is briefly described in the next chapter.

[19] *The Sleepwalkers* (1959), 'Epilogue: 1. The Pitfalls of Mental Evolution', 525.

[20] According to Edward O. Wilson, writing in 1998, 'The notion of a culture unit . . . has been around for over thirty years, and has been dubbed by different authors variously as mnemotype, idea, idene, meme, sociogene, concept, culturgen, and culture type. The one label that has caught on the most, and for which I now vote to be winner, is meme, introduced by Richard Dawkins in his influential work *The Selfish Gene* in 1976' (*Consilience*, 149). If Wilson's chronology is correct, Koestler must have been among the first to arrive at this idea (or meme?).

[21] This word, which probably owes something to Smuts's 'holism', was introduced in *The Ghost in the Machine* (1967): 'It seems preferable to coin a new term to designate these nodes on the hierarchic tree

Though this term has yet to make it into the *Oxford English Dictionary*, it has the great merit of forcing us to recognize the 'Janus-faced' properties of such a component. Every holon is both a part and a whole, but the extent to which it is one or the other is not fixed. Wholeness and partness, or what Koestler called the 'self-assertive' and 'integrative' tendencies (compare the above quotations from Schoenberg and Schenker), are in perpetual conflict.

The best-known Koestlerian coinage is 'bisociation', signifying the process whereby new 'matrices' (roughly corresponding to the Kantian 'schemata') are produced by the association of old ones. A simple example is the contraption, compounded from the typewriter, electronic calculator, and television set, with which I am writing these words. Many inventions, both material and conceptual, do undoubtedly arise in this manner, the only question being whether 'multisociation' would not be a more accurate word. In music, particularly, such processes appear to be ubiquitous. It is not only that, in the old adage, nothing comes from nothing; nothing comes from anything *single*. The antecedents of musical patterns are always multiple—often bafflingly so.

The attractor

The *Naturphilosophen* were struck by the paradoxical way in which orderly processes coexist with the irregularities of nature. Recent theorists have given these processes various names: 'self-regulating open hierarchic orders', 'dynamical systems', 'complex adaptive systems', and so on. Whatever one calls them, they exhibit a form of change quite unlike that of the Newtonian clockwork: a self-regulating irregularity, a 'deterministic chaos', an endless conflict between order and disorder.

What keeps such systems from flying off into total chaos is the 'attractor', a state of complete order which is periodically approached but never quite attained. In the somewhat different form of the 'magnet', this too, goes back to the early musings of the nature philosophers.[22]

In music, the most obvious attractors are certain primordial rhythmic, melodic, and harmonic patterns. Whenever music departs too much from them, whether on the scale of the individual movement or of the entire genre, we begin to feel uncomfortable. In either event, it is time for a return to simplicity.

which behave partly as wholes or wholly as parts, according to the way you look at them. The term I would propose is "holon", from the Greek *holos* = whole, with the suffix *on* which, as in prot*on* or neutr*on*, suggests a particle or part' (p. 48).

[22] 'One of Schelling's most powerful poetic images was that of the magnet, a paradigm for the idea of the coincidence of opposite forces in Nature, for which parallels were found in such phenomena as the contraries of acid and alkali in chemistry' (Roger Cardinall, *German Romantics in Context*, 82).

AMBIGUITY

Music is ambiguous for at least two reasons: first, because the patterns or schemata that we bring to it are never totally precise, and often extremely vague; and second, because the process of matching actual sounds against these patterns is instinctive rather than logical. As Koestler says, 'The so-called law of contradiction in logic—that a thing is either A or not-A but cannot be both—is a late acquisition in the growth of individuals and cultures . . . The unconscious mind, the mind of the child and the primitive, are indifferent to it.'[23] So, too, is the musical mind, which feels no obligation to choose between contradictory patterns. Rather than being either X or Y, a figure may be—and very often is—both X and Y. In addition, all 'holons' are ambiguous—'Janus-faced'—by their very nature. A G major chord in a C major movement, for instance, is *simultaneously* dominant and tonic. Depending on which face is more prominent, we may say that the 'key' is C or G. But this distinction is misleadingly precise. In fact, there is an unbroken range of emphasis between the two.

Ambiguity, far from being an occasional subtlety, is part of the fabric of music. It is what makes music beautiful and musical analysis difficult. Any conceivable system of musical terminology or notation runs the constant risk of making things seem more clear-cut than they actually are. I make no claim to have escaped this danger, but have at least done my best to warn the reader against it. If words like 'tendency' and 'inclination' crop up with irritating frequency, they are a mark not of woolly thinking but, on the contrary, of a regard for accuracy.

One further warning. Music has been aptly described as a 'rum go'. It is a baffling mixture of opposites: of the mathematical and instinctive, the emotional and intellectual, the precise and vague. It would be unreasonable to expect something so odd to be reasonable. In evaluating any musicological theory, it is well to bear in mind the words attributed to the nuclear physicist Wolfgang Pauli, when presented by a colleague with a particularly bright idea: 'It's crazy—but is it crazy enough?'

---

[23] *The Act of Creation*, ch. 15, 'Illusion', p. 305.

2 The Ramellian Paradigm

In the course of a lecture delivered in 1938, Sir Donald Tovey made the following observation:

A modern master of popular scientific exposition—that is to say, an eminent man of science—has remarked that when the phenomena compel a scientific theory to become fantastically complex we may foresee that we are observing the phenomena from the wrong point of view: as, for instance, when the motions of the planets require a tangle of deferents and epicycles, so long as we try to explain them as seen from a fixed earth instead of from a central sun. The whole trouble of the official theory of sixteenth-century harmony lay in the fact that the theorists retained the point of view of purely melodic scales long after these scales had become inveterately harmonic, as well as melodic, phenomena.[1]

It is a great pity that Tovey, exasperatingly and typically, neglects to give the name of the 'eminent man of science', since that gentleman was clearly anticipating Thomas S. Kuhn's theory of 'paradigm shifts' by several decades. As the latter explained in *The Structure of Scientific Revolutions* (1962), scientists, to function at all, need what he called a 'paradigm': that is to say, a frame of reference that can support their theories, plausibly explain their findings, and guide them towards further research. In many respects, such a paradigm is the scientific equivalent of a religious faith.

It is characteristic of a successful new paradigm that it works splendidly. During the phase of what Kuhn calls 'normal science', researchers make rapid advances, all appearing to confirm its validity. But soon gaps begin to appear between theory and observation. Attempts to bridge these deprive the paradigm of its pristine simplicity. Then, as contradictory findings pile up, it becomes ever more elaborate and implausible, till at last the science reaches a 'crisis', to be resolved only by the supervention of a new and radically different paradigm—at which point the cycle begins again.

In the above quotation, Tovey describes just such a crisis in the musical theory of the sixteenth and seventeenth centuries. It was resolved by the 'paradigm shift' that received classic expression in the second sentence of Rameau's *Traité*

[1] *A Musician Talks* (1941), pt. 2: *Musical Textures*, 8–9.

d'harmonie of 1722: 'It is customary to divide music into harmony and melody, though the latter is merely part of the former, and a knowledge of harmony is sufficient for a perfect understanding of every property of music . . .'.[2]

This Ramellian paradigm is with us still. For almost three centuries, theorists have been content, for the most part, to regard melody as 'merely a part of harmony'. Harmony, in the imagery of musical analysis, is a foundation, providing 'an inner skeleton on which varying contours may be draped'.[3] Melody, on the other hand, is merely 'the surface of a series of harmonies'.[4]

It is typical of a Kuhnian paradigm that we take it so thoroughly for granted as to forget its existence. Conventional Western theory has grown so used to interpreting melody in terms of harmony that the very idea of a purely melodic construct has become strange to it. Every mode takes its bearings from harmony; so does every melodic sequence and cadence; so, too, do dissonance, key, and modulation. Yet melody existed for thousands of years without the benefit of harmony, and still manages without it in many parts of the world today. Can it really be relegated to so dependent a status?

For European 'art' music between about 1600 and 1800, the Ramellian paradigm worked tolerably well—best of all, naturally enough, for Rameau's own period, the first half of the eighteenth century. As well as relating melody to harmony in a simple and plausible way, it had the merit, so congenial to the Age of Reason, of reducing ambiguity to a minimum. Melody, being part of harmony, was regulated by the same orderly hierarchic system, revolving ultimately round the tonic triad. The resemblance to Newton's clockwork universe was not entirely coincidental.

Practice, too, seemed to confirm the Ramellian view. With the harmonic accompaniments customary since the late sixteenth century, the melody at first fitted the chords very well. Then the fit gradually became less neat. Triads sprouted sevenths, ninths, elevenths, and thirteenths; appoggiaturas and other non-harmonic notes proliferated. Just as the Ptolomaic theory had needed ever more epicycles (in effect, wheels within wheels within wheels) to cope with advances in astronomical observation, so the Ramellian system demanded ever more complex harmonies to keep up with developments in melody. To be sure, both systems *worked*. As the astronomers would have put it, they 'saved the appearances'. It is perfectly possible to explain the movement of the planets in terms of epicycles, and there is nothing melody can do that cannot be dealt with by an adequate outfit of higher dominant discords, passing notes, changing notes, appoggiaturas, added sixths,

---

[2] 'On divise ordinairement la Musique en Harmonie & en Melodie, quoique celle-cy ne soit qu'une partie de l'autre, & qu'il suffise de connoître l'Harmonie, pour être parfaitement instruit de toutes les proprietez de la Musique . . .' (ch. 1, par. 2)

[3] Henry Jackson Watt, 'Melody', 284; quoted by Alexander L. Ringer in *New Grove II*, 'Melody', xvi. 364.

[4] Tovey, 'Melody', in the *Encyclopaedia Britannica*, 11th edn.; reprinted in *The Forms of Music*, 91.

sevenths, or ninths, inverted pedals, and so forth. But in each case, as the explanations become more epicyclical, they become correspondingly less plausible. Paraphrasing Tovey, we might say that the whole trouble with the official theory of nineteenth-century harmony lies in the fact that theorists retained the point of view of harmonic scales long after they had reverted to being inveterately melodic.

Even without these objections, there have always been strong arguments against the Ramellian paradigm. It completely fails to account for those traditions, many of them impinging on European art music, in which harmony plays little or no part. What happens when a non-harmonic folk tune is harmonized? What about unharmonized melody within the Western classical tradition? And if harmony is so all-important, how is it that we can take pleasure in singing or whistling tunes with no harmonic backing at all?

But the deepest objection to the Ramellian paradigm is that it begs the question. Chords are made up of notes, which is to say of melody. Chords *are* melody, behaving in a special way. To base melody on harmony is therefore to base it on itself. Just as electricity and magnetism are aspects of electro-magnetism, so are melody and harmony aspects of 'melo-harmony'. Harmony is an 'emergent' property of melody, in the same way as life is an emergent property of matter, or mind of life. And, just as one can have life without mind and matter without life, so one can have melody without harmony—but not harmony without melody. There can be no explanation of harmony that does not take into account its melodic component.

Even Rameau implicitly recognized as much when he supported harmony on the extremely important tune known as the 'bass', or more precisely the 'fundamental bass' (*basse fondamentale*), which differs from the actual bass in consisting solely of chordal roots. In some harmonic systems (for instance, those of sixteenth-century dances and much twentieth-century popular music) this makes little difference, since the fundamental and actual basses are virtually or entirely the same. As harmony becomes more complex, this ceases to be true, and for this reason the theory of the fundamental bass has often been unjustly attacked. But here, at least, Rameau was on the right track.

Where he went wrong was rather in his treatment of the upper voices, which he turned into mere appendages to the bass. Their sole duty, in the Ramellian system, is to conform to the harmony, either directly as concords or indirectly as discords. The harmony, in its turn, is generated by the fundamental bass, which itself revolves around the keynote. The whole system has a pleasing neatness, which satisfied the Gallic instinct for order and hierarchy, and worked well enough in actual music to last almost two centuries before being challenged.

SCHENKER'S INSIGHTS

The challenge came mainly from Heinrich Schenker.

Firstly, he gave melody a certain autonomy, though still deriving it from the *harmonic* major triad—*der Klang in der Natur* ('the sound in nature'), as he called it. As Eugene Narmour has pointed out (though not in so many words), Schenker's system is still essentially Ramellian.[5]

Secondly, he sorted out some of the confusion about what constitutes a melody. A defect of Rameau's scheme is that it makes little or no distinction between the upper voices: *the* tune has no special status. Realizing that this would not do, Schenker took the drastic step of reducing the harmonic fabric, in effect, to a two-part counterpoint between a single melody and its bass.

It is strange that this second insight of his has attracted so little attention, since it is arguably the most valuable part of his whole system. Perhaps for the first time, it recognizes the great truth that two contrapuntal voices are graspable in a way that more than two are not. The human ear reacts to polyphony rather as some primitive tribes are said to count: one—two—many. Once the voices get beyond two, the instinctive reaction is to divide them into 'bass', 'main upper voice', and 'other'.

In insisting on this, Schenker was defying not only Rameau, but several centuries of pedagogic tradition. The whole thrust of contrapuntal teaching has been to make as little distinction between the voices as possible. Every voice must be equally tuneful, and every figure must sound equally well throughout the harmony, with only minor allowances for the special function of the bass. Nor does the number of voices make much difference. According to the official view, five-part counterpoint differs in degree rather than kind from the two-part variety. It is merely harder, for both composer and listener.

And, of course, there is a vast quantity of music that seems to bear this out. Since the twelfth century, composers have been turning out polyphony in three or more parts. But if this is closely examined, we find that much of the complexity is illusory. Great contrapuntists like Palestrina and J. S. Bach (or for that matter Wagner) carefully distinguish foreground from background and strictly ration the moments of genuine polyphonic complexity. What the listener hears at such times is a euphonious confusion, which never persists long enough to become wearisome.

In any case, elaborately polyphonic music has always been the exception. From the Middle Ages to the present day, the norm has been a bass, a principal upper

---

[5] 'In Schenkerian theory, the functional factors of harmonic voice leading always assimilate the functions of melody and rhythm; melody and rhythm can never irrevocably modify their harmonic-contrapuntal "origins"' (*Beyond Schenkerism*, 58).

voice, and one or more subordinate voices. In some form or other, composers have always returned to this basic scheme, no doubt because it answers an instinctive human need. In the language of the previous chapter, it is an 'attractor'.

TONAL COUNTERPOINT

This two-voice arrangement is the basis of the analytical system propounded in this book. It differs from Schenker's ideal system in being much freer. Both voices may behave as they please, subject only to following rules:

1. The Melody (note the capital letter) occupies the foreground of the listener's attention.
2. The Melody is heard against the background, actual or implied, of the Bass.
3. The Bass is at the bottom of the harmony, and carries harmonic implications.

In sum, Melody and Bass are in counterpoint, but it is counterpoint of a very special sort.[6] To distinguish it from the familiar textbook variety, I shall use the term 'tonal counterpoint', meaning the interplay between two systems of tonality, one centred on the Melody and the other on the Bass.[7]

In R. O. Morris's handy coinage, all counterpoint involves 'at-oddness',[8] which naturally tends to increase as time goes on. In the earliest tonal counterpoint, Melody and Bass were only very mildly at odds, generally moving in parallel at the distance of a fourth or fifth. By Rameau's time they had diverged to the point where the Melody, while still following the harmonic implications of the Bass, avoids too crass a coincidence of outline—hence, of course, the prohibition of parallel fifths and octaves—while the Bass itself had been simplified to a few stock formulas, so familiar as to be understood even when not explicitly sounded.

This latter development makes it possible for eighteenth-century melody to be 'harmonic' even in the absence of harmony, as we see not only in such things as Bach's suites for unaccompanied violin, but also in much folk music. The bare tune of 'The Bonny Lass o' Fyvie' (Ex. 2.1(*a*)), for instance, implies the chord scheme I I IV · I IV I–V I as clearly as any piano accompaniment. This can easily be seen if it is stripped of its passing notes (Ex. 2.1(*b*)).[9] In Ex. 2.1(*a*), the symbols I, V,

---

[6] Throughout this book the word 'counterpoint' includes all forms of simultaneous musical conflict within an overriding pattern. Thus, cross-rhythm and syncopation are forms of rhythmic counterpoint. For counterpoint in the traditional sense, I use the word 'polyphony'.

[7] As Rudolph Réti points out (see *Tonality, Atonality, Pantonality*, posthumously published in 1958, p. 7) tonality is really 'tonicality'. In his view, 'harmonic tonality' combines with 'melodic tonality' to form 'pantonality', roughly equivalent to my 'tonal counterpoint'.

[8] See *Contrapuntal Technique in the Sixteenth Century*, 18.

[9] This feature is shared by many British songs of the period, e.g. 'Cease your Funning', from *The Beggar's Opera*, and William Boyce's 'Heart of Oak'. In a slightly different category come those tunes that are actual basses, e.g. 'Down among the Dead Men'.

Ex. 2.1. 'The Bonny Lass o' Fyvie' (Scottish ballad tune) (up a 4th)

(*a*) complete tune

(*b*) outline of (*a*) minus passing notes

(*c*) the same, with some notes transposed down an octave and the implied Bass

first inversion of *C* major chord

and IV are a way of indicating that we perceive the Melody as a counterpoint to the Bass *1 1 1 5 · 1 4 1–5 1*, together with its implied chords. And if we transpose a few notes of the tune down an octave (Ex. 2.1(*c*)), it becomes plain that this counterpoint is in fact a sort of heterophonic unison. (Notice, by the way, the sonata-like correspondence of the bracketed figures concluding the two halves.) Such tunes are sometimes said to be, or to contain, 'their own bass'. The Bass is, so to speak, built in: it has no need of being imagined, and to that extent the at-oddness is reduced. Tunes of this sort flourish particularly in places where chordal patterns coexist with pure, unharmonized melody, such as the Britain of the eighteenth century or—as we shall see in Chapter 16—the United States of the early twentieth.

But at the same time as being in counterpoint to an often unheard Bass, tunes like 'The Bonny Lass o' Fyvie' must be melodically self-sufficient. If they were not, they could hardly survive the test of being sung and transmitted without accompaniment. The triadic chords that figure so prominently in them are primarily melodic, and only incidentally harmonic. They are, in fact, *melodic* chords. And as we advance into the nineteenth century, they coincide less and less with those of the Bass.

THE ARCHITECTURE OF MELODY

Ultimately, the laws of melody (which here includes the Bass) rest on the same principles as those of rhythm, but with certain cardinal differences. Rhythm deals with the infinitely plastic medium of time, and can therefore create patterns of extreme regularity and simplicity. Melody, on the other hand, must struggle with the far more refractory element of pitch, with results both more complex and more interesting. Like melody, rhythm exhibits symmetry, hierarchic organization, self-similarity, and ambiguity; but it does so in a manner much harder to analyse.

A large part of the trouble is the roundabout way in which human beings perceive musical pitch. Objectively considered, melodic intervals are ratios of vibration frequency: the octave, for instance, is 1:2, the fifth 2:3, the major third 4:5. Subjectively, we hear these intervals not as ratios but as quasi-linear measurements. Instinctively and unconsciously, we position melody in tone space; and into this tone space, by what can only be called a synaesthetic miracle, we read a quasi-visual symmetry.

The result is a perpetual conflict between objective and subjective ratios. At no precise point does one form of perception end and the other begin. The octave, to be sure, seems inviolate, but even perfect fifths and fourths may be treated now in one fashion, now in the other, while smaller intervals are habitually 'bent'. A violinist (or other performer on an instrument of flexible pitch) will instinctively strive to make the intervals of chromatic and whole-tone scales precisely equal. In Africa and Indonesia, a similar impulse has produced equally spaced pentatonic and heptatonic scales. Also in Africa, the perfect fourth is often divided into three equal, narrow seconds. A familiar feature of the blues is the 'neutral' third, lying midway between the major and minor thirds, and so bisecting the perfect fifth. Less well known, but also quite common, is the 'neutral second', midway between the major and minor seconds.[10]

It is largely this conflict between symmetries that makes it possible to extract such an endless variety of tunes from what would seem at first sight to be such a meagre stock of basic patterns. But the composer's gain is the theorist's difficulty. The pervasive ambiguity, the sheer number of potential meanings, makes melody that much harder to understand. To do so, we must learn not to shun ambiguity but to embrace it, and this is best done by examining purely melodic patterns of the utmost simplicity.

---

[10] It may often be heard in the blues, especially in the form of a neutral *4* bisecting *3* and *5* (e.g. in 'Haunted Road Blues', Ex. 16.19). The blues also possesses, in addition to the 'blue' third bisecting the perfect fifth, an interval of two and a half semitones bisecting the perfect fourth. Generally occurring between *5* and *1*⁺, this may be transcribed as either a flat *7♭* or a sharp *6*.

But where, in a musical culture so thoroughly dominated by harmony, can we find such patterns? As we shall see in the next chapter, the answer is: all around us.

3 The Children's Chant

> For once the ontogenetic law is fully confirmed: the individual sum-
> marizes the evolution of mankind.
>
> Curt Sachs[1]

The best place to reconstruct the evolution of melody is the nursery. As long ago as 1917, a Viennese psychologist by the name of Heinz Werner made a systematic study of infant song, using the recently invented technology of sound recording.[2] Curt Sachs summarizes his findings as follows:

> The earliest attempts of children less than three years old resulted in one-tone litanies and in melodies of two notes a narrow minor third apart, the lower of which was stressed and frequently repeated. At the age of three, children produced melodies of two notes a second apart, and even three-tone melodies. Children three and a half years old sang in descending tetrachords. Continual repetition was the only form.[3]

In other words, the child's first musical discovery is the note of fixed pitch ('one-tone litanies'), which we may call i. Then comes the hierarchic structure of two notes a 'narrow minor third' apart; later, this pattern is refined to a definite $ii-i$. Finally, this major second is combined with the minor third $i-vi^-$ to form the 'descending tetrachord' $ii-i-vi^-$.[4] An important point, not specifically mentioned by Sachs, is that the minor third has now become the main interval and the initial ii a mere upbeat. The whole evolutionary process is summarized in Ex. 3.1.

Ex. 3.1. The evolution of the children's chant

(a) one-note stage   (b) first attempt at   (c) two-note stage   (d) complete
                          two-note patterns   chant

∟ intonation vague
and variable

---

[1] *The Rise of Music in the Ancient World*, 43.

[2] His findings are recorded in the paper 'Die melodische Erfindung im frühen Kindesalter' ('Melodic Invention in Early Childhood').   [3] *The Rise of Music in the Ancient World*, 43.

[4] It may seem puzzling that this *three*-note pattern is called a 'tetrachord', from the Greek for '*four* strings'. The reason is that in ancient Greece it would have been performed on four adjacent strings of the lyre—that is, skipping over the second-to-bottom string. Like many musical terms, it is a useful misnomer.

In its mature form, this chant is not so much a tune as an improvisatory formula, an Indian rāga or Arabic maqām in microcosm. Its core is the descending minor third, which I shall call *g–e*. This may be decorated with an unaccented *a*, or it may be truncated by the omission of the final *e*, as in Ex. 3.2.

Ex. 3.2. Variants of the children's chant

(*a*) plain   (*b*) decorated   (*c*) truncated
    (two–note) form   (three–note) form   form

And, even at this rudimentary stage, these tiny patterns begin to group themselves into larger units. The natural order is plain–decorated, giving the 'classic' form of Ex. 3.3, which is what is generally meant by the unqualified term 'children's chant' in this book.

Ex. 3.3. The 'classic' form of the children's chant

(*a*) simple duple   (*b*) compound duple

It would, however, be a serious mistake to suppose that the children's chant is confined to children. Among adults, too, it has been immensely fertile. Along with the even more primitive 'tumbling strain', it was for thousands of years the basis of most human melody, and this is true in some societies even today, or at any rate was until recently.[5] Even when superseded in everyday use by more complex tunes, it often retains a special ritualistic status, as, for instance, in the western Slavonic 'spring songs', known in Russian as *vesnyanki*,[6] which continued in use well into the twentieth century. Their origins are obviously pagan:

[Various accounts] bear witness to the magic function of the movements, the incessant movements of the springtime songs, whose purpose was to facilitate the quick awakening of nature—the growth of grass, the opening up of the rivers, the flight of birds, and so on. . . . These descriptions make clear *the connection between the performance of the spring invocations and some form of action* [italics original]: they are never declaimed in a stationary manner. . . . Vesnyanki were performed chorally (or, often with choral responses), very

---

[5] See Bruno Nettl, *Folk and Traditional Music of the Western Continents*, 44–6.
[6] Singular: *vesnyanka*. Derived from *vesna*, spring.

loudly, from high places (so that their call carried the better). They took the form of short little phrases, usually repeated several times in a row, like melodic formulas.[7]

Here we catch a glimpse of prehistoric European song. The call-and-response form, the bodily movement, the vocal quality, and the ritual purpose all have analogues in many parts of the pre-industrial world—Africa, in particular, springs to mind. This is music from the dawn of mankind. Later on, I shall be quoting a few more adult examples of the 'children's' chant,[8] but first something further must be said about the children themselves.

While developing their chant, they are also learning to talk and to draw. All over the world, regardless of culture, they begin to produce 'one-tone litanies' at about the same age as one-word sentences. Later, they progress to two-note melodies and two-word sentences: 'Where doggie?', 'Dada throw', 'All dry'.[9] By the time they have reached the children's chant proper, they have also attained something approaching adult language.

This is striking enough. At the very least, it seems to prove that it is more than a mere metaphor to describe music as a language. But in some ways the parallels with the equally universal development of the child's pictorial sense are even more remarkable. This begins with untidy haystacks of lines, indistinguishable from what a chimpanzee would produce if you put a crayon in its hand. The infant artist then goes on to whirling shapes, which gradually resolve themselves into a single, somewhat wobbly but nevertheless recognizable circle. This is next decorated with criss-crossing lines. As the child advances to two-note tunes, the circle becomes a sun-shape, with lines radiating from it. This is then adorned with a face. Finally, as the child masters the mature chant and a semblance of adult speech, the sun is transformed into a human figure.[10]

In both singing and drawing, the stages of development are essentially the same. First comes the maturing, within the child's brain, of the innate mathematical schema: the circle, the straight line, the basic intervals and rhythms, the sense of symmetry. Then the child proceeds to hierarchic ordering, powerfully symbolized by the sun shape. Finally, these abstract patterns are endowed with emotional

---

[7] Izalii Zemtsovsky, *Melodika kalendarnyx pesen* (*Melodic Characteristics of Seasonal Songs*), 78 ff. Quoted (and presumably translated) by Richard Taruskin in 'Russian Folk Melodies in *The Rite of Spring*', 530. In this long essay several other melodies apparently derived from the children's chant are quoted, though the connection is not explicitly made. See his Exs. 10b, c, d, and e, 17b, c, and d, 18, and 20.

[8] See Exs. 3.7 (another spring song), 3.12, and, on p. 423, Ex. 15.29.

[9] See Robert B. McCall, *Babies: The First Three Years of Life*, 144–5, and Steven Pinker, *The Language Instinct*, 268. The latter gives twenty-one of these two-word sentences, adding that 'Children's two-word combinations are so similar in meaning the world over that they read as translations of one another.' Since 95% are in the correct word order, they also reveal a rudimentary grasp of grammar, as well as vocabulary.

[10] The development of the child's pictorial sense can be followed in Desmond Morris's television series *The Human Animal*, available in video form. There is also an accompanying book with the same title.

content—and here we come to the great difference between music and visual arts. As the young artist moves from abstraction to representation, the young musician stays with abstraction. But, at the same time, the chant ceases to be 'absolute music'. Its patterns, while remaining in themselves as abstract as ever, become a channel for emotion—generally the primitive one of childish aggression.

CONSONANCE AND CHORDALITY

In passing from the two- to the three-note stage, the child discovers a new and fundamental pattern: the chord. Over the past century we have become very broadminded about chords. First they were overlaid by towers of thirds, then the thirds were replaced by fourths. Soon the point was reached where any random agglomerations of pitches qualified as chords. For these, it would be better to reserve the word 'harmonies'. Chords are something different: coherent, hierarchic, and, if not always perfectly euphonious, at least always *intelligible*. And they can be successive as well as simultaneous.

What is the source of this coherence, this intelligibility? Evidently it has something to do with concordance. We intuitively feel that thirds, fourths, fifths, and octaves are basic components of both melody and harmony; and here we can learn a great deal from another simple experiment, rather like the one with the clock that told us so much about rhythm. The apparatus is any instrument capable of emitting even, unaccented notes. An organ would be ideal, but any other instrument can be used (or for that matter the singing voice), provided that its notes are equal in length and accent.

The experiment is simply this. Starting with the most consonant intervals, evenly oscillate the constituent notes while trying to decide which is the main one. In the case of the octave, it is immediately clear that neither note predominates; both are exactly equivalent in everything except pitch. That, of course, is why we normally identify them by the same letter, figure, or syllable. But this quality is unique to the octave. With the more dissonant intervals, one note always predominates. In the perfect fifth, it is clearly the lower. In the perfect fourth, it is almost equally clearly the upper; and in this our subjective judgement is borne out by primitive melody, where oscillating fourths are not uncommon.[11]

Proceeding to the major third, we find that the main note is the lower. At least in the specific case of the major mediant, this has long been recognized. As Hans Keller put it, 'if the term "leading-note" hadn't happened to be chosen for the

---

[11] See the four tunes (from Tierra del Fuego, Bulgaria, Russia, and Croatia) consisting solely of a perfect fourth in Wiora, 'Älter als die Pentatonik', 196; also the introduction to the American 'tie-shuffling chant' quoted in *Origins*, 135. In every case, the upper note is clearly the 'tonic'.

seventh degree, nobody would object if the mediant were called the leading-note: innumerable melodies testify to its powerful pull towards the tonic. You only have to sing, inside your head, mediant–tonic in any key to convince yourself of the instinctive truth of my submission.'[12]

With the minor third, matters become a little less clear. This time the bias is towards the upper note, as in many primitive chants,[13] but it is relatively weak.

The experiment can be extended to the still more dissonant major and minor second, but let us stop at this point. A property shared by all the intervals considered so far is that they form part of the major triad, within which *c* predominates over *g* and *e*, and *g* over *e*.

These hierarchic biases are borne out by the many simple tunes that happen to fall into major triads. Thus, *e* is first attracted to *g* and then *g* to *c* in a railway porter's chant noted by Percy Scholes (Ex. 3.4), and *e* is repeatedly attracted towards *c* in an early twentieth-century American 'holler' (Ex. 3.5). (Incidentally, one of the delights of these rudimentary chants is their faithful reflection of the cultures that produced them. Ex. 3.4 is as distinctly English as Ex. 3.5 is unmistakably Afro-American.)

Ex. 3.4. Railway porter's chant (up a 5th)

Change here for Hal-i-fax! all change.

Ex. 3.5. 'Shack Bully Holler' (down a major 3rd)

Raise up, boys, raise up, raise up.   Break-fas' on de ta-ble, an' -a cof-fee's git-ting col', Ef you

CHORUS

don' come now, gon-na throw it out-do's. Ain-cha gwine, ain-cha gwine, boys, ain-cha gwine?

This order of attraction reflects the priority of the same notes within the harmonic series: *c* comes before *g*, and *g* before *e* (Ex. 3.6). These notes possess not only consonance, but the unique property of *chordality*. Octaves, fifths, fourths, and thirds form chords whereas seconds do not: a distinction expressed in everyday language by calling the former 'leaps' and the latter 'steps'.

---

[12] *The Great Haydn Quartets*, 199.

[13] e.g. the Slovakian spring song (Ex. 3.7), the railway porter's chant (Ex. 3.4), and the children's chant itself.

Ex. 3.6. The priority order of the harmonic series

This appears to be another human peculiarity. There is no obvious reason why the major triad (or the first five notes of the harmonic series) should be singled out in this way. Perhaps, in some distant galaxy, there are creatures that hear thirds as steps, or semitones as leaps. But to us humans, the major triad and its component intervals occupy a special 'wired-in' status. Every theorist from the days of Pythagoras to the early twentieth century has recognized this fact, but no one has expressed it more vividly than the German Romantic Wilhelm Heinrich Wackenroder, in a story published in 1797:

For is not half the credit for the divinity of our art due to the eternal harmony of Nature, and the other half to the benevolent Creator that enabled us to exploit this treasure? All those delightful melodies, in their thousandfold variety, arousing in us the most diverse of emotions—do they not spring from the single, wonderful triad which Nature brought into being an eternity ago?[14]

Notice that to Wackenroder the major triad is not merely (as Schenker was later to call it) *der Klang in der Natur*, but *der Klang in der Natur* perceived in a uniquely human, God-given way. This is an acute observation, except that we should now be inclined to substitute for 'the benevolent Creator' that more up-to-date divinity, Evolution. If it is true that organisms evolve towards an ideal 'edge of chaos' between rigidity and flexibility,[15] our perception of melody may well be a case in point.

We can now begin to see why the children's chant develops as it does. The infant first discovers the downward step *a–g*, with *g* as the principal note. The next stage is to expand this into a chord. But what chord? To the child, the regular alternation of stressed and unstressed beats is much more fundamental than any particular melodic contour, and it is on this foundation that the first melodic line is built. It follows the principle whereby musical patterns diverge from the concurrent—

---

[14] 'Das merkwürdige musikalische Leben des Tonkünstlers Joseph Berglinger' ('The Remarkable Musical Life of the Composer Joseph Berglinger'), about three-quarters of the way through. The speaker is the composer-hero. This story, which will be summarized in Ch. 14, was published as part of the *Herzens-ergießungen eines kunstliebenden Klosterbruders* (*Outpourings from the Heart of an Art-Loving Monk*). An English translation may be found in *Source Readings in Music History*, ed. Strunk, v: *The Romantic Era*, 10–23.

[15] See particularly Stuart Kauffman, *At Home in the Universe: The Search for Laws of Self-Organization and Complexity*.

literally 'running together'—to the '*dis*current' (the word is in the *Oxford English Dictionary*, but unfortunately is pronounced to be obsolete). To put it more colloquially, this 'law of divergence' demands that the ups and downs of melody and rhythm evolve from 'in sync' to 'out of sync'. In rhythm, the ups and downs are mainly accentual, though length also plays its part; in melody, they are a matter of pitch and chordal position. High notes predominate over low notes, roots over fifths, and fifths over thirds.

At the same time, the hierarchic sense groups these ups and downs into chords and bars, and these, too, must coincide. By instinct as well as convention, bars begin with accented beats: the natural unit is '*tick* tack', not '*tack tick*'. By the law of divergence it follows that chords must at first do likewise. Putting all this together, we arrive at the child's first real tune:

bars:	strong beat	weak beat	strong beat	weak beat
chords:	strong note	weak note	strong note	weak note
pitch:	high	low	high	low

Since the order of predominance within the chord is root–fifth–third, there are three possible tunes: c^+–g, c^+–e, and g–e. Of these, the second is much too awkward, leaving the falling perfect fourth (c^+–g) and the falling minor third (g–e). Either might conceivably work, but, as we have seen, it is the latter that is actually chosen.

There are several reasons for this. The minor third has several advantages over the acoustically simpler fourth. First, its size: both the minor third and major second come very easily to the human voice (though, again, matters may be different in another galaxy), in particular lending themselves to the oscillation that is the child's most natural form of melody making. Then there is the initial a–g, which fits together with the minor third g–e much better than the perfect fourth g–d (transposed from c^+–g). There is something unsatisfactory about a–g–d. For reasons that I shall come to later, its three intervals make an awkward whole.

Finally, the very simplicity of the perfect fourth makes it too clear-cut, too strongly biased towards its upper note, too deficient in the precious attribute of ambiguity.

AMBIGUITY AND GROWTH

Biologists inform us that cell membranes are poised at the boundary between the solid and the liquid state. In much the same way, the three intervals composing the children's chant maintain a delicate balance between rigidity and dissolution. Like invisible elastic bands, the melodic tensions holding together this 'musical cell' have just enough 'give' to allow new cells to grow out of it.

This ambiguity first becomes evident in the sub-cell *a–g*. Not only is it almost evenly balanced between its two constituent notes; its very identity is in doubt. Is it the 'major tone' between harmonies 8 and 9, or the 'minor tone' between harmonies 9 and 10 (see Ex. 3.6)? Or, to put it in terms of vibration ratios, is it 9/8 or 10/9? The difference is slight, but perceptible. Since *g* is the main note, one would expect the major tone, on the analogy of notes *c"–d"* of the harmonic series. But if a minor third is 'subtracted' from (or, in strict mathematical terms, divided into) a perfect fourth, the result is a *minor* tone:

$$a/g = a/e \div g/e$$
$$= 4/3 \div 6/5$$
$$= 4/3 \times 5/6$$
$$= 10/9$$

In practice, of course, the ear does not trouble itself with the slight distinction between these two forms of major second. Instead, it prefers to regard this basic melodic step as a single, flexible interval, varying according to circumstance and often amounting to no more than a bisection of the major third. Like so many things in music, it is a convenient fudge.

The other sub-cell, *g–e*, is ambiguous in a different way. What is in doubt is not its size or identity—it is a minor third, and no mistake—but its chordal nature. This can clearly be seen from those numerous chants that consist of minor thirds and nothing else. Example 3.7 is a Slovakian relative of the Russian *vesnyanka* ('We carry away the wicked winter, we bring the warm summer') in which the children's chant is reduced to a reiterated *g–e*. Here there is no doubt that *g* is the main note, and as such points to *c*, though this is never actually heard.

Ex. 3.7. Slovakian spring song (down a 5th)

```
Ta  ne - se - mo,  ta  ne - se - mo  tu   kle - tu  zi  -  mu.
Pri - ne - se - mo,  pri - ne - se - mo  to   tep - lo  lé  -  to.
```

Elsewhere the emphasis may shift towards *e*, as, for instance, in the 'closed' relative of the children's chant known to German scholars as the *Rufterz*, or 'call third'[16] (Ex. 3.8). In this extremely flexible melody, both notes may vary greatly in rhythm, the *g* being anything between a single cry (Ex. 3.9(*a*)) and an extended recitation, and the *e* often acquiring an extra beat (Ex. 3.9(*b*)).[17] In addition, the order of the pitches may be varied, giving the patterns *e–g* (Ex. 3.9(*c*)) and *g–e–g*.[18]

---

[16] See Wiora, 'Älter als die Pentatonik', 194.

[17] This is frequently sung to the syllable 'Oh!' in street cries, etc. Cf. 'Hishie Ba' ' (Ex. 4.4).

[18] e.g. in the first part of railway porter's chant (Ex. 3.4), to the words 'Change here for Halifax!'

Ex. 3.8. The call third: 'Let's Play Cops and Robbers!'

Let's play cops and rob-bers!

Ex. 3.9. Variants of the call third

(*a*) (*b*) (*c*)

reciting note

In none of these variants does *e* actually dominate over *g*. The accent may be evenly shared between both pitches, but is never firmly placed on *e*. To do so would be unequivocally to transform the *e–g* from the top half of *c–e–g* to the bottom half of *e–g–b*. Instead, it hovers somewhere between the two. Even in this simplest of melodies, chordal identity is relative rather than absolute.

The children's tetrachord

The combination of the 'cells' *a–g* and *g–e* into the complete three-note chant introduces the interval of the perfect fourth, and with it a potential new chord (Ex. 3.10). Pursuing the biological analogy, we may think of it as an enclosing membrane, and most subsequent developments consist essentially in making it stronger.

Ex. 3.10. The chordal structure of the children's chant

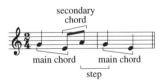

secondary chord

main chord main chord

step

All that is necessary to begin the process is a slight stress on *a*, as in Ex. 3.11. With a little more emphasis this can then lead to such elaborate melodies as Ex. 3.12. Here we see how the pull of the periphery produces a tension between

Ex. 3.11. Andean tune (down a 4th)

the *a* minor and *c* major chords, known to the Russians as *peremennost'*, or 'mutabil-ity'.[19] It may also occur between *a* minor and *g* major, and in either case has obvious links with the children's chant. It is far from confined to Russian music, being in fact inherent in all pentatonic melody.

Ex. 3.12.   'Na more utushka kupalasya' ('On the Sea there Swam a Little Duck'), Russian folk song (down a 5th)

As we can see from melodies such as these, the 'relative' triads of *a* minor and *c* major form a unit, the seventh $a^--c-e-g$, which is almost (but not quite) stable, and almost (but not quite) a chord. Perhaps we might call it a 'compound chord'. The not-quiteness is the great virtue that makes possible *peremennost'* and many other beautiful things. However, this 'pentatonic seventh' (as I shall call it) is a topic for the next chapter. Let me first say something more about its psychological pre-decessor, the 'children's tetrachord' *a–g–e*.

This owes its beauty to the proportions of the 'cells' composing it. As has often been noticed, these fall very nearly into the 'golden' ratio[20] (0.618, to three places of decimals) whereby, of two parts making up a whole, the smaller is to the larger as the larger is to the whole: $x / y = y / (x + y)$, in mathematical shorthand. In fact, the intervals of the children's chant can be made genuinely 'golden' by adopting a tun-ing about midway between equal temperament and just intonation. (In the former tuning, the ratio is 0.600; in the latter, 0.634.)

These proportions are equally pleasing whether the third is above or below the second, or the motion up or down. In every case, this 'knight's move', so called for reasons obvious to chess players, is probably the most beautiful and certainly the most characteristic feature of pentatonic melody.

TOWARDS HARMONY

Chords form a melodic backbone to which non–chordal notes adhere at the distance of a tone (more or less) or semitone. But which is chord, and which attachment? Even in extremely simple melody, it is not always easy to tell. The 'children's

---

[19] See Taruskin, 'How the Acorn Took Root', 198.

[20] Also 'golden proportion', 'golden section', etc.

'mode' may be heard either as an *e–a* chord with an attached *g*, or as an *e–g* with an attached *a*. Moreover, such attached notes are 'Janus-faced' and may themselves serve as roots for chords. For instance, the note *a* sprouts an *a–c*$^+$ chord in both of the passages just quoted (Exs. 3.11 and 3.12).

This point becomes especially important in those offshoots of the children's chant that isolate and repeat the major second *a–g*. In the next three examples (Exs. 3.13–15),[21] the original chant is, as it were, prolonged backwards, with more and more emphasis on the initial *a–g* and less and less on the concluding *g–e*, till at last the latter drops away. We are then left with an unadorned see-saw, in which one note predominates over the other. In Ex. 3.13, the predominant note is *g*, as in the children's chant itself; but in the first part of Ex. 3.14, and still more in Ex. 3.15, the *a* begins to assert itself. While remaining a step-note in relation to *g*, it becomes a potential chordal root in relation to *c* and *e*. Two-note chants of this type readily blossom into the parallel triads of *g* major and *a* minor, which, once they assume harmonic form, are well on the way towards a 'major–minor' system.

Ex. 3.13. 'Guy Fawkes Guy' (English children's song), beginning

Guy Fawkes Guy,   Poke him in the eye,   Hang him on a lamp-post and there let him die.

Ex. 3.14. Song of the Uitoto Indians of Colombia (down a 4th)

Ex. 3.15. Song of the Indians of British Columbia, Canada

But before we go on to examine these harmonic implications, there is still more to be said about pure melody.

[21] Compare Ex. 3.13 with another children's song, the Basque 'Gaur dala biar dala' (Ex. 7.12 on p. 96).

4   The Pentatonic Scale

What makes a tune pentatonic? This is one of those questions, like 'How long is the coastline of Great Britain?', that prove to be much less simple than they appear at first sight. The obvious answer, 'using the five notes of the pentatonic scale, and no others', does not take us very far. 'Auld Lang Syne', for instance, is pentatonic in this straightforward sense, but not all pentatonic melodies are so obligingly regular. All the tunes quoted in the previous chapter are in some sense pentatonic; but one of them, 'Na more utushka' (Ex. 3.12), includes an extra-pentatonic b, and most of the others use fewer than the complete five notes. 'Pentatonic' melody may be, strictly speaking, sub- or super-pentatonic. Moreover, not every sub-pentatonic melody makes an equally pentatonic impression. Triadic tunes like the railway porter's chant (Ex. 3.4) and 'Shack Bully Holler' (Ex. 3.5)—or for that matter any bugle call—seem somehow less pentatonic than those built on the children's chant.

Why should this be? There are several points to consider.

First, melodic hierarchies, like any others, are by their nature ambiguous. The triad is an entity in its own right, but it is also a part of the pentatonic scale. In one sense, it is pentatonic; in another, it is not. At the other extreme, every heptatonic or even chromatic tune will reveal a pentatonic skeleton when its semitones are removed. So deep-seated is the instinct to search for pentatonic underpinnings, that composers of the atonal school had to draw up elaborate rules to frustrate it.

To make matters worse, not all these modal skeletons are equally pentatonic. So it is quite possible to have two tunes, each making full use of all seven notes of the heptatonic scale, that are 'pentatonic' to different degrees.

The next (and most important) point is that it is of no consequence that the pentatonic scale happens to contain five notes; what really matters is the degree of dissonance it permits (or excludes). It is a sort of a musical crystal that grows out of consonance. Interval may be added to interval in any order, and, provided one keeps within a certain limited range of dissonance, the result will always be pentatonic. (This is one reason why attempts to discover *the* origin of the pentatonic scale will always be futile.)

The last point is that this 'range of dissonance' is deliberately ambiguous. It stops with an interval, the major second, which is intermediate between consonance and dissonance. If pentatonicism (or 'pentatony', as East European scholars like to call it) were simply a matter of melodic consonance, the most pentatonic interval would be the octave, and a bugle call would be more pentatonic than 'Auld Lang Syne'. In fact, the 'pentatonic effect' demands a delicate tension between the partially dissonant major second and the more consonant intervals, especially the minor third. Neither the second alone (as for instance in Ex. 3.15) nor the consonant intervals (as in the bugle call) are sufficient in themselves. The pentatonic effect is a playing on the boundary between consonance and dissonance; and, to judge by the children's chant, the human brain is programmed to take a special delight in it.

It will be seen that the word 'pentatonic' can mean several different and even sometimes contradictory things. Unfortunately, this is not a difficulty that can be easily got round. One cannot simply scrap or redefine the word, because the ambiguities and contradictions are embedded within the human mind. In the chapters that follow, I can only hope—perhaps over-optimistically—that the context will make everything clear.

FROM THE CHILDREN'S CHANT TO THE PENTATONIC SCALE

There are two ways of proceeding from the children's chant to the pentatonic scale. One is to extend the chant at either end, or even at both ends, as in Ex. 4.1, where *a* rises to c^+ and *e* sinks to *d*. (Actually, this tune is, strictly speaking, hexatonic, because of the fleeting *b*; but the framework remains unmistakably pentatonic.)

Ex. 4.1. 'The Fause Knight upon the Road' (Scottish ballad tune) (down a 4th)

"Oh, whare are ye gaun," says the fause knight up - on the road.
"I'm gaun to the schule," says the wee boy; and still he stood.

The other way is, as it were, to 'clone' the children's mode. Instead of being extended, the *a–g–e* pattern may be reproduced, in either an upward or downward direction, at the distance of a fourth or fifth (Ex. 4.2). Of the four theoretical possibilities—up a fourth, up a fifth, down a fourth, down a fifth—only the last two,

Ex. 4.2. Replication of the children's chant at the 4th or 5th

(*a*)   (*b*)   (*c*)   (*d*)

given the human preference for descending melodic lines, are of any evolutionary significance. The fifth-down pattern (Ex. 4.2(*d*)) is perhaps the oldest of all, and certainly the most widespread. Ethnomusicologists call it 'fifth-answering', usually with the implication of a more or less sequential (though not always strictly pentatonic) pattern. Its closeness to the children's chant is well illustrated by Ex. 4.3. Like so much African song, this bluesy lament[1] is accompanied by an instrumental ostinato,[2] consisting in this case of a falling minor third doubled by the voice first at the twelfth and then at the octave (Ex. 4.3(*b*)).

Ex. 4.3. 'Ngoneni, ngoneni nebakitsi' (Swazi lament) (up a tone)

(*a*) beginning

(*b*) contrapuntal reduction

---

[1] The words, which even my Swazi informant found cryptic, mean: 'What have I done? What have I done?' Then (unquoted): 'I live in the forest. I am afraid . . .'.

[2] The instrument is the makweyana bow, in which the bowstring is tied back near the middle to form two unequal lengths. These are then tuned to the desired interval and struck with a stick.

This 'fifth-answering' is only one instance of what is probably the greatest complexity-generator in music: the displacement of melodic patterns from one part of the octave to another. But notice the word 'pattern'. We are concerned, not with the *transposition* of a figure, but with the *transference* of the pattern of which the figure is a realization. In the passage just quoted, *a–g–e* is transposed, but the 'children's tetrachord' is transferred. In the same way, an individual tune may be transposed into the dominant key, but that key is itself a transference of the tonic key. Except at the octave, all transpositions imply transference.

Tensions and ambiguities

The pentatonic is sometimes called a 'gapped scale'. Ethnomusicologists dislike the term as suggesting a defective form of heptatonic, but if the word 'gap' is replaced with 'chord', the description becomes quite legitimate. It is indeed a 'chorded scale', consisting of major-second steps interspersed with minor-third chords; but equally it is a 'scaled chord', consisting of a seventh with a bridged third. The former aspect is expressed by the formula $c–d–e\ g–a\ c^+–d^+–e^+ \ldots$; the latter, by $a^-–c–(d)–e–g\ a–c^+–(d^+)–e^+–g^+ \ldots$

Regarded as a chord, it has unique and beautiful properties. As well as forming a coherent whole in itself, the seventh $a^-–c–e–g$ readily breaks into the component triads $a^-–c–e$ and $c–e–g$, each with its own power. The major triad is the bottom of the harmonic series, but the minor triad is the bottom of the pentatonic seventh. In a very real sense, its tonic and dominant notes, *a* and *e*, are the tonic and dominant of all pentatonic music, though to avoid confusion it is better to call them the main and secondary pentatonic poles. (Incidentally, medieval theorists seem to have had an inkling of the cardinal importance of *a*, for why else should they have designated it by the first letter of the alphabet?)

It is the chords that give pentatonic melody its strength. In a well-balanced pentatonic tune the major and minor triads are nearly always in harmonious antagonism. Of course, the details vary enormously, but we can make a few generalizations. Certain patterns constantly recur: the major and minor triads; the pentatonic seventh; and the children's tetrachord and its inversion, which is sometimes called the 'psalm tetrachord' from its frequent occurrence in psalm tones. Very often, these are enclosed in a well-defined 'envelope' consisting of a fourth, fifth, or octave. The medieval word for such an envelope was *ambitus*, here Anglicized as 'ambit'.

Ambit should not be confused with compass. The top and bottom notes may exceed it, provided the sense of enclosure is retained. A tune may, for instance, have the ambit $e–e^+$ but the compass $d–g^+$. Nor should ambits be confused with keys; a tune with the ambit $a^-–a$ is not necessarily in the key of *A* minor. The commonest ambits are those bounded by the pentatonic poles (e–a, a^-–e, a^-–a, and e–e^+), followed in frequency by their 'relative major' equivalents (g–c^+, c–g, c–c^+, and g^-–g). But we should not fall into the trap of assuming that the former are necessarily associated with the minor mode and the latter with the major. It is true that this is often the case, as in the 'authentic' (1–1^+), and 'plagal' (5^-–5) modes of the textbooks. Very often, however, it is not.

In particular, the ambit a^-–a is frequently associated with the key of C major. In unharmonized melody, there is often a division of responsibility between the a minor triad, which *outlines* the melody, and the c major triad, which *accents* it. The archetypal example is the children's chant itself, where the ambit is e–a but the accent falls on g. In more elaborate tunes, it is likely that the ambit will be a^-–a and the accent on both g and c. We have already seen this pattern in 'Ngoneni, ngoneni' (Ex. 4.3), and further examples could be adduced from all over the world. 'Hishie Ba'' (Ex. 4.4) is as characteristic of northern Europe as 'Ngoneni, ngoneni' is of Africa. Instead of the 'saw-toothed' melodic contour we have the typically European arch; instead of end-repetition, a symmetrical binary form. Yet both tunes have the same pentatonic framework, the same a^-–a ambit, and (apart from a few rhythmic differences) the same d–c–a^- drop at the end, derived, of course, from the children's chant. Indeed, the last four bars of the European tune will be found on examination to be a florid variation on the first phrase of the African one.

Ex. 4.4. 'Hishie Ba'' (Scottish folk song) (down a 4th)

A striking feature of 'Hishie Ba'' is the dissonant treatment of d in bar 4, resolved, four bars later, not on a but on c. This is a minor flesh on c major bones. In fact, all that is needed to convert it into a straightforward c major is the removal of the as at the beginning and end. The resulting tune may not be particularly good, but it is perfectly normal and intelligible. It is also very much at odds with orthodox musical theory, especially in its fashionable Schenkerian guise.

A digression on Schenker

Since most of my readers will be familiar with Schenker's system, there is no need to explain it in great detail. Its basis is the *C* major triad, 'arpeggiated' to form an *Ursatz* or 'primordial pattern' (translations vary) consisting of a *c–g–c* (or I–V–I) bass in counterpoint with a descending *Urlinie* (Ex. 4.5). This 'background' is then elaborated (or 'diminished', in Schenkerian parlance) into the 'foreground' that we actually hear.

Ex. 4.5. The Schenkerian *Ursatz* and *Urlinie*

This theory has indubitable merits. Even by the exalted standards of late nineteenth-century Vienna, Schenker was a crank, but a crank with a streak of genius. At a time when other theorists were trying to explain everything in terms of harmony, he saw the importance of melody, and something of its chordal nature. Probably the most fruitful of his ideas was that of 'prolongation', the extension and elaboration of chords or melodic degrees; but here again, his originality lay mainly in his view of melody. Little that he had to say about harmony was particularly novel, though he did show a keen insight in reducing it to two-part counterpoint. His reduction of complex harmonic progressions to a gigantic I–V–I cadence revealed an inkling of self-similarity. And he is hierarchic to a fault.

Unfortunately, these promising insights were cobbled into a grandiose, absurdly mechanistic scheme that takes account neither of the pervasive ambiguity of music nor the limitations of the human mind (a 'background' appropriate to a simple lyric may also do duty for the first movement of a symphony). A perhaps equally fundamental defect is the exclusive concentration on the major triad. To Schenker, the minor triad is merely an inflection of the primordial *c–e–g* to *c–e♭–g*. The pentatonic context has no place in his scheme at all.

Thus, a pentatonic tune like 'Hishie Ba' ' (Ex. 4.4), otherwise an excellent subject for Schenkerian analysis (Ex. 4.6), is disqualified by the *a*s at either end. Both 'background' and 'middleground' make good sense in themselves, but entirely fail to do justice to the *a* minor feeling of the whole. The top *a*s must be explained away as 'neighbouring notes' to *g*; the low *a*s fall out of the scheme altogether.

Ex. 4.6. 'Hishie Ba' ', with a Schenkerian analysis

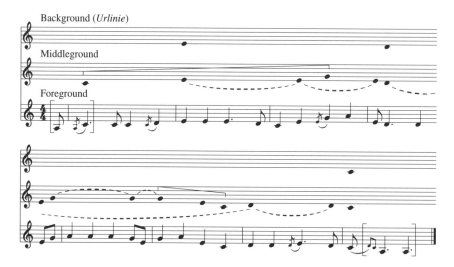

It may be objected that Schenker, who had the loftiest scorn for folk music of all kinds, never intended his analytical methods to apply to non-harmonic harmony. This is true; but, as we shall see in later chapters, melodic lines very like that of 'Hishie Ba' ' were common in the urban and indeed 'serious' music of his own time. Throughout the nineteenth century, the major and minor modes become both more pentatonic and harder to disentangle. Increasingly, the relative keys of *a* minor and *c* major fuse into a compound mode in which the major triad is revealed as what it always really was: a subset of the pentatonic seventh.

THE DIATONIC CONTEXT

A close approach to these nineteenth-century patterns can be found in those folk tunes where the mode is major—in other words, the tonic is *c*—but the ambit is a^--a or $e-e^+$. Here again, Scotland provides good examples. 'Young Johnstone' (Ex. 4.7) is an instance of the former pattern, 'Clyde's Waters' (Ex. 4.8), of the latter.

The first of these tunes is also notable for a small but significant detail in its sixth bar: the passing *f*, which makes it, strictly speaking, not pentatonic but hexatonic. This is by no means the first of the 'pentatonic' tunes quoted in these pages to include non-pentatonic notes; both 'The Fause Knight upon the Road' (Ex. 4.1) and 'Na more utushka kupalasya' (Ex. 3.12) had passing *b*s. But in no case has the interpolation been prominent enough to disturb the pentatonic effect. As it

Ex. 4.7. 'Young Johnstone' (Scottish ballad tune) (down a 5th)

Young John-stone and the young Col' - nel Sat drink-ing at the wine; O gin
1　　　　　　　*2*　　　　　　*3*　　　　　*4*

ye wad mar-ry my sis - ter It's I wad mar - ry thine.
5　　　　*6*　　　　　*7*　　　　*8*

Ex. 4.8. 'Clyde's Waters' (Scottish ballad tune)

Young Wil - lie stands in his sta - ble door, And comb-ing down his steed; And
1　　　　　　*2*　　　　　　*3*　　　　　*4*

look - ing through his white fing - ers, His nose be - gan to bleed.
5　　　　*6*　　　　*7*　　　*8*

happens, there has been no 'pentatonic' tune including all seven notes of the diatonic scale, but such a thing is perfectly possible.

What, then, is the real difference between the pentatonic and heptatonic scales? The answer to this apparently simple question turns out to be surprisingly complicated. Historically, the six- and seven-note scales developed out of their five-note predecessor. They are 'bridged pentatonics' in which an extra note fills either one or both of the minor thirds—incidentally, the reason why naturally occurring modes never exceed seven focal notes. (The 'octatonic scale' of alternating tones and semitones does, as its name suggests, contain eight notes; but in its fully developed form it can hardly be regarded as a natural occurrence.)

How the bridging occurred is an altogether more difficult question. In all probability, the minor third was at first split more or less equally, and only later divided into a clean-cut tone-plus-semitone. But what of the semitone itself? Where did *that* come from? Drones, natural-harmonic instruments, microtonal glides, the inborn tendency to 'bend' a dissonant second towards its goal—all these no doubt played their part. In any case, the semitone was the most important discovery in the history of melody after the pentatonic scale itself. The two minor-third slots could now each be filled in two distinct ways, giving four possibilities in all: $a^-–b^-–c$, $a^-–b\flat^-–c$, $e–f\sharp–g$, and $e–f–g$. In conformity with the diatonic scale, these could then be combined in the following ways:

$a^--b^--c + e-f\sharp-g$, giving $a^--b^--c-d-e-f\sharp-g$, or, transposed, $d-e-f-g-a-b-c^+$;
$a^--b\flat-c + e-f-g$, giving $a^--b\flat-c-d-e-f-g$, or, transposed, $e-f-g-a-b-c^+-d^+$;
$a^--b^--c + e-f-g$, giving $a^--b^--c-d-e-f-g$.

The fourth possible combination, $a^--b\flat-c + e-f\sharp-g$, is, of course, not diatonic. It gives the *heptatonia secunda* scale, which will be discussed in Chapter 11.

The first of these patterns to develop were those in which the semitonal interpolated notes point in the same direction, or, to put it another way, in which they are separated by a perfect fifth. The Phrygian mode of the ancient Greeks (which they themselves called 'Dorian') appears to have evolved out of an earlier pentatonic mode in just this manner. We can form some idea of its origins from a Spanish street cry (Ex. 4.9), in which a $d-e-g-a$ framework, clearly derived from the children's chant, is filled with a dissonant f, resolving on e.

Ex. 4.9. 'Pregón de un vendedor de romances' (cry of a Spanish ballad seller) (down a 4th)

As such fillers became more common and the semitone more clearly defined, the pentatonic scale gradually yielded to the heptatonic; but it was a slow process, largely because musicians were reluctant to give up the advantages of pentatonic patterns. In a great deal of folk melody it is hard to say where one system ends and the other begins. Whereas 'The Fause Knight upon the Road', 'Young Johnstone', and many other Scottish, Irish, and American tunes are clearly pentatonic, the cry of the ballad seller is something of a borderline case, and would become even more so if (as often in Spanish music) the $f-e$ were repeated a fifth higher as $c-b$. Yet this tune, too, has a clear pentatonic framework.

In fact, it is the rule rather than the exception that heptatonic melody should have a definite pentatonic framework. This is true of English as well as Scottish and Irish folk song,[3] of most twentieth-century popular music (including jazz), and even (notwithstanding its elaborate chromaticisms) of classical Indian music. Not only are the pentatonic rāgas regarded as the 'strongest'; as Fox Strangways points out, 'A song may be in a pentatonic scale although more than five distinct notes are touched in it, if it has only five substantive notes and the other one or two are used as passing-notes'.[4] Most pertinently of all for present purposes, it is also

---

[3] For a discussion of the pentatonic patterns hidden within English folk songs, see Herman Reichenbach, 'The Tonality of English and Gaelic Folksong'.   [4] *The Music of Hindostan*, 126.

true, to an ever-increasing extent, of classical European music during the nineteenth century.

The three pentatonic species

One reason why this pentatonic basis has usually been overlooked is that the composer need not confine himself to a single pentatonic framework. There are, in all, three possible 'species', which Hungarian scholars have called 'naturalis', 'obtusa', and 'acuta', after the three hexachords of medieval theory.[5] The *hexachordum naturale*, with its fourth degree removed, becomes the 'pentatonia naturalis'; the *hexachordum molle*, similarly treated, the 'pentatonia obtusa'; the *hexachordum durum*, the 'pentatonia acuta'. In English, we might translate these terms as the 'natural', 'blunt', and 'sharp' pentatonics, though in this book I have preferred to revert to the medieval 'soft' and 'hard' for the last two (Ex. 4.10).

Ex. 4.10. The three pentatonic species

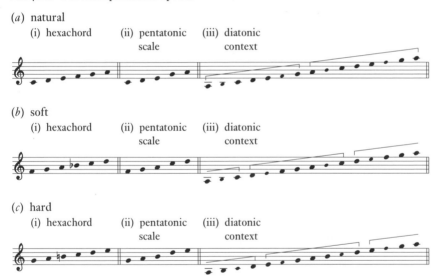

(*a*) natural
    (i) hexachord   (ii) pentatonic   (iii) diatonic
                       scale   context

(*b*) soft
    (i) hexachord   (ii) pentatonic   (iii) diatonic
                       scale   context

(*c*) hard
    (i) hexachord   (ii) pentatonic   (iii) diatonic
                       scale   context

Although it is helpful to think of the 'natural' pentatonic as $a^-\!-\!c\!-\!d\!-\!e\!-\!g$, the 'soft' pentatonic as $d\!-\!f\!-\!g\!-\!a\!-\!c^+$, and the 'hard' pentatonic as $e\!-\!g\!-\!a\!-\!b\!-\!d^+$, the order of the notes is in each case arbitrary. The natural pentatonic, for instance, could just as well take the forms $c\!-\!d\!-\!e\!-\!g\!-\!a$, $d\!-\!e\!-\!g\!-\!a\!-\!c^+$, $e\!-\!g\!-\!a\!-\!c^+\!-\!d^+$, or $g\!-\!a\!-\!c^+\!-\!d^+\!-\!e^+$. For these are *species*, not *modes*. They are, so to speak, angles at which a pentatonic

---

[5] My source for these terms is Lajos Bárdos, 'Ferenc Liszt, the Innovator', 4–5. He leaves it unclear whether these terms are his own invention or common Hungarian currency. The latter seems more likely.

scale may relate to its diatonic background. This background, which in its fully developed form exists only in European music since the Middle Ages, may be visualized as the white keys of the piano (or a transposition thereof), into which the pentatonic species fit in three possible ways (Ex. 4.10(*a* iii), (*b* iii), and (*c* iii)).

The natural pentatonic is, in a sense, the 'tonic' to which the hard pentatonic plays 'dominant' and the soft pentatonic 'subdominant'. Unlike the actual tonic, dominant, and subdominant chords, however, the pentatonic species are composites, fusing *A* minor + *C* major, *D* minor + *F* major, and *E* minor + *G* major into single entities. And just as in Greek myth the two sexes were originally one, and ever after have longed to return to this composite identity, so the individual triads are prone to recombine into their parent, pentatonic forms. This is most obvious in the case of *D* minor and *F* major, which repeatedly merge into the 'added sixth' f–a–c^+–d^+, but it is true also of the *A* minor–*C* major and *E* minor–*G* major combinations. If we are inclined to overlook these tendencies, it is because our notions of 'normal' melody are drawn from precisely that period, between about 1680 and 1760, when the more obviously pentatonic figures were most rigorously banished.

Yet even the tunes of this period have their pentatonic skeletons; even 'The Bonny Lass o' Fyvie' (Ex. 2.1(*a*)), specifically chosen for its sturdily diatonic character, is constructed out of melodic chords that, being triadic, are *ipso facto* pentatonic. If the effect is nevertheless un-pentatonic, it is partly because this tune includes several semitones, and partly because it excludes all 'knight's moves'. If, on the other hand, the Appalachian folk hymn 'Father Get Ready' (Ex. 4.11) *does* sound pentatonic, in spite of its six-note scale, this is because it shifts between pentatonic species in such a way as to combine several knight's moves with a total absence of semitones.

Ex. 4.11. 'Father Get Ready', beginning (Appalachian folk hymn) (down a 5th)

A further important point is that Basses inevitably tend to be more pentatonic than Melodies, since they depend on pentatonically sturdy intervals. If we stipulate that a Bass must possess the degrees *c* and *g* (= *1* and *5*), there are again three possible pentatonic arrangements. Historically, the first to develop was c–$e♭$–f–g–$b♭$, which is, of course, a transposition of the 'natural' pentatonic a–c–d–e–g (Ex. 4.12(a)). The other two are c–d–f–g–$b♭$, common in the sixteenth century, and c–d–f–g–a, for the ordinary major mode (Ex. 4.12(b) and (c)).

Ex. 4.12. The pentatonic Bass modes

(a)   (b)   (c)

or, transposed

CHROMATIC INFLECTION

What, then, of the classical *minor* mode? That, too, has a pentatonic Bass, but in a distorted form: the same, in fact, as that of the major mode, but with the sixth and sometimes also second degree flattened (c–$d(♭)$–f–g–$a♭$). Chromatic inflections such as these may be applied to any of the four notes making up the pentatonic sevenths, in either an upward or a downward direction. Any member of the pentatonic seventh may be raised or lowered by a semitone. This gives the notes $a♭$, $c♯$, $e♭$, and $g♯$, which may form the major thirds $a♭$–c and a–$c♯$, and the minor thirds c–$e♭$ and $c♯$–e. Of all these novelties, by far the most important are the major third a–$c♯$ and the minor third c–$e♭$, since they introduce a new, chromatic major–minor relationship. It is now possible to link c major not only to a minor, but also to c minor; and a minor may similarly be linked to a major. This is of course the familiar 'tonic' or 'parallel' relationship, in which keys share 1 and 5.

Meanwhile, the same inflections make possible a new range of fifth and seventh chords. Raising c to $c♯$ gives the 'dominant seventh' a–$c♯$–e–g (or, transposed, c–e–g–$b♭$ or g–b–d–f). Lowering e to $e♭$ gives the 'half-diminished' seventh a–c–$e♭$–g so beloved of the Romantics. If, in addition to this, g is lowered to $g♭$, the result is the fully diminished seventh a–c–$e♭$–$g♭$. Lowering a to $a♭$, or raising g to $g♯$, gives the augmented fifths $a♭$–c–e and c–e–$g♯$.

A final point is that, by raising or lowering a note or two, pentatonic sevenths can be interlocked to form ninths. For instance, $f♯$–a–$c♯$–e plus a–c–e–g gives $f♯$–a–$c(♯)$–e–g, and a–c–e–g plus c–$e♭$–g–$b♭$ gives a–c–$e(♭)$–g–$b♭$. What is more, the process is repeatable, with stupendously complicated and, on the face of it, very unpentatonic results.

Conclusion

In a way, the word 'pentatonic' is unfortunate. It is incidental that there happen to be five notes in the scale. The real basis of pentatonic melody is consonance, and, ultimately, that 'sound in nature', the major triad. This primordial pattern is so powerful that it provides a frame of reference for all the more elaborate types of melody and harmony, whether heptatonic, chromatic, or, for that matter, atonal. In the end, all music is pentatonic.

PART TWO

The Harmonic Revolution

5 Primitive Harmony

HARMONIC VERSUS MELODIC CHORDS

Once they become harmonic, melodic chords undergo several changes. Most obviously, they acquire a juiciness of which the melodic equivalent gives no inkling. To sound an interval simultaneously is to intensify it: perfect fifths become stronger, major thirds sweeter, minor thirds gloomier. As for dissonant intervals like the minor second or augmented fourth, they develop the stridency that the lay public associates with the words 'dissonance' and 'discord'. Curiously, this view is not shared by the experts:

An interval or chord which, so to speak, enjoys a certain amount of self-satisfaction is a Concord, whilst one which restlessly tries to push on to something in front is a Discord: the words Consonance and Dissonance have similar meanings.[1]

Dissonance. Two or more notes sounding together and forming a discord, or a sound which, in the prevailing harmonic system, is unstable and needs to be resolved to a consonance.[2]

Discord. b. . . . a chord which by itself is unpleasing or unsatisfactory to the ear, and requires to be 'resolved' or followed by some other chord.[3]

Discord is transition; concord is finality.[4]

Given the prevalence of the Ramellian paradigm, it is only to be expected that dissonance and discord (the two words have been more or less synonymous for over a thousand years)[5] should be regarded as peculiarly harmonic. What *is* strange is the absence of any reference to 'discord' in the non-technical sense.[6] Actually,

---

[1] Scholes, *The Oxford Companion to Music*, 'Harmony: 24. Some Definitions of Common Terms in Harmony, (*h*)', 456.

[2] *The Grove Concise Dictionary of Music*, 210.　　[3] *OED*, iv. 747, article on 'discord', definition 3.b.

[4] Tovey, *The Forms of Music*, 'Harmony: III. Modal Tonality', 51. Originally a series of articles in the 11th edn. of the *Encyclopaedia Britannica*.

[5] See the quotation from Hucbald (*c.* 880) on p. 57.

[6] To be fair to Tovey, he does define 'discord', in a glossary at the end of his *Encyclopaedia Britannica* article (xiii. 9), as 'a combination in which both its logical origin in a musical scheme and its acoustic roughness show that it cannot form a point of repose'.

there are two quite distinct aspects to harmonic dissonance: the restlessness or instability that it shares with melody, and the acoustic roughness peculiar to harmony. To distinguish them in this book, I shall use 'dissonance (*dis-sonance*, 'clashing sound') for the former, and discord (*dis-cord*, 'clashing chord') for the latter.[7]

Acoustically, all intervals but the octave are discordant in this sense to a lesser or greater extent; psychologically, the matter is more complicated. As in the case of pure melody, we must make a distinction between intra- and extra-triadic intervals. Again, all the former are concordant (though not to the same degree), the major second is a near-concord, just as it is a near-consonance, and the minor second is as emphatically discordant as it is dissonant.

A further, rather more obvious effect of making a melodic chord harmonic is that it acquires a top and a bottom, and with it a harmonic bias towards the bottom, or 'bass'. This harmonic bias may or may not coincide with the melodic bias (towards, for instance, the *c* in *c–g*, or the *g* in *e–g*). When it does, we say that the chord is in 'root position'; when it does not, that it is in some sort of inversion. Inevitably, ambiguous or intermediate patterns are possible, such as the added-six chord *c–e–g–a*, but such cases are exceptional. In general, harmonic chords are far less ambiguous than their melodic equivalents. Whereas the former need to be defined by contour and rhythmic emphasis, the latter for the most part define themselves. An unambiguous series of triads is the normal condition of Western harmony—so normal, indeed, that we have fallen into the habit of calling it *the* harmony, and endowed it with an identity independent of melody, and even seemingly in opposition to melody. How, one must ask, did this extraordinary situation come into being?

PRIMITIVE CHORDAL PROGRESSIONS

We shall never know for certain how chordal harmony began, but we can be sure that it has existed for a very long time. Primitive music abounds in it, and there is no reason to suppose that matters were different in prehistoric times. Two principal sources are heterophony, which is more natural than strict unison, and organum, or the doubling of the tune at the fourth or fifth, which likewise arises very instinctively:

men and women street-singers in London have occasionally been noticed to be singing in parallel fifths; the boy Mozart and his father, in Venice in 1771, heard 'a duet in pure fifths

---

[7] 'Discord' was originally the opposite of 'accord', later shortened to 'chord'. Both come from the Latin *cor, cordis*, 'heart', the root meanings therefore being 'to differ (or agree) at heart'. The spelling of 'chord' is due to confusion with the Greek χορδη, string.

sung by a man and woman in the street without missing a note' [probably a survival of ancient folk practice]. Sir John Stainer complained at a Church Congress in 1894 that he once had his worship disturbed by an individual singing at the top of his voice 'uniformly a perfect fifth below the trebles'.[8]

Yet another source was the overlapping of call and response, though there is no guarantee that the ensuing harmony will be chordal. And when both call and response consist of the same scrap of tune, the resulting two-part round is an important ancestor of fugal polyphony.

These are all primarily vocal forms, but one should not forget instruments, especially instruments that produce the natural harmonic series. These are undoubtedly of immense antiquity. On the walls of the cave of Les Trois Frères in south-western France (c.15,000 BC), there is a painting of a man apparently playing a mouth-bow of a type still common in Africa.[9] This instrument is sounded by inserting the string into the mouth and twanging it, meanwhile changing the shape of the oral cavity so as to bring out the desired harmonic. The jew's harp or guimbarde works on the same principle, except that the twanging is done on a tongue of metal, cane, or wood instead of a taut string. In either case—and this is what makes the instrument harmonic as well as melodic—the fundamental sounds as a drone bass throughout.

Even apart from this special case, drones are not uncommon in primitive music, but neither are they characteristic of it. The fully developed drone (especially in the bass) is a product of the ancient civilizations of India and western Asia. It has the paradoxical feature of being, strictly speaking, harmonic, yet providing the background for a single thread of melody. As a result, the cultures in which drones are most prominent are also those in which pure melody has been most assiduously cultivated.

The next step after the harmonic chord was the harmonic progression; and here a distinction must be made between a mere *succession* of chords, such as organum automatically produces, and a chordal *progression*. For two chords to qualify as a progression, they must be in a hierarchic relationship. Either one must be subordinate to the other, or both subordinate to a third chord. At this point harmony ceases to be a mere expansion or consolidation of melody and becomes a force in its own right, so it is only natural that the first steps along this road were tentative. The harmonic progressions of recent primitive music are usually confined to two indefinitely repeated chords, and it is reasonable to suppose that this was for a long time the only type. The interval in the bass varies, but it is striking that the seemingly

---

[8] Scholes, *The Oxford Companion to Music*, 'Harmony: 4. The History of Harmony: Phase I. Parallelism and Perfect Intervals', 447.

[9] The performer, presumably a shaman of some kind, is clad in a bison skin and appears to be dancing. For a reproduction, see *The Book of Music*, 18.

natural interval of the perfect fourth is in fact rare,[10] its place being taken by the major second, or something approaching it.

Why should this be? To begin with, the chordal progression, like everything else in harmony, grew out of pure melody. The regular harmonic swing was at first conceived as an amplification of a similar melodic swing, and some intervals swing better than others. The minor third works particularly well, but for harmonic purposes suffers from the disadvantage of producing weakly differentiated chords that all too easily coalesce into pentatonic sevenths (cf. Ex. 4.3(*a*)). The root of the trouble is that the minor third is itself a chordal interval, as, of course, are the major third and perfect fourth. This probably explains why progressions at this last interval are rare in primitive harmony and established themselves in Europe only by a long and devious route.

It is, then, precisely the non-chordal nature of the major second that makes it such a good basis for chords. It would be a small step to build fifths or triads on the oscillating-second tunes of Chapter 3 (see Exs. 3.13–15), and in fact something of the kind frequently happens in primitive harmony. In the two musical-bow tunes quoted here, we see how the harmonics could first stand alone (Ex. 5.1), and then be imitated by the voice (Ex. 5.2). Incidentally, the combination in the latter tune of harmonics 3, 4, and 5 over *c* with harmonics 3 and 4 over *d* is yet another route to the pentatonic scale (g–c^+–e^+ + a–d^+ = g–a–c^+–d^+–e^+).

Ex. 5.1. Tswana musical-bow tune (up a 4th)

Ex. 5.2. Swazi song with musical-bow accompaniment (up a 4th)

---

[10] See e.g. the (native) mouth-organ tune from Borneo in Schneider, 'Primitive Music', 178, Ex. 285.

This oscillating Bass, often miscalled the 'double tonic' ('no tonic' would be more accurate), is one of the great musical archetypes, occupying much the same position in harmony as the children's chant does in melody.

Harmony in Europe

With all due respect to African polyrhythmic drumming, Indian rāgas, or the exquisite subtleties of the Far East, European classical harmony is the most astounding development in music, perhaps even in art. Yet it is comparatively recent. Its roots lie in the folk harmony of early medieval Europe, which from the meagre evidence available to us seems to have resembled that of pre-colonial Africa. As this native harmony fell under the domination first of the Roman Empire and then of the Christian Church, it came into contact with a radically different tradition. Writing half a century ago, Laurence Picken observed that 'it is reasonable to assume that liturgical homophony in Europe was dominant to "barbaric" polyphony, just as Christian culture was dominant to pagan culture in the centres of urban civilisation. It has been suggested before now that folksong elements were absorbed by plain chant; and it is conceivable that the emergence of Church polyphony was due essentially to the same process.'[11] In fact, this is not so much 'conceivable' as 'very likely'. Northern Europeans harmonized religious music because, for them, it was the natural thing to do.

Soon afterwards, another vital ingredient was added to this cultural mixture: that of musical literacy. Alone among the great religions of the world, the Catholic Church developed a musical notation efficient enough for harmonic purposes.

Probably the first extant reference to polyphony occurs in *De harmonica institutione*, a treatise written by the monk, theorist, and composer Hucbald about the year 900: 'Consonance is the calculated and concordant combination of two notes, which will only occur if two notes of different pitch are combined to form a musical unity, as happens when a man and a boy sing the same tune, or in what is generally known as "organizing" [*organizatio*].'[12] The first notated examples, in the *Musica enchiriadis* of about the same time, include both 'strict organum', with the melody in parallel fourths or fifths throughout, and 'free organum',[13] which, like the *podgoloski* of Russian folk music, begins and ends with a unison but branches out in between.[14] There is also evidence that monophonic 'calls' were

---

[11] 'Instrumental Polyphonic Folk Music in Asia Minor' (1954), 83–4.

[12] 'Consonantia . . . est duorum sonorum rata et concordabilis permixtio, quae non aliter constabit, nisi duo altrinsecus editi soni in unam simul modulationem conveniant, ut fit, cum virilis ac puerilis vox pariter sonuerit; vel etiam in eo, quod consuete organizationem vocant.' The translation is that of Dom Anselm Hughes. See 'The Birth of Polyphony', 277. The whole chapter is of the greatest interest.

[13] e.g. 'Rex coeli, Domine' (Ex. 5.10).

[14] For a description of *podgoloski*, see Victor Belaiev, 'Kastalsky and his Russian Folk Polyphony'. For a

answered with polyphonic 'responses', as, for instance, in the dedication of Ramsey Abbey (composed in 991): 'While the Decani side of the choir sang a melodious strain with excellent voices, the Cantoris side laboured at organum parts in joyful songs of praise.'[15] All in all, it seems that the earliest organum was little more than an ecclesiastic adaptation of folk practice.

Then, not long before the year 1000 (that easy-to-remember date generally taken as marking the first stirrings of European revival), the invention of staff notation brought the first radical change. Tentatively at first, then with more confidence, composers began to elaborate the polyphonic web. The two voices expanded, first into three, then into four or more, in the process becoming both more independent and more tightly knit, largely through the agency of chordal progression. The 'double tonic' is already implied (though never explicitly recorded) in the tune of 'O Roma nobilis' (Ex. 5.3). This must have enjoyed considerable popularity during the twelfth century, since it appeared in at least three manuscripts, to two sets of words.[16]

Ex. 5.3. 'O Roma nobilis' (12th-c. song) (down a 5th)

partial example (ending, but not beginning, with a unison), see 'Prialitsa' (Ex. 15.29 on p. 423).

[15] 'Cum dextera pars sonum melodum personaret inclytis vocibus, tum sinister [i.e. sinistra] jubilando organicis desudabat laudibus'. See Hughes, 'The Birth of Polyphony', 279 (his translation). The same pattern is common in African and Afro-American singing.

[16] The other set belongs to a love song, 'O admirabile Veneris idolum'. The three manuscripts are at present housed in libraries at Rome, Montecassino, and Cambridge. See J. A. Westrup, 'Medieval Song', 220–1.

A similar ostinato, this time quite explicit, appears in the celebrated canon 'Sumer is icumen in' (Ex. 5.4), dating from about a century later. In both cases, the oscillating second is of a specifically European type, with the emphasis firmly on the bottom note.[17] Combined with clear-cut, four-bar phrase rhythms, it turns the *C* major triad into a true tonic, and the *D* minor–*C* major progression into a definite cadence. In passages like these we see the beginnings of modern tonality.

Ex. 5.4. 'Sumer is icumen in', beginning (English 13th-c. canon) (up a 5th)

The Irish Washerwoman and the Drunken Sailor

At about the same time, composers were developing a minor-mode version of this ostinato by the simple process of emphasizing its upper chord. In other respects, the major and minor versions were much alike. If *X* and *Y* stand respectively for the main and subsidiary chords, the principal patterns are the following (the rhythm is, of course, subject to a great deal of variation):

(1) ♩ | ♩ | ♩ | ♩ |
   X   Y   X   Y

(2) ♩ | ♩ | ♩ ♩ | ♩ |
   X   Y   X–Y   X

(3) ♩ | ♩ | ♩ | ♩ ♩ |
   X   Y   X   Y–X

Pattern 1, which we have seen in 'Sumer is icumen in', did not die out with the Middle Ages, but lived on in dance tunes like the seventeenth-century English jig 'Dargason' (Ex. 5.5). To this day, tunes based on it may be heard from traditional fiddlers and bagpipers.

But these are the exception. More usually, Pattern 1 is provided with some sort of concluding cadence. Sometimes this is on chord *Y*, as in 'Oft have I Ridden upon my Grey Nag', a version of the 'Dargason' tune recorded by Thomas

---

[17] Cf. the 'Guy Fawkes Song' (Ex. 3.13 on p. 37).

Ex. 5.5. 'Dargason' (English jig, *c.*1600) (down a 4th)

Ravenscroft in 1609 (see Ex. 7.5). The standard practice, however, is to end on the tonic, thereby transferring chord *X* to the end of the strain, as in Patterns 2 and 3. This incidentally causes the harmonic rhythms to diverge from the bar rhythms, as can easily be seen if the chords are represented by unbroken lines over more than one cycle. Here, for instance, is Pattern 2:

bars   —— —— —— —— —— —— —— ——
               1   2   3   4   1   2   3   4, etc.
chords —— —— —— —— —— —— ——
              X   Y   X–Y   X   Y   X–Y   X, etc.

The *X Y X Y* pattern is still there, but its rhythm has been distorted from

                 chords   X Y X Y
                 length in half-bars 2 2 2 2

to

                 X Y X Y
                 4 2 1 1

or, in Pattern 3, to

                 X Y X Y
                 3 2 2 1

In either case, the initial *X* chord straddles two statements of the tune.

This apparently trifling change was nothing less than revolutionary. It introduced a new and potent form of counterpoint, not between rhythm and rhythm, or melody and melody, or even melody and harmony, but between harmony and rhythm. Simple two- or three-chord formulas, combined with equally simple bar rhythms, could now generate forms that were both highly complex and, because of the simplicity, immensely strong; and they could do this merely because they were no longer 'in sync'.

We have already seen the major-mode form of Pattern 2 in 'O Roma nobis' (Ex. 5.3). Tunes constructed on this formula, in either mode, have survived to the present day,[18] but more often the chord scheme was doubled in length and the harmonic cadence moved (as in Pattern 3) to the last two bars:

$$\text{X} \quad \text{X} \quad \text{Y} \quad \text{Y} \quad \text{X} \quad \text{X} \quad \text{Y} \quad \text{X}$$

This 'cadential bunching' is a common occurrence in expanded harmonic schemes, simply because the end of the tune (or strain, or phrase), is otherwise likely to drag. As we shall see in later chapters, it was to play an important part in the waltz.

This expanded form of Pattern 3 is the most common harmonic scheme in traditional Irish and Scottish dance music. Hundreds of examples might be cited, of which probably the best known are (in the major) 'The Irish Washerwoman' (Ex. 5.6), a clear descendant of 'Dargason' (Ex. 5.5), and (in the minor) 'The Drunken Sailor' (Ex. 5.7), a sea shanty adapted from an Irish reel. They may serve as representatives of major and minor double-tonic tunes generally.

Ex. 5.6. 'The Irish Washerwoman' (Irish jig), beginning (down a 5th)

Ex. 5.7. 'The Drunken Sailor' (sea shanty tune, originally an Irish reel), beginning (up a 5th)

It should not, however, be imagined that X and Y must always be double-tonic chords. In countless tunes, including one version of 'The Irish Washerwoman' itself, Y is an ordinary dominant, with or without a seventh; in twentieth-century popular music, it is often the subdominant. The only requirement is that it should be in some way subordinate to X. Nor is it necessary for Patterns 1, 2, or 3 to make

---

[18] See e.g. 'The Barley Corn', an Irish version of the familiar 'John Barleycorn' song, collected in *Irish Street Ballads*, p. 176, no. 89. This consists of a series of minor-mode variations on Pattern 2. It bears a distinct resemblance to 'O Roma nobilis' in rhythm and cadence.

up self-contained tunes. Very often, they form part of some larger design. (Think, for instance, of all those passages, swinging regularly between tonic and dominant in the manner of Pattern 1, to be found in sonata-form movements.) These patterns may not be quite as easily summarized as the children's chant, the pentatonic scale, or the double tonic, but in their way they are just as archetypal.

THE DRONE

Like a great many other Oriental things, the systematic drone reached medieval Europe in the Middle Ages. How far back it goes in its Asian heartland is unclear, though we do know that the bagpipe was already in existence at the beginning of the Christian era, albeit as an extremely humble instrument.[19] At the other end of the social spectrum, it is probable that the brass instruments of ancient temples (including Jewish ones) were sometimes used to sustain drones, as in modern Tibetan Buddhism. Apart from fanfares, there was, after all, little else they could do, and there is something unmistakably numinous about a deep, unbroken, long-continued note.[20] In any case, drones have been important in Christian worship since at least the Middle Ages.

Even today, these contradictory associations are reflected in the words used to describe a persistent bass note: on the one hand, the 'pedal point' of that most respectable of instruments, the organ; on the other, the 'drone' of the bagpipe. It is worth noting, however, that these are both *instruments*. By its very nature, the drone has always been primarily an instrumental effect, and, like so many instrumental effects, has mostly been left to the discretion of the performer. In consequence, it has seldom been written down. Often the only evidence we have for the presence of a drone is the melody it has generated. For a drone is a frozen chord. Even in the absence of further harmony, its overtones will shape any melody it accompanies. If the drone is c, then the poles of attraction will be the notes forming the pentatonic seventh: c, e, g, and, to a lesser extent, a.

The effect of the drone on the melodic c is paradoxical. On the one hand, it attains a new prominence; on the other, the competition of the drone can render it insipid, or even, on some instruments, inaudible. It is much more satisfactory to linger on e or g, which combine melodic stability with harmonic resonance. In a common formula, the tune rises from c, revolves for a while around e, and then sinks back to c. This is the pattern of certain psalm tones found in both the Jewish

---

[19] See Baines, *Bagpipes*, 63–8 for a history of the early bagpipe.

[20] Schneider remarks that 'The long sustained (non-rhythmical) drone . . . appears to represent a particular mystic force' ('Primitive Music', 50), and cites examples from widely separated cultures.

and Catholic liturgies. From the striking similarity of Exs. 5.8 and 5.9,[21] they presumably had a common origin in ancient Jewish practice. We cannot know whether this involved a drone bass, but we do know that a phrase similar to the first half of the Jewish chant was accompanied in this manner as early as the ninth century (Ex. 5.10, bracketed section).

Ex. 5.8. Jewish psalm tone (down a 4th)

Ex. 5.9. Catholic psalm tone no. 6 (down a 4th)

Ex. 5.10. 'Rex coeli, Domine' (sequence, *c*.900)

In tunes such as these the drone has three effects, all quite foreign to the unharmonized pentatonic melody of previous chapters. Firstly, it counteracts the tendency of the human voice to fall, providing instead a basis from which it is natural to rise, and to do so by step. The drone is therefore a parent both of the rising scale and, with the subsequent fall, of the melodic arch. Secondly, it encourages an in-tune *f* at the distance of a perfect fourth, with a strong tendency to resolve on *e*; and since the resulting *e–f* semitone is easily reproduced a fifth higher as *b–c*⁺, this is an important advance towards the complete diatonic scale. Thirdly, it throws into relief the concordant notes *e* and *g*, which when singled out can then serve as tonics, or near-tonics, in their own right.

The consequences of this singling out were momentous. In the case of *e*, it led naturally to an emphasis on the semitone *f–e*, which then became the nucleus of some sort of Phrygian mode, as in Ex. 5.11. This Spanish folk hymn closely resembles the Catholic psalm tone quoted above (Ex. 5.9), except that it is somewhat more elaborate—and ends on *e* instead of *c*.

---

[21] The semibreves indicate reciting notes.

Ex. 5.11. 'La Virgen de los Dolores' (Spanish folk hymn)

A similar emphasis on *g* produces a kind of parallel major mode a fifth above that on *c*. In medieval theory, the word for the continual return to the same note was *repercussio*, 'striking again'—incidentally a term well worth reviving, in the form 'repercussion'. Later it was applied to the repeated note itself, usually but not invariably *g*. In this sense, *repercussio* comes close to being the Western equivalent of the Indian *vādī*. Something of this old sense still attached to the word *dominante*, when introduced by French theorists in the early seventeenth century.[22] Only later did 'the dominant' come to mean merely 'the note a perfect fifth above the tonic', to the puzzlement of generations of music students.

The later history of the drone

By the thirteenth century the drone had become a veritable craze. In the early decades of the century, the composers of the Parisian Notre Dame school produced polyphonic works in which *cantus firmi* were stretched into drones often amounting to the equivalent of sixteen or more bars of 6/8 time; a few decades later, depictions of drone instruments had begun to proliferate. Since many of the instruments were of Near Eastern origin, Arabic influence no doubt had a great deal to do with this, but the response was characteristically Western. In the East, the drone had been valued precisely because it provided a static background to an unrivalled elaboration of mode. In Europe, it became a dynamic force. It is significant that *shifting* drones had existed in Western polyphony from the start, and that the drone mania coincided with the first recorded appearance of the double tonic. In direct contradiction

---

[22] See Alfred Mann, *The Study of Fugue*, 49–50. 'The term *dominante*, the key word of harmonic thought and the modern equivalent for the early meaning of the *repercussio*, had gained currency in France much earlier than in the other European countries (it appeared first in the *Institution harmonique* by Salomon de Caus, 1615)' (p. 50).

to the Oriental experience, the long-term effect was to complicate harmony and simplify mode.

Out of the great wealth of western Asian modes, only those with minor thirds were of lasting consequence in Europe. The classical minor is an amalgam of the pentatonic minor with several Oriental modes, including the Phrygian. To this mixed ancestry it owes its richness, its instability, and, above all, its ambiguous approach to the major, both as a pentatonic 'relative' and a drone-based 'parallel'.

It would, however, be a great mistake to suppose that the creative force of the drone ended with the Renaissance. In a variety of guises—Mediterranean, east European, Scottish, Irish, Oriental, Afro-American—it went on producing new patterns well into the twentieth century. Of all harmonic devices, it is not only the simplest, but probably also the most fertile.

6 The Discovery of Tonality

THE MEDIEVAL BACKGROUND

For half a millennium ecclesiastical polyphony retained the hovering timelessness of the chant from which it had sprung. Then, after 1400, it began to change. The harmony became simpler, fuller, and stronger, in the process developing the powerful organizing force, radiating out from cadences of an entirely new type, that we call 'tonality'. The power depended upon the simplicity, and both came largely from popular music.

An example of late medieval music just touched by tonality in this sense is 'Adieu m'amour', by the northern French composer Binchois (Ex. 6.1). It is for a solo voice, the cantus, accompanied by two counterpoints, the tenor and contratenor, the former (so called because it originally 'held' the main tune) maintaining its own smooth melody while the latter rather awkwardly fills out the harmony. Each of the principal two voices has its own distinct form of cadence: $ii(\flat) \rightarrow i$ in the case of the tenor, and $vi(\flat) \rightarrow i^+$ (the 'Landini'[1] or 'under-third' cadence) in that of the cantus. These always occur together, so that their polyphonic relationship is fixed ($vi/ii \rightarrow i^+/i$ or $vi\flat/ii\flat \rightarrow i^+/i$); but *not*, be it noticed, their position within the mode. Already we see the beginnings of a hierarchic key system. It is worth noticing, too, that these proto-keys conform to the pentatonic seventh (C, G, E, A), and that the under-third cadences greatly strengthen this pentatonic impression.

Against these cadences in the cantus and tenor, the contratenor executes two distinct progressions: $iv(\sharp) \rightarrow v$, when the 'key' is G, E, or A (as in the bracketed Cadences 1, 4, 5, and 6), but $v^- \rightarrow v$ when it is C (Cadences 2, 3, and 7). The first of these progressions gives one of the medieval cadences ('Lydian' or 'Phrygian',[2] depending on the context); the second, a makeshift version of the full close. This cadence, with its queer-looking octave leap, remained in common use for the rest

---

[1] So called after the Florentine composer Francesco Landini (*c.*1325–97), who, though not actually the inventor of this cadence, made much use of it. Strictly speaking, the Landini cadence is a particular type of under-third cadence with the contour (i^+–$vii(\flat)$–$vi(\flat) \rightarrow i^+$, elaborated by Binchois into i^+–$vii(\flat)$–i^+–$vi(\flat) \rightarrow i^+$).

[2] So called because of the 'Lydian' $iv\sharp$ and 'Phrygian' $ii\flat$; otherwise, these cadences have no necessary connection with the modes they are named after.

Ex. 6.1. Binchois, 'Adieu m'amour' (*c.*1450) (up a 5th)

of the fifteenth century and the early years of the sixteenth. To Binchois, it was still evidently a somewhat perplexing novelty, since he confines it to the same rigidly identical form in the same tonic key. On the other hand, he is confident enough to end the movement with it. Behind this rather roundabout full close, one feels, some more straightforward precedent must have lurked.

And, in fact, just such a precedent had existed for at least a generation. Full closes of a much more modern type may be found in a *ballata*, or dance–like part song, composed some thirty, forty, or fifty years earlier by the Italian composer Antonio Zacara da Teramo (Ex. 6.2).[3] Their origin clearly lies in the bagpipe music

---

[3] The source of all my extracts from Zacara is Nino Pirrotta, 'Zacara da Teramo' (in *Music and Culture*

alluded to in the title.[4] In bars 4–7 we hear a sustained drone, and at the bracketed perfect cadences (bars 2–3, 7–8, 10–11, 12–13, 18–19, 21–2), something even more interesting: an *arpeggiated* drone.

Ex. 6.2. Antonio Zacara da Teramo, 'Ciaramella' (early 15th-c. *ballata*), beginning (up a 5th)

in Italy from the Middle Ages to the Baroque, 126–44). He gives 'Ciaramella' and 'Rosetta che non cambi mai colore' in full, as well as fragments of 'Amor né tossa'. All three contain bagpipe imitations. There is also a discussion of the general question of popular influence on early 15th-c. Italian music.

  [4] In the 15th c. the ciaramella was a north Italian form of bagpipe. Dictionaries derive the word from the Latin *calamellus* (Italian *cialamello*), diminutive of *calamus*, 'reed', making it a doublet of *chalumeau* and

For, like any other musical device, the drone grew more elaborate with time: first came the single drone on the tonic, then the double drone on both tonic and dominant, and finally the arpeggiated drone. In recent times, the most usual means of producing this last has been a special bagpipe, known from Poland to northern Serbia, including an additional chanter pierced with a single hole, which is left open for the tonic and closed for the dominant below. Example 6.3 is a specimen of the music it produces.[5] The effect was known both to Beethoven, who imitated it in

Ex. 6.3. Bagpipe *kolo* from Gajda, Slovenia, conclusion (up a diminished 5th)

'shawm' (the present-day meaning). I suspect that the real source is the Arabic *zummara*, 'reed pipe', assimilated to *cialamello* by folk etymology. This *ballata* also plays on the secondary meaning 'flirtatious young woman'.

[5] See Baines, *Bagpipes*, 69–70 and 74–9. For a much more elaborate, Hungarian example, see Ex. 11.85 on p. 210.

the first movement of his Pastoral Symphony,[6] and, centuries earlier, to William Byrd. From its title, one suspects that 'The Bagpipe and the Drone' (Ex. 6.4), from the latter's 'Battle' Suite,[7] was intended to imitate a two-man team, like the modern Italian ciaramella and zampogna.

Ex. 6.4. Byrd, 'The Bagpipe and the Drone' (no. 6 of the *Battle* suite, 1591), beginning

Perhaps the *1–5–1* leaps accompanying Zacara's full closes imitate an independent drone of this type; they certainly imitate an arpeggiated drone of some sort. To judge by their stiff, cautious air, they were still something of a novelty, and it is notable that the main cadences are of an older type. Perhaps to Zacara the full close was not a cadence at all, but merely an effective conjunction of melodic formulas; but it is equally likely that the disposition of the cadences was dictated by the folk-like 'tenor', which remained the principal tune of the movement. This is in a Phrygian mode based on *5*, with *6♭→5* cadences impossible to harmonize with V–I progressions. The effect, to present-day ears, is Spanish, the reason of course being that Spanish popular music has retained many features once current over a much wider area.

Though written a half-century earlier, Zacara's *ballata* sounds much more modern to us than Binchois's chanson. In some respects—the principal cadences, the allocation of the main tune to the tenor rather than the cantus, and the rough-and-ready counterpoint—it is, to be sure, relatively archaic, but in other respects it shows a more advanced harmonic sense. Stiff as they are, Zacara's full closes are less invariable than Binchois's; moreover, they use the plain leading note, not the Landini formula. His contratenor is throughout more 'bass-ic' and his key sense more developed, with distinct modulations to the relative major (bars 10–13) and subdominant (bars 18–19). In a word (and in spite of the minor mode) he is more *tonal*.

But what *is* tonality? Why did it develop at just this place and time? And—perhaps more to the point—why had it not developed much earlier?

---

[6] See the end of the exposition (bars 123–34), and the corresponding part of the recapitulation.

[7] Conjectured to celebrate the victory over the Spanish Armada in 1588. At all events, that dramatic occurrence must have been fresh in people's minds.

THE ESSENCE OF TONALITY

The *New Grove* contains seven definitions of 'tonality'—doubtless an incomplete list, for no musical term has been more argued over. Yet it is not, I believe, such a difficult concept, provided we jettison a few cherished confusions.

To begin with, tonality requires a Bass as well as a Melody. Pure, self-sufficient melody of the kind discussed in Chapters 3 and 4 cannot be tonal. It is therefore unfortunate that the word 'tonal' has come to be extended to everything, from Gregorian chant to Dixieland jazz, that is not *a*tonal.

Since tonality requires both a Melody and a Bass, it is inherently contrapuntal, but not every combination of Melody and Bass is tonal. A special Bass is needed, founded on intervals of the utmost consonance. Apart from the octave, the most consonant interval of all is the perfect fifth, so it follows that this interval is central to tonality. In the Melody, the same leaning towards consonance ensures that the normal mode is the major. Tonal Melody, like the tonal Bass, is distinguished by both intervallic simplicity and self-similarity.

The connection between these two properties may be shown by rearranging the diatonic scale as the pile of fifths $c^-–g^-–d–a–e^+–b^+$, plus the f below c^-, as in Fig. 6.1. We can then at once see why it is only in the major mode that the hexachords on *1* and *5* exactly match, and only in the major and natural minor modes that the three primary triads all have the same shape. In short, we can see how the major comes to be both the most consonant and the most self-similar mode in existence.

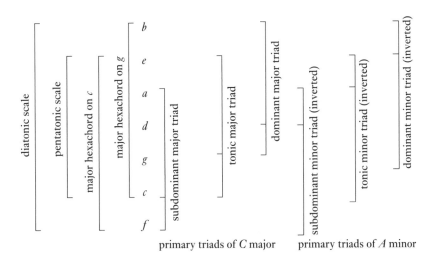

FIG. 6.1. The diatonic scale as a pile of fifths

Tonality, then, is a way of so regulating the counterpoint between Bass and Melody as to maximize consonance and self-similarity. Moreover, as its name (really 'tonicality', as Réti pointed out) implies, it refers everything to a tonic, and this *1* belongs primarily not to the Melody but to the Bass. To put the matter at its simplest, tonality is a method of composition based on interrupted drones.

This reliance on the Bass greatly reduces ambiguity. Directly or indirectly, everything is referred to the tonic; every note, every chord, has a precise function within the tonal hierarchy. This explicitness is both the greatest strength and most conspicuous weakness of the tonal system. On the one hand, it makes possible structures of unrivalled complexity; on the other, it substitutes for the delicious ambiguities of non-tonal music what must at first have seemed a crushing obviousness.

The very simplicity that was to prove its greatest merit made tonality an unpromising infant. The most one can say for the earliest examples is that they are bright and purposeful. Before composers could make much out of tonality, there were several daunting problems to be overcome. An appropriate style of melody had to be developed; the minor mode had somehow to be adapted to tonal purposes; the immense hierarchic potential of tonal harmony had to be explored, bit by tiny bit, and somehow reconciled with chromatic embellishment and polyphonic complexity.

Solving such problems was a long and untidy process. The various features of tonality developed independently, and at greatly differing rates—one reason, incidentally, why it has elicited so many conflicting definitions. Even before Zacara, the major mode and the tonic-and-dominant progression had existed for hundreds of years in popular music;[8] after him, a few more hundred years were to elapse before a fully tonal style of composition arrived in the late seventeenth century—if, indeed, it arrived at all.

THE UNWRITTEN TRADITION OF RENAISSANCE ITALY

It was only to be expected that the principal agents in this long and erratic development should be Italians. For centuries, they have preferred strong melodies, backed by relatively unobtrusive accompaniment, to the polyphonic webs of northern Europe. Compare, for instance, Vivaldi with J. S. Bach, Verdi with Wagner, Puccini with Richard Strauss. As early as the fifteenth century, this national bias was asserting itself in an explicitly populist manner: 'Already in 1429 Ambrogio

---

[8] e.g. the striking arpeggios on both tonic and dominant in the 13th-c. English dance tune quoted in Hughes, 'Music in Fixed Rhythm', 338, Ex. 181.

Traversari praised Leonardo Giustinian for his ability in singing sweet songs to the accompaniment of an instrument, an art which, "contrary to the habit of the ancients, is better known nowadays to the people than to learned men".[9]

Unfortunately, we know little about the music of composers like Giustinian, because they seldom, if ever, troubled to leave any record of it. The cradle of tonality was an 'unwritten tradition', in some ways resembling jazz and related popular genres, in others the classical music of the Orient.[10] Like most popular music, it generally did without musical notation, relying instead on memory, improvisation, and stock formulas; but, unlike popular music, it often enjoyed high cultural prestige. The main instrument was the lute, which like the modern guitar was favoured by amateur and professional alike, both alone and as an accompaniment to the voice.

It was this, and not the late medieval polyphony of the Church, that was the true Renaissance music. Unlike most other artists, musicians had no usable models from the ancient world, so, as Traversari suggested, they looked for inspiration to popular music. This worked surprisingly well, even if it took them a century or more to rival the masterpieces of Raphael or Michelangelo. In its grandeur and elaboration, Baroque music corresponds so exactly to the visual arts of the period that there is a danger of forgetting how fresh it was. The ancients had no hand in it at all.

In fact, it is easy to exaggerate the ancients' hand even in sculpture and architecture. One of the principal reasons for the enormous success of Italian Renaissance art was that it was a hybrid, indebted not only to ancient Greece and Rome, but also to medieval France, to the Arab world, to the Carolingian Empire, and, not least, to the native popular culture. In so far as it *was* a classical revival, the motives were as much political as cultural. Patriotic, populist, and antiquarian impulses were mixed up in a manner that set the pattern for nationalistic movements ever after. And, as inevitably happens in such cases, the spotlight played on a remote, glorious, semi-mythical past, while humbler agencies were thrust into the shadows.

In truth, Renaissance Italy owed less to its ancient heritage than to its fortunate geography. Most of the country was a mountainous peninsula lying squarely between the Arab, Hispanic, Byzantine, Slavonic, French, and German worlds. In the late Middle Ages, when travel was still much easier by sea than by land, this was an unbeatable situation for trade, not only in goods and services, but also in ideas. By the late fifteenth century, these advantages had procured for it an eminence that can only be compared to that of the United States at the present day. On the economic side, this proved to be short-lived; but on the cultural side it endured for several centuries, and nowhere more vigorously than in music.

---

[9] Pirrotta, 'Novelty and Renewal in Italy, 1300–1600' (in *Music and Culture*), 167.

[10] For a detailed account, see William F. Prizer, 'The Frottola and the Unwritten Tradition'.

It is easy to forget how great and long-lasting this pre-eminence was. At the highest cultural level, Italian music remained a model for composers all over Europe at least from 1600 to 1800; at the popular level, its reign was even longer, say from 1500 to 1900. Among the factors that contributed to this astonishing success were the great diversity of Italian popular music, ranging from near-Arab in the south to near-German in the north; a talent for blending these diverse elements into a harmonious and graceful whole; and a related talent for reconciling the popular with the cultivated. Most important of all, however, was the flair, manifested in all the arts, for patterns that were at once simple, pleasing, and powerful.

This transformation of popular song and dance into high art has attracted surprisingly little attention. Sir Hubert Parry and Sir Henry Hadow—neither an iconoclast—might just as well not have written, more than a century ago:

> It was in compositions of a lower order [i.e. *frottole, villanelle,* etc.] that composers were driven to experiment in rhythmical groupings of periods more like modern harmonic forms; for as in these they tried to set their poems directly and simply, they had no choice but to look for successions of chords which were effectively alternated and balanced.[11]

> It is not too much to say that the dances collected in Arbeau's Orchesographie [1588] come nearer to our sense of tonality than all the masses and madrigals that contemporary learning could produce.[12]

And Edward Lowinsky, four decades ago, might have saved himself the trouble of expanding these ideas into the short book *Tonality and Atonality in Sixteenth-Century Music* (1961). Even today, the origins of the European classical tradition are conventionally traced to late medieval polyphony—glorious music, to be sure, but a collateral rather than a direct ancestor.[13]

In this we can no doubt see the workings of piety, together with its close relative intellectual snobbery. And, of course, there is the natural preference of scholars for firm evidence: from their point of view, written traditions are much more satisfactory than unwritten ones. Fortunately, however, the unwritten tradition did eventually find its way onto paper. At first we get fleeting glimpses of it in the semi-popular vocal music of the later fifteenth century; and then, in 1508, it is brilliantly illuminated by a collection of lute pieces published in Venice by Ottaviano Petrucci.

---

[11] Sir Hubert Parry, *The Evolution of the Art of Music* (1893), 113.

[12] Sir Henry Hadow, *Studies in Modern Music, Second Series* (1895), 'Johannes Brahms', 277–8.

[13] See e.g. Carl Dahlhaus, *Studies on the Origin of Harmonic Tonality.* This book, based on a thesis published a few years after Lowinsky's study, gives him only a few grudging references. Even so, Dahlhaus can find nothing substantial to say against his argument.

THE DANCE SUITES OF JOAN AMBROSIO DALZA

Of the composer, nothing more is known than what appears within the publication itself: that is to say, that he was a Milanese lutenist by the name of Joan Ambrosio Dalza, Joan being another form of Giovanni. His compositions, as collected here, include *ricercari*, preludes, and transcriptions of vocal music, but consist mainly of dance movements, most of them arranged in suites made up of a *pavana*, *saltarello*, and *piva*,[14] roughly corresponding to the later allemande, courante, and gigue. These suites are in turn grouped into two sets, the first being described as *alla venetiana*[15] (in the manner of Venice), and the second as *alla ferrarese* (in the manner of Ferrara):[16]

Suites *alla venetiana*
    no. 1 in G
    no. 2 in F
    no. 3 in D
    no. 4 in C
    no. 5 in B♭

Suites *alla ferrarese*
    no. 1 in C
    no. 2 in F, with normal tuning (i.e. G–c–f–a–d'–g')
    no. 3 in B♭, with the two lowest strings tuned down from G–C to F–B♭ (i.e. F–B♭–f–a–d'–g')
    no. 4 in F, with the lowest string tuned down from G to F (i.e. F–c–f–a–d'–g').

As even this bald list shows, the two sets show marked and, in some ways, puzzling differences. It is natural that a Venetian publisher should issue a set of Venetian dances, but why the *ferrarese* set? The simplest explanation is that Dalza moved from his native Milan to Ferrara, composed the *ferrarese* set there, and then, probably in response to the decline of that city at the end of the fifteenth century, moved on to Venice, where he composed the *venetiana* set. This guess is supported by the internal evidence of the pieces themselves. Take the matter of key. Though Dalza's notation, being lute tablature, has no key signatures, he clearly does have key schemes in mind; and these are much less sophisticated in the *ferrarese* than in the *venetiana* set. Among its other relatively primitive features are

[14] This last imitated a now-obsolete north Italian bagpipe, briefly described in Baines, *Bagpipes*, 111–12.

[15] So spelt by Dalza (or Petrucci). The modern spelling is *veneziana*.

[16] Dalza does not specifically describe these series of dances as suites, but does write: 'Nota che tutte le pavane hanno el suo saltarello e piva' ('Note that every *pavana* has its *saltarello* and *piva*'). The keys, like the numbers, are editorial, but implicit in the tablature notation. In the last two suites of the *ferrarese* set, the final movement is for some reason entitled 'Spingardo', though identical in style to a *piva*.

the *scordature*, or special tunings, of Suites 3 and 4 (which remind one of much present-day folk music), the more diffuse form, the less varied and independent harmony, and the thinner texture.

Notable differences occur, too, within the *ferrarese* set. Suites 3 in B♭ and 4 in F, to judge by several peculiarities they have in common—the special tunings, the designation of the final movement as 'Spingardo', and certain thematic and stylistic traits—were composed together, and probably before the others. The likely order of composition is therefore:

Suites *alla ferrarese*
  nos. 3 in B♭ and 4 in F
  nos. 1 in C and 2 in F
Suites *alla venetiana*

Since this is more or less the reverse of the order within the book, it was presumably Petrucci's policy to give the most up-to-date pieces pride of place near the beginning.

The importance of the order of composition is that it provides a key to nothing less than the development of modern tonality out of a folk idiom similar to that of the present-day Balkans. Needless to say, this conjectured order is open to dispute, but seems to me plausible enough to be taken as given in the analysis that follows.

The alla ferrarese *suites*

We begin, then, with nos. 3 and 4 of the *ferrarese* set, with their special tunings. It is often said that Renaissance dance harmony grew out of the ground bass. At least as far as Dalza's dance suites are concerned, this is quite untrue. His technique is essentially a two-chord, drone-and-dominant one. Elsewhere he has a *saltarello* and *piva* accompanied throughout by a drone on a second lute,[17] like the Indian tambura, but in these two suites the drone is provided by specially tuned strings on the same instrument, as in much present-day folk or popular music. In this respect, as in several others, the *pive alla ferrarese* nos. 3 and 4 are the most primitive movements in the whole collection. They employ a 'centipede' form, still to be heard in modern bagpipe music,[18] whereby a handful of basic formulas are repeated, grouped, and varied in more or less random fashion. The favourite formal device is immediate repetition, with or without variation: AA BB . . . , $A_1A_2 B_1B_2$ . . . , AAAA $B_1B_1B_2$ . . . , and so on. This has the double advantage of providing a sem-

---

[17] For the latter see Ex. 7.19 on p. 100.

[18] e.g. the Hungarian bagpipe *verbunkos*, Ex. 7.17. For the phrase ' "centipede" form' I am indebted to Edward J. Dent: 'The principle of alternation once established in Scarlatti's day, the "centipede" type of construction—the stringing together of small consecutive segments—became almost entirely obsolete' ('Italian Opera in the Eighteenth Century', 508).

blance of structure and giving the performer time to think of what to do next. It was out of such crude repetitions that binary form developed.

Ex. 6.5. The bagpipe 'double tonic'

A favourite pattern in bagpipe music was the double tonic on *c–d* (Ex. 6.5). As we can see from another of Zacara's bagpipe imitations (Ex. 6.6), this was known (and probably already old) in the early fifteenth century. By Dalza's time, it had begun to mutate into the tonic-and-dominant of later popular music. We can see this happening, before our very eyes as it were, in two passages from Dalza's *spingardi*. In the first (Ex. 6.7), Melody and Bass retain their primitive distinctness. In the second

Ex. 6.6. Antonio Zacara da Teramo, 'Amor nè tossa' (early 15th c.), extract (down a 4th)

Ex. 6.7. Joan Ambrosio Dalza, 'Spingardo [i.e. Piva] alla ferrarese' no. 3 in B flat (1508), bars 95–104 (up a tone)

(Ex. 6.8), the *d* and *f* of the Melody have begun to merge with the *g* of the Bass to form a series of dominant chords—and dominant-seventh chords at that.

What made this revolutionary development possible was, of course, the

Ex. 6.8. Joan Ambrosio Dalza, 'Spingardo [i.e. Piva] alla ferrarese' no. 4 in F (1508), beginning (up a 5th)

arpeggiation of the Bass. Without it, tunes like that of Ex. 6.8 might have continued unchanged indefinitely—and indeed did, in passages like Ex. 6.9, collected over four centuries later in northern Spain.

Before we leave these primitive bagpipe imitations, there is something more to

Ex. 6.9. Sword dance for bagpipe from Galicia, north-west Spain, beginning

be noticed about Ex. 6.7. In its 'double tonic' progression, the first triad is not *c* major but *a* minor, which functions as a 'dominant' to the ensuing *d* minor triad. The former is really a subset of the 'natural pentatonic', and the latter of the 'soft pentatonic'. An Irish reel with a similar chordal structure makes the same point (Ex. 6.10).

Ex. 6.10. 'The Maid amongst the Roses' (Irish reel), beginning (down a tone)

The evidence of the pavane

This primitive system is, however, restricted to the *pive*. Dalza's other two dance forms are much more sophisticated. Not much need be said about the *saltarello*, which, with its hemiola rhythms and fiddle-like leaps, somewhat resembles a Handelian hornpipe. In form, it is almost as improvisatory as the *piva*, though more regular, with two-bar, self-repeating phrases. The general effect is something between an African 24-pulse cycle and Bach's D minor Chaconne for unaccompanied violin.

The *pavana* is a very different matter. Though we have little information on its origins (Dalza's examples are the first on record) we do at least know that it was a processional dance, which was sometimes performed on wind instruments or even sung. And Dalza's *pavane alla ferrarese* do undoubtedly betray vocal influence,[19] especially from the early *frottola*.[20] This was in some ways a counterpart to the Franco-Flemish chanson,[21] but earthier. 'The *frottola*', it has been said, 'is at best a second-rate form of art, as regards both the texts and the music. It is the work of hack poets and inferior musicians. It is artificial and banal, devoid of technical prowess or serious emotion. It is repetitious, stereotyped, and cliché-ridden.'[22] But, from one point of view, these were precisely its strengths. The repetitions and clichés were the soil in which tonality grew.

A careful comparative study of Dalza's *pavane alla ferrarese* shows how the closed, symmetrical forms of the *frottola* merged with the improvisatory, drone-based patterns of the *piva*. Comparing no. 3 in B♭ (Ex. 6.11) with no. 1 in C (Ex. 6.12), we find the following differences:

[19] Imogene Horsley, in 'The 16th-Century Variation: A New Historical Survey' (1959), proposed that the *pavana alla venetiana* had developed from 'an instrumental origin—a style derived from the practice of improvising above a repeated bass' and the *pavana alla ferrarese* from song (pp. 119–20).

[20] Strictly speaking, the *frottola* belongs to Mantua. Other north Italian cities had their own, related genres, e.g. the Florentine carnival songs. But, in view of the closeness of Mantua to Ferrara, it was probably the actual *frottola* that influenced Dalza

[21] e.g. Binchois's 'Adieu m'amour' (Ex. 6.1).

[22] Everett Helm, 'Secular Vocal Music in Italy (*c*. 1400–1530): The *Frottola* Forms', 391. I should add that this opinion was expressed over forty years ago. Since then, I am told, the *frottola* has risen in critical estimation.

Pavana in B♭: with trivial exceptions (in bars 3 and 5) the bass sticks to the tonic and dominant;

Pavana in C: the bass is much more mobile and the harmony generally more modern.

Pavana in B♭: Theme B is little more than a four-bar appendage to Theme A;

Pavana in C: Theme B has blossomed into an eight-bar, symmetrical tune.

Pavana in B♭: the main ordering device is the recurring cadence (bracketed), as in the *saltarelli* and *pive*;

Pavana in C: in pairs of recurring cadences (bars 3–4 and 7–8, and again 11–12 and 15–16), contrast is beginning to predominate over repetition.

As regards this last, there was nothing new about symmetrically contrasted cadences as such; in one form or another, they had been known for centuries. What was new was to base them on the tonic and dominant chords. And here, we should

Ex. 6.11. Joan Ambrosio Dalza, 'Pavana alla ferrarese' no. 3 in B flat (1508), beginning (up a tone)

Ex. 6.12. Joan Ambrosio Dalza, 'Pavana alla ferrarese' no. 1 in C (1508), beginning

note, Dalza is perfectly at home. It is his treatment of the subdominant, supertonic, and submediant that is primitive, with frequent vestiges of folk organum, as, for instance, in bars 2–3 and 5–7 of Ex. 6.13. As a rule, all three chords are glued to either the tonic or dominant, in the manner of Ex. 6.14.

But there is one interesting exception to this rule. Reduced to essentials, Theme C from Exs. 6.11 and 6.12 is an undulation around *3* over a tonic drone, which

Ex. 6.13. Joan Ambrosio Dalza, 'Pavana alla ferrarese' no. 4 in F (1508), bars 127–41 (up a 5th)

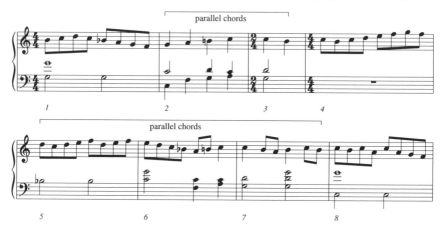

Ex. 6.14. Dalza's treatment of secondary chords

terminates first in I–V and then in I–V–I (Ex. 6.15). No doubt its origin lay in a
medieval pattern similar to Ex. 6.16. As adapted by Dalza, this ancient formula has
the immense historical significance of being the first known instance of a harmonic
binary structure made up of the three primary triads. (In the *melodic* binary of
Themes A and B, the Bass remains the same, or nearly the same, while the Melody
changes; in the *harmonic* binary, the Bass changes too.) As the *passamezzo moderno*,
Dalza's pattern was to become wildly popular later in the century, and in sundry
guises has remained in vigorous use to the present day.

Ex. 6.15. The skeleton of Theme C from Dalza's *pavane alla ferrarese*

Ex. 6.16. Serbian bagpipe tune (down a tone)

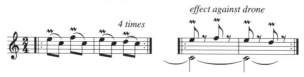

In Dalza, the IV–I progression is still embryonic, the incidental result of harmonizing *f*→*e* in parallel sixths against a static *c* in the bass. It took composers several decades to realize that the polyphonic combination we now know as the 'subdominant' was a chord in its own right.

The alla venetiana *suites*

Turning to the *alla venetiana* suites, we find no more *scordatura*, but the systematic employment in standard lute tuning of five keys systematically arranged in descending order of pitch: G, F, D, C, B♭. These are, of course, keys *avant la lettre*, but none the less astonishing in a publication of 1508.

In these suites, Dalza has gone beyond suggestions of other instruments. The *piva* is no longer a bagpipe imitation, but merely a lively dance in a jig time; the *saltarello*, a straightforward, medium-tempo, triple-time movement, not unlike an early minuet. Gone, too, are the echoes of the *frottola* in the *pavana*. Everything is idiomatically and uniformly adapted to the lute. The movements are much shorter and would seem also to be a little slower, especially the *pavane* and *pive*. The instrumental technique, though still simple, is in general more sophisticated, with fuller and more frequent chords.

The most striking change of all, however, is that the harmonic binary form that played so hesitant a part in the *ferrarese* suites has now taken over almost completely. Apart from short interludes, usually on the IV–V–I progression, these suites are little more than sets of variations on Ex. 6.17. One can see from the second of them (Ex. 6.18) how this worked in practice. There is an obvious resemblance to Theme C of the *ferrarese* set, but without the rhythmical swing between *f* and *e*. Instead, we have a much less regular pattern of embellishment, with the *f*→*e* progression all-important. Here, the subdominant chord has lost any special status it may have enjoyed. Whenever *4* is at all prominent, Dalza feels obliged to harmonize it with a consonant triad, but it matters little whether this is IV, II, or VII♭.

Ex. 6.17. The basic pattern of the *alla venetiana* dances

A further feature of the *alla venetiana* suites, evident in Ex. 6.18, is a subtle technique of melodic variation. The standard sixteenth-century way of varying a tune is to retain the rhythmically stressed notes—the 'pillars', so to speak—but link them in different ways. This is what Dalza does at the beginning of the *pavana* (Ex. 6.18(*a*)), where the 'pillars' (ringed) are *g–e–c*. But then we get something quite different. The bracketed *g–f–e–d–c* scale, repeated in a different rhythm, gives rise

Ex. 6.18. Joan Ambrosio Dalza, Suite *alla venetiana* no. 2 in F (1508) (up a 4th)

(*a*) *Pavana*, beginning

(*b*) *Saltarello*, beginning

(*c*) *Piva*, beginning

to the new figure *f–e–d–c–d*, which is itself similarly varied—different rhythm, same contour—in the remaining two dances.

This form of variation is typically Oriental. On the one hand, it probably owed something to the Near Eastern influence so strong in Venice at the time; on the other, it is an early ancestor of the 'thematic transformation' and 'developing variation' of the nineteenth century.

The mysterious major mode

These suites, *ferrarese* as well as *venetiana*, leave us with a puzzle. Why are the melodic and harmonic patterns so extremely limited? The sensible procedure, from the modern (or for that matter Baroque) point of view, would be to introduce as much variety as is compatible with the various dance styles. And why is everything in such a thoroughgoing major? (With the sole exception of the supertonic, even minor *chords* are rare.) It is not as though Dalza is unacquainted with the minor; elsewhere, he uses it freely. Recall, too, that all this has been sanctioned by Petrucci, who invested a lot of money and effort in the publication of these suites and presumably expected to make a profit out of them.

Part of the answer no doubt lies in the Renaissance passion for variation. To vary movements that were themselves made up of variations was a challenge and delight. To present similar material in different keys was (we may suppose) an exciting novelty. And as long as Dalza confined himself to the major mode, only a few basic formulas were available to him. His harmonic resources consisted of the tonic, the dominant, and a few severely limited secondary chords; his melodic resources, of a small range of concomitant formulas.

But these restrictions make it doubly puzzling that he stuck so exclusively to the major mode. The only possible explanation is that major tonality, combined with a rudimentary binary form, had become so popular in northern Italy as to amount to a craze. One might compare it with the ragtime mania of four hundred years later. Just as early ragtime combined arrangements of banjo pieces and popular songs with standard piano technique, so the *ferrarese* suites combined arrangements of bagpipe pieces and *frottole* (or *frottola*-like passages) with standard lute technique. In both cases, these disparate ingredients were to form the basis of popular music through the rest of the century.

Perhaps this craze, like many another, turned out to be commercially disappointing. At any rate, Italy had to wait twenty-eight years for another such collection.[23] The publication of Dalza's *Intabulatura di lauto* was therefore particularly fortunate. In it we see not only the prototypes of many sixteenth-century dances, but the germ of the entire Classical style. Most important of all was the *pavana alla ferrarese*. Not only does it provide the model for the later pavan;[24] the tune types here labelled Themes B and C also had distinguished careers, of which we shall be hearing much more in later chapters.

It is ironic that the *venetiana* dances owe their archaic charm to a wealth of secondary chords that must once have seemed advanced, while the features that make the *pavane alla ferrarese* seem modern to us were in fact primitive. The square, eight-bar phrases; the alternation of full and half closes; the homophonic texture; the tonic-and-dominant harmony: these were the drastic simplicities of popular dance music. In that simplicity lay enormous strength.

Historians owe a great debt to Joan Ambrosio Dalza. It is an enormous stroke of luck that this obscure Milanese lutenist published such a large collection of dances at just this time. We should be thankful that his intention was not to be clever or original, but merely to turn an honest penny by giving the public what it wanted.

---

[23] Antonio Casteliono's *Intabulaturo de leuto* of 1536. Meanwhile various collections had appeared elsewhere, notably the *Dixhuit basses dances* (1529) and *Quatorze Gaillardes, neuf Pavennes . . . (c.* 1531), published in Paris by Pierre Attaingnant.   [24] See Horsley, 'The 16th-Century Variation'.

7   Rivals to Tonality

It may seem puzzling, in view of the strikingly modern character of some early sixteenth-century dance music, that tonality took so long to develop. But of course the composers of the sixteenth century were not interested in tonality—had, in fact, never heard of tonality. What *did* interest them was *aria*:

> in the sixteenth century . . . the word aria referred to some undefinable quality felt to be present in some pieces of music and missing in others . . . it meant the feeling that certain melodies, or, more generally, certain kinds of music, unfolded phrase after phrase with a coherent sense of direction, with an immediacy that gave to their progress the sense of an inevitable course aimed at a precise goal. . . . One basic element, which sixteenth-century theory was still unprepared to recognize and assess, must have been a 'logical' sequence of harmonies, either fully realized in a polyphonic composition or merely implied in the statement of a melody, a sequence whose logic was not yet necessarily fully consistent with the logic of tonal harmony.[1]

Tonality, then, was a means of procuring *aria*, but not the only one. 'Modal' progressions might equally well provide that 'sense of an inevitable course aimed at a precise goal'. Only very gradually, and never entirely, did tonality supersede them.

It is to these non-tonal progressions that this chapter is devoted. And since our definition of tonality is unusually narrow, their range is correspondingly wide, including not only those progressions conventionally regarded as 'modal', but also such things as the plagal subdominant and even the ordinary minor mode. Modality, like most other things in music, is a matter of degree.

THE DOUBLE TONIC

The most archaic of modal survivals, and the first to disappear from cultivated music, was the double tonic, which, it will be remembered, comes in the basic

---

[1] Nino Pirrotta, 'Willaert and the *Canzone Villanesca*', 195, in *Music and Culture in Italy from the Middle Ages to the Baroque*, 175–97.

forms *A*m–*G* and *C*–*D*m. Of these, the first really belongs with the history of the minor mode, of which more in due course. We begin, then, with the 'Irish Washerwoman' *C*–*D*m pattern, which was also on the whole the more archaic and the first to go.

In sophisticated Italian music, this appears to have happened about 1500. Dalza confines it to the *pive alla ferrarese*, and even there it is set over a tonic-and-dominant bass. In other parts of the world, however, it lived on vigorously, and nowhere more so than in the British Isles, where it was a favourite with the English virginalists. Probably no great composer has been more attached to it than William Byrd. A notable instance, from his programmatic 'Battle' Suite, is 'The Burying of the Dead' (Ex. 7.1)[2]—evidently a well-known dirge, since Thomas Vautor quoted it some thirty years later, in the madrigal 'Sweet Suffolk Owl' (1619).[3] In both cases, the old-fashioned double-tonic progression is soon abandoned for something more modern, and the same is true of Byrd's 'Hornpipe', really a long set of variations (Ex. 7.2).

Ex. 7.1. Byrd, 'The Burying of the Dead' (from 'The Battle', 1591), beginning

Ex. 7.2. Byrd, 'A Hornpipe' (late 16th c.), beginning

But why 'Hornpipe'? The hornpipe is an ancient instrument, still played in a few out-of-the-way places, consisting of a reed pipe to which a horn (real or imitation)

---

[2] He also has a similar but untitled arrangement of the same tune (transposed up from C into F) in 'A Medley', section 5 (*FVB*, no. [CLXXIII], ii. 224).

[3] See *The Oxford Book of English Madrigals*, 303–9. The quotation, to the words 'and sings a dirge for dying souls' appears on pp. 307–8.

has been attached to serve as a bell. Often there are two pipes in parallel, terminating in either one or two horns, and sometimes also a bag at the blowing end. In its most elaborate form, the hornpipe is therefore a droneless bagpipe with a double chanter; and the music of this instrument gives some idea of the origins of the medieval double tonic. Example 7.3, collected in twentieth-century Turkey, is just

Ex. 7.3. Hornpipe tune from north-east Turkey (down a 5th)

such a hornpipe tune, and we can deduce, from Thomas Weelkes's 'ayre' 'Jockey, thine hornpipe's dull' (Ex. 7.4), that similar instruments were producing similar patterns in sixteenth- and seventeenth-century England. The bracketed passage (bars 8–13) parodies a style of piping evidently regarded as rustic and old-fashioned,

Ex. 7.4. Weelkes, 'Jockey, thine hornpipe's dull' (1608), beginning (down a 5th)

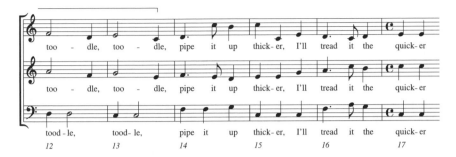

at least among urban sophisticates. It is, in fact, a folk survival of the medieval 'rondellus' (or 'rondel'): in effect, a two-part round over an ostinato bass.[4]

Nor is this the only round over a double-tonic bass to come to us from early seventeenth-century England. There are several more in the publications of Thomas Ravenscroft, the most interesting being 'Hey, Down Down' (Ex. 7.5).

Ex. 7.5. Ravenscroft, 'Hey, Down Down' (1609) (down a 4th)

---

[4] See Ernest H. Sanders, 'Rondellus', in *New Grove II*, xxii. 648–9. Normally all three voices begin together. 'Sumer is icumen in' (Ex. 5.4) is in effect an elaborate rondellus with the upper voices entering in succession. (It is also unique among rondelli in having more than three voices.) For a later example over a drone bass, see the pastoral finale of 'Spring' from Vivaldi's *Four Seasons* (Ex. 7.7, bars 7–8).

Not only does this begin with a bare double-tonic bass; it is also a 'quodlibet' of pre-existing tunes, two of which, 'The Woods so Wild' and 'Dargason' (cf. Ex. 5.5 on p. 60) are well known from other sources.[5]

Here, as in many other Elizabethan and Jacobean tunes, the second II of the I–II I–II progression has been 'tonicized', thereby creating an equal balance between the two keys—a true 'double tonic', in fact. Elsewhere, the harmony simply returns to I at the end, as in countless Scottish and Irish dance tunes. Some of the delightful pieces in the Fitzwilliam Virginal Book stick quite closely to this folk prototype,[6] though others stretch it almost to the breaking point.[7] For the double tonic, though not necessarily crude or primitive, proved to be a dead end. In larger forms, the future belonged to simpler, immensely extendible tonic-and-dominant progressions. The natural home of the double tonic was in popular dance music, where it has continued to thrive to the present day.

THE PENTATONIC SEVENTH

For a long time, both the pentatonic seventh $a^-\!-c\!-e\!-g$ and its close relative the pentatonic triad $a^-\!-c\!-e$ continued to dominate both the Melodies and Basses of Renaissance popular music. They are most prominent in those Bass patterns, still close to the children's chant, that blend major and minor, but in the long run were more important in the Melody. To set a Melody with a strong emphasis on a and e over a Bass squarely founded on c and g is a quintessentially Italian procedure, to be found as early as Zacara's 'Ciaramella',[8] and again in one of Dalza's *pive* (Ex. 7.6).[9] Two centuries later, we see it once more, little altered from Dalza's formula, in Vivaldi's *Four Seasons* (Ex. 7.7).[10]

Later still, it was to become a favourite device of nineteenth-century Italian opera. One example, from Donizetti's *L'elisir d'amore*, will be quoted in a subsequent chapter (Ex. 13.55); another occurs in Verdi's *La traviata* (Ex. 7.8). In both these passages, the bittersweet effect of minor Melody against major Bass is enhanced by

---

[5] For 'The Woods so Wild', see the sets of variations in the *FVB* by Byrd (no. LXVII, i. 263–6) and Gibbons (no. XL, i. 144–8). Other double-tonic Ravenscroft rounds are (from *Pammelia*) 'Oaken Leaves', 'The Nightingale', 'The Old Dog', and 'There Lies a Pudding in the Fire', and (from *Deuteromelia*) 'Hold thy Peace', all published in 1609. 'Oaken Leaves', 'The Nightingale', and 'Hold thy Peace' are reprinted in *The Penguin Book of Rounds*, ed. Rosemary Cass-Beggs, 11, 84, and 59 respectively.

[6] e.g. Bull, 'A Jig: Doctor Bull's Myself' (no. [CLXXXIX], ii. 257); Giles Farnaby, 'Tower Hill' (no. [CCXLV], ii. 371).

[7] e.g. Morley, 'Go from my Window' (no. IX, i. 42–6).

[8] See Ex. 6.2 on pp. 68–9, especially bars 10–13.

[9] For the full harmony, see Ex. 6.18(*c*) on p. 84.

[10] This is, of course, yet another bagpipe imitation; cf. the very similar 'Pifa' from Handel's *Messiah* (Ex. 10.1 on p. 136).

Ex. 7.6. Joan Ambrosio Dalza, *Piva* from the Suite *alla venetiana* no. 2 in F (1508), beginning (down a 4th)

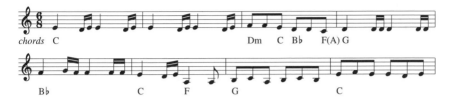

Ex. 7.7. Vivaldi, *The Four Seasons*, 'Spring' (*c.*1725), 3rd mvt. ('Danza pastorale'), beginning (down a major 3rd)

making the context purely minor. The Melody begins in *A* minor, rises to a climax on *e* or *g* in *C* major, and then subsides back into *A* minor. This, too, is an old Italian device. In a discussion of the lute songs of Dowland (who in this respect is only imitating the Italians), Lowinsky points out that he 'loves to modulate from minor to its relative major. In this way both modes illuminate and heighten each other, for a modulation to the relative major is always felt as an upsurge from which the melody sinks back to its minor compass'.[11] By just such means, Verdi is able to wring intense pathos from the plain major mode (bars 3–10 of Ex. 7.8).

[11] *Tonality and Atonality in Sixteenth-Century Music*, 55.

Ex. 7.8. Verdi, *La traviata* (1853), Act III, Scene i, Andante mosso section, 'Addio del passato bei sogni ridenti', bars 11–20

It is also possible to move through the pentatonic seventh in the opposite direction (that is, from major to minor and back again), as in Handel's 'Lascia ch'io pianga' (Ex. 7.9). But this remained comparatively rare until the late eighteenth century.[12] During the Baroque period, the more usual practice was to base the Melody firmly on *1* and *5*, though a great deal depended on the context. Custom dictated not only the rhythm of dance forms, but also many features of melody, harmony, and structure.

It is therefore significant that 'Lascia ch'io pianga' was originally a saraband, since major-mode sarabands placed great stress on *3* and *6*, as may be quickly seen

Ex. 7.9. Handel, *Rinaldo* (1711), Act II, Scene iv, 'Lascia ch'io pianga' (down a 4th)

(*a*) beginning

---

[12] Notice how the melodic contour of the initial theme (Ex. 7.9(*a*), bars 1–7) is reproduced in a condensed form in the middle section (Ex. 7.9(*b*), bars 1–2). Such condensation is very important in later music, occurring between scherzos and trios, introductions and allegros, first and second subjects, etc.

e che so - spi - ri,   e che so - spi - ri   la li - ber - tà!   La-scia ch'io pian-ga

9   10   11   12   13   14   15   16

(*b*) bars 31–4 (beginning of middle section)

Il duo-lo in - fran - ga   que-ste   ri - tor - te

17   18   19   20

from the keyboard suites of J. S. Bach. Of the eighteen sarabands in his 'English',
'French', and 'German' suites, eight are in the major; and of that eight, six begin
on *3* and two on *5*. Of the ten sarabands in the minor, five begin on *3*♭, three on *5*,
and only two, fleetingly, on *1*. Moreover, those that begin on *1* or *5* tend to proceed
to *3*♭, *6*♭, or *7*♭.

The reason is fairly obvious. Sarabands were intended, in the language of the
time, to be 'affecting', so Bach naturally stresses the affecting intervals. There could
not be a greater contrast with his fugal subjects, which almost invariably begin on *1*
or *5*, in the latter event quickly proceeding to *1*. In the entire 'Forty-Eight' there
are only two exceptions, both in Book 2. And, lest one should put this down to the
abstract austerity (real or supposed) of these fugues, the tonic-and-dominant bias
is, if anything, even greater in his fugal gigues.

None of this is peculiar to Bach, whom I mention merely because his works are
so readily accessible. The fact is that the duties of a fugal subject are very different
from those of a self-contained tune. The former must assert itself clearly within
the polyphonic web, and for that a sturdy tonic emphasis is almost indispensable;
the latter, effortlessly standing out against its accompaniment, can indulge in a
luxurious emphasis on the more expressive degrees of the mode. It is an indul-
gence that composers were more and more inclined to yield to.

Melostasis

Throughout 'Lascia ch'io pianga' (Ex. 7.9) one feels the presence of the *a* minor
triad. Even when the Melody departs from it, as in bars 11–14, it continues to lurk
in the background—'prolonged', as the Schenkerians would say, just as the C major
triad is 'prolonged' through the harmony. And the same is true, in their different

ways, of the preceding three examples: all prolong melodic patterns through changes of harmony.

Unfortunately, there is no entirely convenient name for this process. The Schenkerian 'prolongation', while fairly well established, has several drawbacks—for a start, it clashes badly with the ordinary meaning of the word. 'Pitch reinterpretation', used by Anthony Newcomb in connection with Wagner,[13] is accurate but a little too broad. To anyone who feels the need for something more precise, I diffidently offer the terms 'melostasis', for the 'prolongation' of the Melody, and 'harmonostasis', for the corresponding process in the Bass, together with the related adjectives 'melostatic' and 'harmonostatic'.

Harmonostasis is the very foundation of Western musical theory, implicit in words such as 'tonic' and 'key'; but it is not so fundamental as melostasis, to which it bears the same 'emergent' relation as harmony does to melody. However one chooses to describe them, there can be no denying that these bedrock concepts need names of some sort. If any of my readers can improve on my suggestions, please let them do so.

THE MINOR MODE

Nothing could be more misleading than the phrase 'major–minor system', with its implication of two symmetrically opposed but essentially similar modes. The major mode, in practically its modern form, arrived suddenly at the beginning of the sixteenth century. It was a beautifully simple structure, such as might have been devised by a musical mathematician, and after its discovery little was left but the gradual unfolding of the possibilities inherent in this simplicity. The minor, in contrast, began as a composite of several pre-existing modes with not much more than the flat third in common. Two or three centuries were required to shape it into a single, consistent pattern, and even that remained an uneasy hybrid in which older types, both Western and Oriental, lived on.

Influences on the early minor fell into two broad categories: on the one hand, the pentatonic minor of medieval Europe, which only gradually disentangled itself from the major; and, on the other, several drone-based modes of Near Eastern origin. A good example of the former, dating from the later fifteenth century, is the *basse danse* 'Le Petit Roysin' (Ex. 7.10).[14] Sketchily notated, with no harmony and hardly any rhythm, it is more a framework for improvisation than a finished

---

[13] See 'The Birth of Music out of the Spirit of Drama', 53.

[14] The *basse danse* ('low dance'), an ancestor of the pavan, was so called because the feet were kept close to the floor. 'Le Petit Roysin' ('The Little Grape', suggesting alcoholic conviviality) is a tenor, around which other parts would be improvised.

Ex. 7.10. 'Le Petit Roysin' (*basse danse* of *c.*1470) (down a 4th)

melody. But what a framework! Descendants and close relatives of this sturdy but flexible tune may be found through most of Europe and North America, in genres as diverse as 1960s 'folk rock' and the Classical concerto.[15]

Meanwhile, the same potent union of the minor pentatonic with simple binary form was beginning to appear in Italian dance music. In combination with traditional ostinato Basses, it gave birth to a whole range of harmonic formulas, the oldest of which was the *passamezzo antico*. This had grown out of the 'Drunken Sailor' form of double tonic (Ex. 7.11(*a*)) by a series of easy stages. Stage 1, already mentioned in the previous chapter, was to create a 'closed' form of the same pattern (Ex. 7.11(*b*)). The next two steps, which were probably taken concurrently, were the following:

Stage 2   The 'open' and 'closed' forms were so combined as to form a symmetrical binary pattern (Ex. 7.11(*c*)).

Stage 3   In both the 'open' and 'closed' forms, variants developed with V substituted for VII♭ (Ex. 7.11(*d*) and (*e*)).

After this, it was a short step to Stage 4, combining the old and new patterns in I–VII♭, I–V–(I) (Ex. 7.11(*f*) and (*g*)).

There is something deeply satisfying about the resulting bass line, *a–g–a–e–(a)*.

Ex. 7.11. The development of the *passamezzo antico*

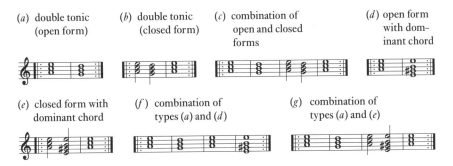

(*a*) double tonic (open form)   (*b*) double tonic (closed form)   (*c*) combination of open and closed forms   (*d*) open form with dominant chord

(*e*) closed form with dominant chord   (*f*) combination of types (*a*) and (*d*)   (*g*) combination of types (*a*) and (*e*)

---

[15] See Salmen, 'Towards the Exploration of National Idiosyncrasies in Wandering Song-Tunes'; Lloyd, *Folk Song in England*, 89–90; and *Origins*, 178. The examples alluded to are Simon and Garfunkel's 'Scarborough Fair', based on an English folk song, and the finale of Beethoven's Violin Concerto, where the Gm episode (bars 127 ff.), follows the first half of the 'Petit Roysin' pattern.

Ex. 7.12. 'Gaur dala biar dala' (Basque children's song) (down a tone)

It will be seen that it is a close relative of the children's chant, and indeed occurs in some actual children's songs (Ex. 7.12, bracketed ending).[16] It also (which brings us closer to the *passamezzo antico*) supplies a ground bass to certain old rounds.[17]

Stage 5 was a second 'binarization' of these childlike patterns (Ex. 7.13(*a*)). Now only one refinement was lacking: the substitution, in Stage 6, of *C* for *A*m at the beginning of the second half (Ex. 7.13(*b*)). With this, we arrive at the mature *passamezzo antico*, or 'old step-and-a-half'.

Ex. 7.13. The basic pattern of the *passamezzo antico*

(*a*) early form

(*b*) later standard form

This, in its turn, gave rise to further 'chord rows' (also known as 'chord strings'), the most important of which were the *romanesca*, where both halves begin with *C* (Ex. 7.14), and the *folia*, where the initial *A–G A–E* progression is switched round to *A–E A–G*. This latter development makes possible a binary scheme twice as long and far more modern (Ex. 7.15)—so much so, in fact, that it has never entirely fallen out of fashion.[18]

---

[16] Sung on St John's Eve (23 June) while leaping over ritual midsummer bonfires. Translation: 'Tomorrow is St John's Day. The day after tomorrow is the second day of St John. There are no witches on our ground. If there are, let them be burnt.'

[17] e.g. 'Hey ho, Nobody at Home', which exists in two versions: Ravenscroft's (in *Pammelia*, 1609) and a traditional variant. Both may be found in *The Penguin Book of Rounds*, 28–9.

[18] See Richard Hudson, 'The *Folia* Melodies'; Scholes, *The Oxford Companion to Music*, 'Folia', 365–6; and *The New Harvard Dictionary of Music*, 323. Later examples include Beethoven, Fifth Symphony, slow movement, bars 167–76 (first half of the pattern only: see Ex. 11.44), and Rachmaninov, 'Variations for Piano on a Theme by Corelli', Op. 42 (1931). A comparatively recent popular song based on the *folia* is

Ex. 7.14. The basic pattern of the *romanesca*

Ex. 7.15. The basic pattern of the *folia*

In all these patterns both Melody and Bass (but more obviously the latter) are founded on the pentatonic seventh, which provides a framework within which the harmony may shift expressively between major and minor. In particular, it makes possible that typically Italian, bittersweet effect of moving the Bass to the relative major while keeping the Melody in the minor. Already a feature of the mature *passamezzo antico*, this becomes even more pronounced in the *folia*.

A near relation to this '*folia* effect' is the practice of following up an *A* minor half close with a *C* major chord, as happens in the middle of the *passamezzo antico*. This occurs so frequently between movements that some theorists regard it as a form of 'Phrygian' cadence, as though the *E* major chord were an actual tonic. In fact, it is no more than yet another instance of what Jan LaRue calls 'bifocal tonality', 'combining major and relative minor to form a broader but not indefinite harmonic arena'.[19] And, like the *folia* effect, it never quite died out.[20]

The classical minor

Few modes can have been more mixed in their origins than the classical minor. Among its ancestors we can trace both the pentatonic minor from Western Europe and a whole family of drone-based minors from the Orient. One of the latter is an Arabic mode, known for over a thousand years, in which the lower tetrachord is minor and the upper tetrachord major: $1-2-3\flat-4-5-6-7-1^+$.[21] In its bare notes, this is identical with the ascending 'melodic minor' of European theory. Even more exotic are the modes employing the 'Oriental' tetrachord $v-vi\flat-vii-i^+$, which of course include the 'harmonic minor' $1-2-3\flat-4-5-6\flat-7-1^+$.

'The Green Leaves of Summer', theme song of the film *The Alamo* (music by Dimitri Tiomkin, words by Paul Francis Webster, 1961).

[19] See 'Bifocal Tonality: An Explanation for Ambiguous Baroque Cadences', 182.

[20] See e.g. the transition to the Andante theme in the overture to Wagner's *Fliegende Holländer*.

[21] The *1* and *5* are printed bold to bring out their cardinal position within the mode. This Arabic mode is the only non-diatonic one in the *Risāla fi'l-mūsīqī* (*Treatise about Music*) of Ibn al-Munajjim (d. 912), the others resembling the diatonic modes of ancient Greece or medieval Europe. See Henry George Farmer, 'The Music of Islam', 448.

In the Orient, modes such as these were kept separate; in the West, they merged into a single, variegated minor in which the upper tetrachord could be anything that occasion demanded. This state of flux has been conventionally reduced to the following neat scheme:

> melodic minor
> (up) 1–2–$3\flat$–4–5–6–7^+–1^+; (down) 1^+–$7\flat$–$6\flat$–5–4–$3\flat$–2–1;
> harmonic minor
> (same in both directions) 1–2–$3\flat$–4–5–$6\flat$–7–1.

In theory, the 'harmonic minor' is used to form chords, and the 'melodic minor' to create melodies; and there is just enough truth in this distinction to lend it a certain pedagogic plausibility. The basic minor-mode chords (Im, IVm, V, V7, V9♭, VI♭) are indeed drawn from the 'harmonic minor'. And it is true that, generally speaking, $7\natural$ is used in upward, and $7\flat$ in downward movement. (Incidentally, this tendency is not confined to the minor mode; one occasionally comes across a 'melodic major'.)[22]

Even so, the exceptions are so numerous as to make one wonder whether the notion of the 'melodic minor' is worth persisting with. Composers often employ the 'rising' melodic minor in descending scales, or vice versa,[23] and they have little fear of the augmented second that the 'melodic minor' was supposedly developed to circumvent. Indeed, when one compares the textbook injunctions against this interval with the practice of real composers, the suspicion grows on one that ethnic prejudice has been at work. Nineteenth-century theorists discovered that the augmented second was characteristically Oriental, and decided that it must therefore be un-European, 'awkward', 'unnatural', 'hard to sing'.

In fact, the classical minor is not a scalar mode at all, but a collection of melodic formulas, like the modes of the East, only much more varied and unstable than any rāga or maqām. Nor is it diatonic; the only truly diatonic minor modes are the Dorian, Aeolian, and Phrygian. What holds it together, and leads us to accord it a quasi-diatonic status, is its intimate association with the major mode. And this, too, was ultimately due to the drone, which made it natural to measure major and minor thirds against a common background. In due course this facility was extended from the drone to the key, making possible 'parallel' as well as 'relative' connections: in other words, *C* minor–*C* major as well as *A* minor–*C* major.

An important consequence was that the dissonance inherent in the minor third could now be resolved up by a semitone. Nowadays, the most familiar way of doing so is to pass directly from one note to another, for instance from $e\flat$ to $e\natural$. In the

---

[22] e.g. the extract from Dalza's *Pavana alla ferrarese* no. 4 in F (Ex. 6.13 on p. 82, bars 1–2 and 6).

[23] My favourite example is the Air from Bach's Partita (or 'German' Suite) no. 6 in E minor, which begins with a 'descending' rising scale, immediately followed by a 'rising' descending one.

sixteenth century, the same effect was more subtly achieved by passing from one *mode* to another. This explains both the major tonic triad known for some reason as the *tierce de Picardie*, the purpose of which is to relieve the tension of a preceding minor passage (and which, notwithstanding dictionary definitions, is as likely to occur in the middle as at the end of a movement), and the modal fluctuations that lend so much charm to the works of the English virginalists and French *clavecinistes*.[24]

THE DRONE BASS

As we saw in Chapter 5, the drones of medieval Europe thrust the dominant into prominence, in extreme cases giving it an almost tonic status. One practical result was that, especially in the German-speaking world, many bagpipes were designed with a 'plagal' ($5-5$) compass. Even without the evidence of Michael Praetorius's *Syntagma musicum* of 1619 (Ex. 7.16), this might be deduced from many of the bagpipe imitations so popular in the seventeenth and eighteenth centuries.[25]

Ex. 7.16. Tunings of the German bagpipes known as the *Hümmelchen* ('little hummer') and *Schäferpfeife* ('shepherd's pipe'), after Praetorius (1619)

Whether 'plagal' or 'authentic', drone-based tunes tended to revolve round a ladder of thirds consisting of *1*, a prominent *5*, and the major or minor thirds overlying these notes. This gives four possible arrangements of the 'rungs', which I list in order of naturalness:

(1) *1–3♭–5–7♭*
(2) *1–3–5–7♭*
(3) *1–3–5–7*
(4) *1–3♭–5–7*

Pattern 1 is, of course, a version of the pentatonic seventh, as also is Pattern 2, with the third raised from minor to major. In Pattern 3, the melodic centre of gravity shifts to the minor triad *3–5–7*, and in Pattern 4 we leave the diatonic scale behind.

---

[24] Larger-scale contrasts are also sometimes found, e.g. Wilbye's exquisite madrigal 'Adieu, Sweet Amaryllis', with its almost Schubertian contrast between a *C* minor opening and *C* major conclusion.

[25] e.g. the 'Fantasie' by Telemann quoted below (Ex. 7.18), or the Musette ('Gavotte II') from Bach's 'English' Suite in G minor.

In all four types, the 7(♭) behaves more like a third to *5* than a seventh to *1*. This is particularly true of the minor (or neutral) 'blue seventh', which is attracted to *5* in the same way as the 'blue third' is to *1*, often (in the case of 7♭, almost invariably) from the apex of the phrase or figure. A more formal designation for the blue seventh would be the 'apical minor seventh'.

Blue sevenths are extremely typical of drone instruments such as bagpipes and hurdy-gurdies. Examples abound both in actual folk music (Ex. 7.17) and in its countless imitations from the fifteenth to the twentieth century (Ex. 7.18).

Ex. 7.17. Bagpipe *verbunkos* (20th c.), beginning (down a 5th)

Ex. 7.18. Telemann, Fantaisie no. 8 (1732–3), beginning (up a major 3rd)

The apical *major* seventh, though very much rarer, also occasionally crops up in music of this type. We are fortunate in having a remarkable early sixteenth-century example from the invaluable Dalza, in a *piva* for two lutes (Ex. 7.19). While one of these spins out an improvisatory melody, the other sustains an open fifth drone in a

Ex. 7.19. Joan Ambrosio Dalza, *Piva* for two lutes (1508), beginning

somewhat bolero-like rhythm. The effect of the whole is distinctly Oriental, to the present-day Western listener suggesting nothing so much as the sitar-and-tambura ensemble of northern India. The likeness extends even to the rhythmic interplay between the two instruments, which go in and out of sync in a thoroughly Oriental fashion.[26] The modal framework, in which it is not hard to hear echoes of the Arabic maqām, is again a ladder of thirds (*6⁻–1–3–5–7*, with the emphasis on *3–5–7*).

Whether major and minor, both apical sevenths contradict the 'leading' third of the dominant chord, and for this reason are rare in strongly tonal contexts. Between the early sixteenth and mid-eighteenth centuries, the major apical seventh disappeared almost completely from the written record,[27] though it may have lingered on in Italian popular music. Over the same period, the minor (or 'blue') apical seventh became gradually rarer, though it never totally vanished. Several ways were found of accommodating it to tonality, the commonest being the so-called 'English cadence', where a *7♭–6–5* progression is set over a normal dominant chord. Though not confined to English composers, it was certainly extremely popular with them. Ex. 7.20 is typical of dozens if not hundreds of such passages in the Fitzwilliam Virginal Book alone.

Ex. 7.20. Anon., 'Praeludium' (no. XXV in *The Fitzwilliam Virginal Book*, *c*.1600), conclusion

The composers of the sixteenth and seventeenth centuries, while relishing these modal conflicts, generally avoided making them simultaneous—but by no means always. When it suited their purpose, they could grind major against minor to great effect. Probably the last first-rank composer to exploit such 'false relations' was Purcell, whose String Fantasia no. 7 (1680) opens with a whole series, embedded in a modulating polyphony of Tristanesque intensity.

By that time, such things were beginning to sound old-fashioned; the taste of the eighteenth century was for something lighter and more euphonious. But, like

[26] Much of the melody is in '12/8' bar rhythms, which coincide with the '9/8' of the drone at carefully spaced intervals. The first of these occurs at the beginning of the last bar of the quoted extract.

[27] A few sporadic examples may be found, e.g. the first Polonaise (bar 5) from J. S. Bach's *Anna Magdalena Bach Book*. A striking case is 'Fairest Isle' (bar 3), from Purcell's *King Arthur*, where early manuscripts give the seventh as both major and minor. This suggests that it may have been performed at a neutral pitch somewhere between the two—which does, in fact, give the most beautiful effect.

many archaic things, these major–minor clashes survived in the popular music of the southern and eastern fringes of Europe. From that fertile source, they found their way back into the works of a line of composers stretching from Domenico Scarlatti to Bartók.[28]

PLAGALISM

Other things being equal, the lower note of a perfect fifth will predominate over the upper. This is the psycho-acoustic basis of the full close, and indeed of V–I progressions in general. But what if things are unequal? Can this relationship be reversed?

It can, but with difficulty. So it is not surprising that plagalism,[29] as we may call this reversal, was a long time establishing itself. The subdominant chord was slow to develop in any form, but especially as an approach to the tonic. Here the history of the *passamezzo moderno* is instructive. After a promising start in Dalza's *ferrarese* suites of 1508, it next appears in a collection of dances published in 1530,[30] but with the *1 4 1 5 · 1 4 1–5 1* Bass replaced by *1 4 7♭–6 5 · 1 45 1*, which of course avoids the IV–I progression altogether. When this did arrive, it was evidently regarded as equivalent to the VII♭–Im of the *passamezzo antico*. From very different starting points, the two *passamezzi* had converged to become variants of the same harmonic pattern (Ex. 7.21), and the names at least suggest that the *moderno* type was modelled on the *antico*.

Ex. 7.21. Basic *passamezzo* patterns

(*a*) *passamezzo antico* (early form, transposed to *C* minor)

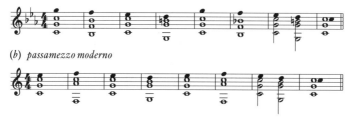

(*b*) *passamezzo moderno*

---

[28] See the quotations from Scarlatti (Ex. 11.29), Beethoven (Ex. 11.30), Haydn (Ex. 11.75), and Liszt (Ex. 11.76(*a*)) on pp. 172–3 and 203–4.

[29] I am indebted to David Brown for this useful word. See the quotation on p. 304.

[30] *Quatorze Gaillardes neuf Pavennes sept Branles et deux Basses Dances . . .* published by the Parisian Pierre Attaingnant. The *passamezzo moderno* pattern appears in the pavan–galliard pair nos. 21 and 21a. See Willi Apel, *History of Keyboard Music*, 241.

At this time, the plagal progression was accompanied by a very limited range of melodic patterns. Already, V–I might be 'melodized' in many ways, but IV–I only in two: *4–3* or, less often, *6–5*. And even here the *4–3* is strongly associated with the serpentine *3–4–3–2* pattern noticed in Chapter 6 (see Ex. 6.15). Increasingly buried under ornamental detail, this continued to weave its way through the elaborate *passamezzi moderni* (or their equivalent, the 'quadrant', or major-mode pavans) that flourished in the late sixteenth and early seventeenth centuries. In the end, this type of tune became so popular as to be something of a joke, acquiring, according to Thomas Morley, the nickname 'Gregory Walker': 'That name in derision they have given this quadrant pavan, because it walketh amongst the Barbars and Fidlers, more common than any other.'[31]

In its primitive form 'Gregory Walker' (surely a handier label than 'the *passamezzo moderno*') lingered on in such out-of-the-way places as Britain, the United States, and (as we know from Schubert's waltzes) the Austrian highlands. Like other plagal patterns, it then enjoyed a great revival in the nineteenth century. In popular music, it continues to flourish to this day.[32]

Another dance form with a similar history was the early saraband—not the stately Baroque dance, but its wild and scandalous predecessor. This had two salient characteristics: a hemiola rhythm alternating bars of 6/8 and 3/4, and a self-repeating *3/I–4/IV–3/I–2/V* pattern like the first half of the *passamezzo moderno*. Unfortunately, the censure of the Church has rendered the origins of the dance even more obscure than usual, so that the slightly anomalous Ex. 7.22, recorded a century or so after its heyday, seems to be the first known Spanish example.[33] Similar tunes, though not always harmonized in this way, have remained popular in Spain ever since.[34]

Ex. 7.22. Gaspar Sanz, Saraband (1674), beginning (down a tone)

---

[31] *A Plaine and Easie Introduction to Practicall Musicke*, 120. The pavan had by this time gone out of fashion in Italy, but was still popular in England. The name 'Gregory Walker' may perhaps refer to a form of wig called the 'Gregory' (see ibid. 214).

[32] Probably the most striking 20th-c. example is the chorus from 'The Lullaby of Broadway' (music by Harry Warren, words by Al Dubin, 1935), which is virtually identical with the 16th-c. original.

[33] The earliest known saraband appears to be one published in Paris almost half a century earlier in 1626. See Devoto, 'La Folle sarabande', 42, and José Castro Escudero, 'Addition à l'article de D. Devoto sur "La Sarabande" ', 122.

[34] e.g. the opening theme of the Entr'acte (based on a Spanish original) preceding Act IV of Bizet's *Carmen*. See Winton Dean, *Bizet*, 196–7.

The 'Black Sheep' pattern

Yet another plagal pattern, intermediate in complexity between a simple progression and a complete tune, is I I · IV I, falling into two distinct phrases and melodized with the outline $3\,3\,·\,4\,3$ or $5\,5\,·\,6\,5$ (Ex. 7.23). The effect is one of stability gently disturbed and then restored. Two examples from about 1600 are, in the major, the wonderfully tender 'Essex's Last Goodnight' (Ex. 7.24)[35] and, in the minor, 'Fuggi, fuggi, fuggi da questo cielo' (Ex. 7.25).[36] The former tune is anonymous; the latter we owe to a Neapolitan musician known to history only as Giuseppino, or 'Little Joe'.[37]

Ex. 7.23. The I I · IV I pattern

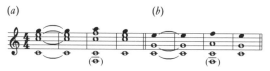

Ex. 7.24. 'Essex's Last Goodnight' (*c.*1600)

Ex. 7.25. Giuseppino, 'Fuggi, fuggi, fuggi da questo cielo' (*c.*1600), beginning (down a 5th)

---

[35] 'This song was popular upon the death of Walter Devereux, first Earl of Essex, who died 22 September 1576. Its popularity was revived in 1601, when on 25 February Robert Devereux, second Earl of Essex and "favorite" of Elizabeth I, was executed.' *Elizabeth Rogers hir Virginall Booke*, ed. Charles J. F. Cofone, 120 n. 13.

[36] Notice the gravity of the words: 'Flee, flee, flee, this harsh, pitiless sky.'

[37] According to *The Grove Concise Dictionary of Music*, he was 'probably Giuseppe del Biabo, an entertainer from Bologna who sang his own songs and played the jew's harp [for which *biabo* is an Italian dialect

For two centuries, this pattern continued to be more or less confined to popular music—but there it throve. Derivatives of 'Fuggi, fuggi' may be found all over Europe, from the big tune in Smetana's 'Moldau'[38] to 'Baa-baa Black Sheep'.[39] We shall be returning to them, along with other modal patterns, but not until we have followed the triumphant course of tonality from the late sixteenth to the mid-eighteenth century.

word] and theorbo' (p. 293). But even this is far from certain, and in any case takes us little further. The initial strain of his melody belongs to an ancient and widespread type. Cf. Exs. 11.96 and 11.97, from India and Spain respectively, on p. 221.

[38] There is controversy about whether Smetana learnt this tune in his native Bohemia or in Sweden, where he lived for several years (see Koestler, 'To Covet a Swallow', in *Drinkers of Infinity*, 277–9). Later it came to be used for the Israeli national anthem.

[39] For the actual 'Black Sheep' tune, under its French name of 'Ah, vous dirai-je, Maman', see Ex. 13.35 on p. 307.

8 Dissonance and Discord

Probably more nonsense has been talked about dissonance than anything else in music. To clear away this inherited confusion, let us start with a few simple principles.

DISSONANCE VERSUS DISCORD

First, a point of terminology. Like heat and cold or light and dark, consonance and dissonance are opposite ways of measuring the same property. Just as, to the physicist, cold is merely the absence of heat, and dark the absence of light, so dissonance is merely the absence of consonance. In strict logic, this chapter might equally well have been entitled 'Consonance and Concord', but there are two good practical reasons for using the negative terms. One is that total consonance and concord are rare, being in fact confined to the unison and octave;[1] and the other is that dissonance and discord, from the point of view of the artist (as opposed to the scientist), are *positive* qualities. They are what gives music its interest and vitality.

Secondly, the words 'dissonance' and 'discord' (at least as used in this book) stand for two quite different things. Dissonance is a property of successive notes; discord, of simultaneous notes.

Thirdly, these two properties are apprehended in very different ways. Dissonance, like the melody of which it forms part, belongs to the select group of symmetrical sense impressions.[2] It is essentially mathematical, and its perception is among the most refined of intellectual achievements. Discord, in contrast, belongs with the less cerebral (and, in evolutionary terms, much older) sense impressions of colour, taste, or touch. We implicitly acknowledge as much whenever we describe a triad as 'bright', a third or sixth as 'sweet', or a diminished seventh as 'velvety'.

Both discord and dissonance contain an element of the subjective. As has often been pointed out, the chord that is startling in Mozart may be soothing in Wagner.

---

[1] Or, of course, multiples of the octave. In the same way, most generalizations about simple intervals hold good also for their compound equivalents, e.g. major tenths behave like major thirds.

[2] The word 'symmetrical' is here used in the scientific sense explained in Ch. 1.

Some theorists have even gone so far as to maintain that discord is *wholly* subjective—that, with deep enough understanding, all chords would seem equally euphonious. This was, notoriously, the opinion of Arnold Schoenberg: 'What distinguishes dissonances from consonances [i.e. discords from concords] is not a greater or lesser degree of beauty, but a greater or lesser degree of *comprehensibility*. In my *Harmonielehre* I presented the theory that dissonant tones appear later among the overtones, for which reason the ear is less intimately acquainted with them.'[3]

But even in Schoenberg's time this idea already had a long history in German music theory. As far back as 1738, the Swiss mathematician Leonhard Euler had suggested that 'the human mind delights in law and order, and so takes pleasure in discovering it in nature. The smaller the numbers required to express the ratio of two frequencies, the easier it is . . . to discover this law and order, and so the pleasanter it is to hear the sounds in question.'[4]

Now, it is true that what Schoenberg calls 'comprehensibility' and Euler 'law and order' is an important aspect of harmony; but it is quite distinct from the gut feeling of discord. And it is certainly not true that the brain, by a mere act of comprehension, can abolish this primitive sensation. We humans have evolved sense perceptions of wonderful flexibility. When we go out into the snow, we adapt to the cold; when we eat a curry, we adapt to the pungency; when we listen to Wagner, we adapt to the relatively high level of discord. Our senses operate, so to speak, on elastic scales. But there is a limit to the elasticity, and the marks on each individual scale always maintain the same order. The *relative* harshness of the intervals is the same whether the composer happens to be Wagner or Mozart, or for that matter Schoenberg or Palestrina.

This is an observation on which every 'naive listener' will surely agree, yet it is far from easy to explain. The most plausible theory is still the one, advanced in the 1860s by the great German acoustician Hermann Helmholtz, that attributes the sensation of discord to the pulsations, known as 'beats', produced by narrow intervals as their vibrations go in and out of phase with each other. With *extremely* narrow intervals, the effect is that of a pleasant shimmering; but as the interval widens and the beats speed up, this rapidly turns into a harsh grating.

Helmholtz further had the brilliant idea of calculating the 'beatiness' produced by the various intervals, including those between the overtones. Using a simple (if somewhat arbitrary) formula, he arrived at a graph (Fig. 8.1)[5] tracing the discord generated between a static middle C—let us call it c—and an upward glide from c to c^+.

---

[3] 'Composition with Twelve Tones (1)', repr. in *Style and Idea*, 214–44, at 216.

[4] Sir James Jeans (paraphrasing Euler's words), *Science and Music*, 155. Cf. also the quotation from Sir Henry Hadow on p. 415 of the present book.

[5] My source is Jeans, *Science and Music*, 159. Though the graph itself has been exactly reproduced, the accompanying scales are new.

just intonation

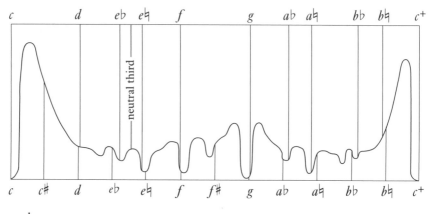

equal temperament

FIG. 8.1. Degrees of discord for the violin, as calculated by Helmholtz

As it happens, Helmholtz based his graph on the overtone spectrum of the violin. Had he chosen another instrument, the result would have been different. With a flute, the peaks would have been lower; with an oboe or trumpet, higher. And there would have been other minor differences as well. In any case, all such calculations must contain an element of the subjective, since one can no more put a precise figure to the acoustic harshness of a jangling semitone than to the 'bite' of a pinch of chilli powder. Nevertheless, the general shape of the graph would be the same whatever the instrument, and a very remarkable shape it is. Forgetting for the moment its musical implications, what do we see?

The first impression is of a series of hills eroded into steep peaks and plunging ravines. Looking more closely, we notice that the peaks are symmetrically ranged on either side of a central valley; every bulge and hollow to the east (as it were) has its fellow to the west. As is usual with natural objects, however, the symmetry is not exact but skewed. It is as though a mathematically regular pattern had first been constructed out of Plasticine and then had its left half pulled out of shape.

Turning to the musical implications, we find that the central ravine corresponds closely, if not quite exactly, to the *g* a perfect fifth above the drone on *c*, and that there is a similar correspondence between the neighbouring gullies and the concordant intervals. We may also notice that, in general, the intervals of just intonation are more concordant than those of equal temperament.

All this is more or less what we would expect *a priori*. But the best evidence for the essential truth of this graph is that it agrees so well (and not only in obvious ways) with musical practice. This is particularly evident in the drone-accompanied tunes that most nearly mimic the behaviour of Helmholtz's two violins. Just as we would expect, such tunes place great emphasis on e, f, g, and a, with the g often acting almost as a second tonic. Meanwhile, both $b\flat$ and $e\flat$ behave as mild dissonances, the former generally resolving on a or g and the latter on $e\natural$, d, or c.

Most striking of all is the manner, precisely reflecting the disposition of hills and valleys around the central ravine of the graph, in which dissonant notes are symmetrically grouped around g. This is most obvious in the traditional music of eastern Europe, where the $a\flat$ above g is often made to correspond to the $f\sharp$ below it. There is even an entire mode—the so-called 'Hungarian scale' $c\ d\ e\flat\ f\sharp\ g\ a\flat\ b\ c^+$— symmetrically arranged around the g. And in the very different (but also, at first, drone-based) idiom of the blues, we find another form of symmetry, in which the $b\flat$ above g corresponds to the e below it. In all such cases, c may replace g as the central note.

One of several surprises in Helmholtz's graph is how concordant the tritone $f\sharp$ is—almost as much so, in fact, as the minor third and sixth. This explains why the diminished seventh, held up by harmonic relativists as a prime example of the dis- cordant-yet-beautiful, is in fact not so very discordant, though certainly complex. The same is true even of the whole-tone chord c–d–e–$f\sharp$–$a\flat$–$b\flat$. To be truly harsh, a discord needs a semitonal clash, represented on the graph by the precipitous peaks at either end.

It is on the summits of those peaks that we find the points of extreme discord, at a distance of about a quarter tone from the upper and lower octaves. As we move down the slope of the graph—in other words, further away from the octave—the discord rapidly subsides. A practical consequence is that, if we wish to emphasize the dissonant nature of a major or minor second, we naturally inflect (or 'bend') it slightly towards the note of resolution. It was no doubt by this path, among others, that the semitone developed, and the semitone itself, as every violinist knows, tends to be slightly squeezed when acting as a leading note. A similar, if less famil- iar, case is that of the e in the progression $e{\rightarrow}c$. Interestingly, the point of maxi- mum dissonance is here reached not with the minor but the neutral third—no doubt one reason why blues musicians are so fond of this interval.

All this is straightforward enough as long as one assumes the background of an actual drone. In real music, matters become more complicated. A violinist will still raise the b in the cadence $b/g{\rightarrow}c^+/c$, even though the accompanying harmony is no longer highly discordant; a blues singer will still flatten the third, even when per- forming without any harmony at all. We feel the discord that goes with dissonance, even when the discord is not present.

Conversely, we feel the dissonant tensions even within an isolated 'concord'. It is yet another instance of the seemingly limitless human capacity for perceiving musical patterns 'as if'. An unaccompanied tune can be heard 'as if' harmonized; a single, solid chord can be heard 'as if' dissolved into its component notes. Without this capacity, it is unlikely that the so-called 'concords' would strike us as particularly euphonious. 'Innumerable theories', as Sir James Jeans pointed out, 'are ready to tell us the origin of the annoyance we feel on hearing a discord, but none even attempts to tell us the origin of the pleasure we feel on hearing harmony; indeed, ridiculous though it may seem, this latter remains one of the unsolved problems of music.'[6] If it were simply a matter of discord, the only entirely pleasing interval would be the octave, followed in order of tolerability by the fifth, fourth, major third, and so on down to the semitone. It is surely not a sufficient explanation for our delight in hearing a major triad that it contains the 'right' amount of discord. Something more positive is needed.

That something, I can only suppose, is the presence of those same fourths, fifths, thirds, and sixths that come so naturally to the human voice. The human brain has an innate feeling for the major triad, in both its melodic *and* harmonic aspects. From the psychological (rather than acoustic) point of view, those intervals that occur within it are concords, and those that fall outside it are discords. This is why the minor third is a 'concord', and the minor seventh a 'discord' (or perhaps a 'semi-concord'), though about equally discordant in strictly acoustic terms.

This special status of the triadic intervals raises a problem of terminology. What is one to call them—'triadic concords', perhaps? For convenience, I have stuck to the traditional practice of terming them simply 'concords', with everything else a 'discord'. The rare uses of the word 'discord' in the strict acoustic sense will, I hope, be evident from the context.

A BRIEF HISTORY OF DISCORD

Earlier in this chapter, I compared the pungency of strong discord to the 'bite' of spicy food. This gastronomic analogy may be carried further. Just as peasant food has usually been more highly seasoned than *haute cuisine*, so marked discord is, on the whole, more characteristic of popular than cultivated music. Till the late eighteenth century, the prevailing view had been that it was better left to the lower orders, except for the special purpose of expressing strong emotion. It was the German Romantics, with their high regard for negative sensations in general, who first began to regard extreme discord as a sign of intellectual superiority.

The next step was to turn discord into an index of musical progress. Throughout the twentieth century, the orthodox view was that, as the harmonic sense became

[6] Jeans, *Science and Music*, 156.

more sophisticated, so Western music grew steadily more discordant. First there were the bare octaves and fifths of medieval organum; then thirds and sixths; then dominant sevenths (popularly imagined to have been invented by Monteverdi); then ninths, major or minor, and so on up to the consummation of the early twentieth century.

Now, it is quite true that, over the centuries, composers became both more skilled and more enterprising in the handling of discords. But this did not mean that the general texture of their music inevitably became more discordant. The trend was in that direction, to be sure, but with many ups and downs. The level of discord does indeed rise in medieval music, largely because of increasing polyphonic complexity (though it is a myth that twelfth- or thirteenth-century composers were afraid of thirds and sixths),[7] reaching a peak in the Ars Nova of the fourteenth century. But thereafter it sinks towards the extreme euphony of the 'Palestrina' style, rises again with the Baroque, dips for a while in the eighteenth century, and then again rises through most of the nineteenth. (I say 'most of the nineteenth', because one could well argue that post-Wagnerians like Mahler and Strauss are less discordant than Wagner himself, at least until the sharp upturn in the early twentieth century.) In the same way, twentieth-century popular music rises to a peak of discordance in the 1940s and then sinks in the 1950s and 1960s.

The pattern, then, is not one of inexorable upward thrust, but of long-term fluctuations between high and low. And this, after all, is what one should expect, on the analogy of similar swings of taste between bland and spicy food, or rounded and pointed shapes, or bright and muted colours. Discordance is, indeed, a special form of harmonic colour, and subject to the same vagaries of fashion as other colours.

Much more important than these passing vogues was the discovery, over the centuries, of ever more complex ways of relating discord to dissonance. Eventually, these very different properties became so intimately associated that Western theory has thoroughly confused them. In fact, there is no inevitable link between, say, the discord f/e and the dissonant progression $f \rightarrow e$. On the one hand, dissonant notes may be harmonized in an entirely concordant way, as in $f/F \rightarrow e/C$ and $f/Dm \rightarrow e/Am$; on the other, discords may have nothing to do with dissonance, as in the parallel sevenths and ninths of many twentieth-century composers, or the added sixths, sevenths, or ninths that jazz musicians like to throw into a final tonic chord. There is no question of such discords resolving. Nor, strictly speaking, do any discords resolve; that is something that dissonances do. There ought really to be another word—'reduction', perhaps—for the stepping-down to a lower intensity of discord that normally accompanies the resolution of a dissonance.

---

[7] See Hughes, 'Music in Fixed Rhythm', 339–41.

Medieval composers were careful managers of both dissonance and discord, but it was only gradually that they brought the two together. In compositions like Binchois's 'Adieu m'amour' (Ex. 6.1), anything more discordant than a perfect fourth or fifth is banished from the extremities of the more important sections, while stronger discords are allowed in between. There is, then, a wave-like oscillation between concord and discord, which goes back to the prehistoric origins of Western polyphony and was to last until the seventeenth century. Except at the cadences, the discords have little connection with the dissonances in the individual voices. They are, rather, a sort of harmonic grit, tolerated as long as they do not become too extreme, and in due course give way to concords.

The gradual linking of discord to dissonance occupied all of the fifteenth and most of the sixteenth centuries. This long period witnessed several interconnected developments. Firstly, dissonance itself became stronger. In the Melody, the old Landini cadence (7–6→1^+) went into decline. It appears to have died out in Italian popular music by 1500,[8] and a few decades later disappeared from church polyphony too. This left the field to stepwise cadences, particularly 2→1 and 7→1^+. In the Bass, the great innovation was of course the discovery of the new, much more dissonant interval of the perfect fifth, and with it the 5→$1^{(+)}$ cadence.

Secondly, dissonant *notes* combined to form dissonant *chords*. The polyphonic cadences of late medieval music had still been composites of individual voices; by the end of the fifteenth century, they were harmonic progressions in their own right.

The culmination of these tendencies was the invention of the dominant chord and the tonal harmony that goes with it. At the same time, there was a third, at first quite independent development: the gradual refinement and control of discord. In most Ars Nova scores, the first thing to strike us is the cross-rhythm, which generates discords in an apparently random manner. There is certainly no question of resolution, except in so far as the discords give way to concords at the cadences. In the course of the fifteenth century, this free-for-all was gradually brought under control. By the time we get to Binchois's 'Adieu m'amour', composed about the middle of the century, most of the discords resolve in one way or another. We could describe them as suspensions or accented passing notes, though of course Binchois knew nothing of these theoretical constructs. His aim was merely to make his harmony as sweet and smooth as possible.

Next, even the accented passing note was refined away, leaving the suspension as virtually the sole form of noticeable discord. Now, what is a suspension? It is a progression consisting of two concords, so arranged that part of the first chord is

---

[8] At least Dalza does not use it, though he does have some related formulas with a passing 7 between 6 and 1^+. See Ex. 6.7, bars 5–6 (p. 77); Ex. 6.13, bar 7 (p. 82); and Ex. 6.18(c), bar 7 (p. 84).

held over, or 'suspended', into the second. Generally the suspended note creates a discord, though this is not obligatory. In any case, it then belatedly joins the second concord, so removing any friction it may have caused. By these simple means, the reduction of discord and the resolution of dissonance are united in one operation.

Another way in which discord and dissonance could be brought together was to give more bite to that most dissonant of chords, the dominant. As this became more familiar and central to the harmony, so it became more discordant. Already in Zacara's 'Ciaramella' the leading note is approached by way of a suspension,[9] and by 1500 this had become a standard procedure in the polyphonic style.

About the same time, the composers of popular music were developing a quite different form of dominant discord. In their harmony, suspensions played little or no part; nor, for that matter, did any form of 'preparation' in the usual sense. What we do find is the superimposition of two pre-existing patterns: the double tonic 1–3 2–4 in the Melody, and the arpeggiated drone 1–5 in the Bass. The result, which may be written $[1$–$3]/1$–$[2$–$4]/5^-$, is of course a version of the I–V7 progression. Dominant sevenths of this type are already common in Dalza's lute music, composed in the first decade of the sixteenth century,[10] so we should not be surprised if the same chord crops up a century later in a much more modern guise (Ex. 8.1).

Ex. 8.1. Bull, 'The Quadran Pavan' (*c.*1600), no. 3 (i.e. Variation 2), bars 3–4 (down a tone)

It was only natural that the composers of popular music, having been the first to set the dominant chord against the tonic, should also be the first to introduce an appropriate measure of discord into that most dissonant of chords. Later, as tonality developed, so too did the dominant discords. To reinforce dissonance with discord seems a human instinct. At any rate, it is surely significant that when the subdominant chord began to behave rather like a dominant in twentieth-century popular music, it too acquired a minor seventh.

Conversely, the tonic chord, being consonant, had also to remain concordant. This explains why cadences on a minor tonic were such a rarity before 1700, and

---

[9] See Ex. 6.2 on pp. 68–9 bars 2 and 10. Here the suspensions are probably still the accidental outcome of cross-rhythm between the bass and the upper parts, though the resulting 6/4s look strikingly modern.

[10] e.g. the *spingardo* in F (Ex. 6.8 on p. 78).

why tonics in general for the most part remained obstinately triadic right through the eighteenth and nineteenth centuries, while dominants sprouted an impressive array of ninths, elevenths, and thirteenths. The one exception is the chord of the added sixth on the major tonic, which had occasionally cropped up as early as the first decade of the sixteenth century.[11] Its reappearance in the nineteenth is closely associated with pentatonic patterns—naturally enough, for a chord that is itself a form of pentatonic seventh—and is a sign that the tension between tonic and dominant was at last weakening.

This is not the place to go into the niceties of dissonance and discord, such as take up many pages in textbooks on harmony and counterpoint. At bottom, they are all variations on a few basic patterns. The indispensable feature is the resolution, which may occur either *within* the chord, as in the suspension, or *on* it, as in the $V_7 \rightarrow I$ progression.[12] Without resolution of some kind, whether immediate or delayed, actual or implied, we are back with mere discord. This is a perfectly legitimate musical resource, but, as we have seen, essentially more primitive than discord-plus-dissonance. It is the smear of mustard on the roast beef, the dash of cayenne pepper in the lobster salad.

Resolution, then, is obligatory if discord is to be bound up with dissonance. Preparation, however, is not. The textbook emphasis on preparation is something of a historical accident, arising out of the treatment of discords in early polyphony. Moreover (as the textbooks seldom bother to mention), it is sometimes the concordant, not the discordant note that is prepared. A dominant seventh, for instance, may be formed by first sounding the triad and then introducing the seventh. As we have seen, this is in fact how the earliest dominant sevenths were obtained. It is also a standard method of forming the 'blue' seventh.[13]

Even when a discord was prepared, there was the possibility that the preparation might subsequently be dropped. By this route, a suspension could turn into an appoggiatura. An intermediate step was to repeat the suspended note on the beat, as often happens in the light vocal music of the sixteenth century. It is more likely, however, that the appoggiatura began as an instrumental grace. Since this was normally left to the discretion of the performer, its early history is obscure, so we are lucky to have such a clear instance as Ex. 8.2.

This appoggiatura happens to be a concord, but a fragile one. If this passage were performed by a solo instrument and continuo, the continuo player would naturally put in the *a* that Byrd so carefully omits. In any case, the urge to reinforce dissonance with discord was soon at work. Not only did appoggiaturas become more discordant over the centuries; they also become very much longer.

---

[11] e.g. in Dalza's *spingardo* in B♭ (Ex. 6.7 on p. 77).

[12] e.g. Bull's 'Quadran Pavan' (Ex. 8.1), where the *f* of the middle voice resolves on *e* at the same moment as the *g* of the Bass resolves on *c*.   [13] e.g. in Telemann's bagpipe imitation, Ex. 7.18 on p. 100, bars 5–6.

Ex. 8.2. Byrd, Variations on 'The Carman's Whistle' (*c.*1600), no. 2 (i.e. Variation 1), beginning

Conclusion

Even more than harmony itself, the complex interaction of dissonance and discord is the great glory of classical Western music. Yet its development appears to have been quite haphazard. As we have seen, the suspension grew out of the partiality of late medieval composers for complicated cross-rhythms. The resulting discord was at first an incidental matter, tolerated within otherwise concordant harmony for the sake of rhythmic counterpoint. But, precisely as it became exceptional, so it also became potentially expressive.

Over the period from about 1450 to 1910, composers explored that potential to the limit. At the same time, they developed ever subtler ways of handling dissonance. If it is true, as I speculated in Chapter 1, that our perception of musical patterns has evolved to an optimal balance between fuzziness and precision, then dissonance and discord are surely a case in point. The human ear is extremely sensitive to the onset of dissonance, but relatively lax about its resolution. This latitude has made possible resolutions of many kinds. Sometimes they are delayed or frustrated; sometimes they resolve on further dissonances, which may link themselves in long chains; sometimes they are merely implied, as a dissonant note breaks off and leaves the ear to finish the rest for itself.[14]

By the early twentieth century, composers hardly needed to provide actual resolutions. Given the slightest hint, audiences would do the job for them. A great deal of early atonal music works on this principle. At the same time, the treatment of discord attained a comparable latitude. Indeed, it seemed as though composers could do anything they liked with discords, but this was an illusion. No amount of familiarity will make a Madras curry taste as bland as a rice pudding.

---

[14] Perhaps the earliest example occurs at the end of Schubert's song 'Die Stadt', where a diminished seventh evaporates in this manner, leaving the bare tonic note in the bass. It has been truly said that this discord does not so much *re*solve as *dis*solve.

9 The Evolution of Tonality

TOWARDS THE BAROQUE

Not so very long ago, Western music was seen as triumphant march from the primitive to the sophisticated. 'Old' modes gave way to 'new' keys, which in turn progressed from the simplicities of Monteverdi to the complexities of Wagner. To the great project of tonality, every major composer contributed his bit.

In fact, there never was such a project. Tonality was not deliberately constructed but just grew, like the giraffe's neck or the human brain, in response to an impersonal evolutionary force. There were, to be sure, periods when composers pursued a common ideal: ease and elegance in the eighteenth century, expressive power in the nineteenth. But their efforts were fitful and uncoordinated, and the results unpredictable. In any case, such ideals were simply the musical expression of the prevailing taste. They could hardly be expected to fit in with long-term tendencies unique to music.

Through every vagary of fashion, the tendency was towards a style of harmony both formally predominant and acoustically simple. It is the simplicity that strikes us in early tonality. There was very little in this unpretentious music to attract the ambitious composer. Its only evident merit was a certain rough vigour, perhaps combined, to the sixteenth-century ear, with an endearing folkiness. The enormous capacity for hierarchic organization had yet to be revealed. And here it should be remarked that harmonic hierarchy, in itself, was far from new to Western music. Primitive key relationships had already begun to appear in mid-fifteenth-century polyphony,[1] but the nearest that early sixteenth-century dance music came to them was the occasional II7/♯–V or I7♭–IV progression. It was only when the cadential hierarchies of the polyphonic style were combined with the harmonic simplicity of popular music that mature key systems became possible.

The merging of these very different traditions was a long and convoluted process. On the one hand, the great masters were loath to relinquish the subtleties of modal harmony; on the other, it took popular composers almost a century to develop even

---

[1] Cf. Binchois's 'Adieu m'amour' (Ex. 6.1 on p. 67).

moderately complex tonal structures. The 'balletts' of Thomas Morley, published in the 1590s and modelled on the dance-like *balletti* of Giovanni Giacomo Gastoldi,[2] were among the first compositions to balance the dominant and subdominant keys in a systematic way:

They [Gastoldi's *balletti*] show none of the modal effects that a composer like Marenzio, say, uses so skillfully, and on the other hand show little awareness of the basic principles on which modern tonality is based. . . . Morley grasped the principle of the dominant relationship as Gastoldi evidently did not; or at least he had a lively sense of the contrast between dominant and subdominant cadences. Almost always Morley's first phrase stays in the tonic, and the second moves to the dominant; almost invariably he modulates more widely than Gastoldi does.[3]

Figure 9.1, as an example, gives the keys of the cadences in Morley's Ballet no. 4.[4]

FIG. 9.1. Modulations in Morley's Ballet no. 4

It was about this time, too, that the *passamezzi* and its relatives were making a similar transition. All through the century they had been getting steadily bigger, and in the process undergoing radical changes. For the growth of a musical pattern is never a simple expansion; every elaboration places a strain on the original framework. As the accretions multiply, they must either group themselves into subsidiary patterns or collapse into a mass of uncoordinated detail. In this conflict, order ultimately prevails over chaos as new, hierarchically grouped patterns develop. Eventually, these become so powerful as to supersede their parent.

This process is particularly well illustrated in the *passamezzo moderno*. Even in the very early form of Dalza's Theme C[5] it had been lightly ornamented, and further elaboration eventually swelled it to about four times its original length. Now this elaboration, though principally a matter of melodic embellishment, also involved the underlying chords, since sixteenth-century composers had yet to learn the art of sustaining long stretches of Melody over a static Bass. (Such occasional exceptions as 'The Trumpets' in Byrd's 'Battle' suite, amounting to the equivalent of twenty-four common-time bars on the chord of C major, 'prove the rule' by their crudity.)

---

[2] Gastoldi's *balletti* were published in 1591 and 1594, Morley's first book of balletts in 1595.

[3] Joseph Kerman, *The Elizabethan Madrigal*, 143.

[4] After Kerman, ibid.; transposed from the original key of G.

[5] See the *pavane alla ferrarese* nos. 3 in B♭ and 1 in C (Exs. 6.11 and 6.12 on pp. 80–1).

The only way to enlarge a harmonic scheme, then, was to introduce new chords. Bull's 'Quadran Pavan' (Ex. 9.1), already quoted for its dominant seventh, shows how far this harmonic efflorescence could go. Here the master pattern (ringed) is showing clear signs of strain. While the *F* and *G* chords blossom into transient keys (incidentally destroying the intervening plagal progression), the Melody avoids straggling only by the introduction of several subsidiary patterns, mostly of a sequential nature.

Ex. 9.1. Bull, 'The Quadran Pavan' (*c.* 1600) (down a 5th)

(*a*) bars 1–9 (first half of Theme)

(*b*) bars 91–5 (second half of no. 5, i.e. Variation 4)

A similar fate overtook the other chord rows. As they reached the limits of intelligibility, the luxuriant harmonic undergrowth began to organize itself into those overriding patterns that we now call keys. The *Ruggiero*, which was coming into fashion at about this time, was from the start based on key contrasts rather than chords. Its structure comes down to the following:

> 1st phrase: relatively unemphatic cadence in the tonic;
> 2nd phrase: emphatic cadence in the dominant;
> 3rd phrase: starts in the dominant and leads back to the tonic;
> 4th phrase: emphatic cadence in the tonic.

Here we have the seeds of the Baroque binary form, and even of the Classical sonata form—at any rate when the mode is major. Meanwhile, minor-mode patterns were following a parallel course.[6] Only gradually, and never quite completely, were the two streams to merge.

It had taken some ninety years to get from Dalza to Morley; it took about as long again to arrive at mature Baroque harmony. This was a synthesis of many disparate elements, old and new, all grouped round a neat and orderly system of diatonically related keys. These may be imagined as six stations on a toy railway network. Three of the stations are in the major (C, F, G), and three in the minor (Am, Dm, Em). The central station, known as 'the tonic', may be either C or Am. Important branch lines link the relatives C–Am, F–Dm, and G–Em. Between stations, the tracks are composed mainly of chords falling by fifths: one may, for instance, get from C to G by the track C–F–Bm–$E_7/\sharp$–Am–$D_7/\sharp$–G. Very often, such tracks are cast in the form of sequences of paired chords, such as C–F Bm–$E_7/\sharp$ Am–$D_7/\sharp$.

In keeping with this metaphor, the prevailing impression is dynamic, purposeful, outward-bound. If the home station is C, our first important destination will probably be G; if it is Am, we may be bound for either C or Em. In every case, we are likely to linger a while in subdominant regions before returning home.

Needless to say, this account of Baroque harmony is drastically simplified. A full description would include chromaticism, modal relics, the use of scales (diatonic or chromatic) as binding devices, and many other refinements. By the first decade of the eighteenth century, the whole system had become rich and flexible enough to sustain the great generation of composers born within five years of 1680.[7]

But, being a living language, it did not stop there, but continued to change. And the change, as it turned out, was in the direction of still further simplicity.

---

[6] See e.g. Byrd's 'Passamezzo Pavana' in the *Fitzwilliam Virginal Book*, no. LVI (i. 203–8).

[7] viz., Vivaldi, 1678; Telemann, 1681; Rameau, 1683; Handel, J. S. Bach, and Domenico Scarlatti, all 1685.

THE CLASSICAL STYLE

The tendency towards simplicity was far from being confined to music. In reaction to the somewhat oppressive magnificence of the previous century, the preference in all the arts was for elegance, ease, and plainness:

Pope's great achievement in English literature was the triumph of simplification. In one of his earliest works, the *Pastorals*, there is simplicity and nothing else . . . —

> O deign to visit our forsaken seats,
> The mossy fountains, and the green retreats!
> Where'er you walk, cool gales shall fan the glade;
> Trees, where you sit, shall crowd into a shade;
> Where'er you tread, the blushing flow'rs shall rise,
> And all things flourish where you turn your eyes.

The lines flow on with the most transparent limpidity—

> But see, the shepherds shun the noon-day heat,
> The lowing herds to murm'ring brooks retreat,
> To closer shades the panting flocks remove;
> Ye Gods! and is there no relief for love?

Everything is obvious. The diction is a mass of *clichés*; the epithets are the most commonplace possible . . . The rhythm is that of rocking-horse; and the sentiment is mere sugar. But what a relief! What a relief to have escaped for once from *le mot propre*, from subtle elaboration of diction and metre, from complicated states of mind, and all the profound obscurities of Shakespeare and Mr. T. S. Eliot! How delightful to have no trouble at all— to understand so very, very easily every single thing that is said![8]

Change a few words, and exactly the same could be said of the fashionable music of the time. What people wanted was something that could be understood very, very easily, with rocking-horse rhythms, sugary sentiment, phrases answering each other in the manner of rhyming couplets, and musical clichés—here an elegant chromatic chord, there an affecting appoggiatura—in place of verbal ones.

In literature, the leading nation was France; in music, it was Italy. Italian opera, which at this time meant little more than a series of solo arias relieved by the occasional duet or ensemble, became the model for progressive spirits all over Europe. In their eyes, it was a vast improvement on the arid complexities (as they saw them) of seventeenth-century polyphony. The new ideal, which was consciously democratic and popular, even 'populist',[9] was an easy cantabile without too much distraction from the accompaniment.

---

[8] Lytton Strachey, 'Pope'. The Leslie Stephen Lecture for 1925, reprinted in *Literary Essays*, 79–93; this extract occurs on p. 88.

[9] See the quotations from 18th-c. composers on p. 134, and also their source, Romain Rolland, 'The Origins of Eighteenth-Century "Classic" Style', in *Romain Rolland's Essays on Music*, 50–68.

The new harmonic simplicity

This unimpeded cantabile proved to be a great simplifier. The endlessly modulating sequences that had been the Baroque norm came to be restricted to passages of deliberate turbulence; elsewhere, their place was taken by long stretches of essentially three-chord harmony in a stable key. In some respects this made things more difficult for the composer: banality, repetition, sheer monotony became that much harder to avoid. So great, indeed, was this difficulty that it took a good half-century—roughly from 1720 to 1770—to resolve it completely.

One way of doing so was, paradoxically, to simplify harmony even further, so that the norm became a tonic-and-dominant texture with the subdominant reserved for special emphasis. It was yet another *recul à mieux sauter*, a return to something not far from the harmonic language of Dalza's *pavane alla ferrarese* (Exs. 6.11 and 6.12), but vastly more sophisticated. For the composers of the mid-eighteenth century enjoyed three great advantages over their remote predecessors. Firstly, they could employ key relationships much wider ranging than anything known to the sixteenth century. Secondly, their melodic vocabulary was much larger. That is to say, they had at their disposal many more melodic figures, which could be combined with even the simplest of harmonic chords, and enabled them to extend these to greater and greater length. Thirdly, they greatly refined the interplay between rhythm and harmony. In the sixteenth century, these had for the most part coincided; in the eighteenth, they increasingly diverged, as tonic-and-dominant patterns long current in popular music took on new meanings. Some, such as I–V I–V and V–I V–I, were centuries old; others, more recent. Most powerful of all was the 'split dominant' I–V V–I, which was essentially no more than the old cadential formula I–V–I with the dominant chord divided between two phrases.

This simple-seeming pattern went back almost as far as tonic-and-dominant harmony itself. Even Dalza hints at it in one or two places, and by the 1580s it had established itself as a feature of the chord row known as the *pavaniglia*, or 'little pavan' (Ex. 9.2). This begins as a *folia* progression with split chords: instead of the plain Im V · I VII, we have Im–V V–Im · Im–VII VII. This new pattern, like the *folia* itself, seems to have come from Spain, since it was also known as the 'Spanish Pavan', 'Pavane d'Espagne', and so forth.[10]

---

[10] See Richard Hudson, 'Pavaniglia'.

Ex. 9.2. Fabritio Caroso, early example of *pavaniglia*, from *Il ballarino* (1581) (up a 4th)

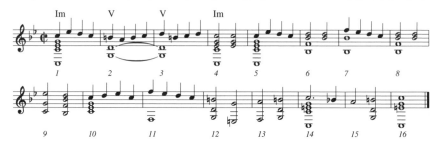

But this promising beginning came to nothing. Already in Bull's variations on 'The Spanish Paven',[11] we can see the typically Baroque proliferation of subsidiary chords beginning to smother the original pattern. Like many another sixteenth-century progression, the split dominant maintained its primitive simplicity only at the folk level. It is tempting to connect the *pavaniglia* with the northern Spanish *jota aragonese*, where the harmony is nothing but a string of split dominants, and it is certainly true that early eighteenth-century examples often have a popular flavour (Exs. 9.3 and 9.4).[12]

Ex. 9.3. J. S. Bach, Cello Suite no. 3 in C (*c.*1720), Bourrée I, beginning

Ex. 9.4. Vivaldi, *The Four Seasons* (*c.*1725), 'Winter', 2nd mvt., beginning (down a minor 3rd)

At the same time, the emerging taste for clear-cut antithesis expressed through simple harmony produced another, quite different type of split dominant, derived

[11] *FVB* ii. 131–4.
[12] For other examples in a more or less popular style, see the Minuet from Domenico Scarlatti's 'Tocata 10' (quoted in Kirkpatrick, *Domenico Scarlatti*, 150), and the Polonaise in D minor from the *Anna Magdalena Bach Book* (no. 17) by J. S. Bach.

Ex. 9.5. Purcell, *Timon of Athens* (1694), Overture, beginning (down a tone)

from the imperious opening gesture of the French overture (Ex. 9.5). One might call it the 'dramatic', as opposed to the 'popular' form of the pattern.[13]

It took an astonishingly long time, however, for composers to attach any importance to the split dominant in either form. In so far as they thought about it at all, they appear to have regarded it as merely another way of harmonizing more or less sequential phrases. The first composer to realize its full potential was Mozart. Not only did he quickly see how it could be varied, decorated, and, especially, extended (Ex. 9.6); he was perhaps also the first to grasp that it *was* a split chord, and that the same principle could be applied to other harmonies.[14]

A close relative of the split dominant is what Robert S. Winter calls the 'bifocal close'.[15] This is merely a half close followed up in the dominant *key*, in other words,

Ex. 9.6. Mozart, String Quintet in C, K. 515 (1787), 1st mvt., beginning

[13] For another early example, see the Sinfonia (i.e. French overture) from J. S. Bach's Partita no. 2 in C minor. The 'dramatic' split dominant had a surprisingly long career. It remained common in Haydn and survived as late as the opening phrase of Beethoven's 'Pathétique' Piano Sonata in C minor, Op. 13 (1797–8).

[14] He is particularly partial to the split subdominant. See e.g. the opening themes of the Piano Concerto No. 17 in G, K. 453, and Don Ottavio's aria 'Dalla sua pace' in *Don Giovanni* (Act I, Scene iii, no. 11).

[15] See 'The Bifocal Close and the Evolution of the Viennese Classical Style'; Mozart is discussed on pp. 299–328. The term 'bifocal close' was inspired by, but should not be confused with, the major–minor 'bifocal tonality' of Jan LaRue (see p. 97 of the present book).

a split dominant in which the section after the split (usually a sonata-form second subject) has been 'tonicized'. This, too, was a great favourite with Mozart, in whose works (notwithstanding the disapproval of certain theorists) it turns up almost 150 times, 'from his first symphony to his last piano concerto'.[16]

It is also a special case of a type of modulation that was coming into frequent use at this time. Here, there is no gradual working round to the new key, but an abrupt leap, often after a brief silence. Such modulations are 'disjunct' rather than 'conjunct', and derive from the square, abruptly juxtaposed strains of dance music.[17] As these became fashionable, so too did their characteristic style of modulation. It was all part of the Classical taste for ease, simplicity, and sharp contrast.

The same might be said of broken-chord accompaniment figures like the Alberti and waltz basses. These 'dummy accompaniments', as they have been disdainfully termed, had a long history in popular music.[18] With the Melody now so predominant, they were called upon to perform two increasingly important tasks: on the one hand, to provide a pleasant and not too distracting background, and, on the other, to fill in the gaps between melodic phrases.

Deep simplicity and surface complexity

To the conservative observer, it must have seemed that the *galant* style of the mid-eighteenth century, with its short-breathed tunes, thin texture, trumpery harmonies, and tinkling accompaniments, was sinking into a morass of irredeemable triviality. We now know that it was instead beginning an ascent to the glories of the Classical school, and that, paradoxical as it may seem, the glories and the trivialities were intimately linked.

At the root of it all lay a reciprocity between the simple and the complex, such as the theorists of complexity describe in gnomic, almost biblical aphorisms:

Simple systems give rise to complex behavior. Complex systems give rise to simple behavior.[19]

Surface complexity arises out of deep simplicity.[20]

---

[16] 'The Bifocal Close and the Evolution of the Viennese Classical Style', 337.

[17] For an early example, see Zacara's 'Ciaramella' (Ex. 6.2 on pp. 68–9), bars 19–20. Cf. also the abrupt transition to the relative major in the middle of the *passamezzo antico*. During the Baroque period this form of modulation continued to be typical of dance forms, e.g. the finale of J. S. Bach's Violin Concerto in E major, and (in the same key) the 'Gavotte en rondeau' from his Sonata No. 6 for unaccompanied violin.

[18] Something like the Alberti bass may be found as far back as the early 16th c. In 'My Lady Carey's Dompe' (anon., *c.*1525; reprinted in the *Historical Anthology of Music*, ed. Davison and Apel, 105), the Alberti-like figure $1-1^+-5-1^+$ (etc.) is repeated throughout the movement.

[19] Gleick, *Chaos*, 304.

[20] 'Murray Gell-Mann has a good phrase for it: Surface complexity arising out of deep simplicity.' Roger Lewin, *Complexity*, 14; see also Gell-Mann's own book, *The Quark and the Jaguar*.

The course of European music between 1600 and 1800 beautifully illustrates these principles, as self-similarity, born of simplicity, gave rise to structures of the utmost complexity.

This is as true of rhythm as of melody or harmony. Self-similarity is a characteristic of Classical rhythm, whether strictly symmetrical—four-beat bars within four-bar phrases within sixteen-bar strains—or dynamically asymmetrical. For an example of the latter, we need go no further than the familiar first movement of Mozart's Serenade for Strings in G, better known as 'Eine kleine Nachtmusik' (see Table 9.1).

TABLE 9.1. *Dynamic bar rhythms in 'Eine kleine Nachtmusik'*

Section	Number of bars	
Opening phrase	4	
Answering phrase	6	
Opening section as a whole		*10*
Transition to dominant key	17	
First group as a whole		*27*
Second group	28	
Exposition as a whole		*55*
Development and recapitulation	82	
Movement as a whole		*137*

It will be seen that each succeeding section is about half as long again as the one before, with one exception. This is the second group, where a 2:3 ratio would overbalance the movement. Instead, the two groups are equally long, though even here the one-bar difference is on the right side.

Is it far-fetched to see in this delight in self-similarity a parallel with neoclassical architecture? The façade of a Palladian mansion is essentially a scheme of rectangles within rectangles, often of the self-similar Golden type, right down to individual bricks, window panes, and door panels. But a structure consisting of nothing but straight lines and right angles would be intolerable (as countless twentieth-century buildings amply demonstrate), so Classical architects were careful to relieve the rectangularity with cunningly placed arches, cupolas, and curlicues of all kinds. Quite likely, too, there would be an artfully irregular garden not far away, with a brand-new ruin in the fashionable Romantick Taste.

In music, too, the danger of excessive symmetry was avoided by carefully calculated irregularity, rhythmic, melodic, or harmonic. It is probably true to say that all genuinely Classical art demands such irregularities. But in music they were more than merely expressive; by the very nature of sound, they were inevitable.

The minor mode

The most important of these challenges to symmetry was the classical minor mode. This adaptation of the natural minor to major-mode harmony had been several centuries in the making. First the major dominant chord was borrowed from the major mode; then the subdominant chord, though still minor, was made to behave like its major-mode equivalent; later, the supertonic and submediant chords underwent similar adjustments. In the end, the chords on *1, 2, 4, 5*, and *6*(♭) (note the pentatonic pattern) all had equivalent functions in both modes:

Major mode	Minor mode
I	Im
II	II5♭
II7	II7/5♭
IV	IVm
V(7)	V(7)
V9	V9♭
VI	VI♭

The minor had become, in effect, a 'dark major'.

By the mid-eighteenth century, however, even this majorized minor had come to seem a disturbance of normality. Different nations reacted to this disturbance in different ways. Whereas the Italians smoothed away its asperities, treated it as a temporary disruption, or simply avoided it, the Germans revelled in its turbulent power. In other words, the Italian response to the minor mode was Classical, and that of the German Romantic. A feature of the Romantic minor found in both J. S. and C. P. E. Bach, in Haydn, and in Mozart, is that it often comes at the end of the movement.[21] It is a procedure that would have seemed to the Italians extravagantly emotional, like finishing on an unresolved discord. In a discussion of a slightly later period, Julian Budden remarks that there was an 'unwritten but very strict law of early Italian romantic opera that *any extended piece in the minor key must end in the major*. To violate this rule as Pacini did in *I Cavalieri di Valenza* is to incur the sinister-sounding charge "abuso dei minori" '.[22]

---

[21] For examples of J. S. Bach's 'Romantic' minor, see the 'Goldberg' Variations nos. 15, 21, and 25, especially the last. Haydn is most Romantic in the 'Sturm und Drang' works of the 1770s, which often end in the minor. Later, he was to make a point of providing a happy ending in the major.

[22] *The Operas of Verdi*, i. 41. Italics in the original.

Two questions arise. The first is why the *galant* composers, if they were intent on lightness, ease, and grace, did not extend this preference to the minor mode itself. Why not bring back the Picardy third and major subdominant, banish diminished sevenths and minor ninths, and generally restore the mode to something like its sixteenth-century form? It is not as if such reversals are unknown; something rather like this did in fact occur in the next century. Why, then, did it not occur earlier?

Probably the best answer is that it would have violated the aesthetic instincts of the Age of Reason. This was a culture that favoured sharp antitheses and neat categories in everything. Just as it objected to the mixture of comedy and tragedy in Shakespeare's plays, so too would it have objected to the mixture of major and minor in the music of his time. Classical taste demanded internal consistency in a mode. Just as the three primary triads of the major mode were all major, so those of the minor mode were all minor—or at least they would have been, if the exigencies of tonality had not overridden this instinct in the case of the dominant.

The second, more fundamental question is whether gloom, however attenuated, is an essential part of the minor mode. Until quite recently, the official answer was 'no'. A passage from a 'music appreciation' textbook of 1955 sums up the orthodox view: 'Is the minor "sadder" than the major? Such connotations exist only in reference to the music of a particular time and place. The nineteenth century seems to have regarded the minor as more somber than the major.'[23] The implication is that other cultures might not share this singular quirk. In the right circumstances, the minor could be ever so much jollier than the major.

One is reminded of the notion, fashionable at the same time, that a six-note Schoenbergian discord could be just as euphonious as a major triad, once you got used to it. Both, I suspect, go back to nineteenth-century German relativism. The relativists pointed on the one hand to the many cheerful Baroque compositions in the minor mode, and on the other to the 'Dead March' from Handel's *Saul* or the lament of Orpheus from Gluck's *Orfeo*,[24] both in the major. In these latter, what they failed to notice was that, though the harmony may indeed be major, the Melody places unusual emphasis on minor intervals. And while the pre-Classical minor mode can show many animated gavottes, bourrées, and so on, it can also show many indisputably sombre sarabands and folias.

The truth is not that early composers were unaware of the mournfulness of the minor mode, but rather, as in the case of the more extreme discords and dissonances, that they had yet to exploit it. In fact, from the strictly scientific point of view, minor intervals *were* a form of discord and dissonance. The emotions

[23] Joseph Machlis, *The Enjoyment of Music*, 192–3. Cf. also the quotation from Sir Henry Hadow on p. 415 of the present book.

[24] 'Che farò senza Euridice?' (Act IV).

expressed, depending on the context, might be gloom, melancholy, tension, resolution in adversity, wistfulness, and a host of others. But they were all in a some sense negative, and nothing could entirely erase the negativity. A jig in the minor mode may well express merriment, but never quite the same unclouded merriment as the same jig in the major.[25]

[25] For a further discussion of this point, see Cooke, *The Language of Music*, ch. 2, 'The Elements of Musical Expression', 34–112, especially 'The Ambiguities of the Minor System', 90–4.

PART THREE

The Melodic Counter-Revolution

10 The Rude, the Vulgar, and the Polite

> The general aim in music is to make other people feel outside it—or outsiders, compared to yourself.
>
> Stephen Potter[1]

'Folk' music (and indeed the 'folk' themselves) was a discovery of that momentous age of discoveries, the late eighteenth century. The earlier attitude is neatly captured in the words of Joseph Addison:

> When I travelled, I took a particular Delight in hearing the Songs and Fables that are come from Father to Son, and are most in vogue among the common People of the Countries through which I passed; for it is impossible that any thing should be universally tasted and approved by a Multitude, tho' they are only the Rabble of a Nation, which hath not in it some peculiar Aptness to please and gratifie the Mind of Man.[2]

Addison's lordly condescension is pre-, or perhaps proto-Romantic. In modern terms, what he is describing here is partly 'folklore' ('come from Father to Son') and partly 'popular culture' ('universally tasted and approved by a Multitude, tho' they are only the Rabble of a Nation'). The distinction between the two was first made clear, some fifty years later, by the German Romantics. To them, the art of the 'common People' came in both deserving and undeserving varieties, like the Victorian poor.

To this day, there remains something faintly Teutonic about this dichotomy, and it is significant that the adjective 'folk', applied to the deserving variety, has never made much headway beyond the Teutonic sphere of influence. In the Latin countries, 'folk music' is still *popular*, *popolare*, or *populaire* (though one also hears of *la musique folklorique*), and even in English, 'popular music' remained the accepted term till late in the nineteenth century.

[1] *Some Notes on Lifemanship*, 85.
[2] *The Spectator*, no. 70, 21 May 1711, first sentence. This is the first in a series of two essays on 'the old song of Chevy-Chase'. Reprinted (with modernized spelling) in *Selections from Addison's Papers Contributed to* The Spectator, 378.

Why should the Germans have made this distinction? No doubt it had something to do with their tendency to take a compartmentalized, even Manichean, view of the universe, but probably the main reason was that popular music was especially highly developed among them. Nowhere in Europe did it come closer to what we should now call 'art' music. This closeness, while encouraging beneficial cultural exchanges, also drove 'serious' composers (as they were beginning to think of themselves) into a defensive snobbery. It is easy to adopt an attitude of benign condescension to a popular musician when he is a peasant bagpiper or blind hurdy-gurdy man; not quite so easy when he is a prosperous bandleader in the house next door.

This uneasy ambivalence was something new. During the seventeenth and early eighteenth centuries, the dealings of 'serious composers' with popular music had been quite unselfconscious. No one regarded such composers as anything other than highly skilled craftsmen, but, on the other hand, no one questioned the superiority of their product. When it suited them, they used the popular idiom without embarrassment, but they felt no obligation to do so. Nor were they troubled by scruples about ethnic authenticity.

The nearest modern parallel may be found in cookery, an art whose inescapably practical nature has protected it from both the Romantic and Modernist movements. Till the mid-eighteenth century, the position of a master composer closely resembled that of a master chef today. It was as normal for a German like Handel to compose Italian music for an English audience, as it would now be for a Hungarian to cook French dishes in a New York hotel. When the foreigner did compose in the native style, it was in the spirit of a chef dressing up a local dish. Handel's English hornpipes are the equivalent of Frenchified bread-and-butter puddings.

The distinction that this age *did* make was between the 'polite' on the one hand (probably the nearest modern equivalent is 'upmarket'), and the 'rude' or 'vulgar' on the other. With the Romantic movement, 'polite' turned into 'serious' or 'classical'; 'vulgar', into 'popular'; 'rude', into 'folk'. And of all these transformations, the most important was the last. In the 1760s, it became chic to be rude. Old ballads, medieval verse, the mostly imaginary Celtic world of Macpherson's Ossianic concoctions, architecture in both the Greek and Gothic styles, were suddenly all the rage.

From the outset, a connection was made between the remote past and the primitive present. The archaisms of peasant art, hitherto merely crude, began to be seen as uncorrupted relics of a glorious antiquity. This is easy enough for us to understand, being, after all, no more than early Romanticism. But there is another strand in late eighteenth-century thought, more puzzling to the modern observer, in which this new respect for the primitive becomes entangled with a still-powerful craving for order:

'The sacred word "nature" is probably the most equivocal in the vocabulary of the European peoples,' wrote A. O. Lovejoy who isolated more than sixty distinct meanings of it. . . . But its primary connotation was 'uniformity' and 'universality' and it was this meaning that made 'nature' a sacred word of the Enlightenment. Since the reason is, it was assumed, identical in all men, anything of which the verifiability or intelligibility is limited to particular periods or conditions must necessarily be without truth or value, at any rate to the man of reason.[3]

One is reminded of Popper's observation, quoted in my Introduction, that 'it is an important postulate of scientific method that we should search for laws with an unlimited realm of validity'.[4] What the Age of Reason did was to extend this principle from matters of fact to matters of taste.

This deep faith in 'natural' law is a bond between early Romanticism and neo-classicism. Just as the architecture of ancient Greece was felt to be more 'natural' than that of Rome because it was earlier and simpler, so the 'noble savage' was assumed to be the superior of a cultivated eighteenth-century gentleman; and so, too, simple folk melody was held to be a great improvement on Baroque polyphony. Of course, it was all self-deception. Very few eighteenth-century gentlemen ever met a savage, noble or ignoble; ancient Greek architecture was far from simple; and the much-admired 'folk melody' was an urban idealization that had little in common with the rustic reality. The bogus has always played a vital part in Romanticism.

Muddled though it might be, however, the universalist ideal exerted a powerful influence. It explains the mystifying but oft-repeated statement that 'music is a universal language', and still colours received notions of 'folk song'. But it was not without rivals. During the same period, a contradictory nationalism was arising on the periphery of Europe. Especially in relatively backward countries still under foreign domination, such as Scotland, Ireland, and Hungary, patriots were beginning to regard peasant music as an expression of the national spirit.

And, in any case, genuinely archaic music was everywhere acquiring the value of rarity. Throughout the more prosperous parts of Europe, ancient traditions were being abandoned or at least modified. In music, as in other things, both the peasantry and the urban poor were becoming more like the gentry, thereby further promoting the trade in musical ideas. And this trade was naturally inclined to be most vigorous where the social gap was narrowest. As a rule, 'folk' influences on the classics come, not from an archaic peasantry, but from a mixed, largely urban society with an important class of professional popular musicians.

In contradiction to this point an elaborate mythology has grown up. The great composer hears a peasant girl singing a 'folk tune' in the fields, or perhaps he recollects it from the lips of his beloved old nurse—at any rate, it comes to him from some such impeccably folky source. Perceiving its great beauty, he makes it the main theme of his new symphony. Such (more or less) is the legend.

---

[3] Hugh Honour, *Neo-Classicism*, 105.   [4] *The Poverty of Historicism*, 103.

Now, while this sort of thing did occasionally happen, as a generalization it is false on every count. In reality, 'folk' influence was a matter not so much of ready-made tunes as of adaptable formulas, which were likely to come, not from simple peasants, but from professional urban musicians. And they were likely to go, not into symphonies, but into dance suites or serenades. If they did make their way into a symphony, it would probably be in some such unobtrusive place as the trio of a minuet or the second episode of a rondo. In short, they passed smoothly from the most sophisticated popular music into the least sophisticated art music.

A new democratic spirit encouraged this exchange. Throughout the eighteenth century, in stark contrast to the twentieth, the ideal of progressives was to be light, simple, and above all easily intelligible.[5] There was a widespread reaction against the stifling grandeur of so much seventeenth- and early eighteenth-century art: compare Pope with Milton, Mozart with J. S. Bach, 'Louis Seize' furniture with 'Louis Quatorze'. Artists were acquiring a new public, bourgeois rather than aristocratic, less inclined towards ostentation and less able to afford it. 'Thinking people' espoused the democratic ideal and, unlike many of their fellows in more recent times, extended it to the arts. To quote a few German artists:

He who can benefit many does better than he who writes only for a small number. (Georg Philipp Telemann)

One should write for all. We live in society. Let us make songs that are neither so poetical that the fair singers cannot understand them nor so commonplace and empty that intelligent folk cannot read them. (Karl Wilhelm Ramler)

[Good melody must have] an indefinite quality with which everybody is already familiar. (Johann Mattheson)[6]

And if this was the prevailing opinion in Germany, it was doubly so in the Latin countries.

These tendencies combined to give the 'polite' music of the later eighteenth century a novel character. Not only did composers make far more use of the popular idiom; they did so in a new spirit. In the Baroque, popular influences had been concentrated in dance music, and usually took the form of recent borrowings from the popular tradition. In general, those gavottes, bourrées, and so forth, placed by convention before the final gigue,[7] were meant to be tuneful and unpretentious. Often, like the later minuet or scherzo, they provided relief between weightier movements. When composers turned them to more serious use, their nature

---

[5] Cf. Strachey's remarks on early 18th-c. poetry (p. 120).

[6] Quoted from Romain Rolland, 'The Origins of Eighteenth-Century "Classic" Style', in *Romain Rolland's Essays on Music*, 50–68 at 63–4. Ramler (1725–98) was a poet who contributed to the development of the early Lied. Mattheson (1681–1764) was a composer and musical theorist.

[7] Nowadays sometimes known as *Galanterien* or 'galanteries', though *The Grove Concise Dictionary of Music* (p. 279) informs us that there is no 'good reason' for this usage.

changed accordingly. The intimate blending of the popular with the serious is foreign to the Baroque.

But it is the lifeblood of the Classical style. We have seen how harmonic simplicities provided the foundation for its majestic tonal hierarchies. In the same way, periods of four, eight, or sixteen bars made possible all manner of contrasts, overlappings, and artful irregularities—and so, too, for melody, form, and instrumental texture. Everywhere the unpretentious formulas of popular music received exquisitely sophisticated treatment.

This was done quite deliberately. In the arts, as elsewhere, the final third of the eighteenth century was a period of restless and perfectly conscious experiment. Nothing pleased the artist of those times more than combining what had hitherto been separate, or even incongruous. Horace Walpole writes a novel in the form of a Shakespearean drama, and so creates the first 'Gothick' romance, *The Castle of Otranto*.[8] Chippendale applies Chinese or medieval European ornament to ordinary Georgian chairs. Wedgwood designs a handsome soup tureen in the form of a Grecian urn. Cabinetmakers apply the details of classical architecture to tables and wardrobes. Benjamin West, in 'The Death of Wolfe', paints a Baroque death scene in modern dress, even including a noble savage in the person of a (quite unhistorical) American Indian.[9]

It is against this background that we should see the Balkan folk tunes, primitive ländler, scraps of Gregorian chant, and fugatos (or even complete fugues) that Haydn inserts into his symphonies and string quartets. In 1760 he was still composing in the *galant* manner; twelve years later, he had produced a body of work that is not merely Classical, but also often Romantic. It is as though, a century and a half before Mahler's celebrated remark to Sibelius, he had decided that a symphony (or sonata, or string quartet) should 'contain the world'. The label *Sturm und Drang*, conventionally applied to this stage in his development, is rather inadequate—and not only because throughout it he continued to compose un-stormy music. It was more that, like many of his lesser contemporaries, he had begun to sense the immense capacity of the sonata style for contrast within unity.

The Germans have another name for the *Sturm und Drang* period (roughly 1770 to 1785): the *Geniezeit*, or 'time of genius'. But there is an obvious conflict between classicism and the cult of genius. The former is moderate, sociable, essentially Latin, and sane; the latter excessive, solitary, essentially Teutonic, and more than a little mad. For almost sixty years, from the early Romanticism of the 1770s till the deaths of Beethoven and Schubert in the late 1820s, the great Viennese masters miraculously reconciled these contradictory ideals.

---

[8] See Marilyn Butler, *Romantics, Rebels, and Reactionaries*, 20–1.

[9] See Honour, *Neo-Classicism*, 107–13 and 150–3.

Of course it could not last. By 1830 Romanticism had triumphed, and with it a fatal estrangement from the popular spirit. A golden age was at an end.

THE CANTILENA STYLE

> One might indeed say with some truth that the classical tradition is nothing more or less than the Italian tradition.[10]
>
> Edward J. Dent

From the late Middle Ages till the early twentieth century, two contrasting strands run through the web of European music. One, originating on the southern and eastern fringes of the continent, is partially Oriental, highly charged, and extremely complex. The other, invented in northern Italy during the fifteenth century, is wholly Western, comparatively restrained, and essentially simple. The simplicity makes it easier to deal with, but no less important. For this was not merely the primary language of Italian composers for several centuries; with slight modifications, it was the musical lingua franca of all Europe. This Italianate idiom formed the starting point for composers as different as Beethoven, Wagner, Chopin, and Glinka. It also formed the basis of Western popular music (at least in its more sentimental moods) throughout the nineteenth and early twentieth centuries.

The pastoral manner

The basis of this Italian style was what might be called (in the idiom of the times) the 'pastoral manner'. This is the musical equivalent of Dresden china shepherdesses, poems celebrating the pretty loves of Strephon and Amaryllis, or the elegantly neoclassical dairy where Marie Antoinette and her courtiers played at being milk-maids.[11] Its principal model is the more soulful type of Italian piping, as imitated, for instance, in the 'Pifa'[12] ('Pastoral Symphony') from Handel's Messiah (Ex. 10.1).[13]

Ex. 10.1. Handel, *Messiah* (1742), Part I, 'Pifa' (the 'Pastoral Symphony'), beginning

---

[10] 'Italian Opera in the Eighteenth Century, and its Influence on the Music of the Classical Period', 504.   [11] See Honour, *Neo-Classicism*, 162–4.   [12] i.e. *Piva.*
[13] Cf. also the 'Danza pastorale' concluding 'Spring' in Vivaldi's *Four Seasons* (Ex. 7.7 on p. 91).

In essentials the musical language is that of the popular dances, but the mood is quite different. Everything—the moderate tempo, the lilting triple time, the slow, drone-like chords, the great emphasis on the 'affecting' *3* and *6*—is directed towards evoking a mood of rustic serenity. Twenty years later, in 'The Dance of the Blessed Spirits' from Gluck's *Orfeo* (Ex. 10.2), the same idiom has shed most of its

Ex. 10.2. Gluck, *Orfeo* (1762), Act II, no. 29, Ballet, 'The Dance of the Blessed Spirits', beginning (down a 4th)

pastoral associations and become merely neoclassical. Later still, this part-pastoral, part-Classical style was to attain the height of refinement in the hands of Mozart. If there is still a hint of rusticity in 'Secondate, aurette amiche' (Ex. 10.3)—and

Ex. 10.3. Mozart, *Così fan tutte* (1790), Act II, Scene iv, no. 21, 'Secondate, aurette amiche', beginning of instrumental introduction (down a minor 3rd)

Ernest Newman does remark on the 'strongly rustic tang of the scoring'[14]—it is rusticity *à la* Watteau. The style of this tune owes as much to bel canto as to popular music. As is clear from the markings habitually applied to it—'espressivo', 'dolce', 'cantabile', 'affetuoso'—it was valued chiefly for its power of tender expression. Let us call it the 'cantilena style'.

The expressiveness of the cantilena style was largely due to the tension between a Bass firmly grounded in *C* major and a Melody in which the pentatonic poles *a* and *e* became ever more prominent. The tendency, well illustrated in the previous two examples, is to extend the Melody upwards to fill the octave $e-e^+$, and at the same time to suppress the extra-pentatonic notes. Mozart's initial phrase (bracketed) must also be one of the first examples of the further expansion of $e-e^+$ to $g-e-e^+-c^+$. The resulting gracefully serpentine curve reappears in probably hundreds of tunes, mostly of a light or popular nature, from the late eighteenth to the mid-twentieth century.

As the *a* minor triad came to be more clearly defined, so too did its 'dominant chord', the *e* minor triad, and *its* 'dominant note' *b* (or *7*), which, in the form of the apical seventh, had long existed in popular music.[15] In the mid-eighteenth century, this was rediscovered by way of the slow descent from 1^+ to 5. Familiar examples are to be found in the middle movement of Bach's Concerto for Two Violins in D minor (1723) and the even better known 'Ombra mai fu', from Handel's opera *Serse* (Ex. 10.4(*a*)).

Here, the leading note has already lost its harmonic function; it no longer 'leads'. The next step was to turn it into an appoggiatura to *6*. This is the sort of thing that would have occurred spontaneously to singers or solo instrumentalists in the days when they were expected to embellish their tunes.[16] Such a phrase as bars 10–11 of Ex. 10.4(*a*), for instance, might easily turn into Ex. 10.4(*b*)—as, indeed, it does in some later arrangements.

Ex. 10.4.   Handel, *Serse* (1738), Act I, Scene i, 'Ombra mai fu' (down a 4th)

(*a*) instrumental introduction, beginning

14 *Opera Nights*, 254.
15 See Dalza's *piva* for two lutes of 1508 (Ex. 7.19 on p. 100).
16 Cf. Byrd's version of 'The Carman's Whistle' (Ex. 8.2 on p. 115).

(*b*) bars 10–11, with appoggiatura

The final step, arrived at about 1760, was to place the 7 at the top of the phrase. When, as often happened, the 6 was itself an appoggiatura to 5, the result was the double appoggiatura 7→6→5. But soon the apical 7 began to grow into something both more independent and even more expressive. Again *Così fan tutte* affords an early example of a pattern which, like the *g–e–e⁺–c⁺* curve, was to become a nineteenth-century cliché (Ex. 10.5). Even here, despite Mozart's obviously parodistic intent, its expressive power is striking.

I must add that these respectable origins have not spared the apical seventh the censure of certain theorists.[17] Their objections to it are, on the one hand, its failure to behave like a well-bred leading note, and, on the other, its associations with what the Germans would call *triviale Musik*. The first of these charges is merely another instance of the Ramellian fallacy; the second has more substance. It is quite true that sevenths of this type occur more often in Franco-Italian opera, Viennese operetta, or American popular music than in the German classics (though one could point to plenty there too),[18] and also that they are likely to degenerate into clichés. But this is merely because the lighter genres led the way in developing the chord of *e* minor.

In any case, clichés are an inescapable part of the evolutionary process. Before a musical pattern can be elaborated, it must first become familiar; and this, in practice,

<hr />

[17] See e.g. Sir Hubert Parry, *Style in Musical Art* (1911), 116–18, and Hermann Rauhe, 'Zum volkstümlichen Lied des 19. Jahrhunderts' (1967), 178–181, 193, and 195. Interestingly, the latter remarks on the strong accentuation, flat pitch ('zu tiefe Intonation'), and impure, 'squeezed' ('gequetschte') articulation given to the apical seventh by German folk or popular singers (p. 193). All this suggests that they treated it as a species of 'blue' seventh.

[18] For a particularly beautiful example, see Beethoven, Fifth Symphony, slow movement, bar 225.

Ex. 10.5. Mozart, *Così fan tutte* (1790), Act I, Scene ii, no. 4, 'Ah, guarda, sorella!', Allegro, bars 13–28 (up a minor 3rd)

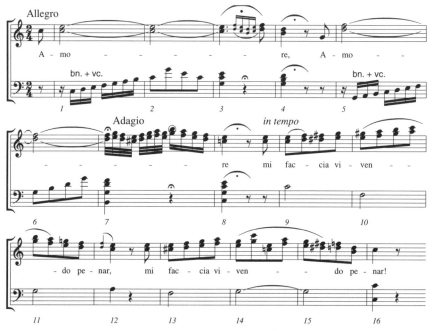

means mechanical repetition, ready-made emotion, and cheap effects generally. If the word had existed in the fifteenth century, critics would no doubt have complained about the irritating new cliché of preceding the tonic chord with the dominant.

Melodic chromaticism

About the same time, the melodic vocabulary was enriched by a type of chromaticism new to Western music. Chromaticism as such was, of course, no novelty. In various guises, it had existed for centuries. One particularly daring type, called by Lowinsky 'triadic atonality',[19] had been invented in the sixteenth century. Others owed their existence to Oriental modes, to compressed modulation, or to the clash of major and minor over a common tonic. But these earlier forms of chromaticism had involved the harmony as a whole. Moreover, they were generally the sign of a troubled or at least a grave spirit, and as such associated with the minor mode.[20]

---

[19] See *Tonality and Atonality in Sixteenth-Century Music*, ch. 4, 'Floating tonality and atonality in sixteenth-century music'.

[20] This is very evident in the keyboard works of J. S. Bach, e.g. the '48', Bk. 1, Fugues in Fm, F#m, and Bm, and Bk. 2, Prelude in Am and Fugue in Dm; the Sinfonia ('Three-part Invention') in Fm; and the

The new chromaticism was quite different: independent of the harmony, light, graceful, and associated primarily with the major.

It developed astonishingly fast. Within a single generation, from about 1755 to 1785, it had evolved from an occasional effect to an indispensable resource. This explosive growth was due partly to the new independence of Melody—for, as *3*, *5*, and *6* began to behave rather like tonics, so they acquired the 'leading notes' *2♯*, *4♯*, or *5♯*—and partly to the simplification of harmony. In the chromatic scale of the Baroque period, each note had normally been harmonized with a separate chord. Later, the chromatic scales were retained while the harmony was smoothed out. And this form of ornament (to recall what was said about clichés) proved to be very easily imitable. Once a chromatic grace had been applied to one degree of the mode, it was a simple matter to transfer it to another.

Mixed up with all this was the chromaticism of the Orient, as transmitted through east European popular music. The chromatic patterns of Ex. 10.6, from one of Haydn's 'Gypsy' finales, are reminiscent of the northern Indian *rāg kedārā*, a popular major-mode rāga which makes a special feature of setting *f♯* off against *f♮*, usually in the contexts of *g–f♯–g* and *a–g–f♮–e*.[21] Incidentally, this is one of those places in Viennese music that make one wonder whether the 'Oriental' influence is generally western Asian or specifically Gypsy—that is to say, northern Indian. But the main point is that none of its chromatic embellishments would be out of place in the most elegant of Mozart's minuets.

Ex. 10.6. Haydn, String Quartet in C, Op. 74 No. 1 (1793), last mvt., bars 270–8 (near end)

'Goldberg' Variations, no. 25 in Gm. The only exception to the generally serious mood is the sparkling Em fugue from the '48', Bk 1.

[21] See the five simple examples collected in Fox Strangways, *The Music of Hindostan*, 303–4. The second of these, Ex. 389, even duplicates the *f♯–g–a–g* figure of Haydn's second bar.

A digression on causation

In music, as anywhere, 'complex systems give rise to simple behaviour'. We could predict from its very simplicity that the cantilena style had a plethora of causes, only a few of which have been touched on in this chapter. One is reminded of the detective story in which every one of the suspects turns out to have dunnit. Time and again, the musical historian is faced with this paradox. All but the very simplest patterns have multiple origins; and, as a rule, the simpler they are, the more multiple the origins will be. This seems as good a place as any to examine this puzzling phenomenon.

Even today, our notions of causation are profoundly influenced by the scientific revolution of the seventeenth century. Newtonian physics gave such satisfying results that later thinkers found it natural to apply its principles to biology. They assumed that nature—including human nature—must proceed by similar chains of cause and effect. One had only to trace the chain backwards to arrive at the ultimate cause: natural selection in Darwin, the economic motive in Marx, the sexual instinct in Freud. People argued about which was the correct 'driving force', but seldom stopped to wonder whether the whole system might be based on a false analogy.

It now appears that no driving force is needed. (That metaphor, I suspect, is a last relic of Aristotelian physics.) Evolution is a process whereby parts combine into wholes, and this happens automatically. A better metaphor would be the mutual attraction of magnetically charged particles.

There is nothing new about this idea. Jan Smuts propounded it as long ago as 1926:

The creation of wholes, and ever more highly organised wholes, and of wholeness generally as characteristic of existence, is an inherent character of the universe. There is not a mere vague indefinite creative energy or tendency at work in the world. This energy or tendency has specific characters, the most fundamental of which is whole-making. And the progressive development of the resulting wholes at all stages—from the most inchoate, imperfect, inorganic wholes to the most highly developed and organised—is what we call Evolution.[22]

And no doubt the German *Naturphilosophen* had said something of the kind long before. More recently, the notion of spontaneous 'whole-making' has been taken up by the complexity theorists. When they tell us that 'complexity is downhill to evolution',[23] they are paraphrasing Smuts.

---

[22] *Holism and Evolution*, 99.
[23] As e.g. Ian Stewart and Jack Cohen do in *The Collapse of Chaos*, 136 and *passim*.

Lest this seem an excessively optimistic notion, I must add that the whole-making is not necessarily benign. Undesirable events are equally holistic. To take a stock example, the fall of the Roman Empire had no single cause, but rather a whole network of mutually reinforcing causes. The same is true of the decline of all systems whatever, whether political, social, or artistic. It is also true that, in relinquishing the orderly piston-rods of linear cause and effect, we are giving up a little more of the beguiling nineteenth-century dream of precise and comprehensive explanation. But this is only to acknowledge the inherent fuzziness of things in general and music in particular.

Returning from this digression, let us proceed to that other great strand in European music: the idiom of its southern and eastern fringes.

11   The Debt to the East

I. THE PHRYGIAN FRINGE

Western Europe has never been comfortable with its debt to the Orient, and especially to the Muslim world. In view of over a thousand years of religious conflict, commercial rivalry, racial prejudice, and mutual incomprehension, this is hardly surprising. But perhaps the real reason is simply that the debt was too huge to be acknowledged. For the simple fact is that, until about six hundred years ago, the European peninsula was little more than a cultural colony of Asia.

The colonization came in two waves. The first, lasting very roughly from 600 BC to AD 400, imposed on Western Europe an essentially east Mediterranean culture, including of course a Semitic alphabet and a Semitic religion. The second, which began, equally roughly, about 800, came from the then much more advanced Islamic world, and affected every aspect of European life, until it at last subsided about the time of the Italian Renaissance. There was, however, at least one art on which Near Eastern culture continued to impinge for several more centuries, and this was music.

'It is a very singular species of music, as wild in modulation, and as different from that of all the rest of Europe as the Scots, and is, perhaps, as ancient, being among the common people merely traditional.' That is Charles Burney on the Neapolitan street singing of 1770.[1] He is clearly describing the near-Arab idiom current till well into the twentieth century over most of southern Italy. Yet Naples was also one of the great centres of Italian opera, and Burney further remarks that in the operative style of singing 'there is an energy and fire, not to be met with perhaps elsewhere in the whole universe: it is so ardent as to border upon fury . . .'.[2] He might be talking about Spanish flamenco singing.

Nor was Naples the only eighteenth-century city where cultivated Western music flourished against a background of semi-Oriental popular music. Among the others were Venice (the second centre of Italian opera), Madrid (where Domenico Scarlatti settled), and, most important of all, Vienna.

---

[1]   *Dr Burney's Musical Tours in Europe*, i: *An Eighteenth-Century Musical Tour in France and Italy*, 254.
[2]   Ibid. 285.

The Oriental Teuton

It was from the East that German Romantic music got its fire and passion. In fact, not only German music but German culture as a whole has always had an Oriental tinge. For well over a thousand years, the Germanic, Slavonic, and Magyar peoples have been trading, fighting, mating, migrating, and, inevitably, profoundly influencing one another. As late as the early eighteenth century, Slavonic languages were being spoken in what is now central Germany; in parts of eastern Germany, they lingered on into the twentieth.[3] And it was the easterners, on the whole, who took the lead in the German cultural renaissance of the eighteenth and nineteenth centuries.

It is, therefore, not surprising that the Germans, compared with their western neighbours, are a partially Orientalized people. This is evident in many national traits: the love of fantasy; the gift for mathematics; the almost Indian delight in complication; the weakness for cloudy mysticism; the fatalism (transmogrified into 'historical necessity'); the tendency to regard abstractions as somehow more real than the sensible world; the obsession with unity, and especially the unity of opposites. This inclination towards the East is especially obvious in the realms of abstract thought, and it is surely not coincidental that so many eminent German thinkers—Marx, Freud, Einstein, Popper, and Schenker, to name only a few—have been Jewish, at least by origin. But it is almost equally evident in music. One cannot but be struck by how many German composers, from the sixteenth century to the present day, have had some sort of contact with the East. A few, like the Bohemian Gluck, were outright foreigners; others had Slav, Magyar, or Jewish blood; still others, like Haydn, Schubert, and Liszt, absorbed the Eastern idiom from their surroundings—so much so, in the case of Liszt, that we tend to forget that he *was* a German.

There were also those who were born in the West but settled in the East, like Beethoven and Brahms; or who acquired a smattering of Eastern culture from their professional wanderings, like Weber and Telemann. The latter is an especially interesting case, because he is one of the few German-born composers who explicitly tells us about his enthusiasm for east European music, discovered on a visit to Silesia during his mid-twenties. The date would have been about 1705:

I got to know Polish and Hanakian music in its true barbaric beauty. In common inns, the band consisted of a fiddle, strapped to the body and tuned a third higher than usual,[4] so as

---

[3] See W. B. Lockwood, *An Informal History of the German Language*, ch. 10, 'German versus Slav in the East', 170–4.

[4] This was no doubt a form of rebec, which survived till the twentieth century in Poland. See Anna Czekanowska, *Polish Folk Music*, 165–7.

to stand out over half a dozen others, a bass trombone, and a regal. In better-class places, however, the regal was absent, but the two leading instruments were reinforced—for instance, I have known thirty-six bagpipes and eight fiddles to be played together. You would hardly believe the wonderful ideas these pipers and fiddlers have, as they improvise while the dancers rest. An observer could pick up enough ideas from them to last a lifetime. In short, this music is brimming with good things, if properly handled. Since that time, I have written various *concerti grossi* and trios in this style, dressing them in an Italian garb with alternating adagios and allegros.[5]

Finally, there were those German composers who absorbed the idiom less directly, either from migrant Easterners or from other Germans. Foremost among these was Telemann's friend and contemporary Johann Sebastian Bach. The Eastern tinge that characterizes much of Bach's work (especially, perhaps, in the minor mode) becomes quite explicit in at least one composition, the 'Peasant Cantata', the east European modes, simple waltzes, primitive polkas, and sixteenth-century relics[6] of which presage similar things in Haydn, Mozart, Beethoven, and Schubert. Like Telemann, these later composers continued to give the music of the East 'an Italian garb'.

In this enterprise the Viennese composers were particularly well placed, for Vienna was both the most Oriental and the most Italianate of German cities. It was the rich and passionate idiom of the East that gave the Viennese the edge over their French and Italian counterparts—and this, incidentally, is as true of rhythm as of melody or harmony. Haydn and Beethoven in particular would be unrecognizable without the rhythmic verve so characteristic of east European popular music and so very uncharacteristic of the older German tradition.

For convenience, I call this part-Oriental idiom 'east European'. Its precise origins are of little relevance to us, and in any case obscure. To the Viennese it was all Hungarian, Gypsy, or Turkish, almost—but not quite—indiscriminately.

The Hungarian Gypsy style

By the late eighteenth century the Gypsies had established a near-monopoly as popular musicians in Hungary, mainly because the Magyars regarded this trade as shameful or even sinful. But the music they played was not Gypsy, for which there was no demand, but Hungarian; and this, again, was not the music of the Hungarian countryside, but a rapidly evolving urban hybrid. Despite the heroic efforts of scholars like Bartók on behalf of the native peasant music, it is this mixed style that the world has always regarded as 'Hungarian', and that German composers meant

---

[5] For the original German, see *Georg Philipp Telemann in Selbstzeugnissen und Bilddokumenten*, ed. Karl Grebe, 95–6. The Hanaks were a Slavonic people, western neighbours to the Poles.

[6] e.g. the aria 'Unser trefflicher lieber Kammerherr', which is based on the *folia*.

by 'Gypsy' music. To Haydn, Mozart, Beethoven, and Schubert, 'Gypsy' ('alla zingarese') and 'Hungarian' ('all'ongarese') were synonymous. The celebrated 'Gypsy Rondo' of Haydn's Piano Trio in G was headed 'In the Gipsies' style' in England, but 'Rondo all'Ongarese' in Vienna, and Beethoven seems even to have conflated the two terms in his Rondo 'alla ingharese', popularly known as 'The Rage over a Lost Penny'.

But at least 'Gypsy' music was performed by Gypsies. The closely related 'Turkish music' had no direct connection with the Turks at all. It was a fantasy style, remotely based on Turkish martial music but inspired mainly by Western notions of the exotic and barbarous East. Its chief distinguishing feature was a battery of percussion instruments, consisting usually of bass drum, cymbals, and triangle (this last, however, being a Western contribution), which contributed a stirring march rhythm. To polite Western ears, it must all have been rather thrilling—the more so in that the Turks, having narrowly failed to take Vienna in 1683, continued to pose a threat for a long time afterwards.[7]

The height of the Turkish vogue was the third quarter of the eighteenth century. Then, as Gypsy music became fashionable about 1780, the distinction between the two rapidly dwindled to the point where little was left of Turkish music but its instruments. In any case, much of what passed for Turkish had really been Hungarian all along; and this was not altogether mistaken, for the Hungarians, in the course of being partially colonized by the Turks, had absorbed many influences from them. As in any colony, this was especially true of the towns, which partly accounts for the marked contrast between the music of urban and rural Hungary.

Such differences as remained between the Turkish and Gypsy styles were smoothed away by the Gypsies themselves, who quickly made any effective 'Turkish' feature their own. Foremost of these was the minor mode, which seems at first to have been regarded as a Turkish speciality. (Thus, Haydn's 'Gypsy Rondo' (Ex. 11.78) is in the major, but Mozart's 'Rondo alla turca' in the minor.) In specifically Turkish contexts, the 'Turkish' style lingered on into the early nineteenth century,[8] but for most purposes it had been subsumed into the 'Gypsy' style by 1800.

To compound the terminological confusion, there was also the *verbunkos*, originally a dance staged by Austrian recruiting officers to lure gullible Hungarian youths into the Imperial Army (hence the name, from the German *Werbung*, 'recruitment'). Since this stratagem continued in use for a century or so, we must presume that it was fairly successful. However, in spite of its martial character, the *verbunkos* did not originate with the army; at first, it was simply the 'magyar', or Hungarian dance. Its chief peculiarity was the contrast between a slow and majestic

---

[7] See Jonathan Bellman, *The* Style Hongrois *in the Music of Western Europe*, ch. 2, 'The Magyars, the Turks, the Siege of Vienna, and the Turkish Style'.

[8] e.g. Beethoven's incidental music to *The Ruins of Athens*.

lassu and a fast and exhilarating *friss*,[9] which could alternate several times in extended performances. Melody, harmony, and rhythm were all typically Hungarian Gypsy, and in fact the term '*verbunkos*' has tended to replace 'Hungarian Gypsy' in musicological parlance. Though far from ideal for this purpose (its range of meaning is actually somewhat narrower), it at least avoids the muddles surrounding the words 'Hungarian' and 'Gypsy'.

Comparisons have often been drawn between the Hungarian Gypsy idiom and jazz. There are, indeed, many points of resemblance, but also important differences—most notably that the African element in jazz is much greater than the Gypsy element in 'Gypsy' music. It is significant that 'Hungarian' tended to replace 'Gypsy' as the normal term during the nineteenth century: Schubert composed a 'Divertissement à la *hongroise*', Liszt a series of *Hungarian* Rhapsodies, Brahms a set of *Hungarian* Dances. In the same way, jazz was 'black' or 'Negro' when still a novelty, but is now generally regarded as simply American. When, in 1859, Liszt published a book arguing that Hungarian Gypsy music really *was* Gypsy, it caused a furore.[10] We now know that he was wrong. There is not much common ground between 'Hungarian Gypsy' music and the actual Gypsy idiom, which is sparingly ornamented, makes little or no use of that 'Gypsy' fingerprint, the augmented second, and, most surprisingly of all, has no traditional instruments.[11] In contrast, the African element in jazz and related forms of popular music is quite genuine, though sometimes exaggerated and often misunderstood.

Both genres, while playing up their exotic side, really belonged to middle-class Western music. How else, after all, could they appeal to middle-class Western audiences? Related genres—the Mississippi blues, the wilder strains of Balkan folk music—might be truly exotic. But it was not these that initially captured the imagination of the great bourgeois public. In their mainstream forms, both jazz and Gypsy music were the products of a double process of assimilation: first *of* 'the folk', and then, with an eye to commercial gain, *by* them. As Bálint Sárosi tells us:

It was through the influence of West European music that the gypsy band playing several parts came into existence. The demand to be able to harmonize the melody more or less in keeping with the taste of West Europe also fundamentally influenced the structure of the melodies, too. In the earliest verbunkos publications . . . it can already be seen that painful attention is being taken that the melody should be harmonizable . . .[12]

---

[9] From the German *frisch*, brisk. The *lassu* is also known as the *lassan*, and the *friss* as the *friska*.

[10] The book, *Des Bohémiens et de leur musique en Hongrie*, was written in collaboration with his mistress, Princess Carolyne Sayn-Wittgenstein. There is still argument about who wrote what in it.

[11] For a description of genuine Hungarian Gypsy music, which has been extensively investigated over the past sixty years, see Bálint Sárosi, *Gypsy Music*, 24–35. Though without instruments, it does use handclaps, finger snapping, etc., in polyrhythmic accompaniments that may well have contributed something to the urban 'Gypsy' style.   [12] *Gypsy Music*, 111.

Eighty or ninety years later, something similar was taking place in the United States. In both cases, the end product was much less alien than it pretended to be.

The importance of the Fringe

Just as jazz was only one small part of a large family of Afro-European hybrids, so Hungarian Gypsy music was only one part of a similar family of Asian–European hybrids, with close relatives in eastern Europe and more distant ones in Italy and the Iberian Peninsula. Within these vast families, influences were carried by a variety of agencies. Chief among these were, on the one hand, nomadic peoples like Gypsies, and, on the other, migrant labourers of all kinds. The latter included both the special and horrific case of the slave, and the itinerant musician. As A. L. Lloyd points out, the 'principal tune-carriers' of past centuries were

the professional minstrels of the Middle Ages, of whatever class, whether their patrons were aristocrats or the back-street inhabitants of towns or the grinning crowds at a country fair. Some of these followed their occupation within a narrow radius of action, more or less tied to a single locality. Others would roam widely, the courtly musicians, as Walter Salmen reminds us, being equally at home in a Scottish baron's fortified farmhouse or an Austrian duke's castle in Vienna or the palace of the King of Catalonia, while their poorer colleagues went on the pilgrim excursion boats to Santiago de Compostela and heard the music of Galician bagpipers, or at the great six-weeks' fair at Leipzig learned from a Polish fiddler a tune he had picked up at last year's fair in Novgorod. A German account of 1552 tells of the fairground meeting of four wanderers from England, Italy, Denmark and Turkey . . . In 1192, King Béla III of Hungary sent one of his minstrels to Paris *ad discendam melodiam* to pick up tunes and polish his technique. Each year, from 1483 onward, Richard III used to bring minstrels over from Bavaria and Austria, five at a time, armed with *laissez-passer* letters to facilitate their journey to and fro via Calais.[13]

These practices did not end with the Middle Ages. The wanderings of so many famous composers—of Handel to London, Beethoven to Vienna, Rossini to Paris, Stravinsky to Los Angeles—are only upmarket, latter-day instances of the same thing. At a humbler level, too, ethnic musical genres have often been spread by wandering musicians over the past two centuries. The Czechs who introduced the polka to Paris in the 1840s, the American minstrel groups who toured Britain during the same decade, the jazz musicians who created a sensation in Europe during the 1920s—these are only a few of the more obvious cases.

Such comings and goings help explain why similar musical patterns so often crop up in widely separated places. They may be melodic or harmonic (for instance the hornpipe pattern of Exs. 7.2–4), but most often they are rhythmic. We know from modern experience how infectious catchy rhythms can be, and the same

[13] *Folk Song in England*, 88.

seems to have been true of earlier times. Probably the most familiar example is the hemiola, known over most of Europe, western Asia, North Africa, and South America, but there are many others—for instance, the anticipation of the first note of the bar by a half-beat, found in Hungary,[14] Scandinavia, the British Isles, and the United States; the slow triple rhythm of the bolero and the polonaise; the three heavy final beats in the polka and Irish hornpipe; and the ♩♩ ♩♩♩ rhythm (or variant) of the French *branle de Poitou* (an ancestor of the minuet, in which the same rhythm often recurs) and many east European dances.[15]

This musical traffic was especially busy in the crescent stretching along the northern shores of the Mediterranean and up into eastern Europe. Many ancient bonds united this vast tract. Greeks and Phoenicians had traded over it; Macedonians, Romans, Arabs, and Turks had in turn conquered great swathes of it, establishing empires that lasted for centuries; and, finally, its eastern extremity, from northern Italy to southern Poland, had fallen under Austro-Hungarian rule.

It is, therefore, hardly surprising that the southern and eastern fringes of Europe were bound together by a deeply interconnected musical tradition. And, as one would expect of a borderland, they had much in common with both East and West. On the eastern side, probably the most widespread and characteristic feature was the Phrygian mode, or rather family of modes. For this reason (and also, admittedly, because it makes a memorably alliterative label), I shall call this vast area the Phrygian Fringe.

We should never forget that the Phrygian Fringe (or Fringe for short) was, up to a few centuries ago, the *civilized* part of Europe. Till the late Middle Ages, it was the Christian West that was backward and the Islamic East that was advanced, and these roles were only gradually reversed. In consequence, the *gesunkenes Kulturgut* of this region is as likely to be Oriental—the relic of some Arab, Turkish, Persian, or Indian court—as Western.

As far as Western classical music is concerned the important parts of the Fringe were southern Spain, southern and north-eastern Italy, and eastern Europe; and in each case circumstances were different. Spanish popular music is unique both in never having made any bones about its Oriental strain and in its extraordinary attraction for foreigners. It is an old joke—and not entirely a joke—that most 'Spanish' music has been composed outside Spain. Gilbert Chase mentions 'Chopin, Corelli, d'Indy, Elgar, Glazunoff, Gluck, Humperdinck, Ibert, Liszt, Carl Loewe, Massenet, Moszkowski, Mozart, Pierné, Rossini, Anton Rubinstein, Saint-Saëns, Schumann, Spohr, Richard Strauss, Stravinsky, Widor, Hugo Wolf',[16] as well as

---

[14] See the bagpipe *verbunkos*, Ex. 7.17 on p. 100, bars 7–8.

[15] See Brahms, Piano Trio in B major, Op. 8 (1st version), end, and Tchaikovsky, Symphony No. 4 in F minor, first movement, *passim*. Both French and east European influences seem to be at work in the minuet of Mozart's Symphony No. 40 in G minor.

[16] See 'The Spell of Spanish Music', in *The Music of Spain*, 289–304. The list quoted here appears on p. 304.

Bizet, Chabrier, Copland, Debussy, Glinka, Gottschalk, Ravel, and Rimsky-Korsakov. But even this formidable list is not complete. One might add Verdi ('The Dance of the Veils' in *Don Carlos*), Balakirev (*Overture on Spanish Themes*), and many others. Nor should we forget those foreigners, like Domenico Scarlatti and Boccherini, who went so far as to settle in Spain.

It is easy to see what attracted this army of foreigners to the popular music of Spain. Like that of Hungary, it had a fire and drive, and, at the technical level, a rhythmic and modal interest lacking in the European mainstream. In nineteenth-century France, particularly, its contribution was enormous, reaching far beyond such obvious cases as Bizet's *Carmen*, Lalo's *Symphonie espagnole*, or Chabrier's *España*. Equally important are those passages where the Spanish tinge is subtle and implicit, such as the 'Scène d'amour' from Berlioz's *Roméo et Juliette*, or the duet 'Mon cœur s'ouvre à ta voix' (generally known in the English-speaking world as 'Softly Awakes my Heart') from Saint-Saëns's *Samson et Dalila*. Significantly, both are love scenes.

The Italians, too, had an Oriental fringe, but made comparatively little of it. If one compares Spanish popular music with such Italian genres as the siciliana, barcarolle, or Neapolitan street song, one is struck by the relative blandness of the latter. All three have a marked family likeness: the rhythm is, as a rule, an even 3/4, 6/8, or 12/8, often interspersed with hemiolas; the mode, an Orientally tinged minor; the mood, a gentle melancholy. And when these mild Orientalisms made their way into opera, they did so in the smooth, gradual, all but unconscious manner typical of Italian music.

A conspiracy of silence

Of all the various elements that went into the German Romantic style, two stand out as particularly important: the Baroque (and, later, pre-Baroque), and the music of the Fringe. But while more than justice has been done to the former, the latter has been almost entirely ignored.

The origins of this conspiracy of silence lie deep in the past. Like Victorian England, early eighteenth-century Germany had been generally regarded as a *Land ohne Musik*—or rather a *paese senza musica*. By the later eighteenth century, the Germans had managed to acquire a reputation as a musical people, and by the mid-nineteenth century they had become *the* musical people. Later still, music itself—or at any rate 'good' music—was widely thought to be a peculiarly Teutonic thing. It was natural that this should go to the Germans' heads, that they should come to regard music almost as an exclusive possession, that they should forget how much they owed to other cultures. And, of course, there were other, more sinister motives.

Mixed up with national pride was a great deal of ethnic prejudice, some of it directed at the French and Italians, but the worst reserved for the east Europeans.

This is one place where the distinction between Germany and Austria *is* relevant. Within the German-speaking world, two sets of prejudices were at work: that of the north Germans against the Austrians, and that of Germans generally against their eastern neighbours. Both prejudices were mixed up, as usual, with ignorance. The east European features in Haydn's music at first struck northern critics as alien and incomprehensible,[17] and similar reactions were later to be provoked by Beethoven, Brahms, and Mahler. But the worst sufferer was undoubtedly Schubert. Hans Gál gives an indignant account of the hostility and condescension with which he was regarded right up to the 1960s.[18] To the present-day reader, some of the things written about him are almost beyond belief, and here it is only fair to add that the British could be as inane as any German. Percy Scholes was an erudite musician and generally sensible fellow, but this is his opinion of the composer of the 'Unfinished' Symphony, the String Quintet in C major, and the *Winterreise*: 'the best of his work will always charm by its melody, its refined harmony, and its easy, happy spirit, or, if more serious, by its not too deep yet sincere expression of more sober feeling'.[19]

Gál is inclined—rightly, I think—to put such stark incomprehension down to 'something like a language barrier'.[20] Quite apart from general hostility on religious, ethnic, or political grounds—and it is worth remembering that Prussia fought and won a war against Austria in 1866—north Germans disliked east European music simply because they could not understand it.

The Austrians were quite different. They thoroughly understood the east European idiom because they were themselves east Europeans; but in other respects they were even more bigoted. The situation rather resembled that of the American Deep South. The Austro-Hungarian Empire was the product of centuries of colonial expansion on the part of the German-speaking peoples, a sort of Deep East, with the same baffling mixture of easy intimacy and virulent prejudice. These eastern Germans enjoyed, understood, and were ever ready to appropriate the music of their non-German neighbours; but, once they had made it their own, they had a trick of speedily forgetting its origins. To be sure, there was nothing unique in this. Something similar has happened in Britain between the English and the Irish, in the United States between whites and blacks, and in many other

[17] See H. C. Robbins Landon, *Haydn: Chronicle and Works*, ii: *Haydn at Eszterháza, 1766–1790*, 281.

[18] See *Franz Schubert and the Essence of Melody*, 11–16.

[19] *The Listener's History of Music*, 7th edn., 1954 (1st edn., 1923), i. 153. Not cited by Gál.

[20] *Franz Schubert and the Essence of Melody*, 33. He observes that it is especially Schubert's most Viennese works, e.g. the 'Trout' Quintet and the finales of the Octet, the String Quartet in A minor, the Piano Sonata in D, and the two Piano Trios, that 'have over and over again aroused annoyance and disdainful rejection'.

places. Seldom, however, can there have been such an outbreak of cultural amnesia as in nineteenth-century Austria.

Both sets of prejudice were at their height towards the end of the nineteenth century, which by an unfortunate accident was also the formative period of modern musicology. Together they explain why, over and above the general neglect of popular roots, the east European strain in German music has been so thoroughly hushed up.[21] In fairness, it should be added that something more than mere prejudice was at work. There was also the notion, always dear to the Germans, that great art is universal. Music, at its most elevated, was an abstract and all-comprehending language, rather like mathematics. This being the case, what part could regional or ethnic preferences have in it? From that point of view, it was not even true that Mozart, Beethoven, Wagner, or Brahms composed *German* music. What they composed was *great* music: great for every culture and period, absolutely and universally great. It was merely a fortunate accident that German happened to be their native tongue.

Shorn of its nationalistic excesses, this way of thinking is far from dead. It is written large over those journals of musical theory that aspire to the abstract universalism, as well as the appearance, of mathematical treatises. The present study, needless to say, takes a different view. And if the eastern end of the Fringe occupies most of the chapters that follow, it is partly because that was where the cultural collisions were at their most fruitful—but also because that is where historical biases most badly need correcting.

The development of a unified language

In any case, the 'polite' Fringe dialects, whether Spanish, Italian, Balkan, Hungarian, Polish, Czech, or Slovak, in time became less and less distinguishable. Examples could be cited almost *ad infinitum*. The Spanish bolero and Polish polonaise were already being conflated in the late eighteenth century:

It was probably the partition of Poland [in 1793 and 1795] which made the *polonaise* or *polacca* fashionable towards the end of the eighteenth century. Cherubini's *Lodoiska* is on a Polish subject, and it was appropriate that the comic servant should sing a polonaise in the first act, and equally appropriate for a girl to dance one in his second Polish opera, *Faniska* (1806). But just the same sort of polonaise occurs in Gaveaux's *Léonore* (1798), the first version of the *Fidelio* story, although here it is evidently intended to sound Spanish [i.e. like a bolero rather than a polonaise].[22]

---

[21] To the best of my knowledge, the few studies of east European influence on German composers that do exist are mostly the work of non-Germans. The best-served composer is Brahms (see Wolfgang Ebert, 'Brahms in Ungarn'—which, however, is based on 'Brahms Magyarorsagon' by the Hungarian Lajos Koch); the worst-served, Beethoven.   [22] Dent, *Opera*, 116–17.

Later, Chopin was to compose a polonaise-like 'Bolero' (Op. 19), and Glinka a 'Polonaise' on a bolero theme; and to confuse matters even further, Hungarian 'polonaises' already existed in the eighteenth century.[23]

Weber's incidental music to *Preciosa* (1820), a play about Spanish Gypsies based on Cervantes, contains music in both the Hungarian and the Spanish styles;[24] conversely, the Spanish violinist Sarasate composed a set of *Zigeunerweisen*. Much of Chopin is a blend of the Polish folk idiom with the southern Italian cantilena of Bellini and Donizetti;[25] Verdi, returning the compliment, sometimes borrows from Chopin.[26] The Russo-Hispanic compositions of Glinka, Rimsky-Korsakov, and others are too well known to need comment. Bizet, according to Winton Dean, had essentially 'only one type of local colour', regardless of whether the setting was Spain, Provence, Egypt, or Ceylon.[27] German-speaking composers such as Brahms and Wolf (himself part Slav) were attracted to the popular music of both Spain and eastern Europe. The Hungarian scholar Ernő Lendvai has pointed out resemblances between late Verdi and Bartók.[28]

In short, a single pan-Fringe dialect had by the late nineteenth century become a commonplace feature of cultivated European music—much too commonplace, indeed, for its importance to be recognized.

II. DRONES AND OSTINATOS

In both south and east European countries, observers were struck by the strangeness of the popular harmony. Here, for instance, is Charles Burney on some Neapolitan street music, performed by two singers accompanied by a violin and calascione (a kind of two-stringed Neapolitan guitar):

The modulation surprised me very much: from the key of A natural [i.e. A minor], to that of C and F, was not difficult or new; but from that of A, with a sharp third [i.e. A major], to

---

[23] They may be found both in Haydn and in anonymous manuscripts. See Bence Szabolcsi, 'Haydn und die ungarische Musik', 166.

[24] See Bellman, *The* Style Hongrois, 142–4.

[25] For a discussion of Donizetti's debt to the southern Italian *canzone popularesco*, see Ashbrook, *Donizetti*, 373, 379–85.

[26] See Budden, *The Operas of Verdi*, i. 398 and 400–1. A particularly Chopinesque passage (Lida's aria 'Quante volte come undono' from *La battaglia di Legnano*) is quoted on p. 401.

[27] See *Bizet*, 146.

[28] 'According to the evidence of Bartók, the historical antecedents of 20th century Hungarian music should be sought in those masters who felt a peculiar attraction towards *modal* variety: polymodality. However astonishing it may sound, the boldest step in this direction was taken by *Verdi*, alongside Mussorgsky and Liszt' (*The Workshop of Bartók and Kodály*, 123). The same book contains many examples of Verdi's 'modernisms'. See especially pp. 96–101, 114–24, 141–56, 159–64, 177–200, and 211–16.

E flat, was astonishing; and the more so, as the return to the original key was always so insensibly managed, as neither to shock the ear, nor to be easily discovered by what road or relations it was brought about.[29]

And here is Liszt on Hungarian Gypsy music:

The civilised musician is at first so astounded by the strangeness of the intervals employed in Bohemian [i.e. Gypsy] music that he can find no other way of settling the matter in his own mind than that of concluding the dissonances to be accidental; that they are mere inexactitudes; or, to be quite frank, faults of execution. He is equally put out by the modulations, which are habitually so abrupt as to defy his most treasured scientific musical tenets.[30]

To Burney, the striking feature of the modulations is their smoothness; to Liszt, it is their abruptness. But in other respects the resemblances outweigh differences. Wherever the popular music of the Fringe came into contact with the cultivated music of the Centre, the upshot was queer harmonies, and especially queer modulations. Of the various reasons advanced for this queerness, three stand out as especially important.

First, that they were due to sheer ignorance. Western harmony was so unfamiliar to popular musicians from drone-based or purely melodic cultures that they could not help producing bold new effects, to say nothing of simple blunders—so, at any rate, runs the argument. There is some truth in it, but not, in my opinion, very much. To begin with, one is faced with the usual difficulty of deriving positive effects from negative causes. Progressions caused by sheer ignorance do not sound striking, beautiful, or exotic, but merely wrong. In any case, Fringe harmony is far from being a collection of arbitrary juxtapositions. It has, as I hope to show, a demonstrable logic.

The second reason, which Liszt was probably the first to advance, was that the strange harmonies were the product of east European modes:

Bohemian music with few exceptions adopts, for its minor scale, the augmented fourth, diminished sixth and augmented seventh. By the augmentation of the fourth, especially, the harmony acquires a strangely dazzling character—a brilliancy resulting only in obscurity. Every musician recognises at once how decidedly and to what an extent this practically constant triple modification of the intervals caused the harmony of Gipsy music to differ from that in use by us.[31]

Though Liszt's description is confused, its gist is clear enough. He is obviously referring to the so-called 'Gypsy' or 'Hungarian' mode $1-2-3\flat-4\sharp-5-6\flat-7-1$. He is quite right about its capacity for engendering novel harmonies, and also about the special importance of $4\sharp$, without which this mode would simply be the

---

[29] *Dr. Burney's Musical Tours in Europe*, i (1773), 244.

[30] *Des Bohémiens et de leur musique en Hongrie* (1859), translated as *The Gipsy in Music* (1881), 299.

[31] Ibid. 301. Quoted, together with the previous extract, in Bellman, *The* Style Hongrois, 124–5.

'harmonic' minor, already reconciled with Western harmony for more than two centuries. But he exaggerates its ubiquity. Many other strange modes existed in Hungary, eastern Europe, and the Fringe generally, all of which had harmonic repercussions.

The third reason advanced for the novel harmonies of the Fringe is that among 'the folk' they were not novel at all, but highly traditional. Some of them (the minor dominant chord, for instance) are a survival of the 'art' music of an earlier age, but most derive from two far more ancient sources, either separately or in combination: drones imported from the East, and ostinatos going back to the very beginnings of harmony.

Drones

Drones, and especially the double drone on *1* and *5*, promote a melodic framework resembling a 'dominant' seventh—in other words, a pentatonic seventh with a major third. The bagpipe *verbunkos* already quoted (Ex. 7.17) is a good example. One's first impression is that a dominant seventh has been set over a tonic drone, but historically this is topsy-turvy. It is rather that many dominant sevenths are really transferred tonic sevenths. A passage from Scarlatti, clearly inspired by flamenco guitar (or its eighteenth-century antecedent), shows how this could happen (Ex. 11.1). In isolation, the first five bars look like straightforward drone-based folk melody; in context, they become a protracted dominant chord. But, even when transferred to the dominant, this drone-based melody retains many of its original characteristics, most obviously the internal resolution of the dissonant seventh.

Ex. 11.1. Domenico Scarlatti, Sonata in G, K337, L26 (mid-18th c.), bars 61–7 (down a major 3rd)

This particular type of transferred drone was especially convenient for composers working in sonata form. At a stroke, it enabled them to accommodate repetitive popular formulas without getting stuck in a groove; to reconcile the modal minor seventh with tonal harmony; and, most important, to make something interesting out of the extended dominant chords that drove the new style.

Ostinatos

What of the oscillating drone, or two-chord ostinato?

We have noticed the vigorous survival of 'double tonics' in early seventeenth-century England. These same ostinato patterns also lived on in Spain, Italy, and eastern Europe, where they came in four varieties: major (*C*–*D*m), as in the Turkish hornpipe tune (Ex. 7.3); minor (*A*m–*G*), as in Ex. 11.2; and two types of Phrygian (*E*(m)–*D*m and *E*(m)–*F*).

Ex. 11.2. Hungarian bagpipe solo (early 20th c.), bars 13–18 (down a minor 3rd)

None of these easily fitted into a strictly tonal system; but by turning one or other of the two chords into a dominant the trick could be managed. In the major (*C*–*D*m) type, the secondary chord of *D*m was easily transformed into *G*7/*d*. To judge by a remarkable passage from one of Beethoven's early serenades (Ex. 11.3),

Ex. 11.3. Beethoven, Serenade for Flute, Violin, and Viola in D, Op. 25 (1801), last mvt., bars 27–42 (down a tone)

this was already happening in the Hungarian Gypsy music of the time.[32] At any rate, his tune strikingly resembles a common type of Hungarian folk melody (Ex. 11.4)—which, however, has nothing to do with the double tonic.

Ex. 11.4. 'Haj, Dunáról fuj a szél' (Hungarian folk song, early 20th c.) (down a 5th)

In the Phrygian (E(m)–Dm and E(m)–F) types, it was the main chord that became a dominant. Essentially, the principle is the same as that of Ex. 11.1: in itself, the ostinato (or drone) remains the same, but its relation to the tonic changes. With equal truth, we could say that the ostinato has been shifted a fifth up, or that the tonic has been shifted a fifth down. By treating the E(m)–Dm progression in this fashion, composers were able to preserve the ancient double-tonic oscillation within a system of strictly tonal harmony. We find it not only in Scarlatti (Ex. 11.5),[33] but even, several decades later and at the other end of Europe, in Beethoven, though unlike Scarlatti he carefully avoids the parallel fifths (Ex. 11.6).[34]

Ex. 11.5. Domenico Scarlatti, Sonata in D, K96, L465 (mid-18th c.), bars 57–66 (up a minor 3rd)

---

[32] It may also be found in Italian folk music of more recent times. See the *saltarello* for ciaramella (shawm) and zampogna (bagpipe) quoted by Anthony Baines in *Woodwind Instruments and their History*, 206, Fig. 47(*b*). The style is reminiscent of Dalza's *pive*.

[33] 'Characteristic of Scarlatti's love of hovering between major and minor are the progressions IV minor and V major in the pieces that imitate popular music'; Ralph Kirkpatrick, *Domenico Scarlatti*, 210. For an example of a similar pattern in its original tonic position, see Ex. 11.14(*a*) on p. 163.

[34] The similarities between Scarlatti and the Viennese composers (cf. also Exs. 11.9–10, 11.21–2, and 11.29–30) are both striking and mysterious, since *direct* influence seems unlikely.

Ex. 11.6. Beethoven, String Quartet in F minor, Op. 95 (1810–11), last mvt., bars 116–23 (down a 4th)

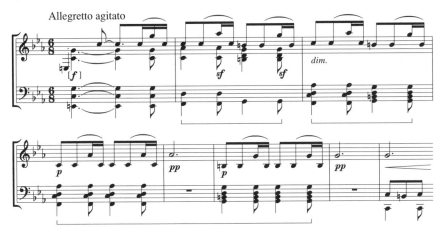

I should add that, from now on, almost all drone-based passages have been so transposed as to place the drone either on *c* (if tonic), or *g* (if dominant). When the passage is in the minor, this may sometimes seem perverse (and indeed, it is always a good practice in such cases to make a mental transposition to the 'pentatonic' version of the mode, for instance from *C* minor to *A* minor). But it is less confusing than skipping from drone-note to drone-note would be—and certainly less confusing than leaving everything in its original key.

The other Phrygian 'double tonic' (*E*(m)–*F*) differs from the patterns considered so far in that the interval is not a tone, but a semitone. This, too, goes back to the primitive oscillations described in Chapter 3. When the lower note predominates, as it usually does in these primeval melodies, the upper note tends to be flattened, first by about a quarter tone[35] and eventually by a full semitone. This is, indeed, the most likely principal origin of that interval. Examples 11.7 and 11.8, again from opposite ends of the Fringe, represent this primitive type.

Ex. 11.7. 'Danza de Palos' (Spanish dance tune)

Ex. 11.8. Bulgarian tune

---

[35] e.g. the American Indian song from British Columbia (Ex. 3.15 on p. 37).

If a series of triads is then built on this simple basis, the result is the *E*(m)–*F* progression. In instruments of the lute or fiddle class, this is easily achieved by shifting the left hand up or down a semitone, as in the flamenco guitar style.[36] Less well known is the practice of rural Turkish fiddlers: 'the music generates a feeling of breathless tension through constantly-changing irregular rhythms[37] and by the most drastic and abrupt modulation possible, namely, by a sudden shift to a half-position—a modulation unthinkable in classical Turkish music'.[38] Similar patterns made their way into the works of Scarlatti and Haydn, in the latter case no doubt through the mediation of Hungarian Gypsy musicians. Not only do both composers use the same formula in Exs. 11.9 and 11.10; they do so in the same parts of the movement, namely, the lead-back to the recapitulation.

Ex. 11.9. Domenico Scarlatti, Sonata in C, K159, L104 (mid-18th c.), bars 37–44

Ex. 11.10. Haydn, String Quartet in D minor, Op. 76 No. 2 (1796–7), 1st mvt., bars 84–90 (up a minor 3rd)

[36] For an imitation of this effect see Rimsky-Korsakov's *Spanish Capriccio*, Ex. 11.16(*c*) on p. 165.
[37] As in the Bulgarian tune (Ex. 11.8 on p. 159).
[38] Laurence Picken, 'Instrumental Polyphonic Folk Music in Asia Minor', 79.

As in the other flamenco-like passage already quoted from Scarlatti (Ex. 11.1), the popular formula has been transferred to the dominant, though with no loss to its original character. To the Classical composer, the resulting tonal ambiguity was one of the great attractions of this pattern. It is strikingly demonstrated in Ex. 11.11, where the same theme serves both as tonic and dominant.

Ex. 11.11. Beethoven, Piano Sonata in B flat, Op. 22 (1800), 1st mvt. (up a 5th)

(*a*) bars 58–68

(*b*) bars 77–83

Drones and ostinatos combined

In this passage we also see something new: the superimposition of a two-chord ostinato over a static drone. Since both these patterns are individually very old, there is no reason to think that the combination of the two is much less ancient. Very likely it occurred, ad hoc and without leading to anything more complex, over thousands of years in countless musical cultures. Only in medieval Europe, where a relatively advanced harmonic sense already existed, did its vast possibilities begin to be exploited, and then only in those southern and eastern regions where both drones and ostinatos were in vigorous use.

The means were simple. By the judicious insertion or omission of a note or two, it proved possible to generate a new series of progressions and chords, to which a further series was later added by alternating the double drone. The main possibilities are summarized in Ex. 11.12 for the static drone, and Ex. 11.13 for the alternating drone. As we can see, the chords generated are the major subdominant (Ex. 11.12(*a* ii)), the minor subdominant (Ex. 11.12(*c* iii)), the ordinary dominant

Ex. 11.12. Two-chord ostinatos over a static drone

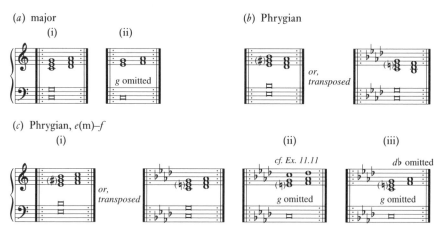

(*a*) major

(*b*) Phrygian

(*c*) Phrygian, *e*(m)–*f*

Ex. 11.13. Two-chord ostinatos over an arpeggiated drone

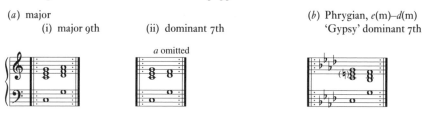

(*a*) major

    (i) major 9th   (ii) dominant 7th

(*b*) Phrygian, *e*(m)–*d*(m)

'Gypsy' dominant 7th

seventh, as already noticed in Chapter 6 (Ex. 11.13(*a* ii)),[39] the dominant major ninth (Ex. 11.13(*a* i)), and the Phrygian or 'Gypsy' dominant seventh (Ex. 11.13(*b*)), to which we may add the formula just noticed in Beethoven (Ex. 11.12(*c* ii)).

Such chords did not arrive immediately, but gradually coalesced out of what was at first no more than a euphonious overlaying of melodic strands. In the case of the Phrygian dominant seventh (Ex. 11.13(*b*)), we can watch this process taking place, 'before our very eyes' as it were, in the 'Gypsy' movement from Rimsky-Korsakov's *Spanish Capriccio* (Ex. 11.14). In this movement, the Russian device of

Ex. 11.14. Rimsky-Korsakov, *Spanish Capriccio* (1887), 4th mvt., 'Scena e canto gitano'

(*a*) bars 1–7 (up a tone)

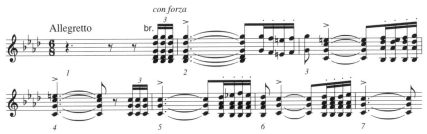

(*b*) bars 124–5 (up a minor 3rd)

(*c*) bars 79–80 (down a tone)

(*continued on next page*)

[39] See the discussion of 'The Dance Suites of Joan Ambrosio Dalza', especially p. 78 (for the dominant 7th) and pp. 81–3 (for the subdominant 6/4).

(Ex. 11.14 *cont.*)

(*d*) bars 62–3 (up a minor 3rd)

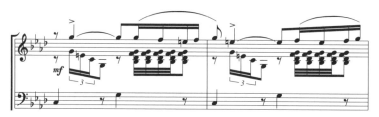

the 'changing background', as pioneered by Glinka, is applied to melodic material of a genuinely Andalusian kind. And what makes the result so interesting is that the background consists almost entirely of various kinds of double tonic or drone.

There are only two themes, both very short, which we may call Tune A and Tune B. At the beginning of the movement, Tune A is announced as a fanfare without any drone at all (Ex. 11.14(*a*)). The harmonic scheme is that of the Spanish double tonic already noticed in Scarlatti,[40] but based on the original tonic instead of the dominant. In various parts of the ensuing movement, this is then set over drones on *c* (Ex. 11.14(*b*)), *g* (Ex. 11.14(*c*)), and *c–g* (Ex. 11.14(*d*)), the last of which produces a 'Phrygian dominant seventh'. It is essentially the same process as generated ordinary dominant sevenths in Italian lute music, and was later to generate dominant major ninths in the waltz and polka. In passing, it may be noticed that the same 'Gypsy' dominant seventh is also found at the other end of Europe (Ex. 11.15).

To return to the *Spanish Capriccio*, Tune B is a fiery upsurge, very much in flamenco guitar style, which is again first announced over a bare double tonic (Ex.

Ex. 11.15. Liszt, Hungarian Rhapsody No. 2 in C sharp minor (1847), beginning (down a semitone)

[40] See Ex. 11.5 on p. 158.

11.16(*a*)) and later set over drones on *g* (Ex. 11.16(*b*)) and *b♭* (Ex. 11.16(*c*)). In spite of (or perhaps because of) their popular origin, these last two harmonizations introduce the modernistic feature of unrelieved discord. So does a fragment of Tune A (Ex. 11.17), with an effect much more Russian than Spanish. In it, one sees the beginnings of the harmonic language of Stravinsky.

Ex. 11.16. Rimsky-Korsakov, *Spanish Capriccio* (1887), 4th mvt., 'Scena e canto gitano'

(*a*) bars 54–7 (up a minor 3rd)

(*b*) bars 71–7 (down a tone)

(*c*) bars 99–103 (up a semitone)

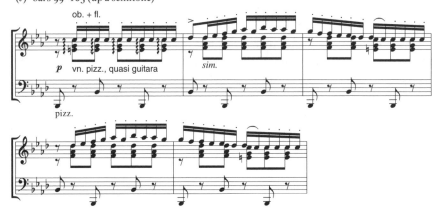

Ex. 11.17. Rimsky-Korsakov, *Spanish Capriccio* (1887), 4th mvt., bars 43–8
(up a minor 3rd)

All these excerpts from the *Spanish Capriccio* have been so transposed as to give
the impression that the Melody remains in place while the drones shift. In fact, the
opposite is true. Except for the initial fanfare, which is a semitone higher than the
rest of the movement, the drone remains static while the Melody moves up and
down. This means that the 6/4 chords of Ex. 11.14(*c*) are really based, not on the
dominant, but on the tonic, as in Ex. 11.18(*a*). In the same way, Exs. 11.16(*c*) and
11.17, though using similar progressions, do so in different parts of the mode (Exs.
11.18(*b*) and (*c*)).[41]

Ex. 11.18. Harmonic schemes of extracts from Rimsky-Korsakov's *Spanish Capriccio*

(*a*) Ex. 11.14(*c*)   (*b*) Ex. 11.16(*c*)   (*c*) Ex. 11.17

The passage summarized in Ex. 11.18(*a*) is almost, but not quite, a modulation
to the subdominant. One essential feature of true modulation is lacking: the V–I
progression. In fact, no such progression occurs anywhere in the movement.[42]
What has happened is that the ostinato theme has moved up a fourth while the
drone has stayed in place. In the same way, the chords of Ex. 11.18(*b*) are those of
Ex. 11.18(*c*) raised a tone in relation to the keynote. A characteristic of Fringe
progressions is their Lego-like capacity for slotting into various parts of the mode
without disturbance to the main key.

Of all the Fringe ostinatos, by far the most important for the purposes of the
Classical composers was 5/3–6(♭)/4. Again, there are several possibilities, depending on whether the drone is single or double, where it is situated, and whether the
mode is major or minor (Ex. 11.19). The double-drone type (Ex. 11.19(*a*)) is particularly characteristic of eastern and central Europe, where it may be found in
both the waltz-polka and Gypsy traditions. As with all these drone-based

[41] For two more ways of treating this ostinato, cf. Ex. 11.11 on p. 161.

[42] With one exception, the few true V chords (always with minor ninths) all proceed to the 7th on VII♭.
The exception is the dominant at the very end of the movement, which closes in the normal way into the
ensuing 'Fandango asturiano'.

Ex. 11.19. The 5/3–6(♭)/4 formula in various positions

(*a*) over *c* + *g* drone   (*b*) over *c* drone   (*c*) over *g* drone

  (i)   (ii)   (i)   (ii)   (i)   (ii)

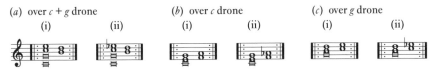

ostinatos, the effect may be one of rustic innocence or passionate gloom, depending on the mode.

As a general rule, this double drone retains much more of its folk associations than the single type, no doubt because the bare fifth is so much more 'drony'. A celebrated example, explicitly alluding to street music, is the haunting final song of Schubert's *Winterreise* cycle (Ex. 11.20).[43]

Ex. 11.20. Schubert, 'Der Leiermann' (no. 24 of *Winterreise*, 1827), beginning of instrumental introduction (up a semitone)

Of the two single-drone patterns, by far the more important is that in which the drone (or 'pedal', as it is usually termed) is on the dominant (Ex. 11.19(*c*)).[44] It proved to be an invaluable way of spinning out the dominant chords so essential to the sonata style. For this purpose, it is often put in the minor, even where the context is major (Exs. 11.21 and 11.22).

Ex. 11.21. Domenico Scarlatti, Sonata in C, K133, L282 (mid-18th c.), bars 14–28

---

[43] Cf. also the 'Dumka' from Dvořák's String Quartet in E flat, Op. 51 (Ex. 16.27 on p. 459).

[44] The type on the tonic (Ex. 11.19(*b*)), being in effect a series of plagal cadences, is particularly at home at the end of the movement. Cf. Ex. 11.61 on pp. 192–3.

Ex. 11.22. Mozart, Piano Sonata in A minor, K. 310 (1778), 1st mvt., bars 16–23

But the same pattern may also make a self-contained tune, such as one is especially likely to encounter in 'Gypsy' finales. When this comes at the beginning of the movement, it is usually preceded by some sort of introductory gesture on the dominant. Schubert, doubtless following popular practice, likes to make this a simple chord in bare octaves.[45] Beethoven, in the finale of his String Quartet in B flat, Op. 130 (his last substantial composition), has a quiet accompaniment figure in skipping octaves, and, in his Seventh Symphony, two loud chords from the full orchestra (Ex. 11.23).

Ex. 11.23. Beethoven, Symphony No. 7 in A (1811–12), last mvt., beginning (down a major 6th)

[45] See the 'Trout' Quintet (Ex. 11.26) and the Piano Sonata in B flat, D960. The finale of the String Quintet in C major begins similarly, except that the initial chord is part of the theme itself.

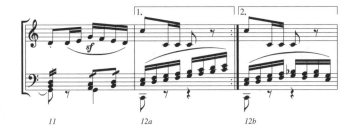

11   *12a*   *12b*

A certain tonal ambiguity clings to these introductory dominants. Is such a drone tonic or dominant? Traditional Western theory is accustomed to settle such matters by looking at the last chord. But ought not the first chord to have some say as well? In hammering out that thunderous first chord, Beethoven is not so much posing this question as knocking the listener over the head with it.

The consonant 6/4

This was not the end of the ambiguities generated by these ostinatos. For instance: when 5/3–6♭/4 is based on the tonic, what is the mode? Is it major with a minor sixth, minor with a major third, or a mode in its own right? This is a question to which we shall be returning when we come to look at the east European modes. And then there is the 6/4 chord itself.[46] Conventionally regarded as a 'discord', this is actually a dissonant concord. All positions of a major or minor triad are equally concordant, but only the root position is completely consonant. Both the first inversion (or 6/3) and the second inversion (or 6/4) are dissonant, in the sense that neither would make an entirely final close to a movement. It is true that, of the two, the 6/4 is the more dissonant, but that is not why it has come to be classed as a discord. The reason is rather that, while no procedure exists for resolving the 6/3, such a procedure *does* exist for the 6/4. By a tradition going back to the fifteenth century, the '4' above the bass must resolve down to a '3'.

This, however, is only one way of dealing with the '4'. Another is to keep it (and the '6') in place and move the bass up a step. Evidently a feature of east European popular harmony, this may be found in an interesting set of *zingaresi* attributed (probably falsely) to Haydn (Ex. 11.24).[47] It also occurs in many of his undoubtedly genuine works—for instance, the finale of 'Surprise Symphony', where it effects a witty return to the main theme (Ex. 11.25). In this, as in so much else, he was followed by Beethoven.

---

[46]   For convenience, I use '6/4' for both major and minor forms, i.e. 6♮/4 and 6♭/4; so, too, with the 6/3 chords.

[47]   It is difficult to believe that Haydn would have passed such crude progressions, except in a spirit of scientific objectivity out of keeping with his times. This, however, only makes these *zingaresi* all the more valuable as historical documents.

Ex. 11.24. *Zingarese* no. 5 in D (late 18th c.), beginning (down a tone)

Ex. 11.25. Haydn, Symphony No. 94 in G (1791), last mvt., bars 142–7 (down a tone)

Yet another way of dealing with the 6/4, springing directly from the 5/3–6(♭)/4 ostinato, is to treat it as a consonance, or at least to grant it the quasi-consonant status of the 6/3. In the theme from Beethoven's Seventh Symphony (Ex. 11.23), the 6/4s can hardly be said to resolve on the ensuing 5/3s. In fact, this passage is little different in harmonic effect from the finale of Schubert's 'Trout' Quintet, where the tonic chords are in root position (Ex. 11.26).

Ex. 11.26. Schubert, Quintet for Piano and Strings in A, Op. 114, the 'Trout' (1819), last mvt., beginning (up a minor 3rd)

The next step is to quit this semi-consonant tonic 6/4 with the same freedom as the 6/3. One pattern is to repeat the 5/3-6(♭)/4 sequentially, as in Ex. 11.27; another, favoured by Italian composers, is to step down from a 6/4 on *c* to a dominant inversion on *b⁻*, and there are several other possibilities. In these anomalous 6/4s, composers discovered a new type of chord, consonant enough to be treated almost as freely the 6/3, but dissonant enough to lend impetus to the harmony. It proved to be a valuable resource.[48]

Ex. 11.27. Haydn, String Quartet in E flat, Op. 33 No. 2 (1781), last mvt., bars 43–55 (up a major 3rd)

III. OUTLINE, REFRAIN, AND SEQUENCE

Imagine a crude graph, outlining the course of a tune in such a way that one has some idea of relative pitch and duration, but not enough to identify rhythm or mode. Is such a graph useless? Not at all. From it, we can learn a great deal. How do the phrases rise and fall? Is the general tendency up or down? Is any figure repeated, and if so how? Does it come at the beginning or end of the phrase? Is the repetition at the same pitch, or at a different one? These are some of the questions such a graph would answer. They all come within the category of what I call 'contour and refrain'.

Contour and refrain—the two, as we shall see, are intimately related—are arguably as fundamental to music as rhythm, for, as we saw in Chapter 1, the 'tumbling strains' of instinctive song probably go back to the cries of our pre-human ancestors. And, because they are so primitive, these tumbling strains are also extremely widespread. We find them, combined with every sort of mode, all over the world, and not least on the European Fringe.

[48] Interesting 6/4s may be found scattered through this book, e.g. in Rimsky-Korsakov's *Spanish Capriccio* (Ex. 11.14(*c*) on p. 163), Chopin's 'Revolutionary' Study (Ex. 11.47 on p. 183), Verdi's *Otello* (Ex. 13.18 on p. 290), and Wagner's *Rheingold* (Ex. 13.22(*b*) on p. 297).

The 'Birch Tree' pattern

Among the most widespread of Fringe tune families is what might be called the 'Birch Tree' pattern, after one of its more primitive members, the Russian folk song 'A birch tree stood in the meadow' (Ex. 11.28).[49] It belongs to an important

Ex. 11.28. 'Vo pole beryoza stoyala' ('A birch tree stood in the meadow', Russian folk song) (up a semitone)

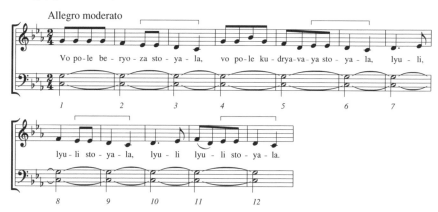

subgroup of tumbling strain, in which the successive phrases 'tumble' from a diminishing height, like a bouncing ball. Often, too, they end with the same figure, in this case the bracketed $e\flat$–$e\flat$–d–c.

This form of tumbling strain is especially associated with Africa and Afro-America,[50] but in a rather different form it is equally typical of western Asia. Here, as a rule, the contour is flatter than in the African type—from *5* down to *1*, instead of an octave or more—and the initial high note is strongly emphasized, either by 'passionate lengthening' (as ethnomusicologists call it), or by the no less passionate repetition of a short figure. Most often, the latter is some sort of decoration of *5*, involving *6♭*, *7♭*, or, very often, both (Exs. 11.29 and 11.30).

Ex. 11.29. Domenico Scarlatti, Sonata in G minor, K121, L181 (mid-18th c.), bars 34–9

[49] The version given here comes from Balakirev's 'Overture on Three Russian Themes' (1858). For others, see Tchaikovsky, Fourth Symphony, last movement, and (complete with words) Taruskin, 'How the Acorn Took Root', 195, no. IIa.

[50] Cf. 'Ngoneni, ngoneni nebakitsi' (Ex. 4.3(*a*) on p. 40) and the 'Joe Turner' blues (Ex. 16.9 on p. 444).

Ex. 11.30. Beethoven, Piano Sonata in D minor, Op. 31 No. 2 (1802), last mvt., bars 43–51 (up a minor 3rd)

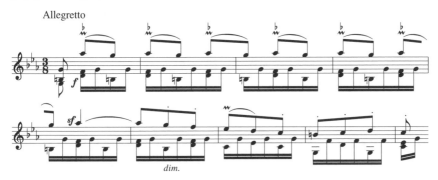

In this pattern, the only really constant detail is the descent through the triad. Everything else may vary. The third may be major as well as minor (though it is usually the latter), the second flat, the fourth sharp. Even the harmony, when present, may differ radically. Tchaikovsky's 'Slavonic March' (based on a Serbian folk tune) and an episode from Chopin's Mazurka in B flat, Op. 7 No. 1 (Exs. 11.31 and 11.32) are clearly variants of the same tune, yet the first is harmonized with a tonic chord, and the second with the augmented sixth on 6♭.

Ex. 11.31. Tchaikovsky, 'Slavonic March' (1876–7), bars 5–8 (up a tone)

Ex. 11.32. Chopin, Mazurka in B flat, Op. 7 No. 1 (1830–1), bars 43–54 (up a tone)

In a related, perhaps even more common formula, the melody descends to the semitone below *1*, as in Exs. 11.33 and 11.34. These are again variations on the same theme; indeed, it is hardly a figure of speech to describe Beethoven's tune as a 'jazzing up' of Mozart's.

Ex. 11.33. Mozart, Piano Sonata in A minor, K. 310 (1778), 1st mvt., beginning (up a minor 3rd)

Ex. 11.34. Beethoven, Piano Sonata in C sharp minor, Op. 27 No. 2, the 'Moonlight' (1801), last mvt., bars 21–8 (beginning of 2nd group) (up a diminished 4th)

The intense mournfulness of this pattern obviously appealed to the Viennese composers. To Schubert, it must have seemed the natural choice in three of his settings of 'Wer nie sein Brot mit Tränen aß', the lachrymose song of the Harper in Goethe's *Wilhelm Meister*.[51] In Beethoven, it is almost a 'fingerprint', as strongly associated with negative emotions as the rising major scale is with positive ones. Among many examples are the 'Klagender Gesang' ('Lament') from the Piano Sonata in A flat, Op. 110 (third movement, from bar 9 on) and the funeral march

[51] 'Wer nie sein Brot mit Tränen aß, / Wer nie die kummervollen Nächte / Auf seinem Bette weinend saß, / Der kennt euch nicht, ihr Himmlischen Mächte.' ('He who has never eaten his bread with tears, who has never sat weeping on his bed through anxious nights—he knows you not, ye heavenly powers.')

from the 'Eroica' Symphony (bars 45–50). The latter, like most nineteenth-century funeral marches, has a specifically Hungarian colour.[52]

The striking thing in the six passages just quoted is the descending line, so different from the arch of the usual 'classical' tune. But we should not forget that other feature of the 'Birch Tree' pattern, the repeated figure. Such figures—or 'refrains', as we can call them for convenience—are so much a part of improvised melody that they can only be the product of a deep instinct. Though varying greatly in length and elaboration, they conform to the following simple rules:

1. The repetition is at the same pitch.

2. Such variation as may occur is slight and incidental; the refrain is always recognizable as such.

3. The refrain always comes at the same place in the phrase: that is, either at the beginning or the end.

In the most primitive and also the most widespread type, the refrain comes at the end, as in the 'Birch Tree' tune itself, or the passage quoted here from Beethoven's 'Razumovsky' Quartet in C (Ex. 11.35). But it is equally possible to place it at the beginning of the phrase. This 'pre-refrain', as we might call it, is particularly common in Oriental music, whether popular or 'art'. For a Western example, we need go no further than the opening bars of Beethoven's Pastoral Symphony. It is as if the whole orchestra had become an improvising peasant bagpipe. In Ex. 11.36 we can see the ultimately Oriental manner in which the pre-refrain divides into interlocking components: the figure *e–f–a–g* (bracketed as A), which

Ex. 11.35. Beethoven, String Quartet in C, Op. 59 No. 3 (1806), slow mvt., bars 20–5 (down a major 6th)

---

[52] For other 'Hungarian' funeral marches, see Beethoven's Piano Sonata in A flat, Op. 26, third movement; Chopin's Piano Sonata No. 2 in B flat minor, third movement (Ex. 11.42); Siegfried's funeral march from Wagner's *Götterdämmerung*; Mahler's First Symphony, third movement, and his Fifth Symphony, first movement; and even, parodistically, the tiny funeral march in Mendelssohn's incidental music to *A Midsummer Night's Dream*, which to present-day ears sounds curiously like Mahler.

Ex. 11.36. Beethoven, Pastoral Symphony, No. 6 in F (1808), 1st mvt. (down a 4th)

(*a*) beginning

(*b*) bars 29–34

introduces each new paragraph and remains unchanged,[53] and the descending scale (*a*)–*g*–*f*–*e* (bracketed as B_1, B_2, etc.), which is constantly being varied, and sometimes (as in bars 5–6 and 7–8) distributed between different octaves.

On a larger scale, the pre-refrain is beautifully, if unwittingly, described by Tovey in his essay on Schubert's *Wanderer* Fantasy: '[the slow movement] is a kind of set of variations on the central tune of one of Schubert's greatest songs, *Der Wanderer* . . . I say "a kind of set of variations" because the variations all arise as so many continuations of a tune that has no end.'[54] This sort of variation was important in Schubert's music from the beginning. In all the thousands of words that have been written about his earliest masterpiece, the setting of 'Gretchen am Spinnrade' from Goethe's *Faust*, little notice has been taken of the strong folk element. Gretchen, after all, is a simple girl of the people, which to Schubert would

---

[53] The same function is performed by the *b♭–g–f–g* figure in the Hungarian bagpipe *verbunkos* (Ex. 7.17 on p. 100) and the *f♯–g* in the Romanian tilincă solo (Ex. 11.95 on p. 220).

[54] *Essays in Musical Analysis*, iv.72.

have meant that she came from a partially Oriental culture. So it is not surprising that her song makes use of several east European devices. One of them is to bind the movement together with the theme announced at the start (Ex. 11.37).[55] The

Ex. 11.37. Schubert, 'Gretchen am Spinnrade' (1814) (down a 4th)

(*a*) bars 2–6

(*continued on next page*)

(*continued on next page*)

[55] The immediately following *a–e* at the beginning and end (Exs. 11.37(*a*) and (*d*)) is a recognized Hungarian mannerism, known as the 'Kuruc fourth'. It is normally repeated, often several several times over, (e.g. 'Rákóczi's Lament', Ex. 11.98 on p. 222). See Bellman, *The* Style Hongroise, 121–2. The word 'Kuruc' (pronounced 'kooroots', with the accent, as always in Hungarian, on the first syllable) refers to the late 17th-c. 'crusade' against the foreign dominant. It presumably derives from the German 'Kreutz'.

(Ex. 11.37 *cont.*)

(*d*) bars 114–20 (conclusion)

Mei - ne Ruh'___ ist hin,   mein Herz ist schwer.

close resemblance of this scrap of tune to the Spanish Gypsy hymn to the Virgin (Ex. 5.11 on p. 64) is surely not entirely coincidental.

For later generations of lieder writers, this form offered a fertile compromise between the strophic and *durchkomponiert* forms. In effect, the strophic repetitions were reduced to an opening phrase (sometimes including text as well as music), while the composer treated the rest of the stanza as he pleased.[56] Nor was the variation technique confined to the melodic line. Much of expressive power of Ex. 11.37 lies in the ever-changing contexts it weaves round note *e*. The accompanying chord may be *A* minor, *E* minor, or *C* major; the note of approach *d*, *f*, *f♯*, *g*, or *a*. This, too, is typically east European—and also typically Schubertian.

Sequences

The Fringe sequence subverts received notions not only about sequences, but about melody in general. Though the ancestral patterns were extremely primitive, consisting mostly of simple figures bounded by a fourth or (more rarely) a third, and swinging between pentatonic intervals (Ex. 11.38), these developed in an extraordinary way. First, the individual steps had chromatic dissonances imposed on them; then, these steps were exactly reproduced, instead of changing with the

Ex. 11.38. Pentatonic frameworks of some typical Fringe sequences

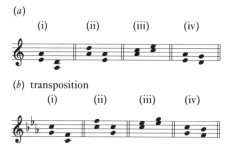

---

[56] Notable late Romantic examples are Brahms's 'Wie Melodien zieht es mir' and Mahler's 'Ich bin der Welt abhanden gekommen', the form of the latter being particularly close to its Oriental origins.

context. In other words, the typical Fringe sequence became both highly chromatic and 'real' rather than 'tonal'. The result, for all its complexity, generally keeps close to its popular origins. Beneath the extravagantly chromatic flourishes, the primitive frameworks of Ex. 11.38 show through, making it convenient to deal with them in the order given there.

At the fifth or fourth

The 'answering' of a phrase or figure at the lower fifth occurs in many ancient traditions, including the oldest, pentatonic stratum of Hungarian peasant music. Very often it takes an at least partially sequential form. The effect is that of a statement and response, which may be repeated as frequently as desired. When first developed, this pentatonic pattern was devoid of harmony, and any 'tonic–dominant' contrast still embryonic. Later, it came to be adapted to various heptatonic modes,[57] and in due course found its way into classical Western music.

In the process it was adapted in various ways. Sometimes the sequence was reduced to a pair of corresponding cadences like those bracketed in Exs. 11.39 and 11.40 (in both of which the correspondence is confined to the Melody).[58] At other

Ex. 11.39. Beethoven, Piano Concerto No. 4 in G (1804–7), slow mvt., bars 6–13 (entry of piano) (down a major 3rd)

Ex. 11.40. Schubert, 'Die Krähe' (no. 15 of *Winterreise*, 1827)

(*a*) instrumental introduction

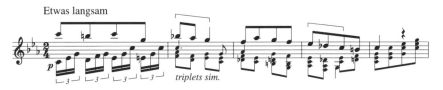

(*b*) outline of Melody

---

[57] Sárosi quotes the pentatonic original and Phrygian derivative of one such tune (*Gypsy Music*, 98). Cf. also Ex. 11.4 on p. 158.

[58] Cf. also the 17th-c. Viennese song 'Nichts Irdisch ewig gewehrt' (Ex. 11.80 on p. 207).

times it was assimilated to rudimentary key contrast, with a simply harmonized 'statement' in the tonic and an exactly corresponding 'response' in the dominant.[59]

Another, less expected assimilation was to the fugal exposition. From the number of occasions when Gypsy-like passages launch into fugatos, there can be no doubt that the Viennese composers somehow associated the fugal texture with the east European idiom. And, occasionally, one may discern a link between the fugal type of 'answer' and the folk variety. The finale of Mozart's last String Quartet, K. 590 in F, includes a fugato (beginning at bar 155) on a positively Bartókian subject answered at the fifth below. This, however, may be a coincidence. But there can be no mistaking the likeness between the passage just quoted from Beethoven's Fourth Piano Concerto (Ex. 11.39) and the opening subject of his C sharp minor String Quartet (Ex. 11.41); the two passages are variations on the same theme.[60] In an analysis of this quartet, Tovey remarked that 'both the beginning and the end of this fugue throw strong emphasis on the flat supertonic (D natural). In the subject the minor sixth (A), with its sforzando, is reflected by D natural in the answer, which has been put into the subdominant (instead of the orthodox dominant) for this very purpose'.[61] This observation is all the more telling in that it shows not the slightest inkling of folk influence.

Ex. 11.41. Beethoven, String Quartet in C sharp minor, Op. 131 (1825–6), 1st mvt., beginning (down a semitone)

Adagio ma non troppo e molto espressivo

At the minor third

For the Romantics, sequences at the minor third were the most fruitful of all. They could take many forms—major or minor, up or down—but the most important type was at the upward minor third. The harmony, in the more primitive examples,

[59]   This effect is imitated e.g. by Beethoven (Serenade for Flute, Violin, and Viola, rondo theme (Ex. 11.3 on p. 157)), Weber (*Freischütz*, Act I, Scene iii, ländler), and Chopin (Mazurka in D, Op. 33 No. 2).

[60]   The east European character of Beethoven's subject becomes even more evident if the *f–a♭–g–f–e♭–f* figure of bars 3–4 is treated as a drawn-out flourish to the ensuing *g*, i.e. with the *e♭* at the beginning of bar 4 unaccented. This accords with Beethoven's bowing instructions.

[61]   'Some Aspects of Beethoven's Art Forms', 290, in *Essays and Lectures on Music*, 271–97.

is limited to the chords *Am–C*, or even to an *Am* drone. This sequence type is characteristically Hungarian. A notable example (in spite of the composer's origins) is Chopin's celebrated funeral march. It has three components: an *a–c–b–a c–e–d–c* sequence in the Melody, a sustained *Am* chord in the Bass, and a repeated *e–f* in the middle,[62] the last two combining to form a wonderfully mournful ostinato (Ex. 11.42).

Ex. 11.42. Chopin, Piano Sonata No. 2 in B flat minor (1839), slow mvt. ('Funeral March'), bars 3–6 (up a major 7th)

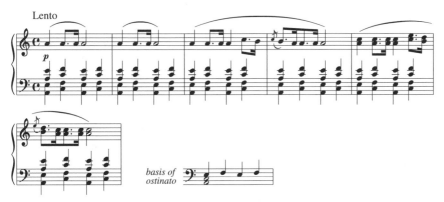

Liszt's Second Hungarian Rhapsody contains what is virtually a florid variation on Chopin's tune, accompanied by a bass of the *folia* type (Ex. 11.43), and the *folia*

Ex. 11.43. Liszt, Hungarian Rhapsody No. 2 in C sharp minor (1847), 'Lassan', bars 2–10 (up a minor 6th)

[62] Hidden ostinatos of this oscillating-semitone type are extremely common from the Viennese classics on. They derive from east European folk music (cf. the two-note Bulgarian tune, Ex. 11.8 on p. 159).

itself may occasionally be found, as in the slow movement of Beethoven's Fifth Symphony (Ex. 11.44). Notice that it again wears a distinctly Hungarian dress.

Ex. 11.44. Beethoven, Symphony No. 5 in C minor (1807–8), 2nd mvt., bars 167–76 (up a semitone)

There was also a more extended sequence, much favoured by the Viennese composers, based on the *folia* progression (*A*m–*G C–B E*m–*D*, etc.), of which Ex. 11.45 is a typical specimen. In view of the east European fondness for strict (or 'real') sequences, it was natural that this, in turn, should engender a variant moving through *A*m, *C*m, *E♭*m, and so on up the diminished seventh chord. Early, relatively tentative examples of this highly chromatic procedure occur in Haydn and Beethoven, but it was not till the early twentieth century that it came to be fully exploited.[63]

Ex. 11.45. Beethoven, Piano Sonata in G, Op. 31 No. 1 (1802), 1st mvt., bars 88–93 (down a tone)

---

[63] This will be more fully discussed when we come to the octatonic scale (pp. 226–30).

At the major second

The folk beginnings of the major-second type may be seen in Ex. 11.46. This already has the Fringe characteristic of being 'real' instead of 'tonal'; and the 'reality', in more elaborate passages like Ex. 11.47, may extend to the harmony.

Ex. 11.46. Romanian folk song (early 20th c.)

Ex. 11.47. Chopin, Study in C minor, Op. 10 No. 12, the 'Revolutionary' (*c.*1830), bars 60–84 (conclusion) (down a minor 3rd)

Because of its strong dissonance and consequent rigidity, the 'Oriental' tetrachord is particularly well adapted to this 'real' treatment (Exs. 11.48 and 11.49). Like a tropical flower so bright and distinctive that it blinds us to the surrounding foliage, this form of tetrachord is both self-assertive and self-*dis*similar. It is the antithesis of the unassuming, fern-like major tetrachord, which, though not very interesting in itself, possesses enormous integrative powers.

Ex. 11.48. Beethoven, String Quartet in C sharp minor, Op. 131 (1825–6), last mvt., bars 349–58 (down a semitone)

Ex. 11.49. Bizet, *Carmen* (1875), Act II, no. 17, 'Fate' theme (down a semitone)

It should not be imagined, however, that these exotic patterns have got entirely away from their diatonic origins. Remove the semitonal dissonances (Ex. 11.50), and the pentatonic frameworks stand revealed.

Ex. 11.50. The melodic skeletons of the previous three examples

(*a*) Chopin (Ex. 11.47, bars 6–9, up a minor 3rd)

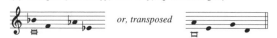

(*b*) Beethoven (Ex. 11.48, bars 1–5)

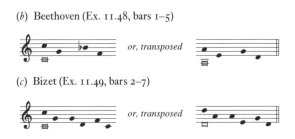

(*c*) Bizet (Ex. 11.49, bars 2–7)

Ruckhafte Senkung

If the folk pattern of Ex. 11.46 is supported by triadic drones moving in parallel with the tune, the result is what German scholars call *ruckhafte Senkung*, or 'abrupt lowering'. As a rule, both chords are in the minor, giving a typically east European 'real' sequence. A typical instance of this pattern is Ex. 11.51, from the late eighteenth-century set of *zingaresi* mentioned earlier.

Ex. 11.51. *Zingarese* no. 8 in A minor/D minor (late 18th c.), beginning

bass 8va lower

This formula seems to have fascinated German composers at least from the time of J. S. Bach,[64] even if, in deference to classical norms, they generally turned it into something like Ex. 11.52. The Viennese composers' attempts to integrate it into the

Ex. 11.52. Adaptation of the 'ruckhafte Senkung' pattern: harmonic skeleton

sonata style are particularly interesting. In Mozart's Fantasia for piano in C minor (Ex. 11.53) the influence of the Hungarian *lassu*—the slow part, it will be recalled, of the *verbunkos*[65]—is easily discernible. This, however, is a fantasia, and a very fantastic one at that. It has little to do with the sonata style, or at any rate with sonata form.

---

[64] e.g. the 'Goldberg' Variations, var. 25, bars 1–3.   [65] See pp. 147–8.

Ex. 11.53. Mozart, Fantasia for Piano in C minor, K. 475 (1785), beginning (down a minor 3rd)

The *verbunkos* influence comes out even more clearly in Beethoven's *Prometheus* ballet music, where the *lassu* (performed by the oboe, in imitation of the Hungarian *táragató*) explodes into a *friss*-like 'allegro molto' (Ex. 11.54) in an unmistakably Gypsy manner.

Ex. 11.54. Beethoven, *Die Geschöpfe des Prometheus* (1800–1), no. 9, Allegro molto section, beginning (down a minor 3rd)

But, again, Beethoven does not use actual sonata form. That had to wait for the somewhat later Piano Sonata in G, Op. 31 No. 1, the first movement of which contains many east European features (cf. the extracts in Exs. 11.45 and 11.84), the most notable being the *ruckhafte Senkung* at the beginning and the casting of the

second group in the mediant later on. The combination evidently fascinated
Beethoven, since he returned to it the following year in the first movement of the
'Waldstein' Sonata (Ex. 11.55). Melodically, this bears a remarkable resemblance
to the *friss*-like Ex. 11.54. The correspondences between the bracketed figures are
obvious enough to make commentary superfluous (though I should perhaps point

Ex. 11.55. Beethoven, Piano Sonata in C, Op. 53, the 'Waldstein' (1804), 1st mvt.

(*a*) beginning

(*continued on next page*)

(Ex. 11.55 *cont.*)

(*b*) bars 35–6 (second subject)

out that, in both cases, Figure D is an augmented version of Figure B). What Beethoven has done, probably quite unconsciously, is to spread the melodic figures of the *friss* over the modulations of the earlier sonata movement. Like Telemann long before him, he has given the traditional music of eastern Europe an 'Italian dress'.

At the minor second

No matter how chromatic they might be in detail, the sequences discussed so far all had some sort of diatonic basis. This ceases to be true of those at the upper semitone. Their connection with string technique has already been touched on.[66] Like other Fringe sequences, but more frequently than most, they may include dramatic silences between the steps. These give the player a moment to slip the hand up or down a semitone, and may also have something to do with the silences in the Muslim

Ex. 11.56. Haydn, String Quartet in F minor, Op. 55 No. 2, the 'Razor' (*c.*1788), 2nd mvt., bars 9–22 (down a 4th)

[66] See p. 160.

call to prayer. Whatever their origins, they are an arresting feature of classical Arabic 'ūd (lute) and qānūn (psaltery) music, where even the naive Western listener can detect an ancestral likeness to the Spanish guitar on the one hand and the Hungarian cimbalom on the other. Probably the first great composer to use this type of sequence, silence and all, was Haydn (Ex. 11.56). But the man who really made it his own was Beethoven.[67]

And here, all too soon, we must leave the Fringe sequence. Much more could be said, for instance, about the length of the step. In contrast to the generally short and propulsive steps of Baroque sequences, those quoted above are long and melodious. In fact, they are tunes, or near-tunes, in their own right, even belonging to discernible tune families in several cases.[68] This is one feature they share with the typical Romantic sequence. Another is harmonic waywardness. Whereas the Baroque sequence had been essentially a chain of cadences, the Fringe sequence is largely or completely uncadential, and often startlingly chromatic. It was one of the great gifts from the Fringe to the Romantics. The other was a vastly enriched range of scales and modes, to which the rest of this chapter is devoted.

IV. MODES AND SCALES

(RELATIVELY) DIATONIC MODES

Oriental modes are much too fluid for the cast-iron categories of Western theory. Modes flower into melodies, and melodies dissolve into modes that themselves combine and recombine in endless, kaleidoscopic variety. In such circumstances, octave-sized modes are better replaced with 'mini-modes' or 'modules', Lego-like components that can be plugged, unplugged, and interchanged at will.

But how are we to classify these modules? In this and the following chapter, I make an imperfect distinction between 'diatonic' and 'chromatic' modes—imperfect, because even the 'diatonic' variety can be pretty chromatic by Western standards. Within these modes, probably the most convenient distinction is not between major and minor, but between seconds and thirds; in other words, between $ii\flat/\natural$, on the one hand, and $iii\flat/\natural$, on the other.

---

[67] The opening theme of the Piano Trio in C minor, Op. 1 No. 3, is an early, if incomplete, example. Complete examples include the impressive openings of the 'Appassionata' Piano Sonata (Ex. 14.4(*a*) on p. 352), the String Quartet in E minor, Op. 59 No. 2, and the String Quartet in F minor, Op. 95.

[68] Cf. Exs. 11.39 and 11.41; 11.40 and 11.80; 11.42 and 11.43; 11.54 and 14.4(*a*).

The variable second

The most dissonant and expressive degree in Fringe melody is *ii*♭, in all its various forms. As *2*♭, it is both the defining interval of the Phrygian mode and the foundation of the 'Neapolitan' chord II♭, better known, in its first inversion, as the 'Neapolitan sixth'.[69] In Ex. 11.57 we see the pre-harmonic *2*♭ of Italian folk music; in Ex. 11.58, from the very dawn of Italian opera, a similar melodic formula is harmonized, but *not* by the Neapolitan chord.[70]

Ex. 11.57. Anon., 'Passione' (Sicilian religious processional song, 20th c.), beginning

Ex. 11.58. Peri, *Euridice* (1600), 2nd episode, Orpheus's lament, beginning

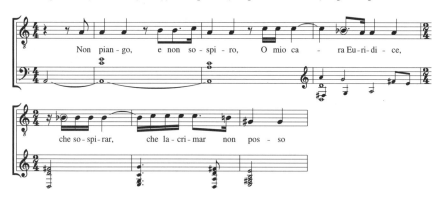

Both these passages demonstrate the impossibility of separating the flattened *2*♭ from plain *2*♮. The former is, in effect, a dissonant version of the latter, and always liable to resolve up to it (*2*♭→*2*♮); and the same is true of other varieties of *ii*, such as *6*♭/♮ and *4*♮/♯. In any case, it is not always easy to distinguish between *2*(♭)→*1* and *6*(♭)→*5*,[71] which already shows the fluidity of these Fringe modes.

---

[69] The very word 'Neapolitan', from the early 18th-c. Neapolitan school of opera composers, hints at the Oriental origin of this chord—for Naples was, of course, in the very middle of the Fringe.

[70] Although II♭ came to be the normal way of harmonizing *2*♭, there have always been many exceptions, e.g. J. S. Bach's 'Goldberg' Variations, var. 25 (Ex. 11.60 on p. 192).

[71] Cf. Beethoven's Piano Sonata in B flat, Op. 22 (Ex. 11.11 on p. 161), and Exs. 11.62–3 on pp. 194–5.

Throughout the eighteenth and early nineteenth centuries, the 'Neapolitan' 2♭ retained exotic or rustic associations for Italian composers. It was especially prominent in the *canzonetta*, described by Dent as 'a popular song of folk-song type, generally in the local dialect, and sung by some very humble character. The Neapolitan songs were generally in six-eight time, and sometimes in old modes, like some of our own folk-songs.'[72] A late example is 'Una volta c'era un re', sung by Cinderella in the opening scene of Rossini's *La Cenerentola*,[73] and given here in full as an example of the *canzonetta* style (Ex. 11.59). Among its popular features

Ex. 11.59. Rossini, *La Cenerentola* (1817), Act I, Introduzione, 'Una volta c'era un re', beginning (up a 5th)

---

[72] *Opera*, 113. The first *canzonette*, in compositions of the so-called Neapolitan school, date from about 1700.

[73] Like many another *canzonetta*, this tells the tale of the opera in which it occurs, in this case the familiar Cinderella story: 'Once upon a time there was a king who was tired of being alone. . . . What was he to do? Despising pomp and beauty, he turned instead to innocence and goodness.' Senta's ballad, in Wagner's *Der fliegende Holländer*, is a late, Germanized adaptation of the same convention.

are the plagal progressions in bars 2–3 and 12–13, the echoes in bars 9–10 and 19–20, the 'la la' refrain, the guitar-like pizzicato accompaniment, the 6/8 time, the 'modal' sevenths, the Phrygian second, and the Neapolitan chord. Later still, Italian opera composers were to turn these last two into hard-worked 'Oriental' clichés.[74]

German and east European composers, though perfectly capable of similar things, generally made something rather different, more ambitious and non-exotic, out of these formulas (Ex. 11.60). Not that their Phrygian mode was any less 'Oriental' than the Italians'. On the contrary, the Viennese and east Europeans even sometimes place the $2\flat \rightarrow 1$ progression *on* the final cadence, rather than before it, as in the 'Gypsy' rondo concluding Beethoven's early Piano Trio in C minor, Op. 1 No 3 (Ex. 11.61).[75]

Ex. 11.60. J. S. Bach, 'Goldberg' Variations (1741–2), Variation 25, bars 14–16 (down a 4th)

Ex. 11.61. Beethoven, Piano Trio in C minor, Op. 1 No. 3 (1794–5), last mvt., conclusion

---

[74] According to Budden, 'There is little [in *I Lombardi*, 1843] to distinguish the idiom of Asians from that of the Crusaders apart from choppy rhythms, tonic pedals and an emphasis on the Neapolitan sixth— devices which, typically, also recur in *Aida* as "orientalisms", though of course enhanced by a far more subtle and sophisticated technique' (*The Operas of Verdi*, i. 123–4).

[75] Cf. also Schubert, String Quintet in C, last movement, end; Brahms, Fourth Symphony, slow movement, end; and Chopin, Mazurka in E minor, Op. 41 No. 2, bars 7–8 and end.

In isolation, the final chord of this passage would seem to be a dominant rather than a tonic. Again we see how delicate the distinction between these chords could be. The same point is made even more forcefully by the next two examples. In the third Entr'acte from Bizet's *Carmen* (Ex. 11.62) the chord of resolution is clearly a tonic;[76] in a similar passage from Beethoven's 'Moonlight' Sonata (Ex. 11.63),[77] it is just as clearly a dominant.

Static Melody over changing Basses

What makes the difference between these two passages is harmonic context. It is simply that in Bizet the drone bass is *1*, and in Beethoven *5*: a special case of the rule that the same melodic pattern takes on different meanings when set over different Basses.

This rule is particularly important in the music of the Fringe. It is a characteristic of Oriental melody, whether drone-based or purely melodic, that it returns again and again to certain degrees of the mode, the return—or 'repercussion', as medieval theorists would have called it—most often taking the form *ii♭→i*. When popular musicians came to harmonize this type of melody, they discovered that a fine effect

---

[76] I should add that both Winton Dean and Gilbert Chase describe this concluding chord as a dominant (see respectively *Bizet*, 197, and *The Music of Spain*, 296). But in that case the same must be true of the Beethoven passage (Ex. 11.61).

[77] Notice the tremolo, surely an imitation of the Hungarian cimbalom.

Ex. 11.62. Bizet, *Carmen* (1875), Entr'acte no. 3 (down a tone)

(*a*) bars 34–41

(*b*) bars 154–63 (conclusion)

Ex. 11.63. Beethoven, Piano Sonata in C sharp minor, Op. 27 No. 2, the 'Moonlight' (1801), last mvt., bars 9–14 (down a semitone)

could be obtained by varying the Bass at the repercussion. And, since the cadence *ii♭*→*i* is most naturally heard as the *f*→*e* of the pentatonic seventh, they further discovered that the most appropriate Basses were those forming the triad *a–c–e* (Ex. 11.64(*a*)). Two harmonizations could then be juxtaposed in six ways: up or down at the minor third (Ex. 11.64(*b* i–ii)); up or down at the fifth (Ex. 11.64(*b* iii–iv)); and up or down at the major third (Ex. 11.64(*b* v–vi)).

Ex. 11.64. The three harmonizations *ii♭*→*i*

(*a*) basic forms

(*b*) combinations of basic forms

(*c*) variations on (*b*)

(*continued on next page*)

(Ex. 11.64 *cont.*)

As ever, all manner of variations were possible. In some places, *ii♭*→*i* might be simplified to *i*; elsewhere, it might be elaborated to the short descending scale (*iv*)–*iii♭*–*ii♭*→*i* or the modified 'knight's move' *iv*–*ii♭*→*i*: where convenient, *ii♭* might be raised to *ii♮*. A few of these possibilities are given in Ex. 11.64(*c*). Common to them all is *i*, or *e* in this case.

The most frequent juxtapositions are those in which the Bass moves by a third. The minor-third type, in particular, is a favourite with east European composers, who seldom fail to endow it with a characteristic, bittersweet melancholy (Ex. 11.65).[78] Often the melodic cadence takes the form of the 'knight's move' (Ex. 11.64(*c* xiii–xiv)), especially, perhaps, where Hungarian influence is strong. Schubert's celebrated 'Serenade' is case in point (Ex. 11.66). Another example,

Ex. 11.65. Schubert, Waltz in A flat, Op. 33 No. 15 (1823–4) (down a minor 6th)

[78] Notice the folk ostinato in bars 1–4, which Schubert also uses in the Gypsy-like finale themes of the String Quintet in C major and 'Trout' Quintet in A.

Ex. 11.66. Schubert, 'Ständchen! ('Serenade') (1828) (down a 4th)

(*a*) bars 11–20

(*b*) bars 29–36

this time definitely not Hungarian, is Chopin's Mazurka Op. 30 No. 2, where the same figure occurs four times in a row with four different harmonizations (Ex. 11.67). Notice that, whereas Chopin keeps his melodic cadence precisely the same, Schubert continually varies his, so that each new variation seems to grow out of the one before. This is characteristic both of Schubert in particular and the Viennese composers in general, and it is also rather characteristic that these variations progressively simplify melodic line, mode, and rhythm.

Ex. 11.67. Chopin, Mazurka in B minor, Op. 30 No. 2 (1836–7), bars 33–48
(up a major 3rd)

Juxtaposition at the *major* third is almost as common, and perhaps even older. In the form *e*/[*C . . . E*], it goes back at least to the late medieval Italian popular music imitated by Zacara da Teramo (Ex. 11.68).[79] Much later, it was employed by

Ex. 11.68. Zacara da Teramo, 'Rosetta che non cançi' (early 15th c.), bars 49–55
(up a tone)

Vivaldi,[80] Domenico Scarlatti,[81] Haydn,[82] and at last Beethoven, who began by putting it into those traditional receptacles for folk influence, the trios of minuets or scherzos,[83] then into the main sections of the same (Ex. 11.69), and finally into sonata-form expositions.

[79] Nino Pirrotta ('Zacara da Teramo', in *Music and Culture*, 128) points out the popular nature of this passage. Notice the alternating drones in bars 2–4 and 6.   [80] See Michael Talbot, *Vivaldi*, 112.

[81] e.g. the Sonatas in G, K241, L180, in F, K366, L119, and in B flat, K442, L319. All have 'second subjects' in the mediant.

[82] e.g. the trio from the third movement of the Symphony No. 36 in E flat, and the main finale themes from the Keyboard Sonata HXVI: 31 in E and the Symphony No. 88 in G.

[83] See the String Trio in E flat Op. 3, first minuet; the String Quartet in F, Op. 18 No. 1; and the Trio for Two Oboes and Cor Anglais in C, Op. 87 (Ex. 11.70 on p. 199).

Ex. 11.69. Beethoven, String Quartet in D, Op. 18 No. 3 (1798–1800), 3rd mvt. (Scherzo), beginning (down a tone)

These last have attracted a great deal of attention. It used to be thought that Beethoven, romantically daring, was 'breaking the rule' that a sonata-form exposition in the major ought to proceed to the dominant. He certainly effected an enlargement of harmonic resources, but what was his actual motive? Tovey, in his discussion of the Piano Sonatas Opp. 31 No. 1 and 53, maintained that the initial modulation to the flat seventh 'makes the dominant ineffective as a key for a contrasted section'.[84] There may be some truth in this, but it misses the point that Beethoven is not thinking primarily in terms of key—that is, of the Bass—but rather of Melody. This is already evident in the trio of the early Trio for two Oboes and Cor Anglais in C (Ex. 11.70). (It is absurd to talk of the trio of a Trio, but never mind.) While the Melody resembles that of the previous example, the Bass is quite different. If one can speak of chords being 'tonicized', the final *e*s of both Exs. 11.69 and 11.70 are 'chordified', but in two distinct ways: in Ex. 11.69 as a tonic, but in Ex. 11.70 as the dominant of *A* minor.

Ex. 11.70. Beethoven, Trio for two Oboes and Cor Anglais in C, Op. 87 (*c.* 1795), 3rd mvt. (Scherzo), Trio, beginning

Interestingly, the first of Beethoven's unorthodox second-subject keys, in the String Quintet in C (Ex. 11.71), is not a mediant but a submediant. It is introduced by a passage of 'dominant preparation' on the *E*7 chord (bars 4–19), which, apart

---

[84] *A Companion to Beethoven's Piano Sonatas*, 115. For the Op. 53 Sonata, see Ex. 11.55 on p. 187.

from its length, is similar to the *E* chord at the end of the previous example. This helps explain why Beethoven chose these unorthodox keys, since his thinking, like that of other composers at the time, was becoming increasingly pentatonic. And the pentatonic poles are *a* and *e*.

Ex. 11.71. Beethoven, String Quintet in C (1801), 1st mvt., bars 22–44

It is no coincidence that the *e*/[*C* . . . *E*] pattern crops up in those composers—Vivaldi, Scarlatti, Haydn, Beethoven, and later Schubert—who were most strongly influenced by Fringe modality. Like its twin *e*/[*E* . . . *C*], it began as a way of harmonizing the Phrygian mode, and in some quarters never got far from these origins. This is particularly true of Spanish music, but by no means confined to it. There is a distinct likeness between the Gypsy music in Falla's *El amor brujo* (Ex. 11.72) and that in Schubert's *Divertissement à la hongroise* (Ex. 11.73), even though

Ex. 11.72. Falla, *El amor brujo* (1915), 'Danza del juego de amor', Poco meno mosso section, beginning

Ex. 11.73. Schubert, *Divertissement à la hongroise* (1824) (down a minor 3rd)

(*a*) beginning

(*b*) bars 70–6

the composers (and Gypsies) come from opposite ends of the Europe.[85] Perhaps the most striking thing about both passages, but particularly the Schubert, is the mixture of keys. Rather as the dabs of blue and yellow in an impressionist painting merge into a shimmering green, so the chords of *C* major and *E* minor merge into a single but compound tonality.

Blue thirds, sevenths, and fifths

Much of what has been said about seconds is true also of thirds. They, too, can slot into various parts of the scale, occur in both major and minor versions, and serve as pivots for changing harmonies. There is, however, one crucial difference: thirds are concordant, seconds are not. Moreover, it is the third that colours the triad, including of course the tonic triad. By inflecting the third, it is possible to juxtapose, interchange, and generally mix up modes over the same tonic. There is much to be said about these devices, but first we must examine the form of minor third described in this book as 'blue'.

The blue third is arguably the most instinctive interval of all, tracing its lineage directly back to the *g–e* of the children's chant. In essence, the 'blueness' amounts to nothing more than the attraction of *iii♭* to *i*. There is the blue mediant *3♭*, where *i* = *1*; the blue seventh *7♭*, where *i* = *5*; and, similarly, the blue fifth (in the minor mode), where *i* = *3♭*, and the blue dominant (in the major), where *i* = *3*. Even blue sixths, fourths, and tonics are not entirely impossible. Undeniably the most important blue notes, however, are those resolving on some part of the pentatonic seventh, in other words:

1. *c*, the blue third of the minor mode, resolving on *a*;
2. *e♭*, the blue third of the major mode and blue fifth of the minor, resolving on *c*;
3. *g*, the blue seventh of the minor mode, resolving on *e*;
4. *b♭*, the blue seventh of the major mode, resolving on *g*.

Translated from alphabetical into numerical notation, these are *3♭* and *7♭* (for both modes) and *5♭* (for the minor).

Of these three blue notes, by far the most important, at least until the advent of the blues itself, was *7♭*. In cultivated music, it enjoyed high popularity in the sixteenth and seventeenth centuries, became increasingly rare in the eighteenth, and returned to favour in the nineteenth. But even at its rarest it was never entirely out of fashion. Many examples, usually of an east European cast, may be found in the Viennese classics. In those days there were two standard ways of accommodating it:

---

[85] Notice that the bass of Ex. 11.73(*b*) is a drawn-out version of the 'Phrygian double tonic', and cf. Exs. 11.9 and 11.10 on pp. 160–1.

Ex. 11.74. Mozart, Piano Concerto No. 22 in E flat, K. 482 (1785), slow mvt., bars 33–6
(beginning of piano solo)

to introduce it as a transient modulation to the relative major, or, as Mozart does in
Ex. 11.74, to turn it into an appoggiatura.

Quite often, the 7♭ occurs over a dominant chord, so that it clashes with an implied or explicit 7♮. This close relative of the old 'English cadence'[86] crops up with
increasing frequency from about the middle of the eighteenth century. In early examples[87] the 7♭ is a mere grace note, but towards the end of the eighteenth century it
begins to become more emphatic. In Ex. 11.75, from one of Haydn's late string
quartets, the dissonance becomes positively Bartókian—which is not altogether
surprising, since Haydn and Bartók were drawing on the same east European
sources.

Ex. 11.75. Haydn, String Quartet in E flat, Op. 76 No. 6 (1796–7), slow mvt.,
conclusion (up a semitone)

---

[86] See p. 101.
[87] e.g. the pair of examples from Scarlatti and Beethoven (Exs. 11.29 and 11.30 on pp. 172–3).

A word should be said about the bracketed four-note scale that occurs in several places in Ex. 11.75. In various modal guises, this crops up again and again from the late eighteenth century on. Perhaps the most celebrated instance is the insistently drumming bass of the middle section of Chopin's Polonaise in A flat, Op. 53 (said to evoke 'the hooves of the Polish cavalry'), but there are countless others.[88] Liszt has an entire movement, the 'Czárdás Obstiné' (Ex. 11.76), consisting of little more than varied harmonizations of this figure—hence, of course, the title.[89] Later in the movement he transforms it from 7♭–6♭–5–4 to 7–6–5–4 (Ex. 11.76(*b*)), thereby conclusively demonstrating the kinship between the major and minor (or 'blue') versions of the apical seventh.

Ex. 11.76. Liszt, 'Czárdás Obstiné' (1884) (up a semitone)

(*a*) beginning

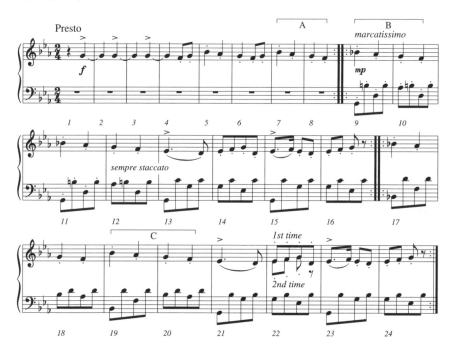

---

[88] Another example that may be mentioned is Beethoven's *Egmont* Overture, where the four-note scale, first introduced at a slow tempo (bar 15), goes on to generate much of the movement.

[89] I owe this example to Alan Walker; see 'Liszt and the Twentieth Century', 359.

(*b*) bars 234–50

(*c*) successive harmonization of the repeated figure

But it would be quite wrong to suppose that these simultaneous clashes between major and minor thirds were confined to eastern Europe. Julian Budden has an interesting passage on similar things in Verdi, which he describes as

merely the survival of a linear way of thinking that goes back to the sixteenth and seventeenth centuries: an extension of the principle whereby both ascending and descending forms of the melodic minor scale could be used simultaneously despite the fierce discord that results for those with vertically trained ears. Such 'bitonality' is much more common in Verdi than modern editions would allow us to suppose.[90]

He then quotes, from *I due Foscari* (1844), a clash between 7♭ and 7♮ which has been bowdlerized in modern editions, adding that 'It is amusing to note that at the very time that he was writing such passages, well-meaning English editors were busy "correcting" similar "audacities" in Purcell.'[91]

---

[90] *The Operas of Verdi*, i. 39.   [91] Ibid. 40.

Nor was Verdi the only Italian composer to indulge in such 'audacities'. Thirteen years before *I due Foscari*, we find a similar clash in Bellini (Ex. 11.77, bar 6). This passage is, indeed, 'bitonal' in another sense as well, since the Melody stands in a 'relative major' opposition to the Bass: *c* major against *A* minor, or, in this transposition, *e♭* against *C* minor.

Ex. 11.77. Bellini, *Norma* (1831), Act I, no. 5, Duet, 'Va crudele', beginning of voice part (down a 4th)

The variable third

Translation between modes

In modern Western music, we take it for granted that a melody can be translated from the major to the minor mode (or vice versa) and remain 'the same tune'. Yet this easy interchange seems to be rather unusual. To the best of my knowledge, it is unknown in the traditional music of sub-Saharan Africa or the Far East. For that matter, there appears to have been nothing like it in the older European music, before it was introduced from western Asia or northern Africa during the Middle Ages.

It is therefore not surprising that it has particularly flourished on the Fringe. In eastern Europe, especially, scraps of melody regularly turn up in both modes. A simple example is the zigzag descending scale in two 'Gypsy rondos' (though only one is identified as such): Haydn's Piano Trio in G (Ex. 11.78) and Beethoven's String Quartet in C minor, Op. 18 No. 4 (Ex. 11.79).

Ex. 11.78. Haydn, Piano Trio in G (1795), last mvt. ('Gypsy Rondo'), beginning (down a 5th)

Ex. 11.79. Beethoven, String Quartet in C minor, Op. 18 No. 4 (1798–1800), last mvt., beginning

Here, it is hard to say which mode came first; elsewhere, one can sometimes be more specific. Among the most interesting of Haydn's borrowings from popular music is the 'Night-Watchman' tune (so called from a song of that name), which he uses in at least seven places,[92] and always differently. Unusually for Haydn's folk sources, it is known from prior examples. A seventeenth-century predecessor is the devotional song 'Nichts Irdisch ewig gewehrt'[93] (Ex. 11.80). As will immediately be seen, it is based on a typically east European 'fifth-answering' pattern.

Ex. 11.80. 'Nichts Irdisch ewig gewehrt' (1686) (down a tone)

Nichts Ir - disch e - wig ge - wehrt wie ein Wet - ter-hahn sich ver - kehrt

---

[92] Symphony No. 60 in C, fourth movement, bars 61–72 (Ex. 11.81) and (in a different form) sixth movement, bars 61–72; Divertimento, Hob. II: 17, eighth movement, bars 1–4; Divertimento in E flat, Hob. II: 21, fourth movement (second Minuet), Trio, bars 6–12; Baryton Trio No. 35, third movement (Minuet), Trio, bars 1–8; Cassation for two Barytons and Bass, Hob. XII: 19, second movement, bars 1–8; Piano Sonata in C sharp minor, Hob. XVI: 36, third movement (Minuet), bars 1–8; and the four-part round 'Wunsch', Hob. XXVIIb: 43, bars 1–4. See Landon, *Haydn: Chronicle and Works*, ii: *Haydn at Eszterháza, 1766–1790*, 280–1.

[93] 'Nothing earthly lasts for ever'; in modern spelling, 'Nichts irdisch ewig gewährt'.

Ex. 11.81. Haydn, Symphony No. 60 in C, 'Il Distratto' (1774), 4th mvt., bars 61–72

To Haydn, its most interesting feature is evidently the initial phrase, which he reproduces exactly in Ex. 11.81, though in dominant rather than tonic position, and followed by an equally ancient rising-scale figure.[94] In a vigorously bucolic, major-mode variant, the same combination appears some forty years later in Beethoven's Pastoral Symphony—incidentally the only tune in the entire symphony of undisputed folk origin (Ex. 11.82).

Ex. 11.82. Beethoven, Pastoral Symphony, No. 6 in F (1808), 3rd mvt., Trio, beginning (up a tone)

Comparing Exs. 11.80–82 tells us several things about the popular melody of eastern and central Europe. Firstly, it shows that modal 'translations' are not limited to the classical major and minor. A 'Lydian' tune like that of Ex. 11.82 may begin life in the 'Hungarian' mode (or vice versa). Secondly, it brings out the almost Oriental fluidity of east European melody, and in particular the way the same figure may occur in different parts of the mode. And finally, it illustrates the tonal ambiguity that such processes could lead to, and which could be heard in popular music long before being taken up by the 'serious' composer. In the 1780s, a minor German composer by the name of Christian Schubart described Hungarian melody as 'totally bizarre' in modulation: 'for instance, it can begin with four bars of G and then finish in C'.[95] Allowing for differences in key and notation, that is just what Beethoven does in Ex. 11.82.

---

[94] Cf. Giuseppino's 'Fuggi, Fuggi' (Ex. 7.25 on p. 104).
[95] *Ideen zu einer Ästhetik der Tonkunst* (1784–5), 352. Quoted in Bellman, *The* Style Hongrois, 64 and (in the original German) 231.

Semitonal fluctuation

Like the Fringe second, but even more so, the Fringe third is prone to the semitonal wavering strikingly illustrated in Ex. 11.83. The effect depends, broadly, on whether the background is major or minor. If it is minor, a fleeting major third will have a gently pathetic effect, like that of the sun peeping for a moment out of a grey sky (Ex. 11.84, bar 4). If, as is more usually the case, it is major, the effect will be one

Ex. 11.83. Bulgarian bagpipe tune (down a minor 3rd)

Ex. 11.84. Beethoven, Piano Sonata in G, Op. 31 No. 1 (1802), 1st mvt., bars 97–108, end of exposition (up a semitone)

of brightness disturbed and then restored (and, on its restoration, all the more wel-
come for having been disturbed). Here, the minor third is likely to come towards
the end of the musical unit, whether this happens to be the phrase, melody, or
movement. Examples may be found in east European folk music (Ex. 11.85, bar 6),
in Vivaldi,[96] in Scarlatti (Ex. 11.86), and, most of all, in the Viennese school, where

Ex. 11.85. Hungarian bagpipe tune, beginning (down a 4th)

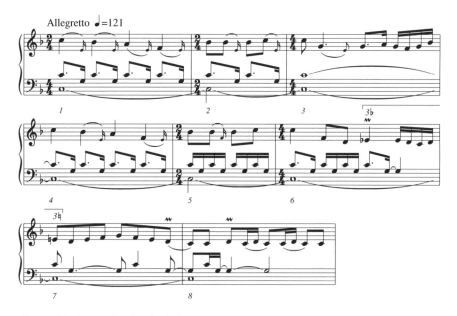

Ex. 11.86. Domenico Scarlatti, Sonata in D, K96, L465 (mid-18th c.), bars 93–103
(up a minor 3rd)

[96] 'Vivaldi is . . . fond of fleeting visits to the parallel minor key . . . especially as a diversion before a final,
clinching phrase' (Talbot, *Vivaldi*, 112).

it becomes almost a mannerism. One is particularly likely to find it towards the end of a sonata-form exposition.[97]

As well as generalized patches of minor-mode turbulence, there is also a more concise formula in which a single $3\flat$ is immediately resolved (Ex. 11.87). The resolution, in this case, is double: first up a semitone to $3\natural$, then down a semitone to 2, or perhaps down a major third to 1 (that is to say, $3\flat \rightarrow 3\natural \rightarrow 2$ or $3\flat \rightarrow 3\natural \rightarrow 1$). As well as $3\flat$, all the other minor degrees of the mode ($2\flat$, $7\flat$, and $6\flat$) may be treated in this fashion. It all turns on the easy-going attitude of the human ear to resolution. Yet again, we see how our perception of musical ambiguities seems designed to yield the richest aesthetic results.

Ex. 11.87. Haydn, String Quartet in D, Op. 50 No. 6 (1787), 2nd mvt., bars 18–22 (down a 4th)

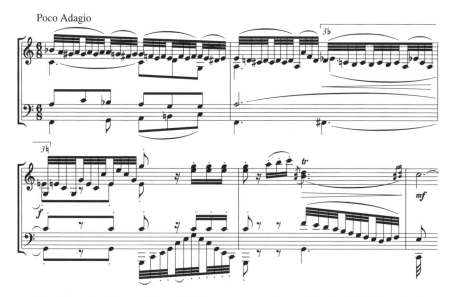

The formula of Ex. 11.87 quickly became popular, and by the third decade of the nineteenth century had become so much a part of Franco–Italian vernacular that its origins were growing hazy. In the *ranz des vaches* from Rossini's *William Tell* Overture (Ex. 11.88), it might equally well be central European or Italian. Later still, it became merged with the American blue third.[98]

---

[97] As in Ex. 11.86. Cf. also Exs. 11.84, 11.87 and, wavering between $2\flat$ and $2\natural$, Ex. 11.11(*a*) on p. 161.

[98] This point will be taken up again in Ch. 16, pp. 456–60.

Ex. 11.88. Rossini. *William Tell* (1829), Overture, bars 209–17 (up a 4th)

On a larger scale, major–minor juxtapositions arise naturally out of the Classical delight in contrast. We have already seen Scarlatti, in Ex. 11.9, follow up a flamenco-like minor-mode theme with a major-mode fanfare,[99] and similar effects may be found in many later composers. The instruments imitated in Beethoven's piano sonatas include the string orchestra, solo violin, horn, bagpipe, and even cimbalom (see Ex. 11.63 on pp. 194–5), and in every case the instrument evoked retains its characteristic style of harmony, melody, *and* mode.

Juxtapositions, fluctuations, and indeed contrasts of every kind between major and minor modes over the same tonic became increasingly common throughout the nineteenth century. In fact, they went so far as to imperil the very distinction between major and minor. At least, that is the opinion of certain theorists. We find Robert Bailey, for instance, writing that

An immediately apparent principle of later nineteenth-century German tonal construction is modal mixture, the use of both the major and minor inflection of a given key. Schoenberg recognized the 'transition from twelve major and twelve minor keys to twelve chromatic keys' and claimed that 'this transition is fully accomplished in the music of Wagner, the harmonic significance of which has not yet by any means been theoretically formulated.'[100] The terms *major* and *minor* remain useful, of course, but only for the purpose of identifying the qualities of particular triads. When we want to identify the tonality of large sections, or that of whole pieces or movements, it is best simply to refer to the key by itself and to avoid specifying mode, precisely because the 'chromatic' or mixed major-minor mode is so often utilized.[101]

In other words, one can no longer talk of major and minor *keys*, only of major and minor *chords*.

[99] See p. 160. Kirkpatrick discusses the influence of instruments other than the harpsichord on Scarlatti's sonatas in *Domenico Scarlatti*, 'Imitations of Other Instruments' and 'The Influence of the Spanish Guitar' (pp. 199–206).

[100] Arnold Schoenberg, *Theory of Harmony*, trans. Roy E. Carter (Berkeley, 1978), p. 389. [Author's footnote.]

[101] 'An Analytical Study of Sketches and Drafts', 116.

This fashionable notion is highly dubious (the admiring mention of Schoenberg should be enough in itself to put us on our guard). To begin with, it is misleading, to say the least, to speak of a single 'chromatic' mode. What in fact developed was a continuum of modes ranging from pure major to pure minor. Whereas the modal palette of the eighteenth century had mainly consisted of primary colours, that of the nineteenth was full of intervening shades. Such composers as Wagner, Brahms, and Mahler (as well as non-Germans like Verdi or Franck) made increasing use of these intermediate hues, but by no means neglected the extremes. Ever since the sixteenth century, an unclouded major mode had been among the composer's most valued resources, as, to a lesser extent, had been an unrelievedly gloomy minor. To abandon them would have been merely silly, and until Schoenberg not even the most avant-garde German was prepared to do so.

Extended tonality

The development of modes that were part-major, part-minor had profound consequences for tonal relationships. As long as keys were 100 per cent *C* major, *A* minor, or whatever, there was no problem. But now they could be, so to speak, 85 per cent *C* major and 15 per cent *C* minor, or 54 per cent *A* minor and 46 per cent *A* major. (The percentages are, of course, spuriously precise, but the principle holds good.) Modal mixture of this kind had the effect of vastly enlarging the range of easily accessible keys, while at the same time destroying the distinction between close and remote relationships.

The consequent 'extended tonality' (which could just as well have been called an 'extended modality') was in some ways too much of a good thing. Such ready access to almost any key could easily degenerate into a shapeless harmonic slush. To guard against this danger, composers instinctively anchored their modulations in the central, modally ambiguous chord of *C* (minor), whence they could smoothly proceed to the immediate relations of both modes. Altogether twelve keys were now within easy reach: *C* major, *C* minor, *D* minor, *E♭* major, *E* minor, *F* major, *F* minor, *G* major, *G* minor, *A♭* major, *A* minor, and *B♭* major. And to these must be added the 'Neapolitan' keys *D♭* major and *B* minor, both of which had been in common use for a century or more.[102]

It may be noticed that these fourteen keys (including the last two) make up seven pairs, one for each note of the diatonic scale, and falling into two classes, depending on whether their tonic notes are identical (*C* major/*C* minor, *F* major/*F* minor, *G* major/*G* minor) or inflected (*D♭* major/*D* minor, *E♭* major/*E* minor, *A♭* major/ *A* minor, *B♭* major/*B* minor). In the latter case, it is the third (respectively *f*, *g*, *c*,

---

[102]   In relation to a tonic *C*, *B*m is the mirror image of *D♭* major, i.e. as *C*m is to *D♭* major, so *B*m is to *C* major.

and *d*) that is common to the two chords. For this reason, key relationships of this kind have been called 'monotertial'.[103]

The source of all this dizzying complexity was the intersection of 'parallel' and 'relative' key-relatedness, or, even more fundamentally, of pentatonic and drone patterns. Given the delight of east European popular musicians in both of these (to say nothing of pungent chromaticism), it is not surprising to find them sometimes coming up with a rudimentary form of extended tonality. In another of those fascinating *zingarese* (Ex. 11.89), a minor tonic is followed first by its parallel, and then by its relative major (*C* minor–*C* major–*E*♭ major–*C* minor), all within the framework of the pentatonic seventh *c–e*(♭)*–g–b*♭.

Ex. 11.89. *Zingarese* no. 6 in D minor (late 18th c.) (down a tone)

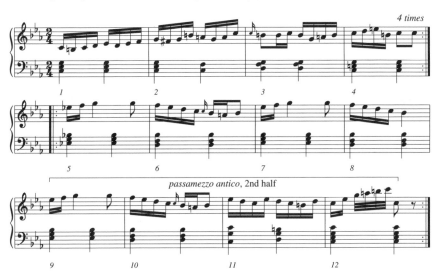

And the interest of this passage does not stop there. The first strain (bars 1–4) owes something both to the European *tierce de Picardie* and the old Arab mode with a minor third and a major sixth and seventh; and the second strain (bars 5–12) is a sort of Gypsy version of the *passamezzo antico*, the second half of which is reproduced in bars 9–12, at least as regards the basic chords. All in all, this little *zingarese* is an object lesson in the fertile collision of musical cultures characteristic of the Fringe.

[103] I owe this word (and indeed the whole concept) to Anatole Leikin (see *The Cambridge Companion to Chopin*, 'The Sonatas', 178). It is a translation of the equivalent Russian term, introduced by Leo Mazel in the article 'K voprosu o rasshirenii ponyatiya odnoimennoy tonalnosti' ('Expanding the Concept of Parallel Keys', 1957).

CHROMATIC MODES AND SCALES

Chromaticism is a matter not only of dissonance but also of structure. The ordinary minor, strictly speaking a chromatic mode, has traditionally been accorded diatonic status because its strongest dissonances are associated with the dominant chord. The so-called 'Gypsy' mode *1–2♭–3–4–5–6♭–7* is almost equally at home in tonal harmony, the only real difficulty being to reconcile its *2♭* with the full close; and this, as we have seen, is easily done by raising it to *2♮* when necessary.

Moreover, the Gypsy mode, in spite of its strong chromaticism, retains the skeleton *1–4–5*. There is a cardinal distinction between modes that share this feature and those that raise *4* to *4♯*. One even encounters modes that lack *5*, but with this last category we leave nature behind. It is a fundamental instinct to provide melody with the backbone of a perfect fourth or fifth, and when this is absent we are pretty sure to find the meddling hand of the theorist.

In compensation, these extremely chromatic modes are generally based on scales of an inhuman regularity. As usual, complexity brings with it a compensating simplicity: the more chromatic the mode, the simpler the scale. Before we tackle these countervailing extremes, however, a word must be said about a mode that might seem at first to belong in the diatonic category.

The Lydian mode

The Lydian mode (*1–2–3–4♯–5–6–7*), though indeed diatonic in the sense of being playable on the white notes of the keyboard, has always stood apart from its fellows. Its affinities are rather with the chromatic modes that share its raised fourth, alongside which it tends to occur in a 'Lydian Fringe' stretching from the Balkans into Scandinavia.

Various origins can be found for it, undoubtedly the most ancient of which is the natural harmonic series. This includes a note intermediate between *f* and *f♯* (see Ex. 3.6), but much more readily interpreted as a flat *4♯* than a sharp *4♮*. And, since instruments producing the harmonic series have existed for a very long time, so too must the tunes played on them. As it happens, instruments of this type have survived especially well in Scandinavia, eastern Europe, and the southern fringe of the German-speaking world. Among them are the jew's harp, the alphorn, and the

---

[104] The jew's harp (or 'guimbarde') was particularly popular in Austria as a serenading instrument (see Klaus P. Wachsmann, 'The Primitive Musical Instruments', 40). A Lydian alphorn tune was collected by Brahms in Switzerland in 1868 and used in the finale of his First Symphony (bars 30–46, marked 'Più Andante'); for a facsimile of his transcription, see Barry Tuckwell, *Horn*, 108. There will be more about the tilincă and its relatives, including the transcription of a solo (Ex. 11.95), on p. 220.

rudimentary flute known in Romania as the tilincă.[104]

No doubt cultural conservatism had much to do with the survival of these instruments, but they would hardly have done so well if they had not suited the prevailing taste in melody. One feature of this was a tendency to emphasize the dominant, which attracted to itself the leading note $4\sharp$, not only in the Lydian mode but also in the 'Hungarian' minor ($1–2–3\flat–4\sharp–5–6\flat–7$). To the purist, the Lydian $4\sharp$ should *not* be a leading note, but so strong is the urge to make it one that entirely Lydian passages are a rarity, at any rate in 'classical' music. The passages quoted here (Exs. 11.90–92) display an impressive geographical and chronological range, from the Austria of the 1780s to the Norway of the 1890s. This makes the family likenesses, not only in mode, but also in harmony, rhythm, and style of accompaniment (notice the drone basses and heavy, often syncopated accents), all the more extraordinary.[105]

Ex. 11.90. Haydn, Symphony No. 88 in G (*c.*1788), Minuet, bars 64–70 (end of Trio) (up a 4th)

Ex. 11.91. Chopin, Mazurka in F, Op. 68 No. 3 (1829), bars 37–44 (up a tone)

---

[105] Another passage very much in this tradition is the Gypsy rondo theme from Brahms's String Quintet in G, Op. 111. See Ex. 13.62(*b*) on p. 324.

Ex. 11.92. Grieg, 'Havet' ('The Sea'), Op. 61 No. 1 (1895), bars 3–14 (beginning of voice part) (down a 4th)

The heptatonia secunda family

Substitute 7♭ for the Lydian 7♮, and you have the 'acoustic mode', extremely common in parts of eastern Europe (according to Bartók, some peasant villages knew no other) and based, like certain other modes from the same region, on the scale named by Hungarian scholars the 'heptatonia secunda'.

Why 'heptatonia secunda'? Owing to the deeply rooted human tendency to interpret all melody in pentatonic terms, the number of really distinct scales is surprisingly small. Firstly, one is limited to tones and semitones. Everything else—the *śrutis* of classical Indian music, the bent notes of the blues, the larger pentatonic intervals—may be related to these intervallic building blocks, either by microtonal inflection or subdivision. And secondly, there must be no adjacent semitones, because these will be heard either as bisections of the tone, or as leading notes with a common focus (for instance, the 5 of the 'Hungarian' mode *1–2–3♭–4♯–5–6♭–7*)—in either case, refinements that belong rather to modes than scales.

With this provision, let us see how many tone-and-semitone scales (or 'basic scales' for short) we can form. The crucial point is that each semitone must be separated from its nearest fellow semitone by at least one tone. This means that the semitones are at their densest in the 'octatonic' scale of alternating tones and semitones,[106] with four of each interval to the octave. All other basic scales must

---

[106] The now-standard term 'octatonic scale' appears to have been invented by Arthur Berger in the early 1960s (see Taruskin, 'Chernomor to Kashchei', 73). The same pattern has also been called, by Rimsky-Korsakov, 'the semitone–whole-tone scale'; by Messiaen, 'the second mode of limited transposition'; by the Russians, the 'Rimsky-Korsakov scale'; by the Dutch, the 'Pijper scale'; by the Hungarians, 'the model 1:2 scale'; also 'the diminished mode', 'the half-step–whole-step scale', the 'whole-step–half-step scale', etc.

have more tones and fewer semitones. There are, in fact, only two possibilities: either five tones and two semitones, or six tones and no semitones at all. The latter is, of course the whole-tone scale.

What, then, of the scales composed of five tones and two semitones? Again, there are only two possibilities, if the semitones are to be kept apart: that in which the tones form alternating groups of two and three, and that in which they form alternating groups of one and four.

To sum up, there are only three tone-and-semitone scales: one octatonic and two heptatonic. The last two, the diatonic and heptatonia secunda scales, may be summed up as follows, with tones represented by '1' and semitones by '½':

diatonic   1 1 1 ½ 1 1 ½ 1 1 1 ½ 1 1 ½ 1 1 1 ½ 1 1, etc.
heptatonia secunda   1 1 1 1 ½ 1 ½ 1 1 1 1 ½ 1 ½ 1 1 1 1 ½ 1, etc.

Two features of the heptatonia secunda immediately stand out: the 'tetratonal' bunching 1 1 1 1, and the alternating tones and semitones 1 ½ 1 ½ 1. Indefinitely extended, these respectively give the whole-tone and octatonic scales.

A less obvious feature of the heptatonia secunda is the wealth of diminished and augmented intervals. Where the diatonic scale has the one dissonant note-pair *f–b*, the heptatonia secunda has no fewer than three: *c–f♯*, *e–b♭*, and *f♯–b♭*; and since these may each be inverted, there are in all two diminished fifths, two augmented fourths, one diminished fourth, and one augmented fifth. Because of all these dissonant intervals, this scale can provide only four modes with proper dominants, namely:

1. the aforementioned 'acoustic' mode *1–2–3–4♯–5–6–7♭*;
2. the 'major–minor' mode *1–2–3–4–5–6♭–7♭*, with a major third and minor sixth;
3. the medieval Arabic mode[107] *1–2–3♭–4–5–6–7*, known to Western theorists as 'the ascending melodic minor' (though it may equally well be used in descent);
4. the modified Phrygian *1–2♭–3♭–4–5–6–7♭*, with major sixth.

Example 11.93 sets out the relationships of these modes to the heptatonia secunda, whole-tone, and octatonic scales.

Ex. 11.93. The heptatonia secunda modes

(*a*) in relation to the parent scale

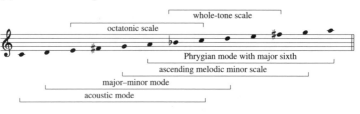

---

[107] See p. 97.

(*b*) with *c* as tonic
  (i) major–minor

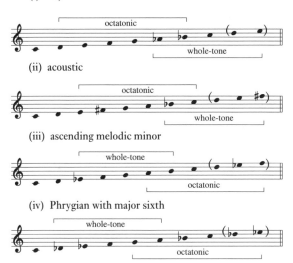

  (ii) acoustic

  (iii) ascending melodic minor

  (iv) Phrygian with major sixth

Now let us take a closer look at them.

The 'acoustic' mode

The oldest is the 'acoustic', so called from its resemblance to numbers 8–14 of the natural harmonic series. However, as Ex. 11.94 shows, this is not so very close. In the harmonic series, the notes marked with arrows are all flat: *f♯* by almost exactly a quarter tone, *a* by somewhat more than this (so that it is actually closer to *a♭*), and *b♭* by just under a sixth of tone).[108] In the harmonic series, the rungs of the ladder get steadily closer together; in the acoustic mode, they are arranged in the ratio of 1 : 2. If the latter is derived from the former, it has undergone considerable adjustment.

Ex. 11.94. Numbers 8–16 of the natural harmonic series

There can be little doubt, however, that the acoustic mode owes its existence to natural-harmonic instruments. Of these, probably the most important (at least for

---

[108] For a precise table of distances between the harmonics (in 'cents', or hundredths of a semitone) see Guy Holdham, rev. Murray Campbell and C. Greated, 'Harmonics' in *New Grove II*, x. 855.

eastern Europe) is a simple flute consisting of no more than a long narrow tube open at both ends. Depending on whether it is stopped or left open, it can produce two harmonic series, one an octave lower than the other, which may then be combined to form an interlocking scale. Flutes of this irreducibly primitive type, though now rare, must once have been extremely widespread. Till recently they were well known in southern Africa,[109] and in eastern Europe have survived in Romania, Poland,[110] and probably elsewhere. Ex. 11.95 is a dance tune performed on the Romanian tilincă.[111]

Ex. 11.95. 'Batuta' (20th c.), beginning

Even this brief extract reveals a veritable folk maqām—perhaps even an ur-maqām. Every degree of the mode has its specialized function, so that *g*, for instance, is a central note and *c* a final (which here means something different from a tonic). And to go with these functions, every degree either has its characteristic form of ornament—a lower chromatic appoggiatura in the case of *g*, an upper mordent in those of *b♭*, *a*, and *f♯*—or, like *e*, is deliberately left plain.

Notice that dissonant intervals are carefully avoided, for the note-pairs *e–b♭*, *f♯–b♭*, and *f♯–c* are never brought into direct contact. Instead, the modules *b♭–a–g* and *g–f♯–e* are kept separate, though united by the common *g*.

The major–minor mode

At least as important as the acoustic mode is the 'major–minor', with its piquant combination of a major third and minor sixth.[112] Though, as we can see from Exs.

---

[109] See Percival R. Kirby, *The Musical Instruments of the Native Races of South Africa*, 111–21 and pl. 41. He plausibly suggests (pp. 119–20) that this African instrument was the ancestor of the ancient Egyptian flute. This, in turn, may well be related to the east European instrument.

[110] See Anna Czekanowska, *Polish Folk Music*, 159–60.

[111] For a discussion of this instrument see Tiberiu Alexandru, 'Tilinca: ein uraltes rumänisches Volksinstrument' ('Tilincă: An Age-old Romanian Folk Instrument'). There is also a short article by the same author under the heading 'Tilincă' in *The New Grove Dictionary of Musical Instruments*. Both include a photograph of the virtuoso performer of Ex. 11.95, Mihai Lacatus.

[112] The same term is sometimes used to mean 'mode with both *3♮* and *3♭*' (see e.g. the passage by Robert

11.96 and 11.97, its geographical distribution is extremely wide, it is again especially characteristic of eastern Europe. In his classic study of English folk song, A. L. Lloyd mentions that the Hungarian scholar Lajos Vargyas 'was delighted to find among our melodies a scale' (described as 'g-a-b-c-d-e flat-f (taking g as keynote)') that was 'rare in the West but frequently met with in Moravia, Hungary and Rumania'.[113] This is, of course, none other than my 'major–minor'.

Ex. 11.96. Indian beggar's song (20th c.) (down a 5th)

etc.

Ex. 11.97. Spanish song (20th c.) (down a 5th)

Its great popularity on the Fringe was largely due to its hybrid character. By combining the dissonant 6♭ of the East with the major triad of the West, it offered musicians something from both worlds. In particular, it had the inestimable advantage of being easily harmonizable. The Gypsy musician's first step in adapting traditional melodies to the middle-class market had always been to harmonize them, and with drone-accompanied tunes the easiest way to do so was to thicken the drone into a full major triad. It was a treatment to which the major–minor lent itself especially well.

Here it is interesting to compare 'Rákóczi's Lament' (Ex. 11.98), an ancestor of the famous 'Rákóczi March', with a modally similar passage from one of Chopin's mazurkas (Ex. 11.99). Both emphasize notes of the *c* major triad, but in different ways. In the lament, the main focus is *g*. In the mazurka, it is *e*, which has the effect of bringing out the dissonances in the mode. One is conscious of the diminished fifth between *e* and *b♭*, and to a lesser extent of the diminished fourth between *e* and *a♭*.

Bailey quoted earlier, p. 212.) Anatole Leikin informs me that the major–minor mode (in my sense) is known to Russian theorists as the 'harmonic major'. I have also seen it described as the 'Hindu scale'.

[113] *Folk Song in England*, 52.

Ex. 11.98. 'Rákóczi's Lament' (1826), beginning (down a tone)

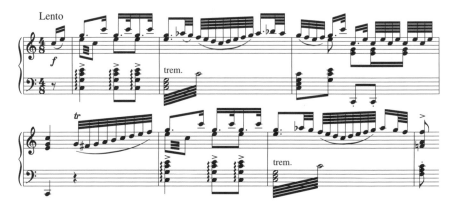

Ex. 11.99. Chopin, Mazurka in C sharp minor, Op. 6 No. 2 (1830–1), beginning (up a diminished 4th)

The emphasis on *e*, which recurs again and again in major–minor tunes, suggests that this mode is, after all, only another variant of the pentatonic seventh. And this is confirmed by Ex. 11.100, which Mahler clearly intended to be heard (like many lullabies) as a variation on the children's chant. Provided we refrain from leaning too heavily on the *a♭*, all the possibilities of the uninflected pentatonic seventh are still available.

Ex. 11.100. Mahler, 'In diesem Wetter!' (no. 5 of the *Kindertotenlieder*, 1904), end of voice part (down a tone)

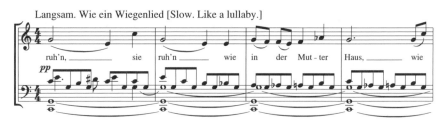

in   der   Mut - ter   Haus! _____

The greater the prominence of *e*, the more complex will be its relation to the dissonant *a*♭. We see something of this in Ex. 11.101, which is cast in an 'octave mode' framed between *e* and *e*⁺. Like the *e*♭s we looked at earlier, that deliciously ambiguous *a*♭ resolves in two directions: both down to *g* in bars 2–3 and 10–11, and up to *a*♮ in bars 2–6 (and there we may notice that the *a*s of bars 6 and 8, though mildly discordant, do not themselves resolve). This ability to resolve upward by a semitone implies that it must also be, in some sense, a *g*♯ (just as the *e*♭ was also a *d*♯); and this second identity is reinforced by that srong *e*. It is really a pity that conventional notation forces us to identify chromatic notes as sharp or flat. Quite often, they are both at the same time: *d*♯ and *e*♭, *g*♯ and *a*♭, even *a*♯ and *b*♭.

Ex. 11.101. Johann Strauss, 'Voices of Spring' (*c*.1882), section in A flat, beginning (down a major 6th)

As composers were quick to see, the double identity of $ab/g\sharp$ in particular made it possible to indulge in harmonies of extreme boldness without impairing the underlying tonality. At a first glance, Ex. 11.102 looks more like Bruckner or Brahms than a composition of the 1770s. On closer examination, one sees that the harmonic audacities are attached to the Balkan mode of the Melody.[114] (Surprisingly, the effect in performance of this passage, especially the highly chromatic bars 8–11, is more neo-Baroque than east European—which again shows how closely the two idioms were associated in the minds of the Viennese composers.)

Ex. 11.102. Haydn, String Quartet in F minor, Op. 20 No. 5 (1771), 1st mvt., bars 135–49 (down a semitone)

---

[114] It is a close relative of the 'Istrian' mode of Croatia (see Ex. 11.107 on p. 227).

It is doubtful whether Haydn could have laid so much harmonic stress on the *a♭* of bars 8–10 if this note had not been enharmonically equivalent to *g♯*. And if this seems far-fetched, consider the end of Chopin's Polonaise in A flat, Op. 53, where the same note (bracketed in Ex. 11.103) simultaneously functions as *a♭* (resolving on *g*) in the Melody and *g♯* in the harmony. If Chopin had been content to be more conventional (if less effective), he might have harmonized the *a♭* with an *F* minor chord. Potentially, the same note belongs to the two monotertially related chords *a♭/f* and *g♯/e*.

Ex. 11.103. Chopin, Polonaise in A flat, Op. 53 (1842), conclusion (up a major 3rd)

This sort of complex and ambiguous dissonance was only one of the resources hidden in the major–minor mode. Another was the symmetrical correspondence of the trichords *e–f–g* with *g–a♭–b♭*, which, when treated (more or less) sequentially, could produce patterns like that of Ex. 11.104. But why stop at these two trichords? Why not not extend them to *b♭–c♯⁺–d♭⁺*, or *c♯–d–e*?—or even both?

Which brings us to our next topic: the octatonic scale.

Ex. 11.104. Brahms, Symphony No. 4 in E minor (1885), slow mvt., bars 5–8 (down a major 3rd)

The octatonic scale

The deceptively simple principle of the octatonic scale is the regular alternation of tones and semitones. It is most easily visualized as a diminished-seventh chord in which all the minor thirds have been filled in the same way. If, for instance, the chord is $c-e\flat-f\sharp-a-c^+$, the filling may be either $c-d-e\flat-f-f\sharp-g\sharp-a-b-c^+$ or $c-d\flat-e\flat-e\natural-f\sharp-g-a-b\flat-c^+$. It follows that the filler notes must themselves make a diminished-seventh chord—but in that case, how can one distinguish filler from framework? The answer is that one cannot, without help from the context. We at once see the immense capacity of this scale for disorientation and confusion.

If, however, the composer manages to establish that the framework is $c-e\flat-f\sharp-a-c^+$, it makes an important difference which of the two filler sevenths is chosen (Ex. 11.105). Both have their advantages, if the intention is to maintain links with the diatonic scale. The strong point of the $c-d-e\flat-f-f\sharp-g\sharp-a-b-c^+$ type is its closeness to the minor mode, since it consists of four interlocking minor tetrachords, each of which comes complete with its own leading note. Transposing down a minor third and making a few enharmonic changes, these tetrachords may be imagined as belonging to the keys of A minor ($g\sharp-a^--b^--c-d$), C minor ($b^--c-d-e\flat-f$), $E\flat$ minor ($d-e\flat-f-g\flat-a\flat$,) and $F\sharp$ minor ($e\sharp-f\sharp-g\sharp-a-b$). This form of octatonic scale is there-

Ex. 11.105. The two types of octatonic scale

(*a*) melodic　　　　　　　　　　(*b*) harmonic

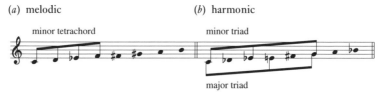

fore sometimes described as 'melodic'.

The strong point of the $c-d\flat-e\flat-e\natural-f\sharp-g-a-b\flat-c^+$ type is that it contains the perfect fifth $c-g$, similarly reproduced at intervals of a minor third. It is consequently full of diatonic triads and sevenths ($c-e-g$, $c-e\flat-g$, $c-e-g-b\flat$, $c-e\flat-g-b\flat$, $e\flat-g\flat-b\flat$, $e\flat-g\flat\flat-b\flat$, and so on), which lend themselves admirably to harmonic purposes. This form of octatonic scale is therefore sometimes described as 'harmonic'.

Needless to say, the connection between these neat scales and actual music is patchy. Although it seems natural to think of modes as particularized scales, in historical fact scales are generalized modes. We may be sure that fragmentary pentatonic modes existed for tens of thousands of years before anyone was conscious of a pentatonic scale; and in the same way, diatonic tunes long preceded the diatonic scale. Before a scale can become a fully realized pattern, it must be grasped as a principle. The pentatonic principle is that of high consonance; the diatonic principle attaches to pentatonic patterns the dissonant interval of the semitone. In the highly chromatic scales of the Fringe (and particularly, perhaps, its eastern extremity), there are several principles at work, or perhaps it would be better to call them tendencies or preferences. The first is towards dissonance. The second, which we can observe in the Gypsy, Hungarian, acoustic, and major–minor modes, is towards symmetry; its ultimate product is the whole-tone scale. The third is to saturate the melody with minor intervals, and it is this that leads to the octatonic scale.

In the ordinary minor mode, the simplest way to indulge this octatonic tendency is to flatten the fifth degree by a semitone—to make it, in fact, a blue fifth. If *a* is the tonic, this gives us, with the leading note $g\sharp^-$, seven of the eight notes of the octatonic scale: $g\sharp^--a^--b^--c-d-e\flat-f$. This is the pattern of Ex. 11.106, incidentally

Ex. 11.106. Klephtic (20th-c. Greek guerrilla) song, 1st verse, 2nd phrase

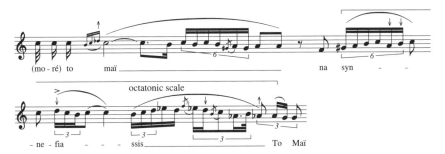

a fine corrective to the notion that 'folk' music is necessarily simple.[115] Bewilderingly chromatic though this passage may seem, it is outdone by the 'Istrian' mode of Croatia (so named after the Istrian Peninsula, which projects towards northern Italy from the Balkan coast), where a similar process is applied to the Phrygian mode (Ex. 11.107). Here the three notes $a–b–c^+$ are flattened to $a\flat–b\flat–c\flat^+$, giving,

Ex. 11.107. The Istrian mode

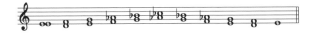

again, seven notes of the octatonic scale. We saw something like this Istrian mode (though without its top note) in the remarkable passage from Haydn's String Quartet

---

[115] Notice, as further evidence of the dual identity of enharmonic equivalents, how $g\sharp$ (resolving on *a*), turns into $a\flat$ (resolving on *g*) at the end.

in F minor, Op. 20 No. 5, and in much the same way, the blue *e♭* of Ex. 11.106 reappears in Schubert's 'Unfinished' Symphony (Ex. 11.108).

Ex. 11.108. Schubert, Symphony No. 8 in B minor, the 'Unfinished' (1822), 1st mvt., bars 13–20 (down a tone)

So much for the 'melodic' form of the octatonic scale. With its perfect fifth between *c* and *g*, the other, 'harmonic' type has a natural affinity with drones. Certain Indian modes come quite close to it. *Māravā*, one of the ten *thāts* or basic modes of northern India, resembles an octatonic with one note omitted and another raised by a semitone; and it can even happen that the *b♮* is changed to *b♭*, as in the southern Indian rāga *rama-pria*:

octatonic	*c*	*d♭*	*e♭*	*e♮*	*f♯*	*g*	*a*	*b♭*
māravā	*c*	*d♭*		*e♮*	*f♯*	*g*	*a*	*b♮*
rama-pria	*c*	*d♭*		*e♮*	*f♯*	*g*	*a*	*b♭*

It is probable that the latter began life as an 'acoustic' mode with a Phrygian second, especially in view of a slight flattening of *f♯* and *b♭*, which brings it close to the natural harmonic series.[116] This Indian mode looks much less exotic if the *d♭* is transposed up an octave. We then have something very like the complete octatonic scale to be found in the slow movement of Beethoven's Piano Sonata Op. 28 (Ex. 11.109)—a sonata, incidentally, which is said to have been a particular favourite of the composer's.

[116] For a song in this mode, together with a flute improvisation on the same melody, see Malm, *Music Cultures of the Pacific, the Near East, and Asia*, 105.

Ex. 11.109. Beethoven, Piano Sonata in D, Op. 28, the 'Pastoral' (1801), slow mvt., bars 71–7 (down a major 6th)

There are two points to be noticed about Beethoven's use of the scale. Firstly, it is based on a diminished seventh; and secondly, within that diminished seventh, the Melody mounts by minor thirds: e–$f\sharp$–g–$f\sharp$ g–a–$b\flat$–a $b\flat$–c^{+}–$d\flat^{+}$–c^{+}. Such sequences were later to take in the Bass as well as the Melody, thereby giving rise to some extremely chromatic modulations.[117]

Many theorists would regard the octatonic patterns in passages like this as 'fortuitous', mere by-products of a decorated diminished-seventh chord.[118] I cannot

---

[117] e.g. in Chopin's Nocturne in G, Op. 37 No. 2 (Ex. 15.4 on p. 385).

[118] e.g. Taruskin, 'Chernomor to Kashchei', 95–6, and Donald Street, 'The Modes of Limited Transposition', 820.

agree. Of course, it is extremely unlikely that Beethoven had ever heard of the octatonic scale, under any of its various names, and it is almost equally improbable that he noticed the alternation of tones and semitones. But it is inconceivable that he was unconscious of the modally complex, semi-Oriental character of this passage. If he was unaware of the octatonic *scale*, he had at least an inkling of the octatonic *principle*.

Most of what has been said about the octatonic is true also of the whole-tone scale. It, too, grew out of a love of symmetrical, dissonant melody; but, compared with the octatonic, it was even more symmetrical (unrelievedly so, in fact), and to that extent even less natural. As fully realized patterns, both the octatonic and whole-tone scales are creations of the mid-nineteenth century. They really belong to the history of Modernism, where we shall be meeting them again in due course.

Conclusion

This chapter has given a necessarily inadequate idea of Fringe influence on the European classics during the eighteenth and early nineteenth centuries—inadequate, because so much of the evidence has disappeared. Even so, I shall probably be suspected of exaggeration. Surely the examples quoted here, striking though they no doubt are, must be exceptional?

There are several answers to this. First, these passages are *not* exceptional. Fringe influence pervaded European music at every level. The lowest, and unfortunately also the most familiar, was a trumpery mass of 'local colour', a depressing world populated by bogus Gypsies, kitsch Neapolitans, and tinselly Orientals. At a much higher level, but still overtly exotic, are such things as the *ongarese* finales of the Viennese composers, the mazurkas of Chopin, or the Gypsy numbers in Verdi or Bizet.

Finally, there are the many places where foreign influence has been completely absorbed, often without the knowledge of the composer himself. This is the most interesting case of all. As one becomes aware of these half-Oriental patterns, large tracts of music take on a new look. What had seemed eccentric, progressive, illicit, perhaps even a 'stroke of genius', becomes perfectly normal.

Next to snobbery and ethnic prejudice, the greatest barrier to recognizing these patterns is what philosophers call the 'genetic fallacy', the feeling that everything somehow carries the taint of its origins. Compositions that draw on trivial sources must themselves be trivial; Oriental patterns must go on sounding Oriental—or so we tend to think. The greater the composer, the more triumphantly will such notions be refuted.

12 The Dances of Central Europe

I. THE POLKA FAMILY

One of the most remarkable features of Western music has been a persistent association, over several centuries, of certain lively dance rhythms with the major mode. At the popular level, these major-mode dances changed remarkably little from the sixteenth to the twentieth century. From Dalza to Strauss, we find the same bright, clear, melodic lines, the same four- and eight-bar phrases, the same tonic-and-dominant harmony, often even the same tunes.

Of course there were local characteristics, as there inevitably are in popular music. The waltzes and polkas of central Europe have a great deal in common with the partly Oriental, east European music of the previous chapter. In fact, the distinction between 'central' and 'eastern' Europe is anything but easy to sustain. As a rule, 'central Europe' spoke German and 'eastern Europe' Hungarian or a Slavonic language, but this is no more than a rough guide. And though, at first sight, the primitive waltz and polka seem to inhabit a different world from the strange modes and sombre harmonies of 'eastern' Europe, but this is due less to cultural origins than to the peculiar nature of the major mode, whose bright, primary tints are at their most effective when kept pure. There is a large family of minor modes, continually hybridizing and mutating, but only one major mode. And when mode is disregarded, we find that the central and east European styles have much in common. Centuries of mutual influence ensured that the same rhythms, drones, ostinatos, and formal procedures appear in both. To a much greater extent than appears on the surface, they belong to the same tradition.

This is particularly true of the polka, which was also much the more folky of the two dances. It is therefore convenient to deal with it first, even though its vogue came three decades later than that of the waltz.

A family history

The term 'polka family', though handy, is somewhat misleading. Both the waltz and polka belong to a succession of similar dances (speaking musically rather than choreographically) going back at least to the beginning of the sixteenth century. The line of descent of the waltz runs through Dalza's *saltarello alla veneziana*, the galliard, the minuet, and the passepied; that of the polka, through the bouncy common-time dance tunes of the Fitzwilliam Virginal Book, the English country dance, the French contredanse, and the écossaise, which means 'Scottish' but by general consent had nothing to do with Scotland. Inevitably, though, these genealogies are both incomplete and over-tidy. Nothing hybridizes more readily than dance music.

A striking instance of how the same pattern could persist over centuries is provided by what one might call the 'Nobody's Jig' family. In the discussion of Dalza's *pavane alla ferrarese* in Chapter 6, I pointed out a tune type consisting in essence of a series of 2/V–3/I cadences so graded as to make a sixteen-bar tune.[1] This is still not quite an independent structure, its purpose being rather to echo and drive home the cadence out of which it probably developed. However, it soon broke free, and, in the slightly altered form of 'Nobody's Jig', became one of the most popular tunes of the seventeenth century (Ex. 12.1).[2]

Ex. 12.1. Richard Farnaby, 'Nobody's Jig' (*c.* 1600), Theme

'Nobody', it should be explained, was a traditional comic figure, depicted with breeches reaching to his neck. In the early seventeenth century, English theatrical troupes appear to have taken both the clown and his signature tune to the German-

---

[1] See 'Theme B' in Exs. 6.11 and 6.12 on pp. 80–1.

[2] If Ex. 12.1 is compared with Dalza's 'Theme B', it will be seen that the basic melodic pattern has been transferred down a third, from 2–3 to 7–1. Transference of this kind is a common feature of 16th-c. popular music.

speaking world, where they were renamed 'Pickelhering', that is to say, 'Pickled Herring'.[3] Much later, Haydn included a minor-mode version of this tune (Ex. 12.2) in the finale of his Symphony No. 60 in C,[4] along with such other popular melodies as 'Night-Watchman' tune (Ex. 11.81) and a version of Byrd's 'Bagpipe and Drone' (Ex. 6.4).[5] In spite of the elaborate Gypsy garb of drone basses, *ruckhafte Senkung*, aggressively parallel fifths, sycopated accompaniment, and irregular bar rhythms, the kinship of Ex. 12.2 to 'Nobody's Jig' is clear enough— and incidentally shows how all was gist to the Gypsy mill.

Ex. 12.2. Haydn, Symphony No. 60 in C, 'Il Distratto' (1774), 4th mvt., bars 82–99 (down a 4th)

This same movement ends with a scrap of melody (Ex. 12.3) in some ways even more interesting for our purposes, since it is a direct musical ancestor of the polka (notice, by the way, the Gypsy rhythm in the accompaniment). Again, the harmony is a series of V–I cadences. Indeed, this pattern is so common in the polka family that it can conveniently be called the 'polka progression'.

Of course, Haydn himself would not have described this tune as a polka, because

[3] For all this information I am indebted to John M. Ward, 'The Morris Tune', 306–9.

[4] This symphony was based on incidental music to the play *Der Zerstreute* (*The Absent-Minded Man*, or, in Italian, *Il Distratto*).

[5] Haydn's version differs in that it is in 2/4 rather than 6/8 time, and has no drone. Otherwise it is virtually identical with Byrd's, down to the two-part counterpoint. The orchestration for high oboes suggest that Haydn, too, had the bagpipe in mind.

Ex. 12.3. Haydn, Symphony No. 60 in C, 'Il Distratto', bars 151–8, near end

that dance had yet to be invented. To him, it would have been a contredanse, originally a lively alternative to the bourrée and gavotte but by this time beginning to be formalized. Unlike the bourrée and gavotte, however, it came, not from France, but from England; hence the name, a French corruption of the English 'country dance'. Its duple time might be either simple or compound (in other words, 2/4 or 6/8), both rhythms often being used in the same movement. It was no doubt for this reason that the simple-duple type came to be notated as 2/4 rather than 2/2 or 4/4, a convention kept up in its descendants till the early twentieth century.

By the time of the French Revolution, the contredanse had become the favourite dance of the urban middle class. Like the minuet, it absorbed a wide range of popular patterns:

in Haydn's time the contredance became an essentially international phenomenon. . . . It proved resistent enough to adopt exotic or Eastern European elements without having given up its fundamental European *contredanse*-character. Wherever its material originated from, the only thing it really needed, was a popular, easily recognizable dance-profile, no matter of its being of Slavonic, Ungarese, Gipsy or Alla Turca character.[6]

A comparison between the main theme from the finale of Haydn's 'Bear' Symphony and one of the liveliest passages in Johann Strauss's *Fledermaus* (Exs. 12.4 and 12.5) shows how remarkably polka-like these eighteenth-century tunes could sometimes be.

Musical characteristics

The ur-polka, like the ur-waltz, was peasant dance music little changed since the sixteenth century. The harmony, with its drone basses and simple ostinatos, takes

---

[6] Dénes Bartha, 'Thematic Profile and Character in the Quartet-Finales of Joseph Haydn', 59.

Ex. 12.4. Haydn, Symphony No. 82 in C 'The Bear' (1786), last mvt., beginning

Ex. 12.5. Johann Strauss, *Die Fledermaus* (1874), Act II, no. 11, finale, bars 33–40 (down a tone)

us back to Dalza, but it was destined to develop quite differently. Where the dance forms of the sixteenth century sprouted new chords, those of the eighteenth and nineteenth expanded existing ones. In later polkas and (especially) waltzes, the musical interest is concentrated in melodic lines of ever-increasing subtlety, while the harmony, for the most part, retains its primitive plainness.

These melodic patterns derived from a wide variety of sources. One, easily overlooked, is the Oriental melody discussed in the preceding chapter. As we saw there, 'translation' between modes was a frequent practice. A tune in some exotic minor mode could reappear, bright and new, in the major.[7] Besides, it is a mere Western prejudice to suppose that major modes were unknown to the East. The northern Indian *bhūpkaliān*,[8] for instance, is a form of the major pentatonic *1–2–3–5–6* with *3* as *vādī* and *6* as *samvādī* (or, put another way, *a̅–c–d–e–g*, with the emphasis on *a* and *e* and *c* as a drone), close relatives of which may be heard in the concluding section of Mozart's 'Rondo alla turca' and the main themes of Beethoven's 'Rondo alla ingharese' and 'Turkish March'.[9]

Similar influences may also be detected in rhythm. Western Asia shares with Africa a rich and ancient tradition of cross-rhythmic accompaniment figures, many of them known to Gypsies and other east European popular musicians. Among these are | ♪♩♪ |, which is extendible to | ♪♩♩♪ |, | ♪♩♩♩♪ |, and so on; the accented half-beat rhythm known in Hungary as *estam*; and the off-beat patterns |𝄾♪𝄾♪♩ |𝄾♪𝄾♪♩ | and |𝄾♩♩♩ |𝄾♩♩♩ | (or notational variants thereof). Accompaniment figures like these came to be associated with polka-like tunes about the same time as the waltz was acquiring its characteristic bass.[10] In Schubert's écossaises (which can sound exactly like polkas), they shed their Gypsy associations and become normal accompaniment figures. By the mid-nineteenth century, the polka and waltz basses had converged towards essentially the same formula of on-beat basses combined with off-beat chords. Only the off-beats differed: 'one *two three*' in the waltz, 'one *two three four*', 'one *two three four*', or 'one *two three* (rest)' in the polka family. In spite of this identity of means, however, the results were very different. While the waltz remained smooth and romantic, the polka, no doubt under the influence of the Hungarian *friss*, sometimes developed a rhythmic drive that can only be called jazzy. A famous instance is Strauss's 'Unter Donner und Blitz' (Ex. 12.6), which incidentally also shows how the form had expanded since its beginnings. If we compare it with Haydn's polka-like tune (Ex. 12.3), we find the same V7–I progressions, but at four times the length.

This music unmistakably *swings*, especially when Strauss reinforces the *estam* rhythm with the drums in bars 40–3. Polkas like these snapped their fingers at decorum in a way that the waltz never did and never could. From the start, the

---

[7] e.g. the 'Night-Watchman' tune (Exs. 11.80 and 11.81), which reappears in the major mode in Beethoven's Pastoral Symphony (Ex. 11.82). See pp. 207–8.

[8] Also known as *bhūpaliān*, or simply *bhūp*.   [9] From incidental music to *The Ruins of Athens*.

[10] Cf. e.g. the | ♪♩ ♪ | rhythms in Schubert's *Divertissement à la hongroise* (Ex. 11.73(*b*), first bar) and the polka-like tune from Haydn's Symphony No. 60 in C (Ex. 12.3 on p. 234).

Ex. 12.6. Johann Strauss, 'Unter Donner und Blitz' (*Polka schnell*, 1868), bars 5–51 (down a 5th)

polka had been less dignified than the waltz. Though the ur-polka had a similar background to the ur-waltz, it was always more likely to be treated in an ostentatiously popular way. Haydn's tune (Ex. 12.4 on p. 235) is a case in point. With those drones, that spare texture, that threefold repetition, it might be Stravinsky expertly wrapping up some Russian peasant tune.

The waltz did, it is true, create a scandal during the second decade of the nineteenth century. But that was due to the dance, which was quite simply the sexiest yet seen in European ballrooms, not the music. In the polka craze of the 1840s, the reverse was true. The dance was respectable, if boisterous, but the music was disreputably catchy. Polkas have made occasional appearances in 'serious' music, usually by Czech composers, but nowhere near as often as waltzes, and in their ballroom form have always been treated more simply. They did not expand to anything like the same extent, continuing to be made up of relatively short, loosely connected strains, usually in a simple ABA form with B in the subdominant. Nor was there any polka equivalent to the waltz 'suite'.

Towards the end of the nineteenth century, while the waltz settled into a languid elegance, the polka became even more impetuous and exciting. Not only did it absorb something from the headlong dances of eastern Europe, as we have just seen; in its turn, it exerted a strong influence on the military march, and, both directly and through the march, on early ragtime. For hundreds of years the middle and upper classes had sought their rhythmic excitement at the periphery of Western civilization. First they had gone to the British Isles, then to eastern Europe. Now it was the turn of the southern United States.

II. THE WALTZ

THE EARLY WALTZ

> Endearing Waltz!—to thy more melting tune
> Bow Irish jig and ancient rigadoon,
> Scotch reels, avaunt! and country-dance, forego
> Your future claims to each fantastic toe!
> Waltz—Waltz alone—both legs and arms demands,
> Liberal of feet, and lavish of her hands;
> Hands which may freely range in public sight
> Where ne'er before—but—pray 'put out the light.' . . .
> Morals and minuets, virtue and her stays,
> And tell-tale powder—all have had their days.[11]

By the time Byron wrote the above lines, the waltz, though still in its riotous youth, was no longer a novelty. Viennese high society had known it since the 1780s, as a substitute for the already old-fashioned minuet. As an economist might put it, there was a 'gap in the market' for a lively dance in 3/4 time. The amusingly rustic

---

[11] Byron, 'The Waltz: An Apostrophic Hymn' (1812), ll. 109–16 and 182–3. This poem may be found in *The Poetical Works of Lord Byron*.

import that filled it went by many names: *Ländler* (country dance), *deutsche Tanz* (German dance), *Steirische* (dance from Styria, in south-eastern Austria), *Dreher* (turner), and so on. Out of this terminological welter *Walzer* (roughly translatable as 'twirler') emerged victorious.

In a different social climate this new dance might simply have revitalized the minuet, as imports from the countryside have so often revitalized ballroom dances. Indeed, for a while this seemed to be happening. On the one hand, the minuets of composers like Haydn and Mozart begin to show clear waltz influence from about 1770. On the other, Mozart's *Sechs deutsche Tänze*, composed in 1791, are closer to being minuets than waltzes. An intelligent observer might have predicted a bright future for this hybrid.

But this was an Age of Revolution, musical and choreographic no less than social and political. Within a few years, the dignified old aristocrat was being rudely shoved aside by the plebeian upstart. To quote Byron again:

> The fashion hails—from countesses to queens,
> And maids and valets waltz behind the scenes;
> Wide and more wide thy witching circle spreads,
> And turns—if nothing else—at least our *heads*;
> With thee even clumsy cits[12] attempt to bounce,
> And cockneys practise what they can't pronounce. (ll. 153–8)

Three years after these lines were written, the Napoleonic Wars came to an end and the golden age of the waltz began. The fifteen years from 1815 to 1830 were a pioneering period for waltzes of all kinds: the several hundred ländler of Schubert; the glittering salon waltzes of Chopin; Weber's 'Invitation to the Dance', which brought to maturity the 'waltz suite'; the classic Viennese type of Strauss and Lanner; and in the 'Ball' movement from Berlioz's *Symphonie fantastique*, the symphonic waltz.

During the following ninety years, from 1830 to 1920, the waltz became respectable, and even posh, but never ceased to be popular. In fact, its sheer popularity, extending to the most austere and intellectual of musicians, is perhaps its most astonishing feature. Within the German-speaking world, composers were virtually obliged to turn out at least a ländler or two; even Wagner was not exempt. Outside it, the form showed an amazing adaptability to local custom. In Spain it became intensely Spanish, in Russia ineffably Russian. The most disparate of composers found something congenial in it. Chopin wrote polished, elegant waltzes, Brahms placid ländler, Scandinavians bleak waltzes in the minor mode. French composers of the smarty-pants school wrote brittle, satirical waltzes. From Haydn to

---

[12] Abbreviation of 'citizen': a rude word for a 'petty bourgeois'.

Shostakovich, virtually everybody who was anybody wrote waltzes. The only notable exception appears to have been Mendelssohn. Perhaps the form offended what Shaw called his 'kid glove gentility'.

Composers were at ease with the waltz. Its characteristic fault was an excessive facility, the very opposite of the sense of struggle and constraint that so often mars pretentious Romanticism. In the absence of all other evidence, the waltz form could be reconstructed by combining the musical effects that came most naturally to nineteenth-century musicians. And, because it carried no burden of tradition, composers could incorporate into it any feature that took their fancy—whether from Italian opera, east European folk music, the symphonic idiom, or anywhere else—with no fear of being reproached for violation of 'the true waltz form'. Furthermore, they could use the hoariest clichés, melodic, harmonic, or rhythmic, and no one would accuse them of being hackneyed or 'derivative'. The waltz was a holiday from the oppressive burden of being original.

Perhaps because of this, it developed in an extraordinarily consistent, almost organic manner. To an astonishing degree, the seeds of the later waltz, especially in its pure Viennese form, are contained in the primitive Tyrolean ländler.

The ur-waltz

The beginnings of the waltz could hardly have been more modest. The earliest known examples appear to be a group of five 'Tänze', of which the first is Ex. 12.7.[13] The feature one immediately notices about this ur-waltz is its extreme, almost caricatural simplicity. Not only are the chords throughout the set limited to the tonic and dominant; these are also treated in an oddly restricted way. They suggest a 'double tonic' of the most primitive 'Irish Washerwoman' kind,[14] in which the secondary chord has been assimilated to the dominant seventh and placed before

Ex. 12.7. *Tanz* no. 1 from the Sonnleithner Collection (down a tone)

[13] They are given in full in Flotzinger, 'Und waltzen umatum . . .' (to which my account of the early waltz is deeply indebted), 507–8. There the date is stated to be 1702, which seems hard to credit. Could it be that the 'o' is a mistake for '6'? Whatever their date, these little dances are extremely primitive.

[14] e.g. the bagpipe tune imitated by Zacara da Teramo in the early 15th c. (Ex. 6.6 on p. 77), or its modern Galician relative (Ex. 6.9 on p. 78).

the tonic.[15] This double-tonic ancestry helps explain the prominence in all waltzes of the chord of the dominant seventh, of sequences, and of repeated rhythms.

Yet another influence on Ex. 12.7 was the *Volkslied*, which formed a neat stanzaic framework for these repeated patterns. Tunes of this type could be sung to the words of Goethe's 'Erlkönig':

Wer reitet so spät durch nacht und Wind?

Es ist der Vater mit seinem Kind.

All this was as true of the ur-polka as the ur-waltz, but in one respect the two dances sharply diverged. In neither the polka nor any of its antecedents does one find the flowing variations of the second half of Ex. 12.7. These are a countrified version of the Baroque 'double' (or 'division' in English),[16] and testify to the slightly greater sophistication of the early waltz. Rude and rustic though it might be, it was at least in touch with Franco-Italian traditions. In cultivated music the *double* proper was going out by the second half of eighteenth century, but in the early waltz it not only survived but flourished. As so often happens, what had begun as 'variation' turned into 'theme'. Soon the flowing rhythm was being used for its own sake,[17] and by the end of the century it had come to typify the rustic waltz.

A step up from these primitive beginnings is taken by our next example, entitled 'Steirische in C'[18] (Ex. 12.8). While the form remains much the same as in Ex. 12.7,

Ex. 12.8. 'Steirische in C'

---

[15] This happened in the polka too. Cf. the polka-like tune from Haydn's Symphony No. 60 in C (Ex. 12.3 on p. 234).

[16] e.g. J. S. Bach's unaccompanied Violin Sonata No. 2 in D, where each of the four movements has its 'double'. This form of variation goes back to the 16th c.

[17] e.g. in two of the five 'Sonnleithner' dances.   [18] Date unknown, probably 18th c.

the melodic line is in every way more complex. Instead of rocking-horse sequences, we have a fluent and beautifully proportioned eight-bar Melody, spread over rather than bound to the same tonic-and-dominant Bass. There is a new, unmistakably Italianate suavity in the graceful curve of the opening phrase[19] and the sweetly sighing appoggiaturas of bars 2–6. Already we see a typically Viennese blend of the easy charm of Italy with the 'divine beeriness'[20] of central Europe.

The waltz bass

In rhythm, as in melody and harmony, the essential features of the waltz existed separately long before being brought together in the late eighteenth century. The waltz bass of Ex. 12.9 differs from the genuine article in only two respects: it reaches into the top part (no doubt the composer regarded it as a variant of the usual saraband rhythm), and it is poorly sustained.

Ex. 12.9. *Sarabanda* for lute (*c.*1645), beginning (down a 5th)

A similar short-windedness characterizes the waltz-like basses that begin to crop up in minuets and their trios from about 1765. As a rule, they expire after four bars.[21] Only gradually did they become more persistent,[22] and one can quite see why the composers of this period would have regarded it as crude and mechanical to prolong these figures unduly. Even such sporadic examples as do occur are confined to passages conspicuously popular in style. For persistent waltz basses, we must go to actual popular music, or at any rate imitations thereof. When we do so, we find another ancestor of the waltz bass: the articulated drone.[23] This is the waltz-time equivalent of the broken-octave bass that provides a counter-rhythmic

---

[19] Cf. the opening phrase of Mozart's 'Secondate, aurette amiche' (Ex. 10.3 on p. 137).

[20] The phrase is Mencken's. See *A Mencken Chrestomathy*, 'Johann Strauss', 539.

[21] e.g. in the trio from Haydn's Symphony No. 49 in F minor ('La Passione', 1768), and the main section of the minuet from his Symphony No. 57 in D (1774).

[22] e.g.: Haydn, the trios of the Symphonies Nos. 76 in E flat, 85 in B flat ('La Reine'), and 86 in D (all composed in the 1780s); Symphony No. 94 in G (the 'Surprise', 1791), first movement, bars 66–73, and main section of minuet; Mozart, Divertimento No. 17 in D (1779 or 1780), main section of minuet; Serenade for Twelve Wind Instruments and Double Bass in B flat (*c.*1783–4), second trio of second minuet; *Così fan tutte* (1790), Act II, Scene i, Despina's aria 'Una donna a quindici anni'.

[23] e.g. Beethoven's 'Sieben Ländler', WoO 11 (*c.*1798), no. 3 (Ex. 12.10 on pp. 246–7). For a more modern waltz bass, cf. no. 5 from the same set (Ex. 12.11 on p. 247).

background to many east European tunes.[24] It is to rhythm what the ordinary drone is to melody: in effect, a 'rhythmic drone'.

Doubling in thirds

Similar origins, part-Italian, part-central European, may be found for the melodic chromaticism of the waltz,[25] as well for the almost equally characteristic doubling at the third or sixth, which existed in the Hungarian Gypsy, Italian Baroque, and, later, Classical styles. No doubt the ultimate source was a widespread tradition of folk organum.[26] Early waltzes were often performed by bands consisting of two violins and a bass,[27] which again shows their closeness to the Italian mainstream, since this was no more than a plebeian version of the Baroque 'trio sonata' line-up. It lasted into the late nineteenth century, when it evolved into the still-popular 'Schrammel quartet'.[28] In popular music, the Baroque continuo-and-solo combination has never gone out of fashion.

In these early waltz bands, the two fiddles would naturally spend much of their time playing in thirds or sixths, but more even-handedly than is customary in 'classical' music. Such bias as there was between the two parts would be shifting and ambiguous. This is still true of Austrian folk music, where the tune is often harmonized at the upper third, just as in the 'Steirische in C'.[29] This 'over-third doubling', as we might term it, has unexpected consequences. Though the upper part (call it the Descant) reflects the contour of the Melody (or Tune), it does so through a distorting mirror in which tones and semitones often change places. With time and familiarity, this distorted version may come to be admired for its own sake—in other words, Descant may turn into Tune. The new Tune may then acquire its own Descant, which again may turn into Tune—and so on, if not *ad infinitum*, at least until there is a different version of the Tune for each of the seven degrees of the mode.

---

[24] For an early example, see the Musette in D (a veritable compendium of east European effects) from J. S. Bach's *Anna Magdalena Bach Book*, composed in the 1720s. Later examples may be found in the finales of Haydn's 'Oxford' Symphony, No. 92 in G, beginning; Beethoven's Symphony No. 8 in F, bars 18 ff.; Beethoven's String Quartet in B flat, Op. 130, beginning, etc.

[25] e.g. the c♯ in bar 5 of the 'Steirische in C' (Ex. 12.8 on p. 241). Cf. the chromaticisms in the finale of Haydn's String Quartet in C, Op. 74 No. 1 (Ex. 10.6 on p. 141).

[26] See Bellman, *The* Style Hongrois, 111. Cf. also the 'Istrian' mode (Ex. 11.107 on p. 227).

[27] Beethoven's 'Sieben Ländler' WoO 11 (*c*.1798), discussed below, are thought to have been originally composed for this combination. Only a piano arrangement survives.

[28] The original Schrammel band, started in 1878, consisted of the brothers Johann and Joseph Schrammel playing violins accompanied by a bass guitar. A clarinet (later replaced by an accordion) was subsequently added.

[29] See Ex. 12.8. In the original notation the relationship between the melodies on the treble stave was made clear by pointing the tails of the lower notes upward, and those of the upper notes downward.

Needless to say, nothing quite like this happened in real life. The descanting is seldom mathematically precise, and there is a limit to the number of times Descant can turn into Tune before the Melody becomes hopelessly estranged from the unchanging Bass. Nevertheless, it is clear that a melody could go through this process at least twice. The e–e^+ ambit of the 'Steirische' (and many other waltz tunes) may well originally have been c–c^+. Moreover, its own Descant looks forward to a whole series of waltz clichés, including the apical *7*, 'waltz *6*', and tritone between *7* and *4*. Other peculiarities derived at least in part from this process are the chromatic figures *3*–*2♯*–*3* and *5*–*4♯*–*5* (reflecting *1*–*7⁻*–*1*), the cadence sweeping down from *7* to *7⁻*, (reflecting *5*–*5⁻*), and the paradoxical resolution of a concordant *5* on a discordant *4*/V7 (reflecting *3*–*2*/V7).

THE BEGINNINGS OF SOPHISTICATION

Meanwhile, the four-bar progression, while remaining the harmonic basis of the waltz, was becoming somewhat more diverse. Throughout its history, waltz harmony has been organized in closed sections—'clauses', one might call them[30]—ending with a V7–I cadence. In the the earlier waltzes, the clause had been nothing *but* the V7–I progression, repeated to make a four-bar phrase. In the rather more sophisticated tunes that succeeded this primitive type, it might also be I I · V7 I, I V7 · V7 I, or I IV · V7 I.

At the same time, the tune as a whole was doubling in length, from eight to sixteen bars. At its most primitive, this sixteen-bar pattern resembles the older theme-and-*double* (from which it no doubt developed) in that the second half is a variation on the first, but differs from it in that the variation is now further from the theme and includes harmonic reinforcement (a plain V7–I cadence, for instance, may be strengthened to IV–V7–I). Let us call this the 'harmonic variation' type. In a second, somewhat more complex type, the sixteen bars fall into a AABA pattern.

But these tunes were still very short, even with repeats. To make any impact, whether on the village green or in the concert hall, the form had to expand even further. There were two courses open to the composer. One was to expand the individual movement, the difficulty here being that symmetry demanded that the next stage should be a thirty-two-bar tune—quite a jump. The other course was to resort to the already ancient form of the medley; in other words, to string a series of short tunes together. It was the latter, much easier path that the composers of the late eighteenth century took. In doing so, they invented the 'waltz suite'.

---

[30] This seems an appropriate term for a *closed* harmonic progression, since 'close' and 'clause' both derive from the Latin *claudere*, to shut.

Beethoven's Sieben Ländler, *WoO 11*

The nearest approach we have to the primitive waltz suite is Beethoven's *Sieben Ländler*, WoO 11, composed in 1799. Earlier sets, such as Mozart's 'Sechs deutsche Tänze' of 1791, had been intermediate in style between the minuet and the true waltz. Beethoven, in contrast, not only imitates the rustic ländler; he positively revels in its limitations.

The most obvious of these limitations is the extreme simplicity of the harmony. The entire set is confined to four chords within a single major key: I (or, on one occasion, I7♭), V7, IV and II7/♯. Moreover, the first halves of all seven numbered sections are confined to I and V7, as also is the 35-bar coda. The formal restrictions are almost as striking. Every one of the seven numbers is a thirty-two-bar melody (including repeats), symmetrically divided into sixteen-, eight-, and four-bar sections. In view of this simplicity, one might suspect the set of being a very early work, or at best a pot-boiler. In fact, it was composed after the 'Pathétique' Piano Sonata, and with an attention to detail evident even in the bare harmonic scheme. In this opusculum, we see Beethoven cultivating the mastery of simple harmony that has caused him to be described as 'the apostle of tonic and dominant'.

The chords making up the first halves are summarized in Table 12.1. There is no need to examine them in detail to grasp three essential points. Firstly, every strain ends with a V7–I close; secondly, the only chords are the tonic and dominant; and thirdly, these chords are in every case differently disposed. To distinguish nos. 3 and 6, the former has both given a tonic drone, which is itself different from the

TABLE 12.1. *The harmonic scheme of Beethoven's* Sieben Ländler, *WoO 11*

Number	Bars							
	1	2	3	4	5	6	7	8
1	I	V7	V7	I	I	V7	V7	I (over *1–5* drone)
2	I———		V7——		V7——		I–V7	I
3	I–V7 I		V7	I	I–V7 I		V7	I (over *1* drone)[a]
4	I———		V7——		I———		V7	I
5	V7	I	V7	I	V7	I	V7	I (over *5* drone, except the last chord)[b]
6	I———		V7	I	I———		V7	I
7	I———		I	V7	V7——		V7	I

[a] See Ex. 12.10.
[b] See Ex. 12.11. This harmonic progression is of east European origin. Cf. the Gypsyish main theme from the finale of Beethoven's Seventh Symphony (Ex. 11.23 on pp. 168–9).

tonic-and-dominant drone of no. 1 and the dominant drone of no. 5. Moreover, this careful differentiation is characteristic of the movement as a whole. The second halves also all have distinctive chord schemes, as do the B sections of the AABA numbers.

This variety would have been impossible if Beethoven had confined himself to the old four-bar clause. Instead, he alternates it with the newer eight-bar type. Nos. 1, 3, and 5 belong to the old type, with archaic features such as the drone bass and flowing *double* rhythm;[31] nos. 2, 4, 6, and 7, to the new. And, as well as being carefully varied, the harmony is so arranged as to build up to a climax towards the end of the movement. This is achieved mainly by husbanding the IV chord, which does not appear at all until no. 4. Thereafter it receives a subtly increasing emphasis, culminating in the big IV–V7–I progression (the only one in the movement) in no. 7. At the same time, the harmonic rhythm becomes broader. Notice especially the expansion of the split dominant:[32]

$$\text{No. 1: } IV_7 \cdot V_7\,I$$
$$\text{No. 2: } I\times2\,V_7\times2 \cdot V_7\times2\,I\times2$$
$$\text{No. 7: } I\times3\,V_7 \cdot V_7\times3\,I$$

In many sets of variations, those coming towards the end are 'prophetic' of later developments, as though the process of evolution had been compressed into a single movement. In just this manner, these prolonged chords foreshadow the later waltz.

Almost equally interesting are the B sections of the numbers in AABA form. In no. 3 (Ex. 12.10), Beethoven indulges in that favourite game of the Viennese composers, 'Dominant or Tonic?' For where V7 is so much the norm, the plain V of bars 9–12 sounds rather like a key; and when the seventh of the chord arrives in bar 12, one has a distinct sense of modulation back to the tonic.

Waltz harmony, faithful to its beginnings, remained essentially cadential—or, more precisely, perfect-cadential. One has only to run one's eye along the Bass of

Ex. 12.10. Beethoven, *Sieben Ländler*, WoO 11 (1798–9), no. 3 (down a tone)

[31] See Ex. 12.10 below.

[32] From now on, multiple bars on the same chord will be indicated by the sign '×': e.g. I×2, two bars on I; V7×3, three bars on V7, etc.

Ex. 12.10 to see the big I–V–I cadence. The II7/♯–V7 progression, later to become so popular in the waltz, merely extends the pattern back a step.

But what if the A section itself begins with V7? How does one lead up to a chord whose essence is that of leading up? Later waltz composers delighted in finding the most diverse solutions to this conundrum. Beethoven contents himself with placing a subdominant in front of that dominant (Ex. 12.11, bars 12–13). An incidental

Ex. 12.11. Beethoven, *Sieben Ländler*, WoO 11 (1798–9), no. 5 (down a tone)

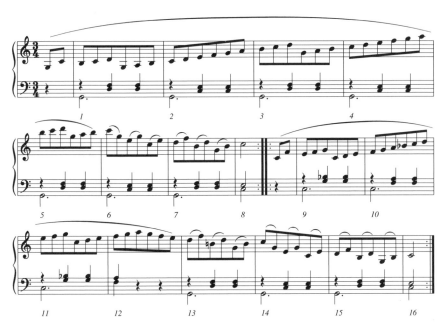

point of interest, and further proof of how seriously Beethoven took these little waltz tunes, is that the initial figure of Ex. 12.11 is the germ of the fugato in the scherzo of his Fifth Symphony.[33]

Modal characteristics

The complete absence from this set of a minor chord—let alone a minor key—is typical of early waltzes, which are invariably and entirely in the major. But it is a special type of major, with strong emphasis on the pentatonic poles *a* and *e*, especially the former. This 'waltz sixth' had several origins. In the double-tonic progression, it formed the fifth of the II chord. It also arose naturally from the harmonization of 4/V7 at the upper third. But perhaps the most important origin is a yodel-like figure on *a–g–e* common in the early waltz (Ex. 12.12). Though almost as primitive

Ex. 12.12. The *a–g–e* waltz figure

as the ur-waltz quoted above (Ex. 12.7), this evidently had a distinct origin, since its first chord is I rather than V7. It is also decidedly vocal—a close relative, in fact, of the children's chant, which it resembles in being closely linked to the pentatonic seventh. It is also, like the children's chant, inclined to repeat itself, often over changing harmonies, as in Exs. 12.13–15.

Ex. 12.13. Haydn, Symphony No. 88 in G (*c.*1788), Minuet, Trio, beginning (down a 5th)

---

[33] See the beginning of the trio. In addition, the 'Fifth Symphony' figure a little later (just before the double bar) occurs in no. 2 in the WoO 11 set. A coincidence?

Ex. 12.14. Beethoven, Bagatelle in A flat, Op. 33 No. 7 (1801–2), bars 9–20 (2nd half of main theme) (down a semitone)

Ex. 12.15. Hummel, *Deutsche* in C, Op. 39 No. 1 (*c.* 1810), Trio, bars 9–16 (2nd half) (down a minor 7th)

A further modal peculiarity, shared by the waltz with much other central and east European melody, is an emphasis on 5. Often this is strong enough to produce a bitonal tension between *C* and *G*. In Ex. 12.16, the key of the first four bars might almost be *G*—in other words, the harmonic progression might be I–IV–G7–I instead of V–I–II7/♯–V.

Ex. 12.16. Haydn, Symphony No. 77 in B flat (1782), Minuet, Trio, beginning (up a tone)

THE LATER WALTZ

Leider *nicht* von Johannes Brahms.   Johannes Brahms[34]

Growth by doubling

To sum up, then, the waltz of about 1800 was still an unpretentious country dance, with, it would seem, very little in its form, harmony, or even melodic line to interest the composer. Yet, thirty or forty years later, this unpromising infant had become in every respect—social, musical, and financial—a dazzling success, generating a host of subspecies and establishing itself, in the form of the 'waltz song', both in the drawing room and on the operatic stage. At the folk level, it continued to flourish in both vocal and instrumental forms. In the concert hall, waltzes, or at any rate waltz-like movements, appeared in the worthiest of compositions. Nevertheless, the most characteristic representative of the genre continued to be the Viennese waltz, and this remained to an astonishing degree a bigger, grander, vastly more sophisticated version of the Tyrolean ländler. The waltz suite had expanded enormously, acquiring an introduction that could swell almost to the size of an overture, a correspondingly weighty coda, and often, too, introductions to individual numbers. But if we strip away these accretions, we find the individual numbers essentially similar to those of the early waltz in all but one respect: they are twice as long. The basic, unrepeated waltz strain (in other words, the bit before the double bar-line) now takes up sixteen bars instead of eight.

This form of expansion was unique to the waltz. With most dance or song forms, the original framework is gradually stretched. This is what happened to the Renaissance chord rows, and, in a very different way, to the twelve-bar blues. But the waltz, being bound to symmetrical phrases of four, eight, or sixteen bars that were also restricted in metre and tempo, could not do this. Apart from stringing together yet more sub-movements, the only way to expand was by repeated doubling, like an organic cell. The germ of the 'ur-waltz' was probably a repeated two-bar phrase (Ex. 12.17(*a*)) not unlike the bagpipe tune quoted by Zacara in the early fifteenth century (see Ex. 6.6 on p. 77). These two-bar phrases would then be combined into four-bar phrases (Ex. 12.17(*b*)), which would in turn be combined into eight-bar phrases (Ex. 12.17(*c*)), and so on.

---

[34] 'Unfortunately *not* by Johannes Brahms.' When Strauss's daughter asked Brahms for his autograph, he wrote in her autograph book the opening bars of 'The Blue Danube' and these words.

Ex. 12.17. Development by doubling in the 'ur-waltz'

(*a*) two-bar stage

(*b*) four-bar stage

(*c*) eight-bar stage

Needless to say, this is a much simplified account; in real life, repetition would be mixed up with variation. Regardless of historical accuracy, however, it does demonstrate the cycle of repetition, variation, pairing, and consolidation by which the waltz developed. A further illustration, this time drawn from actual music, is provided by the next two examples. Whereas Haydn's melody (Ex. 12.18), with no more than a slight variation at the cadence, has only just emerged from the stage of bald repetition, the *volkstümliches Lied* (Ex. 12.19), probably starting from a similar

Ex. 12.18. Haydn, String Quartet in G minor, Op. 74 No. 3, 'The Horseman' (1793), 1st mvt., bars 55–62 (up a tone)

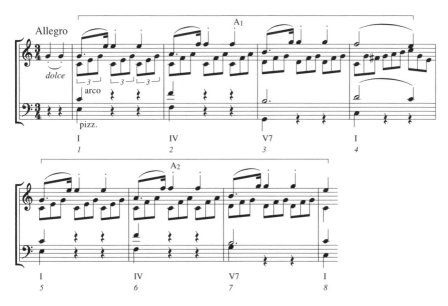

Ex. 12.19. 'Bei Sedan wohl auf den Höhen' (*volkstümliches Lied*, late 19th c.)

tune, has made so many changes to A₂ that one must look fairly hard to see any kinship to A₁ at all. These changes, however, affect only the Melody; the Bass, actual or implied, remains as before. And, while diverging in form, A₁ and A₂ have grown together into a new eight-bar strain, unified by the climax of bars 5–6 and the sonata-like (but purely melodic) correspondence of bars 3–4 and 7–8.

By the 1820s, eight-bar tunes like that of Ex. 12.19 (if not necessarily so harmonically simple) had become the norm. The great majority of Schubert's waltz tunes begin with repeated strains of this type, though sometimes he will write the repeat out in full in order to vary the harmony of the final cadence, usually with one of his marvellous modulations.[35] Meanwhile, this Schubertian type was beginning to appear in early waltz suites such as Lanner's 'Terpsichore-Walzer' (see Ex. 12.23 on p. 256), but with the difference that the sixteen-bar strain is itself repeated and balanced by a further sixteen bars after the double bar-line. A new cycle of doubling had begun.

Harmony

To keep up with this, harmonic progressions also doubled in length, but only after a long time-lag. From the point when the sixteen-bar strain became the Viennese norm, it took the 'split dominant' some thirty or forty years to expand from from I×2 V7×2 · V7×2 I×2 to I×6 V7×2 · V7×6 I×2, via an intervening phase in which the split chord was a subdominant or supertonic. An early example of the mature split-dominant pattern is the famous opening strain of 'The Blue Danube', composed in 1867 (Ex. 12.37 on pp. 267–8). Such patterns soon became extremely popular, and in the light music of the early twentieth century almost inescapable.

The V I · V I pattern of the ur-waltz lagged even further behind, for it was not till the early twentieth century that the sixteen-bar pattern of Ex. 12.20 became at all common. From this we must conclude that the expanses of tonic or dominant

---

[35] e.g. Op. 18 No. 2 and Op. 50 No. 32 both modulate to the diatonic mediant; Op. 9 No. 33 to the flat mediant; Op. 9 No. 14 to the flat submediant. Op. 50 No. 12 appears to be unique among Schubert's hundreds of waltzes in that the variation is of the ordinary 'antecedent–consequent' type, i.e. a half close answered by a full close.

Ex. 12.20. Lehár, *The Merry Widow* (1905), Waltz, 2nd strain, beginning (down a 5th)

harmony in turn-of-the-century waltzes, marches, and ragtime, far from being primitive, were the outcome of a long process of evolution in which more complex harmonies had been repeatedly rejected.

As always in music, simplicity bred complexity. In compensation for this harmonic plainness, composers developed new melodic and rhythmic patterns. One natural effect of these extremely prolonged, drone-like chords is that the melodic cadence assumed a new importance. More and more, we find cadence *within* stretches of unchanging tonic harmonic: 'one-chord cadences', as we may call them. There was also a particular problem at the end of the strain, where rhythmic activity normally continued till the last bar. This is satisfactory with chord rhythms such as these:

I×1 V×1   or   V×1 I×1
I×3 V×1   or   V×3 I×1
I×7 V×1   or   V×7 I×1

but not with these:

I×2 V×2   or   V×2 I×2
I×6 V×2   or   V×6 I×2

where the harmonic cadence arrives a bar too early for comfort. There were two ways of filling the resulting gap: to silence the upper part and transfer the melodic interest to a bass filler, as in Ex. 12.21, or to follow the harmonic cadence with a purely melodic one, as in Ex. 12.22.[36]

---

[36] This form of double cadence may be found as early as Schubert (e.g. the waltz in E flat, Op. 9 No. 13), but later became both more frequent and more elaborate.

Ex. 12.21. Johann Strauss, 'Roses from the South' (1880), no. 4, bars 29–38 (down a minor 3rd)

Ex. 12.22. Tchaikovsky, *Album for the Young* (1878), 'Chanson italienne', bars 17–32 (down a tone)

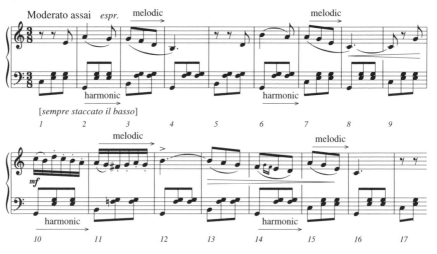

At the same time, the imposition of four-bar rhythms on six- or seven-bar chords gives rise, not only to a new kind of 'split dominant', but also to a 'split tonic':

$$I I I I \cdot I I V_7 V_7 : V_7 V_7 V_7 V_7 \cdot V_7 V_7 I I$$
$$I I I I \cdot I I I V_7 : V_7 V_7 V_7 V_7 \cdot V_7 V_7 V_7 I$$

All these developments are important not so much for the waltz itself as for turn-of-the-century American popular music. In marches and ragtime, the 'bass filler' became the 'bass run'; later, in jazz, it became the 'break'. In the blues, double cadences became a frequent feature, and split tonics and one-chord cadences quite fundamental.

The power behind all these developments was the harmonic simplicity that had always characterized the waltz. It is significant that many of the complexities of Schubert's waltzes are rejected by Strauss, at any rate in the actual numbers (introductions and codas are another matter). He uses the minor mode sparingly,[37] and plagal progressions hardly at all: a restraint all the more remarkable when we recall that, at just this time, 'serious' composers were becoming obsessed with abstruse harmonies. The total number of waltz tunes composed during the nineteenth century must run into many thousands. Strauss alone composed close on 200 waltz suites, each consisting of several numbers, which in turn are nearly always made up of two distinct strains. Yet the composers responsible for this enormous output not only used the same simple harmonic formulas over and over again, but simplified them even further.

Modulation

For all its simplicity, waltz harmony has plenty of scope for modulation, which comes in two types: *disjunct* modulation from number to number, which I had better reserve for the discussion of the waltz suite, and *conjunct* modulation within the individual strain. In this latter type, as in most nineteenth-century modulation, Melody predominates over Bass, or, to put it another way, Bass reinforces Melody. A modulation to the dominant, for example, will usually take the form $g/[C \ldots G]$. Given the great importance of the pentatonic poles a and e in waltz melody, we should therefore expect the corresponding keys to be especially favoured as harmonic destinations. And we do in fact find E minor (or, increasingly, major) steadily gaining on G major in this capacity, till by the end of the century they become about equally common.

As we noticed in Chapter 11,[38] this last type of modulation seems to have been a product of the Oriental fringe. Though it may occasionally be found in close relatives of the waltz before 1800,[39] it was not till the 1820s that it became common in the waltz itself. Ex. 12.23 is typical of this early period. In later examples the mediant harmony ranges from a single, unprepared chord (as in Ex. 12.24)[40] to passages of eight bars or more (as in Ex. 12.25).[41]

---

[37] For a rare exception, see 'Voices of Spring', Ex. 11.101 on p. 223, bars 14–21.

[38] See p. 200.

[39] Cf. the scherzo from Beethoven's String Quartet in D, Op. 18 No. 3 (Ex. 11.69 on p. 199).

[40] Sharp-eyed readers will have noticed that the e of bars 15–17 is not prepared by an earlier e, but introduced as the 'dominant' of a. Strauss does something similar in the 'Tritsch Tratsch Polka' (Ex. 13.72), except that there the progression, instead of being $a/Ge/E$, is $g/Cd/D$.

[41] This is also a fine example of a 'split tonic' (bars 1–8). Both ringed notes are for future reference, and have nothing to do with the present discussion.

Ex. 12.23. Lanner, 'Terpsichore-Walzer', Op. 12 (*c*.1825), no. 4, beginning (down a 5th)

Ex. 12.24. Johann Strauss, 'Wine, Woman, and Song' (1869), no. 3, beginning (down a 4th)

Ex. 12.25. Tchaikovsky, *Eugene Onegin* (1879), Act II, no. 13, Waltz, bars 43–66 (beginning of main theme) (down a tone)

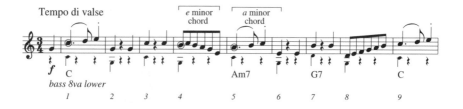

The incidence of other keys as harmonic destinations is proportionate to the pentatonic stability of their root notes, so that *A* minor is far from unknown (Ex. 12.26),[42] even *D* minor occasionally encountered,[43] and only the keys based on *f* and *b* (apparently) ruled out.

Ex. 12.26. Schubert, Waltz in B flat, Op. 33 No. 6 (1823–4), beginning (down a minor 7th)

chords sim.

Melody

In melody, as in harmony, the waltz remained true to its beginnings. Far from withering away, features prominent in the late eighteenth or early nineteenth century became ever more pronounced. I can do no more than list them briefly:

Sequences. Sequential steps expanded from one to four or even eight bars, all the while retaining their elastic, non-harmonic character.

The waltz sixth. The reiterated *a* that first appeared in the yodel-like *a–g–e* pattern (e.g. in Exs. 12.13–15 on pp. 248–9), grew into something not far from an inverted pedal (Exs. 12.27 and 12.28).

The independence of that repeated *a* in Ex. 12.28 is characteristic of the later waltz. Not only *a*, but *e*, *b* and sometimes other notes clash boldly with the underlying harmony. But of all these collisions, the most important was that of *a* against

---

[42] Cf. also Strauss's 'Artist's Life', no. 4, and 'Wo die Citronen blüh'n', no. 2.

[43] e.g. Schubert, Waltz in B major, Op. 67 No. 14.

Ex. 12.27. Schubert, Waltz in C, Op. 9 No. 31 (1821), bars 11–18

Ex. 12.28. Johann Strauss, jun., 'Emperor Waltz' (1889), no. 2, bars 31–46, after double bar-line (up a major 3rd)

C major, here seen in bars 4, 5, 8, and 12. This 'added sixth' is, of course, a harmonic version of the pentatonic seventh; and, just as its melodic equivalent is poised between consonance and dissonance, so is this harmonic seventh poised between concord and discord. In fact, by the time Strauss composed this passage, composers were beginning to think of it as virtually concordant. It would be straining orthodoxy to say that the *a*s of Ex. 12.28 actually resolve.[44]

Pentatonic patterns. Waltz melody, like nineteenth-century melody generally, became steadily more pentatonic; and not only in the sense of laying increasing emphasis on *a* and *e*, but also in the details of individual figures. The yodel-like *a*–*g*–*e* was the predecessor of similar patterns in other parts of the mode, which soon joined up to form extended pentatonic passages. In the sixteen-bar strain of Ex. 12.29, the only extra-pentatonic note is the *f* of bars 8–9.

---

[44] Cf. the subtle passage from 'Voices of Spring' (Ex. 11.101 on p. 223).

Ex. 12.29. Delibes, *Naila* (1866), 'Pas des fleurs', 1st strain, bars 3–20 (up a minor 3rd)

The triad e–g–b. This 'dominant chord' of the pentatonic scale, rare in Schubert's waltzes and far from frequent even in Chopin's, came into its own in the second half of the century. Often it carries a distinct suggestion of the Phrygian mode, as in Ex. 12.30. This is particularly true of waltzes from the Spanish-speaking world, whether of the salon or, *a fortiori*, folk type (Exs. 12.31 and 12.32).

Ex. 12.30. Johann Strauss, 'Artist's Life' (1867), no. 5, beginning (down a 4th)

Ex. 12.31. Rosas, 'Sobre las olas' ('Over the Waves', 1891), 1st strain (up a 4th)

Ex. 12.32. 'Heraclio Bernal' (Mexican ballad tune, 20th c.) (down a 4th)

The note g. By the later nineteenth century, this was receiving an emphasis that sometimes raised it almost to the status of a melodic tonic (Ex. 12.33).

Ex. 12.33. Johann Strauss, 'Accelerationen' (1860), no. 4 (down a 5th)

Scalar patterns. The waltz, true to its popular origins, has a great tendency to descend. And this, combined with the square-cut phrasing, repeated rhythms, and sequential contours that make waltz tunes so easy to follow, often produces descending scales of great elaboration. In Ex. 12.34, the scale is very obvious; later, it became subtler as well as longer, as composers developed a technique of coquettishly withholding the next step down (as we can see from the ringed notes in Exs. 12.25 and 12.30, on pp. 256–7 and 259).

Ex. 12.34. Schubert, Waltz in C, Op. 50 No. 26 (*c.* 1823), 2nd strain

In this manner, countless waltz tunes composed between about 1860 and 1910 fluttered languidly down to clinching final cadences. Often called 'serenades' in their final and most elaborate form,[45] they were a perfect counterpart to the soulfully reclining, diaphanously clad ladies that artists loved to depict during the same period.

Rhythm

As many of the tunes quoted above demonstrate, one of the commonest rhythmic features of the later waltz was the hemiola. Its origins, as usual, were complex. With rare exceptions like the main theme of Weber's 'Invitation to the Dance' (Ex. 12.35), it was not much heard before 1830. What we rather find is a tendency to accentuate the third beat of the bar, which gradually evolved into the hemiola proper during the next decade or two. The process may be followed in Chopin's waltzes, composed between 1827 and 1847. Here there is no *obvious* folk influence, but rather a spontaneous development springing from the form itself, and the same can be said of the Viennese waltz, which went through a similar process about the same time. It is interesting that Berlioz attributed the syncopations in the latter specifically to Johann Strauss, senior:

It is not sufficiently recognized what an influence he has already had on the musical taste of Europe as a whole by introducing cross-rhythms into the waltz. . . . If the public outside Germany is ever brought to appreciate the extraordinary charm that can on occasion result from combined and contrasted rhythms, it will be owing to him. Beethoven's marvels in this line are too exalted to have affected more than a small minority of listeners. Strauss, on the other hand, deliberately appeals to a popular audience; and by copying him, his numerous imitators are perforce helping to spread his influence.[46]

But in truth the decisive factor was probably the expansion of the form against the background of an unchanging bass rhythm. The 'double' hemiola[47] (3/2 against 3/4) provided a way of halving the tempo of the melody without slowing the underlying beat. In many later waltzes, the underlying 3/4 stands in much the same relation to the surface 3/2 as the tonic-and-dominant Bass does to the lushly chromatic Melody. In either case, the background is kept simple and mechanical as a foil to a rich and elegant foreground.

---

[45] e.g. those of Drigo, Toselli, and Braga.

[46] *Memoirs*, 463.

[47] So called to distinguish it from the 'half' hemiola (6/8 against 3/4). The latter played little part in the waltz, though examples may be found in Chopin (e.g. Op. 42 in A flat) and, later, in the jazz waltz.

THE WALTZ SUITE

The Strauss waltzes, it seems to me, have never been sufficiently studied. Consider, for example, the astonishing skill with which Johann manages his procession of keys—the inevitable air which he always gets into his choice.

H. L. Mencken[48]

The element of variation

All music is variation, in the sense of reconciling variety with sameness; only the proportions of the two elements differ. Even in the most primitive music, where sameness overwhelmingly predominates, there will be some variety; and conversely, even the most sophisticated music demands the stiffening of a little sameness.

The relevance of this general principle to the waltz is that there are no firm lines between suites and sets of variations. No one would describe the later Baroque suites as sets of variations, yet they possess many variation-like features. With rare exceptions, the dances are in the same key, follow the same binary pattern, and employ similar rhythmic, harmonic, and melodic procedures. And, as we trace these suites back to their origins, the similarity becomes ever more pronounced. Their early sixteenth-century predecessors are often closer to being sets of variations than many works so designated.[49] Conversely, as variations become more elaborate they begin to resemble suites, as may be seen for instance from Bach's 'Goldberg', Beethoven's 'Diabelli', or Brahms's 'Handel' sets, of the last of which Bernard Shaw remarked that these might 'just as well be called variations on the key of B flat'.[50]

In the waltz, primitive 'suites' like Beethoven's WoO 11 were effectively sets of variations, with a 'theme' consisting of a sixteen-bar tune in two repeated eight-bar sections of 3/4 time, harmonized in the simplest major-mode chords and ending with a V7–I cadence. And there was also, in the '*double*', a more obvious type of variation, where the harmony remains the same while rhythm and melody are varied. As the waltz suite became more genuinely suite-like, this type of variation remained an important resource. Composers seemed to regard it, consciously or unconsciously, as a way of unifying an increasingly elaborate and variegated form. In any case, it was hard to avoid, given the small choice of harmonic patterns—or perhaps the truth is rather that the harmony was kept simple to provide opportunities for variation.

Like all successful musical forms, the waltz suite was a hybrid. At the most fundamental level it derived from the medleys that popular musicians had been

---

[48] *A Mencken Chrestomathy*, 'Johann Strauss', 540. Originally published in *Five Little Excursions, Prejudices: Sixth Series* (1927).   [49] Cf. Dalza's *alla venetiana* suites (Ex. 6.18 on p. 84).
[50] 'A Sentimental Voluptuary'; reprinted in *Shaw's Music*, ii. 917. First published in *The World*, 21 June 1893.

performing for centuries (and, in many places, still do today). On this simple basis was imposed the eighteenth-century ballroom suite, and, later, more complex forms such as that of Weber's 'Invitation to the Dance', which is really a rondo with a superabundance of episodes. Though more complex and varied than any previous waltz suite, this is again unified by repeated harmonic progressions. Thus, three of its principal themes (Ex. 12.35(*a*), (*b*), and (*c*)) are based on the closely related patterns I×4 V7×4 and I×4 V7×3 I. But, in spite of this harmonic similarity, the rhythms could hardly be more different: brilliant and incisive in the

Ex. 12.35. Weber, 'Invitation to the Dance' (1819) (up a semitone)

(*a*) bars 35–42 (first strain of main theme)

(*b*) bars 43–58 (second strain of main theme)

(*c*) bars 95–126 (first strain of second episode)

first theme, elegant and flowing in the second, yet more flowing in the third. This difference in pace is reflected in the length of the strains, which respectively comprise eight, sixteen, and (anticipating the waltz of a half-century later) thirty-two bars.

Key schemes

Apart from sheer size, the great difference between the mature waltz suite and its primitive ancestors is that the 'numbers' are in contrasted keys. The prevailing mode, it is true, continues to be the major. With the notable exceptions of Schubert and Chopin, the greatest waltz composers seldom write entire strains in the minor, and in fact retain the Classical view of that mode as a kind of dissonance, to be resolved by a prompt return to the major. But within these restrictions key relationships are bold and varied, as can be seen from Beethoven's other two waltz suites, WoO 8 and 13, composed about 1795:[51]

Zwölf deutsche Tänze für Orchester, WoO 8:
C A F B♭ E♭ G C A F D G C, followed by a coda in *C*;

Zwölf deutsche Tänze für Orchester, WoO 13:
C A♭ F C E♭ A♭ C F D♭ B♭ G C, followed by a coda in *C*.

A careful examination of these key schemes reveals some basic principles. Firstly, the initial tonic returns at the end (and sometimes also in between, though this is not essential), thereby provided a model for those Romantic sonatas and symphonies where every movement is in a different key.[52]

Secondly, the keys generally descend by thirds or fifths, though they may also rise by the same intervals. Unlike Liszt or Wagner, Beethoven is careful to alternate major and minor thirds: we find *C–A–F* or *C–A♭–F*, but not *C–A–F♯* or *C–A♭–E*. In fact, *C–A(♭)–F* can be regarded as an elaboration on plain *C–F*. With a few exceptions, then, the underlying pattern is a series of falling fifths, with or without an intervening key.

This subdominant-ward drift was to become ever more prominent, not only in the waltz, but in nineteenth-century music generally. There were, to be sure, other possibilities. Like Beethoven, later waltz composers were fond of juxtaposing keys a third apart, and sometimes, as in Strauss's 'Artist's Life' and 'Wiener Blut', they were content simply to alternate tonic and subdominant. But the general rule is that they prefer the placidity of 'flat' keys to the brightness of 'sharp' ones.

To modulate to the subdominant is to reproduce, on a larger scale, the V–I progression of the ur-waltz. Both are falling, passive processes, unlike the dynamic

---

[51] In the WoO 8 set, the original key is C; in WoO 13, it is D.

[52] Cf. the key schemes of these two waltz suites with that of Beethoven's C sharp minor String Quartet, Op. 131: C♯m–D–A–E–G♯m–C♯m (or, transposed, Cm–D♭–A♭–E♭–Gm–Cm).

rise to the dominant characteristic of the Classical style. As Tovey put it, the sub-dominant 'is the key to which the home-tonic is dominant; and beginners in composition are apt, like some seventeenth-century pioneers of tonality, to upset their tonic by a top-heavy subdominant introduced too early in a short piece'.[53]

In fact, not only beginners in composition, but the greatest composers of the nineteenth century are inclined towards this sort of progression. As the summary in Table 12.2 shows, Chopin's 'Grande valse brillante' in E flat, Op. 18 (1831) is a study in falling harmony of every kind.

TABLE 12.2. *The modulations in Chopin's 'Grande valse brillante', Op. 18*

No. of sub-movement[a]	Bars	Key of theme	Initial progression
1	1–20	C	V7–I
2	21–36	F	I–IV♯ dim. 7–V7–I
Nos. 1 and 2 repeated	37–68	C, F	
3	69–116	B♭	V7–I
4	117–64	B♭	I7♭–IVV7–I
5	165–88	E♭	I–IV6/5–V7–I
Nos. 1 and 2 recapitulated, then coda	189–end	C, F, C	

[a] The numbers are my own. Unlike the German-speaking composers, Chopin did not number the sub-movements of his waltzes.

We have only to run our eyes down the third column to see the subdominant-ward drift. Moving to the fourth column, we immediately observe how nos. 1 and 3 begin with V7–I, and No. 4 with I7♭–IV. This last progression contains a subtle ambiguity, similar to that already noticed in a much earlier waltz tune by Haydn (Ex. 12.16 on p. 249). At first it sounds like V7–I, which would imply yet another modulation to the subdominant. Only later do we grasp that it is actually I7♭–IV, and that the key is the same as before (Ex. 12.36).

This 'Grande valse brillante' is, however, far from being an extreme instance of subdominant drift. Strauss's 'Morgenblätter' takes us two steps further. Since each number has a middle section in its own dominant[54] the overall scheme is that

---

[53] *Essays in Musical Analysis*, i, 'Introduction', 6.
[54] The middle section of no. 4 is a slight exception, since it modulates to the dominant only after beginning in the tonic.

Ex. 12.36. Chopin, 'Grande valse brillante' in E flat, Op. 18 (1831), bars 117–32 (down a semitone)

of an undulating descent. Figure 12.1 shows the beginning of this pattern, which continues until D♭ is reached in No. 5, after which a coda gradually works its way back to the home key.

	Intro. 1			2	3
	C	*C*			
		F	*F*	*F*	
			B♭	B♭	B♭
				E♭	E♭

Fɪɢ. 12.1. The modulations in Strauss's 'Morgenblätter'

The subtleties of 'The Blue Danube'

To show something of the subtlety to which the waltz suite can rise, a large-scale example is necessary. For this, we need go no further than the most hackneyed waltz of them all: Johann Strauss's 'Blue Danube'. I quote the first three of its five 'numbers' (Ex. 12.37).

Like all waltz suites, it is essentially a medley, differing from other medleys only in that the 'numbers' are newly composed instead of borrowed.[55] It is, in fact, the highest point attained by that humble form. And, as in any medley, the great difficulty is to produce a unified and purposeful whole, rather than a random string of unconnected fragments; to which must be added, in the specific case of the waltz, the opposite difficulty of drawing variety out of a very limited set of basic patterns.

---

[55] Even this is not always true. Many waltz suites, e.g. Strauss's 'Fledermaus', have been compiled from operetta tunes.

Ex. 12.37. Johann Strauss, 'The Blue Danube' (1867), nos. 1–3 (down a tone)

(*continued on next page*)

(Ex. 12.37 *cont.*)

To take the second of these problems first, Strauss does not, as a rule, attempt to sophisticate the basic patterns, though he is perfectly capable of doing so when necessary. No composer knew better when to break the eight-bar rhythm, to obscure the tonality, to introduce a lush chromatic chord or an unexpected modulation. But, on the whole, it is in the handling of the most commonplace patterns that he shows his mastery. Instead of disguising them, he makes them as clear and obvious as possible, the better to set them off against one another.

This is most evident at the basic level of rhythm. The whole of this extract consists of sixteen-bar strains symmetrically divided into twos, fours, and eights. To bring out the extreme squareness of the underlying rhythm, I have, uniquely in this book, numbered the bars in each strain individually, beginning with the first accented bar, and also slightly thickened the barlines between the four-bar periods. These notational aids bring out the cunningly varied way in which the melodic periods transcend the four-bar compartments. One obvious recourse is the hemiola, which accounts for a good quarter of 'The Blue Danube' as a whole. This comes in several types, sometimes starting on 'odd', and sometimes on 'even' bars (compare 3A, bars 1–2, 5–6, and 9–10, with 3B, bars 2–3, 6–7, and 10–11). Another useful device is that of beginning the tune before the four-bar period, by anything between a single beat and more than a bar. The famous opening theme is a particularly subtle instance, because here the listener is left in some doubt as to where the main accent falls: is it on bar 1 or bar 0? And it is clear, from the way Strauss leads up to this passage, that the momentary rhythmic disorientation is quite deliberate.[56]

The celebrated opening tune is also remarkably repetitive. The same four-bar rhythm recurs six or (if one counts bars 24–5) six and a half times. Schoenberg even had the colossal cheek to point this out as a blemish, which is like regarding Wagner as a boring harmonist on the strength of the *Rheingold* Prelude.[57] In fact, the whole purpose of these repetitions, together with the unrelieved tonic-and-dominant harmony and the rhythmic uncertainty, is to give this passage a preludial character. As a result, the climax at the end (bars 25–32) brings with it a glorious sense of expansion, which carries on into the next strain.[58]

Like all great composers of popular music, Strauss was an expert at turning banalities into subtleties. As we have seen, repeated rhythms are very characteristic of the waltz; so, instead of playing them down, he makes them a special feature. In the same way, he retains the simple tonic-and-dominant formulas, but, like Beethoven in the WoO11 set, varies them from strain to strain, never allowing the four-bar harmonic rhythm to become monotonous, but relieving it from time to time with the older two- or one-bar type (as in 2B and 3B respectively).

It was no doubt the same need to make every pattern as clear as possible to even the most musically obtuse listener that led the waltz composers to hammer on certain degrees of the mode, notably *3* and *6*. This, too, Strauss turns to advantage, by binding the affected notes together into large-scale patterns that cut across the individual numbers (Ex. 12.38). These pentatonic networks are perhaps the subtlest feature of the waltz suite, and it is largely to them that his modulations owe their 'inevitable air'.

Ex. 12.38. Johann Strauss, 'The Blue Danube', melodic emphasis in the first three numbers

[56] The previous introductory section (marked 'Tempo di Valse'), cleverly blurs the boundaries of the four-bar periods. It also ends with an unmeasured silence. One could argue that the question of bar-accent is really only settled in bar 25.

[57] See 'Brahms the Progressive' (in *Style and Idea*, 398–441), 399–400. To do him justice, Schoenberg does describe 'The Blue Danube' as 'otherwise very beautiful'.

[58] This is probably why, following Strauss's own instruction for a vocal arrangement, conductors usually cut the da capo of the first strain (1A). I have done the same in my transcription.

Finally, there is the problem of the waltz cadence, which so readily falls into a few stereotyped forms. Instead of fighting this tendency, Strauss exaggerates it to the point where the cadences recognizably become variations on the same theme, as shown Ex. 12.39. (For further comparison, I include the cadences from the unquoted strain 4B and the introduction to 5A.)[59]

Ex. 12.39. Johann Strauss, 'The Blue Danube', related cadence figures

(*a*) end of no. 1A　　(*b*) end of no. 1B　　(*c*) end of no. 2A　　(*d*) end of no. 4

(*e*) end of introduction to no. 5
　　bars 7–8

And there we must leave 'The Blue Danube', and the waltz generally. It would be easy to go on. It is a great temptation, for instance, to examine Strauss's construction of linking passages, introductions, and codas. But this would be to pass from the pecularities of the waltz to the generalities of nineteenth-century light music. And then comes the question: how far are these generalities confined to light music? What did Strauss have in common with his friend and admirer Brahms? Or with Wagner, another admirer? Or with his almost precise contemporary Bruckner? It is questions such as these that the next chapter will attempt to answer.

[59] Notice the monotertial relationship between the keys of these last two cadences.

13 The Nineteenth-Century Vernacular

> The history of the Victorian Age will never be written: we know too much about it.
>
> Lytton Strachey, *Eminent Victorians*

THE CONTINUING ITALIAN ASCENDANCY

To a musicologist from another planet, gifted with boundless analytical insight but free from earthly prejudice, it would be obvious that Italy was the principal power in nineteenth-century European music. This judgement of course contradicts terrestrial opinion, which awards Germany that honour. Certainly, there is no denying either the great achievements of German composers during this period, or their immense prestige. But prestige is one thing, influence quite another. The German idiom was slow to penetrate beyond the traditional outposts of Teutonic culture in eastern Europe, Scandinavia, the Netherlands, Britain, and the United States. And even within the German-speaking world it faced stiff opposition:

A modern German history of music gives a list of some six hundred German operas produced between about 1830 and 1900; hardly a single one has remained in the ordinary German repertory, apart from a few comic operas and musical comedies of the 1840s which are still popular in their own country, though little known outside. Through the whole of Wagner's lifetime the German theatres were dependent mainly on French and Italian operas, just as they were in the days of Mozart, and indeed right up to 1900 and later certain old French comic operas survived in Germany, which had long been shelved in France.[1]

Moreover, an Italianate strain runs through nineteenth-century German music even at the highest and most self-consciously Teutonic level. Without it, one cannot begin to understand Beethoven, Schubert, Weber, Mendelssohn, Richard Strauss, or for that matter Wagner. With characteristic acuteness, Stravinsky remarks on 'those Italianate melodic figures that curl through his scores from *Das Liebesverbot* to *Parsifal* (and on to *Verklärte Nacht*) without being entirely digested,

---

[1] Dent, *Opera*, 81.

which is to say Germanized'.[2] If this debt was insufficiently acknowledged, it may be because it was too great for comfort. The right-thinking German musician's attitude to Italian opera resembled that of an earnest young aesthete to his rich, lovable, but hopelessly vulgar father.

A popular art

At the popular level there was no such equivocation—and it is important to grasp that Italian opera was emphatically a popular art. At least till about 1860, its traditions remained essentially those of the eighteenth century, its culture insular and conservative. A composr was a skilled craftsman; originality was not greatly prized; the public knew what it liked. And idealism, in so far as it counted at all, reinforced those populist tendencies. The prevailing view, inherited from eighteenth-century Classicism and reinforced by the nationalistic fervour of the Risorgimento, was that great art ought to be accessible to everyone.[3]

For all these reasons, Italian opera was wide open to popular influences. Eighteenth-century *opera buffa* had been an entertainment comparable with twentieth-century musical comedy and quite distinct from the much grander *opera seria*,[4] but gradually the distinction blurred. While *opera buffa* became serious and sentimental, *opera seria* took on a *buffo* vitality, first in Mozart and then in Rossini:

until Rossini the movement of the heroic opera remained somewhat formal and ponderous. It was he who gave elegance and sparkle, as appropriate, to its lyrical style, and who, especially, filled every fibre of the music with a new kind of pulsing vitality, driving along arias and ensembles alike with a texture of dancing or marching orchestral figures, and giving the whole an orchestral colouring so bright and sharply profiled as to be almost garish.[5]

Nor did this tendency stop with Rossini. Though *opera buffa* expired in 1843 with Donizetti's *Don Pasquale*, most of its forms and some of its manner lived on in the hybrid masterpieces of Bellini, Donizetti, and Verdi.

There was also direct folk influence. 'The folk or popular idiom', as Budden points out, 'underlies all that is most deeply felt in Rossini's music',[6] and much the same could be said of his successors. In Italy, the popular idiom was absorbed by a smooth, artless, unreflecting process of cultural osmosis, quite different from the self-conscious folkiness prevalent elsewhere. In spite of the nationalistic ferment of the time, urban professional musicians almost entirely ignored the traditional,

---

[2] *Themes and Conclusions*, 'Wagner's Prose', 246. The original has '*Liebesverbot*' and '*Verklärte*'.

[3] See David Kimbell, *Verdi in the Age of Italian Romanticism*, 15–16.

[4] In Italy, the two genres were produced in different opera houses with separate companies of singers. Outside Italy, a single house and company generally had to suffice for both. This promoted their blending, e.g. in Mozart. See Budden, *The Operas of Verdi*, i. 6–7.

[5] Kimbell, *Verdi in the Age of Italian Romanticism*, 71   [6] Budden, *The Operas of Verdi*, 11.

often extremely archaic music of the Italian countryside,[7] probably because they already possessed a satisfactory national idiom in opera. Elsewhere—in eastern Europe, in Spain, even in the Austria of Haydn, Mozart, and Beethoven—folk music was an escape from the pervasive Italian style. For this the Italians themselves had no need.

Nevertheless, it was only by the continual absorption of popular influences that Italian opera could remain a truly national art. As in the eighteenth century, the main channel for this was the rustic or lower-class character, singing in an idiom subtly different from that of the gentlefolk. Among its characteristics were modal inflections, pentatonic figures, cross-rhythms (especially the hemiola), and repetitive dance basses.[8] As they became familiar, all these features gradually lost their plebeian associations.

The popular features were not always native. Italian composers were anything but puristic (one of their eighteenth-century virtues), and happily drew on foreign genres. It was largely a craving for variety that led them to embrace new dances like the waltz, polka, polonaise, bolero, habanera, or tango, and to cling to old ones like the jig or minuet; and the same motive accounts for much of the picturesque colour of nineteenth-century opera. Peasants and gypsies were not only amusing in themselves; they also presented the composer with an opportunity for jigging rhythms and hemiolas. In the same way, military scenes provided an excuse for marches, church scenes for hymns and chants, old-world ballroom scenes for minuets and gavottes.

Of all these novelties, undoubtedly the most important was the waltz. It is in the opera house that its rise to respectability and international popularity can most easily be traced. In the ballroom scene from *Don Giovanni* (1787), the *deutsche Tanz* represents the Austrian lower classes, in contrast to the middle-class *contredanse* and aristocratic minuet. By the time of Weber's *Freischütz* (1821), it had come to stand for rustic innocence. In Rossini's *Il viaggio a Reims* (1825), though by now well on its way to becoming international property, it served as the musical symbol of Austria. Soon the French, with Chopin and Berlioz in the lead, began to exploit its capacity for glittering elegance, and by the 1830s the Parisian *valse* was a well established subspecies. Not long afterwards it was threatening to become more popular than the Viennese original. In Italy it merged with native popular traditions, as for instance in the demon's chorus from Verdi's *Giovanna d'Arco* (1845), described by his friend and pupil Emanuele Muzio as 'a pretty waltz, full of seductive themes; you can sing it straight away after two hearings . . .

---

[7] See John Rosselli, *Music and Musicians in Nineteenth-Century Italy*, ch. 2, 'The Roots of Musical Life', esp. 23–9.

[8] For an example from a somewhat later period, see Ex. 11.59 (p. 191) from Rossini's *La Cenerentola*, where the humble character is Cinderella.

original, popular, purely Italian'. But, as Budden adds, 'That of course is its fault. It has an innocent vulgarity which reeks of the Neapolitan café.'[9]

It was in *La traviata* (1853) that the operatic waltz reached its apogee, partly because this is a domestic, bourgeois, modern opera, but also because it is set in Paris. Together with *Rigoletto* and *Il trovatore*, it also represents the highest point of international popularity attained by Italian opera. As Verdi himself remarked, 'In the heart of Africa or the Indies you will always hear *Il trovatore*.'[10] But after that high point his populist impulses began to conflict with an increasingly refined technique. Parts of *Un ballo in maschera* (1859) recall Offenbach, but that was his last allusion to current popular music.

In 1901, soon after Verdi's death, Bernard Shaw wrote an obituary largely devoted to attacking the fashionable notion that his last works had been influenced by Wagner:

The real secret of the change from the roughness of Il Trovatore to the elaboration of the three last operas is the inevitable natural drying up of Verdi's spontaneity and fertility. So long as an opera composer can pour forth melodies like *La donna è mobile* and *Il balen*, he does not stop to excogitate harmonic elegancies and orchestral sonorities which are neither helpful to him dramatically nor demanded by the taste of his audience. But when in process of time the well begins to dry up; when instead of getting splashed with the bubbling over of *Ah sì, ben mio*, he has to let down a bucket to drag up *Celeste Aïda*, then it is time to be clever, to be nice, to be distinguished, to be impressive, to study instrumental confectionery, to bring thought and knowledge and seriousness to the rescue of failing vitality.[11]

As usual, Shaw sacrifices pedantic accuracy to rhetorical effect. Harmonic elegancies and instrumental confectionery already exist in early Verdi, and there is no lack of spontaneous tunefulness in the 'Grand March' from *Aida*. But, at bottom, what he says is true, not just of Verdi but of Italian opera in general. Indeed, Shaw's last sentence might be an epitaph for the entire Romantic movement, which excogitated harmonic elegancies and instrumental confectioneries such as the world had never seen.

Waltz, operetta, and the folk mania

While Italian opera was becoming pretentious and respectable, its popular tendencies were carried forward in operetta, which effectively dates from Offenbach's *Orphée aux enfers* (1858). The new genre revitalized the *opéra comique* with a leaven

---

[9]   *The Operas of Verdi*, i. 212.

[10]   From a letter to his friend Count Arrivabene, written in 1862. Quoted in Budden, *Verdi*, 225.

[11]   'A Word More about Verdi', 572. Reprinted in *Shaw's Music*, iii. 570–83. First published in *The Anglo-Saxon Review*, March 1901.

from central Europe, and it is significant that its two greatest masters, Offenbach and Strauss, both came from the German-speaking world. As the following dates make clear, the golden age of operetta coincided with that of the waltz:

Offenbach operettas:
Orphée aux enfers, 1858
La Belle Hélène, 1864
La Vie parisienne, 1866
La Grande-Duchesse de Gérolstein, 1867
La Périchole, 1868

Strauss waltzes:
'Accelerationen', 1860
'The Blue Danube' and 'Artist's Life', 1867
'Tales from the Vienna Woods', 1868
'Wine, Woman and Song', 1869
'Wiener Blut', 1873

And, though only a small selection, this list also gives some idea of the light-music explosion of the 1860s. After 1870 the pace slackens, though it is worth noticing that *Die Fledermaus* dates from 1874, and *Trial by Jury*, the first of the Gilbert and Sullivan operettas, from 1875.

For the origins of this explosive growth we must go back a generation, to the folk-music craze of the 1840s. This had been a pan-European, indeed a pan-Western phenomenon. At one end of Europe, it was the decade of Glinka's *Ruslan and Lyudmila*, most of Liszt's *Hungarian Rhapsodies*, Chopin's last mazurkas and polonaises, and Berlioz's discovery of the 'Rákóczi' March.[12] At the other, it saw a resurgent interest in traditional Spanish music on the part of both natives and foreigners. While the *zarzuela* was returning to favour after being ousted for a time by Italian opera, Glinka was writing his two Spanish overtures, Wallace the Gypsy opera *Maritana*, and Mérimée the novella *Carmen*.

It was also in the 1840s that Félicien David's *Le Désert* (the fruit of several years' stay in Egypt during the early 1830s) inaugurated a long love affair between French composers and the Near East, and that the national dance of Bohemia attained international fame: 'The polka was introduced to Prague in 1837 . . . In 1839 the band of a Bohemian regiment took the polka to Vienna, and that year it also reached St Petersburg. The Prague dancing-master Johann Raab introduced it to Paris in 1840, though it was not until 1843–4 that it became the favourite dance of Parisian society.'[13] Soon afterwards it was to become a craze rivalling the waltz sensation of thirty years earlier.

---

[12] 'The famous orchestral version [of the Rákóczi March] by Berlioz came to life at the time of the composer's stay in Pest, between 9th and 12th February 1846' (Sárosi, *Gypsy Music*, 109).

[13] Gracian Černušák, Andrew Lamb, and John Tyrrell, 'Polka', in *New Grove II*, xx. 36.

Nor was the folk mania restricted to Europe. This was the time when middle-class Europeans got their first taste of Afro-American music:

The classic age of blackface minstrelsy (*c*1840–70) drew appreciably closer by the late 1830s when a modicum of dramatic continuity was introduced and as performers joined together to form duos (most frequently a banjoist and a dancer), trios and finally quartets. . . . The Virginia Minstrels . . . presented the first show of this new type, performing initially with a circus at the Bowery Amphitheatre in New York on 6 February 1843 . . . The Virginia Minstrels met with spectacular success in cities of the eastern USA in the spring of 1843 and in concerts during a brief tour of the British Isles that summer.[14]

Opera, as ever responsive to public taste, was inevitably affected. 'Gypsy' operas were a particular favourite. Seventy-seven of these have been counted between Leo's *Le fente zingare* (1724) and Schmidt's *Notre Dame* (1914),[15] but this is only a selection, and excludes operettas like Strauss's *Zigeunerbaron* or Lehár's *Zigeunerliebe*. The Gypsy element is, admittedly, secondary in many of these operas (for instance Verdi's *Un ballo in maschera* or Smetana's *The Bartered Bride*); but often it is important enough to be advertised in the title, as in *Die Zigeuner*, *La zingarella*, *Les Bohémiens*, *The Bohemian Girl*, and so on. The totals by decade for dated operas (some are undated) are:

1800–1809	0
1810–1819	3
1820–1829	3
1830–1839	10
1840–1849	15
1850–1859	9
1860–1869	12
1870–1879	4
1880–1889	1
1890–1899	2

From this it can be seen that interest in Gypsy operas built up till the 1840s (1844–5 accounted for no fewer than six), fell off somewhat in the 1850s, rallied again in the 1860s, and then declined till the end of the century. Bizet's *Carmen* (1875) was produced at a time when the genre was already on the wane.

To the musicologist from Mars (or for that matter India, Africa, or Japan) the most impressive thing about all these various folk genres would have been less their differences than their similarity. The same features—drones, ostinatos,

---

[14] Clayton W. Henderson, 'Minstrelsy, American', in *New Grove II*, xvi. 737–8.

[15] See Rudolph Angermüller, 'Zigeuner und Zigeunerisches in der Oper des 19. Jahrhunderts', app., pp. 157–9.

pentatonic figures, Phrygian cadences, and so forth—keep on turning up, not only in overtly 'ethnic' music, but also in straightforward Italian operas or Viennese ballroom dances. After all, this is no more than what one should expect from a Europe where communications were better than ever before. Nationalistic enthusiasms notwithstanding, everyday life was becoming ever more cosmopolitan, and it would be surprising if an international musical vernacular had not developed.

Indeed, it might be argued that the real opposition was between this lingua franca and the German tradition of 'serious music'. Composers like Wagner or Brahms were both attracted and repelled by the vernacular. Even when writing waltzes or Hungarian dances, the last thing they wanted was to be mistaken for genuinely popular composers. In their hands, the vernacular idiom was distorted, refined, disguised—but still there. If it had not been, they could hardly have enjoyed the popular success they did.

To sum up, then, the urban middle- and upper-class music of nineteenth-century Europe spoke a variety of mutually intelligible dialects, which, like all dialects, were in a state of flux, constantly changing and constantly influencing one another. A respected group of mostly German composers developed their own distinctively Teutonic variant, but even so the basis of this dialectal family remained Italian.

MELODY

Plain and fancy music

Linguists distinguish between the different 'registers' of a single language. It would, for instance, be unreasonable to expect a memorial service in Westminster Abbey to sound exactly like the conversation in a lorry drivers' café. And in music, too, essentially the same language will take on different registers in the church, the opera house, the concert hall, and the ballroom. That much is obvious enough. What is less obvious is that contrasts of register may occur *within* movements. Ever since the mid-eighteenth century, a feature of Western 'art' music has been the systematic opposition of two such 'registers', distinguished not so much by such basic properties as mode, tempo, or metre, as by general tunefulness. In Italian opera, they were known as 'half music' and 'full music'. Half music was recitative, or at least recitative-like passages. It was rambling, weakly patterned, and asymmetrical—essentially connective tissue. Full music was aria, ensemble, or chorus. It was clear, repetitive, and symmetrical—what we whistle after the show.

Unfortunately, this neat distinction will not do for nineteenth-century music as a whole, because to many composers, especially among the Germans, 'full music' was regarded as not so much full as banal. I therefore propose the words 'plain' for 'full' or strongly patterned, and 'fancy' for weakly patterned. The higher the pretensions of the music, the greater was the preponderance of fancy over plain, though even the most pretentious works have their plain passages. And, conversely, even the lightest genres their fancy ones. The waltz is a case in point. No sooner had it become fashionable in smart society than it acquired introductions, codas, and linking passages, often of symphonic complexity. From Strauss to Bruckner, no composition was felt to be too trivial for a little stiffening, or too serious for a little relief. Within individual works, the tendency was from fancy to plain. Thus, a typical symphony will begin with the fanciness of the slow introduction and wind down to the plainness of the rondo finale. Similarly, the operatic scena proceeds from recitative to aria to cabaletta.

The relevance of this to the nineteenth-century vernacular is that vernacular features most clearly stand out in relatively 'plain' passages, from relatively popular music, of a relatively late date. This, however, is a matter of degree rather than of kind. Probably the most fundamental vernacular feature of all, the independence of Melody, occurs in the most august of compositions.

And, as Melody became more independent, so it became more pentatonic. Any study of vernacular Melody must be at bottom a study in pentatonic patterns: how they were defined, expanded, elaborated, distorted, and, not least, contrapuntally opposed to the Bass.

Diatonic patterns

A multitude of sources, ranging from Gregorian chant to banjo picking, has been found for the pentatonic figures that become more and more frequent in the course of the nineteenth century. But, whatever their precise nature, the assumption has usually been that the source explained the figures. The reverse is nearer the truth. When, towards the end of the eighteenth century, such patterns first began to make regular appearances in music of the Classical school, there was nothing exotic about them. It was not until the folk boom of the 1830s and 1840s that the pentatonic scale acquired overtly picturesque associations, and not until the 1860s that Carl Engel invented the word 'pentatonic' itself.

Early pentatonic figuration was spontaneous to the point of being unconscious, crystallizing out, so to speak, between the pentatonic poles a and e. The first figure to appear was the smallest, the 'knight's move' a–g–e between a and e; as we have seen, it was a feature of the early waltz. Next came the fifth between a^- and e, and finally the whole octave between a^- and a or e and e^+.

Particularly important among these pentatonic figures is the gracefully curving e–a^-–c–e (with or without passing notes to fill in the thirds), which, from the mid-nineteenth to the early twentieth century, wanders like a leitmotif through the most diverse of contexts. It may even have been one of those Italianate melodic figures that Stravinsky described as 'curling' through Wagner's scores from *Das Liebesverbot* on.[16] There is certainly no denying that one of its earlier and more memorable appearances is as the 'Swan Motif' from *Lohengrin* (Ex. 13.1).

Ex. 13.1. Wagner, *Lohengrin* (1846–8), Act II, Prelude, bars 18–21, the 'Swan Motif' (up a minor 3rd)

A few years later, it crops up again, in a form too close for coincidence, in one of Liszt's 'Consolations' (Ex. 13.2).[17] But the treatment is already much more complex. Where Wagner's Melody is confined to a perfect fifth, Liszt's rises to fill the

Ex. 13.2. Liszt, 'Consolation' No. 3 in D flat (1849–50), bars 3–11 (up a semitone)

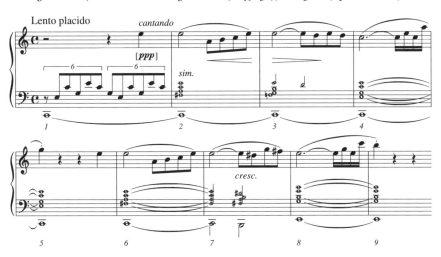

[16] See Deryck Cooke, 'The Musical Symbolism of Wagner's Music-Dramas' (in *Vindications*, 25–36), 30–5, for a penetrating commentary on Wagner's use of this figure, illustrated by quotations from *Tannhäuser* to *Parsifal*. The last of these, from the *Parsifal* Prelude, corresponds to my Ex. 14.13 (p. 370). Cooke argues that, to Wagner, this figure expresses 'man's attachment to false ideals, which erect a barrier between himself and his true ideal' (p. 35).

[17] If Liszt *was* plagiarizing Wagner, wittingly or unwittingly, he was not the only one: cf. the 'Swan motif' from Tchaikovsky's *Swan Lake*. Perhaps this gracefully curving figure should be called the 'Swan Pattern'.

octave, and where Wagner has a single chordal layer, Liszt has three: the *a* minor chord of the Melody, the pedal *c*, and the internal progression *C–D9/♯–G7–C*. He also modulates to the key of *E*, the harmonic dominant of the melodic *a* minor.

In the trio from Sibelius's Second Symphony (Ex. 13.3), composed more than fifty years later, we see the same pattern in yet another guise. Relative to the august environment, Sibelius wishes to strike a popular note, for a trio is after all a traditional point of bucolic repose. But he has no desire to evoke the salon music of the mid-nineteenth century, much less the light music of his own time. He therefore reduces both Melody and harmony to a peasant-like simplicity, while retaining such typical vernacular features as the *e–a⁻–c–e* pattern and its octave-filling extension (though this time down to *e* rather than up to *a⁻*).[18] There is even, in the last, ambiguous chord of this extract, a faint suggestion of Liszt's modulation to *E*.

Ex. 13.3. Sibelius, Symphony No. 2 in D (1902), 3rd mvt., from rehearsal letter E (beginning of Trio) (up an augmented 4th)

By the addition or subtraction of a note or two, the basic *e–a⁻–c–e* formula could be made to yield several further, almost equally fecund patterns. It could, for instance, take in the whole pentatonic seventh by extending backwards to *g–e–a⁻–c–e* or *a–g–e–a⁻–c–e*. The former is the pattern of the 'Valhalla' theme from *Das Rheingold* (Ex. 13.4), and (again fifty years later) of 'La fille aux cheveux de lin' (Ex. 13.5); the latter, of the Forest Bird's song from *Siegfried* (Ex. 13.6).

In their variety and similarity, these passages give some idea of the importance to nineteenth-century melody of the pentatonic seventh. It became, to an ever greater extent, the 'key' in which whole movements were written. As an example,

---

[18] Cf. the similar extension in Exs. 10.2 and 10.3, from Gluck and Mozart (p. 137).

Ex. 13.4. Wagner, *Das Rheingold* (1853–4), Scene ii, beginning (the 'Valhalla' theme) (down a semitone)

Ruhiges Zeitmaaß [Placid tempo]

Ex. 13.5. Debussy, 'La Fille aux cheveux de lin' (1910), beginning (down a diminished 5th)

Très calme et doucement expressif

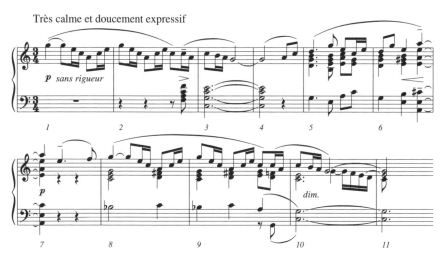

Ex. 13.6. Wagner, *Siegfried* (1856–7), Act II, Scene ii, 'The Song of the Forest Bird', beginning of voice part (up a minor 3rd)

Sehr mäßig [Very moderate]

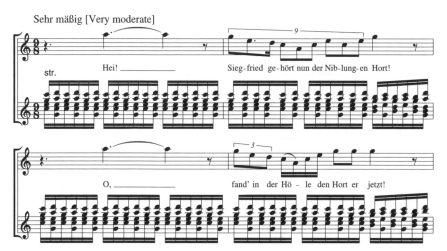

consider Chopin's Study in A minor, Op. 25 No. 11. It begins, like so many Romantic movements, with an unaccompanied melody, in this case a version of the *e–a⁻–c–e* pattern with the *a⁻* omitted (Ex. 13.7). Hearing it, we do not know what the harmonic key will be. It may equally well be *C* major or *A* minor, and in fact Chopin goes on to harmonize this figure first in one of these keys and then in the other. We cannot even be sure which key will conclude the movement (in the event, *A* minor). But we already have a good idea of the *melodic* key.[19]

Ex. 13.7.   Chopin, Study in A minor, Op. 25 No. 11 (1834), beginning

Like its harmonic equivalent, the melodic key is a hierarchic system of great potential complexity. It, too, can flower into chromatic elaborations, or even 'modulations'. Chopin's well-known Nocturne in E flat, Op. 9 No. 2, essentially a set of variations, brings this out very clearly. In Ex. 13.8, I quote three versions of the same tune: (*a*) the 'theme', (*b*) a florid variation, and (*c*) my own simplification of the latter, with chromatic notes omitted. By comparing (*a*) first with (*c*) and then

Ex. 13.8.   Chopin, Nocturne in E flat, Op. 9 No. 2 (1830–1) (down a minor 3rd)

(*a*) beginning

[19] Cf. Liszt's 'Czárdás Obstiné' (Ex. 11.76 on pp. 204–5), in which an initial unaccompanied figure is likewise successively harmonized in relative keys. Only the order differs: in Chopin, *C* major–*A* minor; in Liszt, *A* minor–*C* major.

(*b*) bars 13–16

(*c*) melodic outline of (*b*)

with (*b*), we can see how the note e^+ of bar 1, beginning as a merely detail of the *a* minor chord, goes on to sprout its own *e* minor chord, which is further complicated by chromatic embellishments.

As in much nineteenth-century melody, the notes outside these pentatonic frameworks are at least as interesting as those within it. The more composers came to think in pentatonic terms, the more expressive became their treatment of the extra-pentatonic notes *b* and *f*. Often the effect of these dissonant notes is enhanced by directly juxtaposing them, as in bar 6 of Ex. 13.9,[20] or—a great Romantic formula, not to say cliché—connecting them by a descending scale (Exs. 13.10 and 13.11).

Ex. 13.9. Rossini, *La cambiale di matrimonio* (1810), Scene iii, Duet, 'Tornami a dir che m'ami', beginning (down a major 6th)

A further point to notice about Ex. 13.9 is the fivefold repetition of the bracketed figure *a–g*, always at the apex of the phrase. We have already seen something of the kind in the waltz (compare, for instance, Ex. 12.27 on p. 258), but Rossini's treatment is completely individual. He handles this little figure with a fluidity deriving, through Italian folk music, from the maqām-like processes of the Near East. Everything, apart from the bare melodic contour, is constantly changing: the

---

[20] The significance of the bracketed notes will become apparent in due course.

Ex. 13.10. Mahler, Third Symphony (1895–6), last mvt., bars 9–12 (down a tone)

Ex. 13.11. Elgar, 'Cockaigne' Overture (1901), from rehearsal no. 5 (beginning of 2nd subject) (down a minor 3rd)

harmony, the rhythmic context, the rhythm of the figure itself. And the same is true of the scales in bars 6–7 and 11–12.

Chromatic patterns

We must now return to two closely linked and rather daunting topics, both briefly touched on in previous chapters. One is the chromatic inflection of pentatonic patterns; the other, extended tonality.

To begin with the former. Any note of the pentatonic seventh may be sharpened or flattened, but the favourites are those in which the result is a concordant triad. Most obviously, *c* and *e* may be inflected to give *a⁻–c♯–e* and *c–e♭–g*. Then there are the 'monotertial' *a♭–c–e♭* (against *a–c–e*) and *c♯–e–g♯* (against *c–e–g*). Finally, we should not forget the 'dominant' *e–g–b*, which may similarly be inflected to *e–g♯–b* or *e♭–g–b♭*.

Because it shares two notes with the pentatonic seventh, this 'dominant' is not nearly so sharply distinguished from its 'tonic' as its harmonic equivalent. Often 'tonic' and 'dominant' are combined to form a unit, the 'pentatonic ninth' *a⁻–c–e–g–b*, which, as we have just seen, contains no fewer than nine potential triads. Grouped in threes with the same 'letter names', these are:

$a\flat\text{-}c\text{-}e\flat, a^{-}\text{-}c\text{-}e, a^{-}\text{-}c\sharp\text{-}e,$
$c\text{-}e\flat\text{-}g, c\text{-}e\text{-}g, c\sharp\text{-}e\text{-}g\sharp,$ and
$e\flat\text{-}g\text{-}b\flat, e\text{-}g\text{-}b, e\text{-}g\sharp\text{-}b.$

It will be seen that individual notes are inflected in only one direction: *a* and *e* upwards, and *c* and *g* downwards. Taking into account all its potential inflections, the pentatonic ninth is therefore $a^{-}(\flat)\text{-}c(\sharp)\text{-}e(\flat)\text{-}g(\sharp)\text{-}b(\flat)$: altogether a cornucopia of potential chromatic relationships.

Axial relationships

This brings us to extended tonality, which means, in essence, the unification of strongly contrasted keys within an overriding melodic system. The usual unifying device is a form of pentatonic ninth in which two sevenths interlock around a triad with a variable third: $a^{-}\text{-}c\text{-}e\text{-}g + c\text{-}e\flat\text{-}g\text{-}b\flat = a^{-}\text{-}c\text{-}e(\flat)\text{-}g\text{-}b\flat$. Adapting the terminology of Ernő Lendvai, we can call this the 'double pentatonic axis'[21] (Ex. 13.12).

Ex. 13.12. The double pentatonic axis

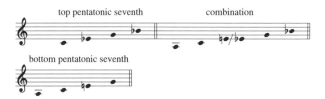

The great power of the axial relationship resides in that chameleon-like third, which, with the minimum of melodic disruption, gives access to two contrasting sets of diatonically related keys. When *e* is natural, *C* major, *G* major, *F* major, *E* minor and *D* minor are all within easy reach; when it is flat, *C* minor, *G* minor, *F* minor, *E*♭ major, and *A*♭ major are equally accessible. It is by such means that Schubert is able to sweep through *C* minor, *E*♭ major, and *C* major in the course of a single eight-bar phrase (Ex. 13.13).[22]

Furthermore, the process is repeatable. It is possible to add more pentatonic sevenths, rooted on *e*♭ and *g*♭/*f*♯, to form a triple or quadruple axis—after which point we are, of course, back where we started. In spite of its chromatic complexity,

---

[21] See *Béla Bartók: An Analysis of his Music*, 'Tonal Principles: The Axis System', 1–16. Lendvai's 'axis' differs from mine (1) in being concerned with harmony rather than melody, and (2) in covering the whole chromatic system, i.e. being 'quadruple' (see below).

[22] Before Schubert, similar patterns already existed in Viennese popular music, e.g. the *Zingarese* no. 6 in D minor (Ex. 11.89 on p. 214).

Ex. 13.13. Schubert, Quintet for Piano and Strings in A, the 'Trout' (1819), 1st mvt., bars 79–84 (up a major 3rd)

the triple axis is far from being an academic fantasy. Example 13.14 shows another natural way of hearing it, as a pentatonic seventh with outgrowths on either side, and it may even retain the diatonic core *a⁻–c*. It is this core, repeated some dozen times, that holds together Wagner's *Tristan* Prelude (Ex. 13.15), though, typically

Ex. 13.14. The triple pentatonic axis

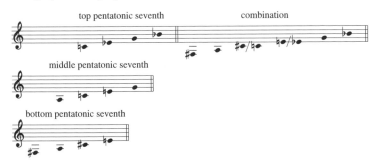

Ex. 13.15. Wagner, *Tristan und Isolde* (1857–9), Prelude, bars 29–36

of this composer, not one of these a^-–c figures (ringed in this extract) is accompanied by an A minor chord.

The quadruple pentatonic axis a^-–c–e–g + c–$e\flat$–g–$b\flat$ + $e\flat$–$g\flat$–$b\flat$–$d\flat^+$ + $g\flat$–$b\flat\flat$–$d\flat^+$–$f\flat^+$ (or the enharmonic equivalent), as used by Bartók and other Moderns, naturally goes further still. It is not so much highly chromatic but *hyper*-chromatic, in the sense that there is no longer the possibility of preserving a single diatonic focus—which, to the Moderns, was of course its great charm. We shall be returning to it in Chapter 15.

Compared with these chromatic extravagances, the double pentatonic axis was simplicity itself, and soon became a standard part of nineteenth-century technique. In particular, it contributed much to the variety and suppleness of Italian harmony, so often caricatured as laughably simple. Example 13.16 demonstrates the flexibility of these axial relationships. It is also, like Ex. 13.9 but in a more elaborate way, a good illustration of Rossini's idiosyncratic variation technique. A

Ex. 13.16. Rossini, *L'italiana in Algeri* (1813), Act II, Scene ix, no. 14, Terzetto, 'A color che mai non sento', beginning (up a tone)

comparison of the bracketed figures reveals how essentially the same pattern can be stretched, contracted, elaborated, simplified, and transposed. Notice particularly the correspondence, so easy to hear but so bewildering to analyse, between bars 6–7 and 10–11. What holds this chromatic tangle together is the note *g*, which, 'monotertially', remains constant while *b♭* and *e♭* are raised to *b♮* and *e♮*.

Chord- or key-relationships of this monotertial type seem first to have appeared in works of the Viennese school.[23] Later, they became a valuable resource of Romantic composers (especially, perhaps, those that had come under Fringe influence), but were far from being confined to them. As a crystal-clear example from Donizetti demonstrates, they were also a native part of the vernacular (Ex. 13.17).

Ex. 13.17. Donizetti, *Lucia di Lammermoor* (1835), Act II, Finale, Chorus, 'Infelice, t'involta', beginning (down a tone)

<hr />

[23] e.g. Haydn, String Quartet in C, Op. 74 No. 1, slow movement, bars 133–56; Beethoven, Fifth Piano Concerto, first movement, bars 151–75, and Eighth Symphony, finale, bars 355–93; Schubert, String Quintet in C, slow movement, episode in Fm (bars 29 ff.) and end, 'In der Ferne' (from *Schwanengesang*), bars 17–21, etc.

Towards the late vernacular

Throughout the nineteenth century, Italian opera became both increasingly penta-tonic and increasingly chromatic. These tendencies culminate in the late works of Verdi, which form a link between Rossini, Donizetti, and Bellini on the one hand and Debussy, Mahler, and Richard Strauss on the other. The final bars of *Otello* (Ex. 13.18) are full of 'advanced' features, even down to the juxtaposition of penta-tonic and whole-tone patterns that Debussy was to make so much his own (bars 14–17). Notice, too, the parallel chords near the end.

Ex. 13.18. Verdi, *Otello* (1887), conclusion (down a major 3rd)

To conclude this brief survey of vernacular melody, it remains to say something about scales and sequences. The sequences that abound in nineteenth-century music fall into two broad types: vernacular and neo-Baroque. Or perhaps it would be truer to describe the latter as not so much neo- as palaeo-Baroque, since its aptness for such purposes as fugato or symphonic development had ensured its survival right through the Classical era. Sequences of this type are dynamic, relatively rigid, and present in both Melody and Bass.

Vernacular sequences, in contrast, are static, relatively elastic, and often confined to the Melody. In addition, they typically move within a framework that is pentatonic, though not necessarily diatonic; chromatic sequences, often of Fringe origin, are very much part of the vernacular. Here one should mention the 'Lisztian' sequence, based on a pentatonic seventh so distorted as to fit symmetrically into the octave. That is to say, the original $a^-\!-c\!-e\!-g$ is turned either into the augmented fifth $a\flat^-\!-c\!-e\!-g\sharp = a\flat$, or the diminished seventh $a^-\!-c\!-e\flat\!-g\flat$ (all sorts of enharmonic alternatives are of course possible). Every step of such a sequence is an exact replica—a 'clone', as it were—of all the others. The result, though exceedingly chromatic, is saved from total confusion partly by its very rigidity and partly by the neatness of the fit within the octave.[24]

Many, probably most, sequences are really elaborated scales, and elaborated scales in general make up a great deal of vernacular melody. Fortunately, not much need be said about them here. They have already been touched on in the discussion of the later waltz,[25] and in any case Schenkerian analysts have taught generations of students to regard music as consisting of little else. We may therefore gratefully allow them to speak for themselves.

HARMONY

A world of mystification blows away as soon as one grasps that words such as 'harmony', 'key', and 'tonality' really describe a tune: that very special and often ambiguous tune we call the Bass. It is to this tune that we now turn.

During the eighteenth century, the Bass had been pretty well confined to a small set of simple, powerful patterns. During the nineteenth, these patterns did not disappear, but they did lose their commanding position. Alongside them (and sometimes in place of them) new patterns grew up. 'Falling' progressions, in which the Bass rises a fifth or drops a fourth (including every type of plagal cadence), became more prominent. So, too, did those based on the most pentatonically primitive intervals: that is to say, thirds, especially the minor third, and major seconds. At the

---

[24] Sequences of this type will be further discussed in Ch. 15, pp. 382–93.   [25] See pp. 260–1.

same time, harmonic organization became generally looser, and it was no longer absolutely essential to maintain the same focus, or 'tonic', from beginning to end.

These new progressions, added to those inherited from earlier times, had enormous chromatic potential. One way or another, almost every chromatic chord of the period is related to them, the main exceptions being those of the Neapolitan family. And here a word should be said about nineteenth-century chromaticism in general. Already in its own time it was something of a fetish, and this since then has lost little of its mystique. It might be said, with little exaggeration, that to many historians nineteenth-century harmony *is* chromaticism. It is seen as a corrosive force, destroying tonality by its 'cancer-like spread through entire movements and works', in the memorable image of Gerald Abraham.[26] But (as Abraham himself points out) this is far from the whole story. Romanticism is only a small part of nineteenth-century European music, and extreme chromaticism only a small part of Romanticism. In any case, chromaticism comes in several varieties, depending on the nature of the Bass. Popular Basses are invariably strong, even when supporting chromatic harmony; conversely, Romantic Basses tend to be weak, even when supporting diatonic harmony. The 'destruction of tonality' would be better described as the weakening of the Bass.

In general, the Germans had always been more interested in harmony than the French or Italians, but in every country harmonic complexity was regarded as a gauge of difficulty. Curiously, though, there seems to have been no corresponding regard for *melodic* complexity. I know of no evidence that composers were any more conscious of the melodic patterns described earlier in this chapter than their sixteenth-century predecessors had been of key relationships. Perhaps because of this, the same melodic patterns crop up in surprisingly diverse contexts, from German symphonies to American ragtime. This is all the more remarkable when one considers the great differences in harmony—at least on the surface. In the pages that follow I intend to dig beneath this surface. The musical examples are calculatedly diverse and incongruous, so that Wagner rubs shoulders with Offenbach, Brahms with Johann Strauss, and Schoenberg with *Hymns Ancient and Modern*; but all have much more in common than one might at first think.

Pentatonic patterns

Throughout the nineteenth century, Basses, just like Melodies, became steadily more pentatonic. Sometimes they trace out an actual pentatonic figure, like that of Ex. 13.19. This type of Bass was especially characteristic of the popular end of the

---

[26] 'The Apogee and Decline of Romanticism: 1890–1914', 43.

Ex. 13.19. Rossini, *William Tell* (1829), Act II, Finale, no. 18, 'Quand l'orgueil les égare de leur sang', beginning

spectrum, where, becoming gradually more prominent, it reached its apogee in early twentieth-century boogie-woogie piano[27] (though this particular example is, unfortunately, rather more reminiscent of the cha-cha).

More important, however, were the poles *a* and *e*—especially *e*. In the major mode, this increasingly asserted itself, sometimes as a starting point but more often as a destination; in which capacity, if it did not replace *g*, it certainly began to rival it. While the 'rising' progression from *c* to *g* became more difficult, especially on a large scale, that from *c* to *e*(♭) or *a*(♭) became easier. Some theorists have even gone as far as to speak of 'dominant avoidance', particularly with regard to the Russian nationalists: 'The most immediately striking characteristic [of the Russian nationalist style of harmony invented by Balakirev in the 1850s and 1860s] is the avoidance of dominant harmony—this at a time when advanced Western (read: Wagnerian) harmonic practice was based on ever more emphatic dominant prolongations.'[28]

---

[27] See Ex. 16.17 on p. 452.   [28] Taruskin, 'How the Acorn Took Root', 200.

But this 'dominant avoidance' was far from being confined to the Russians, or to nationalist composers in general. Even Wagner avoided the dominant as a *destination*. In nineteenth-century music as a whole, movement to the dominant, whether as cadence or modulation, became increasingly rare. This is particularly true of the more popular genres, such as the waltz or Italian opera. According to Julian Budden, 'the traditional move towards the dominant in the first part of a binary structure plays little or no part in Bellinian melody. Whereas Rossini and Donizetti generally have a central cadence on the dominant side of the key, Bellini tends to conclude his first section in the tonic.'[29] So, after him, does Verdi.

Not only *e*, but also *a* gained at the expense of *g*. In the following two examples, an *a* alternates with *c* in the Bass against a children's-chant-like figure in the Melody, but in such a way that the main key may equally well be *C* (Ex. 13.20 and Ex. 13.21(*b*)) or *Am* (Ex. 13.21(*a*)). In passages such as these we see how close the relative keys were coming to merging their identities.

Ex. 13.20. Offenbach, *La Périchole* (1868), no. 3, 'Complainte', beginning of voice part (down a 4th)

Ex. 13.21. Sinding, 'Rustle of Spring', Op. 32 No. 3 (1896) (down a semitone)

(*a*) beginning

[29] *The Operas of Verdi*, i. 14.

(*b*) bars 27–34

molto cresc.

ff

Falling progressions

A further nineteenth-century development was that the I–V–I progression, which had for hundreds of years been the foundation of virtually every musical composition, began to weaken. It was not only that, as we have seen, the journey from I to V become more difficult; the very notion of a 'tonic', in the sense of a base (or Bass) to which one is destined to return at the end of the movement, lost some of its force. Often all that was left was a progression from one chord or key to another a perfect fifth lower (or, what comes to the same thing, a perfect fourth higher): in other words, a falling progression.

Progressions of this type occurred on every possible scale. We have already noticed how waltz suites tend to drift from subdominant to subdominant, and a similar tendency has been observed in movements of a more intellectual type:

When the Romantic composer is not following an academic theory of form—that is, when he is not writing what he felt should be called a 'sonata'—his secondary tonalities are not dominants at all, but subdominants: they represent a diminishing tension and a less complex state of feeling ... Each of the three movements of Schumann's C major Fantasy goes clearly to the subdominant, and all its material is directed towards this modulation. For much of the F minor Ballade, Chopin avoids establishing a secondary key with any degree of clarity: when one arrives, it is astonishingly B flat major. These are two of the most remarkable works of the period, and they are only two instances out of many.[30]

Modulations of this type have a reputation for passivity, or what Rosen here calls 'diminishing tension'. 'Make your first extended modulation to the subdominant,' Tovey says, 'and you deprive your movement of all forward energy and indicate at once that your intention is lyrical and reposeful.'[31]

[30] Rosen, *The Classical Style*, 383.
[31] 'Tonality in Schubert' (in *Essays and Lectures on Music*, 134–59), 137.

That may be true of most Romantic works; it is certainly not true of nineteenth-century music as a whole. One of the most exhilarating devices of the period was a form of introduction that consists of nothing but an extended dominant chord. The idea was, of course, not entirely new. Ever since the seventeenth century, composers had been concluding slow introductions with dominant chords, but it was not till the early nineteenth that they thought of reducing them to nothing *but* a dominant chord. And, as with the perfect cadence or the split dominant, the approach to this seemingly obvious pattern was strangely roundabout. The Viennese composers sometimes permitted themselves one-chord introductions; but the chord is usually a tonic, and the movement usually a finale.[32] The most direct approach, as usual, occurs in movements showing strong popular influence, most of all in those 'Gypsy' finales where the introduction takes the form of a drawn-out dominant *note*.[33] This is still the pattern of Chopin's waltz Op. 18, composed in 1831, except that the note is rhythmically drummed instead of simply held. Thereafter, the full dominant chord quickly becomes the norm. It is especially common in the waltz, Chopin's Op. 34 Nos. 1 and 3, for instance, both beginning with sixteen bars on a skilfully elaborated dominant chord, Tchaikovsky's 'Waltz of the Flowers' (from *The Nutcracker*), with thirty-three bars, and the waltz from *Eugene Onegin* with no fewer than forty-two. But we also find this sort of introductory dominant in polonaises, mazurkas, polkas, and marches,[34] in Saint-Saëns's 'Danse macabre', at the beginning of the second act in Wagner's *Meistersinger*, and in countless other places.

The same principle might also be applied elsewhere. In vernacular harmony (or, indeed, classical harmony in general) no single chord is complete in itself. It is always either a starting point, a destination, or something in between. As a consequence, any opening chord, when dwelt on, sounds like a dominant, in the sense that we confidently expect it to proceed to the chord a fifth below. When east European Gypsies adapted their drone-based music to Western harmony, they found it natural to turn the initial, drone-like tonic into a 'dominant' of this type (see 'Rákóczi's Lament', Ex. 11.98 on p. 222). Wagner, at the beginning of *The Ring*, does essentially the same, even if the 'tonic' chord is characteristically undermined by being made a 6/4 (Ex. 13.22). (Observe, too, how the bare major triad is expanded into a pentatonic seventh as soon as the voice enters. The major triad may indeed be *der*

[32] e.g. Haydn's String Quartet in F, Op. 77 No. 2. The slow movement of Beethoven's Seventh Symphony has a tonic chord in 6/4 position; the first movement of the 'Eroica' two tonic chords. The finale of the same work mixes mediant and dominant chords (cf. Mahler's Fourth Symphony, Ex. 13.62(c) on p. 325). Haydn's String Quartet in C, Op. 74 No. 1, comes closest to later practice with a dominant seventh at the beginning of the first movement, but this resolves on its own tonic before the main theme begins.

[33] See Ch. 11, p. 168. In his Seventh Symphony (Ex. 11.23 on pp. 168–9) Beethoven goes so far as to make the introductory gesture a full dominant chord, but he does so with an air of violent paradox.

[34] e.g. in Chopin, Delibes (cf. Ex. 13.69 on p. 330), Tchaikovsky, Strauss, and Sousa.

Ex. 13.22. Wagner, *Das Rheingold* (1853–4), Prelude and beginning of Scene i
(down a minor 3rd)

(*a*) beginning of Prelude

Ruhig heitere Bewegung [Placidly cheerful tempo]

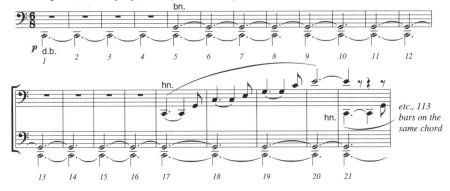

(*b*) end of Prelude and beginning of Scene i

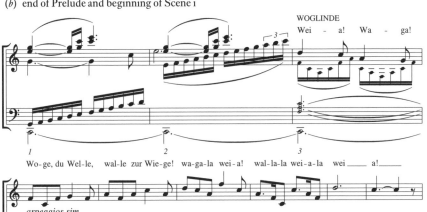

WOGLINDE
Wei - a! Wa - ga!

Wo-ge, du Wel-le, wal-le zur Wie-ge! wa-ga-la wei-a! wal-la-la wei-a-la wei ___ a! ___

arpeggios sim.

WELLGUNDE   WOGLINDE
Wog - lin - de, wachst du al - lein. Mit Well-gun-de wär' ich zu zwei!

arpeggios sim.

Klang in der Natur, the sound in *inanimate* nature; but it is not the sound in *human* nature.)

There could be few more comical contrasts than the one between this awesome passage and the 'Cancan' (or 'Galop infernal', to give it its official title) from Offenbach's *Orphée aux enfers*, composed a few years later (Ex. 13.23). Yet, if we look below the surface, we find a surprisingly similar structure. Here the introductory

Ex. 13.23. Offenbach, *Orphée aux enfers* (1858), Act I, 'Galop infernal' ('Cancan'), beginning (down a tone)

'dominant' is a pair of ordinary tunes instead of a prolonged triad, but by bar 23 there is no doubt, in spite of the absence of signpost discords, that what we have been listening to is essentially a dominant. After such a build-up, nothing could exceed the exhilaration of the main theme where the voices enter, or less resemble the 'diminished tension' conventionally attributed to nineteenth-century sub-dominants.

The ragtime progression

Falling progressions lend themselves to concatenation, one example of which we have already seen in the subdominant-ward drift of the waltz suite. Another is the backward extension of the V–I cadence, sometimes known as the 'ragtime progression' (though I hasten to add that it is no more confined to ragtime than the 'blue seventh' is to the blues). This ragtime progression grew by a process of gradual accretion. First the dominant chord acquired its own dominant, the familiar 'supertonic chromatic chord' II7/♯. This then acquired *its* dominant, which in turn acquired yet another dominant, giving III7/♯–VI7/♯–II7/♯–V7–I. In the popular music of about 1900, even VI7/5♯/♯–III7/♯–VI7/♯–II7/♯–V7–I is not entirely unknown. For practical purposes, however, the ragtime progression is either III7/♯–VI7/♯–II7/♯–V7–I or, rather more frequently, VI7/♯–II7/♯–V7–I, the final tonic being sometimes omitted in both cases.

The first thing to notice about these progressions is the Bass (*e*)–*a*–*d*–*g*–*c*, which differs from the old 'circle of fifths' (in the major mode, *c*–*f*–*b*–*e* . . .) in being clearly pentatonic, since it both conforms to the pentatonic scale and begins on the pole *a* or *e*. Almost always, this pentatonic pattern is mirrored in the accompanying Melody, so that the chromaticism is purely internal. In Exs. 13.24 and 13.25, neither

Ex. 13.24. Rossini, *Stabat Mater* (1841), 'Cujus animam', bars 9–18 (up a major 3rd)

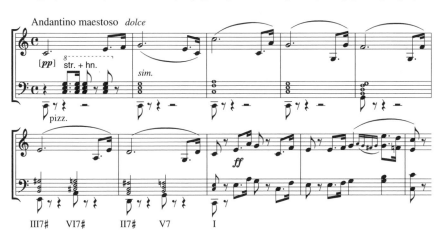

III7♯   VI7♯   II7♯   V7   I

Ex. 13.25. Liszt, 'Liebestraum' (1850), beginning (up a major 3rd)

Melody nor Bass has any significant part in it, the only slight exception being the passing $b\flat$ in bar 8 of 'Liebestraum'. It is typical of the nineteenth-century vernacular that lushly chromatic passages tend to become diatonic when the inner parts are covered up.[35]

As its name suggests, the ragtime progression is especially characteristic of the lighter genres. Its heyday was the first quarter of the twentieth century, when patterns not unlike Liszt's became extremely common in ragtime, jazz, the waltz song, and popular music generally. The only striking innovation was to drop the initial tonic, as for instance in 'Sweet Georgia Brown'[36] (1925). In view of these associations, it was probably inevitable that these patterns should attract the censure of Authority: 'It will be quickly realized that such a common formula as the following [I III7♯–VI7♯–II7♯], however plausible it may sound, has little musical worth; it belongs to the realm of the "salon" at best, or the lowest type of popular dance music, or sentimental "sacred solo".'[37]

---

[35] In bars 13–16 of Ex. 13.25, it looks as though Liszt was unconsciously quoting bars 12–15 of Meyerbeer's 'Robert, toi que j'aime' (Ex. 13.56 on p. 319). If so, he changed the first chord from *F* to *F*m, thereby transforming the sequence from 'tonal' to 'real'—or 'Lisztian'.

[36] By Ben Bernie, Maceo Pinkard, and Kenneth Casey; reprinted in full in *A Hundred Best Songs of the 20's and 30's*, 75–8.

[37] H. K. Andrews *The Oxford Harmony*, ii (1950), 127.

Progressive tonality

As the tonic sense weakened, it became possible to end a movement on a Bass note other than that with which it had begun—or, to use a more conventional phrase, 'in a different key'. This practice, which has come to be called 'progressive tonality' (presumably because it performs a gigantic harmonic progression, instead of sticking to one 'chord'), was neither as bold nor as novel as it is usually claimed to be. Often it is merely a consequence of the enormous size attained by single movements in the late nineteenth and early twentieth centuries. Beyond a certain point, even the most acute listener loses touch with the 'home tonic', leaving the composer free to finish in any key he chooses.

On a smaller scale, 'progressive' Basses usually conform to one of the four patterns of Ex. 13.26, especially the first two. Example 13.26(*a*) is merely a falling

Ex. 13.26. Basses commonly associated with progressive tonality

progression from which no return is made. We can see how this might come about from Offenbach's 'Cancan' (Ex. 13.23 on p. 298), where the return to the initial key might easily have been omitted. In many turn-of-the-century marches and rags, it actually *was* omitted.[38]

The 'progression' to the relative major (Ex. 13.26(*b*)), as well as being more frequent, was much older. It first regularly appears in the second decade of the nineteenth century, but in such a form as to suggest that it must already have had a long unrecorded history. Almost simultaneously, we find it in Schubert's dances (where it accounts for about a quarter of those in the minor mode),[39] and in the Italian *canzonetta*. Probably the first example in all Italian operas is the serenade, near the beginning of *The Barber of Seville*, with which Count Almaviva attempts to woo Rosina. Though the Count is of course not a humble character, his song, to his own guitar accompaniment, is very much in the popular *canzonetta* style. And one of its

---

[38] The first composer to do so seems to have been Sousa, though by his own account he was only formalizing established performance practice. See the quotation on p. 435.

[39] Of Schubert's several hundred waltz tunes, some three dozen are in the minor. Of these, the following end in the relative major: Op. 9 No. 27 in C sharp minor; Op. 18 Nos. 5 in E minor and 8 in E flat minor, as well as the ländler No. 8 in B flat minor; Op. 33 No. 11, in E minor; Op. 5 Nos. 7 in G minor, 24 in G minor, and 31 in A minor. So do the two écossaises, both in B minor, appended to Op. 33.

popular features, one cannot help feeling, is precisely the conclusion in the relative major; which, however, is immediately contradicted by Rosina with two unharmonized bars in the tonic minor. The final tonality therefore remains ambiguous. If this was a scruple, Rossini soon overcame it, since the otherwise similar 'Willow Song' (from the slightly later *Otello*) ends unequivocally in the major (Ex. 13.27).[40]

Ex. 13.27. Rossini, *Otello* (1816), Act III, 'The Willow Song' ('Assisa a' pie d'un salice'), beginning of voice part (up a tone)

[40] The words ('At the foot of a willow sat Isaura, sunk in grief, transfixed with the cruellest love . . .') are a free translation of Shakespeare's 'Willow Song' ('The poor soul sat sighing by a sycamore tree / Sing all a green willow / Her hand on her bosom, her head on her knee . . .'). Notice the strong family likeness to 'Fuggi, Fuggi' (Ex. 7.25 on p. 104).

At least among Italian and French composers, ending a movement in the relative major soon became a perfectly normal procedure—which, in popular music, it remains to this day.

The other tonal 'progressions' are far less important. The only ones worth discussing are those of Ex. 13.26(*c*) and (*d*), where the Bass moves from *c* to *a* or *e*, and even these are far from common. The reason is fairly obvious. Both *c–a* and *c–e* move from major to minor, that is, from relative consonance to relative dissonance. It is true that the *c–a* progression occurs in the *romanesca* (Ex. 7.14 on p. 97), but there the final chord is either the major *tierce de Picardie* or omits the third altogether. Similarly, the finale of Mahler's Fourth Symphony ends in the major mediant key.

All three tertial progressions (*a–c*, *c–a*, and *c–e*) repeat on a large scale modulations we have already seen within the single strain, and like them are generally held together by the repercussion of a persistent Melody note. In Chopin's Second Ballade (Ex. 13.28), which, exceptionally, moves from *C* major to *E* minor, this note is very clearly *e*.

Ex. 13.28. Chopin, Ballade No. 2, Op. 38 (1836–9) (down a 4th)

(*a*) beginning

(*b*) conclusion

Plagalism

The plagal progression IV–I has always been something of a puzzle. From one point of view, it is a mirror image of V–I, with the IV not so much a subdominant as an 'anti-dominant'. But its actual behaviour has never been as straightforward as this simple correspondence suggests. From the start, it has been strongly associated with pentatonic melody. Already in Zacara da Teramo's 'Ciaramella', composed in the early fifteenth century, several plagal progressions occur over an almost entirely pentatonic bass (Ex. 13.29).[41]

Ex. 13.29. Antonio Zacara da Teramo, 'Ciaramella' (early 15th-c. *ballata*), beginning, bass (down a 5th)

These, however, are much less definite than the full closes in the same move-ment—little more, in fact, than ad hoc 'melodizations' of the bass figure d–a^-.[42] The true plagal cadence developed about a century later, by a protracted and roundabout route,[43] and moreover took place in the major mode. In this context the note f, root of the IV chord, was strongly dissonant, so to lay any great emphasis on it was a paradoxical procedure, possible only when the harmonic sense had advanced to the point of hearing IV–I as an inversion of V–I.

Even so, links with the pentatonic scale remained strong—so much so, indeed, that one must conclude that in some sense the plagal progression *is* pentatonic. The association is particularly evident in Russian music. David Brown remarks on 'the plagalism which is conspicuous in certain folk-songs, especially those of an heroic character', and which Glinka (and the later Russian nationalists) made extensive use of. 'Although they may have been conceived entirely without any conscious harmonic background, these tunes very naturally harmonize with a tonic-subdominant-tonic progression (this is true of the one Russian folk-song every Englishman knows, the so-called "Song of the Volga boatmen").'[44]

---

[41] In bars 8–10 the tenor becomes for a while the real bass. To make matters quite clear I give both voices at this point.

[42] See the full quotation of the same passage (Ex. 6.2 on pp. 68–9).   [43] See pp. 102–3.

[44] *Mikhail Glinka*, 116

Now, the main motif of 'The Volga Boatman' (Ex. 13.30)[45] is one of those Russian variations on the children's chant, such as we saw in 'Na more utushka' (Ex. 3.12 on p. 36), where the *a* acquires an accent and often skips directly down to *e*. (The closeness of Ex. 13.30 to the children's chant can easily be seen if it is mentally transposed down a fourth.) To turn this *a–e* into a plagal progression, all that is necessary is to transfer it to the bass as *d–a⁻* (more or less the stage reached by Zacara in his 'Ciaramella'), and then to build triadic chords on it.

Ex. 13.30. 'The Song of the Volga Boatmen' (Russian work song, 19th c.), beginning (down a semitone)

The first Melodies to accompany these plagal Basses almost always resolved downwards by step (Ex. 13.31(*a*) and (*b*)). The few exceptions (Ex. 13.31(*c*) and (*d*)) shared two qualities: they conformed to the pentatonic seventh, and they showed popular influence of one kind or another. In Ex. 13.32 this is Spanish, in Ex. 13.33 central European. By the third decade of the nineteenth century, similar progressions had become fairly common in the Viennese composers,[46] and from then on we find plagalism regularly associated with pentatonicism, whether in Italian opera, the Russian nationalists, or, supremely, twentieth-century American popular music.

Ex. 13.31. Melodic accompaniments to the plagal progression

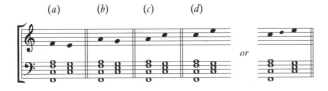

---

[45] The words, roughly translated, mean: 'Heave ho! One more time!'

[46] e.g. Beethoven, String Quartet in C sharp minor, 5th movement (scherzo), bars 118–22; Schubert, String Quintet in C, third movement (scherzo), bars 65–70. Both have the same rising scale as Ex. 13.33. Cf. also the trio from Sibelius's second Symphony (Ex. 13.3 on p. 280).

Ex. 13.32. Domenico Scarlatti, Sonata in C, K420, L2 (mid-18th c.), beginning

Ex. 13.33. Haydn, Symphony No. 53 in D (*c*.1778), last mvt., bars 38–44 (down a 4th)

It need hardly be added that plagal progressions, as they became more common, also became longer and more complex. One possibility was to expand the single note *f* into the melodic chord *f–a* or *f–a–c*⁺; another was to turn the simple progression into a sequence. Both these tendencies can be seen in Ex. 13.34, from the

Ex. 13.34. Mozart, *Così fan tutte* (1790), Overture, bars 29–45

overture to *Così fan tutte*. Over the following century, they were to grow enormously in importance.[47]

The 'Black Sheep' pattern

Yet another outgrowth of the plagal progression was the 'Black Sheep' pattern described in Chapter 7.[48] This had always been associated with popular music, and it retained that character when revived in the late eighteenth century. The *faux-naïf*, Dresden-china-shepherdess rusticity of Exs. 13.35 and 13.36 (the former of course being the 'Black Sheep' tune itself with a French title) is typical. During this early period the pattern was particularly characteristic of dance tunes, appearing first in minuets like Ex. 13.36, and then in waltzes, especially those of Schubert (Ex. 13.37).[49] At a slightly later date, it began to appear (together with other long-submerged folk patterns) in Italian opera (Ex. 13.38).[50] It is a sign of its popular origins that both Schubert and the Italians generally place it over a tonic drone.

Ex. 13.35. Mozart, Variations on 'Ah, vous dirai-je, Maman', K. 265 (probably 1778), Theme, beginning

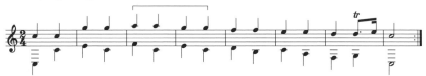

Ex. 13.36. Haydn, Keyboard Sonata in E major, Hob. XVI: 13 (probably 1760s), Minuet, beginning (down a major 3rd)

---

[47] The more or less sequential reproduction of an initial figure at the fourth above, as in Ex. 13.34, was long ago pointed out as a Beethoven 'fingerprint' by Ernest Newman. In *The Unconscious Beethoven* (pp. 11–12), he quotes examples from the Violin Sonata in C minor, Op. 30 No. 2, first movement, bars 1–4, the Piano Concerto No. 3 in C minor, first movement, bars 9–12, and the *Fidelio* Overture, bars 5–12, and there are many others. For a late 19th-c. descendant of Mozart's pattern, see the Prelude to Bizet's *Carmen*, first strain (Ex. 13.74 on p. 335).   [48] See pp. 104–5.

[49] Here the mode need not always be major. For a beautiful minor-mode example, see the waltz in A minor (ending in C major), Op. 50 No. 31.

[50] Cf. also the 'Willow Song' from Rossini's *Otello* (Ex. 13.27 on p. 302).

Ex. 13.37. Schubert, Waltz in C major, Op. 50 No. 1 (*c.*1823), beginning

Ex. 13.38. Donizetti, *Lucia di Lammermoor* (1835), Act II, no. 8, 'Sextet', beginning
(down a semitone)

Observe, too, that Donizetti is already placing it within a pentatonic framework.
Like other folk patterns, it soon diffused through the vernacular as a whole. Even
Wagner uses it, for instance as the song of the Rhine Maidens towards the end of
Das Rheingold—incidentally the only part of that opera to meet with the approval

of Eduard Hanslick.[51] Still, its true home, like that of plagalism in general, continued to be the lighter genres: dances, marches, Italian opera, parlour ballads.

A last, subtle point about the 'Black Sheep' pattern is that, by prolonging the initial I, it brought out the 'dominant' aspect of that chord. This was no doubt one reason why it attained such great popularity. In a single, compact bundle, it united falling, plagal, and pentatonic patterns. No wonder the combination was to prove so irresistible in the totally unexpected form of the twelve-bar blues.

TONAL COUNTERPOINT

During the nineteenth century, the seemingly straightforward entity of 'key' began to play tricks on both listeners and theorists. Individual keys became coy about their true identities, melted together, sometimes seemed to dissolve away completely. What exactly was happening? As a theoretical construct, key rests on the assumption that music is organized around harmonic chords. In the eighteenth century, this had been close enough to the truth to raise few difficulties; in the nineteenth, it ceased to be the case, as *melodic* chords, often sharply at odds with their harmonic accompaniment, came to the fore. Key did not disappear, but became part of the larger system that I call tonal counterpoint.

This, by its nature, is a complex affair, but there is also a compensating simplicity. As harmony becomes more wayward, so melody becomes more pentatonic. Over and over again, we find the familiar 'natural', 'hard', and 'soft' patterns, the novelty being that they now often occur in contrapuntal combination. Let us take them in that order.

The natural pentatonic

The most fundamental of these combinations may be summed up as natural-pentatonic Melody over major-mode harmony. In practice, this generally means the pole *a* or *e* over the diatonic chords *C*, *G*(7), *F*, or *A*m, to which we can perhaps add *D*7/♯. In one case, that of *e* + *F*, the result is astringently discordant; but otherwise it is either concordant (*a* + *F*, *a* + *A*m, *e* + *C*, and *e* + *A*m) or only mildly discordant, and into this last category come a few of the most characteristic chords of the period: the 'tonic added sixth' *a* + *C*, which is of course a pentatonic seventh in harmonic form; the 'dominant thirteenth' *e* + *G*(7), again a form of pentatonic seventh; the 'dominant major ninth' *a* + *G*(7); and the 'supertonic major ninth' e + *D*(7)/♯.

---

[51] See Werner Breig, 'The Music Works', in *Wagner Handbook*, 441.

As we have already seen from the history of the 'waltz sixth' (*a* + *C* or *G*7), these chords came to be treated as virtually consonant. Any dissonance that remained was merely that of the dominant or supertonic chord as such. In spite of their somewhat discordant nature, neither *a* nor *e* was strictly required to resolve, *a* in particular often serving as a point of rest in its own right (Exs. 13.39 and 13.40).

Ex. 13.39. Gounod, 'Sérénade' (1857), beginning of instrumental introduction (down a 4th)

Ex. 13.40. Adam, *Si j'étais roi* (1852), Act II, Finale, Chœur dansé, 'Bondissez et dansez', beginning

Meanwhile the Bass, as we have seen, was also becoming increasingly pentatonic. Its progress in this direction may be measured by comparing the various ways of harmonizing figures built on the triad *c–e–g*. The plain *C* major chord is the obvious choice, resorted to by countless composers over the centuries, but there has always been the option of tonal counterpoint, which in the course of the time became both more frequent and more complex. In Exs. 13.41–3, three operatic overtures all command the listener's attention with the same rising arpeggio, in virtually the same rhythm. Yet each composer harmonizes it differently, Cimarosa's bass (Ex. 13.41) sticking flat-footedly to the tonic, Mozart's (Ex. 13.42) tracing out the *a* minor chord c^+–*a*–*e*, and Berlioz's (Ex. 13.43) descending stepwise from *a* to *e*.

Ex. 13.41. Cimarosa, *Il matrimonio segreto* (1792), Overture, beginning (down a tone)

Ex. 13.42. Mozart, *The Magic Flute* (1791), Overture, beginning (down a minor 3rd)

Ex. 13.43. Berlioz, *Les Troyens* (1856–8), Overture, beginning (down a 4th)

At each successive stage, the Bass diverges a little further from the Melody, so that by the time we come to Berlioz they are effectively in different keys. French composers were particularly attracted to this sort of conflict (Exs. 13.44 and 13.45), which is in fact a direct ancestor of twentieth-century bitonality.

Ex. 13.44. Gounod, *Faust* (1859), Act II, no. 4, Chorus, 'Buvons, trinquons'

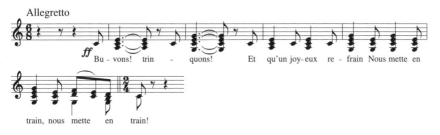

Ex. 13.45. Bizet, *Carmen* (1875), Act I, no. 3, 'Chorus of the Street Boys', end of 1st section (down a tone)

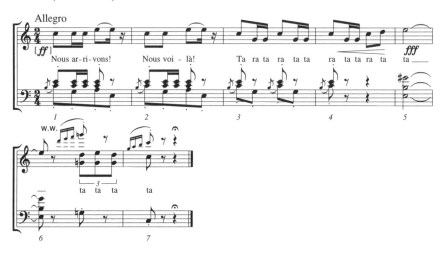

Cadential climax

One of the fundamental changes in nineteenth-century music is that climax gradually replaced antithesis as the chief organizing principle. I must immediately add that the word 'climax' is here used in its original sense of 'a figure in which a number of propositions or ideas . . . [are] set forth so as to form a series in which each rises above the preceding in force or effectiveness of expression . . .',[52] the stock example being Caesar's 'I came; I saw; I conquered'. It is also important to grasp that *repetition* is an essential part of this process. An ordinary crescendo is not a climax, but a Rossinian crescendo, in which the same tune is played over and over again in ever more noisy orchestration, is. Essentially, climax is variation plus intensification.

In its musical form, the repeated element may be anything from a single note to a complete melody; all that is necessary is that the listener should be conscious that it is being repeated. And, in the same way, the intensification may proceed through almost any conceivable parameter. Volume, pitch, instrumentation, and contrapuntal complexity (as in the nineteenth-century round, on which an interesting book could be written) are only the most obvious. Undoubtedly the most fundamental, however, and perhaps also the most important means of organizing tonal counterpoint, is the cadence. Again, there are various ways of grading cadences in order of strength, but whichever way one chooses, a fundamental rule is that

---

[52] *OED*, 'climax', iii. 323, definition 1. The usual sense is sternly ascribed to 'popular ignorance and misuse of the learned word'. From the Greek for 'ladder'.

the repeated element is the *final* note or chord. (Thus, for instance, the familiar pattern . . . I→V . . . V→I is not a climax, but an antithesis.) In general, cadential climaxes may be divided into two classes: 'harmonic', where the repeated element is the final *harmonic* chord, and 'melodic', where it is the final *Melody* note.

Of course, the strength of a cadence depends on a great many things. Most obviously is the harmonic progression: $G→C$, for instance, is stronger than $F→C$. Almost as important is the position within the chord of the final Melody note (let us call it the 'cadential note' for short): $d/G→c/C$, for instance, is stronger than $d/G→e/C$, because the c of c/C is harmonically stronger than the e of e/C, in the sense that the former is a root where the latter is merely a third. This gradation of harmonic strength is the basis of easily the oldest form of cadential climax, . . . $G→e/C$ . . . $G→c/C$. In this *harmonic* form of cadential climax, the chord remains the same but the position of the cadential note changes. It took composers several centuries to work out that the same principle could be applied in reverse, by keeping the cadential note constant but changing the harmony: for instance, . . . e/C . . . e/E. The result was the *melodic* form of cadential climax.[53]

Both types began to develop about the same time, towards the end of the eighteenth century. Of the two, the harmonic variety was by far the simpler, though not, at first, the more important. It clearly fascinated Beethoven, who, as Tovey says, liked to play a 'game of the delicately graded cadences' in his variation themes.[54] At first he played this game with cadences on the dominant chord (Ex. 13.46); but later, in the slow movement of the 'Appassionata' Sonata (Ex. 13.47), he showed that it worked equally well with those on the tonic. In this solemn theme, the harmonic climax of bars 1–4 (. . . $F→C$ . . . $G→C$) is repeated in bars 5–8 with the Melody in a stronger position—a climax of climaxes, in fact.

Ex. 13.46. Beethoven, Piano Sonata in G, Op. 14 No. 2 (1798–9), 2nd mvt., beginning

[53] The familiar . . . $G→e/C$ ... $G→c/C$ type might reasonably be called 'melodic', since it is the Melody that provides the sense of climax. The point to bear in mind is that the harmonic–melodic distinction turns on *the repeated element at the end of the cadence*. Musical terminology is seldom entirely satisfactory.

[54] And 'each time he played it his theme became more subtle and less of a joke' (*A Companion to Beethoven's Pianoforte Sonatas*, 251).

Ex. 13.47. Beethoven, Piano Sonata in F minor, Op. 57, the 'Appassionata' (1804–5), 2nd mvt., beginning (down a semitone)

In the melodic form of cadential climax, the repeated note may be *g* or even *a* (in Ex. 13.40 on p. 310, the *a*/*G* of bar 11 is stronger than the *a*/*C* of bar 7), but undoubtedly the most popular choice is *e*, no doubt because this note lends itself so well to contrasted harmonizations. It is of course strongest in *e*/*E*, rather weaker in *e*/*A*, and weaker still in *e*/*C*. We have already seen several examples of this pattern, including the one just quoted from Bizet's *Carmen* (Ex. 13.45).[55] For further illustration, I offer five more in Exs. 13.48–52. To make the structure even clearer, the cadences have then been abstracted and arranged in chronological order (together with those of Ex. 13.45) in Ex. 13.53. It will be seen that, in spite of the great variety of date, mood, and harmonic detail, the cadential notes are all neatly arranged in ascending order of harmonic strength.

Ex. 13.48. Haydn, String Quartet in B flat, Op. 33 No. 4 (1781), last mvt., bars 13–24 (down a 4th)

[55] The composers are Beethoven (Ex. 11.69), Johann Strauss (Ex. 12.37, no. 3A), Sibelius (Ex. 13.3), and Sinding (Ex. 13.21). Later, there will be further examples from Verdi (Ex. 13.59) and Gounod (Ex. 13.63). In spite of the diversity of style and pattern, if these passages are examined in chronological order it will be seen how the element of climax becomes more and more predominant.

Ex. 13.49. Rossini, *L'italiana in Algeri* (1813), Act I, Scene iv, no. 4, Chorus and Cavatina, 'E un boccon per Mustafà' (down a 4th)

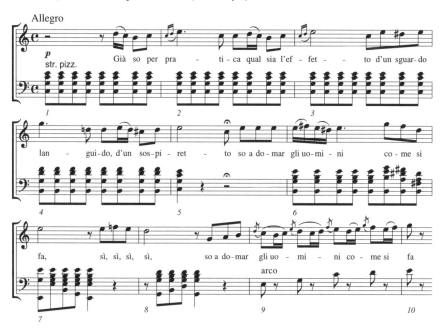

Ex. 13.50. Liszt, *Les Préludes* (1848), bars 47–54

Ex. 13.51. Dykes, 'Horbury' (hymn tune, mid-19th c.) (down a minor 3rd)

Ex. 13.52. Schoenberg, *Verklärte Nacht* (1899), bars 231–5 (down a tone)

A nineteenth-century leitmotif

A further remarkable feature of the cadences in Exs. 13.48–52 is that, contradicting the literal meaning of the word 'cadence', they mostly *rise* to the *e*. In particular, one notices the three-note scale *c–d–e*, bracketed in Ex. 13.53. So common is this little figure in nineteenth-century music, that it is tempting to regard it as a vernacular feature in its own right. Beethoven in particular was so fond of it, along with other rising three-note scales, that it has been pointed out as one of his

Ex. 13.53. Harmonizations of *e* in Exs. 13.45–52 (in chronological order)

(*a*) Haydn, String Quartet in B flat, Op. 33 No. 4 (Ex. 13.48)

(*b*) Rossini, *L'italiana in Algeri* (Ex. 13.49)

bars   2   4   5   6   7

(*c*) Liszt, *Les Préludes* (Ex. 13.50)

bars   1   3   4   7   8

(*d*) Dykes, 'Horbury' (Ex. 13.51)

bars   1   2   3   4   5   7   8

(*e*) Bizet, *Carmen* (Ex. 13.45)

bars   1, 2   4   5

(*f*) Schoenberg, *Verklärte Nacht* (Ex. 13.52)

bars   1   2   3   4   5

'fingerprints'.[56] But, like most of his other idiosyncrasies, this was merely an early manifestation of a general tendency. A proof of the great popularity of this pattern is that, like the cadential climax, there are many examples scattered through this book in passages quoted to illustrate some quite different point.[57]

It is easy to find technical reasons for this popularity. The scale itself is one of the oldest and strongest patterns in music; combining it with a cadence on the pentatonic pole *e* makes it even stronger; it lends itself to many different harmonizations. All this is true, but not enough. Here, surely, is one place where one must also take into account the emotional impact of the pattern. No matter how technically convenient it might be, it would not have become so popular if it had not expressed

[56] See Ernest Newman, *The Unconscious Beethoven*, 71–99. Of the eighty-eight rising scales that he quotes, eight belong to this type.

[57] These include passages from Chopin (Ex. 11.47), Meyerbeer (Ex. 13.56), Wagner (Ex. 13.4), Liszt (Ex. 14.8), Sinding (Ex. 13.21), and Debussy (Ex. 15.26).

the dynamism of the period. Whatever the accompanying emotion—and that can vary enormously—there is always about it a feeling of forward thrust.

Often, too, there is a vaguely religious sense of aspiration, especially when the harmony takes the form of a plagal cadence, and most of all when the subdominant chord is minor (*c–d*/*Fm*→*e*/*C*). Examples may be traced back from Schoenberg (Ex. 13.52, bars 2–3) to Liszt (Exs. 13.50, bars 3–4, and 13.25, bars 13–16), Chopin (the 'Revolutionary' Study, Ex. 11.47 on p. 183, bars 17–21), and Beethoven (Piano Sonata in C minor Op. 111, near the end of the first movement). But perhaps the first fully mature example of this hardy Romantic cliché occurs at the end of the slow movement of Schubert's 'Wanderer' Fantasy (Ex. 13.54(*b*)). It will be seen that this is also an extremely early example—possibly the very first, among movements of substantial length—of 'progressive' tonality.

Ex. 13.54. Schubert, *Wanderer* Fantasy (1822), slow mvt. (down a major 3rd)

(*a*) beginning

(*b*) conclusion

The blue seventh

On the southern and eastern fringes of Europe the blue seventh never quite died out, even in the politest of musical society. The Viennese retained a taste for it,[58] and so did the Italians, usually in the form of relative-major passages that then pathetically sank back into the minor. Long associated with the *canzonette* sung by humble characters, by the 1830s it was making its way up in the world. 'Una furtiva lagrima' (Ex. 13.55) is in many respects a typical *canzonetta* (though Donizetti calls it a *romanza*), performed by the usual country bumpkin, but its rusticity has

---

[58] e.g. in the slow movement of Mozart's Piano Concerto No. 22 in E flat (Ex. 11.74 on p. 203), or the passage just quoted from Schubert's 'Wanderer' Fantasy (Ex. 13.54).

Ex. 13.55. Donizetti, *L'elisir d'amore* (1832), Act II, Romanza, 'Una furtiva lagrima', beginning of voice part (down a semitone)

been refined almost to extinction. Here the blue seventh is no longer archaic, if indeed it ever really was, but merely a source of gentle pathos.

The process of assimilation continued through the century. There is nothing folky, exotic, or archaic about the blue sevenths in Exs. 13.56–8, which are all normal (and beautiful) specimens of the Franco-Italian operatic melody, chosen precisely for their normality. But, like the various harmonizations of the major triad quoted earlier (Exs. 13.41–5), they also reveal an increasingly audacious counterpoint between Bass and Melody. Notice, in particular, how boldly Meyerbeer and Verdi juxtapose the harmonies of the relative major and minor keys. In such cases, we usually find that the bass is triadic or pentatonic.

Ex. 13.56. Meyerbeer, *Robert le Diable* (1831), Act IV, Cavatina, 'Robert, toi que j'aime', bars 4–18 (up a major 3rd)

Ex. 13.57, Verdi. *Don Carlos* (1867), Act II, Part 2, Romanza, 'Non pianger, mia compagna', beginning of voice part (up a major 3rd)

Ex. 13.58. Bizet, *Carmen* (1875), Act I, no. 6, Andantino quasi Allegretto, beginning

Another point to emerge from these passages is the growing importance of the actual as opposed to the 'fundamental' bass. When the chord of *C* major occurs in its first inversion, as in bar 8 of Ex. 13.57 or bar 3 of Ex. 13.58, it matters more that the bass is *e* than that the chord is *C*.[59] In the same way, the ragtime progression is more a Bass ((*3*)–*6*–*2*–*5*–*1*) than a succession of chords. In the sandwich that makes up the nineteenth-century chord, the 'bread' of Melody and Bass was becoming more important than the 'filling' of the internal harmonies. Once we recognize this simple fact, the vernacular harmony of the nineteenth and twentieth centuries becomes much easier to understand: not only unresolved dominant chords, like those in bars 7–8 and 11–12 of Ex. 13.59, but also many anomalous 6/4s,[60] and of course the added sixths, sevenths, and so forth of popular music.

Ex. 13.59. Verdi, *La Traviata* (1853), Act III, no. 10, Scena e Duetto, 'Ah! gran Dio! morir sì giovine', beginning

---

[59] Cf. also the overture to Mozart's *Magic Flute* (Ex. 13.42 on p. 311, bar 3) and the slow movement of Dvořák's 'American' String Quartet, Op. 96 in F (Ex. 13.61 on p. 323, bar 4).

[60] e.g. the one near the end of Verdi's *Otello* (Ex. 13.18 on p. 290, bar 15). Like the unresolved dominants of Ex. 13.59, this is smoothed away by a triadic Bass.

The hard pentatonic

So far, we have looked at (more or less) natural pentatonic passages, but this is a great simplification. To do justice to the full range of vernacular Melody, one must also take into account the other two pentatonic species.

At this stage, not much need be said about the soft pentatonic (d–f–a–c^+), which long remained tentative and unformed. The hard pentatonic (e–g–b–d^+) is quite another matter. It was largely a growing feeling for this pattern that made composers so receptive to the Phrygian or 'e' mode. More and more, vernacular Melody came to be organized round the opposing chords of the natural and hard pentatonic, which became, in effect, omnibus 'tonics' and 'dominants', made up, on the one hand, of a minor + c major, and on the other, of e minor + g major. A few extracts from previously quoted examples will make these patterns clearer (Ex. 13.60). As Melody asserted its independence from harmony, it came more and more to assume pre-harmonic forms, which tended both to group themselves round the three pentatonic species, and (quite apart from any folk influence) to fall into descending contours (Ex. 13.60(*b*) and (*c*)).

Ex. 13.60. Natural versus hard pentatonic: extracts from some previous examples

(*a*) Gounod, 'Sérénade' (Ex. 13.39)

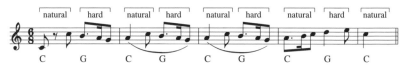

(*b*) Meyerbeer, 'Robert, toi que j'aime (Ex. 13.56)

(*c*) Verdi, 'Ah! gran Dio! morir sì giovine' (Ex. 13.59)

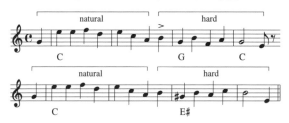

It was, of course, open to composers to make a feature of these primitive patterns, if primitiveness was their object. The lovely slow movement of Dvořák's 'American' String Quartet (Ex. 13.61), for instance, is full of a heavy Slavonic melancholy that might even be called bluesy. One naturally attributes this to the east European folk tradition, or perhaps the Afro-American music that he heard during his sojourn in the United States.[61] But this would be too simple. What Dvořák and similar folk-influenced composers were doing was to bring out the folkiness of patterns already present in the vernacular. When this tune (as distinct from the 'modal' harmonies) is compared with the one from *La traviata* (Exs. 13.59 and 13.60(*c*)), one immediately sees a strong family likeness.

Ex. 13.61. Dvořák, String Quartet in F, Op. 96 (the 'American', 1893), slow mvt., beginning (down a 4th)

---

[61] I leave this second, much-discussed possibility open. What is beyond dispute is that there are both affinities and direct links between east European folk music and the blues. This point will be taken up again in Ch. 16.

So much for pentatonic *melody*. What about the harmony? What happens when a pentatonic seventh is contracted into a harmonic chord? The answer is that we get an 'added sixth', the precise nature of which depends on the species of pentatonic. The natural seventh gives us the tonic added sixth; the soft seventh, the subdominant added sixth; the hard seventh, the dominant thirteenth. But, while theorists have long been aware that the first two of these chords are blends of relative triads—respectively *C* major + *A* minor and *F* major + *D* minor—they have been slower to notice that the same is true of the dominant thirteenth. This becomes particularly clear when it is preceded by the simple mediant; and, as we can see from Ex. 13.62, the tendency was for the mediant element in the compound to become increasingly prominent.[62] In general, the chord or key of *E*m (the difference is really one of emphasis) came to behave more and more like that of *G*. One sees this very clearly near the end of *Les Préludes* (Ex. 14.10 on p. 358, bar 1), where the secondary chords are mediants with no more than a touch of the dominant about

Ex. 13.62. The mediant-to-dominant progression

(*a*) Liszt, Les Préludes (1848), bars 78–80 (down a minor 3rd)

(*b*) Brahms, String Quintet in G, Op. 111 (1890), last movement bars 10–17 (up a 4th)

[62] For the passage preceding Ex. 13.62(*a*), see Ex. 14.9 on pp. 357–8. For a similar but more complex example, see the Prelude to *Carmen* (Ex. 13.74 on pp. 335–6, bars 61–71). Ex. 13.62(*b*) is from one of Brahms's 'Gypsy' finales; cf. its strongly Lydian mode with Exs. 11.90–2 (pp. 216–17).

(*c*) Mahler, Symphony No. 4 (1900), first movement, beginning (down a 5th)

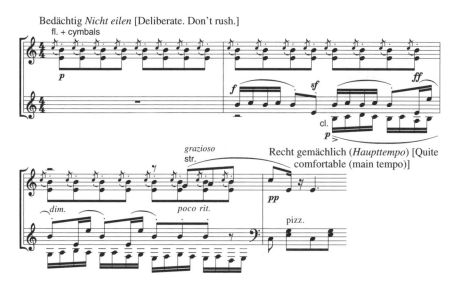

them—and even that vanishes in the next bar. And again one sees it in Ex. 13.63, where the same figure is harmonized first with a *G* and then, by way of a brief modulation to the mediant, with an *E*m chord. Notice, by the way, that this is yet another cadential climax.

None of this, I should at once add, meant that the old dominant chord was losing its importance; but it was certainly evolving into something far more complex.

Ex. 13.63. Gounod, *Faust* (1859), Act V, no. 18, 'Doux nectar dans ton ivresse', beginning of voice part (up a tone)

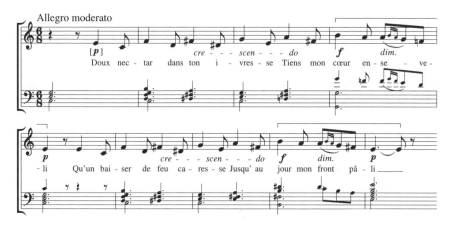

The dominant chord

One of Arthur Koestler's useful coinages was the 'law of infolding', by which he meant the inevitable trend in art 'from the explicit statement to the implicit hint, from the obvious to the allusive and oblique'.[63] Nowhere in music are the workings of this principle more evident than in the dominant chord. By virtue of its simplicity, strength, and familiarity, this chord is uniquely suited to an 'infolding' that was already well advanced in the sixteenth century, and reached their peak in the nineteenth. The latter was the golden age of both the deflected and the oblique cadence. In the former, we veer off from our expected destination; in the latter, we reach it by an indirect path, but in both cases the effect depends on predictability. Only when a formula is thoroughly familiar and predictable—in a word, a cliché—can it be 'folded in'.

Take, for example, that celebrated Victorian ballad 'The Dream', better known as 'I Dreamt I Dwelt in Marble Halls' (Ex. 13.64). This is an early '32-bar song' in a simple AABA form, of which I quote the B section (or what the popular composers of the present day would call the 'middle eight'), followed by the first few bars of the recapitulated A section. Even in Balfe's day, listeners could be sure that A would follow B; and it is this certainty that makes possible the graceful deflection from the key of the major mediant back to the tonic in bars 9–11. Already in bar 9,

Ex. 13.64. Balfe, *The Bohemian Girl* (1843), Act II, Scene i, 'The Dream', bars 31–44 (down a minor 3rd)

---

[63] See *The Act of Creation*, ch. 18, 'Infolding', 339–40. The literal Latin meaning of *implicitus* is 'folded in'.

one is aware that the *b* is very likely going to function as a leading note to c^+. But something is not quite right. The proper harmonic chord for such a leading note would be *G*, and what we are hearing is *E*. In a word, there is a dissonance between Melody and Bass, and it is this that is resolved in bar 10.

No doubt it helps that the discrepant chord is here a mediant, albeit major. (One could even class bars 9–11 with the mediant–dominant fusions of Ex. 13.62.) There is, however, no absolute necessity for this. In Ex. 13.65, the chord is *B*. Nor need the Melody note be *b*. The general formula is $n/[X\text{–}G]$, where *n* is any Melody note compatible with *G* (such as *b, g, d, f*, or even *e*), and *X* is any harmony concordant with *n*. In Ex. 13.66, *n* is *d* and *X* is the 6/5 chord on *F*.

Ex. 13.65. Schubert, Piano Sonata in G, D894 (1826), 1st mvt., bars 10–18 (down a 5th)

It is hard to find a name for this complex and flexible formula. The 'laggard dominant' (in full 'the laggard dominant harmonic chord') is the best I can do. A complete description would take into account not only the Melody and Bass, but the formal context as well. It is significant that all three of the examples just quoted are 'middle eights' (or, in Schubert's case, a 'middle seven') leading up to the recapitulation of the main theme. The very simplicity of the form makes possible the subtlety of the tonal counterpoint. This is one reason why nineteenth-century composers at all levels of sophistication were so fond of clearly defined eight- and sixteen-bar periods. From their point of view, the predictability of such a pattern was its greatest virtue.

Ex. 13.66. Mendelssohn, 'Auf Flügeln des Gesanges' ('On Wings of Song'), Op. 34 No. 2 (1834–7), bars 9–19 (up a major 3rd)

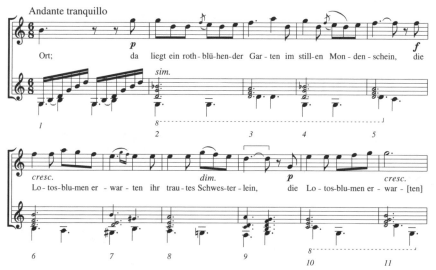

It was also the great virtue of the dominant chord. By the eighteenth century, composers had learnt the power of the preparatory dominant, which instead of closing the present period leads on to the next one. It was largely out of this discovery that the sonata style grew, and an important function of such dominants has always been to lead up to second subjects and recapitulations. There are, however, many variations on this basic formula. The laggard dominant is one, the dominant introduction another. During the nineteenth century, the relation of these preparatory dominants to the melodic context became increasingly tangled. Strangest of all are those cases where the target chord is itself a dominant. When, in the late eighteenth century, composers began to write tunes starting with dominant chords, they faced a problem. What does one do when the tune comes round again? How does one approach a chord as unstable as the dominant, and usually a dominant seventh at that?

The various solutions to this problem are most illuminating. One was to turn the destination dominant into a sort of honorary tonic, to be approached from its own dominant. When Strauss does this in Ex. 13.67,[64] the result sounds so natural that one can easily overlook its audacity—for it blurs the distinctions, not only

---

[64] In the next few examples the note led up to is marked with an asterisk.

Ex. 13.67. Johann Strauss, *Die Fledermaus* (1874), Act III, no. 15, from a bar before the words 'Dies ist Ihr Schlafrock, ich gesteh→' (up a major 3rd)

between tonic and dominant, but also between concord and discord. A yet more paradoxical expedient was to approach the dominant from itself (Ex. 13.68).

Ex. 13.68. Chopin, 'Grande valse brillante' in E flat, Op. 18 (1831), bars 97–104 (down a semitone)

For this trick to work, there are two conditions: the Melody led up to must begin on a note strong enough to serve as a quasi-tonic; and, as this is approached, the Bass must fall silent.[65]

Oblique approaches

Again, it helps if there is a strong sense of expectation. Usually what is expected is the return of a main theme, as in the passage just quoted (and indeed the previous four), but this is not essential. True to the Law of Infolding, the same pattern was soon transferred to the beginning of the movement, as in the Mazurka from *Coppélia* (Ex. 13.69(*a*)). And, having begun the movement in this fashion, Delibes is able, on the return of the main theme, to approach it in a yet more oblique fashion, from the dominant chord of the mediant key (Ex. 13.69(*b*)).

Ex. 13.69. Delibes, *Coppélia* (1870), Act I, Mazurka (down a tone)

(*a*) bars 17–22 (beginning of main theme)

(*b*) bars 49–54 (first return of main theme)

---

[65] It is also possible to interpose a complete silence between the two dominant chords. Cf. the finale of Beethoven's Seventh Symphony (Ex. 11.23 on pp. 168–9).

Ex. 13.70. Johann Strauss, 'A Thousand and One Nights' (*c.*1871)

(*a*) no. 1, end, and no. 2, beginning

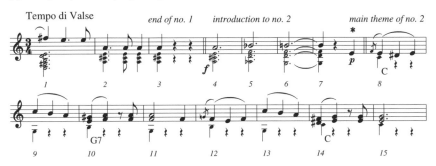

(*b*) no. 2, end of middle section and beginning of recapitulated main theme

In much the same way, the main theme of Ex. 13.70, this time from Strauss, is approached from one angle on its first appearance and another on its return. Though the chord led up to is now the tonic instead of the dominant, the principle is the same. Once again, the first approach is harmonically direct and the second oblique, 'infolded'. What Strauss is really doing in this return, of course, is resolving the *harmonic* chord of *E* on the *melodic* chord of *A* minor.[66]

In all four of the passages just quoted, the Melody has detached itself to a remarkable degree from the Bass. If we hum or whistle the initial figures of their main themes, they strike us as being in a key other than the 'official', harmonic one. This sort of discrepancy, though not entirely new,[67] becomes much more noticeable in the second half of the nineteenth century. In Ex. 13.71 I give Exs. 13.67–70 as heard by the 'naive listener': that is to say (inverting the usual order) with the melodic key as the tonic and the harmonic key as the adjunct.

---

[66] A further, easily overlooked subtlety is that this same melodic chord of A minor (bars 8–11) is an inflection of the harmonic chord of A major in the preceding number (bars 1–3).

[67] Cf. the polka-like theme from Haydn's Symphony No. 60 in C (Ex. 12.3 on p. 234), composed in the early 1770s, where the descent from *f* to *c* sounds more like 1^+–5 than the 4–1 it really is.

Ex. 13.71. The main themes of Exs. 13.67–70 as heard by the naive listener

(*a*) Strauss, *Die Fledermaus* (Ex. 13.67)

melodic key *C,* harmonic key *F*

(*b*) Chopin, 'Grande valse brillante' in E flat, Op. 18 (Ex. 13.68)

melodic key *C,* harmonic key *G*

(*c*) Delibes, Mazurka from *Coppélia* (Ex. 13.69)

melodic key *C,* harmonic key *G*

(*d*) Strauss, 'A Thousand and One Nights' (Ex. 13.70)

melodic key *A* minor, harmonic key *C* major

It was not that the Bass ceased to be important, but rather that its relation to the Melody was becoming ever more oblique and contrapuntal, as composers developed new ways of setting melodic keys against the more familiar harmonic variety. To illustrate the possibilities, which are clearly endless, we must be content with two further examples. The first again shows Strauss's virtuosity in these matters. One of the more problematic key relationships is that between a major tonic and its *major* supertonic, since one naturally tends to hear the latter as the dominant of the dominant. As Tovey puts it: 'If a composer, starting from a major tonic, can persuade the listener that II is a key and not a mere dominant, the effect is one of strange exaltation; unless, of course, the composer is a mere stringer of borrowed tunes whose key-contrasts mean nothing. That is why this is either the most vulgar of modulations or the most sublime.'[68] I am not sure into which of these categories Tovey would have put bars 5–8 of Ex. 13.72, but there is no denying that here Strauss succeeds in making the major supertonic sound like a key in its own right. What one in fact hears, in relation to the preceding phrase (bars 1–4), is not so much the supertonic of *C* as the dominant of *g*.

---

[68] 'Tonality in Schubert', 153. He then cites, as instances of the 'sublime' type, the 'long-delayed return of the main theme in the first movement of the "Eroica" Symphony' (i.e. bars 408–14) and the slow movement of Schubert's String Quintet in C (bars 5–9).

Ex. 13.72. Johann Strauss, 'Tritsch Tratsch' Polka (1858), bars 11–18 (down a major 6th)

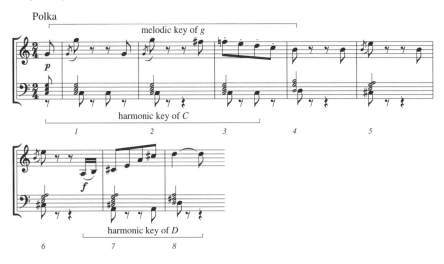

The other example is from Brahms's Second Symphony (Ex. 13.73). Harmonically, it is similar to the extract from Strauss's 'Thousand and One Nights' (Ex. 13.70), but with two further subtleties. The first is that the resolution falls, not on a

Ex. 13.73. Brahms, Symphony No. 2 in D (1877), 3rd mvt. (down a 5th)

(*a*) bars 10–14

(*b*) bars 205–8

note of the tonic triad, but on the 'added sixth' *a*;[69] the second, that in neither of the two approaches is the harmony silent. Both these details are typical of the way 'serious' music (as it was coming to be known by this time) absorbed the devices of the vernacular. Though light by symphonic standards, this movement is hard going when compared with Strauss, Delibes, or Offenbach. But the differences are mostly superficial. At the pentatonic level, the music of the nineteenth-century industrialized West was one.

One last example

As in the case of the waltz, we need a final, large-scale example. What, out of all this unimaginable wealth, is it to be? Obviously, the perfect candidate should be a complete movement of substantial but not unmanageable size. It should be neither too intellectual nor too popular in style, and composed between about 1860 and 1890, when the vernacular idiom had attained full maturity but not yet begun to encroach on the twentieth century. It should illustrate most of the points raised in this chapter. To be fully typical, it should be drawn from French or Italian opera, with perhaps a little Fringe influence. And, ideally, it should be by a composer of genius.

One such movement is the prelude to Bizet's *Carmen*, or more precisely the opening section depicting the bullfighting scene (Ex. 13.74). (A second section, based on the 'Fate' motif, follows after a brief silence.) Some delicate souls regard this prelude as vulgar, but that is a mistake. The vulgarity, if such there be, lies in the object depicted; the music itself is as refined as a poster by Toulouse Lautrec.

The form is extremely simple: merely a rondo with a bustling main theme and two episodes, the first being a Gypsy-like tune in the minor and the second the famous 'Song of the Toreadors'. The bar rhythms are unpretentious, essentially a series of eight-bar periods with here and there a slight expansion or contraction; the general effect, one of the utmost clarity. All is as bright and distinct as a sundrenched Mediterranean landscape. Bizet, as it were, paints in primary colours. He loads his brush, now with red, now with yellow or blue, and applies it to the canvas without attempting to smooth away the brilliant contrasts. In musical terms, this means that the themes follow one another with no more transition than the occasional dominant lead-back, and the same abruptness is evident also on a smaller scale. The dominants of bars 4 and 12 are left without resolution, even to the extent of an 'interrupted' cadence. Similarly, the modulation to the flat mediant key in bars 13–14 is completely disjunct; the music simply jumps in and out of the new key.

---

[69] Cf. Ex. 13.73(*b*) with the recapitulation in Sinding's 'Rustle of Spring' (Ex. 13.21(*b*) on pp. 294–5).

Ex. 13.74. Bizet, *Carmen* (1875), Prelude (down a major 6th)

(*continued on next page*)

(Ex. 13.74 *cont.*)

Such abrupt juxtaposition needs a binding agent, or preferably several. Careful examination of the principal themes reveals the same subtle kinship as we saw in Strauss's 'Blue Danube' (Exs. 12.37–9 on pp. 267–70). If one sings the initial figures of the Main Theme and First Episode in succession, it is at once clear that the latter is a variation on the former, condensed and freely inverted. In rather the same way, the typically Spanish rhythm of the Main Theme is first simplified and then augmented in the two episodes:

Main Theme: | ♫ ♫♫ |

First Episode: | ♫♫♩ | ♫♫♩ |

Second Episode ('Toreadors' Song'): | ♩ ♩. ♪ | ♩ ♩ |

But undoubtedly the most powerful unifier is the grand ladder of thirds that supports the whole movement. The two episodes are in keys a third removed from the tonic, so that the scheme as a whole is:

Main Theme	First Episode	Main Theme	Toreadors' Song	Main Theme
C	*A*m	C	*A*♭	C

If we put together the tonic triads, the result is the monotertial pentatonic seventh $a(♭)^--c-e(♭)-g$, which is extended up to b in the First Episode, and down to f^- in the Toreadors' Song (notice the bracketed pentatonic figures).

This strong leaning towards tertial key relations is typical of the late nineteenth century. There is no extended modulation to the dominant *key*, and even the dominant *chord* is managed with great finesse. Unlike his Russian contemporaries, Bizet does not actually avoid this chord, but he does ensure there is always a subtle twist to lift it out of banality. In bars 1–2 the off-beat dominant sevenths in the accompaniment are contradicted by the Melody. In bars 4 and 8 the dominants are 'laggard', each time in a different way. At the end of the Main Theme in bar 15, the dominant is abruptly approached from the flat mediant. In the First Episode, the dominants of bars 18, 20, and 24 form a subtle cadential climax. In bars 63–70, the dominant and mediant chords are cleverly fused. There is no limit to Bizet's deftness in such matters.

These felicities, and all the others that I must leave my readers to find for themselves, arise directly out of the musical vernacular of the time. I have quoted Martin Cooper on Bizet's instinct, 'which can only be called classical, for the effortless conversion of raw vulgarities into the material for a serious work of art'.[70] This is true and perceptive, but a little misleading in implying that the 'raw vulgarities' underwent some sort of translation. In Mahler, or even in Beethoven, something of the kind does happen; but Bizet, like most French and Italian composers, was much closer to the popular end of the vernacular. With him there is no translation, only selection, refinement, and intensification. But it is doubtful whether even Bizet could have brought off this feat if he had been born a generation later. When he died in 1875, three months after the first performance of *Carmen*, the rift between the popular and 'serious' idioms was already well advanced, and by the end of the

---

[70] See p. 2.

century the vernacular had split into the increasingly irreconcilable dialects of romantic, 'modern', and popular music. It is to these that the rest of this book is devoted.

14 Romanticism

I. ROMANTIC NATIONALISM

The *ancien régime*

By the nineteenth century Romanticism and nationalism had fused to form a single broad movement. It was not only that nationalism, from the start, had been imbued with the Romantic spirit. Romanticism, conversely, was to a large extent a nationalistic movement: a revolt by the Germanic peoples against the cultural hegemony of the Latins, in much the same way as, centuries before, the Italian Renaissance had been a revolt against the Arabs and French. In literature this new revolt was led by the English, in music by the Germans. In both cases, nostalgia for a glorious and largely mythical past was mixed up with a surge of popular culture.

Like any other revolt, it can be fully understood only against the backdrop of the *ancien régime*. The Age of Reason was the last time when Latin culture dominated Europe. The civilizations of ancient Greece and Rome enjoyed enormous prestige, their modern descendants set the tone in all the arts, and the northern Europeans continued to regard themselves as faintly barbaric. And if it was an Age of Reason, it was equally an Age of Rules. The eighteenth-century gentleman's devotion to rules, convention, and correctness in general was like the Fabian socialist's enthusiasm for municipal regulations: they represented progress, order, and the triumph of civilization over chaos and barbarism.

Meanwhile, reverence for the ancient civilizations coexisted with a thoroughly modern outlook. A zest for 'improvement' (that eighteenth-century predecessor of the nineteenth-century 'progress'), common among the aristocracy and upper bourgeoisie, applied not only to technology and science, but equally to the arts, and particularly to music, with its lack of ancient models. With the exception of church musicians and a few 'virtuosi', generally regarded as rather odd, few people took much interest in music more than a few years old.

It was an overwhelmingly agricultural society, in which even the townsfolk, for the most part, had what would now strike us as rustic tastes. 'High' art, which contrived to be at once both classical and up-to-date, was the preserve of a small upper class, who resembled nothing so much as a scattered colonial elite. Often they were as culturally remote from the natives as so many Anglo-Indian nabobs. Literally as well as metaphorically, they spoke a different language, or at least a sharply differentiated dialect. In music, the gulf was just as great, not only in places like Sweden, Ireland, or Poland, but in Italy itself.

This cosmopolitan aristocracy combined great artistic refinement with a hard-headed, down-to-earth, totally unsentimental attitude to the artist himself. Here, as everywhere, money bought quality. The starving genius had yet to be invented. A composer, painter, or sculptor was at best a superior tradesman, in no way distinguished from a cabinetmaker or goldsmith.

The artist as hero

The heyday of this *ancien régime* was the first half of the eighteenth century; or perhaps one should say the half-century from 1690 to 1740, for by 1750 the revolt had already begun. One of its first steps was to invent the artist-as-hero, that strange compound of priest, prophet, philosopher, martyr, and hooligan. Though this wondrous being owed something to the English, his chief creators were the Germans. According to the first edition of the *Oxford English Dictionary*, it was apparently in England that the word 'genius' acquired the sense of 'that particular kind of intellectual power which has the appearance of proceeding from a supernatural inspiration or possession, and which seems to arrive at its results in an inexplicable and miraculous manner'. Thereupon, however, it

came into great prominence in Germany, and gave the designation of *Genieperiode* to the epoch of German literature otherwise known as the 'Sturm und Drang' period. Owing to the influence of Ger. literature in the present [19th] century, this is now the most familiar sense of the Eng. word, and usually colours the other senses. It was by the Ger. writers of the 18th c. that the distinction between 'genius' and 'talent', which had some foundation in Fr. usage, was sharpened into the strong antithesis which is now universally current . . . [1]

Prominent among those 'Ger. writers' was Wilhelm Heinrich Wackenroder. In 1797, a year before his death at the age of 24, he published a short story, 'The Remarkable Musical Life of the Composer Joseph Berglinger', which distils into a concentrated essence several notions current during these formative years of German Romanticism, and is therefore worth retelling in some detail.

The story begins when the young Joseph, son of a good-hearted but narrow-minded and tyrannical physician, is overcome by music heard on a visit to a nearby town. His reactions occupy two pages, of which the following must serve as a sample:

---

[1] vi. 445, article on 'Genius', sense no. 5.

In particular he visited the churches, and heard the holy oratorios, cantatas, and choruses, respendent with trumpets and trombones, ring out beneath the high vaults. At this, an inner devotion would often bring him humbly to his knees. . . . It seemed to him as if his soul had suddenly stretched out great wings; as if he had been lifted up from a barren heath, the cloud-curtain had dissolved before his mortal eyes, and he had soared aloft into the bright heavens. . . . Indeed, at certain passages in the music it appeared at last that a particular ray of light had penetrated into his soul. At that, he seemed to become at once much wiser, and to gaze, eyes shining with a certain exalted and serene melancholy, upon the whole teeming world below.

After this, he naturally has trouble adjusting to everyday life:

For instance, if he was out walking and saw a few people standing around laughing or gossiping, it made a most odd and disagreeable impression on him. He thought: you must remain throughout your whole life, without interruption, in this beautiful poetic rapture . . .

He approaches secular music with the same devotion:

On attending a large concert, Joseph placed himself in a corner, without so much as a glance at the glittering audience, and listened with the same reverence as if in church—just as silent and still, his eyes fixed on the floor in front of him.

Symphonies, in particular,

wrought in his heart a wonderful mixture of gaiety and sadness, so that he seemed equally close to laughter and tears: a mood which so often strikes us on our way through life, and which no art is better fitted to express than music.

After a long battle with his father, Joseph then runs away and becomes a prosperous Kapellmeister. Alas, worldly success turns to ashes in his mouth. His audiences are richly dressed humbugs who secretly regard music as a mere pastime; his fellow composers, time-serving hacks. In a letter to the narrator he pours out his woes:

There is, however, some slight consolation in the thought that perhaps some trifle from my hand may find its way (even if long after my death), in some small corner of Germany, to some person whom Heaven has endowed with the spiritual sympathy to draw from my melodies just what I felt in writing them down, and so much desired to put into them.

It irks him that music is a co-operative effort:

It is a triple misfortune for music to be precisely the art in which so many hands are required merely to bring a work into existence. I gather and lift up my entire spirit to bring forth a great work, only to have a hundred insensitive numbskulls trying to talk me into this or that.

He dreams of chucking it all up:

I'd like to abandon all this culture,[2] take refuge in the mountains with a simple Swiss shepherd, and play with him the Alpine songs that never fail to make him homesick.

In fact

an artist must exercise his art for himself alone, for the exaltation of his own spirit, and for the one or two people who understand him.

The rest of poor Joseph's story is quickly told. He meets a beggarly woman who turns out to be one of his sisters, and informs him that their father is dying. Too late, father and son are reconciled. Shattered by his father's death and the discovery of his sisters' plight, he goes into a decline, rousing himself only to compose a magnificent Easter Passion. Exhausted by this last effort, he sickens further and dies.

How profoundly German this all is, and how unlike anything to be found, either at the time or for long after, in France or Italy! From this story we see how all-important the German contribution was, not merely to Romanticism, but to 'classical music' in general. One can hear just such an 'exalted and serene melancholy' ('erhabenen und ruhigen Wehmut') in a series of German masterpieces dating from Mozart's late works, composed a few years before Wackenroder's story, to Richard Strauss's *Four Last Songs* of 1948.

Throughout that century and a half, the German-speaking world was haunted by the ideal of the *Kunstreligion* in which art, and especially music, attained a religious value. Exported with enormous success, this art-religion has swollen to absurd proportions. All over the Western world, it has acquired its own temples, seminaries, synods, sects, tithes, sacred texts, priests, saints, martyrs, theologians, and heretics, becoming, in the process, more and more a substitute for actual religion. But, to Wackenroder, it was still an *extension* of religion. His hero begins by reacting to sacred but non-liturgical music as though at a religious service, falling to his knees 'in humble devotion'. Later, he transfers this attitude to serious but non-sacred music, throughout which he remains still and silent (though now seated), his eyes fixed on the floor. (Here, incidentally, we see the beginnings of the German ideal, realized by Wagner at Bayreuth, of doing away with the visible presence of the musicians.) In essentials, Joseph's demeanour is exactly what it would be in church—or a present-day concert hall.

---

[2] *Sic.* The original German has 'Ich möchte all diese Kultur im Stiche lassen', thereby antedating by eight years the earliest recorded English use (from Wordsworth's *Prelude*) of 'culture' in this sense. See *OED*, iv. 121, 'culture', def. 5.a.

The rise of Germany as a musical power

A striking feature of this story is its absence of overt nationalism. The only faint approach to it is Joseph's hope of finding a sympathetic listener in Germany, rather than Europe as a whole. At this date, German nationalism was still vague and inchoate, but rapidly developing. Of several broad tendencies that contributed to it, the most important was a new national self-confidence. At the beginning of the eighteenth century, the Germans had inhabited an impoverished backwater, its meagre cultural pretensions confined to mathematics, science, and philosophy. Least of all had they been regarded as a musical people—a judgement in which, on the whole, they humbly acquiesced.

They did, however, possess two great advantages: on the one hand, they were earnest, diligent, and painstaking, with a gift for large-scale composition and elaborate polyphony; and on the other, both their lack of musical chauvinism and their central position within the European continent made it an easy task to as-similate what was best in the music of the surrounding peoples. In the words of Johann Joachim Quantz, Kapellmeister to Frederick the Great: 'If, with due dis-cretion, one were to choose what is best in the musical tastes of the various peoples, the resulting *mixed taste* might, without exceeding the bounds of modesty, be called *the German taste* . . .'.[3] Armed with these advantages, German composers had proved by the middle of the century that they could beat, or at least equal, the French and Italians at their own game. But it was still a Franco-Italian game. Both the international musical idiom and its most admired qualities—grace, wit, polish, ease, fluency, charm—were Italian, or at any rate Latin.

Then, in the third quarter of the eighteenth century, the fashion changed. To be earnest, sensible, and sentimental (as those words were understood at the time) was suddenly in vogue. Here was an environment in which the native German taste could assert itself. And it is important to realize that, below the level of the cosmopolitan upper class, that taste had never succumbed to foreign influences:

to the popular taste Italianism remained all but unknown. The catalogues of the Frankfurt and Leipzig fairs of the eighteenth century afford us proof of this. In these great European markets, in which music occupied an important place, Italian opera, so to speak, scarcely showed itself. Of German religious music there was abundance: Lutheran canticles, ora-torios, Passions, and above all the collections of lieder and liedlein, the eternal and invio-lable refuge of German thought.[4]

---

[3] *On Playing the Transverse Flute* (*Versuch einer Anweisung die Flöte traversiere zu spielen*), final chapter, 'How to Judge Music and Musicians' ('Wie ein Musikus und eine Musik zu beurtheilen sei'), 332.

[4] Romain Rolland, 'A Musical Tour to Eighteenth-Century Germany', 113, in *Romain Rolland's Essays on Music*, 95–120.

In the new atmosphere of national self-confidence, it did not take long for this sturdy independence to spread to the upper classes as well. As we should now put it, the Germans were losing their 'cultural cringe' towards the Latins.

Even so, early German Romanticism was not yet *consciously* nationalistic. Its favourite fictional settings were medieval Christendom and Renaissance Italy, and the folklore that it enthusiastically embraced was at first international rather than particularly Teutonic. A more specifically German Romanticism begins to emerge in Mozart's *Magic Flute* (1791), with its incongruous mixture of neo-Baroque polyphony and Austrian popular song, its un-Italian brand of seriousness, and, of course, its use of the German language. All these features, fused with the Wackenroder style of musical Romanticism, continued into the next century. Indeed, Wackenroder's longer-lived contemporary Ludwig van Beethoven might almost have modelled himself on Joseph Berglinger, not only in his artistic fervour and contempt for the public, but equally in his reverence for the Baroque. The numerous fugal passages in his later works, the experiments with the church modes, the gigantic *Missa Solemnis*—these were neither personal eccentricities nor archaic aberrations, but bang up to date.

Only very slowly was this early Catholic Romanticism superseded by the later nationalistic variety. Its gradual waning may be traced in the settings of Wagner's operas: first, the Renaissance Italy of *Das Liebesverbot* (1836) and *Rienzi* (1840); then, the (Catholic) medieval Germany of *Tannhäuser* (1845) and *Lohengrin* (1848); then the pagan Teutonic world of *The Ring* (1854–76); and, finally, the (Protestant) sixteenth-century Germany of *Die Meistersinger* (1867). In the anomalous *Parsifal* (1882) Wagner was returning, as elderly artists often do, to a preoccupation of his youth, in this case the medieval world of *Lohengrin*.

Classicism, too, lived on, most notably in the figure of Mendelssohn, who would probably have been more artistically successful if he had been born fifty years earlier. (Materially, it is true, he might not have done so well, and would certainly have been well advised to be born into a gentile family.) The Germans never really ceased to be the enterprising eclectics described by Quantz, even if they no longer boasted of it. For one thing, the native popular culture was so limited. The *Volkslied*, for all the fuss that has been made about it, was merely the local form of a song type common to most of western Europe. None of its rather unpromising features were specifically Teutonic. The waltz and polka were more fruitful and distinctive, as well as being more genuinely popular. But that was just the trouble— they were *too* popular. By 1800 German composers had developed a characteristically ambivalent attitude to popular music. Somehow, they managed to exalt *both* the 'folk' *and* the individual genius. Joseph Berglinger, it may be recalled, deplores the communal nature of music, preferring to compose for a select audience of connoisseurs, or even solely for his own satisfaction. Yet he also dreams of making music with a Swiss shepherd, whose own traditions could not be more communal. No wonder the phrase 'internal contradiction' was a favourite with German Romantic thinkers—and not just Marx.[5]

The selfsame contradictions persisted into the twentieth century. Schoenberg was merely echoing Wackenroder when he wrote: 'I believe that a real composer writes music for no other reason than that it pleases him. Those who compose because they want to please others, and have audiences in mind, are not real artists.'[6] For two centuries German intellectuals were troubled by a profound unease about popular culture, often mixed with a sort of guilty fascination. This is one reason why Schubert had to wait so long for his due: they could never quite accept the element of divine café music in him. Even the *Volkslied* was not entirely sacrosanct:

In view of the current veneration of 'the people,' it is necessary to reemphasize that an unbridgeable chasm has always existed and will continue to exist between art and the people. . . . there is an inherent contradiction in the expressions 'popular art' and 'folk art'. . . . Though in the course of centuries certain linear progressions [i.e. those derived from the *Urlinie*] and organic relationships in a masterwork may finally have reached the ears of a considerable number of human beings, this first gleam of understanding cannot be considered a proof that art is based on folk elements. Rather it is Nature that has triumphed, in that Nature has finally made its way to their ears.[7]

This hostility was specifically German. The French revolutionary style that so influenced Beethoven was avowedly popular—an ancestor, in fact, of Soviet efforts to 'bring art to the people'. So was Italian opera, at least until about 1860. In eastern Europe and Scandinavia, it is true, Teutonic notions of folk culture merged with national aspirations, but in a muddled and incoherent way. Eighteenth-century attitudes often lingered on in flimsy disguise, and it is a beautiful irony that Liszt, who did so much to shape east European nationalism, was probably the most cosmopolitan figure in musical history. The more one examines the music of eastern Europe, the less important the purely nationalistic motive seems. Even out-and-out nationalists like Musorgsky were prepared to borrow from alien cultures when it suited their purpose. What really excited them was, as always, the music itself. The true distinction between east Europeans like Musorgsky, Borodin, or Smetana, and Germans like Schumann or Brahms, was not, as is sometimes naively imagined, that the former were nationalists and the latter were not, but that the east Europeans had a much more stimulating native culture to work with. But this was a mixed blessing. On the one hand, it gave their best work

[5] Wagner e.g. complained of the internal contradiction in opera between music and drama.

[6] 'Heart and Brain in Music' (1946), in *Style and Idea*, 53–76 at 54.

[7] Heinrich Schenker, *Free Composition*, i, §263, p. 106. This curious conception of 'Nature' descends from the 18th-c. Enlightenment.

a freshness and vividness exceeding anything the Germans could achieve; on the other, it made the large-scale forms that much more difficult.

Once the first raptures of Romantic nationalism had subsided, its drawbacks quickly became apparent. The command to 'be oneself' can be extremely inhibiting. Still, it was doubtless a good thing on balance—as indeed was the cult of the genius. The music of the past two hundred years would have been a much poorer thing without its Romantic aberrations. Nor have they ever quite disappeared. All the captivating absurdities of both nationalism and Romanticism, theoretically superseded a hundred times over, cling tenaciously to life. To recapture the innocent cosmopolitanism of the eighteenth century, one must go to the popular arts.

II. THE SYMPHONIC TRADITION

In the sonata, musical terminology approaches its formidable worst. Depending on the medium, the same form may be a 'sonata', a 'string quartet' (or other chamber group), or a 'symphony'. The term 'sonata form' itself may describe a single movement or a multi-movement work. Nor is it necessary for a 'sonata' to contain a 'sonata form' movement. In view of this muddle, it seems permissible to stretch the term 'symphonic tradition' to include multi-movement sonata-form works for forces smaller than the orchestra, and there is a certain justification for this in the Romantic tendency to invest all sonata forms with the grand associations of the symphony proper. Whether the work was for orchestra, chamber group, or piano, the composer not only had to manage an increasingly archaic form; he also had to be profound. The wonder is, not that most of the sonata-form works composed after 1830 are stale and academic, but that so many remain fresh and vital.

The expansion of 'first movement' form

It was 'first movement' form that gave the most trouble. There were two principal difficulties. The first was the weakening of the 'drive to the dominant', or indeed in any direction at all, for Romantic harmony does not so much drive as drift. Here the obvious solution was to substitute another key for the dominant, usually some sort of mediant or submediant, including the ordinary relative major. This is one reason, quite apart from the Romantic delight in gloom and turbulence, why so many sonata movements of this period are in the minor.

The second difficulty was the sheer scale of the symphonic movement. To take two representative passages, the finale of Haydn's last complete string quartet, Op. 77 No. 2 in F, is similar in rhythm and tempo to the first movement of Beethoven's

'Eroica' Symphony, which it may well have influenced; but whereas Haydn takes twenty-two bars to reach the dominant key, Beethoven takes forty-four. This means that he must keep up the modulatory impetus for just twice as long— which, of course, he triumphantly does. But even for Beethoven this is a *tour de force*. A simple solution was to keep the movement short, and in fact, after 1830, many of the most successful sonata-form movements are on a small scale.[8] This, however, conflicted both with the Romantic craving for grandeur and the nine-teenth-century belief in progress. It seemed natural that the latest symphony must also be the longest, the most elaborately chromatic, the most richly scored. So, given the requirement to compose on a Beethovenian or super-Beethovenian scale, what was one to do?

The Romantic inclination was to keep the first group short and expand the second, but this tended to produce rambling expositions that contrasted insufficiently with the development and became tedious on recapitulation. One way out of this difficulty was to divide the second group between two keys. The result was the three-key exposition, adumbrated by Beethoven,[9] developed by Schubert, and later taken up by Brahms. After such a long, fragmented, and 'developmental' exposition, however, it was no easy task to make the development proper stand out as something new. The tendency was therefore to turn it into an extended episode, often based on a single, strongly contrasted key and sometimes also in a different tempo.[10]

Even more tricky was the recapitulation. Again there was the danger of prolixity and insufficient contrast, with the added difficulty of contriving an effective finish to the movement. A useful device, going back to Haydn and Mozart and greatly developed by Beethoven, was to repeat the main theme at the end; but this brought its own danger, that of anticlimax. The last return of a much-repeated theme could easily seem like one return too many. Here one solution was to omit the previous return, thereby reversing the order of the exposition. If we call the recapitulated first and second groups A and B, the broad historical sequence was from AB (Mozart) to ABA (Beethoven) to BA (Liszt).

The combined effect of all these innovations was to turn sonata form from a unified, dynamic process into a succession of self-contained tableaux, linked by modulatory transitions or (in Tovey's apt phrase) *coups de théâtre*. For there is something about this later sonata form that is undeniably theatrical, operatic, or (in Mahler's case) cinematic.

[8] e.g. some of Mendelssohn's *Songs without Words* and Brahms's shorter piano pieces.

[9] e.g. in the first and last movements of the Eighth Symphony.

[10] In his analysis of the first movement of Brahms's Piano Quartet in A, Op. 26, Tovey traces the one-key development to 'the later works of Beethoven', adding that it is 'very typical of Brahms. It is an inevitable artistic result of the large scale and manifold thematic material of such works as this quartet' (*Essays in Musical Analysis, Chamber Music*, 196).

Thematic transformation

At the same time, the fragmentation was to some extent compensated for by new unifying devices. 'Thematic transformation' has been the subject of much controversy, some scholars seeing it as a deep and vital principle of composition, others as a dubious trick of little importance. Actually, there is nothing very mysterious about it. Whether one traces it back to the sixteenth-century variation suite,[11] or to the maqām-like processes of the Fringe, it has deep popular roots. We have only to turn back to the Indian beggar's song (Ex. 11.96 on p. 221) to see how humble its social origins could be. The Oriental ability to combine essentially the same melodic line with ever-changing, radically different rhythmic patterns is an ethnic gift, like the African talent for rhythmic counterpoint or the European talent for harmonic counterpoint. It is one of those knacks that must be acquired in childhood, after which they seem perfectly natural.

In the music of Haydn, who no doubt learnt it from Slavs, Gypsies, and Magyars encountered during his earliest years, it is not in the least intellectually pretentious, or even specifically symphonic. In fact, the clearest and most plentiful of his early examples occur within minuets, where their purpose is to link the main section with the trio. Elsewhere, he forges similar thematic links between alternating variations,[12] between slow introductions and subsequent allegros, and between first and second subjects.

As an example of this last, I quote from the finale of one of his early keyboard sonatas the whole of the exposition (Ex. 14.1(*a*)) and the end of the very regular recapitulation (Ex. 14.1(*b*)). Almost everything in this movement flows from the initial eight-bar theme, here broken down into figures A and B, but it does so in a

Ex. 14.1. Haydn, Keyboard Sonata in E, Hob. XVI: 13 (probably 1760s), last mvt. (down a major 3rd)

(*a*) exposition

---

[11] e.g. in Dalza's *alla venetiana* suite no. 2 in F (Ex. 6.18 on p. 84).

[12] In this form, which was a favourite of Haydn's, there are two themes in parallel keys. These are both variations on the same idea, and themselves varied in alternation, i.e. $A_1B_1A_2B_2A_3B_3$, etc.

(b) end of movement

way that makes nonsense of any firm distinction between actual transformation and mere allusion. It is clear that the figure in bars 31–3 is a condensed version of A, and almost equally clear that the descending scale in bars 12–16 is a simplification of B, and that the figure in bars 23–5 is an amalgam of A and B. Such connections are as easy to hear as they are laborious to describe. But is the rapid arpeggio of bar 17 a diminished inversion of A? Is the two-note figure *x* derived from A? Is the figure in bar 34 an augmented, filled-in version of *x*?

One's response to these questions depends on the weight attached to the word 'is'. If it implies fully conscious recognition, the answer is no. But if it merely implies vague identifications, such as the tirelessly pattern-seeking human mind finds in all music, then the answer is yes. When, at the end of the movement, Haydn repeats that initial arpeggio theme (Ex. 14.1(*b*), bars 4–7), it is with the gesture of a conjurer flourishing the top hat from which he has drawn an astounding series of objects.

One reason for quoting this unpretentious little finale at such length is precisely its early date and (at least from the listener's point of view) total lack of sophistication. The thematic correspondences are so easily grasped that it comes as a surprise to discovery how complex and extensive they are. In Haydn's later works, they become even more so. A type deserving special mention is the 'linkage'[13] of the end of one musical idea to the beginning of the next. A particularly neat example occurs in the minuet from the String Quartet in F, Op. 74 No. 2 (Ex. 14.2).

Ex. 14.2. Haydn, String Quartet in F, Op. 74 No. 2 (1793), Minuet (up a 5th)

(*a*) beginning of main section

(*b*) end of main section and beginning of Trio

---

[13] See Walter Frisch, *Brahms and the Principle of Developing Variation*, 15–16 (the term 'linkage technique' is a translation of Schenker's 'Knüpftechnik'). Cecil Grey long ago remarked that 'one of Haydn's favourite methods of melodic construction' was to take 'the last phrase of a theme as the point of departure for a new line of thought' ('Joseph Haydn', 47).

The name usually given to these various metamorphoses is 'thematic transformation'—not an ideal term, since what is transformed is usually not so much a theme as a figure or motif, but probably the best we have. Under whatever name, this has often been adduced as proof of musical 'logic', but in fact is more dreamlike than logical. To an even greater extent than most musical procedures, it acts on the subconscious rather than the conscious mind. It was one of the two principal ways of offsetting the growing fragmentation of sonata form, the other being melodic 'prolongation' (in the Schenkerian sense) over changes of key. In Ex. 14.3,

Ex. 14.3. Mozart, String Quintet No. 3 in G minor (1787), 1st mvt., bars 30–9 (up a tone)

Mozart prolongs the *a* of bars 1–6 through bars 7–10, at the same time raising it by an octave; in effect, the Melody stays in *A*m after the harmonic key has changed to *C*. And Beethoven, in the first movement of the 'Appassionata' Sonata (Ex. 14.4), combines essentially similar methods with thematic transformations not unlike those in Haydn's little finale (Ex. 14.1). Indeed, the kinship between Beethoven's mighty first movement and Haydn's little finale is surprisingly close, especially when one considers that the former is several times longer than the latter. Both begin with an arpeggio theme which is immediately repeated in a contrasting mode and later inverted; both have second subjects that go into the parallel minor; and both end by quoting the initial arpeggio figure.

Ex. 14.4. Beethoven, Piano Sonata in F minor, Op. 57 (the 'Appassionata', 1804–5), 1st mvt. (up a major 3rd)

(*a*) beginning

(*b*) bars 42–9 (beginning of second group)

(*c*) end of movement

And of course both have second subjects recalling the opening theme in a more compact form. This sort of thematic transformation clearly fascinated Beethoven throughout his career. It is too big a subject to go into in detail, but one further example will throw a little more light on his methods. Superficially, the slow movement of the third 'Razumovsky' Quartet (Ex. 14.5) would seem to be very different from the previous example, but closer examination reveals surprising similarities.

Ex. 14.5. Beethoven, String Quartet in C, Op. 59 No. 3 (1806), slow mvt.

(*a*) beginning

(*b*) bars 42–9 (beginning of second group)

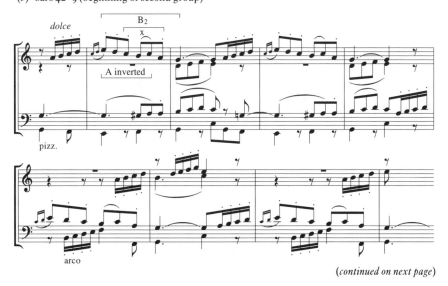

(*continued on next page*)

(Ex. 14.5 *cont.*)

(*c*) end of movement

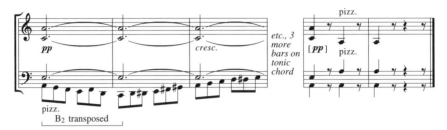

pizz.

B₂ transposed

Again, the two subjects resemble each other in rhythm, in melodic outline, and, most strikingly, in mode; it is hardly too much to say that the wistful little second-subject theme is in an Aeolian or Dorian *a* minor. But melodic line is also important, and, as in the 'Appassionata', this is partially inverted (compare the treatment of Figure A in both cases). Indeed, it was rather a habit with Beethoven to make his second subjects free inversions of his first. Compare, for instance, the corresponding places in the 'Waldstein' Sonata (Ex. 11.55 on pp. 187–8).

Thematic transformation could also take another, more specifically Beethovenish form. Even today, the listener cannot fail to be struck by the bare pizzicato descent of the theme labelled as B₁ (Ex. 14.5(*a*), end), but there is nothing in this bleak passage to suggest that it is of any thematic significance. No further reference is made to it until twenty-seven bars later, when the four-note figure *x* recurs at the beginning of a cadence theme (see Ex. 11.35 on p. 175). Then comes a long transitional passage, with *x* freely inverted, and at last the second subject (Ex. 14.5(*b*)). And here it becomes obvious that figure B₂, of which most of this mournful little theme consists, is none other than a compressed version of B₁.

Obvious, that is, to the eye of the score-reader. But are such coincidences—in Beethoven or other composers—of any significance to the listener? Are they *merely* coincidental, or, at best, a natural consequence of composing a movement in a unified mood? In any case, is it not rash to suppose that they were consciously intended? Is this particular instance not more likely to be a quirk of Beethoven's subconscious, brooding over melodic figures of a particular type? Such questions have been debated for many years, on the one side with scepticism and on the other with something approaching mystic fervour. And, at least in this case, Beethoven gives a clear answer. Yes, such coincidences are formally significant; and yes, they are fully intentional. As we have seen, it was a habit of the Viennese composers, when a motif has proved to be particularly fruitful, to repeat it at the end of the movement. That is just what Beethoven does in the B₂ of Ex. 14.5(*c*). Quite explicitly, he alludes back both to the second subject and the pizzicato cello theme.

What makes this network of thematic connections especially characteristic is that the listener only gradually becomes aware of it, and even then the awareness is probably subconscious. This sort of retrospective understanding, the musical equivalent of the dramatic device whereby a seemingly minor character turns out to be important, is typical of Beethoven. The same impulse lies behind another, even more Beethovenish form of thematic transformation (it is, as far as I know, his own invention, though perhaps suggested by Haydn's 'linkage'), in which an apparently meaningless figure is seized on and then gradually modified— 'morphed', as we should now say—until it assumes the shape of an important theme. The *locus classicus* is the first movement of the Piano Sonata Op. 90 in E minor, where the lead-back to the recapitulation takes this form.

With the exception of these specifically dramatic devices, the thematic transformations of sonata form are merely variants of common practice, differing in no essential respect from what we should find in da capo movements, operatic scenes, waltz suites, or medleys. As the nineteenth century advances, we find an ever more complex network of melodic links, regardless of form or genre. These links, it must be clearly understood, may be absolutely anything the composer can persuade that indefatigable pattern-seeker, the human ear, to accept. But one pattern stands out as especially important. In this, the relation of main to secondary theme reverses that of the ordinary theme and variation, since it is the main theme that is elaborate and diffuse, and the secondary theme that is simple and compact. And again, the categories 'main' and 'secondary' transcend relationships of form or key. They may be found, not only in first and second subjects, but also in minuets (or other short movements) and trios, in slow introductions and ensuing allegros, and so on.[14] Always, the secondary theme brings with it a relaxation of tension. It is, in a word, more tuneful.

There remain two closely related questions: how clearly are these correspondences meant to be perceived by the listener, and how far were the composers themselves conscious of them?

The first is easier to answer than the second. There are plenty of places where the correspondence is perfectly explicit, and others, like the first movement of the 'Appassionata' (Ex. 14.4) where even a casual listener can hardly fail to be aware of them. On the whole, however, composers show their greatest skill in keeping them just below the level of conscious recognition. Which brings us to the second question: how far was the exercise of this skill itself conscious? Here direct evidence appears to be completely lacking. Until the twentieth century, the composers themselves seem to have had nothing to say on the matter—at least, nothing has

---

[14] Something of the kind may be found even in the da capo movements of the early 18th c., e.g. the Bourrée of J. S. Bach's 'English' Suite in A, or Handel's 'Lascia ch'io pianga' (Ex. 7.9 on pp. 92–3).

come down to us. But then, with few exceptions such as Rameau on harmony or Berlioz on orchestration, they had little to say on any aspect of their technique. My own guess is that these subtle correspondences were not only for the most part consciously intended, but also the subject of a considerable body of unwritten lore. Surely so expert and inveterate a transformer of themes and motifs as Haydn must have known perfectly well what he was about. And if so, it is equally implausible that he maintained a complete silence on the matter in conversation with his friend Mozart or his pupil Beethoven. But this, as I say, is only a guess.

Liszt

Liszt, more than any other composer, showed what sonata form might become when released from academic scruple. For an example we need go no further than *Les Préludes*, always one of his most popular, familiar, and influential works. This manages to include virtually all the features of 'advanced' sonata form: modulation to a key other than the dominant, in this case the mediant; a long development, amounting virtually to a movement in itself and grouped around a single key; a reversed recapitulation; and, not least, the sort of thematic and modal unity we saw in the previous two examples. The following is a summary of its main features:

Introduction. Theme A, on a pentatonic seventh nicely balanced between *C* major and *A* minor. Silence. Sequential repetition a tone higher (Ex. 14.6).

Ex. 14.6. Liszt, *Les Préludes* (1848), bars 1–14, beginning of introduction (Theme A)

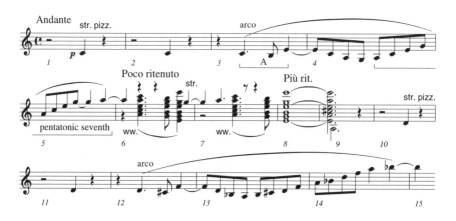

Dominant chord, closing into

First group. Theme B (Ex. 14.7). Theme C (still in *C* major tinged with *A* minor) immediately repeated in *E* major (Ex. 14.8).

Ex. 14.7. Liszt, *Les Préludes*, bars 35–6, beginning of 1st group (Theme B)

Ex. 14.8. Liszt, *Les Préludes*, bars 47–62, continuation of 1st group (Theme C)

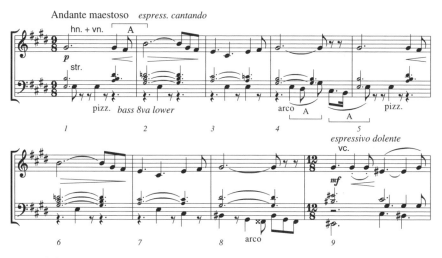

Modulatory transition to

Second group. Theme D in *E* major (Ex. 14.9), immediately repeated in decorated form.

Ex. 14.9. Liszt, *Les Préludes*, bars 70–9, beginning of 2nd group (Theme D)

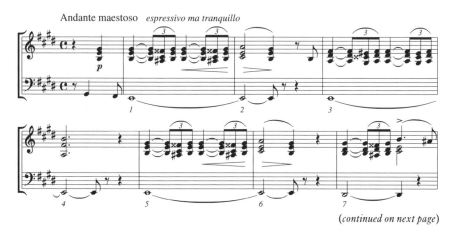

(*continued on next page*)

(Ex. 14.9 *cont.*)

Rich modulations. Reference back to Theme C. Conclusion of the exposition on a diminished-seventh chord. Silence. Then

Development. A stormy episode, marked 'Allegro ma non troppo'. A pastoral interlude ('Allegretto pastorale'), leading into

Recapitulation and coda. Theme D, appearing first in an anomalous A major (bar 260) then in the orthodox tonic key of C major, which prevails for the rest of the movement (bar 296). Theme C, marked 'Allegro marziale animato' (bar 346). Theme D again, transformed into a brisk march ('Tempo di marcia', bar 370). Finally, a grandiose recapitulation of Theme B ('Allegro maestoso', bars 405–19), with a final reference to Figure A of Theme A (Ex. 14.10).

Ex. 14.10. Liszt, *Les Préludes*, bars 416–19 (end of movement)

It will be seen that this movement is in a surprisingly orthodox sonata form, with dramatic 'first subject', transition, and lyrical 'second subject' complete with modulatory digression. Liszt even works in, towards the end of the exposition, the customary backward glance to the first subject, and, just before the final cadence, a last allusion to the opening figure (Ex. 14.10). The most eccentric feature is the commencement of the recapitulation in a foreign key, but even that is not without Classical precedent.[15]

Yet the effect is quite unlike that of sonata form as understood by Haydn, Mozart, or Beethoven. It resembles a rubber sheet stretched to the point of losing its elasticity. The modulations completely lack the true symphonic drive; instead, they drift. This is largely because Liszt's natural inclination is to base his harmony on drones, which are often implied beneath the restlessly chromatic surface even when not actually present. The 'Allegro ma non troppo' of the development section is a case in point. Its initial twenty bars at first strike us as positively atonal, yet when the harmony gravitates back to *A* minor we feel that we have never really left it. Later, in the 'Allegretto pastorale' the drones become explicit, stepping down a ladder of thirds to produce a floating, almost equally atonal sensation.

Another reason for the sense of drift is the sparing use of the dominant chord. There are only two clear-cut full closes, one occurring fleetingly in the transition (bar 64) and the other at the end of the movement. Elsewhere, the dominant chord is always leading up to something; and whenever it does so with any vigour, that something, true to the centripetal tendencies of vernacular harmony, is in the key of *C* major, *A* minor, or *A* major. This paucity of full closes gives the music great fluency; it may meander or stagnate, but never halts. There could hardly be a greater contrast with the closed, 'antecedent–consequent' formulas so loved by his German contemporaries.

It is remarkable, too, how much of this movement is foreshadowed in its first few bars. As in classical Indian music, Liszt begins with a slow, arrhythmic, unharmonized introduction designed to establish the modal and melodic characteristics of the ensuing movement. Its two salient features are Figure A (Ex. 14.6, bar 3), with its downward step and rising fourth, and an ascending pentatonic seventh (bars 4–5). The latter serves as a melodic foundation for the entire movement; for, as we afterwards learn, everything is to be organized around the ladder of thirds $a(\flat)–c(\sharp)–e–g(\sharp)–b$. Modulation, for the most part, is effected by moving from one rung of this ladder to another. It is as natural for Liszt to proceed to the mediant as for Mozart to proceed to the dominant; and just as Mozart has dominants of dominants, so Liszt has mediants of mediants (see Ex. 14.8, bar 8).

There was nothing new about beginning a slow introduction with an unharmonized melody. Half a century earlier, Haydn had done the same in his 'Drum Roll' Symphony (No. 103 in E flat), even down to the subsequent thematic

---

[15] e.g. in the first movement of Beethoven's Piano Sonata in F, Op. 10 No. 2, where the recapitulation likewise begins in the major submediant.

transformations. What *was* new was to develop almost the entire movement out of this opening idea. Here Gypsy influence must surely have been at work. Several of the Hungarian Rhapsodies, composed about the same time as *Les Préludes*, begin in a similar fashion, and No. 13 in A minor, especially, is not so very far from actual Oriental practice. We should recall that Liszt was both a renowned improviser and a student of east European improvisatory technique. To him, the 'maqām principle' was not an ethnomusicological curiosity, but something felt in the fingers.

On the other hand, it must be admitted that in the symphonic poems any such influences lie deeply hidden. The effect of *Les Préludes* is rather that of a one-act Italian opera without words, complete with storm, pastoral idyll, love scene, and martial interlude—this last the equivalent, perhaps, of the moment when the tenor and baritone swear undying vengeance. There is even, towards the end, a march tune that bursts in with all the bathetic jauntiness of Bellini or Donizetti. In fact, this work was first planned as an evocation of the Mediterranean landscape,[16] and its pentatonic figures belong, not to eastern Europe, but to a pastoral tradition running from Rossini to Debussy.[17]

Though far from perfect, *Les Préludes* was an original, effective, and extremely influential piece. Among the composers who probably owed something to it, directly or indirectly, were Tchaikovsky (all the stormy passages), the Dukas of *The Sorcerer's Apprentice* (the swirling chromatic scales of the 'storm'), Richard Strauss (the remarkable chromatic digression of bars 89–100, towards the end of the exposition), and Sibelius (the modal chords of Ex. 14.10). But the greatest debt of all, as we shall presently see, was Wagner's.

Later forms

Sonata form confronted the later Romantic composers with a dilemma. On the one hand, it rested on a type of tonal opposition that no longer came naturally to them. On the other, it contained formal devices that still did, such as strong thematic contrast, rhapsodic development, and large-scale recapitulation. How was one to make use of the latter without shackling oneself with the former?

One solution was to resort to some kind of variation form. Here, as so often, Beethoven had led the way, with the finales of his Third and Ninth Symphonies. A very striking example is the passacaglia concluding Brahms's Fourth Symphony, which is organized on the following sonata-like lines:

---

[16] The complicated history of *Les Préludes* is summarized by Humphrey Searle in 'The Orchestral Works' (in *Franz Liszt: The Man and his Music*), 288–9.

[17] See e.g. the sunrise in Act I of Rossini's *William Tell*; the sunrise and 'Chorus of Hebrew Elders' in Act I of Saint-Saëns's *Sampson and Delilah*; Debussy's *Prélude à l'après-midi d'un faune* (Ex. 15.17 on pp. 400–1); and the 'eclogues' of various composers, including Liszt himself.

Theme and Variation 1: assertive 'first subject'.

Variations 2–3: 'transition'.

Variations 4–11: lyrical 'second subject', which, in the usual Romantic manner, begins fluently, works up to a high point, and then dies away.

Variations 12–15: episodic 'development' in a slower rhythm.

Variation 16–30: 'recapitulation' and 'coda'.

Where it differs from sonata form, of course, is that nowhere does it depart from the tonic key. Instead, Brahms suggests the appropriate modulations by the clever use of tonal counterpoint. The 'first subject', for instance, has a subdominant tinge which makes the clear-cut tonic of the 'second subject' sound a little like a dominant.

It is significant that this feat of key mixture is a finale. In many post-Classical sonata-form works, we can almost hear the composer's sigh of relief at having got over the stern obligations of the first movement. Now he is free to indulge in dances, marches, intermezzos, rhapsodies, rondos, variations, or anything else that takes his fancy—in a word, to be himself. And that self is often rather different from the model of Teutonic severity suggested by the word 'symphony'. After about 1850, it is striking how seldom the composers of enduring sonata-form works are German, as distinct from Austrian. They may be French, like Saint-Saëns; Belgian, like Franck; or English, like Elgar. But more often they are Russian, like Borodin, Tchaikovsky, Prokofiev, and Shostakovich; Czech, like Dvořák and Smetana; Scandinavian, like Grieg, Sibelius, and Nielsen; Austrian, like Bruckner, Mahler, and (by naturalization) Brahms; or Franco-German-Italian-Hungarian, like Liszt.

In other words, they are mostly east European, in the musical if not always in the geographical sense. There will continue to be arguments about the merits of the late Romantic symphony. But at least it was alive; and for that, we must mainly thank this eastern influx.

III. WAGNER AND THE VERNACULAR

There can hardly be any doubt that Wagner's works have survived,
not because they are 'music dramas', but because they are operas.

Hans Gál, *Richard Wagner*, 196

Millions of words have been written on the uniqueness of Richard Wagner. By way
of a change, we are concerned here with his normality. Our Wagner is the composer who began as an imitator of Weber, Auber, Bellini, and Meyerbeer, and never
entirely outgrew those origins. Here it is useful to list his major works, with the
dates when they were first completed—that is, disregarding later revisions:

Opera	Date
Die Feen	1834
Das Liebesverbot	1836
Rienzi	1840
Der fliegende Holländer	1841
Tannhäuser	1845
Lohengrin	1848
Das Rheingold	1854
Die Walküre	1856
Siegfried (first 2 acts)	1857
Tristan und Isolde	1859
Die Meistersinger	1867
Siegfried (last act)	1869
Götterdämmerung	1874
Parsifal	1882

First comes the Weberian *Feen*, then the Bellinian *Liebesverbot*, then the
Meyerbeerian *Rienzi*, then the three 'Romantic operas', in which the mature
Wagner is patchily visible. Five years intervene, during which he plots revolution,
dodges the police, develops a radical theory of 'music-drama', projects great
works, and composes next to nothing. Then at last come the four masterpieces of
his maturity: *The Ring*, *Tristan*, *Die Meistersinger*, and *Parsifal*, spread over almost
three decades.

The operatic background

Even from this bald account several facts stand out: the sheer length of his career;
its unsurpassed breadth, from the second-hand Weber of *Die Feen* to the near-

Schoenberg of *Parsifal*; but also, if less obviously, the extreme slowness of his development. Leaving out the break between 1848 and 1853, it took him fifteen years to attain maturity—fifteen years during which he remained under the strong influence of French and Italian opera. And even then *Lohengrin*, which has been described as standing 'tremulously balanced on the brink of music drama',[18] conforms to most of the traditional patterns. An old Novello score of this opera contains not only parallel texts in German, English, and Italian (with the Italian on top), but an Italian contents page on which a 'Romanza (La visione d'Elsa)', 'Preghiera', 'Marcia religiosa', 'Coro della chiesa', and 'Gran Duetto (D'amore)' are all duly listed.

In the first two-thirds of *The Ring*—that is, *Das Rheingold*, *Die Walküre*, and Acts I and II of *Siegfried*—Wagner made a determined effort to get away from this sort of thing, banning, or at least severely restricting, choruses, duets, and other concerted pieces. But the old Adam insisted on asserting himself. Choruses reappear in *Tristan* and gigantic love duets in both Tristan and Act III of *Siegfried*. As for *Die Meistersinger*, it has arias, dances, marches, choruses, a *pezzo concertato* (in the celebrated quintet), and a spectacular procession towards the end. And when we come to the climax of the *Ring* tetralogy, it can only be said that

Die Götterdämmerung, like the end of Siegfried, is opera. In it we have choruses and *finales*; we have a great *scena* for the *prima donna* with the chorus looking on very much as they used to do when Semiramide was singing *Bel raggio*; above all, we have the tenor stabbed to death and then coming to life to sing pretty things about his love before he expires, just like Edgardo in Lucia di Lammermoor.[19]

It is true that Wagner made these Italianate features entirely his own. Still, the backsliding raises questions about his commitment to music-drama. Why, one is bound to ask, did he impose on himself restrictions that evidently violated his deepest instincts?

At the bottom of it all was a determination to naturalize a genre that had always been rather alien to the German temperament. (Mozart is an obvious exception, but then the composer of *Le nozze di Figaro*, *Don Giovanni*, and *Così fan tutte* was virtually a German-speaking Italian.) Even before Wagner, German composers had preferred the intimate, lied-like aria[20] to the more usual extrovert variety, the chorus to the solo voice, and instruments to voices of any kind. If there had to be voices, they sometimes preferred them to speak rather than to sing. 'Melodrama',

---

[18] Barry Millington, *Wagner*, 183.
[19] Bernard Shaw, 'Bassetto at Bayreuth: IV', 378; repr. in *Shaw's Music*, iii. 360–82. First published in the *Star*, 22–5 July 1896.
[20] e.g. 'Leise, leise', in Weber's *Freischütz*, Act II, no. 9.

in the original sense of dialogue spoken against an orchestral background, was a German speciality, used to thrilling effect in the dungeon scene in *Fidelio* and the Wolf's Glen scene in *Der Freischütz*. Both of these made a great impression on Wagner, and much of his mature work is really melodrama with the speech elevated to recitative. Another route to the same destination was *recitativo obbligato*, a dramatic, orchestrally accompanied recitative that can sound strikingly Wagnerian to modern ears.[21] One of its devices, the recurring unison figure, was seized on by Wagner in his very first dramatic work, the fragment *Die Hochzeit*.[22] Together with the operatic 'reminiscence theme' and the thematic transformations of Liszt and others, it became one source of the Wagnerian leitmotif.

This multiplicity of sources is typical of Wagner. Even among great composers, he is distinguished by his assimilative powers. No one has more often been 'anticipated', 'foreshadowed', or 'prophesied'. A full list of his influences would include virtually every important composer of the early nineteenth century, as well as many unimportant ones.[23]

But it would include little else. With few exceptions, Wagner's style was compounded of elements drawn from his contemporaries. Throughout his life he revered Beethoven, but more as an inspiration than a model. And in any case Beethoven was still a modern, whose Ninth Symphony was first performed when Wagner was already eleven years old. It is true that, when already in his late forties, Wagner became interested in J. S. Bach and derived much of *Die Meistersinger* from him, and there is no doubt a touch of Palestrina in *Lohengrin* and *Parsifal*. But even Beethoven, Bach, and Palestrina put together were not as important to him as Franz Liszt.

The debt to Liszt

It is hard to exaggerate Wagner's debt to Liszt, especially during the 1850s. Reminiscences of *Les Préludes*, in particular, are everywhere. In *Das Rheingold*, one of its main tunes is appropriated for the 'Valhalla' theme,[24] and part of the 'storm' for

---

[21] e.g. the introduction to Donna Elvira's aria 'Mi tradì quell'alma ingrata' in *Don Giovanni*, and several places in *William Tell*.

[22] Deryck Cooke points this out in 'Wagner's Musical Language', 249–53. (The passage in question is quoted on p. 250.) He specifically connects Wagner's insistence on this figure with 'the way that Mozart used an idea to bind an orchestral recitative together' (p. 249).

[23] For details see John Warrack, 'The Musical Background', in Burbige and Sutton (eds.), *The Wagner Companion*, 85–112; Thomas S. Grey, 'Musical Background and Influences', in Millington (ed.), *The Wagner Compendium*, 63–92; and Deryck Cooke, 'Wagner's Operatic Apprenticeship', in *Vindications*, 37–42.

[24] Cf. Ex. 14.8 (Liszt) with Ex. 13.4 (Wagner) on pp. 357 and 281 respectively.

Loge's leitmotif.[25] A few years later, the 'Allegretto pastorale' was plundered for the 'Forest Murmurs' in *Siegfried*. Later still, something of the opening bars went into the Prelude to *Tristan*, where we find the same dialogue between unison strings and chordal woodwind, the same sequence interrupted by dramatic silences, and a similar harmonic ambiguity.[26] Finally, Sieglinde's theme in *Götterdämmerung* is about equally indebted to the 'love theme' from *Les Préludes* (Ex. 14.9 on pp. 357–8) and the duet 'Cara luce, soave conforto' from Donizetti's *La favorita*.[27]

Add the 'borrowings' from such works as the *Faust* Symphony and the First Piano Concerto,[28] and one has some idea of how much Wagner owed Liszt: not just a tune here or a progression there, but entire formal procedures. It was from Liszt that Wagner at last acquired the fluency that he had always aspired to. From the beginning, he had hated the disjointed forms of Italian opera, designed largely to give the responsive Italian audience an opportunity to display its pleasure. A showy cabaletta, for instance, would be followed by a noisy orchestral tutti, which the composer expected (or at least hoped) would be drowned by applause. That sort of thing was anathema to German composers, and to none more so than Richard Wagner. In any case, he had the usual Teutonic fondness for long, uninterrupted periods. Already in his early works he began running the conclusion of each number into the beginning of the following one. The next step was to avoid coming to a conclusion at all, and here Liszt, with his blurring of formal divisions, proved to be a useful model.

At the opposite extreme, it was mainly from Liszt (perhaps with a little help from Beethoven) that Wagner learnt the value of the dramatic silence. As we saw in Chapter 11,[29] this was ultimately Oriental in origin, though long absorbed into east European popular music. A specifically east European pattern was the sequential step that begins with bare melody and then blossoms into harmony.[30] Just such a pattern occurs in Liszt's Hungarian Rhapsody no. 8 in F sharp minor,

[25] Cf. Loge's entry in Scene ii of *Das Rheingold* (just before the words 'Wie? welchen Handel hatt' ich geschossen?) with bars 155–9 of *Les Préludes*.

[26] In addition, Christopher Headington points out a strong resemblance between the *Tristan* Prelude and Liszt's song 'Die Lorelei'. See 'The Songs' in Walker (ed.), *Franz Liszt: The Man and his Music*, 231–2.

[27] If anything, Wagner's tune is closer to Donizetti's, which he knew well from making a piano arrangement of *La favorita* during his impoverished Paris days. It is also possible—indeed likely—that Liszt himself was influenced by it. The resemblance between these tunes (and several others) was pointed out by Henri de Saussine in 'De la Favorite à Saint-Christophe'.

[28] Cf. the chromatic scale in the second movement, bars 137–8, with those in the extract from *Götterdämmerung* quoted in the next chapter (Ex. 15.16 on pp. 399–400).

[29] See the discussion of sequences at the minor second on pp. 188–9.

[30] Earlier examples include the opening bars of Mozart's Fantasia for Piano in C minor (Ex. 11.53 on p. 186) and Beethoven's 'Appassionata' Sonata in F minor, Op. 57 (Ex. 14.4(*a*) on p. 352).

which brings us close to the *Tristan* Prelude even without the intervening stage of *Les Préludes*. The dates fit too, since the Rhapsody was published in 1853 and Wagner began the composition of *Tristan* in 1857. Are we to imagine Wagner eagerly scanning the Hungarian Rhapsodies for cribbable details?

In the matter of harmony, we have his own testimony that the study of Liszt's music turned him into 'a completely different chap as a harmonist'.[31] Unfortunately, he did not elaborate, but we may suppose that he had in mind unusual chordal juxtapositions, 'Lisztian' sequences, and new ways of using chromatic scales, diminished sevenths, and augmented triads. What most of these novelties had in common was the symmetrical division of the octave into 2×6, 3×4, 4×3, or 6×2 semitones.[32] This had two attractions. The first was that it added to the harmonic palette a whole range of new colours, especially apt (like that old symmetrical chord, the diminished seventh) for the depiction of the supernatural and the uncanny. The second was the oddly static effect it produced, which, depending on the circumstances, could be anything from a serene timelessness to a nightmarish sense of getting nowhere fast. Total stasis did not interest Wagner, but its close relative, an extreme slowing of the harmonic pulse, certainly did. It was largely from Liszt that he learnt to achieve it.

The Wagnerizing of the vernacular

This debt to Liszt, and, via him, to the east European folk idiom, is deeply ironic. To all external appearances, Wagner had little use for the folky or exotic—a very considerable sacrifice for an opera composer. The nearest approach in his mature works to the peasants, Gypsies, and Orientals that abound in nineteenth-century opera, are the sturdy burghers of *Die Meistersinger*. In contrast to composers like Smetana or Musorgsky, he created a national style of opera with no aid from the national folk music; and for east European folk music in particular, he had nothing but a frankly racist contempt. Almost always, he avoids anything obviously smacking of it, the only important exceptions being Siegfried's funeral march in *Götterdämmerung*, which has the customary Hungarian tinge, and one or two anti-Semitic caricatures.[33] Yet it was principally from the east that he obtained the defining features of his mature style: the fluency, the suppleness, the 'unendliche

---

[31] In the original, 'ein ganz anderer Kerl als Harmoniker'. The remark was made shortly after the completion of *Tristan*, in a letter written to Hans von Bülow on 7 Oct. 1859. An English translation may be found in *Selected Letters of Richard Wagner*.

[32] For folk origins, see the discussion of the octatonic and whole-tone scales on pp. 226–30.

[33] e.g. 'Als zullendes Kind', sung by the dwarf Mime in *Siegfried*, Act I, Scene i, and Beckmesser's song in *Die Meistersinger*, Act III, Scene v.

Melodie' (which has a distant but real kinship with the endless melody of the Orient), the transformation of themes, the harmonic novelties. In all this, Liszt served as a filter, extracting from the raw folk stuff what was usable in Wagner's ultra-German art. And, by a further irony, it was largely these east European features that removed Wagner from the vernacular. In the words of Richard Capell, 'The idea of fluidity always presents itself when we think of Wagner's music. One thing melts into another, tune into tune, key into key, mood into mood.'[34] This fluidity, so utterly different from the sharp contrasts of a composer like Bizet, is an Oriental characteristic.

Apart from this, the feature of Wagner's style that most distinguished it from the vernacular was its rhythm:

in the nineteenth century a regular 4/4 pulse became more and more confined to German music. At the moment when Italian and French opera had become obsessively delighted with triple pulses of every kind, Wagner composed *Lohengrin* with only the King's Prayer in 3/4, and even that was originally sketched in 4/4. Wagner may have felt that in the *Tannhäuser* overture he had strayed too close to the throbbing 9/8 of Parisian opera, even though he resolutely notated it in 3/4. Significantly, the return of the Pilgrims' March in the overture is fashioned into a broad *alla breve*, refusing to reprise in 9/8.[35]

Wagner seems to have felt a genuine distaste for one feature of Meyerbeer's style (or Berlioz's, for that matter): the frequent alternation of triple and compound metres with common duple time. While *Rienzi*, like *Lohengrin*, maintains a stolid 4/4 for nearly the entire duration of its five acts, Act I alone of *Les Huguenots* includes sections in 12/8, 4/4, 3/4, 2/4, 3/8, and 9/8.[36]

Presumably Wagner objected to triple pulses because they were too dance-like. For similar reasons, he shuns repetitive accompaniment figures, substituting for them counter-melodies, block harmonies, pedal points—or, quite often, nothing at all, for no nineteenth-century composer made more use of totally unaccompanied melody.

It was not that he despised lighter genres such as the waltz—quite the contrary. In his youth, he had been a great admirer of the music of Johann Strauss, senior, which he first encountered in Vienna at the age of 19:

'I visited the theatres, heard Strauss, went on excursions and had altogether a very good time.' . . . He used to go along to a public-house, the Sträusslein, where Strauss, with his fiddle, made everyone frantic with delight. 'When he started to play a new waltz this demon of the Viennese musical spirit shook like a Pythian priestess on her tripod.'[37]

[34] 'Richard Wagner', 230.

[35] Hugh Macdonald, 𝄞, 234.

[36] Thomas S. Grey, 'Musical Background and Influences', 73.   [37] John Chancellor, *Wagner*, 36.

Later, he went so far as to make an arrangement of the waltz 'Wine, Woman, and Song' by Johann Strauss, junior,[38] whom he declared to have the best musical brains in Europe (his own no doubt excepted).

In itself, this is not so very odd. Among highbrow German musicians, a liking for Viennese popular music served the same purpose as an enthusiasm for baseball among American intellectuals: it showed that that one was, after all, a good fellow. But Wagner was a special case, a voracious eclectic who soaked up influences like a sponge and integrated them into his style without effort and apparently without thought. So we find that, though he might banish the rhythm of the waltz from his early operas, he could not help retaining much of its melodic line. Elizabeth's entry in Act II of *Tannhäuser*, to take one instance, occurs to a tune powerfully reminiscent of the parlour or music hall (Ex. 14.11(*a*)). No doubt his avoidance of triple measures was in part due to a secret dread of sounding like Ex. 14.11(*b*). Though he later unbent so far as to compose waltzes (or at any rate waltz-like songs) for the Rhine Maidens in *Das Rheingold*, the Apprentices in *Die Meistersinger*, and the Flower Maidens in *Parsifal*, he never ceased to regard them as a symbol of mindless pleasure.

Ex. 14.11. Wagner, *Tannhäuser* (1843–5), Act II, Scene i (down a 5th)

(*a*) bars 71–84 (end of Prelude and entrance of Elizabeth)

[38] See Millington (ed.), *The Wagner Compendium*, 324.

(*b*) waltz, founded on (*a*)

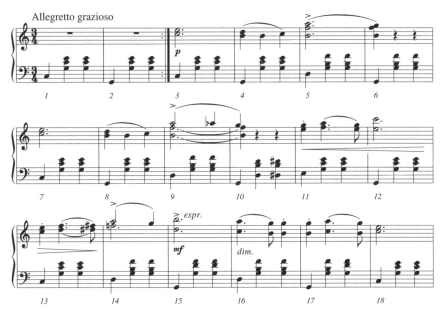

Another way of Wagnerizing vernacular melody was to reduce or even eliminate its accompaniment. The sailor's song in *Tristan* is compounded of much the same melodic elements as the *Tannhäuser* tune, but acquires an archaic, Phrygian quality by being performed, first with no harmony at all, and then over a bare mediant pedal (Ex. 14.12(*a*)). Later, when the tune is taken up by the orchestra, Wagner

Ex. 14.12. Wagner, *Tristan und Isolde* (1857–9), Act I, Scene ii

(*a*) bars 8–20 ('Sailor's Song') (up a major 6th)

(*b*) bars 93–7 (orchestral version of (*a*)) (up a major 5th)

transfers the pedal to the dominant, thereby reverting to something closer to the musical language of *Tannhäuser* (Ex. 14.12(*b*)).

In much the same way, the most awe-inspiring of all Wagner's unharmonized melodies, the opening theme of the *Parsifal* Prelude (Ex. 14.13), turns out to consist of two hoary melodic formulas: the rising pattern *1–3–5–6*,[39] and the downwardly looping *3–6⁻–7⁻–1*,[40] here transposed up a fifth to *7–3–4♯–5*. Even the combination of these two clichés was not original, as we can see from Ex. 14.14, by the minor Italian composer Giovanni Pacini. Yet in Wagner's hands it becomes a passage of wonderful power and originality. Any of his contemporaries, seeking

Ex. 14.13. Wagner, *Parsifal* (1877–82), Prelude, beginning (up a major 3rd)

Ex. 14.14. Pacini, *Saffo* (1840), Act II, no. 6, 'Il cor non basta a reggere', beginning (down a major 3rd)

---

[39] By Wagner's own admission, its immediate source was Liszt's choral work 'Excelsior!', but cf. also bars 5–6 of *Les Préludes* (Ex. 14.6 on p. 356). For further discussion, see Warrack, 'The Musical Background' (in *The Wagner Companion*), 111, and Alan Walker, 'Liszt's Musical Background' (in *Franz Liszt: The Man and his Music*), 72.   [40] See pp. 278–9.

to conjure up the 'dim religious light' of the Middle Ages, would surely have gone to the 'old modes'. It is somehow typical of Wagner that he gives us instead a melody *in the major*, with a deviation to the mediant derived, not from Palestrina or Gregorian chant, but from Italian opera.

Ladders of thirds

Especially in his later work, Wagner's tunes and leitmotifs are nearly always based on a ladder of thirds of one sort or another. Sometimes the gaps between the rungs are filled in to form scales, but more often the ladder-like structure is left exposed. As we have seen, such patterns were anything but unusual at this period; what *was* unusual was Wagner's astonishing faculty for transforming them. Rungs are continually being added or subtracted, squeezed together or stretched apart. More literally, sevenths are stripped down to triads, and triads expanded to sevenths, ninths, or even elevenths, any of which may be diatonic, diminished, or augmented.

The great object lesson for these transformations is, of course, *The Ring*. This begins by building up the major triad that Wagner himself called the *Naturmotiv*;[41] but it is significant that, on the entry of the human voice, this triad expands into a pentatonic seventh (see Ex. 13.22(*b*) on p. 297). And the same, generally speaking, is true of most of Wagner's triadic themes. It is hard to conceive anything more emphatically major-triadic than the beginning of the *Meistersinger* Overture (Ex. 14.15), yet it is already blossoming into a pentatonic seventh by the third bar (or, in the bass, the second bar). This partiality towards the pentatonic seventh runs right through Wagner. Several of his strongest themes consist of little or nothing else;[42] in

Ex. 14.15. Wagner, *Die Meistersinger* (1862–7), Overture, beginning

[41] See Grey's article on the 'Nature motif' in *The Wagner Compendium*, 'A Wagnerian Glossary', 237. This *Naturmotiv* belongs to a German tradition stretching from Wackenroder to Schenker.

[42] e.g., from *The Ring*: 'Ride of the Valkyries' (first four bars); 'Valhalla' motif (Ex. 13.4 on p. 281); 'Forest Bird' motif (Ex. 13.6 on p. 281). The first is confined to the notes of the natural pentatonic seventh, i.e. *a*, *c*, *e*, *g*; the other two add a passing *d*.

others, the pentatonic framework is lightly disguised with passing notes. It need not be of the 'natural' type; often, a 'soft' pentatonic Melody is set over a dominant Bass (in other words $d–f–a–c^+$ over G), as in Ex. 14.16. Here, the autonomy of the Melody is such that one can no longer talk of a simple 'dominant discord'. In effect, Wagner has divided the ladder of thirds into two sections, in such a way that the bottom (consisting of the dominant triad $g^-–b^-–d$) provides a characteristic dominant-harmony restlessness, and the top (consisting of the soft pentatonic seventh $d–f–a–c^+$) an independent melodic framework.

Ex. 14.16. Wagner, *Götterdämmerung* (1869–74), Prelude, bars 337–40 (the 'Brünnhilde' motif) (down a minor 3rd)

In the 'Hunting Horn' theme from *Tristan* (Ex. 14.17(*a*)), Wagner further complicates this structure by the addition of a tonic pedal, thereby anticipating some of the the harmonic experiments of the early twentieth century. In effect, three perfect fifths have been piled on top of one another: first $c^-–g^-$, then $g^-–d$, and finally $d–(f)–a$. Later in the movement, the triad $d–f–a$ conclusively proves its independence (and, by implication, the bitonality of the whole structure) by turning into a tonic in its own right (Ex. 14.17(*b*)).

Ex. 14.17. Wagner, *Tristan und Isolde* (1857–9), Act II, Scene i (up a tone)

(*a*) beginning

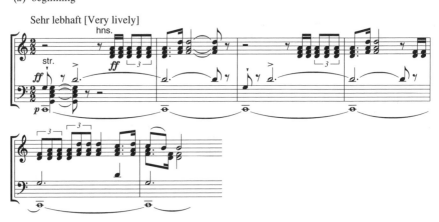

(*b*) bars 74–81

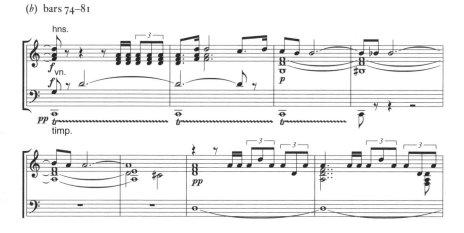

Tonality

Wagner profoundly believes that to travel hopefully is a better thing than to arrive. In his mature works, the Melody remains in a perpetual state of becoming till the very end of the act or movement. There must always be a tonic in the offing, even if endless deflections prevent his dominants from ever reaching it. For this reason, he is careful to ensure that the distinction between tonic and dominant, no matter how weak it may become, never quite disappears.

His tonal ambiguities are those of the vernacular, but exercised over enormous time spans. What has been called his 'bipolar tonality'[43] is generally a matter of hesitating between adjacent rungs of a ladder of thirds: between, for instance, the *a*⁻ and *c* of *a*⁻–*c*–*e*–*g* (as in the Prelude and much of the first act of *Tristan*), or the *c* and *e* of *c*–*e*–*g*–*b* (as in the first act of *Götterdämmerung*). He also makes great use of chromatic inflection, of the type demonstrated on a small scale in 'Elsa's Vision' (Ex. 14.18(*a*)). The effect is highly chromatic—too much so, according to Wagner himself, for anything but dramatic music—but perfectly smooth and comprehensible. Wagner works this miracle, firstly by constructing his bold modulations on a Lisztian framework of rising minor thirds, and secondly by casting his Melody in a series of overlapping pentatonic sevenths (Exs. 14.18(*b*) and (*c*)).

Much of the mystification surrounding Wagner's tonality, whether bi- or uni-polar, springs from attempts to interpret it in symphonic rather than operatic terms. Long before his day opera composers had mastered the art of incorporating modulatory digressions into extended scenes without disturbing the central key.

[43] See Robert Bailey, 'The Structure of the *Ring* and its Evolution', 59–60.

Ex. 14.18. Wagner, *Lohengrin* (1846–8), Act I, Scene ii

(*a*) 'Elsa's Vision' (up a semitone)

(*b*) skeletal outline of Melody and Bass

(*c*) melodic and harmonic chords

    (i) melodic chords   (ii) harmonic chords

       (corresponding to   (corresponding to

       numbered brackets)   ringed notes in (*b*))

Among examples well known to Wagner himself are the overture and opening
scene of *Don Giovanni*,[44] the Wolf's Glen scene from *Der Freischütz*, and the finale
to Act I of *William Tell*. To the symphonic composer, the end of a movement is the
goal towards which everything else is directed; to Wagner, it is not much more than
a necessary inconvenience. Without being perfunctory or ineffective, his concluding

---

[44] 'At sixteen, he was . . . trying to master orchestration by wrestling with the full score of Mozart's *Don
Giovanni*' (Cooke, 'Wagner's Musical Language', 248). Later, he conducted three performances of his own
arrangement of the same opera (see *The Wagner Compendium*, 100 and 324).

passages are far from being preordained, as a study of his key relationships makes clear. For instance, most of the last act of *Der fliegende Holländer* is in C major, but the actual ending consists of a mere forty-nine bars of D major. Similarly, the last half hour or so of *Götterdämmerung* is again grouped around C (both major and minor) but finishes with a brief passage in D flat major. It is significant that in each case the tonic rises by a tone or semitone. (A similar procedure in twentieth-century popular music is sometimes known as the 'truck-driver modulation': you ram in the clutch and shift up to a higher key.) The new key is sustained long enough to impart a feeling of finality, but not long enough to allow the sense of elevation to pall.

Conclusion

The reader may wonder why, in a book that is meant to be about musical patterns rather than individual composers, Wagner alone has such a large section to himself. One reason, I must frankly confess, is that to the musical historian he is enormous fun. In a manner characteristic of the times, he combines genuine greatness with a touch of genuine absurdity.

But there are also more serious reasons. In addition to being a musical genius of unsurpassed originality, Wagner was uniquely influential—and not only among musicians. Beethoven may have become a cult, but only Wagner became an ism, almost as important for what he was supposed to have done as for what he actually did. More than any other artist of the nineteenth century, he embodied the Romantic (and later Modernist) paradox of the individual–communal. On the one hand, the Romantics revered the lone genius, with his scorn for convention and ruthless egotism; on the other, they yearned for the communal, utterly unindividualistic life of the peasant village or the Catholic Middle Ages. So it came about, after Wagner's death in 1883, that his intensely personal idiom turned into a sort of Modernist vernacular.

As such, it was bound to fail, for a true vernacular must be truly communal. In the late Romantics and early Moderns, Wagner's influence is most beneficial where it is least obvious, as for instance in Debussy. The man generally regarded as his successor, Richard Strauss, was really (as we can now easily see) a rather more old-fashioned composer. Yet even the limited successes of the Wagnerian pseudo-vernacular would have been impossible if it had not been deeply rooted in the real vernacular. In spite of all the talk about 'the music of the future', Wagner was very much a man of his time. And that was part of his greatness.

15 Modernism

The Modernist attitude towards popular art has generally been a mixture of hostility and wary flirtation. One thinks of the 'Dance of the Flower Maidens' in *Parsifal*, the waltzes and marches in Mahler and Richard Strauss, the ragtime movements in Debussy and Stravinsky. Even Schoenberg had a brush with jazz.

It is tempting to put this ambivalence down to business rivalry. There was no competition between Mozart and a Gypsy bandleader; they inhabited different economic worlds. But Wagner *was* competing with Johann Strauss, in the sense that a well-to-do burgher might equally well spend his money on *Tristan* or *Die Fledermaus*. This explains why the waltzes, marches, or rags of 'serious' composers usually have an ironic tinge: economists call it 'product differentiation'. It explains, too, why Italian opera composers, whose own product was so commercially successful, could afford to take a more tolerant view of popular music, and why Continental composers could be friendly towards jazz at a time when it was still an exotic and commercially unimportant novelty.

This economic insight provides perhaps the most satisfactory distinction between 'popular' and 'folk' music: while popular music is in commercial competition with 'serious' music, folk music is not. (Hence, too, the promotion of popular genres such as the early blues or jazz to the 'folk' category once they cease to be commercially viable.) And it explains the 'serious' composer's combination of hostility, or its milder cousin condescension, with surreptitious thefts—for this is exactly the attitude of a business rival. But of course there was more to it than that. If the motives of Wagner, Debussy, Stravinsky, et al. had been purely economic, they would have become popular composers themselves. If they did not, it was partly for fear of losing professional caste, but also because they felt themselves to be entrusted with the high mission of Modernism.

But what was Modernism? Evidently a complex phenomenon—almost as resistant to definition as the Romanticism out of which it grew. Its germ can be detected in the hostility of Joseph Berglinger, Wackenroder's ideal composer, towards his public and professional colleagues.[1] It is worth noting, however, that

---

[1] See pp. 340–2.

while Joseph is at odds with his contemporaries, he is not in advance of them. That came later. Indeed, the very notion of being 'in advance', in this special sense, belongs to the nineteenth century. Its roots lie in a peculiarly German conception of progress, articulated mainly by Hegel: not the prosaic, step-by-step improvement of the Victorians, but a mystical force that, like a great wave, carries humanity continuously and ineluctably forward. A more dignified name for it is History. Hegel's influence was enormous, both directly and through his disciples; and it was one of these, Feuerbach, who popularized the phrase 'of the future' ('der Zukunft', in the original German) in his book *Grundsätze der Philosophie der Zukunft* (*Principles of the Philosophy of the Future*). This suggested Wagner's 'artwork of the future' ('Kunstwerk der Zukunft'), which in turn became 'the music of the future'.

The music of the future! What an intoxicating notion—and what a marvellous excuse for obscurity! No wonder it proved so popular. Yet its practical effects were surprisingly limited. To sloganize and pamphleteer was one thing; to put notes on paper, quite another. Composers soon discovered that being 'in advance of one's time' is more easily said than done. The real innovations were rather the outcome of stylistic cross-fertilization, mainly between east and west, than of any striving after novelty. The greatest successes of early Modernism were on the propaganda front, where it defeated the conservatives so resoundingly that their cause has remained a persecuted heresy ever since, at least in the Western democracies. And if Nazi Germany and Communist Russia remained artistically conservative, the long-term effect has been to reinforce the *bien pensant* view that conservatism, in itself, is somehow morally reprehensible.

At first, Modernism was an aspiration rather than a style, an ideological receptacle adaptable to any aesthetic content. Already in the mid-1890s, it was the aim of the intellectually fashionable to be 'ultra-modern—not merely up to date, but far ahead of it'. The speaker is that compendium of late Victorian advanced thought, George Bernard Shaw, and the man he is describing is William Morris: 'his wall papers, his hangings, his tapestries, and his printed books have the twentieth century in every touch of them'.[2] Today this may seem a startlingly inept prophecy, but at the time, and for ten more years, nobody would have seen anything strange in it. The 'modern style' was, if not Morris's delicate neo-medievalism, then its immediate successor, the 'art nouveau'; and there seemed no reason why this should change in the following century.

We generally associate the term 'art nouveau' with small-scale decorative arts such as jewellery, ceramics, glassware, and bookbinding, but in fact its spirit

---

[2] 'William Morris as Actor and Playwright', 211; first published in the *Saturday Review*, 10 Oct. 1896; repr. in *Pen Portraits and Reviews*, 210–17. A year later Shaw made a rather more successful prediction about 20th-c. music (see p. 466 of the present book).

pervaded the avant-garde of the period, not only in the visual arts, but also in literature and music. Debussy was really much closer to the French art nouveau than to Impressionism, and Ravel was closer still. Mahler, Puccini, Rimsky-Korsakov, and even Schoenberg were all, to some degree, art nouveau composers. This was a time when the various arts were particularly close in spirit, and the qualities uniting them, even when difficult to put into words, are easily felt. Perhaps the most striking is what we should now call their elitism. This was exquisite art for exquisite people, a refuge from the horrible nineteenth century. It was everything that contemporary popular culture was not: organic rather than mechanical, aristocratic rather than bourgeois or plebeian, dainty rather than robust, languid rather than energetic, feminine rather than masculine. Think, on the one hand, of Debussy at his most delicate ('Clair de lune', say, or the 'Syrinx' for unaccompanied flute), and, on the other, of a Sousa march.

Popular legend presents the early Modernists as a band of embattled heroes, but one must go to the documents of the period to see how totally insignificant they were to the vast bulk of the population. Even to the cultured classes (themselves a small minority), up-to-date art meant late Romanticism in music, Impressionism in painting, neo-Classicism in architecture, and realism in fiction or drama. The avant-garde were a tiny coterie with many of the characteristics of a religious sect, including a conviction of rectitude and a jealous exclusiveness. Most were socialists, like Shaw and Morris, and as such democratic and internationalist in intention, but they were sufficiently the children of their time to be elitist and nationalist in practice. One of the delights of the art nouveau—and this is true of every art form—is in fact its strongly national character.

The art nouveau phase of Modernism lasted some ten or fifteen years—very roughly, till 1905. Then came a transitional period of another ten or fifteen years, by the end of which the 'modern art' of the twentieth century had attained full maturity. On the face of it, this was the complete antithesis of everything that the art nouveau had been, but in fact the two phases of Modernism form a single broad movement. Most of the gods of later Modernism began as exponents of some sort of art nouveau, and though their styles changed radically, their attitude to society, and to 'art', remained much the same. The ivory tower was not vacated, merely refurnished.

Modernism is therefore both a very large and a very diverse phenomenon, and in discussing it I have had to leave out a great deal. The least unsatisfactory arrangement seemed to be to concentrate on the quarter-century straddling the year 1900: that is, from 1888 to 1912. This is a less arbitrary period than may at first appear. At its beginning, the generation born in the early 1860s was finding its voice. Mahler's First Symphony, Richard Strauss's *Don Juan*, and Debussy's *La Damoiselle élue* were all composed in 1888; Wolf's Mörike and Eichendorff songs, in 1889. By the end of this quarter-century, the Modernists had accomplished their revolution. Bartók's *Allegro barbaro* was composed in 1911; Stravinsky's *Rite of Spring*, Schoenberg's *Pierrot Lunaire*, and Berg's *Altenberg Songs* in 1912.[3] Simply setting down these names and dates tells us a great deal about the hectic innovation of the time. 'If your ear can assimilate and tolerate the music written in 1913 and earlier, then there is nothing in post-war music that can conceivably give you an aural shock.' That observation, made by Constant Lambert in 1934,[4] has lost little of its truth with the passing of seven decades and the intervention of another war.

Moreover, the truly revolutionary phase of Modernism was concentrated into the last few years of this amazing quarter-century. Broadly speaking, the first pre-monitory rumbles could be heard by 1904, the earthquake began in 1907, and the worst of the shocks were over by 1914. (At least, this is true of music and painting; literary Modernism lagged behind by about a decade.) In this chapter, I shall be dealing first with the art nouveau period and its antecedents, some of which go back as far as the late eighteenth century, and then with the few revolutionary years. And since there was far too much going on during either phase for a comprehensive account, I have further narrowed the field to France, eastern Europe, and the German-speaking world, especially Vienna. If it is objected that this leaves out a great deal of important music, I can only agree. As I say, it is merely the least unsatisfactory arrangement.

I. EARLY MODERNISM AND ITS ANTECEDENTS

LADY HUNSTANTON. Music makes one feel so romantic—at least it always gets on one's nerves.
MRS. ALLONBY. It's the same thing, nowadays.

(Oscar Wilde, *A Woman of No Importance*, Act IV (1894))

THE GERMANS

As the nineteenth century approached its end, the Germans found themselves in an uncomfortable position. They were, by general consent, the pre-eminent European power in music. This was a heavy responsibility in itself; and, to make matters worse, the strains inherent in Romanticism were beginning to tell. An early sign of trouble had been the feud between the Schumann–Brahms and Liszt–Wagner factions (or 'the virtuous and the virtuosi', as Ernest Newman called them). That

---

[3] The date of 1913, often given for the *Rite*, is that of first performance, not composition.
[4] See *Music Ho!*, 20.

epic struggle had ended in a truce at the close of the century, but the 'internal contradictions' remained. Tradition and progress, nationalism and individualism,
freedom and discipline: with characteristic single-mindedness, the Germans
strove to do justice to all these conflicting ideals. One result was the reactionary
avant-garde, personified in the figure of Arnold Schoenberg.

Nevertheless, the outward aspect of German musical culture was complacent to
the point of fustiness. Even its avant-garde is in some ways less 'advanced' than late
Wagner. The harmonic conservatism of both Strauss and Mahler has long been
remarked on. Both are fond of basing long passages on tonic pedals (here following
Liszt rather than Wagner), and neither has any fear of simple full closes, even in
works of the most self-consciously progressive sort. Tovey even described
Mahler's harmony as 'the most diatonic that has been heard since classical times,
though it has no inhibitions whatever'.[5] As for Strauss, Mencken correctly pointed
out that his bold-seeming chromaticisms have a way of turning out to be 'no more
than our stout and comfortable friend, the highly well-born *hausfrau*, Mme. C
Dur—with a vine leaf or two of C sharp minor or F major in her hair'.[6]

It is significant that both these composers, and Wolf too, came from the fringes
of the Teutonic world. In all of them, the German tradition is adulterated by a foreign strain: east European in the case of the Bohemian-Jewish Mahler and the
part-Slovenian Wolf, Italian in that of the *Münchner* Strauss:

Strauss's melody was so Donizettian that we could almost believe that the forgotten composer had risen from his marble chair in Bergamo, like the commander in Don Giovanni,
and resumed operations with a German training . . .[7]

It would not be difficult to prove . . . that the melodious and expressive language of Richard
Strauss is, to a great extent, fundamentally Italian.[8]

The melody of Strauss is not German at all. It is Italian.[9]

Both Mahler and Strauss have frequently been accused of vulgarity, with some
justice. Not only are they prone to lapse into the usual late Romantic bombast;
they are also, in Michael Kennedy's words, 'quick to seize on features of popular
music to forge their styles',[10] and this, I suspect, is what really annoyed the critics.

---

[5]   *Essays in Musical Analysis*, vi. 82.

[6]   *A Mencken Chrestomathy*, 'Richard Strauss', 542 (originally published in *Virtuous Vandalism, Damn!
A Book of Calumny* (1918), 56–7). See e. g. the quotation from the end of *Salome* (Ex. 15.27 on pp. 417–18).
Despite its chromatic airs, it is really a big I–IV–V–I cadence, like many of Strauss's most impressive passages.

[7]   Bernard Shaw, *Old Men and New Music*, 751, an unpublished fragment collected in *Shaw's Music*, iii.
748–52.

[8]   Romain Rolland, 'A Musical Tour of Eighteenth-Century Germany', 120, in *Romain Rolland's Essays
on Music*, 95–120.

[9]   Sir Thomas Beecham, quoted in Charles Reid, *Thomas Beecham*, 94.

[10]   *Richard Strauss*, 142–3.

In Mahler especially this popular strain goes deep. Not only does he subject the east European folk modes to an almost Indian elaboration; he is equally at home, and equally ingenious, in his handling of the popular idiom of his time. And it is this, more than anything else, that gives Mahler's melody the characteristic tinge that strikes some people as vulgar. Deryck Cooke defended him against this charge in a radio talk,[11] in the course of which he quoted the länder-like second movement of the Second Symphony, the waltz-like scherzo of the Fifth Symphony, and the hymn-like finale of the Ninth Symphony. It was easy to prove that, in spite of their popular associations, these were all extremely elaborate compositions; which, to Cooke, demonstrated that the supposed vulgarity was ironically meant. On the contrary—so a hostile critic might retort—in themselves, waltzes, marches, or hymn tunes are not vulgar, merely popular. It is only when you dress them up in bizarre forms, weird orchestrations, and recondite harmonies that they become so.

Whatever the truth may be, at least both sides in this argument would agree on the conflict between popular material and elaborate treatment; and the same, to a lesser extent, is true of Mahler's contemporaries. Early Modernism, quite apart from abounding in waltzes, marches, habaneras, boleros, and passages reminiscent of hymns or parlour ballads, speaks a language not so very far from the vernacular. More than that: the Modern idiom largely derives from the vernacular, in both its mainstream and Fringe versions. The latter, in particular, proved to be an invaluable source of novelties.

EASTERN EUROPE

If by 'modern' one means dissonant, discordant, chromatic, and generally bizarre, it is easy to see why Modernism came so easily to east European composers. For generations, they had a ready source of such effects in the local popular music. We have seen how chromatic and dissonant composers like Haydn and Schubert could be when they chose. All that was necessary was to travel a little further along the same road.

Here the most valuable resource was modal symmetry.[12] East European popular musicians have always been partial to symmetry of all sorts. In particular, the reflective type occurs in many of their modes, most obviously when the tonic or dominant is flanked by the same interval:

semitone–TONIC–semitone

semitone–DOMINANT–semitone

[11] An edited version appears in *Vindications*, 95–107, under the title 'Mahler's Melodic Thinking'. The date of the original talk (for the BBC) is not given, but the date of composition is conjectured as '1972?'.

[12] For a discussion of the partially symmetrical folk modes of eastern Europe, see Ch. 11, pp. 217–30.

major third–TONIC–major third

major third–DOMINANT–major third.

It is a feature of the Oriental tetrachord, which fills the scale in the following manner (reading from the bottom up):

TONIC–semitone–augmented second–semitone–SUBDOMINANT

DOMINANT–semitone–augmented second–semitone–TONIC

and it culminates in the 'Hungarian' mode (1–2–$3\flat$–$4\sharp$–5–$6\flat$–7–1^+), which is entirely symmetrical about its dominant:

semitone–augmented second–semitone–DOMINANT–

semitone–augmented second–semitone

Incidentally, it is worth remarking that reflective symmetry is also a feature of many favourite east European rhythms, such as ♪♩ ♪, ♩. ♪♪♩., and ♪♩♩♩♪.

But not all symmetry is reflective. There is also parallel symmetry, such as we find in the diatonic modes. In a more extreme form, this is the symmetry of the octatonic and whole-tone scales, both of which were full of modernistic potential.

Minor-third sequences and the octatonic scale

For the background to these patterns, one must go back a century. As we saw in Chapter 11,[13] parallel symmetry at the minor third occurs in two of the commonest folk modes of eastern Europe, the acoustic and the major–minor:

acoustic mode (notes 3–7)   tone–semitone–DOMINANT–tone–semitone

major–minor mode (notes 3–7) semitone–tone–DOMINANT–semitone–tone

Such modes lent themselves to 'real' minor-third sequences, such as we often find in east European folk music,[14] and these, in turn, were taken up by the Viennese composers and built into more complex patterns. A remarkable example occurs in Haydn's String Quartet in G, Op. 54 No. 1 (Ex. 15.1).

Ex. 15.1. Haydn, String Quartet in G, Op. 54 No. 1 (*c*.1788), 2nd mvt., bars 34–52 (beginning of second group) (up a 4th)

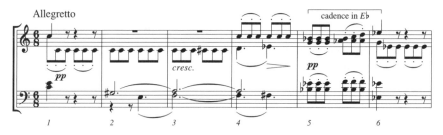

---

[13] See the discussion of the 'heptatonia secunda' family of modes (pp. 217–25), and especially Exs. 11.95–8 on pp. 220–2.

[14] See e.g. the figure in the second halves of bars 12 and 13 of the Romanian *Batuta* (Ex. 11.95).

In their unearthly glow, these modulations recall Schubert, who has a somewhat similar passage in one of his *Winterreise* songs (Ex. 15.2).[15] The main differences are that Schubert's harmony is more elliptical, and that the sequence is in the minor. In fact it is saturated with minor intervals. The words are significant:

> Einen Weiser seh' ich stehen
> Unverrückt vor meinem Blick;
> Eine Straße muß ich gehen,
> Die noch keiner ging zurück.

'I see a signpost standing immovably before my gaze. I must walk a street by which no one has returned.' Virtually from the start, real minor-third sequences in slow tempos have been associated with death. Perhaps the first composer to make the connection explicit was Beethoven, in the 'Marcia funèbre' of his Piano Sonata in A flat, Op. 26.

But these funereal associations were far from compulsory. Depending on tempo, pitch, and instrumentation, such sequences, often in conjunction with the octatonic scale, could express anything from an eerie radiance to the demonic drive of the scherzo from Beethoven's Fifth Symphony (Ex. 15.3).

---

[15] The cadences in bars 5–6 and 10–11 of Ex. 15.1 are also very reminiscent of 'Irrlicht' (*Winterreise*, no. 9), bars 3–4, 7–8, 19–20, and 42–3.

Ex. 15.2. Schubert, 'Der Wegweiser' (no. 20 of *Winterreise*, 1827), bars 55–67 (down a 5th)

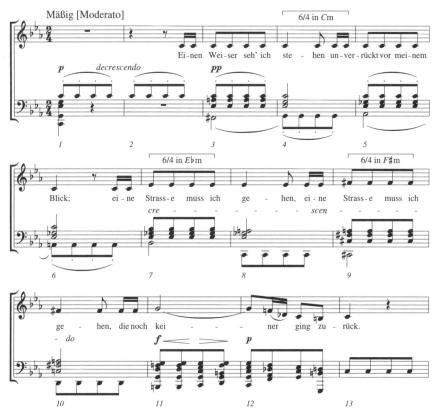

Ex. 15.3. Beethoven, Symphony No. 5 in C minor (1807–8), 3rd mvt., bars 19–48 (down a minor 3rd)

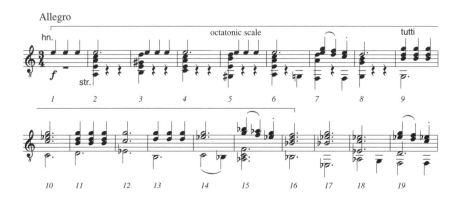

In all three of the passages just quoted, the Viennese masters observe the rule that a real harmonic sequence should never go through more than two unvaried steps. From about 1830, this rule began to be broken, most famously by Liszt, but also on occasion by Chopin, who in Ex. 15.4 takes us from tonic to tonic in four highly chromatic steps, at the same time tracing out a perfect octatonic scale.[16] This passage is typical of its composer in combining the melodic patterns of eastern Europe and Italy, in the respective shapes of the octatonic and pentatonic scales. It also demonstrates the close links between these seemingly antithetical patterns, for the diminished seventh that forms the backbone of bars 1–4 is simply the pentatonic seventh of bars 8–11 with *e* and *g* flattened. Admittedly, the latter is here notated as *f♯* instead of *g♭*, but enharmonic muddles of this type are inevitable in symmetrical divisions of the octave. Whatever else they may do, they always sound far more natural than they look.

Ex. 15.4. Chopin, Nocturne in G, Op. 37 No. 2 (1839), bars 130–40 (conclusion) (up a 4th)

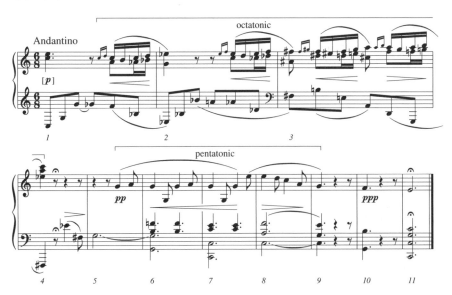

---

[16] I am indebted to Anatole Leikin for pointing out this example to me.

Major-third sequences and the whole-tone scale

Like the octatonic, the whole-tone scale grew out of the heptatonia secunda family of modes, particularly the old Arabic mode resembling an 'ascending melodic minor' (*1–2–3♭–4–5–6–7*),[17] which must have reached eastern Europe by the eighteenth century at the very latest. We have already met an example in a *zingarese* quoted earlier (see Ex. 11.89 on p. 214, bars 1–4), and another occurs in one of Haydn's 'Gypsy' slow movements (Ex. 15.5).[18] It will be seen that Haydn treats it as

Ex. 15.5. Haydn, String Quartet in D, Op. 50 No. 6 (1787), 2nd mvt., beginning (down a tone)

a kind of 'major–minor' mode, but with the minor tetrachord at the bottom and the major tetrachord at the top. The tetrachordal contrast extends to the harmony, since bar 1 is entirely in *C* minor, and bar 2 entirely in *G* major. This pattern of harmonization was no doubt invented by east European popular musicians, who had never heard of the academic rule that 'the key standing in a dominant relation to a minor tonic must itself be minor'. The effect, as developed by later composers, is one of mysterious radiance. In Schubert's song 'Der greise Kopf' (no. 14 from *Winterreise*) it attains an almost hallucinatory quality, nicely reflecting the words:

minor tonic:	Der Reif hat einen weißen Schein
	Mir über's Haar gestreuet;
major dominant:	Da glaubt ich schon ein Greis zu sein,
	Und hab' mich sehr gefreuet.[19]

---

[17] See p. 97, and Exs. 11.93(*a*) and (*b* iii) on pp. 218–19.

[18] Notice the 'fifth answering' between bars 2 and 4, and cf. Exs. 11.39, 11.40, and 11.80 (pp. 179 and 207). Haydn's tune is particularly close to the one in Beethoven's Fourth Piano Concerto (Ex. 11.39).

[19] 'The frost spread a white sheen over my head. I believed that I was already an old man, and was very pleased.' Other instances of this modulation are: Schubert, 'Muth' (*Winterreise*, no. 22), bars 8–11; Beethoven, String Quartet in F, Op. 59 No. 1, slow movement, bars 91–7, and Piano Sonata in A flat, Op. 110, second movement, bars 5–8 (suggested by an Austrian folk tune quoted in Cooper, *Beethoven: The Last Decade, 1817–1827*, 190); Weber, 'Invitation to the Dance', episode in Fm; Chopin, Waltz in A minor, Op. 34 No. 2, bars 177–88.

At the same time, this Oriental mode provided an easy approach to the whole-tone scale. All that was necessary was to flatten the second, as Schubert does in Ex. 15.6.

Ex. 15.6. Schubert, 'Der Müller und der Bach' (no. 19 of *Die schöne Müllerin*, 1823), beginning (down a 5th)

The result is a curious hybrid, with a major upper tetrachord (g–a–b–c^+) over a Phrygian lower tetrachord ($d\flat$–$e\flat$–f–g), the latter resolving on c. Omitting this c gives us the whole-tone scale of Ex. 15.7(a). And, as with other Phrygian modes, there is a twin resolving on 5, with *its* whole-tone scale Ex. 15.7(b). It will be seen that these two whole-tone scales between them cover all twelve semitones of the octave. One can perhaps think of them as the two whole-tone 'keys', between which Debussy, for one, liked to 'modulate'. But how is one to distinguish them? Probably the best plan is to call 1–2–3–$4\sharp$–$5\sharp$–$6\sharp$ the 'tonic' and $2\flat$–$3\sharp$–4–5–6–7 the 'dominant'.

Ex. 15.7. The two whole-tone modes of eastern Europe

(a) 'dominant' type   (b) 'tonic' type

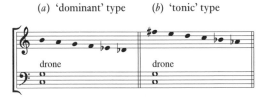

Needless to say, the complete and unbroken whole-tone modes of Ex. 15.7 represent an ideal which was rarely, if ever, attained in folk music or its immediate imitations. What we are likely to find instead is a tentative approach to the whole-tone scale, as in Ex. 15.6, or (bringing us even closer to folk origins) Ex. 15.8. Even

Ex. 15.8. Haydn, String Quartet in B flat, Op. 76 No. 4 (1796–7), 3rd mvt.
('Menuetto'), Trio, beginning (up a tone)

so, passages such as these are the direct ancestors of a distinctively east European or
even Viennese species of whole-tone scale, perhaps the earliest (and certainly the
most quoted) wholly satisfactory example of which occurs in Schubert's Octet
(finale, bars 172–6). It can be found as late as the first decade of the twentieth century, in composers as different as Mahler (Ex. 15.9) and Kreisler.[20]

Ex. 15.9. Mahler, 'Um Mitternacht' (1901), bars 30–4 (down a major 6th)

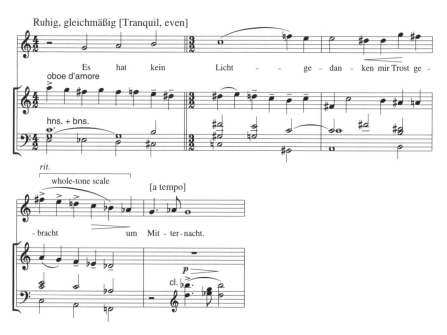

Unlike the octatonic, the whole-tone scale does not lend itself to melodic
sequences—as opposed, that is, to sequential treatment of the harmony. Sequences
at the whole-tone interval of the major second are more likely to be in the minor

---

[20] A beautiful (and appropriately Viennese) example occurs in the unquoted introduction to the
'Caprice viennois' (Ex. 16.1 on pp. 427–8), bar 9, repeated in bar 11.

mode, whether their direction is downward, as in the Balkan *ruckhafte Senkung*,[21] or, more rarely, upward. In a decidedly Lisztian passage from Haydn's 'Oxford' Symphony (Ex. 15.10), it is possible, by straining one's ears, to detect a whole-tone pattern in the accented notes of the Melody (c–$f\sharp$–d–$g\sharp$–e–$a\sharp$). But what really strikes one is the way the minor thirds bite *against* the sequence—and that was no doubt just what the composer intended.

Ex. 15.10. Haydn, Symphony No. 92 in G (the 'Oxford', 1789), last mvt., bars 120–33 (shortly after the beginning of the development)

The genuine whole-tone sequence was a much more self-conscious development, and it occurred, at first, not in the Melody but the Bass. The one in the 'Sanctus' from Schubert's Mass in E flat (Ex. 15.11) has been described as 'surely one of the very earliest seriously intended whole-tone scales in the history of European music'.[22] True enough—but let us not overlook the almost equally interesting Melody, which is a version of the ancient tune that some will associate with the Lutheran chorale 'Wachet auf, ruft uns die Stimme', and others with the Victorian hymn 'Holy, Holy, Holy! Lord God Almighty' (Ex. 15.12)—which is, of course, a translation of Schubert's liturgical text.

By altering the top note of this tune from *a* to *a*♭, Schubert (or perhaps some unknown village composer) has changed the mode from the plain major to the major–minor, which includes all but one note of the whole-tone scale ($a\flat^-$–$b\flat^-$–c–d–e). So even in this consciously modernistic passage we have not left the east European folk tradition entirely behind. The same is true, *a fortiori*, of a later whole-tone passage, from Liszt's Hungarian Rhapsody no. 9 (Ex. 15.13). Again, but much more conspicuously, the Melody is a major–minor tune.

[21] See the Romanian folk song (Ex. 11.46 on p. 183) and the *Zingarese* no. 8 in Am (Ex. 11.51 on p. 185).
[22] Taruskin, 'Chernomor to Kashchei', 84–5.

Ex. 15.11. Schubert, Mass in E flat (1828), Sanctus, beginning (down a 5th)

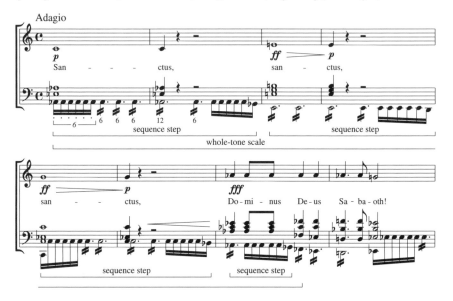

Ex. 15.12. Dykes, 'Nicaea' (hymn tune, mid-19th c.), beginning (down a major 3rd)

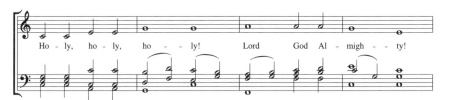

Ex. 15.13. Liszt, Hungarian Rhapsody no. 9 ('The Carnival in Pest', 1853), Finale, bars 111–28 (down a minor 3rd)

About the time that this rhapsody was published, Wagner composed the opening scene of *Das Rheingold*, the Lisztian scales and sequences of which make it a lesson in symmetrical division of the octave (Ex. 15.14). Here Wagner completes

Ex. 15.14. Wagner, *Das Rheingold* (1851–2), Scene i (down a minor 3rd)

(*a*) from 15 bars before the direction 'Allmählich etwas langsamer' to 12 bars after 'Gleichmässig im Zeitmass'

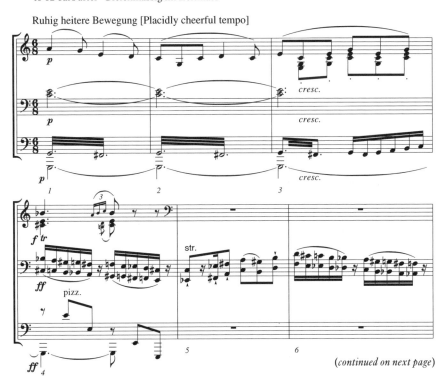

(*continued on next page*)

(Ex. 15.14 *cont.*)

(b) the Melody of bars 9–12, with chromatic scales omitted

the task, begun by Liszt in such works as *Les Préludes* and the First Piano Concerto, of obliterating the folk associations of these patterns. Their purpose, instead, is to evoke the frantic but unavailing efforts of Alberich to catch hold of the Rhine Maidens; and in this Wagner shows his unsurpassed genius for musical symbolism, for the essential point of such patterns is that they provide no purchase for the ear.

Once the whole-tone scale had become firmly established, it was possible to ally it with its natural harmonic companion, the 'French' augmented sixth $6\flat$–1–2–$4\sharp$, or a similar chord on some other degree of the mode. A celebrated example, in which the chord is based on 2, occurs towards the end of Liszt's late piano piece 'Sursum Corda' (Ex. 15.15).

Ex. 15.15. Liszt, 'Sursum Corda' (*c.*1870), bars 63–75 (down a major 3rd)

The importance of Liszt

A word—or rather several words—should be said about Liszt's influence on composers other than Wagner.[23] Among those heavily indebted to him were Franck, Richard Strauss, Bartók, and several of the Russian nationalists. Brahms, too, learnt a great deal from him, not only about thematic transformation (as is generally

---

[23] For his influence on Wagner, see 'The Debt to Liszt' in Ch. 14, pp. 364–6.

acknowledged), but also about harmony. 'Brahms the progressive' is often Brahms the Lisztian. Webern praised the *Gesang der Parzen* (*Song of the Fates*) for its supposed near-atonality: 'The cadences found here are astonishing, and so is the way its really remarkable harmonies already take it far away from tonality!'[24] In fact, this passage is just a Brahmsian elaboration on a typically Lisztian sequence. If we add Liszt's less direct influence—for example, on Schoenberg and his school via Brahms and Strauss, or on the French Impressionists via Franck, Wagner, and the Russians—we begin to grasp something of his historical importance.

Liszt was a strange mixture of ancient and modern. In many ways—his career as composer-performer, his improvisation, his reworking of other men's music, his cosmopolitanism and openness to influences of all kinds—he belongs rather to the eighteenth than the nineteenth century. (At any rate, this is true of 'serious' music, since in all these respects he has a great deal in common with twentieth-century popular musicians.) But, at the same time, he was a self-conscious modernist, tirelessly experimenting with new scales, modes, progressions, and forms.[25] This cerebral approach, so much at odds with his romantic persona, belongs to an east European tradition reaching back to Haydn[26] and forward to Rimsky-Korsakov, Bartók, and Ligeti.

Liszt's boldest harmonic novelties are associated either with diablerie, as in all those *Totentänze*, Infernos, Mephisto Waltzes, *Malédictions*, and *Csárdás macabres* (it is said that he 'feared God but loved the Devil'),[27] or else with scenes of fragrant holiness, as in the passage just quoted from 'Sursum Corda' (Ex. 15.15). And the same, broadly speaking, is true of other composers. Concentrated minor thirds, by their very nature, will tend to sound gloomy; similarly, concentrated major thirds will sound mysteriously bright. Indeed, *any* symmetrical division of the octave, if at all emphasized, will suggest the uncanny.

The accommodation of the chromatic

Nineteenth-century composers were well aware of this fact, and it made them cautious. Not only did they restrict extreme chromaticism to passages where the mood was appropriate; they also took care to integrate it into a diatonic context.

---

[24] See *The Path to the New Music*, 46. The passage referred to (from the double bar and Dm key signature to the end) consists of a broad sequence through *A*m–*C*♯m–*F*m–*A*m, with (another Lisztian device) cadences rising by a major third in the bass.

[25] See Zoltan Gárdonyi, 'Neue Tonleiter- und Sequenztypen in Liszts Frühwerken (Zur Frage der "Lisztschen Sequenzen")' ('New Types of Scales and Sequences in Liszt's Early Works: On the Question of the "Lisztian Sequence"'), and Lajos Bárdos, 'Ferenc Liszt, the Innovator'. Both these studies are packed with musical examples.

[26] e.g. in the cancrizans minuet of the Symphony No. 47 in G.

[27] Louis Kentner, 'Solo Piano Music (1827–61)' (in *Franz Liszt*), 100.

For this purpose they had several devices at their disposal, the most ancient being the drone. Like other musical patterns, this developed in two directions; on the one hand it was elaborated, and on the other 'infolded', so that often it became intermittent or implied.[28] Another device, sometimes combined with the drone, is to treat the chromatic passage as a prolonged dissonance—almost, one might say, as a highly elaborated dominant chord. The natural positions for such dissonances are either at the beginning of a movement or towards the end. Building on Classical precedent, the Romantic composers made extensive use of both.[29]

A third integrating device, and perhaps the most important of all, was to make the chromatic pattern an inflection of its diatonic surroundings. For centuries composers had flattened the third of the major triad. Later they extended the flattening to other parts of the pentatonic seventh, so that $a^-\!-c\!-e\!-g$ might become $a^-\!-c\!-e\flat\!-g\flat$ or $a\flat\!-c\!-e\!-a\flat$ (or, spelt another way, $g\sharp\!-c\!-e\!-g\sharp$). These chords could then be elaborated into octatonic or whole-tone scales, so bringing together the extremes of diatonic and chromatic melody.[30]

The conventional assumption that 'art' music developed from the diatonic to the chromatic is therefore a half-truth. In fact, it became both more chromatic *and* more pentatonic—which is almost to say more diatonic. In composers as diverse as Mahler, Debussy, and Stravinsky, we find pentatonic patterns intertwined with an often extreme chromaticism. In fact, the distinction is not so much between diatonic and chromatic as between single and multiple focus. In the course of the nineteenth century, music became increasingly multi-focal; and multi-focalism was a property shared by the pentatonic scale on the one hand, and the octatonic and whole-tone scales on the other. All that was needed to switch between the diatonic and chromatic types was a semitonal inflection or two.

This helps explain how the Russian nationalists could be equally at home in two apparently antithetical idioms, one extremely diatonic and the other extremely chromatic. The former, an amalgam of genuine folk music and neo-modal harmony[31] compounded of pentatonic figures, drones, the 'old modes', and plagal

[28] e.g. in Wagner, *Das Rheingold* (Ex. 15.14 on pp. 391–2) and Liszt, 'Sursum Corda' (Ex. 15.15 on p. 393).

[29] For introductory chromatic passages, see e.g. Haydn, *Creation*; Mozart, 'Dissonances' String Quartet in C, K. 465; Beethoven, String Quartet in C, Op. 59 No. 3; Wagner, *Tristan* Prelude; Brahms, Piano Quartet in F minor, Op. 34, finale. For digressions towards the end, see Haydn, String Quartet in F minor, Op. 20 No. 5, (Ex. 11.102 on p. 224); Schubert, 'Wegweiser' (Ex. 15.2 on p. 384); Chopin, 'Revolutionary' Study in C minor, Op. 10 No. 12 (Ex. 11.47 on p. 183) and Nocturne in G, Op. 37 No. 2 (Ex. 15.4 on p. 385).

[30] e.g. Chopin's Nocturne, Op. 37 No. 2 (Ex. 15.4 on pp. 385) and *Das Rheingold* (Ex. 15.14 on pp. 391–2).

[31] The neo-modal tradition goes back at least as far as the harmonizations of Gregorian chants in Haydn's mid-period symphonies. Later examples include the 'Heilige Dankgesang' from Beethoven's String Quartet in A minor, Op. 132, the middle theme from Chopin's Nocturne in G minor, Op. 37 No. 1 (bars 41–64), and religious scenes from operas of every description.

progressions, served for scenes of everyday Russian life. The latter, full of strange scales and harmonic progressions largely derived from Liszt, was reserved for the realm of the supernatural. Both, like virtually everything else in the Russian nationalist school, go back to Glinka. Their later development was mainly due to two men: Balakirev, who perfected the diatonic idiom,[32] and Rimsky-Korsakov, who elaborated the chromatic patterns. The latter, by his own account, first used the octatonic scale in the symphonic poem 'Sadko' (1867), under the influence of Liszt and Glinka.[33] Later, he was to explore the theoretical possibilities of extreme chromaticism with a blend of boldness and pedantry that recalls Schoenberg.

The diatonic idiom made much of the ambiguity known to the Russians as *peremennost'*.[34] Often we are left in doubt whether the tonic is *A* or *G*, *A* or *C*, or perhaps *G* or *C*. As we have seen, this sort of thing was far from unusual in nineteenth-century music, but nowhere else was it as prominent, probably because no other national school was as close to the pentatonic origins of melody. In addition, Russian composers often preferred to avoid the dominant chord, and were the first to make cadences such as *G–A*m and *Em–A*m a standard part of their technique. In all these respects, the diatonic idiom had much in common with its chromatic counterpart. Both were composed of brightly coloured chordal strands; both 'undermined' tonality, or at least diffused it.

The Russian national style developed with extraordinary speed. Beginning with Glinka's precocious experiments in the 1830s, it was fully mature by the 1870s. Indeed, that decade may well be regarded as the culmination, not only of Russian nationalism, but of Romanticism in general. The range, variety, and sheer profusion of enduring music composed during those ten years is astounding.[35] At the same time, they mark the beginning of Modernism, even if only a small pro-portion of this music is genuinely modernistic. The materials were all there, but it was to be another two decades before they were put to revolutionary use.

THE FRENCH

When this did at last happen, it was chiefly the work of the French. The striking thing about the French composers of the *fin de siècle*, compared with their German

[32] See Taruskin, 'How the Acorn Took Root', 198–200, where several of Balakirev's harmonizations of Russian folk songs are quoted.

[33] See *My Musical Life*, 78; also Taruskin, 'Chernomor to Kashchei', 93.

[34] This has been touched on in Ch. 3, pp. 35–6.

[35] e.g. Brahms's first two symphonies, Bruckner's symphonies nos. 2–5, Franck's Piano Quintet in F minor, Tchaikovsky's Violin Concerto, Dvořák's *Slavonic Dances*, Grieg's *Peer Gynt* music, Musorgsky's *Boris Godunov*, Wagner's *Götterdämmerung*, Verdi's *Aida*, Saint-Saëns's *Sampson and Delilah*, Bizet's *Carmen*, Strauss's *Fledermaus*, and Sullivan's *Trial by Jury*—and this is only a small sample.

contemporaries, is their sheer modernity. To take two characteristic works of the mid-1890s, Debussy's *Prélude à l'après-midi d'un faune* (1894) inhabits a different world from Strauss's *Till Eulenspiegel* (1895); and what is true of these two works is true of French and German music in general. Even relatively conservative composers like Fauré habitually used a harmonic language bolder than the Germans'.

This remains something of a puzzle. The French had never been regarded as an especially musical nation, either by themselves or by others. On the whole, their musicians had been respectable rather than brilliant, and, with the sole exception of Berlioz, anything but subversive (and even Berlioz eventually revealed himself to be a classicist at heart). It tells us much about the French attitude to music that they were content to import so many of their leading composers: Lully, Piccini, Spontini, Cherubini, and Rossini from Italy; Gluck, Meyerbeer, and Offenbach from Germany; Chopin from Poland; Franck from Belgium. And the same eclectic outlook is evident in those French composers who managed to be born in France. Earlier in the century, they had absorbed influences from Italy, Spain, German Romanticism, and even the Near East. In the 1880s, Wagner was *le dernier cri*; in the 1890s, it was the turn of the Russians. This openness to foreign influences was undoubtedly a great strength. But, for a full explanation of the French triumph, we must also take into account the taste of the *fin de siècle*. By a fortunate accident, it so happened that a general trend in music towards diffuseness of focus and looseness of form exactly coincided with the French vogue for the bright, beautiful vagueness of impressionism.

Debussy and impressionism

All the musical tendencies of the 1890s are united and exaggerated in the person of Debussy. Like Wagner, he started with the musical vernacular of his youth, the *'lingua franca* of la Belle Epoque', as it has been called.[36] And, again like Wagner, he never entirely got away from it, in spite of the extravagant eclecticism of his later style, in which it has been said that 'the church modes, Borodin, Grieg, a dash of Massenet and a dash of Franck, the music of the gypsy orchestras and the Javanese *gamelang* are all traceable'[37]—not to mention Palestrina, Wagner, Musorgsky, and ragtime. Every one of these disparate influences was grafted onto the pallid stem of the Conservatoire tradition.

---

[36] 'Debussy's earliest compositions speak the *lingua franca* of *la Belle Epoque*, a common style owing less to Gounod, Massenet, Saint-Saëns, Lalo, or Franck than to forgotten figures such as Auguste Georges and Benjamin Godard, composers uninspired except by the Conservatoire' (Arthur B. Wenk, *Claude Debussy and Twentieth-Century Music*, 21).

[37] Martin Cooper, *French Music*, 93. The reference is specifically to the String Quartet in G minor, 'the first work of his maturity'.

This elegant exoticism had a long history in France, and not just in music. Parallels for almost everything in Debussy can be found among the welter of influences that went into art nouveau: for the Wagner of *Lohengrin* and *Parsifal*, the Pre-Raphaelites; for Massenet, the salon painters; for the Far Eastern pentatonic, *japonisme*. A little latter, his borrowings from ragtime were to have a similar parallel in the *africanisme* of art deco. On the whole, however, the most important of Debussy's influences were those that came from the east: not only the Javanese gamelan, the Gypsy bands, and the Russians, but also, less obviously, Gregorian chant and Grieg. (The Scandinavian peninsula, for most musicological purposes, may be regarded as an extension of eastern Europe.)

Unlike most French composers, Debussy had little interest in local colour for its own sake. What attracted him in Oriental music was a timeless tranquillity, allied to a sense of mode that seemed to him vastly superior to the crass machinery of Western harmony. Only by understating the harmonic cadences almost to the point of extinction could he achieve the impressionistic ideal of a music

> Plus vague et plus soluble dans l'air,
> Sans rien en lui qui pèse ou qui pose[38]

This was a road down which Wagner had already travelled some way, especially in his later works. There is a passage in *Götterdämmerung*, depicting the innocent delights of the Rhine Maidens, that would fit without incongruity into *L'Après-midi d'un faune*. For what it tells us about both composers, it is worth quoting at some length (Ex. 15.16).

It would be fun to make a list of the 'Debussian' features in this passage: the disguised whole-tone scale in bars 3–4; the combination of pentatonic and whole-tone figures in bar 6; the bracketed scale in bars 2–3, so like the one at the beginning of *L'Après-midi* (Ex. 15.17), the parallel seventh chords in bars 9–10, and so on. More important than any individual detail, however, is the sense that time has been suspended, and with it harmonic progression. Probably acting under the influence of Liszt, Wagner here applies his famous 'dominant harmony' to a tonic, within which sevenths and ninths come and go without actual resolution. When the bass shifts up to $c\sharp$ in bar 10, it colours rather than supports the new theme (on the 'hard' pentatonic seventh $e–g–b–d^+$), and then disappears without making any attempt to explain itself. This is a technique not so much of dissonance and resolution, as of diffusion and consolidation.

Debussy continued where Wagner left off. His Bass is even more sluggish; his Melody, in compensation, even more pentatonic. But it is a shifting, evasive

---

[38] Verlaine, *Art poétique*, first stanza, lines 3–4: '[Music] vaguer, more soluble in the air, containing nothing heavy or emphatic.' The poem was written in 1874 and published in *Jadis et naguère*.

Ex. 15.16. Wagner, *Götterdämmerung* (1869–74), Act III, end of Scene i (down a 4th)

Lebhaft, doch mäßig im Zeitmaß [Lively, but moderate in tempo]

(*continued on next page*)

(Ex. 15.16 *cont.*)

pentatonic, for ever expanding and contracting as if reflected in the rippling water that the impressionist painters so loved to depict. For illustration, we need go no further than *L'Après-midi* itself (Ex. 15.17). This movement, and especially its

Ex. 15.17. Debussy, *Prélude à l'après-midi d'un faune* (1894), beginning (down a major 3rd)

celebrated opening section, has been described as 'the beginning of modern music', and there is enough truth in this description to make it worth examining in some detail. We can then see that Debussy's modernistic audacities, however much they may owe to exotic influences, really grow out of vernacular practice.

This is especially true of the pentatonic scale. But Debussy's pentatonic is a highly idiosyncratic one, habitually blurred with chromatic embellishments and mixed up with whole-tone patterns. The exquisitely languid opening figure is a typical case. At first, it seems to be entirely chromatic, but its later development (compare Ex. 15.18(*a*)) shows that there is in fact a pentatonic framework, *a–g–e*; and at the very end of the movement, this is further reduced to the bare poles *a* and *e* (Ex. 15.18(*b*)).

For all his virtuosity in chromatic transformation, Debussy never loses sight of the pentatonic substructure, and on the whole is most original when most pentatonic. Throughout the movement, he shows his distaste for the plain triad, avoiding it almost entirely in the Melody, and hastening to adorn it with a sixth or seventh in the harmony. In Debussy, everything tends towards complex pentatonic patterns. Not content with the ordinary pentatonic seventh, or even the pentatonic ninth

Ex. 15.18. Debussy, *Prélude à l'après-midi d'un faune* (down a major 3rd), end

(*a*) bars 99–101

(*b*) bars 107–109 (conclusion)

(Ex. 15.19(*a*)), he invented his own oblique version of the latter, in which the central triad is displaced from *c* to *a* (Ex. 15.19(*b*)).

Ex. 15.19. Pentatonic ninths

(*a*) vernacular   (*b*) Debussian

It is this Debussian pentatonic ninth that underlies the opening section of *L'Après-midi*, but this is not immediately apparent to the listener. What we hear, at first, is Ex. 15.20. Only later does it gradually dawn on us that the first note was not *c*, but *a*. The first hint of the true key comes with the unobtrusive *G7–C* cadence of bar 11 of Ex. 15.17, and it is only with the third statement of the opening theme in bar 18 that the matter is put entirely beyond doubt.

Ex. 15.20. Debussy, *Prélude à l'après-midi d'un faune* (1894), beginning (down a semitone)

This gradual unveiling of the tonality is reminiscent of what happens in the *Tristan* Prelude, which must surely have served as Debussy's principal model for *L'Après-midi*. Both begin with the same impression of lifting mist, even if it is the cold, grey fog of the northern seas in the former, and the golden haze of the Mediterranean in the latter. Both build up to richly orchestrated climaxes and then die away to nothing. Both employ a similar range of melodic, harmonic, and even rhythmic effects. But in Debussy these Wagnerisms have been grafted onto a vernacular, and specifically a *French* vernacular stem. In repeating his main theme three times, first unharmonized, then in the wrong (harmonic) key, and finally in the right one, Debussy is doing essentially what Chopin did in his Study in A minor, Op. 25 No. 11.[39] A comparative summary of the two passages (Ex. 15.21) encapsulates the tendencies of the late vernacular. Debussy is more spacious, more chromatic, more discordant (though in a discreet way), above all more oblique. His *real* tonic is the pentatonic seventh that first appears, in the guise of an added-sixth chord, at the third statement of opening theme (Ex. 15.17, bar 18) and is spelt out by the harp at the close of the movement (Ex. 15.18(*b*)).

Unlike Mahler in the famous case of *Das Lied von der Erde*, Debussy does not actually end on an added sixth; his final chord is a tonic triad, though a very understated one. Still, he comes extremely close to doing so, and even this has precedents in the French vernacular (Ex. 15.22).[40]

---

[39] See Ex 13.7 on p. 282.   [40] In Ex. 15.22(*a*), notice the contrast of pentatonic species.

Ex. 15.21. Harmonic climaxes in Chopin and Debussy

(*a*) Chopin, Study in A minor, Op. 25 No. 11 (Ex. 13.7)

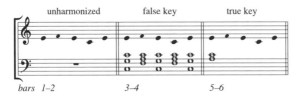

(*b*) Debussy, *Prélude à l'après-midi d'un faune* (Ex. 15.17)

Ex. 15.22. Delibes, 'Le Rossignol' (*c.*1885) (down a 5th)

(*a*) beginning of instrumental introduction

(*b*) end of movement

Once we grasp the central place of the pentatonic seventh in Debussy's art, it becomes much easier to understand his harmony, much of which is derived from the $a^-–c–e–g$ chord by the inflection of one or more of its notes (Ex. 15.23). These inflected chords, together with inversions and enharmonic equivalents, account for a good part of his harmonic vocabulary. They include the ordinary 'dominant seventh' type, in Ex. 15.23(*b*) and (*c*), the 'half-diminished' seventh in (*d*) and (*f*), the fully diminished type in (*e*), and the 'whole-tone' seventh in (*g*). This last is especially interesting, since it brings us back to the fascinating and confusing question of whole-tone patterns in general.

Ex. 15.23. Chromatic inflections of the pentatonic-seventh chord

Debussy's whole-tone scale

By Debussy's time such patterns had long ceased to be a novelty. Unobtrusive whole-tone patterns, whether between *4* and *7*, *1* and *4♯*, or even *2♭* and *5*, were an established feature of the vernacular. French composers, in particular, had long been attracted by the elegant acidity of the augmented fourth.[41] The complete scale had been consciously employed since the 1840s. But no one, either before or since, ever made greater or more varied use of it than Debussy. The Debussian whole-tone scale may be limited to a few notes or extend to an entire movement; it may be subtle or emphatic, languid or vigorous, harmonic or melodic. Nevertheless, there are a few generalizations to be made about it. One, already mentioned, is that it is linked to pentatonic patterns. In the lush middle section of *L'Après-midi*, for instance, the added sixth chord is simply inflected from *c–e–g–a* to *c–e–g♭–a♭* (Ex. 15.24).

Another is that it grows out of the harmony—by no means a matter of course at this period.[42] The chord itself varies. It may be a 'French sixth' on *d*, as in Ex. 15.25,[43] the ordinary French sixth on *a♭*, the whole-tone chord of Ex. 15.23(*g*), or various dominant discords ($g^-–f–b–e♭^+$, $g^-–b–c♯–f$). Except for the purpose of making contact with the diatonic surrounding, the exact identity does not matter.

[41] Leslie Orrey attributes this in part to the peculiarities of the French language: 'There is at least some affinity between it [the interval of the augmented fourth] and the nasal quality of spoken or sung French' ('The Songs of Gabriel Fauré', 76). He also quotes several passages where Fauré 'anticipates' Debussy in the use of the augmented fourth and whole-tone scale (ibid. 76–7, Exs. 1–7).

[42] Cf. Mahler's 'Um Mitternacht' (Ex. 15.9 on p. 388).

[43] Cf. Liszt's 'Sursum Corda' (Ex. 15.15 on p. 393).

Ex. 15.24. Debussy, *Prélude à l'après-midi d'un faune* (1894), bars 55–66 (down a semitone)

Ex. 15.25. Debussy, *Prélude à l'après-midi d'un faune*, bars 29–34 (up a semitone)

Internally, all whole-tone chords are identical, and fall into one of the two 'whole-tone keys' (*c–d–e–f♯–g♯–a♯* and *d♭–e♭–f–g–a–b*, or the enharmonic equivalents), which Debussy likes to play off against one another.

A third generalization is that Debussy's whole-tone passages are modal, in the sense of being constructed around clear-cut and frequently recurring melodic focuses. The classic example is the Piano Prelude 'Voiles' (no. 2 in the first book), which consists almost entirely of one enormous whole-tone chord. In all its sixty-four bars, the only exception is a six-bar pentatonic episode, which, curiously, hardly stands out from its surroundings. In contrast to Schoenberg, who grimly strives to erase all traces of tonality from essentially diatonic patterns, Debussy manages to make the whole-tone scale sound reasonably tonal—or at any rate modal.

If this movement is so transposed that the pentatonic episode lies on the 'white notes',[44] one can see how he manages this. The opening (Ex. 15.26(*a*)), though highly concordant, is indeed atonal. The first hint of what the key might be comes

[44] For the reader's convenience, I have enharmonically respelt some of the notes.

Ex. 15.26. Debussy, 'Voiles' (1909) (up an augmented 4th)

(*a*) beginning

(*b*) bars 39–43

(*c*) conclusion

in bar 5 with the drone *e*, which then persists almost to the end of the movement. Only after some two-thirds of the movement have passed in euphonious vagueness does Debussy reduce the whole-tone chord to a dominant minor thirteenth, which then closes into the pentatonic interlude (Ex. 15.26(*b*)). Nothing could be smoother; the most one could say is that the veils have lifted somewhat. Soon they are back in place, and the movement expires in the tonal obscurity with which it began (Ex. 15.26(*c*)).

The smoothness of these transitions is assisted by the euphony of the whole-tone sections, which revolve round the poles *d* (for starting) and *b♭* (for ending): notes discordant against the drone *e*, but consonant against each other. Whatever Debussy may have said, it was never his intention to banish tonality, but rather to shatter it into a multitude of glittering, kaleidoscopic fragments. Or perhaps a better image would be those strangely interconnected, weirdly disorienting staircases in the pictures of Maurits Escher. 'Such characteristically French movements as impressionism, symbolism, and surrealism', it has been said, 'all began from disorientation.'[45] And it was probably this capacity for disorientation, even more than its sensuous beauty, that drew Debussy to the whole-tone scale. Any few steps seem perfectly normal, but the whole defies rational comprehension. It is beautiful but inhuman. The mind is for ever trying to make sense of it, and for ever being baffled.

One consequence is that the whole-tone scale, like the octatonic, shows best against a diatonic background. The more these artificial patterns come to the fore, the more the composer must compensate with correspondingly primitive ones. This blend of the primitive and sophisticated is a characteristic of the times. We find it not only in fellow Frenchmen like Fauré and Ravel, or fellow impressionists like Delius, but also in east Europeans like Mahler, Bartók, Rimsky-Korsakov, and Stravinsky. With the abandonment of traditional tonality, composers were thrown back on age-old patterns: not just modes or scales, but drones, parallel chords, or those on-the-spot repetitions of which Vaughan Williams protested, 'I can never understand why it is "old fashioned" to have exact repetitions arranged in an

[45] Robert Graves and Alan Hodge, *The Reader over your Shoulder*, 189.

architectural order, while it is "modern" to arrange the repetitions in pairs. To my mind the one is like an architect designing an arch, while the other is like an orator who habitually repeats the last sentence while he is thinking what to say next.'[46]

And of course it was characteristic of art nouveau as a whole to combine the primitive with the sophisticated, or, more fundamentally, the organic with the artificial. Never was a school of artists more in love with the natural, and never were they less capable of being natural themselves.

NEOCLASSICISM

Here we may detect a spiritual affinity with the second half of the eighteenth century, another period when people revered nature while remaining obstinately artificial in their tastes and behaviour. It is not difficult to trace a neoclassical strain in the art, music, and literature of the late nineteenth and early twentieth centuries. Not, indeed, that Classicism had ever entirely gone out of fashion. During the entire century and a half between 1770 and 1920, Romanticism and Classicism were the yin and yang of European music, locked in a creative conflict in which neither could ever be completely victorious. Even the German heartland of Romanticism produced, if not a steady stream, at least a fitful trickle of neoclassical works from Beethoven's Eighth Symphony to Mahler's Fourth.

But it was in the Latin countries that the Classical flame burnt brightest. The origins of the late nineteenth-century neoclassical revival should be sought, not in symphonies, sonatas, or string quartets, but on the operatic stage. In Italian and especially in French opera, the dances of the eighteenth century scarcely had time to go out of fashion before being revived. The line of descent passes from the minuet in Verdi's *Rigoletto* (1851) to the gavotte in Thomas's *Mignon* (1866) to Delibes's dance suite for *Le roi s'amuse* (1882),[47] which began a fashion for old-world dances that lasted for over two decades. Examples include those in Massenet's *Manon* (1884), Satie's three 'Sarabandes' (1887), Ravel's 'Menuet antique' (1895), Chausson's 'Quelques danses' (including *sarabande*, *pavane*, and *forlane*, 1896), Ravel's 'Pavane pour une infante défunte' (1899), and the 'Sarabande' from Debussy's 'Pour le piano' (1901). It is easy to see in this the musical counterpart to the rococo element in French art nouveau, but the vogue was far from being confined to France. There were also Grieg's neo-Baroque 'Holberg' Suite (1884), Verdi's *Falstaff* (1893), which, like *Rigoletto*, contains a minuet, and Richard Strauss's *Rosenkavalier* (1911).

---

[46] 'Some Thoughts on Beethoven's Choral Symphony', 104. In *National Music and Other Essays*, 83–120. For a passage close to the folk roots of this practice, see the finale of *Spring*, from Vivaldi's *Four Seasons* (Ex. 7.7 on p. 91).

[47] The movements are entitled 'Gaillarde', 'Pavane', 'Scène de Bouquet', 'Lesquercade', 'Madrigal', and 'Passepied'.

Neoclassicism was both a reaction against late Romantic opulence and a Latin counter-attack against Teutonic earnestness. It also reflected a new openness to popular influences. In the queerest way, the art nouveau movement (if anything so heterogeneous can be called a movement) contrived to be both populist and elitist. It set out to abolish the distinction between the 'fine' and 'minor' arts, bestowing the same care on ceramics, jewellery, typography, advertising posters, or book illustration as on easel painting or sculpture. The same self-conscious artifice was extended by novelists to popular genres like the ghost, adventure, or detective story (as for instance in virtually the entire output of Robert Louis Stevenson), and by composers to marches, waltzes, and later also ragtime. Quite often, there seems to have been a vague association in their minds between contemporary dance forms and eighteenth-century revivals. Satie's well-known 'Gymnopédies' (1888) are at once neoclassical, modernistic, and a set of three slow waltzes. In fact, it is not always easy to tell the difference between a slow waltz and a minuet or a saraband, and even a gavotte is likely to have a touch of the polka about it.

There is an obvious reason for this affinity. Quite simply, the popular arts, and popular music in particular, were still relatively close to the eighteenth century. Offenbach has been called 'the Mozart of the boulevards', and the same could be said of Johann Strauss (that is, if Vienna contains boulevards). So it was perfectly natural that the early Modernist, when in a neoclassical mood, should cast a wary eye in the direction of popular music.

II. REVOLUTIONARY MODERNISM

> I sometimes wonder whether what is wrong with modern music may not be just this—that composers are putting more brains into their job than it really needs: too much brains and too little music.
>
> Ernest Newman[48]

> If I had a quid for every 'contemporary' work I have listened to the first couple of minutes of . . .
>
> Kingsley Amis[49]

The modernist ferment

An observer of the present day, transported back the Europe of 1900, would find the music surprisingly old-fashioned. The most recent compositions were such

---

[48] 'A Wodehouse Story and Some Reflections' (1931).
[49] 'Rondo for my Funeral' (1973), first published in *The Sunday Times*, 1 July 1973; reprinted in *The Amis Collection*, 388. Ellipsis original.

things as Puccini's *Tosca*, Rimsky-Korsakov's *Tsare Saltane* (including 'The Flight of the Bumble Bee'), Rachmaninov's Piano Concerto in C minor (or at least its first two movements), Elgar's *Dream of Gerontius*, Strauss's *Heldenleben*, Sibelius's *Finlandia*, Mahler's Fourth Symphony, and Schoenberg's *Verklärte Nacht*. Only in France was there a true avant-garde. A few years later matters had changed dramatically. Strauss's *Salome*, described by Dent as 'the foundation of the "modern" style in Germany',[50] dates from 1905; Schoenberg's *Kammersymphonie* from 1906; Bartók's first String Quartet from 1907. What is more, *Salome* enjoyed a success (admittedly *de scandale*) that made its composer a fortune and confirmed his guess that a violent form of Modernism was the coming thing. At the same time, German Expressionist painting, French Fauvism, and starkly unadorned architecture all made their appearance. Twentieth-century Modernism had arrived.

It would be a great mistake, however, to suppose that it made much of a stir at the time. What seems in foreshortened retrospect a cultural revolution was really an abrupt change in taste on the part of a tiny coterie. Whatever had been characteristic of art nouveau was out, and the precise opposite in. Out went cool greys, greens, and lilacs; in came hot reds, yellows, and oranges. Out went sinuous curves; in came straight lines, jagged angles, and checkerboard patterns. Out went lush, seductive harmonies; in came harsh discords. Out went the organic; in came the mechanical. Out went the feminine; in came the masculine.

With this change in taste went a change in mood. Instead of retiring from the world, the fashion was now to go out and engage with it. What had been a mere 'modern style' developed into a quasi-political 'modern movement'.[51] This, like any other political movement, was a coalition of distinct and often conflicting factions, in which we can discern two broad groupings, one Latin and the other Teutonic. Latin Modernism, which was primarily French and above all Parisian, was all about posturing, excitement, theatrical conflict. It grew out of the late nineteenth-century 'art world', with its epigrammatic bitchiness ('Everything is metal— *except* the breastplates'),[52] its undiscovered geniuses, its conventional scorn for convention, its glamorous bohemians and baffled bourgeoisie. Beneath it all lay the mellow cynicism of a culture that had seen fashions come and go for three thousand years; the recognition that, whatever the *dernier cri* might be, sooner or later there would be another *cri*, and then another after that.

The Teutonic strain in Modernism (stretching the word 'Teutonic' to include the Dutch and Scandinavians) was quite different: earnest, didactic, and above all

---

[50] *Opera*, 144.

[51] 'As for England, the aforesaid modern movement has been confined mainly to furniture and smaller articles of decoration . . .' *The Studio* (1907), 3.

[52] Degas on the historical painter Jean Louis Ernest Meisonnier.

organizing. It was the Germans who, beginning in 1907, first institutionalized Modernism in the schools-cum-trade associations known as *Werkbünde*.[53] Other typically Germanic features were an enthusiasm for technology, a fascination with the morbid, and a weakness for pushing ideas to extremes. Of course, the distinction between Latin and Teutonic Modernism is far from neat. Other nationalities were involved, and both attitudes were often combined in a single person. Still, it is an instructive exercise to divide Modernists into 'Latins' and 'Teutons'. Picasso and Stravinsky, for instance, are obviously Latin, and Schoenberg an almost pure Teuton. Richard Strauss, in so far as he is a Modernist, is mainly a Latin. On the other hand, Le Corbusier, a French Swiss, is mainly a Teuton, though with a Latin gift for self-promotion. As a rule, the Latin strain predominated in painting, and the Teutonic in music and architecture.[54]

It is mainly to the complementary strengths of these two strains that the astonishing success of the Modern Movement is due. While the Latins made Modernism exciting, the Teutons made it both impressive and, at least seemingly, practical. While the Latins composed manifestos, the Teutons were drawing up syllabuses. It was the latter who infiltrated educational institutions and cultural bodies, and it was thanks to them that, even in conservative England, the early British Broadcasting Corporation 'put on the air a great deal of Stravinsky, Hindemith, Schönberg, Sibelius, Bartok, of the Parisian experimentalists, "Les Six", and such British composers as Sir Arnold Bax, Frederick Delius, Constant Lambert and William Walton . . .'.[55] But the most munificent state patron of Modernism was, naturally enough, the Weimar Republic of 1919–33.[56]

To be fair, the Modernists were devoted, cunning, and, in a few cases, hugely talented. But they were also extraordinarily lucky. They were lucky in their friends; for, contrary to legend, the early twentieth-century art public was made up for the most part of singularly open-minded people, accustomed by a century of Romanticism to being 'challenged'. They were lucky, too, in their enemies, the most eminent of whom were Hitler and Stalin. Two world wars, encouraging intelligent young people to build a new world and sweep away the vestiges of the old (which, of course, had been responsible for the catastrophe), were another stroke of luck. But most of all they were lucky in the proliferation of 'public sector art', in

[53] The first was the Deutscher Werkbund in Munich; the most famous, the Staatliches Bauhaus in Weimar, was founded in 1919. See Pevsner, *Pioneers of Modern Design*, 35–6.

[54] Literature, for obvious reasons, was much more inclined to keep within national boundaries. In any case, literary Modernism was a relatively feeble affair.

[55] Robert Graves and Alan Hodge, *The Long Week-End: A Social History of Great Britain, 1918–1939*, ch. 14, 'Sport and Controversy', 237.

[56] See Paul Johnson, *A History of the Modern World*, ch. 3, 'Waiting for Hitler', 112–16.

the shape of broadcasting corporations, educational bodies, and cultural bureaucracy in general. At least in the bourgeois democracies, the 'long march through the institutions' proved to be a walkover.

Except in old-fashioned, out-of-the-way places like universities, fundamentalist Modernism has now been extinct for several decades. We live, by general agreement, in a postmodern age. The statement, in the sober pages of *The International Cyclopedia of Music and Musicians* (1964 edition) that Schoenberg 'almost single-handedly . . . ensured the continuation of the art of music in the twentieth century'[57] seems now to come from the scriptures of some ancient sect. But, to continue the metaphor—and it is rather more than a metaphor—Modernism, like other defunct religions, has left behind a legacy of myths, superstitions, and taboos that still show little sign of disappearing.

It is not my intention here to demolish these hoary relics—that task, if possible at all, would require another full-length book—but rather to follow up the trends adumbrated in earlier chapters. Since even this undertaking demands a great deal of selection, it again seems best to concentrate to the leading national schools, in this case German and Russian.

THE GERMANS

The German aptitude for harmony, acknowledged as early as the eighteenth century, had by the early twentieth grown into an obsession. To certain German composers and critics, harmonic complexity had come to be regarded as an end in itself, even as the chief index of musical progress. In this, too, they were merely carrying forward a long-established trend. It is astonishing to find the following sentiments expressed as early as 1824:

Laws, inviolable laws for the regulation of harmony have been made and violated. The rules for the preparation and resolution of chords are only now obeyed, when it is not found preferable to disobey them. A Haydn trembles at his own boldness; his hands recoil even at the sounds himself has made; but still he goes on: more fearless, steps in a Mozart; and, at length, a Beethoven plunges into a congregation of sounds, that might raise from the very grave the spirits of his early predecessors. The audience keeps pace, but it is a lagging one, with these innovations; first wondering what they mean, and lastly wondering at their former insensibility. Such is the progress of human ears . . .[58]

---

[57] pp. 1921–2. The author is George Rochberg.

[58] *Macculloch's Letters to Sir Walter Scott, on the Highlands and Western Isles of Scotland*, ii. 385. John Ramsay Macculloch, described in *The British National Biography* as a 'statistician and political economist', lived from 1789 to 1864. This passage is quoted in Robbins Landon, *Haydn: Chronicle and Works*, v: *Haydn: The Last Years, 1801–1809*, 413.

But the following remarks, made by Sir Henry Hadow in 1895, are in their way perhaps even more surprising:

Now, there is not a single chord in common use at the present day which has not been at some time condemned as a dissonance. The major third was once held to be a discord; so, later, was the dominant seventh; so, within living memory, was the so-called dominant thirteenth.[59] Fifty years ago Chopin's harmony was 'unendurable'; thirty years ago the world accepted Chopin, but shrank in terror from Wagner and Brahms; now, we accept all three, but shake our heads over Goldmark. And the inference to which all this points is, that the terms 'concord' and 'discord' are wholly relative to the ear of the listener. The distinction between them is not to be explained on a mathematical basis, or by any *a priori* law of acoustics; it is altogether a question of psychology.[60]

The date is important. Sir Henry Hadow, MA, BMus, Hon. DMus, later editor of *The Oxford History of Music* and Vice-Chancellor of the University of Sheffield, was anything but a revolutionary firebrand. Born in 1859, he had studied in Germany like so many Victorian musicians, and what we read here is without doubt an echo of the forward-thinking German opinion of the 1880s and 1890s. He is, however, British enough to add that

At the same time, it may be held, fairly enough, that a composer is bound to write in a manner intelligible to his generation. . . . at the present day, a composer who should end a piece on a minor second would be deliberately violating the established language of the time; and would be reprehensible, not because a minor second is ugly—for it will be a concord some day—but because, in the existing state of Music, it could not be naturally placed at the close of a cadence.[61]

These passages contain two ideas, both deeply rooted in German philosophy. One, which derives from the subjectivism of Kant, is that concord and discord are merely 'a question of psychology' rather than acoustics. Later in the same chapter Sir Henry says much the same about the major and minor modes: 'There is no reason *in rerum naturâ* why the minor mode should be sad, but our first ancestors noticed that a cry sank in tone as the power of its utterance failed, and hence established a connection between depression of note and waning strength. So began an association of ideas to which, by transmission and inheritance, the pathos of our minor keys is mainly due.'[62]

The other idea, which derives from the historicism of the then very fashionable Hegel, is that the human race, or at any rate the sophisticated Western portion

---

[59] A strange observation, considering that these last two chords are still so regarded. Presumably Sir Henry meant something like 'held to be intolerably discordant'.

[60] 'Outlines of Musical Form', in *Studies in Modern Music*, second series (1895), 18.

[61] 'Outlines of Musical Form', 18–19.   [62] Ibid. 22.

thereof, is inexorably advancing towards a greater tolerance of discord. And there is no denying that History seemed to bear out this notion. In the early Middle Ages (so the argument ran), composers confined themselves to fifths, fourths, and octaves. Later they advanced to thirds and sixths; then, about the time of Monteverdi, to sevenths of a very timid kind. Then came ninths, elevenths, and thirteenths. Extrapolating into the future, who could doubt that the time would soon come when every conceivable discord, in every conceivable situation, would be equally acceptable?

One should, however, understand that in the 1890s this farrago of bad history and worse logic was still very much in the realms of theory. The actual music was hardly more discordant than it had been forty or fifty years before. Here it is important to distinguish between the intensity of a discord and the regularity of its resolution. Broadly speaking, the composers of 1900 use the same chords as Wagner and Liszt had in the 1850s, but it is true that they feel far less obligation to resolve them.

Several tendencies contributed to this free and easy attitude. One was the psychological detachment of discord from the melodic dissonance of which, for centuries, it had been a by-product. It had now become, at least potentially, a mere harmonic colouring with no need of resolution. Another, equally powerful tendency was the growing independence of Melody in relation to the Bass. A third was the fusion of the chords of *C* major and *A* minor into a consonant pentatonic seventh. All these tendencies go back at least to the early nineteenth century, and belong as much to the vernacular (and later to jazz) as to the avant-garde. At the same time, there were certain procedures that naturally appealed to composers intent on pushing back the bounds of the harmonically possible. Extreme discord, obviously, was one. Another was the broadening of the process of dissonance and resolution from single chords to entire passages.

Bearing all this in mind, we can begin to understand what was happening in the mid-1900s. The excesses of discord and chromaticism that entered German music during these few years were not, as Modernist propaganda would have it, the outcome of inexorable historical pressure. They were rather a matter of fashion, the musical equivalent of the glaring colours and distorted outlines of expressionist painting, and they were associated with appropriately strong emotions. Strauss's *Salome*, already cited as 'the foundation of the "modern" style in Germany', is a horror story of beheading and necrophilia[63] in which the harmonic idiom faithfully reflects the nightmarish atmosphere. Even so, the musical language of *Salome* is for the most part perfectly traditional, and it is precisely by playing this off

---

[63] Salome's final words (see Ex. 15.27) translate as: 'They say that love tastes bitter. But what of it? I have kissed your mouth, Jochanaan'—after the head to which it belonged has been severed from his body, of course.

against a near-atonal chromaticism that Strauss gets his creepiest effects. The sickly horror reaches its height at the very end, when the music, after a long phase of eerily lurching into and out of focus, soars into the purest Viennese-Italian cantilena (Ex. 15.27). In its diseased way, this is one of the great moments of twentieth-century opera.

Ex. 15.27. Richard Strauss, *Salome* (1905), from 7 bars after rehearsal no. 357 (near end) (down a semitone)

(continued on next page)

(Ex. 15.27 *cont.*)

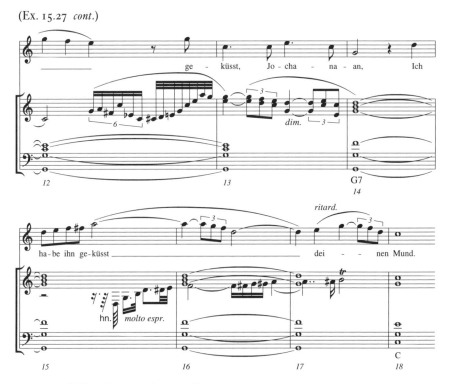

Schoenberg and atonality

As we can tell from both his earlier and later works, this Grand Guignol was not really natural to Strauss. During five years or so, in *Salome* and *Elektra*, he was happy to play the outrageous avant-gardiste and did very well out of it, but then returned to the more congenial world of *Der Rosenkavalier*.

It *was*, however, natural to Schoenberg, who must have quickly seen how he could trump Strauss's ace. All that was necessary was to exaggerate the chromatic idiom even further, while altogether abandoning the diatonic one. This might seem a somewhat perverse proceeding, but Schoenberg had a theory to justify it, called 'the emancipation of dissonance':

What distinguishes dissonances from consonances is not a greater or lesser degree of beauty, but a greater or lesser degree of *comprehensibility*. . . . Closer acquaintance with the more remote consonances—the dissonances, that is—gradually eliminated the difficulty of comprehension and finally admitted not only the emancipation of dominant and other seventh chords, diminished sevenths and augmented triads, but also the emancipation of Wagner's, Strauss's, Moussorgsky's, Debussy's, Mahler's, Puccini's, and Reger's more remote dissonances.[64]

[64] 'Composition with Twelve Tones (1)' (1941), 216–17, in *Style and Idea*, 214–45.

This is not the place for a detailed discussion of Schoenberg's theories, or for that matter of his compositions. After all, not even his worst enemy ever suggested that he had much to do with popular music. Still, he has at least a negative relevance, for no one else did as much to cut 'serious' music off from its popular roots. His ideas became first an intellectual fashion (so that, as early as 1934, Constant Lambert could write of 'Schönberg and the Official Revolution'),[65] and then, for the quarter-century from about 1955 to 1980, attained almost the status of holy writ in musical academia. Even today, they exert a powerful influence, often (as in the parallel cases of Marx and Freud) among people unaware of their origins. So it is worth briefly pointing out what is wrong with them.

First, they rest on a confusion between discord and dissonance, as those words are used in the present book. In reality, it is only dissonances that are *understood*; discords are *felt*.[66] Schoenberg's own compositions bear this out. As Deryck Cooke put it, 'The more "used" one gets to a work by Schoenberg, the more one understands its inherent grimness: familiarity does not bring about a change in the emotional connotation of the sounds, but only a comprehension of the way in which they function as a coherent expressive whole.'[67]

In fact Schoenberg's intention was not really to emancipate dissonance, but to suppress consonance. As theories, his ideas were no good at all; as slogans, they were brilliant. The word 'emancipation', in addition to its exciting and fashionable political overtones, conjured up a wealth of chords quite eclipsing the meagre resources of traditional harmony.[68] And, as with every other variety of 'modern art', the insistence on understanding effected a convenient transfer of responsibility. The implication was that any failure of avant-garde art to achieve public acclaim must be due, not to insufficient skill on the part of the artist, but to insufficient brains on the part of the public.

Consonance and concord were not the only victims of Schoenberg's destructive campaign. Another, more celebrated victim was tonality. Here, broadly the same arguments applied. Music was inevitably becoming more chromatic, just as it was becoming more discordant. Like dissonance, harmonic relationships could be emancipated, the ultimate freedom being a complete absence of tonality. Again, Schoenberg pushed a tendency of his times to what seemed to him its logical conclusion, and again, any dissatisfaction with the result could be put down to incomprehension.

---

[65] The title of Part Five, Section (b) of *Music Ho!*

[66] This point was discussed in Ch. 8, pp. 106–7.

[67] 'The Future of Musical Language', 213, in *Vindications*, 208–14. Originally intended as the final chapter of *The Language of Music*.

[68] Cf. the quotation from Erwin Stein on p. 11.

By the mid-twentieth century these notions had hardened into academic dogma. If a survey were to be made of books and articles on recent musical history published between 1955 and 1980, it would probably be found that most of them mention the collapse of tonality. The following quotations must serve as a small sample:

we shall never be sure when tonality as a concept began to crumble.[69]

The story of twentieth-century music is in great part the story of how different composers coped with the annihilation of tonality . . .[70]

Harmonic tonality, which broke down about 1910, had dominated the scene for three centuries.[71]

Now, whatever it might be, tonality was not a thing. It could not crumble or break down, nor could it be annihilated. The worst that could happen was that composers might stop making use of it. But was even that true? On purely empirical grounds, 'the breakdown of tonality' is as much a fallacy as 'the emancipation of dissonance'. Tonality, however you define it (and the definitions kept shifting, often in the middle of the argument), has retained an important place in the works of relatively conservative composers, to say nothing of popular music.

In fact, the whole 'official revolution' was a pernicious nonsense, and the worst of it was probably the rancour it generated. Reading over the passages quoted earlier, one cannot but be struck by the overcharged language. Composers tremble at their own boldness, tonality is annihilated, audiences shrink in terror. Especially after 1900, there is much talk of battle and conquest, breaking of fetters, smashing of moulds. The violence of the imagery reached its height in the poisonous atmosphere of Hitler's Germany, as witness the following remarks from one of Schoenberg's celebrated pupils:

Today we shall examine tonality in its last throes. I want to prove to you that it's really dead. . . . Relationship to a keynote became ever looser. This opened the way to a state where one could finally dispense with the keynote. The possibility of rapid modulation has nothing to do with this development; in fact, just because all this went on to safeguard the keynote, to extend tonality—precisely because we took steps to preserve tonality—we broke its neck![72]

[69] Edward Lockspeiser, 'Schönberg, Nietzsche, and Debussy' (1961), 210.
[70] Joan Peyser, *Twentieth-Century Music* (1971), p. xi.
[71] Carl Dahlhaus, 'Harmony', §3.iv, in *New Grove II* (1980), x. 866.
[72] Anton von Webern, *The Path to the New Music* (1933), 47–8.

I have read that last sentence many times, and am still unclear as to its meaning. But it seems a strange way to talk about an art.

THE EAST EUROPEANS

As the Modernist craze swept through Europe, east European composers found themselves at a great advantage. Strange scales, queer modes, outlandish harmonic progressions were theirs by birthright. For over a century, dissonant patterns such as these had been contained within a relatively consonant context. To outdo the Westerners in modernistic audacity, all that was necessary was to increase the dissonance while removing the context.

Here the east European Modernists owed much to Debussy. Broadly speaking, he provided the forms and procedures while the native folk music provided the colour. In the French impressionists, drones, parallel chords, and pentatonic passages had been hothouse products; in many parts of eastern Europe, they were vigorous natural growths. So were whole-tone patterns, though east Europeans generally preferred the octatonic, partly because they liked its darkness and partly because it was closer to the diatonic scale. The Russians, in particular, took it to their hearts. The first man to make a serious study of it was Rimsky-Korsakov (in whose honour the Russians called it the 'Rimsky-Korsakov scale'), and the twentieth-century composer who exploited it to greatest effect was his pupil Stravinsky.[73] Altogether, it is hardly too much to describe the octatonic scale as a Russian trade secret.

As we saw in Chapter 11, the octatonic scale comes in two modes, one 'melodic', with the tone at the bottom of the tone–semitone grouping, the other 'harmonic', with the semitone at the bottom. Example 15.28 gives the 'harmonic' mode, in two spellings. Both modes contain all the familiar diatonic chords (Ex. 15.28(*b*)), as well as various fragmentary scales or modes (Ex. 15.28(*c*)), all in regular groups of four to the octave.

But these familiar patterns, like the objects in a Cubist painting, are set at odd and unexpected angles to one another. Tuneful details, while easily isolated, can be sequentially repeated only at intervals made up of multiples of three semitones, such as the minor third, the major sixth, or the augmented fourth. As the bisector of the octave, the last of these intervals had a special status, and deserves a few paragraphs to itself.

---

[73] See Taruskin, 'Chernomor to Kashchei', to which I am much indebted for what follows.

Ex. 15.28. Diatonic patterns in the octatonic scale

(*a*) the source scale

(*b*) chordal patterns
    (i) major triads

    (ii) minor triads

    (iii) 'dominant' or pentatonic seventh

(*c*) scalar patterns
    (i) the first four notes of the minor mode

    (ii) the children's mode

    (iii) the acoustic mode, minus its second note

The tritone as a chromatic 'dominant'

The augmented fourth, or its enharmonic equivalent the diminished fifth (for convenience, the word 'tritone' can be stretched to cover both), had deep roots in east European folk music, where it even occurs in songs close to the children's chant (Ex. 15.29).

For Russian composers, this made its incorporation into 'art' music a relatively simple matter, but in any case it was bound to become prominent in extremely chromatic textures. The basses of Debussy and other turn-of-the-century composers sometimes have tritones in place of the traditional tonic-and-dominant,

Ex. 15.29. 'Prialitsa' ('The Spinning Woman', Russian folk song)

and that was only the beginning.[74] Not only individual notes, but chords or entire keys could be opposed in this manner. So common did such opposition become, that a long line of theorists (beginning, according to Taruskin, with the Russian Boleslav Yavorsky in the late nineteenth century)[75] have seen the tritone as a sort of chromatic equivalent to the dominant. The following quotations, separated by seventy years, are typical:

With the dodecuple system [i.e. the full use of all twelve notes of the chromatic scale] . . . if there is any secondary centre in addition to the chief Tonic hold, it is the diminished fifth or the augmented fourth . . .[76]

The tritone became the cornerstone of polytonality and atonality, accepting the function of a dominant in classical harmony.[77]

But the tritone has a split personality lacking in the true dominant. It may be heard either as an augmented fourth or a diminished fifth, and by switching between the two the composer can instantly modulate to what Ernő Lendvai calls a 'counterpole': 'if the B–F relationship is converted into an F–B one (as is frequently the case with Bartók) then the F (= E♯) assumes the role of the leading note, pulling towards the F♯ instead of E, while the seventh B pulls towards A♯ or A instead of C. So, instead of the expected tonic C major, the *counterpole*, the equally tonic F♯ major (or minor) emerges.'[78] In such a system, the old 'tonic' disappears. Instead of one main key and a group of subordinate keys, we have two looking-glass keys, each the exact reflection of the other. Symmetrical octave division generates symmetrical key schemes.

Hints of counterpolarity may be found as early as Haydn.[79] Later Schubert, and of course Liszt, took it much further; but its full development was mainly the work of the Russians. We can see precisely what Lendvai means from a passage in

[74] e.g. the whole-tone passage from *L'Après-midi*, Ex. 15.24 on p. 406, bars 1–4 and 9–12. See also A. Eaglefield Hull, *Scriabin*, 111, for examples from Scriabin and Rachmaninov.

[75] 'The concept of a stable, consonant, and harmonically static diminished fifth is recognized in Russian theory by Boleslav Yavorsky's formulation of the "diminished mode" (*umenshionny lad*)—his name for the whole-tone-semitone or octatonic scale' ('Chernomor to Kashchei', 111).

[76] Eaglefield Hull, *Modern Harmony* (1914), 39.

[77] Nicolas Slonimsky, introduction to Richard Burbank, *Twentieth Century Music* (1984), p. xii.

[78] *Béla Bartók: An Analysis of his Music*, 12.

[79] e.g. the String Quartet in G, Op. 54 No. 1, second movement, bars 34–52 (Ex. 15.1 on pp. 382–3), the String Quartet in C, Op. 74 No. 1, second movement, bars 133–56, and the Symphony, No. 104 in D, second movement, bars 98–114.

Rimsky-Korsakov's *Sheherazade*, in which a triadic fanfare (but with a 'blue' third) is tritonally bandied about (Ex. 15.30(*a*)). As a glance at Ex. 15.30(*b*) tells us, the result is automatically octatonic.

Ex. 15.30. Rimsky-Korsakov, *Sheherazade* (1888), 2nd mvt.

(*a*) 12 bars after rehearsal letter E (up a 4th)

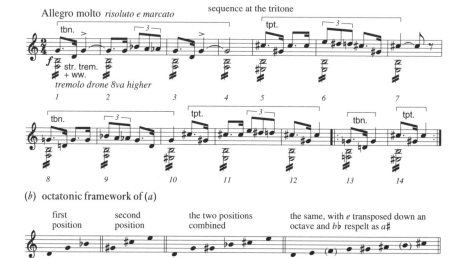

(*b*) octatonic framework of (*a*)

There is just enough coherence in the octatonic scale to bind these counterpolar figures together and make possible an extended modality not unlike Debussy's, but even more chromatic. Where Debussy, in *L'Après-midi d'un faune* (Ex. 15.17 on pp. 400–1), unites the pentatonic sevenths on *f♯* and *a* around the perfect fifth *a–e+*, Stravinsky, in *Petrushka*, unites the 'dominant sevenths' *c–e–g–b♭* and *f♯–a♯–c♯+–e+* around the tritone *e–b♭/a♯* (Ex. 15.31). His methods are similar to (and probably derived from) those of Rimsky-Korsakov in the previous example,[80] but

Ex. 15.31. Stravinsky, *Petrushka* (1911), Part 2 ('Chez Pétrouchka'), bars 34–43

[80] As well as *Sheherezade*, Stravinsky very likely had *L'Après-midi* itself at the back of his mind. Cf. Ex. 15.17, bars 2, 11, and, especially 19, with the sequential figure in bars 6–9 of Ex. 15.31.

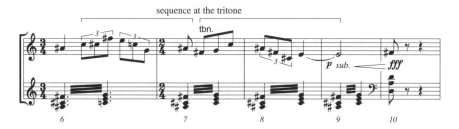

in two respects go further. One is that he substitutes for Rimsky's tritonal drone the famous 'Petrushka chord'. The other, more radical innovation is that the counterpolar melodic chords, instead of being kept apart, are fused into single, faintly bluesy compound mode.

The seductions of symmetry

Of all possible symmetrical divisions of the octave, the octatonic scale is the closest to nature. Because its many diatonic patterns include the pentatonic seventh (see Ex. 15.28(*b* iii) on p. 422), it can serve as a link between complex chromaticism and primitive folk melody. It is not, however, asymmetrical enough to exert any forward thrust. That is one reason why Stravinsky's music—*The Rite of Spring* is a prime example—relies so heavily on pulsating rhythms to generate a sense of movement. For when all is said and done, rigidly symmetrical divisions of the octave are intellectual constructs, not natural growths. They lack the irregularity characteristic of living things.

They also defy the hierarchic sense, just as Schoenberg's atonality does. Schoenberg himself preferred to describe his system as employing 'twelve tones related only to one another'—that is to say, not subordinate to any overriding pattern. Is it fanciful to see in this a reaction against the art nouveau delight in living organisms, which must, by their nature, be hierarchic? Was it the same instinct as led Schoenberg's friend Adolf Loos to develop his stark, unadorned, rectilinear style of architecture?

However that may be, symmetrical divisions of the octave, since the discovery of the diminished seventh, have been associated with the fantastic, the morbid, the inhuman. To cling exclusively to such patterns is to bind oneself with fetters that would have appalled the fiercest martinets of the Paris Conservatoire. One thing we learnt during the twentieth century was that it is precisely revolutionary regimes that turn into the most devoted guardians of the status quo. So it has been with 'modern art'. For a hundred years it has inhabited a strangely unchanging world. Fashions have come and gone, but there has been little real growth. How could it be otherwise, with forms so defiantly inorganic? Meanwhile, a stream of novelties has issued from the popular arts, and from none more so than music.

16 The Popular Style

Extraordinary how potent cheap music is.

Noel Coward, *Private Lives*[1]

I. THE LATE VERNACULAR

Throughout the alarms and excursions of early Modernism, Western popular music continued undisturbed on its way. Though already a separate world from 'serious' or 'classical' music—terms then coming into common use—it was still, in essentials, a late version of the nineteenth-century vernacular. This point needs emphasizing. So stunning has the impact of jazz, blues, and other Afro-American genres been that they have almost obscured the native European strain, which in fact continued to dominate Western popular music till the early 1950s, developing all the time but never quite cutting itself off from its Italian and central European roots. With a light Afro-American tinge, it is the musical language of Cole Porter, George Gershwin, Richard Rodgers, Harry Warren, and the other great songwriters of the 1920s and 1930s. Without even that admixture, it survived in continental Europe well into the second half of the century, attaining perhaps its greatest heights in French *chanson*s such as 'J'attendrais', 'La Vie en rose', or 'Non, je ne regrette rien', none of which owe anything obvious to the United States.[2]

In any case, 'Afro-American' music was itself extremely hybrid, ranging all the way from the near-African to the near-European; and it was inevitably the European end that had most impact on middle-class taste. If this last chapter concentrates on American developments, it should never be forgotten that they took place in a European setting.

The European background

In essence, the musical vernacular of the early twentieth century is that of the late nineteenth century intensified. Melody grows yet more independent of the Bass,

---

[1] Act I, original version. The first word was later altered to the less Cowardly 'Strange'.

[2] 'J'attendrai' was composed by Dino Olivieri in 1938, to words by Louis Poterat; 'La Vie en rose' by Louiguy (pseudonym of Louis Guillaume, originally Luis Guglielmi) in 1946, to words by Edith Piaf; 'Non, je ne regrette rien', by Charles Dumont in 1960, to words by Michel Vaucaire.

and in compensation bar rhythms become even squarer; but, to compensate in turn for this squareness, local rhythms become more syncopated. Harmonically, the norm remains the major mode, but of an increasingly complex type. Just as in the rhythm large-scale squareness is balanced against small-scale irregularity, so in the harmony broad underlying patterns are balanced against superficial elaboration. In Kreisler's 'Caprice viennoise' (Ex. 16.1), the main chords are very simple—much more so than in the average Mozart minuet, for instance. The first sixteen bars:

$$\text{IV II} \cdot \text{I I II II} : \text{II II V V} \cdot \text{V V I I (over a I + V pedal)}$$

are really no more than a big I–II–V–I cadence, with the first three chords split

Ex. 16.1. Kreisler, 'Caprice viennoise' (1910), bars 20–39 (main theme) (up a semitone)

(*continued on next page*)

(Ex. 16.1 *cont.*)

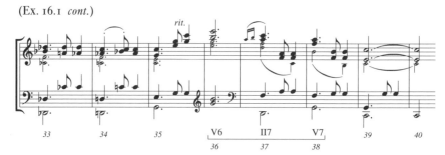

across the four-bar phrases. And the rest, notwithstanding the luscious chromaticisms of bars 23–6 and 33–4, is little more complicated.

Late vernacular harmony, which continued to develop up to the early 1950s, can be very complicated—often much too complicated, in fact. But it becomes easier to understand once we notice that, reversing what had been the usual state of affairs, the subsidiary chord tends more and more to replace the beginning rather than the end of the main chord. Till about the mid-nineteenth century, the normal way of elaborating the chord X had been to turn it into X–Y (so that I IV, for instance, might become I–VI IV). In the late vernacular, the order is more likely to be Y–X. Another favourite device is to replace the normal harmonization of a Melody note by a substitute chord. A good example is the $B\flat$ in bars 23–4 of Ex. 16.1, which replaces the normal dominant as a harmonization of d. The 'laggard dominant' described in Chapter 13 is a form of 'Y–X' progression in which Y is a substitute chord and X a dominant.

Undoubtedly the most striking feature of late vernacular harmony, however, is its chromatic chords. The noticeable thing about these chords, apart from their sheer profusion, is the way they are semitonally glued to their surroundings. Once more, the underlying pattern is often Y–X (as in bars 25–6 and 33–4 of Ex. 16.1), but it may also be X–Y–X. This sort of harmonic sandwich was of course no novelty, nor was it necessarily chromatic; but, again, the tendency was to divide it up as X Y–X rather than X–Y X. One result was a development of the split dominant in which V V becomes V II–V. This 'supertonic sandwich' may be found as far back as Wagner's *Tannhäuser* Overture (Ex. 16.2), but it was not till the 1880s that it became

Ex. 16.2. Wagner, *Tannhäuser* (1843–5), Overture, bars 142–9 (Tannhäuser's song) (up a semitone)

common. To waltz composers, in particular, it was an invaluable way of variegating long stretches of dominant harmony (Ex. 16.1, which is essentially a waltz, contains an instance in bars 36–8). By the early twentieth century, it had become commonplace in popular music of all kinds.

Like most other harmonic progressions, it could be elaborated. One might, for instance, give the II of the V7–II–V7 progression its own dominant, as Tchaikovsky does in Ex. 16.3. The result is somehow impressionistic and 'modal', not because Tchaikovsky has expanded the progression, but because he has detached it from its harmonic context. Where Kreisler's chromatic chords rest firmly on a

Ex. 16.3. Tchaikovsky, 'Valse sentimentale', Op. 51 No. 6 (1882), bars 35–54 (2nd theme) (down a minor 6th)

simple diatonic foundation, Tchaikovsky's hover in the air. This makes them much subtler, though also much less complex. If Kreisler is sophisticated-popular, Tchaikovsky is popular-classical—not that anyone bothered about such distinctions at the time. Both pieces are fine specimens of 'light music', a class of composition highly characteristic of its period and now quite extinct.

At the other end of the great, amorphous swell of popular music, we find a mass of songs, dances, and marches in which the harmony is simpler, the bar rhythms squarer, the melodic framework more regular, and the general effect much more highly patterned—none of which, one should immediately add, precludes its own form of subtlety. The grand old music-hall song 'A Little of What You Fancy Does You Good' (Ex. 16.4(*a*)) is notable not only for the bold sweep of its tune, but also for a new and important type of variation form, which becomes evident when we compare bars 1–8, 17–24, and 33–40, in other words, the first halves of the three sixteen-bar sections (Ex. 16.4(*b*)).

Ex. 16.4. Fred W. Leigh and George Arthurs, 'A Little of What You Fancy Does You Good' (1915) (up a tone)

(*a*) verse and chorus

In these variations the harmony, a simple split dominant, remains the same. And, in addition, all three tunes fit into an identical 'hard' pentatonic e–g–a–b–e^+ framework. This, whether consciously or not, is the composer's true 'theme', and it is notable that it extends to the contrapuntal interjections here given in small notes. Essentially the same technique, greatly expanded, is characteristic of early jazz and the blues, except that there the variations are mostly improvised rather than worked out beforehand.

Before we tackle that formidably complex topic, however, we must take a closer look at *fin de siècle* American music in general.

The United States

> The twentieth century is only the nineteenth speaking with a slight
> American accent.[3]
>
> Philip Guedalla (attributed)

Till almost the end of the nineteenth century, American popular music was a
rather wild and wayward extension of its European counterpart. Even the fashion
for 'nigger minstrel' shows was part of an international craze for ethnic music. The
songs of Stephen Foster, Daniel Emmett, Henry Clay Work, and James Bland (the
first commercially successful black American composer) were little more than the
American equivalent of the German *volkstümliches Lied*, and as such become
extremely popular. By the late nineteenth century, 'plantation songs' were an
internationally recognized genre,[4] but, charming as they often are, their most
striking characteristic to the modern observer is their fraudulence. An Afro-
American atmosphere is sedulously promoted, but there is little that is genuinely
Afro-American in the music. The main influences are Italian opera and Scottish or
Irish traditional music, the forms and harmonies simple in the extreme, and the
result, if remote from the plantation, at any rate thoroughly American.

But why should this white American popular music, at most lightly touched by
African influence, be so enthusiastically attributed to the blacks? There is a parallel
here with the 'Gypsy' music of eastern Europe. It is not only that the Gypsies were
in so many ways the blacks of eastern Europe. There were also larger historical
forces at work in both regions, and indeed throughout the Western world.

One was nationalism, in the sense not so much of ethnic assertiveness as of a
longing to be different and distinctive, to lay claim to one's own unique voice and
ancient traditions. Another was a general rise in living standards. As the poorer
classes prospered, their music changed accordingly. Vaudeville theatres, music
halls, and similar places of entertainment flourished, as did amateur bodies such as
choral societies, brass bands, or ceilidh groups. At the same time communications
improved beyond recognition. Travel, postal services, and printing all became
cheaper and more efficient, while literacy, both verbal and musical, came to be
taken for granted where previously it had been unknown. All this made it possible
for popular music to be 'commercialized'—a misleading term, since much of it
had been commercial all along. What *did* change was the scale of both operations
and profits.

---

[3] Although it appears in more than one dictionary of quotations, I have not been able to find a satisfactory source for this observation. The date is most likely some time in the 1920s. Later the American accent
became more pronounced.

[4] e.g. *The Scottish Students' Song Book* (1891), a representative and influential collection, has a section
of sixteen 'Plantation Songs', five of them by Foster.

All three factors must be borne in mind if we are to understand the history of American popular music. The craze for the 'nigger minstrels' of the 1840s set a pattern that was later to be repeated several times over. First, genuine Afro-American music is introduced to the white, middle-class public as a shocking novelty. Then it is adapted to their tastes, principally by white musicians. Once this relatively bland, commercial product has won acceptance, the public is ready for a new, darker influx, and the cycle begins again.

One must be careful to specify Afro-*American* rather than simply African, because from a very early date black Americans created a unique musical language that drew equally on African and European traditions. In the words of a historian of the slave trade:

The African cultural heritage is somewhat weaker and more diffuse in North America than it is elsewhere on the continent. The peak in the importation of slaves to North America was reached during the two decades on either side of 1750. This means that the African population in this country arrived, on the whole, much earlier than did the majority of settlers from Europe. Afro-Americans have therefore had many generations in which to assimilate general American culture, and the African culture they brought with them has been diffused very widely throughout the population, both black and white, of the Southern states.[5]

A further important point is that the whites encountered by this black influx were themselves mostly humble country folk. During the same period (and in response to the same labour shortage) a wave of 'Scotch-Irish' immigrants arrived from northern Ireland and the Scottish Lowlands. Their predominantly Scottish music was taken up and Africanized by the blacks. Dance music became 'jigs' and 'reels' of the American rather than the Scottish or Irish type, while folk hymns turned into spirituals. A little later, ballads and songs were incorporated in the blues.

This Africanization was largely a negative process. Slowly but surely, black musicians rejected everything that was un-African in white folks' music: the ABA form, the melodic arch, 3/4 time, modulation, and many chordal progressions. It might seem that there was not much left, but, in fact, Africa and the British Isles had much in common. At the most primitive level, there were formal and melodic patterns that might be found pretty well throughout the world, such as the descending contour, the tapering form, the end-repeating variation, the pentatonic scale. Hardly less primitive was the double-tonic ostinato; and finally, there were more complex rhythmic features, such as the hemiola and the accented off-beat, which no doubt went back to a common Afro-Asian source.

---

[5] Philip D. Curtin, 'The Slave Trade and the Atlantic Basin', 93.

Meanwhile, a relatively pure African strain survived in those places (notably the Mississippi Delta) where the black workforce was densely concentrated and supplemented by latecomers. The number of slaves illegally imported between the abolition of the official trade in 1808 and the outbreak of the Civil War in 1861 is difficult to gauge, but was probably substantial; Curtin, in what he admits is 'a shot in the dark', puts it at 54,000.[6] It is probably to this late influx that we owe the near-African patterns that again and again revitalized the paler commercial product.

Ragtime

'Minstrel' music, always relatively European and further Europeanized by composers of the Foster school, had been an enormous success. But by the 1890s a public now thoroughly accustomed to 'Old Black Joe', 'Eliza Jane', and 'Oh! Susanna' was ready for something a little stronger. This demand was met by a new influx of songs and dances. The former, known in those innocent days as 'coon songs', perpetuated the Fosterian tradition of the grinning, banjo-picking, watermelon-munching darkie, but with a significantly blacker input. Many of them had actual Afro-American tunes, often with a distinctly blue tinge.[7] Among the dances, the most popular was the cakewalk, which had originally parodied the airs and graces of the white masters. More important than any individual song or dance, however, was the new performing style known as 'ragtime'.

In essence, this was little more than a method of syncopation—'ragged time', in fact—and the material to which it was applied changed considerably during the first few years of its existence. The early rags, which began to appear in sheet-music form from 1897, shared with the coon songs many folk-like characteristics, such as the alternation of the chords of C major and A minor,[8] pentatonic figures often delicately balanced between the relative major and minor,[9] and the minor mode itself, at that time a comparative rarity in mainstream popular music. There is even at least one double-tonic tune.[10] The style, which often has great charm, is in essentials still the mid-century Afro-Celtic mixture.

Then, some two years later, ragtime developed into a national craze and accordingly changed its character. Published rags became, for the most part, little more than

---

[6] *The Atlantic Slave Trade*, 74–5. This figure includes 'the slave trade to Texas before it joined the union' (in 1845).

[7] e.g. Ben Harney's 'Possumala Dance' (1894), related to the nursery song 'Froggie Went a-Courting'; Irving Jones's 'Mister Johnson' (1896), a close relative of the bluesy spiritual 'Motherless Children'; and the verse section of Hughie Cannon's 'Just because She Made dem Goo-goo Eyes' (1900), which is probably the first recorded member of the 'Frankie and Johnny' tune family (see Ex. 16.12 on p. 448).

[8] This is a feature of the general European vernacular (cf. Exs. 13.20 and 13.21 on pp. 294–5), but the main source of the ragtime version was almost certainly Irish dance music.

[9] e.g. 'Shake yo' Dusters!', by W. H. Krell (Ex. 16.25 on p. 458).

[10] 'Impecunious Davis', by Kerry Mills (1899). It is of the 'Drunken Sailor', *Am–G* type.

syncopated marches, and are usually so described on the title page. This was natural enough, since the late nineteenth-century American march, which we now inseparably associate with John Philip Sousa, had itself absorbed several folk influences. Firstly, there was the polka, through which the march (in both Europe and America) had picked up certain central or east European features. Secondly, there was the Irish march, which, like many of Sousa's, was in 6/8 time. Finally, there was an Afro-American influence transmitted through black bandsmen, and evident both in frequent syncopations (though here it is not always easy to distinguish between Afro-American and east European influences) and in call-and-response patterns between treble and bass (the so-called 'dogfight'). It may be significant that Sousa was an early enthusiast for ragtime.

The ragtime of the 1900s closely resembles the march in its harmonic and melodic style, the only important differences being that its harmony tends to be more plagal and the Melody even more independent. It was also from the march that ragtime acquired the habit of ending in the key a fifth lower than the starting one. As Sousa himself tells us, this was suggested by the practice of actual marching bands:

In my childhood in Washington [this would have been in the 1860s] I noticed that the band parading with the regiments in nearly every instance, although the composition called for a da capo, would finish playing on the last strain of the march; therefore, if it was done practically in the use of the march I could not understand why it should not be done theoretically in the writing of the march. Accordingly, in composing my marches, I ignored the old established rule and wrote with the idea of making the last strain of the march the musical climax, regardless of the tonality.[11]

He does not explain *why* bandmasters did this, but the main reason was no doubt that the trio had become so weighty that a return to the previous theme would seem an anticlimax. An important factor in this weightiness was the 'tonality', which was normally subdominant.[12]

In most other respects, the march closely resembled the polka (or for that matter the waltz) in its melody and harmony. We find the same drawn-out $V7$–I or I–$V7$ · $V7$–I progressions, the same chromatic passing notes, and the same emphasis on 3 and 6. All these features are illustrated in 'The Teddy Bear's Picnic' (Ex. 16.5), best known as a popular song but also a march, and they are equally characteristic of the 'classical' ragtime of Scott Joplin and his lesser contemporaries.

---

[11] 'A Letter from Sousa', *Etude* (Aug. 1898), 231. Quoted in Berlin, *Ragtime*, 100–1.

[12] Cf. the so-called 'Cancan' from Offenbach's *Orphée aux enfers* (Ex. 13.23 on p. 298), composed about the time Sousa is speaking of. Though it does have a da capo, this might well be omitted.

Ex. 16.5. Bratton, 'The Teddy Bear's Picnic' (1907), Trio, beginning (down a 4th)

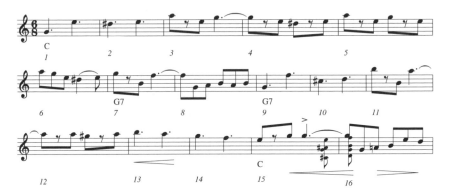

It is fascinating to compare the title pages of the published rags.[13] The early ones are full of Afro-American 'old plantation' imagery, much of it (to our eyes) startlingly racist. Then, about 1900, the tone changes. The caricatures become less crude, the scene may be urban as well as rustic, photographs begin to replace drawings, but the iconography remains predominantly Afro-American. A few years later, even this begins to fade. The human element, now as likely to be Euro- as Afro-American (pretty white girls are a great favourite), often disappears altogether. In accordance with the now popular art nouveau taste, its place is often taken by flowers, both on the title page and in the title, examples of the latter being Scott Joplin's 'Sunflower Slow Drag', 'The Chrysanthemum', and 'Heliotrope Bouquet'.

All this shows how quickly ragtime was being absorbed into the mainstream of American popular culture, but it is only part of the story. Genuine black music continued to fascinate the middle-class public. While in some respects the classical rags became more European, in others, notably rhythm, they became more Afro-American. And of course published ragtime represented only a tiny fraction of black American music-making. From time to time, even within the published corpus, there are tantalizing hints of what was being pounded out on the pianos of thousands of barrelhouses and juke joints. Among these, by far the most interesting are occasional glimpses of the early blues.

---

[13] Invaluable collections for this purpose are *Classic Piano Rags*, *Ragtime Rarities*, and *Ragtime Rediscoveries*, the first selected by Rudi Blesh, the last two by Trebor Jay Tichenor. Between them they contain facsimile reprints of the music and title pages of several hundred rags published between 1897 to 1922, including all those quoted in the present book.

II. THE BLUES AND EARLY JAZZ

As can be seen from its family tree, crudely summarized in Fig. 16.1, there are few musical genres as hybrid as the blues. Here we are mainly concerned with the bottom right-hand corner, where the folk blues merges with the European vernacular to form the mature blues. For the earlier history of the genre, and especially the all-important African contribution, I refer the reader to *Origins*, where these topics are dealt with at great length (I dare not say 'fully').

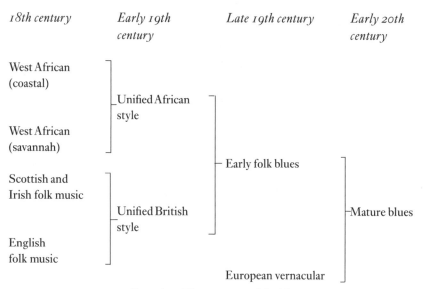

FIG. 16.1. The ancestry of the blues

Still, what happened at this late stage cannot be fully understood without at least a sketchy knowledge of what happened earlier on. Let us therefore retreat a few decades to the middle of the nineteenth century.

Antecedents

It is fortunate that Dan Emmett, founder of the Virginia Minstrels, was also something of a folklorist. 'Old Dan Tucker' (Ex. 16.6), one of his early hits, gives every indication of being a genuine Afro-American tune—'Afro-American', mind you, not 'African'. By this time, at least a century and a half of Afro-British interaction had produced a uniquely American amalgam. Many of the features of this tune, such as the pentatonic melody, descending contour, and open-ended form, are

Ex. 16.6. 'Old Dan Tucker' (1843) (down a tone)

common to both cultures. Some, like the call-and-response pattern in the chorus, or the conclusion of each four-bar phrase with the same figure, are more typical of Africa; others, like the harmony, incline more towards Europe. But not one is purely African or purely European. All are hybrid.

For the historian of the blues, the harmony is particularly interesting. At a slightly earlier stage, it would have been a simple $c + g$ drone, which might have come from the British Isles, the Arab-influenced West African savannah, or—most probably—from both. As we see it here, it has the rough-and-ready air typical of transitions from drone accompaniments to fully chordal systems.[14] It also shows a strong plagal bias. This, in a way, is surprising. In view of the ancestry of this hybrid form—African on the one hand, predominantly Scottish and Irish on the other—one would expect it to develop the double-tonic patterns common to both parent cultures. And, in fact, these did survive in the United States till at least the beginning of the twentieth century. But in the long run it was plagal progressions that prevailed, no doubt because they belonged to a style of folk harmony that was

---

[14] Cf. Dalza's *spingardi* (Ex. 6.7 and Ex. 6.8 on pp. 77–8) and 'Rákóczi's Lament' (Ex. 11.98 on p. 222).

both more international and more fashionable. This did not, however, mean that drone accompaniment died out. On the contrary, thickened into a major triad it lived on vigorously in countless 'one-chord blues', to which we shall return. Example 16.7, from one of the folkier rags, is a step towards this later form.

Ex. 16.7. Johnson, 'A Black Smoke' (1902), bars 9–12 (up a 4th)

The blues mode

The main reason why the creators of the blues were content with such simple harmony was that most of their invention went into the Melody. As it developed in the 1880s and 1890s, the blues form drew to itself all the pentatonic patterns that had flowed through American music over the past century. Many, both African and European, were still close to the children's chant.[15] Others derived from more recent musical strata, including the European vernacular. All, regardless of origin, were wrapped around the c–$e(\flat)$–g triad, which in harmonized blues (for many were still purely melodic) corresponded to the tonic chord of the accompaniment. It was to this solid but flexible core that the blues mode owed its power. Thanks to the variable third it could accommodate the two quite separate pentatonic systems a^-–c–d–e–g, and c–$e\flat$–f–g–$b\flat$. In essence, this was just another form of the double pentatonic axis so important in the European vernacular. But it did have several distinguishing features.

Firstly, the blues mode lays enormous emphasis on the interval of the third, and especially the minor third. This is particularly evident at cadences, where the direction may be upward ($a^-\rightarrow c$ or $e\rightarrow g$) or downward ($e(\flat)\rightarrow c$ or $b\flat\rightarrow g$). In the latter case, the dissonant or 'blue' third may assume a vast array of forms. It may be major or minor, blossom into an entire melodic figure,[16] or even resolve on itself ($e\flat\rightarrow e\natural$). But what it will never do, in the genuine blues style, is to destroy the structure of interconnected thirds on which the whole force of the mode depends. However complex it may become, blues melody never ceases to be pentatonic.

A second, related characteristic is microtonal fluctuation. Whenever possible, blues performers like to 'bend' their blue thirds. On instruments of flexible pitch,

---

[15] Cf. 'Ngoneni, ngoneni, nebakitsi' (Ex. 4.3(*a*) on p. 40). Black American songs with a similar contour include the bluesy 'holler' 'Another Man done Gone' and the spiritual 'Religion So Sweet', the latter collected in *Slave Songs of the United States*, ed. W. F. Allen, C. P. Ware, and L. McKim Garrison (1867).

[16] e.g. the $d\sharp$–e–$d\sharp$–e $d\natural$–e–$d\natural$–e in 'A Black Smoke' (Ex. 16.7, bars 3–4).

such as the voice, violin, or trombone, this is a simple matter. On others, such as the harmonica, it requires a certain ingenuity. On keyboard instruments, it is an impossibility in any literal sense. Yet, so important are bent notes to the blues, that pianists developed ways of suggesting them by striking both the minor and major third at the same time. In every case, what this 'bending' comes down to is the attraction of the dissonant note towards its goal. Sometimes, this amounts to no more than the barely perceptible flattening of the major third. At other times, the blue note may be 'neutral' (intermediate between major and minor) or fully minor, and to complicate matters there is always the possibility of glides, shakes, or mordents. In any case, the degree of flattening will reflect the strength of the pull towards the note below, and probably also the emotional intensity.

The third peculiarity of the blues mode is that it shares to the full the tonal ambiguity (or *peremennost'*, as the Russians would call it), of all pentatonic music. Especially in the early, unharmonized blues, it can be a moot point whether c or a is the tonic. This means that a blue e is potentially not only a blue third in relation to c, but also a blue fifth in relation to a. Though this 'blue fifth' has distant relatives in eastern Europe,[17] it is without any real parallel. Certainly nothing so chromatically bold had been heard before in Western popular music.

The twelve-bar form

Next to its unique mode, the most remarkable thing about the blues is its famous 'twelve-bar' form. (The term, as we shall see, is unsatisfactory,[18] but it is sanctioned by custom, and we may as well stick with it.) The twelve-bar form is both a paradox and a puzzle. Why was it so much more popular than the symmetrical eight- or sixteen-bar form, and where did it come from? It certainly had no connection with the international vernacular, where the trend, if anything, was *away* from asymmetrical phrasing. Nor did it come from Africa. It is true that black Africa has a liking for asymmetrical patterns (and not only in music), and that this was decisive in the development of the twelve-bar form. But the form itself appears to have no direct ancestors in Africa.

It came, rather, from the popular song of Europe, where tunes of more or less this shape have been known at least since the Middle Ages. The two commonest types developed by extending the four-line stanza, or 'quatrain', to six lines, either by repeating the second pair of lines (call this the ABB type) or by adding an independent refrain (the AAB type). In either case, the first four lines would normally be sung by a solo voice, and the last two by a chorus. German scholars,

---

[17] Cf. in the first movement of Schubert's 'Unfinished' Symphony (Ex. 11.108 on p. 228).

[18] Many early blues have only six bars, many later blues twenty-four. Also, two-bar phrases are often irregularly lengthened, e.g. 'Haunted Road Blues' (Ex. 16.19 on p. 453), where the twelve bars are expanded to sixteen (2 + 3; 2 + 3; 2 + 4).

misinterpreting the Meistersingers' terminology, have called the AAB type the *Bar*, and, by analogy, the ABB type the *Gegenbar*, or 'counter-*Bar*'.[19] Both found their way into 'art' music, especially, perhaps, the compositions of the Viennese school. The most famous example must be the 'Ode to Joy' in the finale of Beethoven's Ninth Symphony,[20] which even reverts to the solo-and-chorus structure:

Baritone solo:

> Freude, schöner Götterfunken, Tochter aus Elysium,
> Wir betreten feuertrunken, Himmlische, dein Heiligtum!
> Deine Zauber binden wieder, was die Mode streng geteilt;
> Alle Menschen werden Brüder, wo dein sanfter Flügel weilt.

Chorus:

> Deine Zauber binden wieder, was die Mode streng geteilt;
> Alle Menschen werden Brüder, wo dein sanfter Flügel weilt.[21]

As the words suggest (but is often forgotten), this tune is in a deliberately popular style, and the verse-and-chorus structure is one aspect of it. From about the middle of the eighteenth century, the process of tacking anything from one to eight bars onto the end of a regular period acquired definite popular associations. Sometimes the addition is merely the echo of a bar or two, as for instance in Rossini's *canzonetta* 'Una volta c'era un Re' or Schubert's 'Serenade'.[22] At other times, a whole four- or eight-bar phrase might be repeated, as in the 'Ode to Joy'. The next step up the scale of formal complexity was to add an independent period instead of a mere repetition, as in the main theme from the finale of Haydn's String Quartet in C, Op. 74 No. 1. This, as we noticed in Chapter 11, is one of Haydn's most colourful Gypsy finales, and in his mind the twelve-bar structure of this theme was no doubt just another 'Gypsy' feature. Even more integrated are certain *canzonette*, such as the 'Willow Song' from Rossini's *Otello*:[23]

> Assisa a' pie d'un salice, immersa nel dolore [4 bars]
> Giacea traffita Isaura dal più crudele amore; [4 bars]
> (Refrain:) L'aura fra i rami flebile ne ripeteva il suon.[24] [4 bars]

---

[19] See Horst Brunner, 'Bar form'. In neither case need A be the same length as B.

[20] See bars 241–64. Cf. also the finale of the First Symphony and the slow movement of the Seventh, both of which have twenty-four-bar main themes of this type.

[21] Translation: 'Joy, fair spark of the gods, daughter of Elysium: drunk with fire, O heavenly one, we approach thy sanctuary. Thy spells bind again what fashion has harshly parted. All men become brothers in the presence of thy gentle wing.'

[22] See Exs. 11.59 and 11.66(*a*) respectively (pp. 191 and 197). At this time, the title 'Serenade' (or 'Ständchen'), like 'Canzonetta' and 'Romanza', usually implied that a song was popular in style.

[23] For the tune, see Ex. 13.27 on p. 302.

[24] Translation: 'At the foot of a willow tree sat Isaura, sunken in grief and transfixed with the cruellest love. (Refrain): Through the branches the breeze repeated the mournful sound.'

or, from the same opera, the haunting fragment sung by the gondolier:

> Nessun maggior dolore, nessun maggior dolore [4 bars]
> che ricordarsi del tempo felice nella miseria, [5 bars]
> che ricordarsi del tempo felice nella miseria.[25] [6 bars]

In passages like these, and especially the latter, we come close to genuine Italian folk melody. If far from being Italian blues, they nevertheless have strikingly bluesy features, which it will be well to bear in mind when we come to the later history of the genre.

Another place where the twelve-bar form flourished was the British Isles, especially Scotland, and it was from here that the blues type was mainly derived. The Scottish ballad tune 'Harlaw' (Ex. 16.8) represents a particularly influential sub-

Ex. 16.8. 'Harlaw' (Scottish ballad tune) (down a 4th)

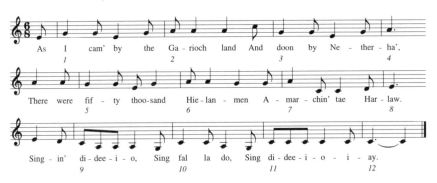

group, with six sections together making an $A_1A_2A_3B\,C_1C_2$ pattern. At the same time, the pentatonic melody is of a notably archaic type, with repeated figures, a cyclical, asymmetrical form, and a descending contour. All these features would seem to be congenial to African ears; and so apparently they were, for by the early twentieth century this tune type had engendered a vast, bluesy progeny. Though varying enormously in detail, these early blues tunes always retain the verse-and-refrain form, and usually also the six-line form. The best known are 'blues ballads' of the 'Frankie and Johnny' and 'Boll Weevil' families, but there are many others, running to literally hundreds of distinct melodies.

This blues type carried further the tendency, already well advanced in its Scottish ancestors, of fusing verse and refrain into a unit of three paired sections, which we may call the 'statement' (bars 1–4), 'counterstatement' (bars 5–8), and 'conclusion' (bars 9–12). The object was both to weaken the finality of the

---

[25] The words are of course from Dante's *Inferno*. Translation: 'There is no greater sorrow than to recall a happy time while miserable.'

counterstatement and to bind it more tightly to the conclusion, and the means
might be melodic, harmonic, rhythmic, or even verbal:

> Corinna, Corinna · where'd you stay last night?
> Tell me, Corinna · where'd you stay last night?
> Your shoes ain't buttoned, girl · don't fit you right.[26]

This typical example of the 'classic' blues stanza, now compressed into three
lines instead of six, reflects a real metrical difference. The stanzas of British ballads
like 'Harlaw' are made up of metrical 'feet', each of which consists of first an unaccented and then an accented syllable. The musical equivalent (bearing in mind that
one can always substitute ♪♪ for ♩) is approximately:

♪ | ♩ ♪♩ ♪ | ♩ ♪♩
♪ | ♩ ♪♩ ♪ | ♩. ♩
♪ | ♩ ♪♩ ♪ | ♩ ♪♩
♪ | ♩ ♪♩ ♪ | ♩. ♩

But these regular 'feet' have no place in African or Afro-American song. As an
early observer put it:

The negroes keep exquisite time in singing, and do not suffer themselves to be daunted by
any obstacle in the words. The most obstinate Scripture phrases or snatches from hymns
they will force to do duty with any tune they please, and will dash heroically through a
trochaic tune at the head of a column of iambs with wonderful skill.[27]

This is, after all, no more than what one should expect from a culture in which
melody and rhythm are so artfully opposed. In Afro-American song, the accent
that counts is the one at the beginning of the four-beat bar; how many syllables
intervene is immaterial. The result is a four-bar line containing two pairs of metrical accents separated by a caesura. Here, for instance, is the accentual scheme of
the bluesy Appalachian lyric 'Single Girl':[28]

> Síx little chíldren · all fór to retáin,
> Náry a one is lárge enough · to hélp me one gráin.
> Bóo-hoo, I wísh I was · a síngle girl agáin.

and here is that of 'Corinna':

> Corínna, Corínna · where'd you stáy last níght?
> Please téll me, Corínna · where'd you stáy last níght?
> Your shoes ain't búttoned, gírl · Don't fit you ríght.

[26] For the tune, see Ex. 16.14 on p. 450.
[27] William Francis Allen, in the preface to *Slave Songs of the United States* (1867), p. iv.
[28] From *English Folk Songs from the Southern Appalachians*, collected by Cecil Sharp, ii. 33, variant C.
The tune is apparently of Scottish origin. See *Origins*, 185–6.

even though the printed page may suggest the more regular

> Your shóes ain't búttoned, gírl.

But this metrical loosening was much more than a mere corruption. British-American singers would not have taken to it so readily if they had not found it congenial. In doing so, they were returning to the instinctive origins of English verse, as seen in Anglo-Saxon alliterative poetry and in many nursery rhymes:

> Síng a song of síxpence · a pócket full of rýe;
> Fóur and twenty bláckbirds · báked in a píe.

and even in the rhetorical prose of the King James Bible and Book of Common Prayer, for instance Psalm 121:

> I will líft up mine eyes unto the hílls · from whénce cometh my hélp.
> My hélp cometh from the Lórd · which máde heaven and éarth.

Conversely, black musicians would not have adopted the twelve-bar structure if it had not appealed to them. But what was the appeal? For an answer, we must go to the most African of all Afro-American vocal genres, the so-called 'holler', also known as the 'field blues'. In its form, the holler was probably as old as song itself: a series of improvised, constantly varied strains, all descending to the same low point and often to the same figure. This is true 'endless melody', without any further organizing principle beyond the grouping of the strains into irregular waves, which themselves taper from high to low. Fortunately, the survival of the holler well into the twentieth century enables us to trace its later evolution. In transcriptions and recordings, we can see how the waves begin to approximate first to loosely grouped stanzas, and then to definite tunes.

The end of this process can be clearly seen in 'Joe Turner', one of several claimants to the title of 'the first blues' (Ex. 16.9), and in effect a holler remodelled on the British-American blues stanza. Its tumbling strains, though grouped into threes, are still recognizably African. In particular, they are very compact; this is a three-, not a six-part form. It was only later, by a further process of remodelling, that a blues form of six descending strains was to develop (as in Ex. 16.19 on p. 453.)

Ex. 16.9. 'Joe Turner' (early 20th-c. blues)

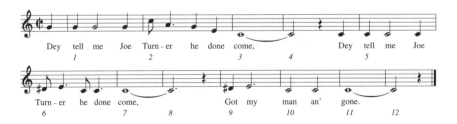

The same partial remodelling may be seen in the words. In the holler, the same line had been repeated over and over, often interspersed with wordless humming or vocalizing. In the most primitive holler-blues, the stanza often consists of the same line sung three times over. 'Joe Turner', no doubt influenced by the British-American stanza-and-refrain form, introduces a new third line, delicately poised between half-rhyme and casual refrain:

> Dey tell me Joe Turner he done come;
> Dey tell me Joe Turner he done come;
> Got my man an' gone.

From this it was a small step to the mature blues stanza, which is simply a rhyming couplet with the first line repeated.

Harmony

Americans of all complexions treated the international vernacular in much the same way as black Americans treated the folk music of the white population. That is to say, they selected from it and then exaggerated whatever was useful to them. For melodic purposes, this meant pentatonic patterns of a special kind; for harmonic purposes, it meant the primary chords and simpler cadences. As we have seen from 'Old Dan Tucker' (Ex. 16.6), plagal cadences were particularly favoured, and a great deal of American popular music can be summed up as pentatonic melody over plagal harmony, the latter often in the form of the *passamezzo moderno* ('Gregory Walker') or one its close relatives. A typical instance is Foster's 'plantation song' 'Massa's in de Cold, Cold Ground' (Ex. 16.10).

Ex. 16.10. Foster, 'Massa's in de Cold, Cold Ground' (1852), verse (down a tone)

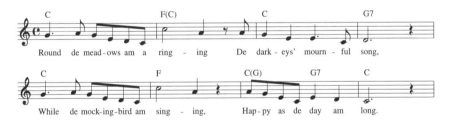

This is already quite close to blues harmony, and replacing the initial I–IV with I I · IV I brings it even closer. One reason for the sudden popularity of this ancient 'Black Sheep' pattern was no doubt that it happened to suit the international fashion for Y–X progressions.[29] It is therefore natural that its first appearances should be nearer to the 'commercial' than the 'folk' end of the American popular music

---

[29] For the distinction between 'X–Y' and 'Y–X' progressions, see p. 428.

spectrum, in such things as the rousing march tune 'Marching through Georgia' (Ex. 16.11(*a*)), which, incidentally, has another *Y–X* progression (II7/♯V) in bar 4. Again, as we can see from Ex. 16.11(*b*), the Melody is essentially pentatonic.

Ex. 16.11. Work, 'Marching through Georgia' (1865) (up a tone)

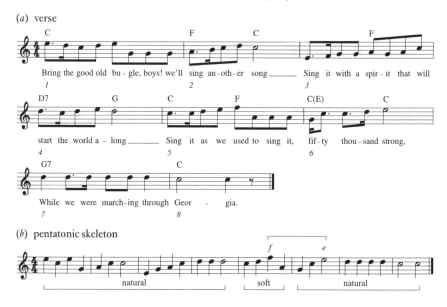

In the actual blues, and particularly the 'blues ballads' popular about the beginning of the twentieth century, we can discern a gradual adaptation of these traditional harmonic schemes to the twelve-bar form. The most primitive type is the one usual in the 'Railroad Bill' ballad, commemorating a black desperado whose real name was Morris Slater, and who died, prosaically shot by a storekeeper, in 1897.[30] This gives a date for the tune, which however can only be approximate, since it is likely that Slater was only the last of a series of bad men associated with it. The harmonic pattern:

I I I I · I I IV V IV · I V I I

is simply a tonic chord (bars 1–4) followed by the second half of 'Gregory Walker' (bars 5–12).[31]

Four years after Railroad Bill's demise, in 1901, came the assassination of President

---

[30] See Norman Cohen, *Long Steel Rail*, 122–31.

[31] For convenience, I shall pretend that we are dealing with regular twelve-bar tunes, though (as has already been pointed out) this is often not the case.

McKinley. This, too, was commemorated in a ballad, with a similar tune but more blues-like harmonic rhythm:

I I I I · IV IV IV I · I V I I

Meanwhile, the vast 'Frankie and Johnny' family (at first known as 'Frankie and Albert') went a little further:

I I I I · IV IV IV I · V V I I

This is very close to the standard I I I I · IV IV I I · V V I I formula, the only difference being that the middle section is IV IV IV I instead of IV IV I I. The reason for this discrepancy is that ballad metre, to which 'Frankie and Albert' still (more or less) conforms, places the accent on the syllable corresponding to the last bar of the four-bar group:

bars:	1	2	3	4
words:	As I cam' by the	Garioch land And	doon by Nether-	*ha'*.

bars:	1	2		
words:	Frankie and Albert were	lovers.		
	3	4		
	O, lordy, how they did	*love!*		

and the change of harmony reflects this ultimately verbal accent. Once more we see how intimate was the connection between words and music in the early blues.

The blues and the international vernacular

The more one studies the early blues (or, *a fortiori*, early jazz), the more one sees in it the influence of the international musical vernacular. If this chapter is to be kept within bounds, all I can do is to touch on a few of the most obviously affected features. Let us begin with its form.

The twelve-bar form

Probably the earliest recorded member of the 'Frankie' tune family is the coon song 'Just because She Made dem Goo-goo Eyes', published in 1900 (Ex. 16.12). The tune is undoubtedly of British folk origin,[32] but somewhere along the line it has been adapted to the twelve-bar harmonic scheme. This, as usual in early examples, is somewhat anomalous: reduced to essentials, the middle section is neither the 'Frankie' IV IV IV I, nor the standard IV IV I I, but I IV I I, with the final tonic chord in 6/4 form.

[32] It is close to that of 'Josie', a hillbilly blues collected in the 1920s. This in turn can be traced back to the Appalachian lyric 'Single Girl' (the words of which were quoted on p. 443), and thence to a Scottish ballad tune. All three tunes are quoted in *Origins*, 185–6.

Ex. 16.12. Hughie Cannon, 'Just because She Made dem Goo-goo Eyes at Me' (1900), verse (down a minor 3rd)

It seems that the standard twelve-bar harmonic pattern was already well known by 1900, but that the composer, Hughie Cannon, decided to smarten it up for the benefit of the big-city audience. Other early twelve-bar blues give the same impression. Composers evidently felt that not only the harmonic scheme, but also the asymmetrical form needed to be adapted. This might be done by turning two twelve-bar strains into a binary structure of twenty-four bars:[33]

I I I I · IV IV I I · four bars ending on V(7)
I I I I · IV IV I I · V V I I

or by extending the twelve bars to sixteen:

I I I I · IV IV I I · extra four bars · V V I I.

---

[33] e.g. 'One o' them Things!' (1904), composed by James Chapman and Leroy Smith, reprinted in *Ragtime Rarities*, 64–7, and quoted in *Origins*, 285–6; 'The Original Chicago Blues' (1915), by James White, also reprinted in *Ragtime Rarities*, 277–80; and 'Over in the Gloryland', recorded by the Sam Morgan Jazz Band (an old-time New Orleans group) as late as 1927, and discussed by Gunter Schuller in *Early Jazz*, 76–7.

as in the chorus of an even earlier coon song, 'I'd Leave ma Happy Home for You', composed by Harry Von Tilzer and published in 1899.[34] If bars 9–12 are omitted, the following (somewhat simplified) harmonic scheme is left:

I V7 I I · IV IV I I · I V7 I I.

the tune it goes with is reminiscent of the 'white blues' made famous two or three decades later by Jimmy Rogers.

Further evidence that the standard harmonic pattern was known in the 1890s is provided by no less a witness than the 'father of the blues' himself, W. C. Handy:

> The melody of *Mr. Crump* [the original title of 'Memphis Blues', published in 1912] was mine throughout. On the other hand, the twelve-bar, three-line form of the first and last strains, with its three-chord basic harmonic structure (tonic, subdominant, dominant seventh) was that already used by Negro roustabouts, honky-tonk piano players, wanderers and others of their underprivileged but undaunted class from Missouri to the Gulf, and had become a common medium through which any such individual might express his personal feelings in a sort of musical soliloquy.[35]

The inventors of the standard twelve-bar harmonic pattern were most likely the 'honky-tonk' (or 'barrelhouse') pianists mentioned here. In spite of their raffish image, many of these were relatively sophisticated musicians, accustomed to catering for a wide range of musical tastes.[36] What could be more natural to these resourceful entertainers than to 'jazz up' the I I · IV I progression? In fact, there is no need to speculate on this point, since a raggy piano version of Foster's 'Old Black Joe' (chord scheme of first four bars: I I IV I · I I IV V) was published as early as 1877.[37]

The uniqueness of the early blues—at least, those that have come down to us— lies not so much in individual details as in the way these fit together. If we compare the English music-hall song 'I'm Henery the eighth, I am' (Ex. 16.13) with the 'hillbilly' blues 'Corinna' (Ex. 16.14), we can immediately see a strong family likeness in both the melody and harmony of their first eight bars. Except for a slight difference in rhythm, the I IV–I progression is the same, and so are the outline and pentatonic framework of the tune.

Why, then, is it so hard to hear 'Henery the Eighth' as the beginning of a twelve-bar blues? The reason is that, as has already been pointed out, the twelve-bar blues is really a *six*-part form, consisting of three main sections, each of which is subdivided into two. In 'Henery the Eighth', the four-bar phrase is a single unit:

---

[34] In *Song Hits from the Turn of the Century*, 119–22.   [35] *Father of the Blues*, 99.

[36] See Giles Oakley, *The Devil's Music*, Part Two, 'The Barrelhouse Circuit and the "Piney Woods" ', 68–74.

[37] The title was 'Old Black Joe . . . [*sic*] Paraphrase De Concert', and the composer Charles Gimble. Reprinted in *The Ragtime Songbook*, ed. Ann Charters, 23–4.

Ex. 16.13. Fred Murray and R. P. Weston. 'I'm Henery the eighth, I am' (1911), chorus, beginning

Ex. 16.14. 'Corinna' ('hillbilly' blues, early 20th c.) (up a 4th)

> I'm Henery the Eighth, I am!
> Henery the Eighth I am! I am!

but in 'Corinna' it is double:

> Corínna, Corínna · where'd you stáy last níght?
> Please téll me, Corínna · where'd you stáy last níght?

Of course, it is highly unlikely that there was any direct connection between these two songs. But that does not affect the argument. The same combination of melodic outline, mode, and harmony may be found in innumerable popular compositions of the period; and, similarly, the six-part structure of 'Corinna' may be found in countless early blues. The development of the classic twelve-bar form was a matter of putting the two together. But notice that the result was a cadential climax (I→I IV→I V→I), itself a typical feature of the international vernacular.[38]

The pentatonic species

American popular melody was in every way more pentatonic than its European equivalent. Not only were the pentatonic figures more clear-cut; they were also used with greater enterprise. In particular, there was a tendency to pair the pentatonic species with the corresponding harmonic triad. Thus, the natural pentatonic goes with the tonic chord, the hard pentatonic with the dominant, and the soft pentatonic with the subdominant—or vice versa. Given the great importance in American music of plagal progressions, this also means that we hear much more of

[38] See pp. 312–16.

the soft pentatonic. It is already conspicuous in waltz songs like 'A Picture from Life's Other Side' (Ex. 16.15)—incidentally a close relative of 'Corinna' and 'Henery the Eighth'—and becomes even more so in many blues tunes, especially those of the 'Frankie' family. If we compare 'Frankie and Albert' (Ex. 16.16)[39] with

Ex. 16.15. 'A Picture from Life's other Side' (early 20th c.), chorus (down a tone)

Ex. 16.16. 'Frankie and Albert' (early 20th-c. blues)

[39] I give the refrain in two versions: as it was originally notated, and then as it was probably sung (more or less).

the roughly contemporary coon song 'Just because She Made dem Goo-goo Eyes' (Ex. 16.12 on p. 448), we find that whereas bars 7–12 almost match, bars 1–6 are completely different. Where 'Goo-goo Eyes' remains close to its Scottish ances- tors, 'Frankie' blossoms out into a sequential pattern that owes something to Africa but much more to the European vernacular.[40]

It is perhaps significant that the collector of this tune, Dorothy Scarborough, regarded it as relatively sophisticated,[41] for it belongs to a type that flourishes on the borderland between pure and harmonized melody. As in many eighteenth- century British tunes,[42] the harmonic basis is spelt out so clearly and sturdily as to render accompaniment redundant. Such tunes 'carry their harmony with them'. With a little adjustment, bars 1–6 could serve as a bass, which is precisely what happened in boogie-woogie. In Ex. 16.17, the primary triads and pentatonic spe- cies do not merely coincide; they become one.

Ex. 16.17. Boogie-woogie bass

The double cadence

American popular music had two forms of double cadence with quite different ancestries. One, which may be labelled the 'waltz' type, developed out of the enlargement of stock harmonic patterns to the point where the final chord arrived inconveniently early for the Melody.[43] The other—call it the 'blues' type—was the inevitable result of a clash between two pre-existing cadential systems, one melodic and the other harmonic. The 'waltz' type is well represented in early rags like Ex. 16.18, where, just as in the waltz itself, the melodic cadence lags a bar behind the

---

[40] Cf. the opening themes of the overtures to Mozart's *Così fan tutte* (Ex. 13.34 on p. 306) and Bizet's *Carmen* (Ex. 13.74 on pp. 335–6).   [41] See *On the Trail of Negro Folksongs* (1925), 83–4.
[42] e.g. 'The Bonny Lass o' Fyvie' (Ex. 2.1(*a*) on p. 24).   [43] See the discussion on pp. 253–4.

Ex. 16.18. Hoffman, 'A Dingy Slowdown' (1900), bars 5–16 (up a tone)

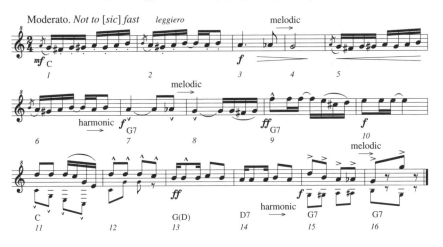

Ex. 16.19. 'Haunted Road Blues', performed by Gwen Foster (1931), instrumental interlude

harmonic one. The 'blues' type is illustrated by Ex. 16.19, which can also serve as an example of an extremely common form of blues tune. In it, the six segments of the British folk ballad have been assimilated to the tumbling strains and blues cadences of the holler, at the same time being set over the twelve-bar harmonic scheme. The result is the following pattern of double cadences:

melodic   melodic

melodic   melodic

harmonic

melodic   melodic

harmonic

But it would be wrong to think of the 'waltz' and 'blues' forms of double cadence as entirely separate. Though quite different in origin, they were similar enough in effect to influence each other. As its title, 'A Dingy Slowdown', suggests, Ex. 16.18 is already beginning to sound faintly bluesy, especially in its cadences.[44] The bluesiness is due partly to outline (compare, for instance, bars 15–16 with bars 13–14 of Ex. 16.19) and partly to a characterisic, slithery form of chromaticism—which, as we shall presently see, brings us back to the European vernacular.

The g mode

A further attribute of these early rags and blues, also illustrated by 'A Dingy Slowdown', is the remarkable development of the *g* mode. Strauss's 'Accelerationen' Waltz (Ex. 12.33 on p. 260) makes clear the ancestry of this pattern, which by the turn of the century was well established in American popular music.[45] In the blues, this *g* mode generally has a minor colour, with *7♮* replaced by a blue *7♭* which bears the same relation to *5* as the blue *3♭* as does to *1*. Just how close this correspondence is can be seen from Exs. 16.20 and 16.21, where the same scrap of tune occurs in both positions.

Ex. 16.20. W. C. Simon, 'Sponge' (ragtime blues, 1911), beginning (up a 5th)

---

[44] The *OED* defines 'dinge' or 'dingy' as '*U.S. slang* ... A derogatory term for a Negro. Also *attrib.* or as *adj.* esp. with reference to a jazz style developed by Negro musicians' (iv. 682). With 'Slowdown', this suggests a deliberate, 'bluesy' tempo.

[45] Another fine example is the chorus of 'Give my Regards to Broadway', composed by George M. Cohan in 1904, and reprinted in *Favorite Songs of the Nineties*.

Ex. 16.21. W. C. Handy, 'Yellow Dog Blues' (1920), beginning of voice part (down a 4th)

But this was not the end of the bluesy *g* mode. An even more advanced example may be found in the 1950s hit 'That'll be the Day' (Ex. 16.22). The harmonic basis of the chorus is still just the same as in the 'Accelerationen' waltz, except that one bar of the former corresponds to two of the latter.

Ex. 16.22. Holly, Petty, and Allison, 'That'll be the Day' (1957), beginning (down a minor 3rd)

(*continued on next page*)

(Ex. 16.22 *cont.*)

What is new and remarkable, apart from the bluesy colouring, is the way the *g* at the beginning of the chorus (bar 9) is approached exactly as if it were a true tonic—that is, from the *harmonic* chord of *D*7.

The chromatic blue third

Mainstream African melody has no precedents for the elaborate chromatic embellishments that are such a striking feature of the blues. Rather, they came from western Asia, by several routes: firstly, the floridly chromatic, semi-Arab melody of the west African savannah; secondly, the related tradition of Scotland and Ireland, which by the early nineteenth century had merged with the African strain to form the 'old way of singing'; and thirdly, the Fringe streak in the European vernacular. In the formative years of ragtime and blues all three came together, and of the three, the most important (at least in the printed sources available to us) was the last. Almost all the chromaticisms in the early blues, including the passages quoted above,[46] are of this type.

One pattern demands special mention. Let us call it the 'chromatic blue third'. Of course, most blue thirds are chromatic by their nature, but this type is more chromatic than most. It consists essentially of *3♭* resolving on *3♮*. In the simplest cases, the resolution takes the form of an immediate appoggiatura, but elsewhere it may be artfully delayed.[47] By the late nineteenth century, this more complex pattern had attained almost the status of a cliché, and, like all the best musical clichés, had greatly expanded. Towards the end of his Cello Concerto in B minor, Dvořák

---

[46] See 'Just because She Made dem Goo-goo Eyes' (Ex. 16.12), 'Corinna' (Ex. 16.14), 'Frankie and Albert' (Ex. 16.16), and, especially, 'A Dingy Slowdown' (Ex. 16.18).

[47] For the earlier history of this formula, see pp. 211–12.

makes a veritable jazz break out of it (Ex. 16.23). Two years later, it turns up in one of Sousa's best-known marches (Ex. 16.24). There is already a faint whiff of the blues about this passage, and this becomes much stronger in the rags that were beginning to appear about this time (Ex. 16.25).

Ex. 16.23. Dvořák, Cello Concerto in B minor (1895), last mvt., bars 385–98 (up a semitone)

Ex. 16.24. Sousa, 'The Stars and Stripes Forever' (1897), bars 53–68 (2nd half of 3rd strain) (up a major 3rd)

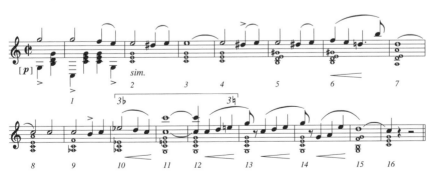

Ex. 16.25. Krell, 'Shake yo' Dusters!' (early rag, 1898), beginning (up a 5th)

Ten years later, the same chromatic mannerism occurs in one of the earliest twelve-bar blues, the significantly titled 'I Got the Blues' (Ex. 16.26), attributed to one 'A. Maggio' and published in New Orleans in 1908. This appears to be the first recorded instance of the word 'blues' in the musical sense, and from the two inscriptions on the title page, 'Respectfully Dedicated to all those Who have the Blues'

Ex. 16.26. Maggio, 'I Got the Blues' (ragtime blues, 1908), bars 5–16 (1st strain) (up a 4th)

(but in what sense?) and 'An up-to-date rag', it seems that the blues style was already becoming fashionable in New Orleans. The tune, a precursor of Handy's famous 'St. Louis Blues', published six years later, consists of little more than a series of cadences from a blue *3* to *1*, against which the twelve-bar chord scheme appears in very nearly its standard form. The one harmonic anomaly is the strange diminished seventh in bar 6—significantly, the same chord as in the corresponding part of 'Shake yo' Dusters!'.

Such passages raise the broader question of European influence on the blues. A bluesy undertone may be heard in many more or less east European composers: not only Russians like Borodin and Stravinsky, or Czechs like Dvořák, but also Scandinavians like Grieg, Nielsen, and Sibelius. Probably the bluesiest of all is Dvořák. I have already quoted the slow movement from his 'American' String Quartet and the jazzy 'break' from his Cello Concerto.[48] Another passage worth quoting is the 'Dumka' (or 'Lament') from his String Quartet in E flat, Op. 51 (Ex. 16.27), if only to show that he was capable of this sort of thing long before setting foot on American soil.

Ex. 16.27.   Dvořák, String Quartet in E flat, Op. 51 (1879), 2nd mvt. ('Dumka'), beginning (down a 5th)

Whether Dvořák was directly influenced by Afro-American music in his 'American' compositions is probably an insoluble question, but his French contemporaries undoubtedly were. There is a touch of the blues in the 'Habanera' from *Carmen*, and much more than a touch in Saint-Saëns's 'Havanaise' (Ex.

[48] Respectively Ex. 13.61 (on p. 323) and Ex. 16.23 above. Both were composed in the United States.

Ex. 16.28. Saint-Saëns, 'Havanaise' (1887), bars 21–34 (up a semitone)

16.28). Now, the habanera (or *havanaise* in French) is a Cuban dance, named after the capital city of Havana, and musically much the same thing as the Argentinian tango. Both these dances belong to a broad Afro-Iberian strain of Latin American popular music, which in turn forms part of an Afro-European culture common to the Americas as a whole. Their bluesiness is therefore not coincidental, but a matter of not-so-distant kinship. Just as there are touches of the blues in tangos or habaneras, so a 'Latin tinge' has often been noticed in both the blues and jazz. Handy's 'St Louis Blues', published in 1914, even has a section in habanera style.

Nor did Fringe influence end there. Between about 1880 and 1920, a wave of immigrants from southern and eastern Europe gave the popular music of the United States a tinge not only Latin, but Mediterranean and east European—a 'Fringe tinge', in fact. It is remarkable how often white jazz musicians or popular songwriters turn out to be of Italian, Jewish, Latin American, or even, like Django Reinhardt, Gypsy origin. Inevitably, this influx left its mark on the blues. That indestructible jazz 'standard', Gershwin's 'Summertime', is surely closer to Dvořák than to Bessie Smith.

A word about jazz

We cannot leave the blues without a page or two on jazz. This has always been a slippery subject. What precisely was its relation to the blues—or to 'classical' music? What *was* it, anyway? In a history of almost a century, the word 'jazz' has meant many things. In the 1920s, it seemed to include virtually any syncopated popular music of American origin. Later it became narrower, but inconsistently so, and more recently broader again. Probably the best definition is: music performed by people who regard themselves as jazz musicians.

Its relation to the blues is equally fuzzy. The blues, everyone agrees, is an essential component of jazz, but also a genre in its own right. That is to say, all real jazz is to some extent bluesy, but a great deal of blues is not jazz. The game of jazz-versus-blues can be played endlessly. Jazz is rhythmic; the blues is melodic. Jazz is fast; the blues is slow. Jazz is instrumental; the blues is vocal. Jazz is sophisticated; the blues is folky. Jazz is innovative; the blues is traditional. That exceptions can be found to every one of these generalizations only adds to the fun.

During the great jazz hullabaloo of the twenties, Ernest Newman wrote that 'jazz is not a "form" but a collection of tags and tricks'[49]—and, by implication, of no use to the serious composer. There is a grain of truth in this accusation. Reduced to essentials, jazz is a method of varying and improvising on pre-existing music. Almost any raw material will do: a march, a popular song, a hymn, a folk tune, a Gem from the Classics. The blues, on the other hand, has its own well-defined form, or rather family of forms. And perhaps that is the best distinction of all: jazz is a method; the blues is a form.

There was, after all, nothing new about this. Since the Middle Ages, and no doubt long before, popular musicians had combined a stock of traditional forms with a bag of tricks applicable to whatever material might come to hand, the only requirement being that the tricks should be immediately effective and place no great strain on the performer's invention. This is certainly true of the popular genres discussed in this book. The 'unwritten tradition' of the Italian Renaissance, the Gypsy music of the eighteenth and nineteenth centuries, the blues and jazz of recent times—however these might differ in other respects, all used a similar mixture of pre-existing material, stock formulas, and improvisation.

In fact, Gypsy music and jazz had so much in common that it is tempting to see them as successive stages in a single historical process. Both were vigorous forms

---

[49] Article in *The Sunday Times*, 6 Sept. 1927.

of urban popular music, in touch with folk tradition but assimilated to the Western mainstream. Both were created mainly, though far from exclusively, by outcast races with dark skins. Both specialized in exhilarating syncopation on the one hand and minor-mode gloom on the other.[50] So close, indeed, was the resemblance, that in the Germany of the 1920s Gypsy (or at any rate east European) musicians were able to fabricate an ersatz jazz out of little more than instruction books and scores, both imported from the United States. It was this Teutonic 'jazz', rather than the genuine American article—least of all the *black* American article— that captivated both bright young things and composers like Krenek, Hindemith, Weill, and Berg.

The story is told in fascinating detail by J. Bradford Robinson,[51] who further points out the particular importance of the rhythmic pattern | ♫♩ ♫ | or | ♫♩ ♩ ♩ |, which he calls the 'shimmy figure'. Quoting numerous examples, he traces this back to the American popular song 'Papa Loves Mama, Mama Loves Papa', which, translated into German as 'Vater liebt Muttern, Mutter liebt Vatern', was all the rage in Germany during the years 1923–4.[52] He might have added that this same figure already had a long history in central Europe. Mahler, for one, had used it, in the first movement of his Fourth Symphony;[53] and so had Beethoven, over a century earlier, in the Gypsy-like rondo theme of his First Piano Concerto (Ex. 16.29). Similar east European pedigrees could be found for all the

Ex. 16.29. Beethoven, Piano Concerto No. 1 in C (1795), last mvt., beginning

---

[50] More or less jazzy rhythms can be found in many east or central European passages quoted in this book. The following is a small sample. Beethoven, Serenade for Flute, Violin, and Viola, finale (Ex. 11.3 on p. 157): anticipation of entire phrases by a half-beat. Strauss, 'Unter Donner und Blitz' (Ex. 12.6 on p. 237): accented off-beats in the accompaniment. Rimsky-Korsakov, *Spanish Capriccio*, 'Scena e canto gitano' (Ex. 11.14 on p. 163): division of twelve-pulse pattern into 7 + 5.

[51] See 'Jazz Reception in Weimar Germany: In Search of a Shimmy Figure', ch. 7 (pp. 107–34), in *Music and Performance during the Weimar Republic*.

[52] Ibid. 121. 'Papa Loves Mama' was composed by Cliff Friend and Abel Baer.

[53] See bars 58 ff., at the direction 'Plötzlich langsam und bedächtig'.

other syncopations and cross-rhythms, the accented off-beats, the blue sevenths and wavering thirds, produced by the jazz musicians of the Weimar Republic. From their standpoint, true jazz must have seemed a sort of Americanized Gypsy music.

But whether the popular influences came from Africa, Asia, or both simultaneously, they proved to be increasingly difficult to absorb. By the 1920s and 1930s, popular music had become something that the 'serious' composer approached warily, from behind the ever-dependable guard of irony. One is somehow reminded of the struggles during the same period of socialist old Etonians to make contact with the working classes. 'Serious' music fell into a long crisis of self-consciousness, of which the word 'serious' was itself a symptom. From that crisis, it is only now beginning to recover. What will be left of 'the classical' when the recovery is complete, is, of course, quite another question.

Epilogue

It is said that all systems contain the seeds of their own destruction. As I write these words, peering into the vast, empty abyss of the twentieth-first century, Western classical music would seem to be a case in point. One way of grasping the full measure of its decline is to make a list of those twentieth-century works that are both genuinely modern and genuinely popular. This excludes two important classes of composition: on the one hand, those that make use of old or folk music, such as Vaughan Williams's *Fantasia on a Theme by Thomas Tallis*, Respighi's *Ancient Airs and Dances*, Copland's *Appalachian Spring*, or Britten's *Young Person's Guide to the Orchestra*; on the other, the dubious category of the 'modern but not *too* modern', the kind of thing that gets put on between, say, the 'Hebrides' Overture and Beethoven's Fifth Symphony, in the hope of not frightening the public away. Bartók's *Concerto for Orchestra* is perhaps an example.

Setting aside these two categories, what is left? In Chapter 15, I mentioned some of the works composed in or just before 1900: Puccini's *Tosca*, Mahler's Fourth Symphony, Sibelius's *Finlandia*, Rimsky-Korsakov's 'Flight of the Bumble Bee', and so on. Clearly, there is little here to frighten the concert-goer, and during the next two decades music of a similar broad appeal continued to be composed. The following list, though far from complete, is probably a fair sample:

1901–1910:
    Elgar, 'Cockaigne' Overture (1901)
    Rachmaninov, Piano Concerto No. 2 in C minor (1901)
    Ravel, String Quartet in F (1902)
    Sibelius, Symphony No. 2 in D (1902)
    Mahler, Symphony No. 5 (1902)
    Sibelius, Violin Concerto (1903)
    Puccini, *Madam Butterfly* (1904)
    Debussy, *La Mer* (1905)
    Elgar, Introduction and Allegro for Strings (1905)
    Strauss, *Salome* (1905)
    Sibelius, Symphony No. 3 in C (1907)

Elgar, Symphony No. 1 in A flat (1908)

Rachmaninov, Piano Concerto No. 3 in D minor (1909)

Mahler, *Das Lied von der Erde* (1909)

Elgar, Violin Concerto (1910)

Stravinsky, *The Firebird* (1910)

1911–1920:

Strauss, *Der Rosenkavalier* (1911)

Ravel, *Mother Goose* Suite (1911)

Elgar, Symphony No. 2 in E flat (1911)

Ravel, *Daphnis et Chloé* (1912)

Sibelius, Symphony No. 5 in E flat (1915)

Holst, *Planets* Suite (1916)

Prokofiev, *Classical* Symphony in D (1917)

Puccini, *Gianni Schichi* (1918)

Elgar, Cello Concerto (1919)

But, as a glance at this list should tell us, all was not well. The composers who figure most prominently—Elgar, Rachmaninov, Mahler, Strauss, Sibelius, Puccini—are all late Romantics of one sort or another, and no longer young. Even the compositions of the coming generation, such as Prokofiev's *Classical* Symphony, tend to be backward-looking. The best the avant-garde can do is Strauss's *Salome*, the more modernistic (and less popular) bits of Holst's *Planets*, and the impressionistic works of Debussy, Ravel, and Stravinsky.

In any case, the flow begins to dry up after 1905. For the period 1901–5 there are ten works; for 1906–1910, six; for 1911–1915, five; for 1916–1920, four. Now, I must disclaim any scientific rigour in compiling this list. Obviously, there will be borderline cases; many people, for instance, would add Stravinsky's *Rite of Spring* (1912), which I prefer to regard as an unusually enduring *succès de scandale* (and in any case greatly indebted to Russian folk music). Nevertheless, the general trend is clear, and it continues into the 1920s:

1921–1930:

Puccini, *Turandot* (1924)

Gershwin, *Rhapsody in Blue* (1924)

Ravel, *Boléro* (1928)

Gershwin, *An American in Paris* (1928)

In the 1930s, interestingly enough, there is a slight rally:

1931–1940:

Prokofiev, *Lieutenant Kijé* (1933)

Rachmaninov, *Rhapsody on a Theme of Paganini* (1934)
Barber, 'Adagio for Strings' (1936)
Prokofiev, *Peter and the Wolf* (1936)
Orff, *Carmina Burana* (1937)
Prokofiev, *Romeo and Juliet* (1938)
Kabalevsky, Overture to *Colas Breugnon* (1938)
Rodrigo, *Concierto de Aranjuez* (1939)

But after this point the flow ceases almost completely. One might make a case for the popularity of a few later compositions, such as Britten's *Peter Grimes* (1945), or Strauss's *Four Last Songs* (1948), but the only unquestionable example I can think of is Khachaturian's 'Sabre Dance' (1942). And in any case these are all works of the 1940s. For the general public, 'classical music' belongs mainly to the eighteenth and nineteenth centuries, carries on with rapidly diminishing vigour into the first few decades of the twentieth, and has ceased to exist by 1950.

Well, popularity is not everything. But by any reckoning an art that has lost touch with its public to this extent is in serious trouble. What went wrong? Perhaps the best answer is contained in the following remarks made by George Bernard Shaw in 1897:

The composers of the XX century! What an easy time they will have, compared with their predecessors in the XIX! There lies the whole material of music before them to do just what they like with. No more forbidden progressions; no more prescribed forms; any chord or discord or no-chord you please, without preparation or resolution . . . false relations at a premium, lest any two simultaneous parts should seem to be insipidly in the same key . . . [1]

The most astonishing thing about this eerily accurate prediction is its date. In May 1897, the avant-garde sensations were Strauss's *Also sprach Zarathustra*, produced the year before, and Debussy's slightly earlier *Prélude à l'après-midi d'un faune*. Schoenberg was a youth of 22 writing Brahmsian chamber music. Brahms himself had died a month previously, at the not very advanced age of 63. In short, we are still in the high tide of late Romanticism, yet here is Shaw confidently describing the modernism that was to take shape some ten years later.

This is an indication that the Modern Movement in music (as in the other arts) was a product not so much of the artists themselves as of critics, theorists, brilliant journalists like Shaw himself, and intellectuals generally. The artists, simple souls that they were, merely carried out a programme laid down for them long before. And while the artists revelled in the dubious delights of the new freedom,

---

[1] 'Composers and Professors in the Coming Century', 391, in *Shaw's Music*, iii. 391–6. First published in *The Musician*, 19 May 1897.

those same intellectuals were setting up a benevolent despotism on their behalf. Articles and books were being written, committees formed, laws passed, syllabuses drawn up, cultural commissars appointed, money extracted from the pocket of the taxpayer, for the benefit of art in general and modern art in particular.

Though it is still not a fashionable opinion, it seems to me that all this well-meant effort was a disastrous mistake. Not only did it totally fail to persuade the public of the charms of modern music; it also grievously—perhaps fatally—weakened the classical tradition at what would in any case have been a time of crisis. The sheer richness of late Romantic music, to say nothing of its hubristic ambitions, must surely have brought on a reaction. In the arts, just as in business, boom is likely to be followed by bust. The classical tradition had been through several such cycles in the past. Late medieval church polyphony, the High Baroque, the Viennese Classical school—all had collapsed in their turn. But, in every case, bracing popular influences had ensured that the tradition as a whole eventually revived.

One might expect something similar to have happened after 1910, and, in fact, the ghostly outlines of such a reaction may be discerned in much of the music composed between 1920 and 1940. Apart from a few late Romantic works (Puccini's *Turandot*, Barber's 'Adagio for Strings', Rachmaninov's *Paganini* Rhapsody), the classical compositions that were most successful with the public all show popular influence of one kind of another, and this tendency would be far more marked if the 'classical' category were broadened to include such things as Gershwin's *Porgy and Bess* or the sophisticated jazz of Duke Ellington.

For the nineteenth-century vernacular did not stop in 1900. It continued to develop for another fifty years, generating patterns that mixed easily with those of late Romanticism and Impressionism. As we are only now beginning to see, classical and popular music had enough in common during the early decades of the century to make a great deal of cross-fertilization possible. But this, apart from a few ironic experiments, was all on the popular side; and after 1950 even the ironic experiments tend to fall away. Whatever the merits of 'serious' music during the 1950s and 1960s may have been, openness to popular influence was not among them. There were two reasons for this. On the one hand, popular music was itself evolving away from its European origins; on the other, classical music was changing too, not so much in itself as in the way it was viewed. As recently as 1940, middle-aged music-lovers had been able to remember when audiences had flocked to hear the latest work of Elgar, Mahler, Sibelius, Ravel, Puccini, Rachmaninov, or Strauss. Not only was this a living tradition; it was also unified. For most practical purposes, it consisted of Bach, Handel, and an unbroken series of masterpieces from Haydn to the recent past, all performed on the same instruments, by the same orchestras, with the same technique.

A mere fifteen years later all that had changed. As a source of enjoyable new music, the classical tradition was dead, or on its last legs; but as a source of *old* music, it was thriving as never before. The radio and the long-playing record, supported by the long economic boom, were bringing 'good music' within the reach of a huge new public. At the same time, the repertoire was being extended to include such masters as Monteverdi, Purcell, and Vivaldi. Moreover, these earlier composers were being treated with a new historical scrupulousness. Performance of their music might still be far from 'authentic', but at least it was no longer shamelessly Romantic.

The result was to make classical music richer, more varied, more interesting, certainly more accessible, but also much more remote from the present. And this tendency was aggravated by a new cultural establishment. The generation that had been born around the beginning of the century, imbibed the progressive notions of the 1920s and 1930s, and at last found itself in a position of power, brought with it a utopian Modernism that now seems curiously unreal. Those were the days when ancient towns had their hearts ripped out and replaced with concrete edifices in the International Modern style; when Pound, Eliot, and Joyce were the gods of Eng. Lit.; when self-respecting painters hesitated to depict a recognizable object; when the ideal composer was a bizarre cross between a Romantic poet and a laboratory worker. The last consideration to cross the mind of such a personage was the approval of the public.

That phase lasted till about the mid-1970s. Since then, three things have happened. First, Modernism has itself at last become old hat. Everyone agrees that we now live in a 'postmodern' era, even if no one can quite agree on what was 'modern', or in which sense we are 'post' it.

The second development is that the classical repertoire, though of course more distant in actual time than ever before, now somehow seems less remote. Its main connotation, to the unsophisticated public, is not so much 'old' as 'posh'. The best proof of this paradoxical contemporaneity is the vogue for classical snippets as background music to radio or television commercials, almost always to advertise perfectly modern products. One is reminded of those Victorian architects who saw nothing odd in employing the neo-Renaissance style for a town hall, the neoclassical style for a museum, the neo-Gothic style for a church, and the latest glass-and-steel construction for a conservatory.

The third development is that composers are again attempting to produce works that the public actually likes, and in the process re-establishing contact with popular music. Whether anything lasting will come of this, it is still too early to say. It may well be that the classical tradition, as a creative force, is finished for good. Probably the greatest difficulty facing composers is summed up in Shaw's words, now true to an extent that even he could not have foreseen: 'There lies the whole material of music before them to do just what they like with.' It is hard to imagine a more painful predicament for a creative artist.

But let us be optimistic. Let us suppose that, some time during this century, 'the classical' does revive. We cannot say what form it will take, since the innovations of art are just as unpredictable as those of science and technology. But we can at least lay down some conditions for its success. Firstly, it must be economically sound. That is to say, it will need to pay its way without the prop of government subsidy; and this can only happen with the support of a real and enthusiastic public, for whose favour composers compete as vigorously as singers, violinists, or pianists do today. The occupation of 'serious' composer must be a potentially lucrative one. Secondly, the revived tradition must reduce 'the whole material of music' to something unified and manageable. To do so, if history is any guide, it will need to go beyond the great works of the past. It will also need to draw on the popular genres of the present, and, through them, on the archetypal and indestructible patterns that give meaning to all music.

In other words, it will need roots.

List of Musical Examples

Note that where both primary and secondary sources are mentioned, the one given first has been used in this book.

3.15 Song of the Indians of British Columbia, Canada. In Wiora, 'Älter als die Pentatonik', 190 (words omitted in this source). Collected by O. Abraham and E. M. von Hornbostel and first published in the *Sitzungsberichte für vergleichende Musikwissenschaft*, 1 (1922), 293–310.

4.1 'The Fause Knight upon the Road' (Scottish ballad tune). Sung by Miss M. Macmath. In *The English and Scottish Popular Ballads*, ed. Francis James Child, v. 411, Ex. 3C.

4.2 Replication of the children's chant at the fourth or fifth

4.3 'Ngoneni, ngoneni nebakitsi' (Swazi lament). Sung by Rosalina Ndlhole and Juana Nkosi, two Swazi women, at Mataffin, Nelspruit, Transvaal, South Africa. Transcribed from the long-playing record *Music of Africa: GALP 1041. Awards III: Osborn Awards 1958*, side 2, track 4, where the title is given as 'Ngoneni, ngoneni bakithi?': (*a*) beginning; (*b*) contrapuntal reduction.

4.4 'Hishie Ba" (Scottish folk song). From the singing of Jeannie Robertson. In *The Scottish Folksinger*, ed. Norman Buchan and Peter Hall, 81.

4.5 The Schenkerian *Ursatz* and *Urlinie*

4.6 'Hishie Ba'', with a Schenkerian analysis

4.7 'Young Johnstone' (Scottish ballad tune). In *The Oxford Book of Ballads*, ed. James Kinsley, 212, no. 54. First published in *Minstrelsy, Ancient and Modern*, ed. William Motherwell (1827), appendix no. 18.

4.8 'Clyde's Waters' (Scottish ballad tune). In *The Oxford Book of Ballads*, 331, no. 87. From the Gavin Greig MSS, University Library, King's College, Aberdeen, I. 76.

4.9 'Pregón de un vendedor de romances' (cry of a Spanish ballad seller). In Donostia, 'El modo de *mi*', 157. From *Cancionero popular de Extremadura*, ed. Bonifactio Gil García, 196.

4.10 The three pentatonic species: (*a*) natural: (i) hexachord, (ii) pentatonic scale, (iii) diatonic context; (*b*) soft: (i) hexachord, (ii) pentatonic scale, (iii) diatonic context; (*c*) hard: (i) hexachord, (ii) pentatonic scale, (iii) diatonic context.

4.11 'Father Get Ready' (Appalachian folk hymn), beginning. In Ritchie, *Folk Songs of the Southern Appalachians as Sung by Jean Ritchie*, 50.

4.12 The pentatonic Bass modes

5.1 Tswana musical-bow tune. In Kirby, *The Musical Instruments of the Native Races of South Africa*, 213. Repeat signs as in original.

5.2 Swazi song with musical-bow accompaniment. Ibid. 200. Words omitted in the original. Repeat signs as in original.

5.3 'O Roma nobilis' (12th-c. song). The tune is from a 12th-c. MS housed in the Cambridge University Library (which, however, has a different set of words, beginning 'O admirabile Veneris idolum'). The better-known words given here are those associated with the two other surviving versions of the tune, one in the Vatican and the other in Montecassino. See Westrup, 'Medieval Song', 221, for full details, including a transcription of the tune given here. The alternative ending comes from the Montecassino version, reproduced in facsimile on the facing page.

5.4   'Sumer is icumen in' (English 13th-c. canon), beginning. From a manuscript in the British Library. Countless facsimiles may be found in reference books and histories of music.

5.5   'Dargason' (English jig of *c.*1600). In *The Complete Country Dance Tunes from* Playford's Dancing Master (*1651–ca. 1728*), ed. Jeremy Barlow, 34, no. 90, under the title '(The) Sedany or Dargason'. First appeared in the earliest edition of *The English Dancing Master*, published by John Playford, 1651.

5.6   'The Irish Washerwoman' (Irish jig), beginning. Based on the tune in *The Dance Music of Ireland*, ed. Francis O'Neill, 67, no. 317, where it is called 'The Irishwoman'. To reproduce what was doubtless an earlier (and still common) version, I have substituted *a* for *b* (at the original pitch, *f♯* for *e*) in bar 3.

5.7   'The Drunken Sailor' (sea shanty tune, originally an Irish reel), beginning. In *The Oxford Song Book*, ed. Thomas Wood (1928), ii. 83.

5.8   Jewish psalm tone. In Werner, 'The Music of Post-Biblical Judaism', 319, Ex. 298.

5.9   Catholic psalm tone no. 6. Ibid.

5.10   'Rex coeli, Domine' (sequence). In Hughes, 'The Birth of Polyphony', 279. From the *Musica Enchiriadis*, *c.*900.

5.11   'La Virgen de los Dolores'. In Donostia, 'El modo de *mi*', 156. Collected from a Spanish Gypsy woman in Somontín, Almería, by Marius Schneider.

6.1   Binchois, 'Adieu m'amour' (*c.*1450). In *Die Chansons von Gilles Binchois* (*1400–1460*), 3. Notation modernized.

6.2   Antonio Zacara da Teramo, 'Ciaramella' (*ballata*, early 15th c.), beginning. In Pirrotta, *Music and Culture in Italy from the Middle Ages to the Baroque*, ch. 9, 'Zacara da Teramo', 135–7, Ex. 9.2. From a MS in the Archivo di Stato di Lucca.

6.3   Bagpipe *kolo* from Gajda, Slovenia, conclusion. In Brömse, *Flöten, Schalmeien, Sackpfeifen Südslawiens*, 93–4. Quoted (with slightly altered notation) in Baines, *Bagpipes*, 77.

6.4   Byrd, 'The Bagpipe and the Drone', beginning. No. 6 of the suite entitled *The Battle* (original spelling *The Battell*), first recorded in the MS collection of Byrd's keyboard music entitled *My Ladye Nevells Booke* and presented to that lady (about whom little else is known) in 1591.

6.5   The bagpipe 'double tonic'

6.6   Antonio Zacara da Teramo, 'Amor nè tossa' (early 15th c.), extract. Source as for Ex. 6.2, p. 138, Ex. 9.3b.

6.7   Joan Ambrosio Dalza, 'Spingardo [i.e. Piva] alla ferrarese' no. 3 in B flat (1508), (original) bars 95–104. In the *Intabulatura di lauto*, fo. 32ᵛ.

All the extracts from Dalza in this book are my own transcriptions from a facsimile edition of Petrucci's original publication of 1508. This is in lute tablature, which gives precise indications for plucking and stopping on a staff representing the six strings of the instrument (thereby obviating all problems of *musica ficta*), but says nothing about how long a note is to last. Nor are there any key signatures or accidentals.

There *are* time signatures and barlines, the latter of a strikingly modern kind, the only difference being that they tend to occur more often than their present-day equivalents, e.g. Dalza's *pive* are notated in '3/8' rather than '6/8' or '9/8' time.

6.8   Joan Ambrosio Dalza, 'Spingardo [i.e. Piva] alla ferrarese' no. 4 in F (1508), (original) bars 1–22. In the *Intabulatura di lauto*, fo. 36ᵛ.

6.9   Sword dance for bagpipe from Galicia (north-west Spain), beginning. In *Cancionero musical de Galicia*, ed. C. Sampedro y Folgar and José Filgueira Valverde, ii: *Melodías*, 122, no. 370.

6.10   'The Maid amongst the Roses' (Irish reel), beginning. In *The Roche Collection of Traditional Irish Music*, ed. Francis Roche, i. 63, no. 159. Bowing marks omitted.

6.11.   Joan Ambrosio Dalza, 'Pavana alla ferrarese' no. 3 in B flat (1508), (original) bars 1–40. In the *Intabulatura di lauto*, fo. 28ʳ⁻ᵛ.

6.12   Joan Ambrosio Dalza, 'Pavana alla ferrarese' no. 1 in C (1508), (original) bars 1–48. Ibid., fo. 21ᵛ.

6.13   Joan Ambrosio Dalza, 'Pavana alla ferrarese' no. 4 in F (1508), (original) bars 127–41. Ibid., fo. 34ᵛ.

6.14   Dalza's treatment of secondary chords

6.15   The skeleton of Theme C from Dalza's *pavane alla ferrarese*

6.16   Serbian bagpipe tune. In Brömse, *Flöten, Schalmeien, Sackpfeifen Südslawiens*, 87.

6.17   The basic pattern of the *alla venetiana* dances

6.18   Joan Ambrosio Dalza, Suite *alla venetiana* no. 2 in F (1508). (*a*) *Pavana*, beginning. In the *Intabulatura di lauto*, fo. 12ʳ, (original) bars 1–16. (*b*) *Saltarello*, beginning. Ibid., fo. 13ʳ, (original) bars 1–8. (c) *Piva*, beginning. Ibid., fo. 14ʳ, (original) bars 1–16.

7.1   Byrd, 'The Burying of the Dead', beginning. This piece, omitted from the earliest source of the *Battle* suite (see note to Ex. 6.4), appears in a later version to be found in *Elizabeth Rogers hir Virginall Booke* (p. 40 of the modern publication edited by Charles J. F. Cofone).

7.2   Byrd, 'A Hornpipe' (original spelling 'Hornepipe'; late 16th c.), beginning. In *Will Forster's Virginal Book* (1624). Collected in *William Byrd: Forty-five Pieces for Keyboard Instruments*, 31 ff. Barring modernized.

7.3   Hornpipe tune from north-east Turkey. In Baines, *Bagpipes*, 47, Ex. 3. Recorded and transcribed by Laurence Picken. The repeat signs are as in the original. However: (1) the note here transposed as *e* has no arrow, but is described in the accompanying text as 'inclining towards a neutral third'; (2) the staves are transposed, i.e. the right pipe is on top.

7.4   Weelkes, 'Jockey, Thine Hornpipe's Dull' (1608), beginning. In *Ayeres or phantasticke spirits for three voices*, 3–5.

7.5   Ravenscroft, 'Hey, Down Down' (1609). In Thomas Ravenscroft, *Pammelia: Musicks Miscellanie*, 13, no. 30. Notation modernized.

7.6   Joan Ambrosio Dalza, 'Piva' from the Suite *alla venetiana* no. 2 in F (1508), beginning. In the *Intabulatura di lauto*, fo. 14ʳ, (original) bars 1–16.

7.7   Vivaldi, *The Four Seasons* (*c.*1725), 'Spring', third mvt. ('Danza pastorale'), beginning

7.8   Verdi, *La traviata* (1853), Act III, Scene i, Andante mosso section, 'Addio del passato bei sogni ridenti', bars 11–20

11.88 Rossini, *William Tell* (1829), Overture, bars 209–17. I have omitted the counterpoint for flute, as well as the chords for other winds.

11.89 'Zingarese' no. 6 in D minor (late 18th c.). Source as for Ex. 11.24.

11.90 Haydn, Symphony No. 88 in G (*c.* 1788), Minuet, bars 64–70 (end of Trio). Drum part omitted.

11.91 Chopin, Mazurka in F, Op. 68 No. 3 (1829), bars 37–44

11.92 Grieg, 'Havet' ('The Sea', 1895), Op. 61 No. 1, bars 3–14 (beginning of voice part)

11.93 The heptatonia secunda modes: (*a*) in relation to the parent scale; (*b*) with *c* as tonic

11.94 Numbers 8–16 of the natural harmonic series

11.95 'Batuta', beginning. Performed on the tilincă by Mihai Lacatus in 1951. Collected by Tiberiu Alexandru, and quoted by him in 'Tilinca', 115–17. Pitch as originally transcribed, but up a tone relative to the performance. No key signature in original.

11.96 Indian beggar's song. Quoted in Schneider, 'Primitive Music', 72, no. 99; attributed simply to 'Schneider'

11.97 Spanish song. Ibid., no. 100; attributed to 'Torner'

11.98 'Rákóczi's Lament' (1826), beginning. In Sárosi, *Gypsy Music*, 104–6. First published by Gabor Mátray in 1826.

11.99 Chopin, Mazurka in C sharp minor, Op. 6 No. 2 (1830–1), beginning. Pedal note on *c* above Melody omitted.

11.100 Mahler, 'In diesem Wetter!' (no. 5 of *Kindertotenlieder*, 1904), end of voice part. I have omitted a heterophonic doubling of the voice by the 1st violins.

11.101 Johann Strauss, 'Voices of Spring' (*c.* 1882). Section in A flat, beginning. I have omitted a fluttering figure in the flutes and clarinets in bars 14–21.

11.102 Haydn, String Quartet in F minor, Op. 20 No. 5 (1771), 1st mvt., bars 135–49

11.103 Chopin, Polonaise in A flat, Op. 53 (1842), conclusion. In the original, the Melody is doubled at the octave below.

11.104 Brahms, Symphony No. 4 in E minor (1885), slow mvt., bars 5–8

11.105 The two types of octatonic scale: (*a*) melodic; (*b*) harmonic

11.106 Klephtic (modern Greek guerrilla) song, 1st verse, 2nd phrase. In Baud-Bovy, 'La Chanson clephtique', *Journal of the International Folk Music Council*, 1 (1949), 44 ff. Quoted in Sachs, *The Wellsprings of Music*, 148.

11.107 The Istrian mode. In Bezić, 'Yugoslavia, §II,3: Folk music, 3. Croatia, (I) The narrow-interval style', *New Grove*, xx. 594, Ex. 9 (where it is given at the same pitch, and called 'The Istrian Scale').

11.108 Schubert, Symphony No. 8 in B minor (the 'Unfinished', 1822), 1st mvt., bars 13–20

11.109 Beethoven, Piano Sonata in D, Op. 28 (the 'Pastoral', 1801), slow mvt., bars 71–7

12.1 Richard Farnaby, 'Nobody's Jig' (*c.* 1600), Theme. In *The Fitzwilliam Virginal Book*, ii. 162–5, no. [CXLIX]. At the beginning, rests have been omitted and a barline added.

12.2   Haydn, Symphony No. 60 in C ('Il Distratto', 1774), 4th mvt., bars 82–99. Oboe part doubling 1st violins omitted.

12.3   Ibid., bars 151–8 (near end). Drum, trumpet, and horn parts omitted.

12.4   Haydn. Symphony, No. 82 in C ('The Bear', 1786), last mvt., beginning

12.5   Johann Strauss, *Die Fledermaus*, Act II, no. 11, Finale, bars 33–40 .

12.6   Johann Strauss, 'Unter Donner und Blitz' (*Polka schnell*, 1868), bars 5–51

12.7   *Tanz* no. 1 from the Sonnleithner Collection, UÖ III/17. Quoted in Flotzinger, 'Und walzen umatum', 507, Musical Example 1. Date given as 1702, though this seems improbably early.

12.8   'Steirische in C'. In Flotzinger, 'Und walzen umatum…', 511, Musical Example 9. From the Hausa Schmidl Collection, in *Aus österreichischen Tanzbüchln*, ed. Edi Rauter and Walter Deutsch, part 2, p. 16. In the original the notes for the main tune point upward and those for the descant downward.

12.9   *Sarabanda* for lute (*c.*1645), beginning. Ibid., 513, Musical Example 10. From the 'Lautenbuch Kremsmünster', I.81, fo. 48ʳ.

12.10   Beethoven, *Sieben Ländler*, WoO 11 (1798–9), no. 3. This set of waltzes may be found in *Bagatelles, Rondos and other Shorter Works for Piano*, 121–4.

12.11   Ibid. no. 5

12.12   The *a–g–e* waltz figure

12.13   Haydn, Symphony No. 88 in G (*c.*1788), Minuet, Trio, beginning

12.14   Beethoven, Bagatelle in A flat, Op. 33 No. 7 (1801–2), bars 9–20 (2nd half of main theme)

12.15   Hummel, *Deutsche* in C, Op. 39 No. 1 (*c.*1810), Trio, bars 9–16 (2nd half). From the *Tänze für den Apollo Saal*, in the *Harmonicon*, ix.

12.16   Haydn, Symphony No. 77 in B flat (1782), Minuet, Trio, beginning

12.17   Development by doubling in the 'ur-waltz': (*a*) two-bar stage; (*b*) four-bar stage; (*c*) eight-bar stage

12.18   Haydn, String Quartet in G minor, Op. 74 No. 3 ('The Horseman', 1793), 1st mvt., bars 55–62

12.19   'Bei Sedan wohl auf den Höhen' (*volkstümliches Lied*, late 19th-c.). In Rauhe, 'Zum volkstümlichen Lied des 19. Jahrhunderts', 188, Ex. 30[b]. From *Mariechen saß weinend im Garten*, ed. H. Goertz, 74.

12.20   Lehár, *The Merry Widow* (1905), Waltz, 2nd strain, beginning

12.21   Johann Strauss, 'Roses from the South' (1880), no. 4, bars 29–38

12.22   Tchaikovsky, *Album for the Young* (1878), 'Chanson italienne', bars 17–32

12.23   Lanner, 'Terpsichore-Walzer', Op. 12 (*c.*1825), no. 4, beginning. In Denkmäler der Tonkunst in Österreich, Band 65, 3–13. Date given as 'vor 1825' (but *New Grove* conjectures '1827').

12.24   Johann Strauss, 'Wine, Woman, and Song' (1869), no. 3, beginning

12.25   Tchaikovsky, *Eugene Onegin* (1879), Act II, no. 13, Waltz, bars 43–66 (beginning of main theme). The original has choral parts omitted here.

12.26   Schubert, Waltz in B flat, Op. 33 No. 6 (1823–4), beginning

12.27   Schubert, Waltz in C, Op. 9 No. 31 (1821), bars 11–18

13.18   Verdi, *Otello* (1887), conclusion

13.19   Rossini, *William Tell* (1829), Act II, Finale, no. 18, 'Quand l'orgueil les égare de leur sang', beginning. Male voice parts omitted.

13.20   Offenbach, *La Périchole* (1868), no. 3, 'Complainte', beginning of voice part

13.21   Sinding, 'Rustle of Spring', Op. 32 No. 3 (original title: 'Frühlingsrauschen'; 1896): (*a*) beginning; (*b*) bars 27–34. The Melody (mostly in the bass) has been extricated from a complex pianistic texture.

13.22   Wagner, *Das Rheingold* (1853–4), Prelude and beginning of Scene i: (*a*) beginning of Prelude (in the original both pedal notes are doubled at the octave below); (*b*) end of Prelude and beginning of Scene i

13.23   Offenbach, *Orphée aux enfers* (1858), Act I, 'Galop infernal' ('Cancan'), beginning

13.24   Rossini, *Stabat Mater* (1841), 'Cujus animam', bars 9–18

13.25   Liszt, 'Liebestraum' (1850), beginning. Officially 'Notturno no. 3', this is the 3rd of three arrangements of previously composed songs, in this case 'O lieb'' (1847; words by F. Freligrath). In the original the Melody is in the middle of the harmony, with the arpeggios above.

13.26   Basses commonly associated with progressive tonality

13.27   Rossini, *Otello* (1816), Act III, 'The Willow Song' ('Assisa a' pie d'un salice'), beginning of voice part

13.28   Chopin, Ballade No. 2, Op. 38 (1836–9): (*a*) beginning; (*b*) conclusion

13.29   Antonio Zacara da Teramo, 'Ciaramella' (early 15th c. *ballata*), beginning, bass. Source as for Ex. 6.2.

13.30   'The Song of the Volga Boatmen' (Russian folk song, originally entitled simply 'Eye ukhnyem!', i.e. 'Heave ho!'), beginning. Accompaniment omitted. First appeared in *A Collection of Russian Folksongs*, compiled by Balakirev and published by A. Johansen, St Petersburg, precise date unknown but evidently in the late 1860s. For full details, see Fuld, *The Book of World-Famous Music*, 520.

13.31   Melodic accompaniments to the plagal progression

13.32   Domenico Scarlatti, Sonata in C, K420, L2 (mid-18th c.), beginning

13.33   Haydn, Symphony No. 53 in D (*c.*1778), last mvt., bars 38–44

13.34   Mozart, *Così fan tutte* (1790), Overture, bars 29–45

13.35   Mozart, Variations on 'Ah, vous dirai-je, Maman', K. 265 (probably 1778), Theme, beginning

13.36   Haydn, Keyboard Sonata in E major, Hob. XVI: 13 (probably 1760s), Minuet, beginning

13.37   Schubert, Waltz in C, Op. 50 No. 1 (*c.*1823), beginning

13.38   Donizetti, *Lucia di Lammermoor* (1835), Act II, no. 8, Sextet, beginning

13.39   Gounod, 'Sérénade' (1857), beginning of instrumental introduction

13.40   Adam, *Si j'étais roi* (1852), Act II, Finale, Chœur dansé, 'Bondissez et dansez', beginning. I have omitted a choral accompaniment in the rhythm of the orchestral bass. The same tune appears in the well-known overture.

13.41   Cimarosa, *Il matrimonio segreto* (1792), Overture, beginning

13.42   Mozart, *The Magic Flute* (1791), Overture, beginning

15.26 Debussy, 'Voiles' (1909): (*a*) beginning; (*b*) bars 39–43; (*c*) conclusion

15.27 Richard Strauss, *Salome* (1905), from 7 bars after rehearsal no. 357 (near end). Even with 3 staves, many details of Strauss's complex score have had to be omitted, but this reduction gives a fair idea of it.

15.28 Diatonic patterns in the octatonic scale: (*a*) the source scale; (*b*) chordal patterns: (i) major triads, (ii) minor triads, (iii) 'dominant' or pentatonic seventh; (*c*) scalar patterns: (i) the first four notes of the minor mode, (ii) the children's mode

15.29 'Prialitsa' ('The Spinning Woman', Russian folk song). In Gordon D. McQuere, 'The Theories of Boleslav Yavorsky', 154, Fig. 43, with words omitted.

15.30 Rimsky-Korsakov, *Sheherazade* (1888), 2nd mvt.: (*a*) 12 bars after rehearsal letter E (as originally notated the drone is on the same augmented fourth throughout); (*b*) octatonic framework of (*a*)

15.31 Stravinsky, *Petrushka* (1911), Part 2 ('Chez Pétrouchka'), bars 34–43

16.1 Kreisler, 'Caprice viennoise' (1910), bars 20–39 (main theme). The piano accompaniment has been somewhat simplified where it clashes with the violin part.

16.2 Wagner, *Tannhäuser* (1843–5), Overture, bars 142–9 (Tannhäuser's song). Cello and viola arpeggios omitted.

16.3 Tchaikovsky, 'Valse sentimentale', Op. 51 No. 6 (1882), bars 35–54 (2nd theme)

16.4 Fred W. Leigh and George Arthurs, 'A Little of What You Fancy Does You Good': (*a*) verse and chorus; (*b*) variations within (*a*). In *Music Hall Song Book*, ed. Peter Gammond, 140–2. First published by Francis, Day & Hunter in 1915.

16.5 John W. Bratton, 'The Teddy Bear's Picnic', Trio, beginning. Published by the composer as a 'characteristic two-step' in New York, 1907.

16.6 'Old Dan Tucker'. Arranged by Dan. D. Emmit. Introduction and interlude omitted. In *Popular Songs of Nineteenth-Century America*, ed. Richard Jackson, 160–2. Facsimile reprint of the original publication of 1843.

16.7 Charles L. Johnson, 'A Black Smoke', bars 9–12. In *Classic Piano Rags*, 42–6. Facsimile reprint of the original publication of 1903 (copyrighted by the composer in 1902).

16.8 'Harlaw' (Scottish ballad tune). From the singing of Jeannie Robertson. In *The Scottish Folksinger*, ed. Norman Buchan and Peter Hall, 132–3.

16.9 'Joe Turner' (early 20th-c. blues). In *The American Songbag*, ed. Carl Sandburg (1927), 241, but undoubtedly much older. Accompaniment omitted.

16.10 Foster, 'Massa's in de Cold, Cold Ground', verse. In *Stephen Foster Song Book*, ed. Richard Jackson, 63–6. Facsimile reprint of the original publication of 1852.

16.11 Henry Clay Work, 'Marching through Georgia': (*a*) verse; (*b*) pentatonic skeleton of (*a*). In *Popular Songs of Nineteenth-Century America*, 126–9. Facsimile reprint of the original publication of 1865.

16.12 Hughie Cannon, 'Just because She Made dem Goo-goo Eyes at Me', verse. Words by John Queen. In *Song Hits from the Turn of the Century*, ed. Paul Charosh and Robert A. Fremont, 141–4. Facsimile reprint of the original publication of 1900.

16.13 Fred Murray and R. P. Weston. 'I'm Henery the Eighth, I am', chorus, beginning. In *Music Hall Song Book*, ed. Peter Gammond, 113–14. First published by Francis, Day & Hunter in 1911.

Glossary

Of the words and phrases defined below, some are my own coinages, others the invention of earlier scholars (to whom I have tried to give due credit), and yet others standard musical terms with a change of meaning.

In addition to elucidating what would otherwise be puzzling in the text, this glossary may serve as a tentative contribution to the much-needed reform of our ramshackle musical vocabulary. Many of the terms listed below are, quite frankly, makeshifts, but they are at least makeshifts into which a great deal of thought has gone. If anyone can improve on them, please do so.

acoustic mode. The mode c–d–e–$f\sharp$–g–a–$b\flat$, so named, apparently by east European scholars, from a resemblance to the fourth octave of the natural harmonic series. It is based on the HEPTATONIA SECUNDA SCALE.

alphabetical notation. A notation employing the letters a–g or A–G, used to describe music in which the position of the TONIC (if present at all) is of secondary importance. Cf. NUMERICAL NOTATION.

ambiguity. The multiplicity or vagueness of PATTERN present in all music.

ambit. The range between the focal notes bounding a melody; usually comprises an octave (from the Latin *ambitus*, used by medieval theorists). See also OCTAVE PATTERN.

apical seventh. A prominent 7 at the apex of a melodic phrase. It differs from the conventional LEADING NOTE precisely because it does not 'lead'. Instead, it bears the same relation to 5 as 3 does to 1. Cf. BLUE SEVENTH.

attractor. In complexity theory, a simple pattern to which an evolving system recurs between episodes of greater complexity.

Bar **form.** A melodic form consisting of three strains in an AAB pattern (mistakenly adopted by German scholars from sixteenth-century Meistersinger usage). It is one of the ancestors of the TWELVE-BAR BLUES. Cf. *GEGENBAR* FORM.

bass, Bass. (1) With a small 'b': the deepest melodic line of a polyphonic passage. (2) With a capital 'B': the melodic line supporting the harmony. In the latter sense, it often (but not invariably) coincides with the FUNDAMENTAL BASS, and is in TONAL COUNTERPOINT with the MELODY.

bass filler. A bass figure filling the gap between the end of the Melody and the end of the strain. Cf. BASS RUN.

bass run. A showy BASS FILLER found especially in Sousa-type marches, ragtime, and jazz.

bending. Microtonal INFLECTION. Chiefly associated with the blues, but also an important feature of much Oriental music, as well as such European music as has come under Oriental influence.

bifocal close. Robert S. Winter's term (suggested by Jan LaRue's BIFOCAL TONALITY) for a half close immediately followed by a passage in the dominant.

bifocal tonality. Jan LaRue's term for a form of KEY MIXTURE 'combining major and relative minor to form a broader but not indefinite harmonic arena'.

bipolar tonality. A form of tonality moving between two contrasted 'poles', e.g. *C* major and *A* minor, or *C* major and *E* minor, without being committed to either of them. Applied by Robert Bailey specifically to Wagner, but common also in other mid- or late nineteenth-century composers.

'Birch Tree' pattern. A predominantly east European tune type, related to the primitive TUMBLING STRAINS and the African SAW-TOOTHED MELODY, in which the phrases first descend from *5* to *1* and then taper off. (From the Russian folk tune 'A birch tree stood in the meadow'.)

bisociation. Koestler's term for the process whereby a new pattern is created out of the fusion of two pre-existing ones.

'Black Sheep' pattern. The initial formula 5/I 6/IV–5/I or 3/I 4/IV–3/I, generally in two halves of two or four bars each. (From the nursery song 'Baa-baa Black Sheep'.)

blue dominant. A rare form of BLUE NOTE on *5* of the major mode. Not to be confused with the BLUE FIFTH.

blue fifth. A BLUE NOTE on *5♭* of the minor mode. Not to be confused with the BLUE DOMINANT.

blue note. A MELODIC DISSONANCE characteristic of the BLUES, though not confined to it. It is normally attracted to the note a third lower (e.g. blue *3→1*, blue *7→5*). Though conventionally indicated as flattened by a semitone (e.g. *3♭*, *7♭*), blue notes are usually 'bent' in some way (see BENDING). See also the preceding and following entries.

blue seventh. A BLUE NOTE on *7♭*, bearing the same relation to *5* as the blue *3♭* does to *1*. It is also the inflected equivalent of the APICAL SEVENTH. See also ENGLISH CADENCE.

blue third. (1) Any BLUE NOTE a third above the note to which it is attracted. (2) More usually, a blue note on *3♭*. See also CHROMATIC BLUE THIRD.

blues. An Afro-European genre originally of the southern United States, characterized by a uniquely chromatic use of the PENTATONIC SCALE. See also TWELVE-BAR BLUES and ONE-CHORD blues, as well as the preceding and following entries.

blues ballad. A form of ballad, popular in the late nineteenth and early twentieth centuries, made up of loosely connected blues stanzas describing some sensational event.

cadence. A progression marking the end of a musical statement. Whether harmonic (i.e. in the BASS) or melodic (in the MELODY), it usually involves the RESOLUTION of DISSONANCE. See also ONE-CHORD CADENCE, UNDER-THIRD CADENCE, ENGLISH CADENCE, DOUBLE CADENCE, CLAUSE, CADENTIAL CLIMAX.

cadential climax. A series of cadences forming a climax in the original, rhetorical sense of the word, i.e. graded from weak to strong. Depending on whether the common element in the cadences is a harmonic chord or Melody note, a cadential climax may be harmonic (e.g. 4/IV→3/I 2/V→1/I or 3/I→2/V 1/II7/♯→7⁻/V) or melodic (e.g. 2/V→3/I 2♯/VII5♯→3/III).

call third. A translation of the German *Rufterz*, given to the chant g–e, with g sustained as a reciting note (so called because often used for calling at a distance). It differs from the closely related CHILDREN'S CHANT in being closed rather than self-repeating.

central European. See EAST AND CENTRAL EUROPEAN.

children's chant. A simple, repetitive chant sung by children (and many adults) all over the world. It consists of an indefinitely repeated g–e, with an optional offbeat a before g. Its notes form the children's mode or tetrachord (cf. PSALM TETRACHORD). See also CALL THIRD.

children's mode. See CHILDREN'S CHANT.

children's tetrachord. See CHILDREN'S CHANT.

chord. A group of notes in consonant relation to one another (see CONSONANCE, sense 3), which, however, may also include dissonance through overlapping or superimposition (e.g. g–b⁻–d + d–f, c–e⁻–g⁻ + c–e♭–g, b⁻–d + d–f, c–e + e–g♯). Though any chord may take a melodic or harmonic form, depending on whether its notes are sounded successively or simultaneously, it is convenient to distinguish between 'harmonic chords' (associated with the BASS) and 'melodic chords' (produced by the MELODY). See also DUAL-LEVEL CHORD, HARMONIC COALESCENCE, HARMONY.

chord row, or **chord string.** A traditional harmonic formula supporting an eight- or sixteen-bar tune, first used in sixteenth- and seventeenth-century Italian dance music. Among the most popular chord rows are the PASSAMEZZO ANTICO, PASSAMEZZO MODERNO, and FOLIA.

chordality. The property by which notes cohere to form a CHORD.

chromatic blue third. A form of BLUE THIRD, of predominantly European origin, in which 3♭ resolves to 3♮.

classical, Classical. (1) With a small 'c': the 'serious' or 'concert hall' music of the Western world from about 1650 on. (2) With a capital 'C': the predominantly Viennese school of the late eighteenth and early nineteenth centuries.

classical minor mode. The MINOR MODE (sense 1) of classical Western music, with variable sixth and seventh degrees.

clause. A period ending in a full close, especially important in the waltz.

conclusion. See TWELVE-BAR BLUES.

concord. (1) A simultaneously sounded CONSONANCE (sense 3). (2) The euphony characteristic of such an interval.

conjunct modulation. See MODULATION.

consonance. (1) The relative absence of DISSONANCE. (2) An interval displaying this quality. (3) More specifically, the consonant intervals are those contained within the major triad, including the octave (the only absolutely consonant interval). The major second occupies an ambiguous category between consonance and dissonance. Consonance may be either melodic or harmonic, in the latter case forming a CONCORD. Cf. DISSONANCE.

coon song. During the 1890s, an American popular song of a purportedly (and sometimes genuinely) Afro–American type.

counterpoint. The controlled conflict of simultaneous patterns. It refers to any aspect of music, not just melody. For example, counterpoint may occur between one rhythm and another, between rhythm and melody, between melody and harmony (see TONAL COUNTERPOINT), etc. For counterpoint in the traditional sense, the word 'polyphony' is used in this book.

counterpoles. Ernő Lendvai's term for the chords or keys a TRITONE (sense 2) apart.

counterstatement. See TWELVE-BAR BLUES.

diatonic. Of melodies, figures, etc., based on the DIATONIC SCALE.

diatonic background. A DIATONIC context for some sub- or super-diatonic pattern, e.g. the PENTATONIC, OCTATONIC, or WHOLE-TONE SCALE, q.v.

diatonic scale. A SCALE of seven notes to the octave, consisting of two semitones and five tones, the tones being arranged in alternate groups of twos and threes. See also HEPTATONIA SECUNDA SCALE.

discord. (1) A simultaneously sounded DISSONANCE (sense 3). (2) The roughness characteristic of such an interval.

disjunct modulation. See MODULATION.

dissonance. (1) The attraction between notes of different pitches. (2) A note attracted in this manner. (3) An interval through which such attraction is exerted: specifically, all those that are augmented or diminished, the minor second, and, in an ambiguous category between dissonance and CONSONANCE, the major second. When a dissonant interval occurs simultaneously, the result is a DISCORD. Cf. CONSONANCE.

divergence, law of. States that the natural tendency of musical patterns is to begin by being concurrent and subsequently to diverge.

dominant chord. The (usually major) chord a perfect fifth above the TONIC. See also INTRODUCTORY DOMINANT, LAGGARD DOMINANT, PREPARATORY DOMINANT, POLKA PROGRESSION, SUPERTONIC SANDWICH, BIFOCAL CLOSE.

double cadence. A CADENCE in which the harmonic and melodic elements, instead of coinciding as usual, are separated. Generally the harmonic cadence comes slightly before the melodic one.

double drone. A DRONE on a perfect fifth. Cf. SINGLE DRONE.

double pentatonic axis. See PENTATONIC AXIS.

double resolution. The resolution of the same DISSONANCE in two ways; e.g. $3\flat$ may resolve both down to 2 and up to $3\natural$.

double tonic. An OSTINATO consisting of two alternating triads with basses a major second apart. Usually the upper triad is minor and the lower major. Depending on which triad is predominant, it may then take either the 'DRUNKEN SAILOR' or 'IRISH WASHERWOMAN' form.

downward leading note. A DISSONANCE (sense 2) a semitone higher than the note to which it is attracted. Cf. LEADING NOTE.

drone. A sustained note or chord, in this book always in the bass. Also called a 'pedal', especially in more sophisticated music, though there is no real distinction. At its most primitive, the drone is (as its name suggests) a single, uninterrupted note. But more developed examples may be rhythmically articulated, melodically or harmonically interrupted, or expanded into a chord. (The TONIC triad is a specialized form of triadic drone.) See also SINGLE DRONE, DOUBLE DRONE, TRANSFERRED DRONE

'Drunken Sailor'. The form of the DOUBLE TONIC in which the upper, minor triad predominates (from the well-known sea shanty of that name).

dual-level chord. A chord combining an upper and lower element, respectively associated with the MELODY and the BASS. Usually the melodic element consists of a single note (e.g. the *3* of the dominant thirteenth or the *6* of the tonic added sixth), but it may also be expanded into a third, or even a full triad (e.g. *2–4–6* in the dominant ninth). The two levels have a tendency to fuse into one by a process of HARMONIC COALESCENCE.

east and central European. The distinction is musical rather than ethnic, geographical, or political. The main difference is that ORIENTAL influence, in the form of complex modes, syncopated rhythms, drone effects, etc., is far more marked in eastern than in central European music.

emergence. The development of complex phenomena out of simpler but radically different ones, e.g. life out of matter or harmony out of melody.

English cadence. A type of full close, popular with English composers in the sixteenth and seventeenth centuries, in which a BLUE SEVENTH clashes with the dominant chord. (So named by twentieth-century English scholars.)

extended modality. The interlocking of more than one pentatonic seventh to form a pentatonic axis. It is effected by the INFLECTION of one or more notes, e.g. $a^- \!\!-\!c\!-\!e\!-\!g + c\!-$ $e\flat\!-\!g\!-\!b\flat$, where e is inflected.

extended tonality. A vague term for the unification of boldly chromatic harmonies around a single TONIC (or group of tonics), especially in nineteenth- and twentieth-century music. It often involves EXTENDED MODALITY.

falling progression. A progression in which the BASS falls by a perfect fifth or a series of such fifths, e.g. POLKA PROGRESSION, RAGTIME PROGRESSION. Cf. RISING PROGRESSION.

fancy music. See PLAIN AND FANCY MUSIC.

field blues. See HOLLER.

fifth. For convenience, used for the interval of the perfect fifth where the 'perfection' is evident from the context.

fifth-answering. An ethnomusicological term for the ancient and widespread practice of 'answering' a phrase at the perfect fifth below. Usually the 'answer' is sequential.

figure. A short section of melody occurring in actual music. Cf. PATTERN, and see also PENTATONIC FIGURE.

first group, first subject. Both terms are used in this book, the former (coined by Tovey) for the entire main-key section of a sonata-form exposition, the latter for its principal theme. Similarly with 'second group', 'second subject'.

focus. In a MODAL FRAMEWORK, a relatively stable (or 'focal') note to which others are attracted.

folia. A CHORD ROW consisting of the chords Im V Im VII♭ · III♭ VII♭ Im V : Im V Im VII♭ · III♭ VII♭ Im–V I. While the BASS is thus modulating to the relative major, the MELODY stays in the minor. The resulting TONAL COUNTERPOINT (minor Melody against relative-major harmony) is the '*folia* effect'.

folia effect. See the preceding entry.

folk music. A vague and loaded term, theoretically denoting something more traditional and less commercial than POPULAR MUSIC. In practice, the distinction is hard to sustain.

fourth. For convenience, used for the interval of the perfect fourth where the 'perfection' is evident from the context.

framework, modal. See MODAL FRAMEWORK.

Fringe. See PHRYGIAN FRINGE; LYDIAN FRINGE.

fundamental bass. Rameau's term for a bass made up of harmonic roots. In early music it coincides with the actual bass, but later increasingly diverges.

Gegenbar **form.** The 'counter-*Bar*' form, consisting of three strains in an ABB pattern. Cf. BAR FORM.

Gregory Walker. See PASSAMEZZO MODERNO.

Gypsy mode. (1) Usually, the ORIENTAL PHRYGIAN MODE. (2) Sometimes, the HUNGARIAN MODE.

hard pentatonic. See PENTATONIC PATTERN.

harmonic. As a general rule, indicates the involvement of the BASS, as in most of the following entries, but notice the special meanings of HARMONIC COALESCENCE, HARMONIC OCTATONIC.

harmonic binary form. That in which the two endings differ in the BASS, e.g.: first ending –V; second ending: –I. Cf. MELODIC BINARY FORM.

harmonic cadence. See CADENCE.

harmonic cadential climax. See CADENTIAL CLIMAX.

harmonic chord. (1) Any simultaneously sounded CHORD. (2) The lower part of a DUAL-LEVEL CHORD.

harmonic coalescence. The process by which a DUAL-LEVEL CHORD turns into a purely HARMONIC CHORD, e.g. V + 4 becomes the dominant seventh V7, or I + 6 becomes the added sixth I6/5.

harmonic octatonic. The form of OCTATONIC SCALE with a semitone at the bottom of each tone–semitone pair. So called because harmonic chords are easily formed from it. Cf. MELODIC OCTATONIC.

harmonic sequence. A SEQUENCE involving the BASS (and usually, but not necessarily, also the MELODY).

harmonic strength. The strength of a MELODY note in relation to the BASS. It depends on the position of the note within the chord, being strongest when it is the root.

harmonize. To provide a MELODY with a BASS (and the accompanying chords). Cf. MELODIZE.

harmonostasis. The persistent reference to a single BASS note, plus the triad it supports, through an extended MELODY. Cf. MELOSTASIS.

harmony. Simultaneous melody, regardless of whether it produces a CHORD. See also HARMONIC.

heptatonia secunda scale. A heptatonic SCALE consisting, like the diatonic scale, of two semitones and five tones, but with the tones in alternate groups of ones and fours. Among the patterns based on it are the ACOUSTIC and MAJOR MINOR modes.

hierarchy. A system with co-ordinated and subordinated sub-systems. See also HOLON, INTEGRATION, SELF-ASSERTION, SELF-SIMILARITY.

holler. An unaccompanied, improvisatory Afro-American song, typically TUMBLING STRAINS. It is both close to Africa and an important ancestor of the BLUES. Also called 'field blues'.

holon. Koestler's term for a sub-system within a HIERARCHY. It is at once a part and a whole, with tendencies towards both INTEGRATION and SELF-ASSERTION.

Hungarian mode. A mode consisting, like the ORIENTAL PHRYGIAN MODE, of two ORIENTAL TETRACHORDS, but on *2* and *5* rather than *1* and *5*, i.e. *1–2–3♭–4♯–5–6♭–7–1*⁺. It possesses the unusual property of reflective SYMMETRY around *5*.

inflection. Change of pitch without loss of modal identity. In Western classical music, it usually involves a semitone, e.g. *e* may be inflected to *e♭*, or *f* to *f♯*; but see also BENDING.

infolding, law of. According to Koestler, this states that the patterns of art tend to become more implicit (literally, 'folded in') as they develop.

integration. In a hierarchy, the subordination of the part to the whole. Cf. SELF-ASSERTION.

introductory dominant. A preparatory DOMINANT CHORD at the beginning of a movement.

'Irish Washerwoman'. The form of the DOUBLE TONIC in which the lower, major triad predominates (from the well-known jig 'The Irish Washerwoman').

key. A harmonic pattern based on a single TONIC. See also MODULATION, RELATIVE MODES, KEY MIXTURE, MELODIC KEY.

key mixture. The merging of two (or occasionally more) harmonic keys, usually in association with a unifying MELODIC KEY. See also BIFOCAL TONALITY, BIPOLAR TONALITY.

knight's move. A PENTATONIC PATTERN made up of any combination of the major second and minor third moving in the same direction. (From the knight in chess, which moves in an L-shape of 1 + 2 or 2 + 1 squares.)

ladder of thirds. A modal pattern with the focal notes (see FOCUS) in a series of thirds, e.g. *a⁻–c–e–g–b♭* (suggested by Curt Sachs). See also PENTATONIC SEVENTH, PENTATONIC AXIS.

laggard dominant. A DOMINANT CHORD that belatedly harmonizes the MELODY note associated with it. It usually leads up to the return of a previously heard theme.

Landini cadence. See UNDER-THIRD CADENCE.

leading note. A DISSONANCE (sense 2) separated by a semitone from the note towards which it is attracted. Not confined to *7*, which moreover does not always 'lead' in this sense. The direction may be upward or downward, but normally the upward leading note is implied. Cf. APICAL SEVENTH, DOWNWARD LEADING NOTE.

linkage. An immediate form of THEMATIC TRANSFORMATION, linking the end of one passage to the beginning of the next (a translation, in the form 'linkage technique' of Schenker's 'Knüpftechnik').

Lisztian sequence. A SEQUENCE, usually of the 'real' type, with steps symmetrically dividing the octave (from the partiality of Franz Liszt to sequences of this type).

Lydian Fringe. The part of Europe, stretching from Scandinavia to the Alps, where the traditional music makes great use of the Lydian mode. Cf. PHRYGIAN FRINGE.

major mode. As a rule, the mode *1–2–3–4–5–6–7*; depending on the context, however, it may also include other modes with a major third.

major–minor mode. The mode combining a major third and minor sixth, i.e. *1–2–3–4–5–6♭–7*(♭). It is based on the HEPTATONIA SECUNDA SCALE.

major tetrachord. The TETRACHORD *1–2–3–4*.

major-third sequence. A LISZTIAN SEQUENCE with steps separated by major thirds.

melodic. (1) Pertaining to melody in general. (2) More usually, indicates patterns involving the MELODY rather than the BASS, as in most of the following entries.

melodic binary form. That in which the two endings differ in the MELODY but not the BASS, e.g. first ending: *–3*/I, second ending *–1*/I. Cf. HARMONIC BINARY FORM.

melodic cadence. See CADENCE.

melodic cadential climax. See CADENTIAL CLIMAX.

melodic chord. (1) Any successively sounded CHORD. (2) The upper part of a DUAL-LEVEL CHORD.

melodic chromaticism. Chromatic decoration of the MELODY independent of the harmony.

melodic dissonance. Dissonance in the MELODY independent of the harmony.

melodic key. A pattern based on a sustained MELODIC TONIC.

melodic octatonic. The form of OCTATONIC SCALE with a tone at the bottom of each tone–semitone pair. So called because it naturally falls into minor tetrachords (e.g. *a–b♭–c–d, c–d–e♭–f*). Cf. HARMONIC OCTATONIC.

melodic progression. See PROGRESSION.

melodic sequence. A SEQUENCE in the MELODY independent of the harmony.

melodic tonic. A persistent melodic FOCUS, analogous to the harmonic TONIC.

melodic vocabulary. The range of melodic figures that can be combined with a given set of harmonic chords.

melodize. To provide a BASS (and accompanying chords) with a MELODY. The opposite of HARMONIZE.

melody, Melody. (1) With a small 'm': any musically meaningful set of consecutive notes. (2) With a capital 'M': the melody in the foreground of the listener's attention, usually (but by no means always) at the top of the harmony. Especially in nineteenth- and twentieth-century music, there may sometimes be more than one melody competing for this status. The interplay between MELODY and BASS constitutes TONAL COUNTERPOINT.

melostasis. The persistence of a MELODY note or group of notes through varied harmonies. Cf. HARMONOSTASIS.

meme. Richard Dawkins's term for a mental construct capable of evolving in a manner analogous to a biological gene.

minor mode. (1) A mode containing the notes *1–2–3♭–4–5*. (2) Any mode with a minor third. See also CLASSICAL MINOR MODE.

minor tetrachord. The tetrachord *1–2–3♭–4*. Cf. PHRYGIAN TETRACHORD, ORIENTAL TETRACHORD.

minor-third sequence. A LISZTIAN SEQUENCE with steps separated by minor thirds.

modal. (1) Pertaining to MODE in the general sense. (2) Pertaining to the non-TONAL modes.

modal framework. A group of focal notes (see FOCUS), usually separated by highly consonant intervals such as the octave, fourth, or fifth.

modal translation. The conversion of one MODE into another by the INFLECTION of its third. See also PARALLEL MODES.

mode. A melodic PATTERN (not confined to the 'old' or 'church' modes) with a distinct set of intervals and degrees of DISSONANCE. Sometimes it has a TONIC (e.g. MAJOR MODE, PHRYGIAN MODES, ACOUSTIC MODE) and sometimes not (e.g. the mode of the CHILDREN'S CHANT). It is distinguished by the varied functions of its notes from a SCALE, which is defined purely by its intervals.

modulation. Change of KEY. If smooth and gradual, it is 'conjunct'; if abrupt, 'disjunct'.

module. A self-contained sub-section of a mode (from the Latin *modulus*, 'little mode'). Usually contained within a TETRACHORD.

monotertial. Anatole Leikin's term, translated from the Russian, for chords or keys linked by a common third, e.g. *C* major and *C♯* minor (common third *e*) or *E* minor and *E♭* major (common third *g*).

mutability. See PEREMENNOST'.

natural pentatonic. See PENTATONIC PATTERN.

neutral third. A third (more or less) intermediate in pitch between major and minor.

nineteenth-century vernacular. The VERNACULAR of nineteenth-century Western composers. Though at its clearest in light music such as dances, marches, etc., it is also found in more pretentious compositions.

note. A musical sound of definite pitch. It may occur in both actual music and abstract patterns. Often a handy synonym for a degree of a SCALE or MODE.

numerical notation. A notation using the numbers *1–7* to describe MODAL (sense 1) patterns in relation to a definite TONIC. Cf. ALPHABETICAL NOTATION.

octatonic scale. This consists of alternating tones and semitones, e.g. $a^-–b^-–c–d–e♭–f–g♭–a♭$, so called because it has eight notes to the octave. It comes in two 'modes', depending on whether the tone or semitone forms the base of the tone–semitone pair (see HARMONIC OCTATONIC and MELODIC OCTATONIC).

octave pattern. A MODAL (sense 1) pattern with the AMBIT of an octave. It is distinguished by the bounding note, e.g. *e* octave, *a* octave.

one-chord blues. A primitive form of BLUES with the harmony restricted to a major-triad DRONE.

one-chord cadence. A melodic CADENCE occurring over an unchanging harmonic chord.

Oriental. Used in this book in a musical rather than geographical or ethnic sense. It includes the cultures of a vast area stretching from Morocco to India, but excludes those of the Far East.

Oriental Phrygian mode. A form of Phrygian mode, often called the 'Gypsy mode', common in ORIENTAL music (as also, however, is the ordinary Phrygian). It consist of two Oriental tetrachords (see next entry) on *1* and *5*, i.e. *1–2♭–3–4–5–6♭–7*. Cf. HUNGARIAN MODE.

Oriental tetrachord. The TETRACHORD *1–2♭–3–4*, common in ORIENTAL music. It differs from the PHRYGIAN TETRACHORD in having a major third.

ostinato. A simple, indefinitely repeated pattern (from the Italian for 'obstinate' or 'persistent'). In this book confined to harmonic ostinatos of two or three chords, e.g. the DOUBLE TONIC. But see also RHYTHMIC DRONE.

over-third doubling. The doubling of a MELODY at the third above.

parallel modes, or **parallels** for short. Major and minor modes with the same TONIC. Cf. RELATIVE MODES.

parallel symmetry. See SYMMETRY.

passamezzo antico. A CHORD ROW consisting of the chords Im VII♭ Im V · III♭ VII♭ Im–V I. The minor-mode equivalent of the PASSAMEZZO MODERNO.

passamezzo moderno. A CHORD ROW consisting of the chords I IV I V · I IV I–V I. The major-mode equivalent of the PASSAMEZZO ANTICO. According to Morley, nicknamed 'Gregory Walker' in Elizabethan England.

pattern. An abstract design that gives meaning to musical sounds. Unlike a SHAPE, it has a psychological as well an acoustic aspect. (The same shape may therefore suggest different patterns to different listeners.) The realization of a pattern in actual music is a FIGURE.

pedal. See DRONE.

pentatonic. Of melodies, figures, etc., based on the PENTATONIC SCALE.

pentatonic axis. A chromatic LADDER OF THIRDS consisting of two or more interlocking pentatonic sevenths. It may be double, triple, or quadruple, depending on the number of sevenths comprising it. I owe the term to Ernő Lendvai, who, however, used it in a rather different sense. See also EXTENDED MODALITY.

pentatonic figure. Any especially distinctive PENTATONIC PATTERN, typically involving the KNIGHT'S MOVE.

pentatonic pattern. There are degrees of pentatonicism. At their strictest, pentatonic patterns are confined to the PENTATONIC SCALE, and to be really characteristic combine a major second with some larger interval (see KNIGHT'S MOVE). Elsewhere, they may include extra-pentatonic passing or dissonant notes. In this case, they come in three species, depending on their relation to the DIATONIC BACKGROUND: the natural pentatonic ($a^-–c–d–e–g$), which is implied unless the contrary is stated, hard pentatonic ($e–g–a–b–d^+$), and soft pentatonic ($d–f–g–a–c^+$). The adjectives are derived from the three hexachords (*naturale*, *durum*, and *molle*) of medieval theory. See also the preceding and following entries.

pentatonic poles. The notes a^- (the main pentatonic pole) and e (the secondary pentatonic pole). They serves as the 'tonic' and 'dominant' notes of the PENTATONIC SEVENTH.

pentatonic scale. The pattern consisting of a PENTATONIC SEVENTH with an extra note bisecting the major third, i.e. $a^-–c–d–e–g$. It is actually ambiguously poised between being a scale and a CHORD.

pentatonic seventh. A chord consisting of two interlocking triads, one major and one minor, i.e. $a-c-e-g$ ($= a-c-e + c-e-g$).

pentatonic species. See PENTATONIC PATTERN.

peremennost'. Modal ambiguity (literally 'mutability') in Russian folk song. It generally involves a subtle shift of focus between a and c or g in pentatonic melody.

Phrygian Fringe. The part of Europe where the traditional music has come under strong Oriental influence, as shown by a partiality for the PHRYGIAN MODES. It stretches from the Baltic down to the Balkans, and then along the northern Mediterranean coast to the Atlantic. Cf. LYDIAN FRINGE.

Phrygian modes. Those modes in which the tonic is approached from the flattened (or 'Phrygian') second. They include the diatonic Phrygian mode ($1-2\flat-3\flat-4-5-6\flat-7\flat$), the ORIENTAL PHRYGIAN MODE ($1-2\flat-3-4-5-6\flat-7$), and the mode (based on the HEPTATONIA SECUNDA SCALE) combining the diatonic Phrygian mode with the major sixth ($1-2\flat-3\flat-4-5-6-7\flat$).

Phrygian tetrachord. The TETRACHORD $1-2\flat-3\flat-4$. Cf. MINOR TETRACHORD, ORIENTAL TETRACHORD.

plagal progression. The harmonic progression IV–I. It forms an essential part of many harmonic formulas, e.g. the 'BLACK SHEEP' PATTERN, PASSAMEZZO MODERNO, and TWELVE-BAR BLUES.

plagalism. Frequent use of, or partiality for, the PLAGAL PROGRESSION. (Adopted from David Brown.)

plain and fancy music. Two categories of nineteenth-century music, roughly corresponding to the 'half' and 'full' music of Italian opera (recitative and arioso), but broader. The patterns of 'plain' music are strong, simple, and regular; those of 'fancy' music weak, complex, and irregular.

pole of attraction, or **pole** for short. A particularly strong FOCUS. Poles typically occur in pairs separated by a perfect fifth, e.g. the $c-g$ of TONAL harmony or the PENTATONIC POLES $a-e$. But see also BIPOLAR TONALITY and COUNTERPOLES.

polka family. A family of musically similar dances in lively $2/4$ time. Apart from the polka itself, it includes the contredanse, ecossaise, galop, etc.

polka progression. A V(7)–I progression, occurring at the beginning of a strain and often repeated thereafter. So named because especially characteristic of the POLKA FAMILY.

polyphony. Melodic COUNTERPOINT.

popular music. A class of music in theory more commercial and less ethnically rooted than FOLK MUSIC, but in practice not always easily distinguishable from it. See also VERNACULAR.

preparatory dominant. A DOMINANT CHORD leading up to a new (or recapitulated) theme.

preparatory emphasis. The preliminary prominence, in the MELODY, of a note that is later to be prominent in the BASS, e.g. the e of C major before a modulation to E minor.

pre-refrain. See REFRAIN.

primitive. It is perhaps necessary to point out that this is not (or at any rate not usually) a term of disparagement. In this book, the principal meanings are: (1) prior in order of development (e.g. 'primitive tonality', 'primitive sonata form'); (2) of music generally, close to its instinctive origins.

priority order. The order of notes in the harmonic series disregarding repetitions in higher octaves, i.e. *c*, *g*, *e*, etc.

progression. A purposeful movement from one note to the next, or a series of such movements. When in the BASS it is harmonic, but otherwise melodic.

psalm tetrachord. A pentatonic tetrachord with a minor third above and a major second below, e.g. *g–a–c*⁺. So called from its frequent use in psalm tones, where the top note is used for recitation. It is the inversion of the children's tetrachord (see CHILDREN'S CHANT).

quadruple pentatonic axis. See PENTATONIC AXIS.

ragtime progression. A FALLING PROGRESSION that works its way to a full or (more rarely) half close by a series of dominants, usually with sevenths, i.e. (III7/♯)–VI7/♯–II7/♯–V7–(I). So named because of its frequency in ragtime and kindred genres, though it goes back much further.

reduction. The release of tension brought about by passing from high to low DISCORD. It is usually, but far from invariably, associated with the RESOLUTION of DISSONANCE.

reflective symmetry. See SYMMETRY.

refrain. A recurring figure at the beginning or end of an otherwise varied melody. If at the beginning it is a 'pre-refrain'. (The ordinary refrain might be regarded as a 'post-refrain', with the 'post' understood.)

relative modes, or **relatives** for short. Major and minor modes belonging to the same PENTATONIC SEVENTH. Cf. PARALLEL MODES.

repercussion. A medieval term (in the form of the Latin 'repercussio') for the repetition of a melodic FOCUS through different contexts. Well worth reviving.

resolution. The release of tension brought about by passing from high to low DISSONANCE. Cf. REDUCTION, and see also DOUBLE RESOLUTION.

rhythmic drone. A rhythmic OSTINATO that serves as a background to broader and more varied rhythms in the MELODY. So named because analogous in function to a melodic drone.

rising progression. A progression in which the BASS rises by a perfect fifth, or a series of such fifths. Cf. FALLING PROGRESSION.

ruckhafte Senkung. A German term for the 'abrupt lowering' of a drone bass by a major second, especially common in east European music.

Rufterz. See CALL THIRD.

saw-toothed melody. A primitive melodic type, particularly common in Africa, consisting of TUMBLING STRAINS arranged in high-to-low groups, like the teeth of a rip saw. It is a direct predecessor of the HOLLER, and, through it, of many BLUES tunes. Cf. the 'BIRCH TREE' PATTERN.

scale. A PATTERN of intervals from which a MODE may be formed by differentiated DISSONANCE. See also PENTATONIC SCALE, DIATONIC SCALE, HEPTATONIA SECUNDA SCALE, OCTATONIC SCALE, WHOLE-TONE SCALE.

second group, second subject. See FIRST GROUP, FIRST SUBJECT.

self-assertion. In a HIERARCHY, the detachment of the whole from the part, or the growth of the whole at the expense of the part. Cf. INTEGRATION.

self-similarity. In complex, and especially in hierarchic systems (see HIERARCHY): (1) the similarity of the larger to the smaller; (2) more specifically, the similarity of the whole to the part.

sequence. A melodic pattern in which a FIGURE, in this book called a 'step', is immediately transposed to another part of the octave. The transposition may be free or strict ('real'), and may be repeated any number of times. See also HARMONIC SEQUENCE, MELODIC SEQUENCE, MAJOR-THIRD SEQUENCE, MINOR-THIRD SEQUENCE, LISZTIAN SEQUENCE.

shape. A musical construct regarded purely as a set of acoustic relationships. Cf. PATTERN.

single drone. A DRONE on only one pitch (which, however, may be doubled at the octave). Cf. DOUBLE DRONE.

soft pentatonic. See PENTATONIC PATTERN.

split chord. A harmonic chord divided between consecutive phrases. Usually the dominant, but any chord may be treated in this manner.

split dominant. See SPLIT CHORD.

statement. See TWELVE-BAR BLUES.

step. See SEQUENCE.

supertonic sandwich. A harmonic pattern in which II(7) is 'sandwiched' between two statements of V(7).

symmetry. The reproduction of a PATTERN in some different position. It may be parallel (in the same direction) or reflective (with reversed direction, as in a mirror).

tetrachord. (1) Any modal pattern bounded by the perfect fourth, whether or not it consists of four notes (e.g. the tetrachord of the CHILDREN'S CHANT, or the PSALM TETRACHORD). (2) The first four notes of a MODE (e.g. MAJOR TETRACHORD, PHRYGIAN TETRACHORD).

thematic transformation. A type of variation, common in nineteenth-century music, that preserves the general outline of a melody (possibly in a stretched, compressed, or inverted form) while changing such features as rhythm, harmony, and mode.

tonal. Of the many possible meanings of this word, the most important in this book is 'founded on the opposition of the tonic and dominant chords'. See also the following entries.

tonal counterpoint. The COUNTERPOINT of MELODY and BASS.

tonality. A word with a notorious number of meanings, often tendentiously applied. In this book, it is mostly limited to the system of melody and harmony organized around the tonic and dominant chords. But broader senses are sometimes hard to avoid, especially in discussing harmonically complex music. See also EXTENDED TONALITY.

tonic. (1) A triadic DRONE, explicit or implicit, forming the harmonic basis of a movement. It is usually but not invariably interrupted by other chords. (2) Its root note. See also MELODIC TONIC.

transference. The duplication of a PATTERN elsewhere in the octave. To be distinguished from transposition, which is the duplication of a specific FIGURE.

transferred drone. A DRONE transferred (see the previous entry) from its original tonic position to another part of the mode, usually the dominant.

translation, modal. See MODAL TRANSLATION.

triadic drone. See DRONE.

triple pentatonic axis. See PENTATONIC AXIS.

tritonal. See WHOLE-TONE PATTERNS.

tritone. (1) Strictly, the interval comprising three tones , i.e. the augmented fourth. (2) In very chromatic music, the augmented fourth or diminished fifth interchangeably.

tumbling strains. In primitive melody, descending phrases repeated in endless variation. Typically, the strains conclude with the same figure and are grouped in cycles tapering from high to low. See also SAW-TOOTHED MELODY.

twelve-bar blues. A BLUES form, usually but by no means always twelve bars long. It comprises six sections grouped into three pairs, in this book called the 'statement', 'counterstatement', and 'conclusion'. The usual harmonization is I–I($7\flat$) · IV–I · V(7)–I, though there are many variants.

under-third cadence. A melodic cadence in which the dissonance is a minor (or, much more rarely, major) third below the note of resolution. Usually it takes the form $6{\rightarrow}1^+$, in which case it may also be known as the 'Landini cadence', after the fourteenth-century Florentine composer of that name.

vernacular. The musical 'language' spontaneously and unselfconsciously employed by the composers of a particular time and place. See also NINETEENTH-CENTURY VERNACULAR.

waltz sixth. The prominent 6 of major-mode waltz tunes. It often clashes with the underlying harmony.

whole-tone patterns. Melodic patterns based on adjacent major seconds ('whole tones'). When confined to only three tones, they are said to be 'tritonal'. See also the next entry.

whole-tone scale. A SCALE consisting exclusively of major seconds ('whole tones'). It comes in two 'keys', differing only in their relation to the diatonic background: the 'tonic' 1–2–3–$4\sharp$–$5\sharp$–$6\sharp$, and the 'dominant' $2\flat$–$3\flat$–4–5–6–7 (or their enharmonic equivalents).

X–Y, Y–X, and X–Y–X progressions. If a principal harmonic chord, designated X, is partially replaced by the subsidiary chord Y, there are three possible positions for Y: at the beginning (Y–X), in the middle (X–Y–X), and at the end (X–Y). In all three cases, the elaborated progression occupies the same rhythmic space as the original chord X.

Bibliography

With the exception of some out-of-the way items and one or two literary classics, the following is a complete list of the works cited, however tangentially, in the text of this book. In addition, it contains the sources for some of the less accessible musical examples. It is merely intended to amplify fragmentary citations and makes no claim to do justice to the subject. That, for a book of this nature, would require a volume in its own right.

Note that collections of works by various authors are entered under title rather than editor or compiler.

ABRAHAM, GERALD, 'The Apogee and Decline of Romanticism: 1890–1914', in *NOHM* x, ch. 1 (pp. 1–79).

ADDISON, JOSEPH, *Selections from Addison's Papers Contributed to* The Spectator, ed. Thomas Arnold (Oxford: Clarendon Press, 1894).

ALDRICH, PUTNAM, *Rhythm in Seventeenth-Century Italian Monody: With an Anthology of Songs and Dances* (London: Dent, 1966).

ALEXANDRU, TIBERIU, 'Tilincă', in *The New Grove Dictionary of Musical Instruments* (London: Macmillan, 1984), iii. 585.

—— 'Tilinca: ein uraltes rumänisches Volksinstrument', in *Studia Memoriae Belae Bartók Sacra*, 107–21.

American Ballads and Folk Songs, ed. John A. Lomax and Alan Lomax (New York: Macmillan, 1934).

The American Songbag, ed. Carl Sandburg (New York: Harcourt, Brace, 1927).

AMIS, KINGSLEY, 'Rondo for My Funeral', in *The Amis Collection: Selected Non-fiction, 1954–1990* (London: Penguin, 1991), 384–9. First published in *The Sunday Times*, 1 July 1973.

ANDREWS, H. K., *The Oxford Harmony*, ii (London: Oxford University Press, 1950).

ANGERMÜLLER, RUDOLPH, 'Zigeuner und Zigeunerisches in der Oper des 19. Jahrhunderts', in Heinz Becker (ed.), *Die 'Couleur locale' in der Oper des 19. Jahrhunderts* (Regensburg: Gustav Bosse, 1976), 131–59.

APEL, WILLI, *History of Keyboard Music to 1700*, trans. and rev. Hans Tischler (Bloomington: Indiana University Press, 1972). First published in German as *Geschichte der Orgel- und Klaviermusik bis 1700* (Kassel: Bärenreiter, 1967).

ASHBROOK, WILLIAM, *Donizetti* (London: Cassell, 1965).

Aus österreichischen Tanzbüchln, ed. Edi Rauter and Walter Deutsch, ii: *Kärnten* (Vienna: Doblinger, 1972).

BAILEY, ROBERT, 'The Structure of the *Ring* and its Evolution', *19th Century Music*, 1 (1977–8), 48–61.

—— 'An Analytical Study of the Sketches and Drafts', in id. (ed.), *Wagner: Prelude and Transfiguration from* Tristan und Isolde (Norton Critical Scores; New York: Norton, 1985), 113–46.

BAINES, ANTHONY, *Bagpipes* (Occasional Papers on Technology, 9; Oxford: Oxford University Press, 1960).

—— *Woodwind Instruments and their History*, 3rd edn. (London: Faber and Faber, 1967).

—— *The Oxford Companion to Music Instruments* (Oxford: Oxford University Press, 1992).

BÁRDOS, LAJOS, 'Ferenc Liszt, the Innovator', *Studia Musicologica Academiae Scientiarum Hungaricae*, (1975), 3–38.

BARTHA, DÉNES, 'Thematic Profile and Character in the Quartet-Finales of Joseph Haydn', *Studia Musicologica Academiae Scientiarum Hungaricae*, 11 (1969), 35–62.

BARTÓK, BÉLA, 'The Folk Music Dialect of the Hunedoara Rumanians', in Benjamin Suchoff (ed.), *Béla Bartók Essays* (London: Faber and Faber, in association with Faber Music, 1976), 103–14.

—— 'The Folklore of Instruments and their Music in Eastern Europe', ibid. 239–84.

—— 'Some Problems of Folk Music Research in East Europe', ibid. 173–92.

BAUD-BOVY, SAMUEL, 'La Chanson clephtique', *Journal of the International Folk Music Council*, 1 (1949), pp. 44–5.

BEETHOVEN, LUDWIG VAN, *Bagatelles, Rondos and other Shorter Works for Piano* (New York: Dover, 1987). A reprint of *Serie 18. Kleinere Stücke für das Pianoforte*, in the Breitkopf & Härtel collected edn. of Beethoven (1862–5).

BELAIEV, VICTOR, 'Kastalsky and his Russian Folk Polyphony', in *Music & Letters*, 10 (1929), 378–90.

BELLMAN, JONATHAN, *The* Style Hongrois *in the Music of Western Europe* (Boston: Northeastern University Press, 1993).

BERLIN, EDWARD A., *Ragtime: A Musical and Cultural History* (Los Angeles: University of California Press, 1980).

BERLIOZ, HECTOR, *The Memoirs of Hector Berlioz*, trans. and ed. David Cairns (London: Granada, 1970). First published by Gollancz, London, in 1969.

BEZIĆ, JERKO, 'Yugoslavia, §II, 3: Folk music, Croatia', *New Grove*, xx. 594–9.

BINCHOIS, GILLES, *Die Chansons von Gilles Binchois (1400–1460)*, ed. Wolfgang Rehm (Akademie der Wissenschaften und der Literatur in Mainz: Musikalische Denkmäler, 2; Mainz: B. Schott's Söhne, 1957).

The Book of Music, ed. Gill Rowley (London: Macdonald Educational, 1977).

BREIG, WERNER, 'The Music Works', in Ulrich Müller and Peter Wapnewski (eds.), *Wagner Handbook* (Cambridge, Mass: Harvard University Press, 1992), 397–482.

BRÖMSE, PETER, *Flöten, Schalmeien, Sackpfeifen Südslawiens* (Veröffentlichungen des Musikwissenschaftlichen Institutes der Deutschen Universität in Prag, 9; Brünn: Verlag Rudolph M. Rohrer, 1937).

BROWN, DAVID, *Mikhail Glinka* (London: Oxford University Press, 1974).

BRUNNER, HORST, 'Bar Form', *New Grove II*, ii. 725–6.

BUDDEN, JULIAN, *Verdi* (The Master Musicians; London: Dent, 1985).

—— *The Operas of Verdi*, i: *From* Oberto *to* Rigoletto, rev. edn. (Oxford: Clarendon Press, 1992).

BURBIDGE, PETER, and SUTTON, RICHARD (eds.), *The Wagner Companion* (London: Faber and Faber, 1979).

BURNEY, CHARLES, *Dr Burney's Musical Tours in Europe*, i: *An Eighteenth-Century Musical Tour in France and Italy*, ed. Percy A. Scholes (London: Oxford University Press, 1959). First published in 1773.

BUTLER, MARILYN, *Romantics, Rebels, and Reactionaries: English Literature and its Background, 1760–1830* (Oxford: Oxford University Press, 1981).

BYRD, WILLIAM, *My Ladye Nevells Booke of Virginal Music*, ed. Hilda Andrews, with a new introduction by Blanche Winogron (New York: Dover, 1969). First published by J. Curwen and Sons, London, in 1926. Dated 1591 in the original MS.

—— *William Byrd: Forty-five Pieces for Keyboard Instruments*, ed. Stephen Davidson Tuttle (Paris: Éditions de l'Oiseau-Lyre, 1939).

BYRON, GEORGE GORDON, LORD, *The Poetical Works of Lord Byron* (London: Henry Frowde, 1907).

Cancionero popular de Extremadura: contribución al folklore musical de la región, ed. Bonifacio Gil García (Badajoz: Excma. Diputación, 1956).

Cancionero musical de Galicia, ed. C. Sampedro y Folgar and José Filgueira Valverde (Pontevedra: Museo de Pontevedra, 1942).

Cancionero popular vasco, ed. R. M. de Azkue, 2nd edn. (Bilbao: Biblioteca de la Gran Enciclopedia Vasca, 1968).

CAPELL, RICHARD, 'Richard Wagner (1813–1883)', in Hubert J. Foss (ed.), *The Heritage of Music: Essays by R. R. Terry . . . [et al.]* (London: Oxford University Press, 1927), 214–48.

CARDINALL, ROGER, *German Romantics in Context* (London: Studio Vista, 1975).

CASTRO ESCUDERO, JOSÉ, 'Addition à l'article de D. Devoto sur "La Sarabande"', *Revue de musicologie*, 47 (1961), 119–25.

ČERNUŠÁK, GRACIAN, LAMB, ANDREW, and TYRRELL, JOHN, 'Polka', *New Grove II*, xx. 34–6.

CHANCELLOR, JOHN, *Wagner* (Boston: Little, Brown & Co., 1978).

CHASE, GILBERT, *The Music of Spain*, 2nd edn. (New York: Dover, 1959).

CHESTERTON, G. K., *Orthodoxy* (London: The Bodley Head, 1908).

Classic Piano Rags: Complete Original Music for 81 Rags, ed. Rudi Blesh (New York: Dover, 1973).

CLOSSON, ERNEST, *Le Manuscrit dit des Basses Danses de la Bibliothèque de Bourgogne*, ed. E. Closson (Brussels: Société des Bibliophiles et Iconophiles de Belgique, 1912).

COHEN, NORMAN, *Long Steel Rail: The Railroad in American Folksong*, ed. David Cohen (Music in American Life; Urbana: University of Illinois Press, 1981).

The Complete Country Dance Tunes from Playford's Dancing Master *(1651–ca. 1728)*, ed. Jeremy Barlow (London: Faber Music, 1985).

COOKE, DERYCK, *The Language of Music* (Oxford: Oxford University Press, 1963). First published in 1959.

—— *Vindications: Essays on Romantic Music* (London: Faber and Faber, 1982).

—— 'Wagner's Musical Language', in Burbidge and Sutton (eds.), *The Wagner Companion*, 225–68.

COOPER, MARTIN, *French Music from the Death of Berlioz to the Death of Fauré* (Oxford: Oxford University Press, 1961). First published in 1951.

—— *Beethoven: The Last Decade, 1817–1827* (London: Oxford University Press, 1970).

—— 'Stage Works: 1890–1918', in *NOHM* x. 145–207.

Corpus di musiche populari siciliane, comp. A. Favara and ed. O. Tiby, 2 vols. (Palermo: Accademia di Scienze, Lettere e Arti di Palermo, 1957).

CURTIN, PHILIP D., *The Atlantic Slave Trade: A Census* (Madison: University of Wisconsin Press, 1969).

—— 'The Slave Trade and the Atlantic Basin: Intercontinental Perspectives', in Nathan I. Huggins, Martin Kilson, and Daniel M. Fox (eds.), *Key Issues in the Afro-American Experience* (New York: Harcourt Brace Jovanovich, 1971), i. 74–93.

CZEKANOWSKA, ANNA, *Polish Folk Music: Slavonic Heritage—Polish Tradition—Contemporary Trends* (Cambridge Studies in Ethnomusicology; Cambridge: Cambridge University Press, 1990).

DAHLHAUS, CARL, *Studies on the Origin of Harmonic Tonality*, trans. Robert O. Gjerdingen (Princeton: Princeton University Press, 1990). First published in German as *Untersuchungen über die Entstehung der harmonischen Tonalität* (Kassel: Bärenreiter, 1968).

—— 'Harmony', *New Grove II*, x. 865–77.

DALZA, JOAN AMBROSIO, *Intabulatura di lauto* (Venice: Petrucci, 1508).

The Dance Music of Ireland: 1001 Gems: Double Jigs, Single Jigs, Hop or Slip Jigs, Reels, Hornpipes, Long Dances, Set Dances, etc., ed. Francis O'Neill, arr. James O'Neill (Dublin: Waltons, 1986). First published in 1907.

DEAN, WINTON, *Bizet* (The Master Musicians; London: Dent, 1948).

DENT, EDWARD J., *Opera*, Rev. edn. (Harmondsworth: Penguin, 1949).

—— 'Italian Opera in the Eighteenth Century, and its Influence on the Music of the Classical Period', *Quarterly Magazine of the International Musical Society*, 14 (1913), 500–9.

DEVOTO, DANIEL, 'La Folle sarabande', *Revue de musicologie*, 45 (1960), 3–43.

DONOSTIA, JOSÉ ANTONIO DE, 'El modo de *mi* en la canción popular española', *Anuario musical*, 1 (1946), 153–79.

DRYDEN, JOHN, *Fables Ancient and Modern, Translated into Verse from Homer, Ovid, Boccace, & Chaucer; with Original Poems* (London: Jacob Tonson, 1700), in *The Poems of John Dryden*, ed. John Sargeaunt (London: Oxford University Press, 1910), pp. 263 ff.

EBERT, WOLFGANG, 'Brahms in Ungarn: Nach der Studie "Brahms Magyarorsagon" von Lajos Koch', *Studien zur Musikwissenschaft*, 37 (1986), 103–63.

Elizabeth Rogers hir Virginall Booke: 112 Choice Pieces for Harpsichord by Byrd, Gibbons, Lawes, and Others, ed. Charles J. F. Cofone, 2nd, rev. edn. (New York: Dover, 1982). Dated 1656 in the original MS.

ELSCHEK, OSKÁR, 'Czechoslovakia, §II, 2: Folk music, Slovakia', *New Grove*, v. 131–6.

The English and Scottish Popular Ballads, ed. Francis James Child, v (New York: Cooper Square, 1965). First published in 1898.

English Folk Songs from the Southern Appalachians, collected by Cecil Sharp, ed. Maud Karpeles, 2 vols. (London: Oxford University Press, 1932).

The English Folksinger, ed. Sam Richards and Tish Stubbs (Glasgow: Collins, 1979).

FARMER, HENRY GEORGE, 'The Music of Islam', in *NOHM*, i. 421–77.

Favorite Songs of the Nineties: Complete Original Sheet Music for 89 Songs, ed. Robert A. Fremont (New York: Dover, 1973).

The Fitzwilliam Virginal Book, ed. J. A. Fuller Maitland and W. Barclay Squire (New York: Dover, 1963). Facsimile reprint of the original publication by Breitkopf & Härtel, Leipzig, 1899.

FLOTZINGER, RUDOLF, 'Und waltzen umatum... : Zur Genealogie des Wiener Walzers', *Österreichische Musikzeitschrift*, 30 (1975), 505–15.

Folk Music and Poetry of Spain and Portugal (Música y poesía popular de España y Portugal), collected by Kurt Schindler (New York: Hispanic Institute in the United States, 1941).

The Folk Songs of North America in the English Language, ed. Alan Lomax, 2nd edn. (London: Cassell, 1963).

FOSTER, STEPHEN, *Stephen Foster Song Book: Original Sheet Music of 40 Songs by Stephen Collins Foster*, ed. Richard Jackson (New York: Dover, 1974).

FOX STRANGWAYS, ARTHUR HENRY, *The Music of Hindostan* (London: Oxford University Press, 1914).

FRISCH, WALTER, *Brahms and the Principle of Developing Variation* (Berkeley: University of California Press, 1984).

FULD, JAMES J., *The Book of World-Famous Music: Classical, Popular and Folk*, rev. and enlarged edn. (New York: Crown Publishers, 1971).

GÁL, HANS, *Richard Wagner*, trans. Hans-Hubert Schönzeler (London: Gollancz, 1976). First published in German by Fischer (Frankfurt, 1963).

—— *Franz Schubert and the Essence of Melody*, translated by the author (London: Gollancz, 1974). First published in German as *Franz Schubert, oder die Melodie* (Frankfurt: Fischer, 1970).

GÁRDONYI, ZOLTAN, 'Neue Tonleiter- und Sequenztypen in Liszts Frühwerken (Zur Frage der "Lisztchen Sequenzen")', *Studia Musicologica Academiae Scientiarum Hungaricae*, 11 (1969), 169–99.

GELL-MANN, MURRAY, *The Quark and the Jaguar: Adventures in the Simple and the Complex* (London: Abacus, 1995).

Georg Philipp Telemann in Selbstzeugnissen und Bilddokumenten, ed. Karl Grebe (Reinbeck bei Hamburg: Rowohlt, 1970).

GLEICK, JAMES, *Chaos: Making a New Science* (London: Sphere Books, 1988).

GRAVES, ROBERT, and HODGE, ALAN, *The Long Week-End: A Social History of Great Britain, 1918–1939* (London: Reader's Union, by arrangement with Faber and Faber, 1941).

GRAVES, ROBERT, and HODGE, ALAN, *The Reader over your Shoulder: A Handbook for Writers of English Prose* (London: Jonathan Cape, 1943).

GRAY, CECIL, *Predicaments; or, Music and the Future: An Essay in Constructive Criticism* (London: Oxford University Press, 1936).

—— 'Joseph Haydn (1732–1809)', in Ralph Hill (ed.), *The Symphony* (Harmondsworth: Penguin, 1949), 22–54.

GREY, THOMAS S., 'Musical Background and Influences', in Millington (ed.), *The Wagner Compendium*, 63–92.

—— 'A Wagnerian Glossary', ibid. 229–41.

The Grove Concise Dictionary of Music, ed. Stanley Sadie and Alison Latham (London: Macmillan, 1988).

HAASE, RUDOLF, 'Leibniz, Gottfried Wilhelm', *New Grove II*, xiv. 500–1.

HADOW, SIR HENRY, *Studies in Modern Music, Second Series: Frederick Chopin, Antonin Dvořák, Johannes Brahms* (London: Seeley, Service & Co., 1895).

HANDY, W. C., *Father of the Blues: An Autobiography*, ed. Arna Bontemps (New York: Macmillan, 1941).

—— *Album of Songs & Pictures from Paramount's VistaVision production* St. Louis Blues (London: Francis, Day & Hunter, n.d.).

HARCOURT, RAOUL and MARGUERITE, *La Musique des Incas et ses survivances* (Paris: P. Geuthner, 1925).

HAYDN, FRANZ JOSEPH (attr.), *Contredanse und Zingarese, für Klavier zu zwei Händen*, ed. Otto Erich Deutsch (Vienna: Strache, 1930).

HEADINGTON, CHRISTOPHER, 'The Songs', in Walker (ed.), *Franz Liszt: The Man and his Music*, 221–47.

HELM, EVERETT, 'Secular Vocal Music in Italy (c. 1400–1530)', in *NOHM*, iii. 381–405.

HENDERSON, CLAYTON W., 'Minstrelsy, American', *New Grove II*, xvi. 736–40.

Historical Anthology of Music, ed. Archibald T. Davison and Willi Apel, 2 vols., 2nd edn. (Cambridge, Mass.: Harvard University Press, 1949).

HOBSBAWM, ERIC, *The Age of Revolution: Europe, 1789–1848* (London: Abacus, 1977). First published by Weidenfeld & Nicolson (London, 1962).

—— *Age of Extremes: The Short Twentieth Century, 1914–1991* (London: Michael Joseph, 1994).

HONOUR, HUGH, *Neo-Classicism* (Style and Civilization; Harmondsworth: Penguin, 1968).

HORSLEY, IMOGENE, 'The 16th-Century Variation: A New Historical Survey', *Journal of the American Musicological Society*, 12 (1959), 118–32.

HUDSON, RICHARD, 'The Folia Melodies', *Acta musicologica*, 45 (1973), 98–119.

—— 'Pavaniglia', *New Grove II*, xix. 252–3.

HUGHES, DOM ANSELM, 'The Birth of Polyphony', in *NOHM*, ii. 270–86.

—— 'Music in Fixed Rhythm', ibid. 311–52.

HULL, ARTHUR EAGLEFIELD, *Modern Harmony: Its Explanation and Application* (London: Augener, 1914).

—— *Scriabin*, 2nd half of *The National Music of Russia: Musorgsky and Scriabin* (London: Waverley Book Company, n.d.).

A Hundred Best Songs of the 20's and 30's (New York: Bonanza Books, 1973).

A Hundred Golden Oldies (London: Wise Publications, 1977).

Hymns Ancient and Modern, for Use in the Church, ed. William Henry Monk, rev. and enlarged edn. (London: William Clowes and Sons, 1875).

Irish Street Ballads, ed. Colm O Lochlainn (Dublin: At the Sign of the Three Candles, 1939).

JEANS, SIR JAMES, *Science and Music* (Cambridge: Cambridge University Press, 1937).

JOHNSON, PAUL, *A History of the Modern World: From 1917 to the 1980s* (London: Weidenfeld & Nicolson, 1983).

JONSON, BEN, *Timber, or Discoveries Made upon Men and Matter*, in Ben Jonson, *The Poems; The Prose Works*, viii (Oxford: Clarendon Press, 1947), 555– 649.

KAUFFMAN, STUART, *At Home in the Universe: The Search for Laws of Self-Organization and Complexity* (London: Penguin, 1996).

KELLER, HANS, *The Great Haydn Quartets: Their Interpretation* (London: Dent, 1986).

KENNEDY, MICHAEL, *Richard Strauss*, rev. edn. (The Master Musicians; London: Dent, 1988).

KENTNER, LOUIS, 'Solo Piano Music (1827–61)', in Walker (ed.), *Franz Liszt: The Man and his Music*, 79–133.

KERMAN, JOSEPH, *The Elizabethan Madrigal* (American Musicological Society: Studies and Documents, 4; New York: Galaxy Music Corporation, 1962).

—— *Musicology* (London: Fontana Paperbacks and William Collins, 1985).

KIMBELL, DAVID R., *Verdi in the Age of Italian Romanticism* (Cambridge: Cambridge University Press, 1983).

KIRBY, PERCIVAL R., *The Musical Instruments of the Native Races of South Africa* (London: Oxford University Press, 1934).

KIRKPATRICK, RALPH, *Domenico Scarlatti* (Princeton: Princeton University Press, 1953).

KOESTLER, ARTHUR, *The Sleepwalkers: A History of Man's Changing Vision of the Universe* (London: Penguin, 1964). First published by Hutchinson (London, 1959).

—— *The Act of Creation* (Danube edn.; London: Pan, 1970). First published by Hutchinson (London, 1964).

—— *The Ghost in the Machine* (London: Arkana, 1989). First published by Hutchinson (London, 1967).

—— 'To Covet a Swallow', in *Drinkers of Infinity: Essays, 1955–1967* (London: Hutchinson, 1968), 277–9. First published in *The Observer*, July 1960.

KUHN, THOMAS S., *The Structure of Scientific Revolutions*, 2nd edn., enlarged (Chicago: University of Chicago Press, 1970).

LAMBERT, CONSTANT, *Music Ho!: A Study of Music in Decline*, rev. edn. (London: Faber and Faber, 1937). First edn. published in 1934.

LANDON, H. C. ROBBINS, *Haydn: Chronicle and Works*, 5 vols. (London: Thames and Hudson, 1978).

LANNER, JOSEPH, *Ländler und Walzer*, ed. Alfred Orel (Denkmäler der Tonkunst in Österreich, Jahrg. 33/2, Band 65; Graz: Akademische Druck- und Verlaganstalt, 1960). First published in Vienna in 1926.

LaRue, Jan, 'Bifocal Tonality: An Explanation for Ambiguous Baroque Cadences', in *Essays on Music in Honor of Archibald Thompson Davison by his Associates* (Cambridge, Mass.: Harvard University Press, 1957), 173–84.

Leikin, Anatole, 'The Sonatas', in Jim Samson (ed.), *The Cambridge Companion to Chopin* (Cambridge: Cambridge University Press, 1992), 160–87.

Lendvai, Ernő, *Béla Bartók: An Analysis of his Music*, rev. reprint (London: Kahn & Averill, 1979). First edn. published in 1971.

—— *The Workshop of Bartók and Kodály* (Budapest: Editio Musica, 1983).

Levy, Kenneth J., Foreword to Oliver Strunk, *Music in the Byzantine World* (New York: Norton, 1977).

Lewin, Roger, *Complexity: Life at the Edge of Chaos* (London: Phoenix, 1993).

Leydi, Roberto, 'Italy, §II, Folk music, 3: Style areas, (i) The Mediterranean area', *New Grove*, ix. 382–91.

Liszt, Franz, *The Gipsy in Music*, trans. Edwin Evans (London: William Reeves, 1960). First published in 1881. A translation of *Des Bohémiens et de leur musique en Hongrie* (1859).

Lloyd, A. L., *Folk Song in England* (London: Panther, 1969). First published by Lawrence & Wishart (London, 1967).

Lockspeiser, Edward, 'Schönberg, Nietzsche, and Debussy', in Felix Aprahamian (ed.), *Essays on Music: An Anthology from 'The Listener'* (London: Cassell, 1967), 209–12. First published in *The Listener*, 9 Mar. 1961.

Lockwood, W. B., *An Informal History of the German Language*, 2nd edn. (London: André Deutsch, 1976).

Lowinsky, Edward E., *Tonality and Atonality in Sixteenth-Century Music* (Berkeley and Los Angeles: University of California Press, 1961).

McCall, Robert B., *Babies: The First Three Years of Life* (Cambridge, Mass.: Harvard University Press, 1979).

Macdonald, Hugh, ♯♯♯♯, *19th Century Music*, 11 (1987–8), 221–37.

McQuere, Gordon D., 'The Theories of Boleslav Yavorsky', in Gordon D. McQuere (ed.), *Russian Theoretical Thought in Music* (Russian Music Studies, 10; Ann Arbor: UMI Research Press, 1983), 109–64.

Machlis, Joseph, *The Enjoyment of Music: An Introduction to Perceptive Listening*, shorter edn. (New York: W. W. Norton, 1957).

Malm, William P., *Music Cultures of the Pacific, the Near East, and Asia*, 2nd edn. (Englewood Cliffs, NJ: Prentice-Hall, 1977).

Mandelbrot, Benoit B., *The Fractal Geometry of Nature*, rev. edn. (New York: W. H. Freeman, 1983).

Mann, Alfred, *The Study of Fugue* (New York: Dover, 1987). First published by Rutgers University Press (New Brunswick, NJ, 1958).

Mariechen saß weinend im Garten, 171 Lieder aus der Küche, ed. H. Goertz (Munich: Ehrenwirth, 1963).

MAZEL, LEO, 'K voprosu o rasshirenii ponyatiya odnoimennoy tonalnosti', *Sovetskaya muzyka*, 2 (1957).

MENCKEN, H. L., *A Mencken Chrestomathy* (New York: Knopf, 1949).

MILLINGTON, BARRY, *Wagner* (The Master Musicians; London: Dent, 1984).

—— (ed.), *The Wagner Compendium: A Guide to Wagner's Life and Music* (London: Thames and Hudson, 1992).

Minstrelsy, Ancient and Modern, with an Historical Introduction and Notes, ed. William Motherwell (Glasgow: Wylie, 1827).

MORLEY, THOMAS, *A Plaine and Easie Introduction to Practicall Musicke* (London: Humfrey Lownes, 1608). First published by Peter Short (London, 1597).

MORRIS, DESMOND, *The Human Animal: A Personal View of the Human Species* (London: BBC Books, 1994).

MORRIS, REGINALD OWEN, *Contrapuntal Technique in the Sixteenth Century* (London: Oxford University Press, 1922).

Music Hall Song Book: A Collection of 45 of the Best Songs from 1890–1920, ed. Peter Gammond (Newton Abbott: David & Charles, and London: EMI Music Publishing, 1975).

NARMOUR, EUGENE, *Beyond Schenkerism: The Need for Alternatives in Music Analysis* (Chicago: University of Chicago Press, 1977).

Narodni pesni ot Timok do Vita (Chants populaires bulgares du Timok à la Vita), ed. Vasil Stoin (Sofia: Ministerstvo na Narodnoto Prosvljshenie, 1928).

NETTL, BRUNO, *Folk and Traditional Music of the Western Continents*, 2nd edn. (Prentice Hall History of Music Series; Englewood Cliffs, NJ: Prentice-Hall, 1973).

The New Grove Dictionary of Music and Musicians, ed. Stanley Sadie (London: Macmillan, 1980).

The New Grove Dictionary of Music and Musicians, 2nd edn., ed. Stanley Sadie and John Tyrrell (London: Macmillan, 2001).

The New Harvard Dictionary of Music, ed. Don Michael Randel (Cambridge, Mass.: Belknap Press, 1986).

The New Oxford History of Music. i: *Ancient and Oriental Music*, ed. Egon Wellesz (London: Oxford University Press, 1957); ii: *Early Medieval Music up to 1300*, ed. Dom Anselm Hughes, rev. edn. (London: Oxford University Press, 1955); iii: *Ars Nova and the Renaissance, 1300–1540*, ed. Dom Anselm Hughes and Gerald Abraham (London: Oxford University Press, 1960); x: *The Modern Age, 1890–1960*, ed. Martin Cooper (London: Oxford University Press, 1974).

NEWCOMB, ANTHONY, 'The Birth of Music out of the Spirit of Drama', *19th Century Music*, 5 (1981–2), 38–66.

NEWMAN, ERNEST, *Opera Nights* (London: Putnam, 1943).

—— *The Unconscious Beethoven: An Essay in Musical Psychology*, rev. edn. (London: Gollancz, 1968). First edn. published in 1927.

—— 'A Wodehouse Story and Some Reflections', in Felix Aprahamian (ed.), *From the World of Music: Essays from 'The Sunday Times'* (London: John Calder, 1956), 181–4.

OAKLEY, GILES, *The Devil's Music: A History of the Blues*, rev. edn. (London: British Broadcasting Corporation, 1983).

OLDHAM, GUY, CAMPBELL, MURRAY, and GREATED, C., 'Harmonics', *New Grove II*, x. 854–6.

ORREY, LESLIE, 'The Songs of Gabriel Fauré', *Music Review*, 6 (1945), 72–84.

The Oxford Book of Ballads, ed. James Kinsley (Oxford: Oxford University Press, 1982).

The Oxford Book of English Madrigals, ed. Philip Ledger (Oxford: Oxford University Press, 1978).

The Oxford English Dictionary, 2nd edn., ed. J. A. Simpson and E. S. C. Weiner (Oxford: Clarendon Press, 1989).

The Oxford Song Book, ii, collected and arr. Thomas Wood (London: Oxford University Press, 1928).

PARRY, HUBERT, *The Evolution of the Art of Music* (London: Kegan Paul, 1893).

—— *Style in Musical Art* (London: Macmillan, 1911).

The Penguin Book of Rounds, ed. Rosemary Cass-Beggs (Harmondsworth: Penguin, 1982).

PEVSNER, NIKOLAUS, *Pioneers of Modern Design: From William Morris to Walter Gropius*, rev. edn. (Harmondsworth: Penguin, 1960). First edn. published as *Pioneers of the Modern Movement* by Faber and Faber (London, 1936).

PEYSER, JOAN, *Twentieth-Century Music: The Sense behind the Sound* (New York: Schirmer Books, 1971).

PICKEN, LAURENCE, 'Instrumental Polyphonic Folk Music in Asia Minor', *Proceedings of the Royal Musical Association*, 80th session (1953–4), 73–86.

PINKER, STEVEN, *The Language Instinct: The New Science of Language and Mind* (London: Penguin, 1994).

PIRROTTA, NINO, *Music and Culture in Italy from the Middle Ages to the Baroque: A Collection of Essays* (Cambridge, Mass.: Harvard University Press, 1984).

POPPER, KARL RAIMUND, *The Open Society and its Enemies*, ii: *The High Tide of Prophecy: Hegel, Marx, and the Aftermath*, 4th edn. (London: Routledge & Kegan Paul, 1962).

—— *The Poverty of Historicism*, 2nd edn. (London: Routledge & Kegan Paul, 1961).

Popular Songs of Nineteenth-Century America: Complete Original Sheet Music for 64 Songs, ed. Richard Jackson (New York: Dover, 1976).

POTTER, STEPHEN, *Some Notes on Lifemanship* (London: Rupert Hart-Davis, 1950).

PRAETORIUS, MICHAEL, *Syntagma musicum* (Wolfenbüttel, 1619).

PRIZER, WILLIAM F., 'The Frottola and the Unwritten Tradition', *Studi musicali*, 15 (1986), 3–31.

QUANTZ, JOHANN JOACHIM, *Versuch einer Anweisung die Flöte traversiere zu spielen; mit verschiedenen, zur Beförderung des guten Geschmackes in der praktischen Musik dienlichen Anmerkungen begleitet, und mit Exempeln erläutert*, 3rd edn. (Breslau: Johann Friedrich Korn, 1789).

Ragtime Rarities: Complete Original Music for 63 Piano Rags, ed. Trebor Jay Tichenor (New York: Dover, 1975).

Ragtime Rediscoveries: 64 Works from the Golden Age of Rag, ed. Trebor Jay Tichenor (New York: Dover, 1979).

The Ragtime Songbook, ed. Ann Charters (New York: Oak Publications, 1965).

RAMEAU, JEAN-PHILLIPE, *Treatise on Harmony*, trans. Philip Gossett (New York: Dover, 1971). First published in French as *Traité de l'harmonie* by Jean-Baptiste-Christophe Ballard (Paris, 1722).

RAUHE, HERMANN, 'Zum volkstümlichen Lied des 19. Jahrhunderds', in Carl Dahlhaus (ed.), *Studien zur Trivialmusik des 19. Jahrhunderts* (Regensburg: Gustav Bosse, 1967), 159–98.

RAVENSCROFT, THOMAS, *Pammelia: Musicks Miscellanie* (London: William Barley, 1609).

REICHENBACH, HERMAN, 'The Tonality of English and Gaelic Folksong', *Music & Letters*, 19 (1938), 268–79.

REID, CHARLES, *Thomas Beecham: An Independent Biography* (London: Gollancz, 1961).

RÉTI, RUDOLPH, *Tonality, Atonality, Pantonality: A Study of Some Trends in Twentieth Century Music* (London: Rockliff, 1958).

RITCHIE, JEAN, *Folk Songs of the Southern Appalachians as Sung by Jean Ritchie* (New York: Oak Publications, 1965).

RIMSKY-KORSAKOV, NIKOLAY ANDREYEVICH, *My Musical Life*, trans. from the 5th rev. Russian edn. by Judah A. Joffe, 3rd edn., ed. Carl Van Vechten (New York: Knopf, 1942).

RINGER, ALEXANDER L., 'Melody, §3, General concepts', *New Grove II*, xvi. 363–73.

ROBINSON, J. BRADFORD, 'Jazz Reception in Weimar Germany: In Search of a Shimmy Figure', in Bryan Gilliam (ed.), *Music and Performance during the Weimar Republic* (Cambridge Studies in Performance Practice, 3; Cambridge: Cambridge University Press, 1994), 107–34.

ROCHBERG, GEORGE, 'Schönberg's "American" Period', in *The International Cyclopedia of Music and Musicians*, 9th edn., ed. Robert Sabin (New York: Dodd, Mead & Co., 1964), 1915–22.

The Roche Collection of Traditional Irish Music, ed. Francis Roche (Cork: Ossian, 1993). One-vol. reprint of the original three vols. of 1911–27.

ROLLAND, ROMAIN, *Romain Rolland's Essays on Music*, ed. David Ewen (New York: Dover, 1959). First published by Allen, Towne & Heath (New York, 1948).

ROSEN, CHARLES, *The Classical Style: Haydn, Mozart, Beethoven* (London: Faber and Faber, 1971).

ROSSELLI, JOHN, *Music and Musicians in Nineteenth-Century Italy* (London: Batsford, 1991).

ROTH, ERNST, *The Business of Music: Reflections of a Music Publisher* (London: Cassell, 1969).

RUSSELL, BERTRAND, *History of Western Philosophy and its Connection with Political and Social Circumstances from the Earliest Times to the Present Day*, new edn. (London: George Allen & Unwin, 1961). First edn. published in 1946.

SACHS, CURT, *The Rise of Music in the Ancient World, East and West* (New York: W. W. Norton, 1943).

—— *Rhythm and Tempo: A Study in Music History* (London: Dent, 1953).

—— *The Wellsprings of Music: An Introduction to Ethnomusicology*, ed. Jaap Kunst (The Hague: Martinus Nijhoff, 1962).

SALMEN, WALTER, 'Towards the Exploration of National Idiosyncrasies in Wandering Song-Tunes', *International Folk Music Journal*, 6 (1954), 52–5.

SANDERS, ERNEST H., 'Rondellus', *New Grove II*, xxi. 648–9.

SANZ, GASPAR, *Instrucción de música sobre la guitarra española* (Saragossa: Institución 'Fernando el Católico', 1966). Facsimile, with prologue and notes by Luis Garcia-Abrines, of the original edition (Saragossa, 1674).

SÁROSI, BÁLINT, *Gypsy Music*, trans. Fred Macnicol (Budapest: Corvina Press, 1978). First published in Hungarian as *Cigányzene* in 1970.

SAUSSINE, HENRI DE, 'De la Favorite à Saint-Christophe', *Revue musicale*, 2/10 (Aug. 1921), 156–9.

Sbornik Russkikh Narodnykh Pesen (*One Hundred Russian Folk Songs*), ed. Nikolai Rimsky-Korsakov (St Petersburg: Bessel, 1877). Numbered as Op. 24.

SCARBOROUGH, DOROTHY, *On the Trail of Negro Folk-Songs* (Hatboro, Pa.: Folklore Association, 1963). Facsimile reprint of the original publication by Harvard University Press (Cambridge, Mass., 1925).

SCHENKER, HEINRICH, *Free Composition (Der freie Satz)*, trans. and ed. Ernst Oster (New Musical Theories and Fantasies, 3; New York: Longman, 1979).

SCHNEIDER, MARIUS, 'Primitive Music', in *NOHM*, i. 1–82.

SCHOENBERG, ARNOLD, *Theory of Harmony*, trans. Roy E. Carter (London: Faber and Faber, 1978). First published in German as *Harmonielehre* by Universal Edition (Vienna, 1911).

—— *Style and Idea: Selected Writings of Arnold Schoenberg*, ed. Leonard Stein, with translations by Leo Black, rev. edn. (London: Faber and Faber, 1984). First published in 1975.

SCHOLES, PERCY, *The Listener's History of Music: A Book for any Concert-Goer, Gramophonist or Radio Listener*, 7th edn. (London: Oxford University Press, 1954). First edn. published in 1923.

—— *The Oxford Companion to Music*, 9th edn. (London: Oxford University Press, 1955). First edn. published in 1938.

SCHUBART, CHRISTIAN FRIEDRICH DANIEL, *Ideen zu einer Ästhetik der Tonkunst*, ed. Fritz and Margrit Kaiser (Hildesheim: Georg Loms Verlagsbuchhandlung, 1969). Written in 1784–5 and first published in 1806.

SCHULLER, GUNTER, *Early Jazz: Its Roots and Musical Development* (New York: Oxford University Press, 1968).

The Scottish Folksinger: 118 Modern and Traditional Folksongs, ed. Norman Buchan and Peter Hall, new edn. (Glasgow: Collins, 1978).

The Scottish Students' Song Book (London: Bayley and Ferguson, 1891).

SEARLE, HUMPHREY, 'The Orchestral Works', in Walker (ed.), *Franz Liszt: The Man and his Music*, 279–317.

SHAW, GEORGE BERNARD, *Pen Portraits and Reviews* (London: Constable, 1931).

—— *Shaw's Music: The Complete Musical Criticism in Three Volumes*, ed. Dan H. Laurence, 2nd rev. edn. (London: The Bodley Head, 1989).

SIEPMANN, JEREMY, *Chopin: The Reluctant Romantic*. London: Gollancz, 1995.

Slave Songs of the United States, ed. W. F. Allen, C. P. Ware, and L. McKim Garrison (New York: A. Simpson, 1867).

SLONIMSKY, NICOLAS, introduction to Richard Burbank, *Twentieth Century Music* (London: Thames and Hudson, 1984), pp. xi–xxi.

SMUTS, JAN CHRISTIAAN, *Holism and Evolution* (Cape Town: N & S Press, 1987). First published by Macmillan (London, 1926).

Song Hits from the Turn of the Century: Complete Original Sheet Music for 62 Songs, ed. Paul Charosh and Robert A. Fremont (New York: Dover, 1975).

Source Readings in Music History. V: *The Romantic Era*, ed. Oliver Strunk (London: Faber and Faber, 1981). First published in 1952.

Sousa, John Philip, *Sousa's Great Marches in Piano Transcription: Original Sheet Music of 23 Works by John Philip Sousa*, ed. Lester S. Levy (New York: Dover, 1975).

—— 'A Letter from Sousa', *Etude* (Aug. 1898), 231.

STEWART, IAN, and COHEN, JACK, *The Collapse of Chaos* (London: Viking, 1994).

—— and Golubitsky, Martin, *Fearful Symmetry: Is God a Geometer?* (London: Penguin, 1993).

STRACHEY, LYTTON, 'Pope' (The Leslie Stephen Lecture for 1925), in *Literary Essays* (London: Chatto and Windus, 1948), 79–93.

STRAVINSKY, IGOR, 'Wagner's Prose', in *Themes and Conclusions* (London: Faber and Faber, 1972), 242–7. First published in April 1965 as a review of *Wagner on Music and Drama*, a selection of Wagner's prose works.

STREET, DONALD, 'The Modes of Limited Transposition', *Musical Times*, 117 (1976), 819–23.

Studia Memoriae Belae Bartók Sacra (Budapest: Aedes Academiae Scientiarum Hungaricae, 1956).

SZABOLCSI, BENCE, 'Haydn und die ungarische Musik', in *Bericht über die internationale Konferenz zum Andenken Joseph Haydns* (Budapest: Akadémiai Kiadó, 1961), 159–75.

TALBOT, MICHAEL, *Vivaldi* (The Master Musicians; London: Dent, 1978).

TARUSKIN, RICHARD, 'Russian Folk Melodies in *The Rite of Spring*', *Journal of the American Musicological Society*, 33 (1980), 501–43.

—— 'How the Acorn Took Root: A Tale of Russia', *19th Century Music*, 6 (1982–3), 189–212.

—— 'Chernomor to Kashchei: Harmonic Sorcery; or, Stravinsky's "Angle"', *Journal of the American Musicological Society*, 38 (1985), 72–142.

TELEMANN, GEORG PHILIPP, *Telemann in Selbstzeugnissen und Bilddokumenten*, ed. Karl Grebe (Reinbeck bei Hamburg: Rowohlt, 1970).

—— *The 36 Fantasias for Keyboard* (New York: Dover, 1987). First published as *Drei Dutzend Klavier-Fantasien* by Martin Breslauer (Berlin, 1923).

THOMPSON, SIR D'ARCY WENTWORTH, *On Growth and Form*, 2 vols. (Cambridge: Cambridge University Press, 1961). First published in 1917.

TOVEY, SIR DONALD FRANCIS, *A Companion to Beethoven's Pianoforte Sonatas* (London: The Associated Board of the Royal Schools of Music, 1931).

—— *Essays in Musical Analysis*, 6 vols., with a further volume on *Chamber Music* (London: Oxford University Press, 1935–44).

—— *A Musician Talks*, pt. 2: *Musical Textures* (London: Oxford University Press, 1941).

Tovey, Sir Donald Francis, *Essays and Lectures on Music* (Oxford: Oxford University Press, 1949).

—— *The Forms of Music: Musical Articles from the Encyclopaedia Britannica* (London: Oxford University Press, 1957).

Tuckwell, Barry, *Horn* (Yehudi Menuhin Music Guides; London: Macdonald, 1983).

Van der Merwe, Peter, *Origins of the Popular Style: The Antecedents of Twentieth-Century Popular Music* (Oxford: Oxford University Press, 1989).

Vargyas, Lajos, 'Die Wirkung des Dudelsacks auf die ungarische Volkstanzmusik', in *Studia Memoriae Belae Bartók Sacra*, 503–40.

Vaughan Williams, Ralph, *National Music and Other Essays*, 2nd edn. (London: Oxford University Press, 1987).

Wachsmann, Klaus P., 'The Primitive Musical Instruments', in Anthony Baines (ed.), *Musical Instruments through the Ages* (Harmondsworth: Penguin, 1966), 23–54.

Wackenroder, Wilhelm Heinrich, *Herzensergießungen eines kunstliebenden Klosterbruders* (1797), in *Sämtliche Schriften*, ed. K. G. Conrady (Munich: Rowohlt, 1968).

Wagner, Richard, *Selected Letters of Richard Wagner*, trans. and ed. Stewart Spencer and Barry Millington (London: Dent, 1987).

Walker, Alan, 'Liszt and the Twentieth Century', in id. (ed.), *Franz Liszt: The Man and his Music*, 350–64.

—— 'Liszt's Musical Background', ibid. 36–78.

—— (ed.), *Franz Liszt: The Man and his Music* (London: Barrie & Jenkins, 1970).

Ward, John M., 'The Morris Tune', *Journal of the American Musicological Society*, 39 (1986), 294–331.

Warrack, John, 'The Musical Background', in Burbidge and Sutton (eds.), *The Wagner Companion*, 85–112.

Watt, Henry Jackson, 'Melody', *Music & Letters*, 5 (1924), 272–85.

Webern, Anton, *The Path to the New Music*, ed. Willi Reich (Bryn Mawr: Theodore Presser, in association with Universal Edition, London, 1963). A translation from the German of 16 lectures originally given in Vienna, 1932–3.

Weelkes, Thomas, *Ayeres or Phantasticke Spirites for Three Voices* (London: William Barley, 1608). Reprinted in *The English Madrigal School*, 13, ed. Edmund Horace Fellowes (London: Stainer & Bell, 1916).

Wenk, Arthur B., *Claude Debussy and Twentieth-Century Music* (Boston, Mass.: Twayne, 1983).

Werner, Eric, 'The Music of Post-Biblical Judaism', in *NOHM*, i. 313–35.

Werner, Heinz, 'Die melodische Erfindung im frühen Kindesalter', *Philologische-Historische Klasse, Sitzungsberichte*, 182 (1917), no. 4.

Westrup, J. A., 'Medieval Song', in *NOHM*, ii. 220–69.

Williams, Leonard, *The Dancing Chimpanzee: A Study of the Origin of Music in Relation to the Vocalising and Rhythmic Action of Apes*, rev. edn. (London: Allison & Busby, 1980).

Wilson, Edward O., *Consilience: The Unity of Knowledge* (London: Little, Brown & Company, 1998).

WINTER, ROBERT S., 'The Bifocal Close and the Evolution of the Viennese Classical Style', *Journal of the American Musicological Society*, 42 (1989), 275–337.

WIORA, WALTER, 'Älter als die Pentatonik: Über die zwei- bis vierstufigen Tonarten in Alt-Europa und bei Naturvölkern', in *Studia Memoriae Belae Bartók Sacra*, 185–208.

Index

Italics indicate the page numbers of musical examples. **Bold** type signifies passages of particular importance (e.g. acoustic mode 217, 218, **219–20**). Dashes within cross-references precede sub-entries (e.g. '*see* accompaniment patterns—syncopated' means '*see the sub-entry* syncopated *within the entry* accompaniment patterns). Chords, keys, etc., are presumed to be major unless the contrary is stated. Square brackets expand a chord into a key (e.g. III♯ is the mediant major triad, [III♯] the key of the major mediant).